Reducing Inequalities in Europe

Reducing Inequalities in Europe

How Industrial Relations and Labour Policies Can Close the Gap

Edited by

Daniel Vaughan-Whitehead

Senior Economist, International Labour Office, Geneva, Switzerland and Professor, Sciences Po, Paris, France and University of Geneva, Switzerland

Edward Elgar
PUBLISHING

Cheltenham, UK • Northampton, MA, USA

International Labour Office

Geneva, Switzerland

Published by
Edward Elgar Publishing Limited
The Lypiatts
15 Lansdown Road
Cheltenham
Glos GL50 2JA
UK

Edward Elgar Publishing, Inc.
William Pratt House
9 Dewey Court
Northampton
Massachusetts 01060
USA

In association with
International Labour Office
4 route des Morillons
CH-1211 Geneva 22
Switzerland
ISBN 978-92-2-130006-9 (paperback)

A catalogue record for this book
is available from the British Library

Library of Congress Control Number: 2017959998

This book is available electronically in the **Elgar**online
Economics subject collection
DOI 10.4337/9781788116299

MIX
Paper from
responsible sources
FSC® C013056

ISBN 978 1 78811 628 2 (cased)
ISBN 978 1 78811 629 9 (eBook)

Typeset by Servis Filmsetting Ltd, Stockport, Cheshire
Printed and bound in Great Britain by TJ International Ltd, Padstow

Contents

Contributors

Dominique Anxo Professor of Economics at the Department of Economics and Statistics, Linnaeus University, Sweden and Director of the Centre of Ageing and Life-course Studies.

Branko Bembič PhD candidate at the Faculty of Arts, University of Ljubljana and Early Stage Researcher at the Faculty for Social Sciences, University of Ljubljana, Slovenia.

Gerhard Bosch Professor of Sociology and Senior Professor in the Institute of Work, Skills and Training (IAQ) at the University of Duisburg-Essen, Germany.

Pierre Courtioux Researcher at EDHEC Business School and Associate Researcher at the Centre d'Economie de la Sorbonne, France.

Christine Erhel Director of Employment and Labour Research Centre (CNAM, Paris) and Associate Professor in Economics at the University of Paris 1, France.

Kerly Espenberg Project Manager and Analyst, Centre for Applied Social Sciences, University of Tartu, Estonia.

Giuseppe Fiorani Professor of Economics and Institutions of the Industrial Districts at the University of Modena and Reggio Emilia, Italy and Member of the Economics Department's Public Policy Analysis Centre.

Stefanos Giakoumatos Professor of Statistics and Quantitative Methods, Department of Accounting and Finance, Technological Educational Institute of Peloponnese, Greece.

Damian Grimshaw Director of Research Department, International Labour Office, Geneva, Switzerland.

Mat Johnson Research Associate at the European Work and Employment Research Centre at the University of Manchester, United Kingdom.

Maria Karamessini Professor of Labour Economics and Economics of the Welfare State at Panteion University, Athens and Governor of the Greek Public Employment Agency, Greece.

Ive Marx Professor of Social Policy at the Herman Deleeck Centre for Social Policy, University of Antwerp, Belgium.

Jaan Masso Senior Research Fellow, School of Economics and Business Administration, University of Tartu, Estonia.

Inta Mierina Senior Researcher, Institute of Philosophy and Sociology, University of Latvia, Riga, Latvia.

Rafael Muñoz de Bustillo Professor of Applied Economics at the University of Salamanca, Spain.

Brian Nolan Professor of Social Policy and Director of the Employment Equity and Growth research programme at the Institute for New Economic Thinking, University of Oxford, United Kingdom.

Fernando Pinto Hernández Assistant Researcher at the University of Salamanca, Spain.

Wiemer Salverda Professor of Labour Market and Inequality, Amsterdam Centre for Inequality Studies (AMCIS) and Director Emeritus of the Amsterdam Institute for Advanced Labour Studies (AIAS), Netherlands.

Annamaria Simonazzi Professor of Economics, Department of Economics and Law, Sapienza University, Rome, Italy.

Maryna Tverdostup Research Fellow, School of Economics and Business Administration, University of Tartu, Estonia.

Lien Van Cant Doctoral researcher at the Herman Deleeck Centre for Social Policy at the University of Antwerp, Belgium.

Daniel Vaughan-Whitehead Senior Economist, Inclusive Labour Markets, Labour Relations and Working Conditions Branch, International Labour Office, Geneva, Switzerland and Professor at Sciences Po, Paris, France and the University of Geneva, Switzerland.

Rosalia Vazquez-Alvarez Econometrician and wage specialist, Inclusive Labour Markets, Labour Relations and Working Conditions Branch, International Labour Office, Geneva, Switzerland.

Foreword

On 24 February 2017 I had the great privilege to host eight ministers and state secretaries in a round-table discussion organized by the International Labour Organization (ILO) and the European Commission aimed at identifying best practices and policy solutions to reduce inequalities. In particular we asked our honourable guests to answer two basic questions:

1. Do you have the feeling that inequalities are increasing in your country; and if so, what type of inequalities?
2. What policy reforms can help, and in particular how can industrial relations (social partners in cooperation with the State) help to limit, or even reduce, inequalities? Are there some recent good examples from your country?

We reproduce below selections of the answers provided by such high-level government representatives, and decided to complement them by reproducing a number of key contributions by representatives of employers and trade unions during the same event, to further identify the particular role that social dialogue and collective bargaining could play in addressing the sources of inequality identified in the present volume.

Mr Joe Camilleri, Permanent Secretary, Ministry for Social Dialogue, Consumer Affairs and Civil Liberties, Malta
It is realistic to say that, yes, inequalities are increasing and it is difficult sometimes to understand what is really the [root cause] of these inequalities. We see more people moving into poverty. We have to address these inequalities.

What are we doing? We have been working as a government to make work pay, and we have introduced a number of initiatives like in-work benefit schemes [and] the reform of our social security system, to help people return to the labour market.

We have also worked on a number of other types of benefits, like free childcare services and also the maternity trust benefit, that ensures the payment of women going on maternity to avoid to have them discriminated against when applying for jobs, especially because we have in Malta the lowest female [labour market] participation rate. This also helps families to increase their income and . . . improve their financial situation.

We have also addressed the precarious employment situation: now any person employed [on service contract] with government has to receive the equivalent salary of a person who is working in government in that job; and now, through tripartite discussions, we are working to see how precarious employment can also be addressed in the private sector. Within the Malta Council for Economic and Social Development we have faced a number of issues together, and we have included not only the employers and the unions in the discussions, but even civil society at large.

This is one of the reasons why the industrial situation is relatively calm in Malta, and we have found that this type of system has always helped to produce the best policies.

Mr Nicolas Schmit, Minister, Ministry of Labour, Employment, the Social Economy and Economic Solidarity, Luxembourg

I was a bit surprised by the first question; you asked 'do you have the feeling?' It is right that the issue of inequality is not only an issue of statistics; beyond statistics there is also the feeling that indeed [even] in a traditional and quiet society such as Luxembourg, inequalities are increasing. And the statistics confirm this feeling; the Gini coefficient for Luxembourg is around 0.28. There is an increased gap between those who earn the minimum wage – 16 per cent of [all workers in Luxembourg], one of the highest [rates] in the EU – and those who [receive] the highest incomes. Even if Luxembourg has the highest minimum wage, it is close to the poverty rate, and poverty is increasing. Temporary and precarious work is also on the increase, particularly for young people. We can also witness a form of polarization of the labour market due to technological changes.

We have a tripartite system which regularly discusses salaries . . . but also tax measures, social measures and other things to limit the extent to which inequalities are increasing. Social transfers are also truly vital because they have an impact on inequalities. The progressive tax system also contributes to this. . . . Collective bargaining is also part of the solution; 50 per cent of workers are covered by collective agreements and they have a quite favourable income situation. We also have a system of wage indexation to price increases that enables those who do not have a collective agreement to at least see their income stabilized and any price increases reflected in their salaries. We are often criticized for maintaining this indexation system, but this is a truly important tool to tackle inequalities.

Ms Yasmin Fahimi, State Secretary, Federal Ministry of Labour and Social Affairs, Germany

Yes, in Germany there is also a trend towards greater inequality. We have economic growth, economic stability and an increase in real wages but, [and] now comes the big 'but', since the mid-1990s up to the mid-2000s, there was an increase in income inequality because the number of low-earners has increased, especially in the hotel and logistics sectors.

It concerns not only specific sectors but also specific groups. Those who are unemployed in the long term are exposed to a very high risk – single parents, these are mostly women of course, and then further, those who are less skilled and those who have a migration background. There is an unequal development here, and we need to think about what has not worked properly and how we can further develop our country in a positive direction.

We looked at different policies to stabilize income in Germany. . . . Collective agreements [developed positively] after German reunification, but since then have decreased somewhat. We have thus implemented a series of measures to strengthen the social partners, we introduced a minimum wage and also made collective agreements easier to conclude. We have also included a new principle in our legislative process that defines standards to protect employees while having clauses to allow more flexibility for companies.

We have also worked on a concept to reach specific target groups, notably for those who receive pensions . . . to see those who work in independent/liberal professions . . . be able to receive better pension benefits. . . . or to have a state solidarity pension for those who have worked many years but still have not been able to make enough before retirement. This is one of the measures against poverty in old age and to reduce the feeling of inequality.

But we must also look at the distribution of wealth, we must reform the taxes on inheritance, for example, to ensure the more equitable transfer of wealth from one generation to the next, which is an issue of major importance in Germany.

Mr Jose Antonio Vieira da Silva, Minister, Ministry of Labour, Solidarity and Social Security, Portugal

We can say that we face two different movements. Until 2008 we experienced a very positive and long-term movement toward the correction of inequalities thanks to the development of the welfare state and the improvement of education in our society. The second movement, after the financial and economic crisis began in 2009, is characterized by a deepening of inequalities.

Austerity policies have had a profound impact on growing inequalities in Portugal: unemployment at a higher level, never reached before, a substantial decrease of families' disposable income also due to real wage decline, a freeze in the minimum wage, wage cuts in the public sector and increased income taxes, escalation of poverty levels, including among workers, especially those in non-permanent positions – Portugal is in the top three in terms of the incidence of temporary workers.

We are trying to reverse these trends and to increase the disposable income of families while continuing to work on the correction of macro-economic and budgetary imbalances.

In this context, let me emphasize three main priorities of our country. The first one is the minimum wage increase on the basis of a national social dialogue, which we did in 2016 and 2017 without any negative effect on employment.

The second priority is the recovery of collective agreements, which have declined since 2009 in both numbers and coverage of workers. The third priority is lifelong learning, especially in a context of emigration from Portugal to other European countries, and paying special attention to young people.

Governments cannot do all these things by themselves. We need strong social dialogue. But I also believe that it is not possible without recovering collective bargaining to talk about wages or working time, which allows employers and employees to adjust to economic and social reality. When those two dynamics are combined, decisive movement is achieved.

Ms Ourania Antonopoulou, Alternate Minister, Ministry for Combating Unemployment, Greece

Three important shifts have contributed to increased inequalities in Greece. First, collective bargaining does not exist in Greece at the moment, due to the laws passed as part of our agreement in 2011–12 with our international lenders. We went from general agreements to sectoral, and even further to firm level agreements; there have been only four sectoral collective bargaining agreements since 2011 and over 250 agreements at firm level. Second, there was the shift to part-time and precarious forms of employment. In 2013 alone, full-time contracts declined by 21 per cent, and correspondingly, part-time and rotational and precarious forms in general increased by the same percentage. The third phenomenon was the reduction of the minimum wage by 22 per cent and therefore also of the starting wage in the public sector, leading to a general reduction of earned income by roughly 28–30 per cent.

If you combine these three shifts, all types of red alarms should start ringing. Not surprisingly, if you have such sudden reductions in earned income, it is impossible to prevent hundreds of thousands of small and medium-sized companies from shutting down. From 2007–08 the unemployment rate increased from 7 per cent to 10 per cent in 2010 and 27.7 per cent in 2013, before slightly declining to 23 per cent in 2015. So, there was a snowball effect and one has to pick up the thread somewhere for it to start reversing itself.

I would like now to move to our priorities. One concerns the employed and the other concerns the unemployed. On the first, we are trying to reinstate collective bargaining, in particular by reversing the suspension of the extension mechanisms[1] and also reversing the suspension of the favourability principle.[2] To support the unemployed, we put in place, together with the social partners, a skills-enhancement programme to match the needs of the private sector – for instance putting horizontal emphasis on ICT [information and communication technology]. We have also put in place the 'Public Work Plus' scheme, whose aim is to provide the unemployed with temporary jobs in useful work that benefits local communities, both in rural and urban areas, so that they can re-use the skills they have not used for years, while being able to respond to future labour market opportunities.

In order to help fight unemployment and emigration among young people, we also have a 90-day guarantee rotating programme, meaning that they can stay outside employment, education or skill-enhancement programmes only for 90 days a year, after which the state will find them a job either in the private sector or the public sector, or possibly a further educational opportunity.

Mr Pat Breen, Minister, Ministry for Employment and Small Business, Ireland

The year 2008 affected us very much indeed when the banking sector and the property sector collapsed in Ireland. Wages in the public sector decreased by 14 per cent. But in Ireland as in other European countries, those inequalities that were there during the difficult times of the recession are there now as we recover. We also face a challenge from Brexit, which has put huge pressures on our small to medium-sized enterprises that mainly export to the EU and make up 97 per cent of workers in the private sector. There are also many women on the minimum wage, and we have sub-minimum rates for young people under 18.

To ensure that inequalities do not increase, we went through changes in legislation and employment conditions, and we have seen the greatest reforms in our employment and industrial relations laws. We have re-enacted joint labour committees and registered employment agreements as well. We have seen the reform of the law on employees' rights for collective bargaining. The recent establishment of the Low Pay Commission in relation to the minimum wage made it possible to take the minimum wage away from the government and make it more inclusive by bringing on board the unions, business partners and academics to decide on the best recommendations for the minimum wage. I am also going to ask them to examine in detail why so many people stay on the minimum wage all their life. We also tried to bring in a tripartite system again, and we brought a number of agreements, starting with the Croke Park Agreement (2010–14), the Haddington Road Agreement (June 2013) and the Lansdowne Road Agreement (May 2015). Those agreements have been very successful and they have achieved financial adjustments and promoted industrial peace as well. We saw a new forum established, the National Economic Dialogue, where we brought in all the social partners, including also research institutes and the academic community, to deal with the challenges – we recently discussed the Labour Employment Economic Forum, and Brexit and its challenges.

Ms Egle Radišauskiene, Deputy-Minister, Ministry of Social Security and Labour, Lithuania
I would like to bring to your attention the picture [on the cover of the book] because in Lithuania, when we look at the OECD [Organisation for Economic Co-operation and Development] data presenting Lithuania as the eighth [worst] country with regard to income inequality, we have exactly the feeling of walking [in such] big shoes with the awareness that we are still far away from . . . good leather shoes. So, what are the reasons?

I think the main challenge is to change wage policy and we have started to do it in the public sector (where the average wage is at about the same level as the minimum wage in Luxembourg and Ireland). We should also pay attention to low wages and the low minimum wage, which, although very low is received by about 20 per cent of all employees.

We also have a problem of domestic migration from rural to urban areas, with very different conditions between people employed for instance in our capital, Vilnius, and those in the regions. We also have a lot of measures in our government programme regarding taxation policy, changes in social security contributions, combined with social assistance policy. For those unemployed who are at the biggest risk of poverty, we are introducing quite a lot of active labour market measures, together with changing industrial relations.

The involvement and influence of the social partners are considerable through the tripartite council, and all the reform packages mentioned earlier went through the tripartite council and the Parliament. This shows that a new social model has been introduced in Lithuania and that we are willing to change.

Mr Claude Jeannerot, Ambassador, Delegate of the French Government at the Governing Body of the ILO, France
Although France is a very socially protective country, and its citizens are attached to this characteristic, social inequalities in France have increased in recent years.

First, certain groups within the workforce are marginalized. Young people are particularly affected by unemployment, but also the elderly. Second, there is a wage gap (of 28 per cent) between men and women in the private sector. Third, there is an increased duality in the labour market, with insiders – who receive a salary within an enterprise and have a stable and long-term contract, which also enables them to have access to training and education – and those who are unemployed or have short-term contracts, and who have real difficulties getting integrated within the labour market. According to the OECD, France is one of the countries in which making the transition from a temporary contract to a permanent one is most difficult. We are using two levers to tackle inequality: the fight against unemployment and the modernization of our institutions and social dialogue instruments. Among the concrete measures, I would like to give three succinct examples.

The first is the personal activity account, which is a type of savings account linked to the individual person and not to the company, which enables employees to receive training throughout their life. It also allows when the person retires, to take into account different forms of work he/she did including volunteer's activities.

The second measure is an exceptional commitment to training of most vulnerable to new forms of employment, such as in ICT and the energy sector, notably through the influence of social dialogue on training at regional level (unions and employers with representatives of regions and of the state).

The third measure is the youth guarantee, which aims at supporting young people between 16 and 20 years of age so that they can actively seek a job. Finally, the French government is also committed to provide a greater space for social dialogue; employees have been represented on the boards of companies so that representatives of five million people employed in very small enterprises have participated in regional consultative bodies.

Nuno Biscaya, Employers' representative CIP, Portugal
We have different models of industrial relations throughout Europe, but we can find common ground on the need to have these two types of social

dialogue, one which is bipartite towards collective bargaining – which can be at sectoral, national or company level – and tripartite social dialogue, which fosters social cohesion and social peace, and which I think is particularly important in times of crisis. We have also seen some erosion of social dialogue, with the crisis playing a role. Collective agreement coverage was reduced in many European countries; in Portugal, the annual renovation of collective agreements suffered a decrease. We also witness wage compression. This wage compression, however, is not due to collective agreement trends but rather the outcome of the restructuring process, with many enterprises also going bankrupt, leading to unemployment and of course social exclusion and poverty.

The minimum wage is also relevant. Here the first thing to consider is whether to have it or not, and when you have it, to consider whether to have it with criteria or without criteria. In my country, the government sets the minimum wage after consulting the social partners, but it does not have any criteria to fix it, so this can be a problem. Finally, another important trend, when talking about how labour relations can influence inequalities, is the digitalization of work, and we should really ask the question: will the instruments we have been using to monitor and manage the labour market – such as law, labour standards and collective agreements – be up to the task of doing that in the future?

Sławomir Adamczyk, NSZZ Solidarnosc, Poland
From the experts' contributions, we can clearly see at a glance the process of undermining traditional industrial relations schemes. Someone says that the UK is a very specific example, but at one time the British model was also more trade-union friendly, not 'perforated' as it is described here. I also remember that Ireland, a couple of years before the crisis, represented for the Polish social partners a kind of pattern example of how to build social peace through national tripartite agreements. As far as Spain is concerned, it cannot be repeated too often how destructive the Troika's intervention in the collective bargaining landscape has been. Many collective agreements disappeared and those that survived were often emptied of content. Slovenia was another country that represented the 'best pupil in the class' among the so-called new EU Member States, but now the erosion of sectoral negotiations, for sure, does not help in maintaining stable industrial relations.

I would like to draw your attention to three elements: (1) decentralization or even marginalization of collective bargaining; (2) the spontaneous increase in atypical labour contracts: precarious, sometimes external labour contracts, zero-hours contracts or micro-jobs; and (3) flexible arrangements. These trends put trade unions under pressure especially since they are not only a European but a worldwide phenomenon, with the same situation for instance in Australia and in New Zealand. We are also witnessing great uncertainty with regard to the future of the world of work, with a variety of factors: technological change, globalization, financialization, climate change and energy transition, which are also important because they affect sectors that were traditionally at the heart of the industrial relations systems. How can self-employed economically dependent people who voluntarily chose such forms of work be covered by collective bargaining? How can we guarantee social standards to crowd-workers and for those in subcontracted microdata operations working through online internet platforms?

Mr Chariton Kyriazis, Hellenic Federation of Enterprises (SEV)
Part of inequality can be explained by segmentation between, notably, the tradable sector – which exports goods and services and has to be internationally competitive to survive – and the non-tradable sector (composed of inward-looking activities including the largest part of state activities, not to mention banking and other services). If you somehow help the non-tradable sector, it tends to attract human capital, financial capital and resources, it takes the form of a bubble, which has to break down at some point because it is not sustainable. This has been the main reason for the crisis in Greece.

The tradable sector is Greece's economic growth champion, and this is reflected also in wages and incomes. To compete on the basis of high-value added goods, it needs not low-wage personnel but rather highly skilled and better-paid ones. So you have a dichotomy here, and inequality cuts across the statistics because this segmentation, and this sort of more 'constructive' inequality have not been researched yet.

This dichotomy is why we also believe that in Greece, at least temporarily, we need to have decentralized wage bargaining systems, because within the same internationally competitive sector, you have certain companies that are very much advanced and internationally competitive, exporting for example, to Germany, using specialist materials, and you have others that have lagged behind and are at the brink of closing down. The challenges and the problems in each sector are entirely different, and this escaped the discussion we are having on inequalities.

Josef Bugeja, GWU, Malta
In Malta, collective bargaining coverage is good, at around 60 per cent of all employees, and we have mainly collective agreements at organizational level, while social dialogue is carried out between civil society, government, employers and trade unions. Today, unemployment is at its lowest level in Malta, at around only 2800.

However, precarious employment must be tackled . . . the principle of equal pay for jobs of equal value must be widened to include multiple employers, and by lobbying – notably the European Union, [and] other nations – to have the Posted Workers Directive amended, so that local labour law applies to all local workers, even if they come from Poland or Bulgaria.

Re-employment and reintegration are also discussed in Malta with my colleagues' employers. And we agree that any policy should aim at helping people reintegrate in the labour market and at making work pay. Otherwise, it will be difficult to motivate someone to get a job when they do not receive enough wages or salaries to make ends meet.

Extension, at firm level, in Malta applies to everyone, trade union members and non-members; since the basis is equal pay for jobs of equal value. Where there is a collective agreement, disparities between wages have been eliminated, because we talk only about grades, scales and the value of work. If you take that out, then workers' rights and obligations change totally. Without such dialogue, without trade unions, there would be no level playing field, but a very disrupted playing field, which would definitely not lead to sound industrial relations.

Renate Hornung-Draus, BDA, Germany
I have three messages. The first on the notion of inequality, because I have a kind of implied trust in the discussion saying that inequality, per se, is bad – and more equality, per se, is good and I would simply like to introduce some nuance into this reflection.

I remember my own childhood in a socialist economy – where there was a strong accent on equality of treatment – and I remember that many doctors or teachers really complained about the fact that they earned only as much as a factory worker, and they perceived this as unfair because they had higher responsibility, they had spent much longer in education and so on. So the notion of fairness and core inequality is not just a one-way street.

The second point is that a lot depends on the institutional context, and I heard the argument being made that deregulation has led to more inequality. The German chapter mentions the Hartz reforms, but obviously those reforms were precisely aimed at allowing for a low-wage sector to emerge, because the issue in Germany at that time was ever-increasing long-term unemployment. So, opening up and deregulating certain things helped people back into the labour market but of course at the same time, it made wage inequality more visible.

My third point concerns the role of social dialogue in reducing inequalities. Multi-company collective agreements, at regional, sectoral or even national level are of course more efficient to limit inequalities than, for instance, completely decentralized company bargaining or no bargaining at all. But the coverage of collective agreements has decreased so that both employers and trade unions should focus on how to change it back to increase coverage. There is no point in saying that multi-company agreements are wonderful if the coverage goes down and down.

Another issue I would like to address, which is currently a black hole, is the entire digital economy. Both employers and trade unions have to demonstrate how added value could be found through social dialogue, including in sectors that today are very unorganized, where we have very low coverage or hardly any coverage at all.

Catelene Passchier, FNV, the Netherlands
The present experts' report shows that the past 15 years of developments have benefited capital more than labour; employers' prospects more than trade union ones. Moreover, the austerity programmes – with the support of the EU and the IMF [International Monetary Fund] – have focused on destroying some of the social fabric – as in Ireland, the Balkans, the Baltics, Spain and Greece. This has put trade unions in a critical situation. Some said that those countries will perform better if they decentralize collective bargaining, if they stop recognizing the importance of social partnership, if they compete with other countries on lower wages and that to have lower wages they need to destroy their previous systems of collective bargaining. But we did not believe them. Today, a lot of evidence says that we were right. It does not mean that all these systems were perfect, they probably needed to improve, but dismantling them has put us in a situation where we have to rebuild – although some things cannot come back, they have been destroyed for ever. Rebuild requires the support of governments and employers and the understanding that they will have to support social dialogue and even trade union membership.

One respect in which the Netherlands were ahead of any other country was recognizing that part-time work was on the rise. We regulated part-time work at a very early stage, introducing equal pay, equal coverage by social security and even a right to work part-time, so that we would not only see women working part-time but also men who wanted to reduce their working hours. That was at the beginning of the 1990s. It seems that we integrated the rise in the female workforce very well. But, of course we have experienced a part-timeization of our economy, and at some stage that led also to flexiblization and precarization. The question now for the Netherlands, is whether we can solve this problem by social partnership. In 2012–13, there was extreme political instability and the employers were very worried. That was an important moment, because they decided we needed a negotiated solution . . . we came to an agreement, the social pact of 2013.

We also see better outcomes when we have multi-employer and sectoral agreements. At the same time, we need the government – but also the EU – to ensure a balance of power and to make sure that there will be social dialogue and social agreements to move forward in certain areas, such as digitalization and the platform economy, which we will need to regulate. If we do not, it will blow up in our faces.

* * *

The answers reproduced above bear witness to the richness of contributions, but also confirm the complexity of inequality issues.

Similar root causes behind inequalities have been reported in numerous European countries, such as the growing category of workers who remain confined to low-paid jobs and also to less optimal forms of labour contract, or have lower access to social security and pensions. This clearly requires extended protection, collective bargaining and labour rights. On the other hand, the contributions presented above also highlight that unemployment remains a major form of exclusion and source of inequality so that incentives are required to maximize the level of employment. At the same time, globalization is also bringing new phenomena, such as the influx of migrant labour, the emergence of outsourced jobs and subcontracting, along with the development of global supply chains. Digitalization and automation, which will cause some jobs to disappear but others to appear, are bringing new opportunities but also potential new sources of inequality.

It is in this complex context that high-level government representatives and social partners have shared their policy solutions to the problem of inequalities, which we hope will incentivize other policy-makers to find the right mix of policy options. Among the solutions, collective bargaining and social dialogue emerged as important levers to stimulate employment and production, while limiting the growth of inequalities. They provide a level playing field for all workers, while also making it possible to negotiate more flexibility and security in accordance with national, sectoral or local circumstances, something that is confirmed by concrete best practices presented in this volume. They also represent precious tools for addressing current and future trends in the world of work. We hope that the present volume can help all those concerned to provide appropriate and original responses to the growth of inequality and to stop its root causes in a permanently evolving world of work.

Heinz Koller
Assistant Director-General,
Regional Director for Europe and Central Asia, ILO

NOTES

1. It allows a collective agreement when signed to cover all employees within its territorial and industry scope.
2. It ensures that when there are multiple collective agreements, for instance at firm and sectoral level, the most favourable applies.

1. Curbing inequalities in Europe: The impact of industrial relations and labour policies

Daniel Vaughan-Whitehead and Rosalia Vazquez-Alvarez

1. INTRODUCTION

A key focus of international debate in recent times has been increased income inequalities and their adverse effects both socially and economically. According to the Organisation for Economic Co-operation and Development (OECD, 2015) income inequality is at its highest level for the past half-century and for the International Monetary Fund (IMF, 2015) growing inequalities hamper economic growth. The reduction of inequalities was recently asserted by the international community (2030 Agenda for Sustainable Development; United Nations General Assembly, 2015) and European organisations as an important policy target. It has also been highlighted that the sources of growing inequality emerge from mechanisms in the world of work (ILO, 2014, 2016; Berg, 2015; EC, 2015a; OECD, 2015). The purpose of this volume is to address the question of income inequalities from its root causes, by highlighting that inequalities may be generated from different labour market and industrial relations systems.

Particular attention is thus paid in this volume to how industrial relations – the various interactions that employers, worker representatives and the state may have on a number of issues – and, in particular, collective bargaining (bilateral negotiations between employer and worker representatives, which the European Commission (EC) calls 'autonomous social dialogue' (Andor, 2012: 3; see also EC, 2015b)) and tripartite social dialogue (dialogue and perhaps negotiations between the three sides) may contribute to limiting or even reducing different possible forms of inequality. We also highlight how this relationship may have changed over time. All European countries have put in place a number of labour market reforms that have led to the emergence of new forms of employment contracts and relations that have affected working conditions. Collective bargaining coverage, mechanisms and contents have been progressively transformed together with the changes in the labour market, legal and policy reforms and the evolving economic and social context. The roles of actors – in particular workers' and employers' representatives – have been challenged and transformed.

This volume presents research to further explore the link between social dialogue indicators (collective bargaining coverage, trade union density, collective agreements, tripartite consultations and so on), social dialogue mechanisms (extension mechanisms, renewal of collective agreements and so on) and indicators of inequalities in the world of work.

The key aim is to identify elements of a response to a number of questions: which countries have succeeded in carrying out the necessary reforms (for instance, in the labour market) without generating further inequalities? What type of industrial relations systems seem to perform better in this respect? What type of policy measures, institutions and actors play a determinant role, in particular the social partners and social dialogue to achieve more balanced outcomes? How far could social dialogue help to address the future transformations of the world of work while limiting inequalities?

The scope of this volume goes beyond pay inequalities to address also other types of inequality, such as inequality in the distribution (and perhaps payment) of working time; access or re-access to jobs; access to training and career opportunities; and access to social protection or to pensions. It also looks at inequalities that may affect particular groups of workers, such as women or young people, or those under certain types of work arrangements, such as part-time workers, temporary workers and the self-employed.

This introductory chapter presents some major lessons from the national studies and their contributions to the existing research on the link between industrial relations and inequalities. Countries have been selected to ensure geographical balance and according to their different models of industrial relations as well as differentiated trends in both industrial relations and inequalities. The experts followed a common framework and were tasked with presenting national industrial relations systems and how these systems have addressed inequalities over time, before systematically identifying their possible effects on various inequalities that may be developing in their respective countries. The experts have used databases whenever possible and have also carried out qualitative research and case studies to illustrate their national stories.

The second aim of this introduction is to review some concrete outcomes of collective bargaining at national, sectoral and firm level that may have helped to reduce inequalities. For this purpose we extend the number of countries (beyond those covered by national chapters) in order to provide the most extensive overview of such outcomes.

Third, we complement the national stories with a comparative statistical analysis from the European Structure of Earnings Survey (SES, Eurostat) to more accurately identify specific effects of collective pay agreements on pay inequality, working time distribution and work contracts.

Finally, this leads us to a number of policy considerations, which are presented briefly in the closing section and further developed in the national chapters.

2. SOME LESSONS FROM THE NATIONAL STUDIES

2.1 Overview of Recent Studies on the Role of Industrial Relations on Inequalities

Before turning to the contents of collective bargaining presented in this volume, we briefly summarise some of the research on the role of industrial relations in inequalities from various perspectives.

The research has focused mainly on testing the effects on wage inequalities of the presence of collective agreements. These studies generally test the impact of collective agreements on intra-firm wage inequality, as generally measured by the Gini index or other indexes of inequality (P90/P10 for the differences between the top and bottom deciles or P90/P50 and P50/P10 to check disparities in the first or second half of the distribution). This is what is proposed, for instance, in the Spanish chapter and in section 4 below.[1]

A number of studies also test how the level at which collective agreements are signed may influence the same indicators of inequality. The literature on the subject suggests that firms with enterprise-level collective agreements have lower wage increases and also higher wage inequality compared with firms with collective agreements at regional or sectoral level.[2] A number of studies also show that centralised bargaining arrangements are associated with lower wage inequality (for a review see Hayter, 2011: 141–52; 2015). For instance, Blau and Kahn (1996) found lower wage dispersion being associated with a higher level of centralisation. Canal Domínguez and Rodriguez Gutiérrez (2016) also found that firm-level collective bargaining led to more wage dispersion compared with a higher level of bargaining.

The role of extension mechanisms has also been analysed. Blau and Kahn (1996) found that extension mechanisms played a significant role in compressing the wage structure. For the period from 1970 to 1990, countries such as Germany, Italy and the Netherlands, which were practising the extension of collective agreements, could limit the growth of wage inequality.

Bargaining coverage is another indicator that was found to influence wage inequality: for instance, Visser (2015) finds a strong negative association between collective bargaining coverage and wage inequality measured by the P1/P10 earnings ratio, and concludes through a study on 32 OECD member states, that coverage would account for 50 per cent of the variance in wage inequality.

Other researchers examined the impact of coordination between different levels of collective bargaining on pay inequality. The evidence is rather convergent and points to a positive correlation.[3] According to the OECD, 'overall earnings dispersion tends to fall as union density and bargaining coverage and centralisation/coordination increase' (OECD 2004: 166). The evidence confirms that more centralised and more coordinated wage bargaining has a negative relationship with the level of wage inequality.[4]

A number of studies have also shown some effect of collective bargaining on gender wage inequality. Blau and Kahn (2003) found a significant effect of collective bargaining coverage and the gender pay gap examining 22 countries from 1985 to 1994 (see also Blau and Kahn, 1992; Rubery et al., 1994, 2005; Rubery, 2015). Negative effects on the gender pay gap were also identified along collective bargaining curtailing and public sector adjustments within austerity measures (Karamessini and Rubery, 2015). Firm-level agreements compared with higher level agreements have also shown to be associated with a higher gender wage gap (De la Rica and González, 2007).

A number of researchers have also demonstrated the relationship that might exist between collective bargaining, on the one hand, and low paid workers, on the other (Gautié and Schmitt, 2010; Salverda and Mayhew, 2009).

The different national chapters in this volume measure the above effects through both quantitative and qualitative analyses. Some of the major findings are summarised below.

2.2 A Possible Role on Low Pay

The first lesson from this comparative volume – which is in line with the literature on this aspect – concerns the bottom of the wage scale. The erosion of collective bargaining in a number of countries has coincided with the increase in the low-pay segment (composed of those workers paid below two-thirds of the median wage), often stimulated by labour market reforms not always adopted with the involvement of social partners, and sometimes adopted despite opposition by the social partners. Income inequality increased rapidly in Germany once the wage-setting system was eroded after the Hartz reforms. The development of so-called 'mini-jobs' outside the scope of collective bargaining contributed to increasing the incidence of low pay in Germany to the highest level in the European Union (EU) and, since there was formerly no minimum wage (until 2015) to put a floor under pay levels, wages plunged to a greater extent than in any other EU member state.

A similar process has also been witnessed in the Netherlands, where the number of low paid and their distance from the average income have increased. This was owing to government pressure since the mid-1990s on unions and employers to lower existing wage scales in collective agreements or to introduce new scales much closer to the minimum wage[5] as a means of enabling the employment integration of worker categories with a weak labour market position.

Also noted in a number of European countries covered in this volume is the increased proportion of part-time jobs – including those with a very low number of working hours – among the low paid, something that may also be explained by weak collective bargaining coverage for this category of workers (and which some collective agreements presented in section 3 and Tables 1.2 and 1.3 will try to address).

Conversely, in Sweden, a centralised and coordinated collective bargaining system and a still compressed wage structure have prevented the development of low-paid/low-skilled jobs, but instead have boosted policies favouring an upgrading of skills and have led to the lowest wage dispersion among OECD countries (followed by Finland and Denmark). Similarly, multi-level bargaining, and extension mechanisms, gave Belgium the lowest share of low-paid workers and made it among the top three best performers on wage equality (see Chapter 3 on Belgium).

2.3 Minimum Wage Acting as the Wage Floor of Collective Bargaining

A second lesson from the country stories in this volume is that the minimum wage – which is the result of social dialogue in most EU countries – clearly contributes to limiting wage inequality (since it makes it possible to increase starting wages at the end of the wage scale thus reducing the pay difference with the top), but only if combined with collective bargaining (that brings with it additional negotiation levels to build more floors).

The minimum wage in the United Kingdom, for instance, has contributed to limiting the rise in low pay, but this is not enough considering that there are no additional bargaining rounds. Moreover the proliferation of various types of work contracts with different wage levels and working conditions has increased inequality. By contrast, the minimum wage in Ireland has helped to reduce inequalities because it has intervened within the framework of a stronger social dialogue framework (at national level) that has limited fragmentation in terms of work contracts and pay conditions.

The case of the Baltic States also shows that progressive adjustment and increases of the minimum wage decided by the social partners have helped to raise wages at the bottom, but have not led to much spillover effect in the absence of collective bargaining. This might explain why trade unions have not had much effect on wage inequalities. The wage premium owing to trade unions' presence is reduced from 7.6 per cent to less than 2 per cent when other variables, such as skills, location and other features, are taken into account. Belgium offers a contrasting example, with low pay scales in some industries that can be, thanks to additional sectoral collective bargaining, 20 to 30 per cent higher than the nationwide minimum. The chapter on Belgium also shows how higher minimum wages help to reduce the lower-tail and overall wage dispersion.

The minimum wage introduced in January 2015 in Germany has also made it possible to address the difficulties in concluding collective agreements in a number of sectors and regions, and has acted as a floor to further promote collective bargaining. It is revealing that the Minimum Wage Act was part of a legislative package entitled the Act on the Strengthening of Free Collective Bargaining (Gesetz zur Stärkung der Tarifautonomie) which, besides introducing the minimum wage, is also intended to expand collective agreement coverage. In fact, derogations from the minimum wage are possible through collective agreements that are declared generally binding.

Conversely, an active collective bargaining process in a context of overall moderation of the minimum wage, as has happened in the Netherlands for the past two decades, can increase rather than decrease wage inequalities.

2.4 Role of Multi-level Collective Bargaining in Wage Disparity

Taking the minimum wage as the wage floor makes it possible, first, to avoid too low wages, while building collective bargaining on it allows wage evolution in terms of a consistent and negotiated wage grid that prevents too high wage differentials. This consistency is strengthened by multi-level bargaining, with wage bargaining at national and/or sectoral level, complemented by wage bargaining at firm level. This effect on wage compression is the third lesson from the different chapters of this volume.

The Spanish system of collective agreements, for instance, based on higher than firm level bargaining, until the crisis had a compressing effect on wage dispersion, contributing to lower levels of wage inequality. Similarly in Sweden, collectively agreed high wage floors, combined with wage agreements at sectoral and enterprise level, have favoured a relatively compressed wage structure which has prevailed, despite decentralisation of wage fixing in recent years which has brought more wage differentiation. This more balanced outcome in terms of inequality is not limited to wage structure but also concerns working and employment conditions (see Chapter 12 on Sweden).

Collective bargaining only at firm level, without some common framework negotiated at higher levels, may lead to fairly diversified wage outcomes and thus to higher inter-firm and sometimes also inter-sectoral disparities, even if it might reduce within-firm inequality.

Moreover, as observed for instance in the Netherlands, wage agreements at firm level seem to have brought a number of additional bonuses on top of the basic wage, which are particularly important for higher-ranking employees, thus increasing inequalities over time, even if part of that rise cannot be attributed to collective negotiations but, rather, to enterprise wage policies. In the Netherlands, collective agreements have seen their grip on wage formation as a whole diminish, so that wages have not followed the pace of productivity growth. Nonetheless, the structure of wage scales that they impose continues to limit the growth of within-firm inequalities. Belgium is a good example where multi-level bargaining starts with inter-professional agreements followed by negotiations in joint committees or subcommittees in individual sectors that then lead to firm-level agreements, a process that led to 90 per cent collective bargaining coverage and which placed Belgium as one of the very few countries where wage disparity did not increase.

While multi-level bargaining – especially within a coordinated system – would help in reducing wage disparity, this might change if the hierarchy between the different levels is modified. In particular, the fact that there are increasingly more derogations or deviation clauses that allow deviation from general rules – as witnessed recently in Spain, but also in Italy, the Netherlands and others – means that the coordination effect might be disrupted in terms of effects on, for instance, wage disparities (Visser, 2016).

2.5 Promoting More Equal Conditions for Groups Less Covered by Collective Bargaining

By its effect of boosting wages at the bottom end of the wage scale, collective bargaining is helping those categories of workers who are generally under-represented there, such as women, but also other categories of workers, such as migrants. National and sectoral agreements in particular make it possible to extend standards to employees with weaker bargaining power, particularly those working in small firms.

This is another lesson from this volume that confirms previous studies mentioned earlier, on the effect of collective bargaining on gender wage inequality. According to the statistical analysis presented in the Spanish chapter, firms with more women not only have lower wages, but also higher wage inequality; a similar process is observed in firms with a high proportion of temporary and part-time jobs. Firm-level agreements (without upper-level bargaining) are also found to be associated with higher wage disparity and a wider gender pay gap. Collective agreements – especially at higher levels – by fixing the same rules for all, represent a way of avoiding discrimination (Pillinger, 2016).

Chapter 2, on the Baltics, confirms that collective agreements have had an impact at the bottom of the scale, and an identified effect on the gender pay gap. Chapter 7, on Ireland, shows that wage inequality fell for Irish men between 1994 and 2001, and for women between 1997 and 2001, the latter in particular being partly attributed to the introduction of the minimum wage in 2000 within a social dialogue framework, as noted earlier (see also McGuinness et al., 2009).

Problems of youth inequality are also presented in this volume. In the Netherlands, enterprises have developed student low-pay schemes that somehow escape from the influence of collective bargaining. Similarly in Slovenia companies in the retail trade, especially supermarkets, have built their business model on the use of young workers at very low levels of pay and with minimum working hours and little use of social dialogue. In Spain, firms with a higher percentage of young employees (under 30 years of age) that were also found to rarely have a collective agreement have experienced more wage inequality.

In Italy, the crisis seems to have led to a substantial worsening of the quality of existing jobs, pay levels and inequalities across socio-economic groups, which has mainly affected young people and low-skilled workers. These are found to have not only the lowest performance in terms of employment and unemployment rates, but also the worst outcomes with respect to job quality, with lower earnings and considerably higher labour market insecurity and higher job strain. They are often confined on temporary contracts and are less covered by collective bargaining. The interest of young workers in trade unions and social dialogue is also very limited.

Collective bargaining can thus also help cover vulnerable groups. For instance, a multi-employer agreement at sectoral or national level can cover more workers since it can be extended to all employers, including those outside the employers' organisations that negotiated the agreement.

Moreover, if they know that an agreement may be extended and become binding, both employers' associations and trade unions will be more engaged in discussions. By contrast, single-employer bargaining at enterprise level may often cover only a limited number of workers, and some groups of workers – for instance, those on non-standard contracts – may not be included. In this sense, multi-employer bargaining is more inclusive and helps to limit inequalities between categories of workers.

The econometric exercise presented in the chapter on Spain shows that firms with a higher proportion of employees with temporary contracts also have higher wage inequality, which indicates that there should be more collective bargaining to cover this type of employee.

2.6 Redistributing Working Time More Equally

By fixing a set of standards, collective agreements might also help to improve equality of working time, in terms of number of working hours, access to overtime and payment of working hours. This is another conclusion of this series of national chapters.

Massive use of zero-hours contracts in the United Kingdom shows how intimately working hours may be related to low pay. Insufficient working hours for part-time workers might also represent a source of inequality, as shown in the Netherlands and other countries. We see in section 3 how collective agreements may address and help to better regulate this area. We also test from our comparative database, in section 4, whether collective agreements do help promote a better redistribution of working hours among all employees.

2.7 Contributing to Lower Inequality in Disposable Household Income

The correlation between industrial relations and inequality in terms of disposable household income has not been studied much. Household income is influenced by wages from individual earners in the household – in which collective bargaining plays a role. Wage inequality was found to explain a very important part of incomes inequality (Visser, 2015).

Disposable household income is also very much influenced by tax policy and social security. The social partners in a number of EU countries – for instance in France and Belgium – also manage social protection, a role that they may further increase along with the progressive withdrawal of the state in a number of countries from its function of providing social security and benefits, particularly pensions. The social partners through their participation in tripartite councils can also influence the distribution process. Social dialogue and industrial relations can thus play a role in disposable household income through different levers, directly through collective bargaining that influences wages or indirectly through their influence on major reforms currently ongoing in many countries, for example, with regard to the labour market, social security, pensions and taxes. This aspect is further investigated in some chapters in this volume.

2.8 The Important Role of the State

From the evidence provided in this volume, another lesson is that the role of the state has generally remained very important. First to set the rules and also promote collective bargaining and social dialogue (for instance, to sign or renew tripartite pacts or agreements) and, second, because the state often decides to develop mechanisms in order to extend some agreements, also to cover workers not initially included in the bargaining agreement. This was the case in countries with inter-sectoral (Belgium and Ireland) and sectoral wage bargaining (Austria, France, Germany, Spain and parts of Belgium), a process that made it possible to maintain high collective bargaining coverage in a number of countries. In other cases, the government also played a major role in developing some mechanisms, such as wage indexation (in Italy in the 1980s, in Greece in the early 1980s and in Belgium until now). The state also remains the initiator of most labour market reforms, but also social protection, pensions and training reforms. In France, even if social dialogue has accompanied flexibility at least to a certain extent, the initiative for reforms came almost entirely from the state. A good example of coordination with the social partners is given by Sweden, where following the agreements during the crisis and follow-up tripartite talks initiated by the government in 2011, a new law was decided on short-time working in December 2013 that subsidises the short-time working system in case of a severe economic recession while further encouraging collective bargaining.

Social dialogue at national level also cannot be maintained without strong support from the state, to keep it alive, to foster it, and also to use it when major reforms must be decided and implemented. The examples of Ireland and Greece here confirm that, however strong tripartite bodies might be, they will lose influence if the state is not directly supporting them. The nature and format of institutions certainly counts but they may be influenced by the evolving power and willingness of the actors, and by the wider political, economic and social context. Just as public policies can support the role that collective bargaining institutions play in wage policy, discontinuous changes in public policies can erode collective wage setting (Hayter and Weinberg, 2011; Eurofound, 2014; Keune, 2015).

As shown in Chapter 6 on Greece, the decision to remove extension mechanisms, the suspension of the 'favourability clause' (given the prevalence of higher level agreements), the greater difficulties introduced for the renewal of collective agreements, combined with the unilateral decision to cut the minimum wage (traditionally established bilaterally by the social partners) clearly resulted in a rapid reduction in the number and coverage of collective agreements. The number of sectoral or occupational agreements fell from 101 in 2009 to 23 in 2015, while collective bargaining coverage was reduced from 83 per cent in 2008 to 40 per cent in 2013 (a mere 10 per cent in the private sector). This had negative effects on middle-income earners in 2008–10, while the minimum wage reforms also hurt those at the bottom, with increased wage inequality from 2012. The state can also influence inequalities through its policy in the public sector. A number of chapters in this volume also show that the employment and wage cuts, but also the shift towards more fixed-term, less secure contracts in the public sector have led to a radical transformation, making public sector employees in general more vulnerable.

The role of the state is also crucial in ensuring that the mechanisms continue to work, as in Sweden where the state is a major player in promoting training mechanisms that support strong external flexibility, combined with rapid re-employability of workers who have been dismissed. Similarly, it can intervene to set a framework on emerging issues. As an example, in Spain a bill was proposed in September 2016 aimed at guaranteeing equal working conditions for employees working in subcontracted firms in respect of the employees of the subcontracting firm. This is likely to encourage collective bargaining to discuss further the modalities of this, in the sectoral or enterprise context.

The important role of the state explains why we decided in this volume to extend the impact on inequalities beyond just collective bargaining and social dialogue to cover industrial relations more generally, also involving the state and not only workers' and employers' representatives.

3. SOCIAL DIALOGUE OUTCOMES ON INEQUALITY: EXAMPLES OF COLLECTIVE AGREEMENTS

This section – and the various chapters in this volume – presents a series of concrete outcomes of social dialogue at national level, but also of collective bargaining at the lower level of the sector, region or enterprise that has managed to reconcile flexibility and security. In Tables 1.2 and 1.3, later in this section, we have complemented the work of the experts with examples of collective agreements in other EU countries that generally confirm the trends described by the experts for their countries.

This picture allows us to see the trends in terms of collective bargaining on emerging issues in the world of work, and to highlight that the effects of social dialogue and collective bargaining on inequality might derive from this capacity of bargaining to reach agreements that reflect the interests of both employers and workers.

Examples of collective agreements show that flexibility with security can be reached in very different ways. An outcome can be reached in the same area or same policy reform with various elements bringing some flexibility and others ensuring some security; this was the case, for instance, in the national agreement on the labour market reforms in the Netherlands, which improved the contractual position of temporary workers on the security side in exchange for shortened dismissal procedures on the flexibility side.

An agreement on flexibility and security can also be struck in a more general framework – generally negotiated at national or sectoral level – where some elements of flexibility introduced in one area, for instance, wages, can be compensated with some elements strengthening workers' security in another area, for instance, better coverage of temporary workers with regard to employment.

Finally, an agreement can be promoted in a more general model where some flexibility can be introduced within companies (for instance, to make dismissals easier), but in exchange for security outside companies, as represented by the Swedish case where more external flexibility with fewer obstacles to dismissal has been accepted in exchange for more security for workers to receive the necessary training to find another job after dismissal.

3.1 Seeking Balanced Outcomes through National Consultations on Major Reforms . . .

The various chapters of this book – for instance, on Greece, Italy and France – converge in describing how adversarial relations between employers and the workers in the 1970s and 1980s were converted into more consensual industrial relations in recent decades with, as a consequence, a clear reduction in social conflicts and days lost owing to strikes. This has also corresponded to the development of tripartite consultations and negotiations and the emergence of social dialogue at national level, with also a number of tripartite pacts (Freyssinet, 2010). All studies suggest that pacts have had the effect of moderating wages, as these pay outcomes grew less than in countries without a pact.

Similarly in Belgium, social partners negotiate upper limits of wage growth – as a way to balance the automatic indexing of wages – on the basis of the weighted average of pay developments in neighbouring countries, namely, Germany, France and the Netherlands. Social partners then discuss in joint committees in each sector within those boundaries.

Ireland is also a good example, where a high level of tripartite partnership for years made it possible to limit wage inequalities by providing a frame of wage progression in line with competitiveness, while the minimum wage, also introduced in 2000 after considerable social dialogue, made it possible to establish a floor to avoid an increase in the low-pay segment. These wage guidelines were then implemented by more sectoral and enterprise-type collective agreements, even if those levels remained less developed than in other EU countries. The collapse of that social partnership, as stated in the Irish chapter, led to conditions being decided unilaterally by the employers, a process that led to wages and working conditions less favourable for the workers.

In Germany, there have never been national collective agreements as in most other EU countries. Nevertheless, there have been a few agreements, for example, to establish a productivity-based wage policy through so-called 'concerted action' (*Konzertierte Aktion*) in 1967–77, or the Schröder government's 'Alliance for Work' (*Bündnis für Arbeit*) in 1998–2003 and the regular national agreements on vocational training for young people. There can be some informal agreements, such as that between the government and the collective bargaining partners during the financial crisis in order to avoid redundancies (see Chapter 5 on Germany).

In the Netherlands, the Wassenaar Agreement of the early 1980s (Hemerijck et al., 2000) was a long-term agreement between unions and employers to restrain wage growth in order to achieve low unemployment rates and inflation. National bodies – mainly the bipartite Labour Foundation (StvdA) and tripartite Social and Economic Council (SER) – and pacts advise the industry-level (and company-level) unions and employers, who are the parties legally permitted to take measures on wages and other aspects of employment in their collective agreements, and on occupational pensions.

Beyond the conclusion of pacts, social partners are often involved in a number of policy-making areas. In Sweden, the industrial relations system plays a fundamental role in regulating the labour market and shaping the development of employment, wage structures and vocational training, but also social protection systems, such as pensions (complementary pension) and unemployment benefits. In France and Belgium (where they are part of governing boards of institutes or agencies in those fields), the social partners are heavily involved in the management of social security, especially public health insurance and unemployment benefits, and participate in the design and delivery of vocational training. Furthermore, the 2007 Act on Modernisation of Social Dialogue makes it compulsory for the French government to consult national trade unions and employers' organisations when proposing reforms of industrial relations, employment and vocational training.

In Ireland, one agreed programme, 'Towards 2016', set out a framework within which the key social challenges facing individuals at each stage of life are tackled, focusing on the needs of children, young adults, people of working age, older people and people with disabilities, and proposing government actions across policy domains ranging from health and education to transport, housing, regional and rural development, tourism, energy, enterprise and sustainability. In this respect, social partnership might be seen as 'settling the distributional questions' (Chapter 7, s. 3, in this volume).

In those countries in which such levels and forms of dialogue are the most developed, more balanced reforms could generally be achieved that have also contributed to limiting the growth of inequalities.

In France, although the state maintains a strong role, several important reforms have been carried out on the basis of social bargaining and national agreements that were then transposed into law. In recent years, there has been an increased participation of social partners in labour market reforms, especially in the recent crisis, with agreements that provide more labour security for workers in exchange for increased labour market flexibility: in 2008 agreement was reached on the possibility for workers to keep their health and training entitlements in case of layoffs (in exchange for the possibility to agree on the termination of indefinite contracts); in 2013 on setting minimum working hours for part-time employees (in exchange for eventual layoffs and wage cuts in case of economic difficulties); and in 2015 on individual training accounts to improve lifelong learning (in exchange for a reduction of employers' vocational training contributions). The recent Act on 'Rules relating to labour, social dialogue modernisation and secure occupational trajectories' (July 2016) was also intended to develop this negotiation process by reforming social dialogue, but the bill was passed without sufficient social dialogue and thus led to strikes and public demonstrations.

In Slovenia, the strength of industrial relations (with tripartite mechanisms through the tripartite Economic and Social Council, minimum wages, collective bargaining at different levels and strong trade unions and employers' organisations) made it possible early in the transition to follow a type of restrained negotiated incomes policy that allowed some wage moderation in exchange for more trade union involvement in reforms, such as on social protection and pensions. The progressive erosion of the bargaining power of trade unions, which coincided with the growth of non-standard employment somehow changed that balance and progressively led both employers and the government to use social dialogue less, something that was further accelerated by the economic crisis. The weaker involvement of the tripartite council in many cases ended in imbalanced outcomes in favour of flexibility and that often led to strikes to reject them (see Chapter 10 on Slovenia).

For example, the introduction of a new law on mini-jobs without social dialogue in Slovenia led to a reform that gave priority to flexibility without security measures. However, the minimum wage increase in 2013 did not incorporate major employers' demands either.

With the crisis, many other governments implemented interventions hurriedly and often without proper consultation with the social partners.

These conflicts in a number of countries also led in some cases to the fall of the government, thus leading to political instability as well.

In Spain, although there is a tradition of national tripartite social dialogue with the conclusion of national pacts or national agreements, in 2010 the reform of collective agreements was decided without effective consultation and agreement with the social partners. This led, for instance, to the decision that when a collective agreement expires, its conditions will only be applicable for one year. The lack of social dialogue in labour market reforms also led to 'imbalanced' reforms in favour of flexibility and to the detriment of security. For instance, the first of the labour reforms eased the terms on which firms can modify working conditions (Article 41 of the Labour Code), an option that is widely used by firms to change working conditions, further strengthened by the possibility of having a derogation from upper-level collective agreements at company level.

In this context, flexibility might have gone too far – as documented in this volume – without compensating security, for instance, with the rapid growth of self-employed who receive very low income and lack social protection, as in the Netherlands, Slovenia and many other signatory countries.

At the same time, social dialogue at national level has brought some innovative outcomes (see Table 1.1), for instance, introducing some security to the trend towards more flexibility in the use of temporary contracts. In France, for instance, tripartite dialogue has led to better coverage of fixed-term workers through a decrease in the minimum number of months to obtain entitlement (four months since 2008) and the recent creation of cumulative rights (*droits rechargeables*) in 2015.

Table 1.1 Examples of innovative agreements at national level, selected EU countries

Items/country	Wages and working conditions	Working time	Employment	Training	Gender equality/ NSFE equality	Private social protection	Social dialogue
Belgium	2009–10 inter-professional agreement on tackling the crisis, including premiums (above indexation) of 125 euros in 2009 and 250 euros in 2010, without increasing costs for employers; higher benefit for temporarily unemployed; employers' new social tax reductions to recruit long-term unemployed	2016 cross-sectoral agreement on working time (No. 35), on temporary agency work (No. 36), and on Leave for compelling reasons (N0. 45)			2008 agreement for gender neutrality in job-grading systems		
Croatia	Dec. 2016 agreement on basic salary increase for civil servants and public employees (by 2% in 2017)						
Estonia	Dec. 2016, agreement on minimum wage for cultural workers with higher education						

Finland	Oct. 2011–13 Framework agreement (covering 94% of workers) to ensure competitiveness and employment, which offers a pay increase of 4.3% over the period Aug. 2013 Employment and growth agreement (covering 90% of workers) provided for modest wage increase over a two-year period and also covered non-pay issues, such as changes in social insurance contributions and unemployment benefit rules	Feb. 2016 Competitiveness Pact stipulated an increase in annual working time of 24 hours, wage freeze for 2017, and holiday bonuses of public sector employees would be temporarily reduced. It also provides for job creation measures					
France		2008 and 2009 inter-sectoral agreements about short-time working and some reintegration schemes for workers 2013 agreement on health setting minimum working hours for part-time	2008 agreement on agreed termination of indefinite contracts 2013 agreement on eventual layoffs and wage cuts in case of economic difficulties	2015 agreement on training individual accounts to improve lifelong learning 2015 reduction of employers' vocational training contributions		2008 agreement with the possibility for workers to keep their health and training entitlements in case of layoffs	Social partners approve Workplace health plan for 2016–20

Table 1.1 (continued)

Items/country	Wages and working conditions	Working time	Employment	Training	Gender equality/ NSFE equality	Private social protection	Social dialogue
Germany	Productivity-based wages (*Konzertierte Aktion* in 1967–77) *Dec. 2016 agreement in* Railway and Transport on innovative one-off payment of €550 between October 2016 and March 2017	Agreement to avoid redundancies through reduced working time during the financial crisis Dec. 2016 agreement in Railways for every employee to choose between a pay rise, working one hour less per week or an additional six days of holiday	'Alliance for Work' (*Bündnis für Arbeit*) in 1998–2003	Vocational training for young people	In 2014, standards governing the working and employ-ment conditions of all agency workers		
Greece		National General Collective Labour Agreement (EGSSE) signed by social partners for 2016 on inclusive labour					

		markets and unemployment, on the refugee immigration problem (but not on minimum wage)		
Ireland	2011 IBEC–ICTU national protocol for orderly industrial relations and local bargaining in the private (unionised) sector, renewed for 2012 and 2013		2013–16 (the Lansdowne Road agreement in the public sector to limit (restore) employment and wage cuts)	
Lithuania	2009 national agreement provided for measures to combat the recession, including cuts in public administration expenditure and an obligation not to reduce basic salaries of civil servants			
Luxembourg	2016–19 new wage agreement in the public sector on wage increase of 1.5%	2016–19 new agreement in public sector for more flexible part-time work arrangements. Possibility to reduce working		Feb. 2016 social partners' agreement for quality at school and training for teaching

Table 1.1 (continued)

Items/country	Wages and working conditions	Working time	Employment	Training	Gender equality/ NSFE equality	Private social protection	Social dialogue
		time by increments of 10% to between 90% and 40% of full working time					
Malta	Malta's tripartite national social dialogue institution, commissioned studies on low pay that recommended the minimum pay to be pegged to a ratio related to the basic average or median wage						
Portugal	2016 tripartite commitment on the minimum wage						2016 debate on the revitali-sation of collective bargaining

Spain	2013 agreement on labour conflicts, mediation and arbitrage	2014 agreement on (extending means tested) unemployment assistance	2008–10 fifth national collective agreement for temporary agency workers	2011 agreement on the reform of public system of pensions	2015–17 agreement on employment and collective bargaining
Slovenia	2017–19 wage agreement for wages in the central public sector	Social Agreement 2015–16 signed in Feb. 2015, after six years without a pact. The agreement covers 12 areas and enumerates 140 goals: finance, sustainable economic development, new investment cycles, public sector, etc. However, a dispute over the Minimum Wage Act led to the withdrawal of employers' support in Nov. 2015			In Dec. 2016, government and social partners signed new rules on the functioning of the main national body for social dialogue, the Economic and Social Council of Slovenia (ESSS)

Table 1.1 (continued)

Items/country	Wages and working conditions	Working time	Employment	Training	Gender equality/ NSFE equality	Private social protection	Social dialogue
Sweden			Number of framework agreements signed by various sectors in 2009/10 on temporary layoffs and short-time working schemes, in response to the crisis			From 2007, national agreement provided for three years (last one in 2016) an 'equality allowance' for low pay among women to be further negotiated at sectoral level	

3.2 . . . and through Innovative Collective Agreements

Collective bargaining at intermediary and firm level is used to complement national social dialogue and agreements in most EU member states, where two-thirds of workers are covered by some form of collective agreement (Van Gyes, 2012), with a general rule widespread in European countries that more decentralised agreements (for instance, at company level) must improve wages and working conditions agreed in higher agreements at sectoral and national levels. Over recent years, however, we have seen that a number of derogation clauses have been added to allow enterprise agreements to define their own standards by negotiation, even below higher negotiated standards, something that might distort the previous hierarchy and coordination of standards between levels.

3.2.1 At sectoral/regional level

Table 1.2 presents a sample of selected agreements in various countries to illustrate the rich process of collective bargaining at intermediate (sectoral/regional) level on a diversified range of topics. The issues discussed very often include inequality either to better extend coverage to groups of workers that were excluded or to negotiate some flexibility/security outcomes.

In the Netherlands the process is fairly extensive because collective agreements are the core instrument for unions and employers to influence labour market outcomes, and there is a possibility – at the prerogative of the Minister of Social Affairs and Employment – to declare industry-level collective agreements generally binding for non-organised employers and employees. It is interesting that in the crisis collective agreements were extended to workers in a number of sectors, such as contract cleaning, security services, waste disposal and personal care. Since these sectors have a large share of temporary agency workers and of migrant workers, this process could certainly help to level up working conditions and reduce the inequalities faced by these groups.

Trade unions and employers' organisations in Sweden are also structured along sectoral/industry lines, and the Swedish bargaining system remains fundamentally a two-tier system – which thus remains centralised and coordinated – where bargaining takes place first at the industry/sectoral level and afterwards at the company level. These collective agreements at the industry level, and even at the company level, are often extended and improve the statutory universal basic social protection in the form of higher replacement/compensation rates or a longer period of entitlement, for example, regarding unemployment and sickness benefits, parental and training leave and pensions (occupational pensions).

Similarly in Slovenia, the fact that sectoral collective agreements cover a relatively wide array of issues appears to be conducive to package deals that include several elements of flexibility and security.

The case studies in the metal and trade sectors (see Chapter 10 on Slovenia) show that collective bargaining can significantly adjust the combination of flexibility and security to sectoral circumstances. Moreover, the collective agreements in those two sectors have managed to put more emphasis on internal flexibility (and especially on working time and functional flexibility, but less on wage flexibility) rather than on external flexibility, which is often not good for workers' security, nor for factories, which generally prefer to maintain a motivated labour force and a good social climate in order to increase their prospects of growth. In the electrical industry, provisions for the elimination of wage supplements that were previously included in the minimum wage were inserted in the collective agreements until the legal redefinition of the minimum wage in 2015.

While the law of 2013 introduced some possible derogation at enterprise level from higher-level – mainly sectoral – agreements, it also enabled the unions to start negotiating various security provisions in other areas of the 'bargaining package', and in some cases to use them to bring reluctant employer organisations to the bargaining table.

In Germany, because of the trade union structure, the industry level has emerged as the dominant bargaining level. However, income inequality in Germany has increased dramatically owing to the erosion of its wage-setting system, which followed the inclusive model until the mid-1990s. This increase was particularly noticeable in those industries and companies in which workers were neither covered by a collective agreement nor represented by a works council. They therefore found themselves in wage negotiations without the protection of the two main institutions – free collective bargaining and codetermination – that constitute the German model of industrial relations.

At the same time, a number of issues have been developed at sectoral level. For instance from 2014, an agreement was reached in the metal industry between IG Metall and the employers to entitle employees to a training agreement with a maximum time horizon of seven years, during which they will be able to work part-time, or take leave, eventually going to study for a degree while saving up certain elements of their pay in a training account to cover the period of absence (see Table 1.2). This agreement seems to take into account the various phases of the life course and should be beneficial both for the employees, who can better manage work and their personal life, and for the companies, which can benefit from a more motivated and better trained labour force. In Austria, since 2013 a new, innovative element was introduced in collective bargaining – the so-called free time option. Two sectoral-level collective agreements concluded in

Table 1.2 Examples of innovative agreements at sectoral, regional and enterprise level, selected EU countries

Extension of sectoral/ firm collective agreement	Wages and working conditions	Working time	Employment	Training	Gender equality/ NSFE equality	Private social protection/ pensions
Austria	2016 agreement in the private health and social care, on pay increase, increase on standby rates, allowances for dirty, arduous or dangerous work	2013 free-time option agreements in electronics and mining and steel (to improve work–life balance and to reduce working hours instead of pay increases) 2016 agreement in the ceramic and stone industries on wages and also free-time option 2016 agreement in metal industry on new working time model	2015 agreement for service providers in data processing and data technology (on employment, working conditions and flexitime accounts)	2016 sectoral collective agreements on educational leave and/or time off for other further training purposes	2009 agreement for 'in-sourcing' self-employed couriers 2011 agreements on extending parental leave (16 months in stone and ceramics, 16 months in metal industry)	2015 agreement for emergency and medical workers on guaranteed six weeks' annual leave

Table 1.2 (continued)

Extension of sectoral/ firm collective agreement	Wages and working conditions	Working time	Employment	Training	Gender equality/ NSFE equality	Private social protection/ pensions
Belgium		Agreements on short-time working			Sectoral agreements also applied to agency workers Joint committees for gender neutrality, including on career breaks 2016 agreement for hairdressing and beauty care against gender discrimination 2016 charter for diversity in banking sector	
Denmark	Agreements in manufacturing and banks on possibility to pay profit-related pay	2014–17 agreement in manufacturing to open 'free choice' accounts for	Series of agreements for the building of the Metro and the Greater Copenhagen	2016 agreement in postal sector on breaks, paid leave but also on a skill development	2014–17 agreement for commercial and clerical workers on maternity protection for	2014–17 company agreements such as at Danske Bank group, including on pensions and

	bonuses Then company agreements on such bonuses Agreement in construction against social dumping and to ensure similar wages and collective bargaining coverage for foreign workers	employees funded by the employers	Light Rail to ensure foreign workers have rights equivalent to those of local employees for the same type of work	fund to develop workers' skills	agency workers 2014–17 agreement for shops that includes continuous training and cooperation fund 2014–17 agreement in manufacturing to ensure that temporary agency workers are not abused compared with full-time workers	social provisions
Finland	2016 agreement in the IT sector	November 2016 agreement on wages and extension of annual working time in technology industry	2017 agreement in commercial sector on paid leaves		2012–14 agreement at Akava to reduce gender pay gap by allocating 0.5% of total wage costs	
France	More than 700 sectoral agreements per	Firm agreements on short-time working	2016 agreement unemployment insurance regime	September 2016 first company-level agreement	2012–14 agreement at EDF for equal	Agreements on early retirement

Table 1.2 (continued)

Extension of sectoral/ firm collective agreement	Wages and working conditions	Working time	Employment	Training	Gender equality/ NSFE equality	Private social protection/ pensions
	year, many of them defining occupational and wage grids (including starting wage/ legal minimum wage) Firm agreements mainly on wages and working time	Also on modalities of 35-hour working week 2013 agreements at Renault and Peugeot to avoid lay-offs in exchange for working time flexibility and wage moderation	for artists (*intermittents*) 2016 agreement at Peugeot with 2000 new young recruits with the 'generational contract', with new forms of flexibility	on digital transformation signed at Orange, including to prepare employees for future changes	pay between men and women and also for part-timers 2011–14 agreement at France Telecom to reduce gender pay gap and promote equal pay etc.	Agreements on early retirement
Germany	Collective agreement in the steel industry in 2010, providing for equal pay for equal work for all temporary agency	Sectoral agreements (for example, in the chemical industry on a working time corridor of 40–35 hours a week and in the metal industry	Agreements on recruitment of trainees/ apprentices even during the crisis	Training agreement in 2014 in the metal sector on a maximum 7 years' training account for employees, to be used also	2012 agreement in the metal and electrical industry to secure a shift to regular employment for temporary agency workers after 18 months	Agreement in the metal sector on employer-subsidised partial retirement scheme

	workers Similar agreement in metal and electric industry in 2012 granting seniority bonuses to temporary agency workers ThyssenKrupp Steel AG Europe agreement to cover subcontractors	35–30 hours) Company agreements on working time flexibilisation (reduction of working time)		outside the company Can also be fed by partial retirement scheme	2012 agreement in metal industry giving works councils right to set limits to the use of temporary agency workers (and also subcontracted)
Hungary					2013 agreement in water sector to motivate companies to sign equality plans (for women and Roma) 2014 agreement in railways for equal pay

Table 1.2 (continued)

Extension of sectoral/ firm collective agreement	Wages and working conditions	Working time	Employment	Training	Gender equality/ NSFE equality	Private social protection/ pensions
Ireland	2016–19 new pay agreement for contract cleaners 2016 local pay agreements bargaining; majority of companies awarded pay increases	2015 agreement for home helpers and workers in retail to ensure a minimum number of working hours				
Italy	November 2016 agreement for wage increase in the public sector Agreement on the distribution of bonuses related to companies' results at SKF			July 2014 agreement in the commercial sector on vocational training that will be provided by sectoral parity institutions; also provided broader	Sectoral and company agreements to represent non-standard workers and those in-between dependent and autonomous employees (*parasubordinati*)	'Inter-generational' pact at company Luxottica to encourage workers close to pension to take 50% part-time work to allow young workers to be hired on a permanent basis

		protection for working mothers and on contract termination	Extension of December 2015 agreements in telecoms and also in the research sector
Latvia	As part of a 2016 cooperation memorandum in construction aimed at halving the shadow economy by 2019, new electronic identification card systems managed by social partners to ensure the selection of qualified workers and to record worked time		
Luxembourg		2016 new collective agreement in the financial sector also	

Table 1.2 (continued)

Extension of sectoral/ firm collective agreement	Wages and working conditions	Working time	Employment	Training	Gender equality/ NSFE equality	Private social protection/ pensions
				aimed at adapting the collective agreement to the 'generation Y'		
Netherlands	2013 agreement in postal and parcel delivery sector to improve working conditions of self-employed deliverers by converting them into employment contracts					
Slovenia		2016 agreement in hospitality and tourism industry for			Collective agreements at sectoral level promoting equal	

		temporary rearrangement of working time 2016 agreement in trade on weekly schedules for workers			pay (and also extra pay) for women and training for this 2014–15 agreements in electrical and metal industry for regularisation of fixed-term work
Spain		2013 agreement in the region of Catalonia to foster competitiveness and reduce unemployment and non-standard employment 2013 agreement in mass catering, notably to increase minimal hours of part-time monitors	Agreement on conversion of temporary into permanent contracts (10%) or limiting percentage of temporary work 2011 agreement of offices, Salamanca, setting minimum of 60% of employees with open-ended contracts Similar limit (65%) in 2015 sectoral agreement for security firms		2016 agreement in the cleaning sector on non-discrimination and equal treatment for all workers (with specific initiatives in favour of equal pay, training, promotion of women)

Table 1.2 (continued)

Extension of sectoral/ firm collective agreement	Wages and working conditions	Working time	Employment	Training	Gender equality/ NSFE equality	Private social protection/ pensions
Sweden		400 companies in engineering industry short-time working agreements on reduction in working hours and in wages	Framework agreement on temporary layoffs, wage adjustments and training in metal industry in March 2009 Temporary redundancy pay agreement on 2 March 2009 in chemical, steel and metal, mine and welding engineering industries, enabling local partners at the firm level to conclude agreements on temporary layoffs	2010 new job security agreements between municipal and county council employees with professional training path aimed at enhancing their employability and promoting their occupational mobility	Sectoral agreements on an 'equality allowance' in sectors dominated by women and with low pay (largest increases in retail and municipal sectors)	

2013, in the electronics and mining and steel sectors, included for the first time the option of converting pay rises into extra time off work, a practice that further developed in 2016 (see Table 1.2).

The chapter on France also shows that sectoral agreements are numerous (more than 700 per year). They focus mainly on wages, and sectoral collective agreements seem to have enabled a better wage progression (+2.5 per cent in 2015) over recent years. The recent agreement in the culture sector is a good illustration of how a better balance can be achieved between flexibility (required considering that most tasks in this sector are short term) and security (with the need to compensate such flexibility with access to unemployment benefits once in inactivity) after months of negotiations.

In Spain, once a collective agreement is signed, its provisions are extended automatically to all employees working in the relevant area, beyond those belonging to the signatory organisations. As a result, nearly 75 per cent of Spanish employees used to be covered by collective agreements. This broad coverage of collective bargaining, together with this combination of levels, was found to have an equalising impact in terms of wages and working conditions.

Some innovative agreements were also signed at regional level, for instance, on fostering competitiveness while reducing unemployment and non-standard employment in Catalonia. These agreements also aim at developing the transition of temporary workers into permanent employment and facilitate working-time flexibility. The Spanish authors point to the fact that only 10 per cent of firms, affecting roughly a quarter of employees (with intermediate-level agreements), include provisions on the conversion of fixed-term contracts into open-ended contracts, and less than 3 per cent of collective agreements establish limits on the ratio between temporary employees and overall labour force. However, a few regional (Salamanca) or sectoral agreements (for security workers) set a clear minimum of 60–65 per cent open-ended contracts in contracts overall (see Table 1.2).

Interestingly, some sectoral collective agreements in a number of countries also set a minimum number of hours for part-time workers, which is important in a context of growing involuntary part-time working reported in most EU countries (for example, this applies to 60 per cent of part-time employees in Spain), a major source of income inequality. For instance, the collective agreement for security workers in 2015 in Spain set a minimal limit of ten hours per week for monitors – who earlier tended to work only 45 minutes a day – thus leading to more equality, and to lower the gender gap, given that most monitors are women. In France, a minimum of 24 hours a week was also set in some sectors.

The above examples of multi-level bargaining contrast with the United

Kingdom, which has opted instead for a decentralised system of collective agreements at enterprise level. However, a continuous deterioration of trade unionisation, a decrease in the number and coverage of collective agreements, especially in the private sector, increasingly fewer representative bodies to enable workers to have a say, has been accompanied by increased wage inequality, with the exception of the public sector, which has maintained more centralised agreements and good coverage in terms of trade union members and collective agreements. Interestingly, Ireland, which is characterised by a similar collective bargaining system decentralised at enterprise level, was able to limit inequality growth with more success, thanks to an overall social dialogue framework at national level, at least until the financial crisis.

Greece is an example of a country that has been shifting since the crisis from a multi-level to a decentralised collective bargaining system. The Greek chapter documents that this shift, including the interruption of social dialogue in areas such as the minimum wage, has led to a number of reforms that promoted flexibility without much security. This is particularly striking for young workers who have incurred more wage inequality through a minimum wage fixed at a lower level for those aged under 25, combined with a new inequality in the distribution of working time, with a growth in the number of young workers stuck in involuntary part-time status.

3.2.2 At enterprise level

An increasing number of issues While some decentralisation of collective bargaining towards the enterprise level is reported in most EU countries (see section 4), it is also important to note that collective bargaining at this level is being rapidly extended to new topics and policy areas (see Table 1.2). Agreements are developing on issues such as equal pay for work of equal value (often called by social partners as 'equal pay for equal work' agreements) and notably to reduce gender inequalities, but also on working time – with a number of agreements on how to improve the quality of part-time employment – and possible solutions to increase the capacity of companies to be flexible while allowing layoffs.

In France, while new rules tend to favour the development of decentralised social bargaining and to simplify the organisation of the industrial relations system, there has been an increase in social partners' commitment to negotiate at the firm level on wages and other topics, such as working time, work organisation, collective health insurance and gender equality, with a recent trend to oblige companies to reach an agreement on some issues. In case of failure to reach an agreement at the company level, an action plan has to be implemented: that principle applies to gender equality (since 2006) and to seniors' employment at companies employing 50 or more people (since 2008).

At the same time, a number of chapters in this book highlight the lack of negotiation on flexibility and security issues at firm level, probably indicating a lack of coordination between national and enterprise level collective bargaining.

By contrast, the second case study in the chapter on Slovenia shows how the good coordination between upper-level and enterprise collective bargaining could improve the working conditions of agency workers in a major electric company. This innovative agreement was first facilitated by the law, which demands equal treatment and does not allow for deviations in this area. Second, the fact that the sectoral collective agreement set the establishment of parity committees at firm level as mandatory gave the union in the company an opportunity to raise the issue with the management relatively easily. The articulation between different levels thus represents an indispensable element for ensuring equality outcomes, in this case on equal treatment for agency workers compared with other workers. It is also relevant in terms of trade union strategy to observe that the union was able to unionise the agency workers only after their efforts to stand up for them and their rights.

In Germany, the range of topics covered by collective agreements has also been expanded significantly in recent years, for instance, promoting unified pay scales or inter-firm mobility, and lifelong learning to respond to new requirements by technological change, as well as gender equality and work–life balance. In particular, collective agreements seem to play an activating function for training within the companies, and the presence of works councils seems to boost training, as shown in the chapter on Germany.

A number of agreements have emerged in a number of countries to help to reduce inequality faced by workers in non-standard employment, in terms of securing them regular employment, improving their wages, bonuses and non-wage benefits, scheduling working hours and improving the work environment (ILO, 2016a). Agreements have been concluded in, for example, Germany to secure regular employment for temporary agency workers, for instance in the metal and electrical industry after a period of 18 months, in the absence of any objective reasons to continue the temporary contract. Another 2012 agreement in the metal sector also grants social partners the possibility to set negotiated limits on the proportion of the workforce that can be temporary or subcontracted. In Ireland collective agreements were also concluded to ensure a minimum number of working hours to home helpers and workers in the retail sector, as a way to introduce more equality in the scheduling of hours for part-time and on-call workers. In the Netherlands, an agreement led to the conversion of 80 per cent of self-employed deliverers (who were paid well below the legal minimum wage) into employment contracts (Drahokoupil, 2015: s.4, para. 2). In Italy, trade unions (the Italian General Confederation of Labour, CGIL, the Italian Confederation of Workers' Trade Unions, CISL, and the Italian Labour Union, UIL) since 1998 have put in place special structures and social dialogue mechanisms for representing non-standard workers, including those in dependent self-employment, which led to some innovative agreements to regulate the relationship between the employer and such workers (a relationship called 'co.co.co' for '*collaborazioni coordinate e continuative*') as in the telecommunications, credit and research sectors, and nearly 100 000 individual contracts.

There are also innovative agreements at firm level in some countries (see Table 1.2) for addressing the wages and working conditions of workers of subcontracted firms (and to extend the contents of the collective agreement to those firms), who often face worse working conditions (Zimmerman Verdejo et al., 2010). The rapid increase in subcontracting (not only in some sectors, such as construction, but in almost all) thus represents a major source of growth of inequality, in terms of wages and working conditions, that could be addressed and limited through collective bargaining.

Collective bargaining can also help to improve the wages and working conditions of women. In Sweden, it was decided by national agreement in 2007 that women would be allowed an 'equality allowance' with the purpose of equalising wages, especially in low-pay sectors dominated by women. This led to collective agreements signed in individual sectors, the largest allowance being achieved in the retail and municipal sectors, most dominated by women.

Collective agreements at firm level also aim to promote employment and growth. In France some innovative agreements took place in 2013 and 2016 in the car industry (Renault, Peugeot) that made it possible to avoid layoffs and boost recruitment in exchange for a number of new flexibility measures (see Table 1.2 and also Chapter 4 on France).

The chapters in this volume also try to identify the issues that negotiations at enterprise level should develop further. The Spanish authors for instance attract attention to the fact that a very low percentage of firms have agreements to improve the wages and working conditions of temporary workers, even though Spain has one of the highest percentages of temporary contracts (25 per cent of total work contracts). Although the role of temporary contracts on the 'flexibility' side has been clear during the crisis – with a reduction only in 2009 of temporary employment, which affects almost 1.1 million people, while open-ended employment was still growing[6] – they were not accompanied by sufficient 'security' measures through social dialogue and collective agreements.

At the same time, the possible derogation to higher-level agreements introduced in a number of countries – such as Spain, Italy and, more recently, France – has affected the link between higher-level (national, sectoral or regional) and firm-level collective agreements. As indicated in the chapter on Italy, because contracts can derogate from higher-level collective agreements, except for the pay structure, 'representation has been pulverised, and within each firm, there is a variety of contracts'. The case of FIAT, for instance, breaking away from national representation and from the national contract in order to activate a new tailor-made contract, seems to have influenced industrial relations in Italy (see Chapter 8 on Italy).

Negotiated solutions in the crisis Collective bargaining has also made it possible to achieve negotiated responses to the crisis (Vaughan-Whitehead, 2011), even if win-win outcomes may be more difficult to reach in such a context because it may exacerbate the diverging interests of employers and workers.

Several countries, such as France, Austria, Belgium and the Netherlands, expanded their short-time working arrangements (or 'work-sharing'), and Germany used these schemes intensively – through intensive collective bargaining and a series of agreements at both sectoral and company level, as shown in Table 1.2 – so that they avoided most layoffs and unemployment in the crisis, a process that the German authors in this volume call the 'German employment miracle'. These arrangements are good illustrations of win-win agreements because they allowed employees to keep their jobs (of course by accepting lower working time and also often wages), while helping the companies to preserve their internal human capital and safeguard their industrial capacities. In Germany agreements between trade unions and employers to continue the recruitment of trainees even within the crisis also turned out to be a successful way of avoiding youth unemployment while maintaining human capital. Germany is a good example of successful joint management of the financial crisis based on the mobilisation and coordination of all bargaining levels (national, industry, region and company).

In Sweden, wage moderation, and not wage cuts as in some other EU member states, characterised collective bargaining during and after the crisis. At the same time, Sweden, following its tradition, has adjusted to the 2008 global economic crisis through a mix of negotiated numerical flexibility and active support for dismissed workers through active labour market policy measures and/or negotiated agreements helping redundant workers to find new jobs rapidly or to enhance their employability. Since

2015, nine out of ten dismissed workers have found a new job or became self-employed within seven months following their first contact with the Job Security Foundations (presented as one case study on Sweden). Furthermore, around 70 per cent of the displaced workers obtained an equal or higher salary in their new job.

In other cases, however, the crisis also led in other directions, with social dialogue being minimised or even avoided.

In Spain the massive increase in unemployment resulting from the economic recession of 2008–13 led to a revision of many of the core elements of the system of industrial relations, including collective agreements. The 2012 reform gave priority to firm-level collective agreements in most of the items bargained (wage, overtime, working time and work–life balance). While the intention behind this change in regulation was to adjust bargaining – and the resulting collective agreement – to the individual firm and its economic circumstances, these changes also led to the reduction in the number of workers benefiting from collective agreements. Moreover, the wage growth bargained in collective agreements signed after the 2010 reform was found to be lower than that bargained before it. A similar outcome is reported in Greece after deep transformation of national social dialogue, collective bargaining and minimum wage fixing.

Moreover, all the examples of sectoral, regional and enterprise agreements covering both flexibility and security issues presented in Tables 1.1 and 1.2 confirm the importance of collective bargaining at those three complementary levels in order to find the right equality balance. This also confirms Marginson and Galetto's (2014) demonstration (from the example of the metal sector in a few EU countries) of 'the capacity of collective bargaining to address issues of flexibility and security at sectoral and company level'. At the same time, they conclude that so far 'package agreements addressing forms of flexibility and security are not unknown at sectoral level but they are less widespread at company level', even if we can see from our examples in Table 1.2 that an increasing number of firm collective agreements – although, so far, in a limited number of countries – are addressing equal pay for work of equal value and some new issues, such as non-standard employment and subcontracting. More examples are provided in the chapters that also develop in-depth illustrative examples on the impact of social dialogue on inequalities (see Table 1.3). The case studies presented by the experts have been chosen to illustrate national stories about industrial relations and inequalities, while at the same time providing a good picture of best practices in terms of collective agreements at national or sectoral level (banking, public sector, cultural sector and automobile) or regional or enterprise level. More generally, the case studies present industrial relations initiatives that cover issues relevant to

Table 1.3 Case studies in selected European counties (presented in individual chapters)

Country	First case study	Second case study
Baltic States (Chapter 2)	Inequality issues in a few enterprise collective agreements in Estonia	Collective agreements and inequality in micro-enterprises in Latvia
Belgium (Chapter 3)	Social dialogue to reduce the gender pay gap	Collective bargaining effects on inequality through a better work–life balance
France (Chapter 4)	Inequality in private social protection at workplace	Innovative collective agreement in the cultural sector
Germany (Chapter 5)	Boosting minimum wages and collective bargaining	Enterprise agreement (ThyssenKruppSteel AG Europe) to manage steel subcontractors
Greece (chapter 6)	Public–private sector divide and inequalities	Security and flexibility measures to improve youth employment and wages
Ireland (Chapter 7)	Inequality, social dialogue and public sector pay	Managing macroeconomic shocks through social dialogue: what effects on inequality?
Italy (Chapter 8)	Flexibility and security in public employment services: comparing Lombardy and Marche	Outcomes of two different labour relations models: Ferrari and Lamborghini
The Netherlands (Chapter 9)	Inequalities, collective bargaining and youth minimum wage	Negotiations to address pay inequality in the banking sector
Slovenia (Chapter 10)	Flexibility/security and inequality in collective agreements in trade and metal sectors	Social dialogue and collective bargaining effects on inequality in a large metal company
Spain (Chapter 11)	Tackling low hours through collective agreement in mass catering	Innovative way to reduce accidents at work in construction
Sweden (Chapter 12)	Role of industrial relations and flexicurity for promoting technological change and skills upgrading	Job Security Councils and transitional agreements to illustrate the Swedish flexicurity regime
United Kingdom (Chapter 13)	Initiative for improving working conditions among the subcontracted social care workforce	Use of agency work and inequalities

inequalities (equality of conditions in terms of pay, working hours, health and safety, access to social protection, and work–life balance) and/or are relevant to specific categories of workers (gender pay gap, youth employment, working conditions of social care workers, public sector employees, agency workers and workers employed by subcontractors).

4. COMPARATIVE RESULTS AT EUROPEAN LEVEL: WHAT EFFECTS ON INEQUALITIES?

Having reviewed theoretical expectations and plunged into some of the national stories and contents of collective agreements on inequality in a number of EU countries, this section provides some statistical facts. What are the trends in collective bargaining and collective agreements, and how interrelated are they with inequality trends? What is the impact of collective agreements on different types of inequality? We test the impact of the presence of a collective agreement and the level of such agreements on three types of inequality: wage inequality (and we take this opportunity also to check the impact of collective bargaining on the gender pay gap); inequality in the conditions associated with different types of work contract; and, finally, inequality in the distribution of working time (with a particular focus on the gap between part-time and full-time workers).

The objective is to use data representative of wage employees in Europe – the Structure of Earnings Survey (SES)[7] – in a number of selected countries[8] to analyse the relations between social dialogue and labour market outcomes that reflect both inequalities and job security. We first review the dynamics of collective pay agreements (CPAs) as identified in the data, and then we provide estimates of the correlation between collective pay agreements and measures of (1) hourly wage inequality; (2) the gender pay gap; (3) contractual agreements; (4) full-time versus part-time prevalence; and (5) work intensity by means of 'working hours'.

Overall, the empirical estimates confirm a positive effect of collective pay agreements on the reduction of inequalities, including the gender pay gap, and on the working conditions associated with employment contracts, such as temporary and part-time work.

4.1 Dynamics of Collective Pay Agreements in Europe and Inequalities (2002–10)[9]

4.1.1 Overall changes

Using the SES, Figure 1.1 shows the distribution (proportional representation) of enterprises in two groups: those that claim to have a collective pay

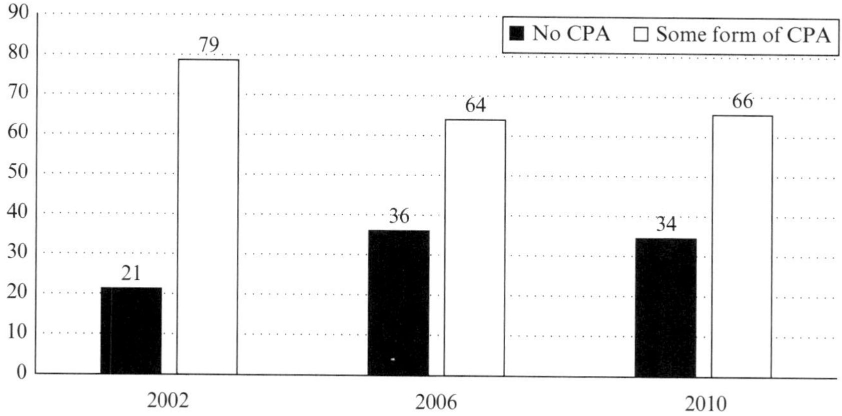

Source: International Labour Organization (ILO) estimates based on the SES from 16 countries.

Figure 1.1 Enterprises with collective agreements, 16 EU countries, 2002–10 (percentage)

agreement – any type, from national to enterprise type of agreement – and those that claim that none of their wage employees are covered by collective pay agreements.[10] Figure 1.1 – as for all those that follow in this section – is based on the weighted average of 16 countries in Europe, as provided by the data.[11] The figure shows that between 2002 and 2010 there was a considerable decline in the proportion of enterprises claiming to have some form of pay agreement: whereas in 2002 about 79 per cent of all enterprises were covered by some form of collective pay agreement, in 2010 the estimates had declined to 66 per cent, a 13 per cent drop. A similar picture emerges when we look at the proportion of employees covered by pay agreements, with a decline from 71 to 66 per cent.

This means that in the period from 2002 to 2010 each percentage drop in the fraction of enterprises covered by some form of collective pay agreement resulted in a 0.38 per cent drop in the fraction of wage employees covered by some form of agreement. The fact that the value of the elasticity is below 1 (0.38) would imply that in 2010 the mix of firms that remained under some form of collective pay agreement was larger in size than in 2002; that is, the evidence would suggest that it is the smaller establishments that are most likely to have lost coverage from the different types of collective pay agreements over the period.

The Appendix (Figure 1A.1) shows similar estimates to those presented above, but using only eight countries – Belgium, Bulgaria, Cyprus,

Estonia, Hungary, Latvia, Lithuania and the United Kingdom – because the dynamics of 'types of collective' pay agreements in these countries is consistent with the information provided by the ICTWSS dataset. Therefore, a similar analysis can be completed as above, but distinguishing six categories of enterprise: those covered by (1) national pay agreements; (2) sectoral agreements; (3) enterprise agreements; (4) other, but with some sort of agreement; and a category (5) of enterprise that 'is not covered by any type of collective pay agreement' (used in the analysis as the default category).

The results show that the proportion of enterprises with a sectoral agreement remained fairly stable (increasing in 2006 and declining in 2010), but that there was a significant decline of enterprises covered by enterprise agreements: whereas in 2002 about 28 per cent of all enterprises were covered by a collective pay agreement at enterprise level, in 2010 the estimates had declined to 16 per cent. Instead, the proportion of enterprises without any collective pay agreements had increased dramatically, from 45 per cent in 2002 to 60 per cent in 2010.

Figure 1A.2 in the Appendix shows the same dynamics, but based on individuals rather than on enterprises as the measurement unit. The figure shows that, proportionally, employees have also lost coverage, with less enterprise collective agreement in favour of more 'sectoral' types and even more towards 'no coverage at all'. It is interesting that the change occurred well before the global financial crisis: in 2006 the proportion of enterprises (and individuals) covered by collective pay agreements at enterprise level had already declined to levels also observed in 2010. What continued to change between 2006 and 2010 is an overall (across-Europe) increase in the number of enterprises and individuals who are now classified as without a collective pay agreement. This leads to a first conclusion that the decentralisation described in previous sections does not systematically mean a collective agreement at enterprise level, but may mean instead a shift to no collective agreement at all.

In order to further understand the relationship between collective pay agreement coverage and the size of establishments, and how such a relationship has changed over time, we carry out the same estimates but disaggregating by size. The SES distinguishes between small (between 10 and 49 wage employees), medium (between 50 and 249 employees) and large enterprises (500 or more employees).[12]

Using these three categories, and on the basis of the weighted average of our larger sample of 16 selected countries in Europe as provided by the data, Figure 1.2 shows that the fraction of small enterprises covered by some form of collective pay agreement has declined by 27 percentage points: from 71 per cent in 2002 to about 44 per cent in 2010. This is

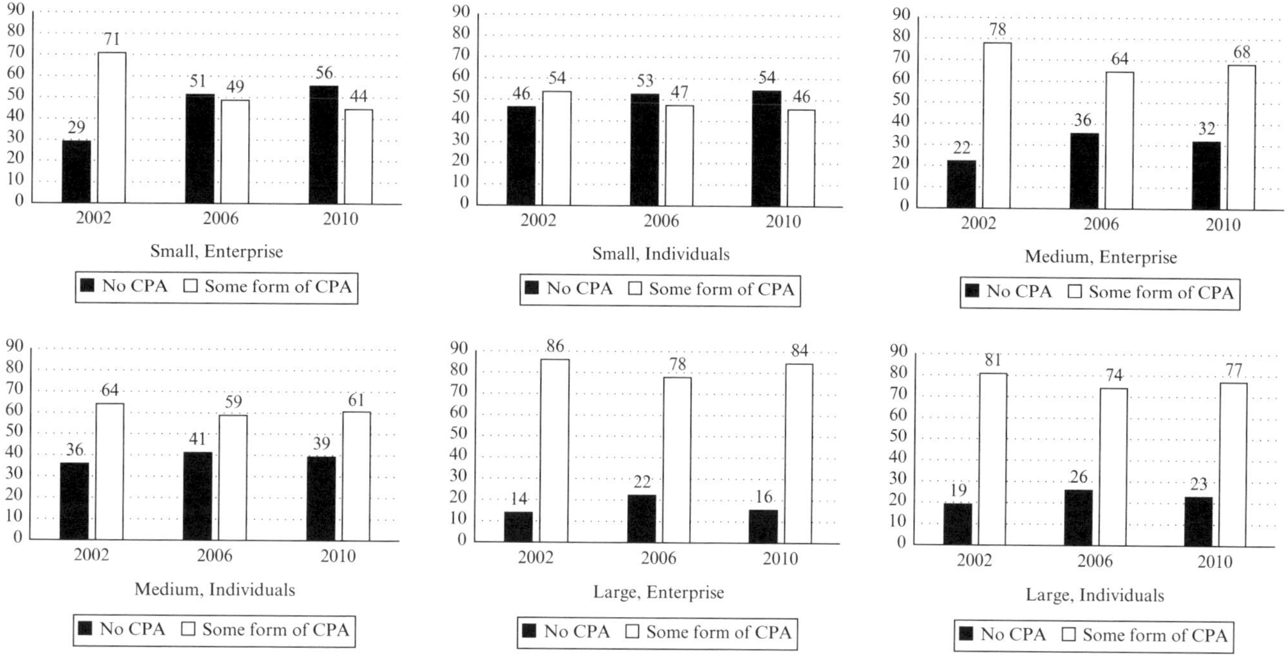

Note: The size of enterprises is between 10 and 49 employees (small), between 50 and 249 (medium) and 250 or above (large). Enterprises with nine or fewer wage employees are not included in the survey (by Eurostat definition).

Source: ILO estimates based on the SES for 22 countries, period 2002 to 2010.

Figure 1.2 Collective pay agreements and enterprise size, 16 EU countries, 2002–10 (percentage)

considerable if we compare it with the decline among medium-sized enterprises (10 percentage points, from 78 to 68 per cent) or the almost negligible decline in the fraction of large enterprises covered by pay agreements (1.5 percentage points, from 86 per cent to 84.5 per cent).

4.1.2 Changes in the coverage of collective pay agreements by economic sector

Collective pay agreements changed over the period – in terms of enterprises and individuals – for the nine sectors identified in the dataset: mining and quarrying, manufacturing (light and heavy), construction and utilities, trade (retail and wholesale), hotels and restaurants, transport and communications, real estate and financial services, social services (services to public administration, health and education) and other (private sector) services.

It is also interesting to analyse at what level (national, sectoral or company) collective pay agreements may have declined the most. Over the period observed, the coverage of national collective pay agreements declined in all sectors. There was a significant increase in sectoral pay agreements, but in some sectors (in particular trade, as well as hotels and restaurants) an increasing number of enterprises opted for no collective pay agreement.

4.2 How Related Are Trends in Collective Agreements and in Inequalities?

The second step consisted in showing the correlation between collective agreements and measures of inequality in the labour market, in particular, wages, hours worked and contractual conditions.

4.2.1 Wage inequality: lower where social dialogue is stronger

We started by exploring trends in wage inequality using the ratio of various percentiles. As defined in the latest version of the *Global Wage Report* (ILO, 2016b), measuring wage or income inequality should not stop at a comparison between the 10th versus the 90th decile, in order not to miss the fact that inequality – and therefore wage inequality – seems to be very much driven by what happens starting at the top 10 per cent, and in particular at the top 1 per cent. Because of this, we review the following ratio-based measures of inequality: using real gross hourly wages we estimate the value of these at the 1st, 10th, 50th, 90th and 100th centiles and estimate the ratios P100/P1, P100/P10, P90/P10, P50/P10 and P90/P50.

Figure 1.3 plots the ratios for each of the two groups of enterprises, those with and those without collective pay agreements, comparing the movement for the period 2002–10. We observe that for all periods wage

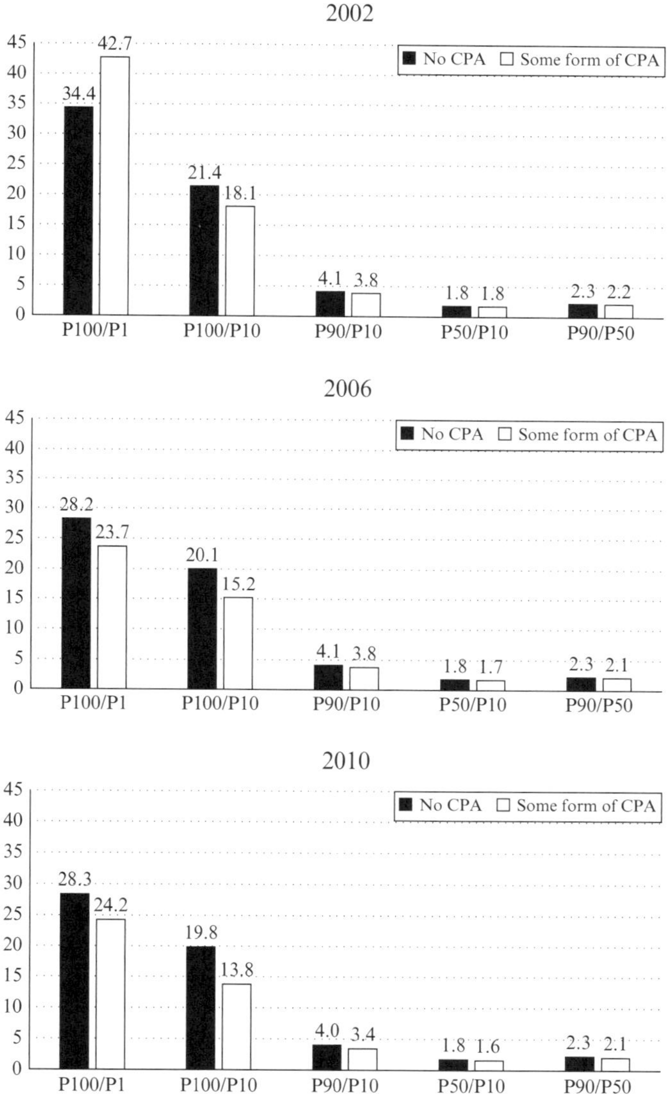

Note: Estimates are based on real hourly wages which includes contractual wages, overtime payment and non-regular bonus and benefits. All measures are based on real values with base year 2010. We estimate the ratios on a country-by-country basis – for each of the 16 economies and for each of the three periods – and use group-specific weight to find the weighted average according to the two groups. All values are based on a representative sample of the 16 economies with data collected in October of each of the years.

Figure 1.3 Wage inequality and collective pay agreements, 2002–10 (percentage)

inequality is consistently lower if there is some form of collective pay agreement – the only exception is the ratio P100/P1 for the year 2002, which may be the result of an outlier (among those with a collective pay agreement).

A comparison between 2006 and 2010 also confirms two points: first, the wage distribution for enterprises with some form of pay agreement is clearly more compressed than that estimated in enterprises without a collective pay agreement; that is, for all ratios estimated we find that these are always larger among enterprises without a collective pay agreement. The picture is consistent over time: social dialogue helped to maintain lower levels of inequality over the period. Second, comparing 2006 and 2010 shows that there was not much change in terms of wage inequality over time, neither for those with nor those without a collective pay agreement. Considering the evidence described before (from Figure 1.1, an increase in the proportion of enterprises and wage employees without coverage) this would suggest that, overall, there was an increase in wage inequality in the population (overall), because those that show greater inequality (not covered by collective pay agreements) weigh more in 2010 compared with their relative weight in 2002.

4.2.2 Gender inequality: declining and influenced by social dialogue institutions

It has been recognised that in the presence of strong industrial relations – which embodies the presence of minimum wages and collective bargaining – the gender pay gap (GPG) is lower. As discussed in previous sections, it is reasonable to suppose that at enterprise level, the existence of social dialogue institutions would result in a smaller gender pay gap. We saw in the previous section that some collective agreements promote equal pay for work of equal value, which may contribute to lower gender inequalities. However, to what extent does the evidence at enterprise level point towards lower gender inequality in the presence of collective pay agreements?

Figure 1.4 shows the estimates of the gender pay gap based on the weighted average of the 16 countries from the SES dataset, using real gross hourly wages for the period 2002–10 with the base year in 2010.

The results confirm that the gender pay gap among wage employees who benefit from collective pay agreements is smaller than in enterprises without collective pay agreements. It is important to note that both groups display considerable gaps in wages between male and female. Nevertheless, over the period, the decline in the gap was greater among those enterprises with collective agreements than those without. Also, in 2010 the gap among wage employees without collective pay agreements was about 40 per cent

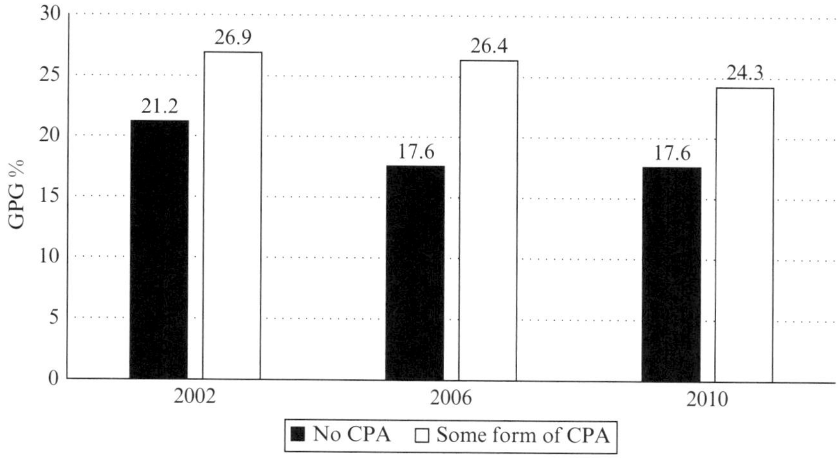

Note: Estimates are based on real hourly wages, which includes contractual wages, overtime payment and non-regular bonus and benefits. All measures are based on real values with base year 2010. The gender pay gap is based on taking the difference between the average wage of males and females, relative to the average wage of males, on a 100 per cent basis. We estimate the gaps on a country-by-country basis – for each of the 16 economies and for each of the three periods – and use group-specific weight to find the weighted average according to the two groups.

Figure 1.4 Gender pay gaps and collective pay agreements, 2002–10 (percentage)

higher than the gender pay gap among wage employees in enterprises that had some form of collective pay agreement.

4.2.3 Work contracts: temporary work higher when social dialogue lower

The SES provides individual base information on contractual agreements: individuals are identified with either a temporary or an indefinite contract. This allows us to extend to the topic of collective agreements the comprehensive analysis completed recently on the use of temporary contracts by Aleksynska and Berg (2016) and the ILO (2016a). We use the information in the SES to construct a variable that identifies each establishment in the data with one of the following six categories: (1) establishments where all wage employees have an indefinite contract; (2) where 75 per cent or more wage employees have indefinite wage contracts; (3) between 50 and 75 per cent have indefinite contracts; (4) between 25 and 50 per cent; (5) between some and 25 per cent; and (6) all workers are temporary. By default, all who are not indefinite contract wage employees are temporary workers.

Figure 1.5 shows the results over time and for both establishments and

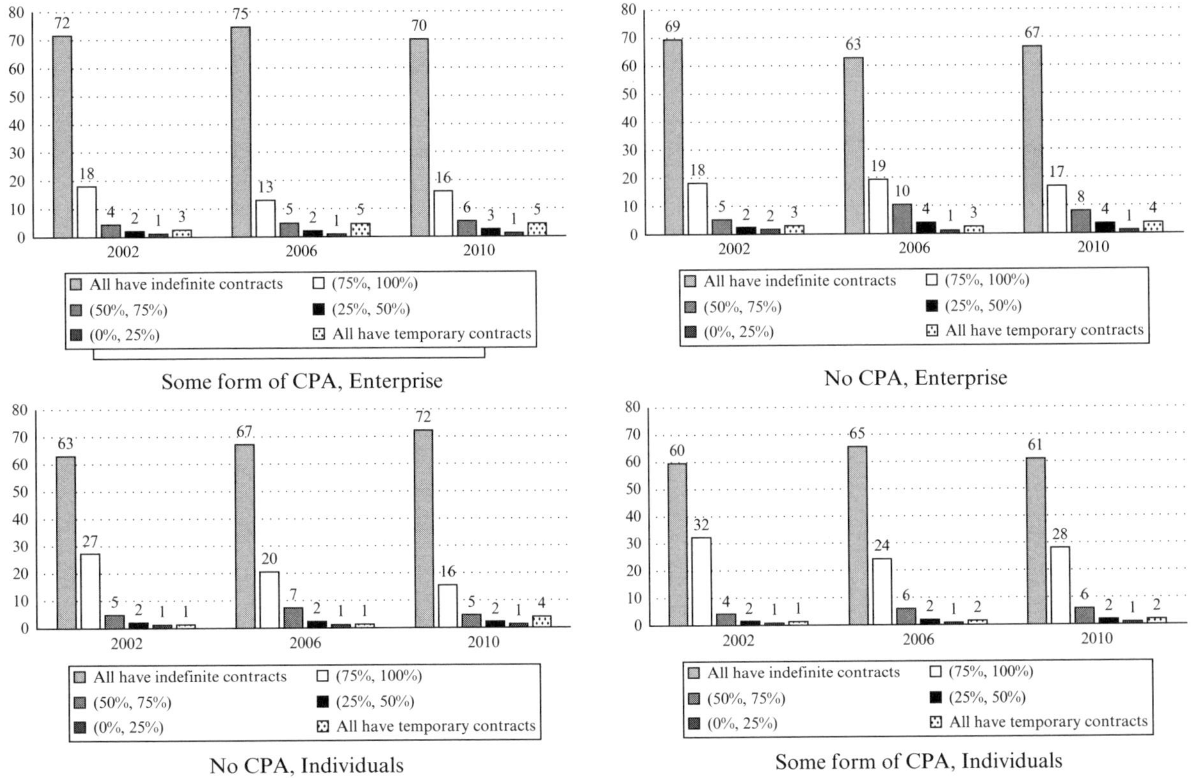

Figure 1.5 Categories of contractual agreement and collective pay agreements, 2002–10 (percentage)

individuals, comparing establishments with and those without some form of collective pay agreement. First, the proportion of enterprises that fall in the first category (that is, all employees have an indefinite contract) is higher in the two groups: 70 per cent in the enterprises with a collective pay agreement and 67 per cent (that is, slightly lower) in the enterprises without a collective pay agreement. Over time, the proportion of enterprises with all employees having an indefinite contract is declining, while the percentage of enterprises with all workers on a temporary contract is increasing. These trends are confirmed in the national case studies presented in this volume, which show an even sharper increase of temporary contracts in most recent years.

4.2.4 Part-time: industrial relations securing more working hours

Together with hourly wages, working time is the variable that ultimately determines overall work-related earnings for each individual. Therefore, a review of inequality would be incomplete without providing estimates of hours worked (per week) according to the strength of social dialogue institutions, as well as by type of collective pay agreement.

The SES provides information on hours worked, so that for each employee we know how many hours they worked per week, how many of these were contractual hours and how many were overtime work. Likewise, the survey identifies whether the workers are classified as full-time or part-time at the enterprise where they work.

Using this information, Table 1.4 shows average hours worked per week by all employees, distinguishing between full-time and part-time workers. The table disaggregates the information to compare the two groups according to the type of collective pay agreement.

Table 1.4 Work intensity by type of collective pay agreement (2010)

	All employees		Full-time employees		Part-time employees		Percentage of part-time wage employees
	Average hours worked per week	% of which are overtime	Average hours worked per week	% of which are overtime	Average hours worked per week	% of which are overtime	
By type of collective pay agreement:							
Some form of CPA	35.1	2.9	38.2	2.8	21.4	3.0	18.7
No CPA	35.3	2.3	39.2	2.2	18.5	2.9	21.2

Note: ILO estimates using the 2010 SES. Absolute values reflect hours worked per week; proportions show the fraction of hours worked per week that count as overtime.

According to Table 1.4 there is great similarity in terms of hours worked per week between full-time workers: on average they work about 38 to 39 hours per week. Where we find more discrepancy is among part-time workers. In enterprises with collective pay agreements the average number of hours worked part time is on average about 21 hours per week, declining to 18 hours among enterprises without a collective pay agreement. Considering that the proportion of 'overtime' is similar between the two groups (about 2.9 or 3 per cent), this would imply that the number of contractual hours offered to part-time workers in enterprises with no collective pay agreement is significantly lower than the number offered to part-time workers in enterprises with some form of collective pay agreement. Collective agreements thus seem to guarantee part-time employees a higher number of working hours, which will then ensure them a higher income. This effect of collective agreements on the number of working hours thus makes it possible to limit rises in wage disparity.

Finally, we observe that the proportion of wage employees who work part-time in enterprises without a collective pay agreement is also higher (at 21.2 per cent) compared with the proportion in enterprises with some form of collective pay agreement (18.7 per cent), which seems to limit, too, systematic recourse to part-time working.

5. POLICY CONSIDERATIONS

Our statistical analysis is in line with some of the most recent trends in collective bargaining and industrial relations, and with a number of relationships with inequalities found in several chapters of this volume and in the relevant literature.

First, our analysis confirms that a decentralisation is taking place towards more collective bargaining at enterprise level, but also the progressive disappearance of collective agreements in some companies and some sectors, such as hotels, catering, cleaning and retail. Countries with a low level of social dialogue institutions are also witnessing a further decline in the coverage rate of collective agreements.

While some decentralisation is also observed in countries with strong social dialogue institutions – with notably a decrease in national consultations and negotiations – the sectoral level remains strong. This level of bargaining is also rich in terms of issues discussed and outcomes negotiated on flexibility and security, as shown by the series of agreements we presented at that level. We can also find innovative agreements concluded at firm level on emerging issues, such as equal pay for equal work, to reduce inequalities faced by women, but also on measures to better cover non-standard forms of employment and how they combine with more flexibility in the labour market. New agreements also appear on the emerging issue of subcontracting or outsourcing to avoid differentiated wages and working conditions, and thus increased inequalities. No doubt, in the current transformations in the world of work, with increased automation, changing tasks and increased mobility, it will be necessary to negotiate similar agreements to ensure balanced outcomes in terms of employment, training, wages and working conditions.

This direct impact of collective bargaining on the nature of the world of work certainly explains the correlation we also found in our analysis between collective agreements and inequalities, not only pay inequality but also inequality in terms of working time distribution and the probability of having certain forms of work contract. First, collective agreements – especially at the higher level, according to national studies – were found to play a role in curbing pay inequalities. Countries with high social dialogue institutions, such as Belgium and Sweden, have managed to keep wage inequalities at relatively low levels. The impact of collective bargaining on low pay – especially in combination with the minimum wage – and on wage compression (especially when there are multiple levels of negotiation) are some of the mechanisms at work identified in this volume. Second, the presence of a collective agreement was also found to reduce the gender pay gap. We saw that an increasing number of collective agreements at different levels promote equal pay for equal work, something that contributes to lower gender inequalities. Third, the proportion of enterprises with all workers holding a permanent contract is higher where there is some sort of social dialogue (with a collective agreement), as highlighted in the chapters of this volume. Fourth, the presence of a collective agreement does not seem to generate a lower or higher proportion of part-time workers, but to ensure, where there are part-timers, that they will receive sufficient working hours. We have provided examples of this type of collective agreement in this introductory chapter. We also saw – notably through the multiple examples of collective agreements in Tables 1.2 and 1.3 but also in national chapters – that collective agreements can improve the working conditions of workers under non-standard forms of employment.

The assessment provided in this volume of a continuous decline of collective bargaining, despite its positive effects in limiting inequalities and generating innovative outcomes in terms of flexibility and security, requires a strong policy agenda. Inequalities are increasingly found to have an adverse effect on economic growth and social cohesion (IMF, 2015; OECD, 2015), so collective bargaining to curb such inequalities represents an important lever that must be maintained and even strengthened. This policy agenda requires the commitment of all actors.

Trade unions have to find new strategies, and this volume presents some innovative initiatives to tackle emerging trends in the world of work, such as the growth of non-standard forms of employment or the increasing recourse to subcontracting. Some interesting developments can be observed, with trade unions overcoming some deterioration of the balance between flexibility and security by influencing the bargaining process. For instance, in Germany, trade unions were confronted with the introduction of derogation clauses in their collective agreements, but managed nevertheless to increase their influence in sectors with high density rates by involving members in company-level bargaining.

Similarly in Italy, trade unions started to organise in order to be able to provide a necessary framework for a number of non-standard forms of contract. Trade unions are also meeting other challenges, such as extending the coverage of collective bargaining to non-standard forms of employment, or taking part in training programmes or training accounts that would help employees to develop lifelong learning, which is particularly important considering that with automation many jobs will disappear and new jobs will be created.

Employers could also benefit from an increased use of collective bargaining to influence flexibility and security outcomes in the enterprise, and thus to implement the necessary reforms and introduce the necessary flexibilities without compromising, but rather increasing, workers' security. Employers might also discuss the possible consequences of a move to a world with no collective agreements and examine the value added that multi-level bargaining with a combination of higher agreements (at national and sectoral level) and enterprise agreements could offer them in terms of employment, human capital, social climate and economic growth.

This volume clearly emphasises that the social partners are dealing with a range of inequalities and that social dialogue mechanisms, such as collective agreements that include issues related to flexibility, security, employment status, training and so on, can be effective in addressing the various forms of inequality, which have deepened over the recent past.

Finally, the role of the state remains central. National social dialogue and collective bargaining institutions could be strengthened where the state decides to play a supportive role and to use social dialogue effectively as a policy tool. This is especially important because in this way the social partners could contribute to policy reforms on issues such as taxation, insurance and social protection, which will determine future inequality outcomes.

By contrast, the recent weakening of social dialogue institutions – often with the motive of lowering labour costs and boosting competitiveness – has not necessarily led to the expected effects on economic growth, while they have seriously aggravated inequalities along with a rapid decline in collective bargaining coverage. The influence of collective bargaining and social dialogue on key aspects of reforms (such as pensions, social security, working time, wages and subcontracting) and on inequalities – which we identify in this volume – should thus give additional motivation to policy-makers and social partners to sustain and strengthen, rather than to weaken, social dialogue and collective bargaining, and to put them among their policy priorities. Forthcoming transformations in the world of work will require increasingly more negotiated outcomes and policy solutions so that they better match the changing aspirations and needs of social and economic actors in Europe.

NOTES

1. See, for example, Aidt and Tzannatos (2002, 2008), Blau and Kahn (2002), Fernández-Macías and Vacas-Soriano (2015) and Wallerstein (1999).
2. See, for example, Rowthorn (1992), OECD (1997, 2004), Blau and Kahn (1999, 2003), Elvira and Saporta (2001) and Aidt and Tzannatos (2002).
3. See, for example, Aidt and Tzannatos (2002, 2008), Blau and Kahn (2002), Teulings and Hartog (1998), Wallerstein (1999), Fernández-Macías and Vacas-Soriano (2015).
4. See, for example, Rowthorn (1992), Dahl et al. (2013), Dell'Aringa and Pagani (2007), Salverda and Mayhew (2009) and Jaumotte and Buitron (2015). For an analysis of the impact of level of bargaining and level of coordination on nominal and real wage increases and on macroeconomic performance, see Eurofound (2015).
5. The average level of the lowest scale in the ministry's monitoring sample of collective agreements has clearly declined, falling by more than 10 per cent, which has had an impact on inequalities.
6. The authors also explain that the burden will then be placed on open-ended contracts, concluding also with the lack of full job security among open-ended employees.
7. The quantitative analysis in section 4 is based on data from the SES, an employer–employee match dataset provided by Eurostat and representative of enterprises (and their wage employees) for all EU and European Economic Area (EEA) member states. Each of the national statistical offices from these countries is obliged to provide survey data representative of the population of enterprises; the data include variables that describe the characteristics of the enterprise (for example, size, economic sector or regional location, among others), the characteristics of the workforce (for example, age of wage employees, education, gender or occupational skill, among others) and the wage structure of all wage employees in the given enterprise (contractual wages, overtime earnings, bonuses and benefits, number of hours worked per week, weeks worked per year and general information on the working conditions of each wage employee working in the surveyed enterprise at the time of the survey). The data are collected every four years (with the first wave starting in 2002) and reflect information from October and up to October of the given year. The last available wave at the time of writing is that of 2010. The data include all (private) economic sectors (that is, they exclude civil service entities and their employees) representing enterprises with ten employees or more; that is, it excludes micro-enterprises. Eurostat collects and consolidates the information so that the final product is a homogeneous set of variables across countries and time periods. Therefore, the data can be used on a country-by-country basis, but also as a unique dataset that reflects the average wage structure in Europe. Whether the data are used for a given country or for all countries to obtain Europe-wide estimates, the analysis relies on the use of frequency weights (also provided in the data by Eurostat) so that the sample is representative of

the population. In total, there are more than 30 countries in the data. However, not all countries are provided to all researchers: each project proposal is reviewed by each of the countries, which then decide on a discretionary basis to provide the data for analysis. For the ILO, a total of 22 countries were provided for all periods available (2002, 2006 and 2010). These countries are Belgium, Bulgaria, Cyprus, Czech Republic, Estonia, Finland, France, Greece, Hungary, Italy, Latvia, Lithuania, Luxembourg, Netherlands, Norway, Poland, Portugal, Romania, Slovakia, Spain, Sweden and the United Kingdom. The data supplied provide information on about 22 million wage employees and about 1.1 million enterprises. For more information on the SES, see http://ec.europa.eu/eurostat/web/microdata/structure-of-earnings-survey (accessed 10 November 2017).

8. We selected the countries for which we have a collective pay agreement distribution that is consistent with industrial relations dynamics over the given period (2002–10) and consistent with the Jelle Visser industrial relations dataset.
9. At the time of writing, data from the SES were not yet available for 2014 (latest survey conducted). Information provided by the experts in their chapters seems to confirm for the most recent period the trends identified in this section.
10. The SES provides information about the type of collective pay agreement that predominates at the enterprise. Each enterprise is asked to declare 'if the enterprise operates under some type of pay agreement, or not'. For those that declare that they operate under some type of collective pay agreement the question is then 'what type of collective pay agreement covers at least 50% of the employees in this local unit?' The responding enterprise can select one of six categories, namely, a collective pay agreement at national level, or at sectoral level, or at sectoral-regional level, at enterprise level including all the units of the enterprise, at enterprise level but covering some units of the enterprise, or 'any other type of collective pay agreement' not covered above. In the results presented, we have grouped these six categories into one: has some form of collective pay agreement. This is compared with enterprises without collective pay agreement. On the other hand, the Appendix shows the grouping of the six categories into four: national collective pay agreements, sectoral collective pay agreements, enterprise collective pay agreements, and 'other (but with some sort of agreement)'.
11. The SES provides the variable 'collective pay agreements' for all 22 countries. However, the estimates we present includes only seven of these countries (Belgium, Bulgaria, Cyprus, Estonia, Hungary, Latvia and Lithuania). Owing to data anomaly in the indicator for collective pay agreement, we have dropped the following countries from our sample: Italy, The Netherlands, Norway, Poland, Spain and Sweden. In the Appendix the selection is based on a comparison of the dynamics of the variable on collective pay agreements in the SES with external sources that provide a comprehensive qualitative description on collective bargaining and pay agreements in several countries (see http://www.uva-aias.net/en/ictwss, accessed 11 November 2017).
12. Approximately 1 million enterprises were surveyed in the 22 countries over the three periods covering 2002 to 2010. The proportional representation of small enterprises for 2002, 2006 and 2010 was 42 per cent, 39 per cent and 40 per cent, respectively; of medium-sized enterprises, 29 per cent, 22 per cent and 25 per cent, respectively; and of large enterprises, 28 per cent, 38 per cent and 35 per cent, respectively. In terms of what proportion of employees belong to each category we observe that these proportions remain relatively constant over time: about 26 per cent for small enterprises, about 20 per cent for medium-sized enterprises and about 54 per cent for large enterprises.

REFERENCES

Aidt, T.S. and Z. Tzannatos (2002), *Unions and Collective Bargaining. Economic Effects in a Global Environment*, Washington, DC: World Bank.

Aidt, T.S. and Z. Tzannatos (2008), 'Trade unions, collective bargaining and macroeconomic performance: a review', *Industrial Relations Journal*, **39** (4), 258–95.
Aleksynska, M. and J. Berg (2016), 'Firms' demand for temporary labour in developing countries: necessity or strategy?', Conditions of Work and Employment Series Working Paper No. 77, ILO: Geneva.
Andor, L. (2012), 'Foreword', in European Commission, *Social Europe Guide*, vol. 2, *Social Dialogue*, Luxembourg: Publications Office of the European Union, p. 3.
Berg, J. (2015), *Labour Markets, Institutions and Inequality: Building Just Societies in the 21st Century*, Cheltenham, UK and Geneva: Edward Elgar and ILO.
Blau, F.D. and L.M. Kahn (1992), 'The gender earnings gap: learning from international comparisons', *American Economic Review*, **82** (2), 533–8.
Blau, F.D. and L.M. Kahn (1999), 'Institutions and laws in the labor market', in O.C. Ashenfelter and D. Card (eds), *Handbook of Labour Economics*, vol. 3, pt B, Amsterdam: North-Holland, pp. 1399–461.
Blau F. and L. Kahn (1996), 'Wage structure and gender earnings differentials: an international comparison', *Economica*, **63** (250), S29–62.
Blau, F.D. and L.M. Kahn (2002), *At Home and Abroad: US Labor-Market Performance in International Perspective*, New York: Russell Sage Foundation.
Blau, F.D. and L.M. Kahn (2003), 'Understanding international differences in the gender pay gap', *Journal of Labor Economics*, **21** (1), 106–44.
Canal Domínguez, J.F. and C. Rodríguez Gutiérrez (2016), 'Collective bargaining, wage dispersion and the economic cycle: Spanish evidence', *Economic and Labour Relations Review*, **27** (4), 471–89.
Dahl, C.M., D. Le Maire and J.R. Munch (2013), 'Wage dispersion and decentralization of wage bargaining', *Journal of Labor Economics*, **31** (3), 501–33.
Dell'Aringa, C. and L. Pagani (2007), 'Collective bargaining and wage dispersion', *British Journal of Industrial Relations*, **45** (1), 29–54.
De la Rica, S. and A. González (2007), 'The impact of firm-level contracting on wage levels and inequality: Spain 1995–2002', Department of Foundations of Economic Analysis II Working Paper No. 7, University of the Basque Country, Lejona.
Drahokoupil, J. (ed.) (2015), *The Outsourcing Challenge: Organizing Workers Across Fragmented Production Networks*, Brussels: European Trade Union Institute.
Elvira, M.M. and I. Saporta (2001), 'How does collective bargaining affect the gender pay gap?', *Work and Occupations*, **28** (4), 469–90.
Eurofound (2014), *Impact of the Crisis on Industrial Relations and Working Conditions in Europe*, Dublin: Eurofound.
Eurofound (2015), *Pay in Europe in Different Wage-Bargaining Regimes*, Luxembourg: Publications Office of the European Union.
European Commission (EC) (2015a), *Research Findings – Social Situation Monitor – Income Inequality in EU Countries*, Employment, Social Affairs and Inclusion, Brussels: European Commission.
European Commission (EC) (2015b), *A New Start for Social Dialogue*, Brussels: European Commission.
Fernández-Macías, E. and C. Vacas-Soriano (2015), *Recent Developments in the Distribution of Wages in Europe*, Eurofound, Luxembourg: Publications Office of the European Union.
Freyssinet, J. (2010), 'Les réponses tripartites à la crise économique dans les

principaux pays d'Europe occidentale', Working Paper No. 12, Department of Labour Relations and Employment Relations, ILO, Geneva.
Gautié, J. and J. Schmitt (eds) (2010), *Low-Wage Work in the Wealthy World*, New York: Russell Sage Foundation.
Hayter, S. (2011), *The Role of Collective Bargaining in the Global Economy: Negotiating for Social Justice*, Cheltenham, UK and Geneva: Edward Elgar and ILO.
Hayter, S. (2015), 'Introduction: what future for industrial relations?', *International Labour Review*, **154** (1), special issue, 1–4.
Hayter, S. and B. Weinberg (2011), 'Mind the gap: collective bargaining and wage inequality', in S. Hayter (ed.), *The Role of Collective Bargaining in the Global Economy*, Cheltenham, UK and Geneva: Edward Elgar and ILO, pp. 136–86.
Hemerijck, A., B. Unger and J. Visser (2000), 'How small countries negotiate change: twenty-five years of policy adjustment in Austria, the Netherlands and Belgium', in F.W. Scharpf and V.-A. Schmidt (eds), *Welfare and Work in the Open Economy*, vol. 2, Oxford: Oxford University Press, pp. 175–264.
ILO (2014), *Global Wage Report 2014/2015: Wages and Income Inequality*, Geneva: ILO.
ILO (2016a), *Non-Standard Employment around the World: Understanding Challenges, Shaping Projects*, Geneva: ILO.
ILO (2016b), *Global Wage Report 2016/2017: Wage Inequality in the Workplace*, Geneva: ILO.
IMF (2015), 'Causes and consequences of income inequality: a global perspective', IMF staff discussion note, June, SDN/15/1, pp. 1–39.
Jaumotte, F. and Buitron, C. (2015), 'Linkages between labour market institutions and inequality,' IMF, accessed 17 November 2017 at http://www. imf.org/external/pubs/ft/survey/so/2015/int071015a.htm.
Karamessini, M. and J. Rubery (2015), 'Women and austerity: the economic crisis and the future for gender equality', *Work, Employment and Society*, **28** (6), 1036–9.
Keune, M. (2015), 'The effects of the EU's assault on collective bargaining: less governance capacity and more inequality', *Transfer*, **21** (4), 477–83.
Marginson, P. and M. Galetto (2014), 'Engaging with flexibility and security: rediscovering the role of collective bargaining', *Economic and Industrial Democracy*, **37** (1), 95–117.
McGuinness, S., F. McGinnity and P. O'Connell (2009), 'Changing returns to education during a boom? The case of Ireland', *Labour Economics*, **23** (S1), 197–221.
OECD (1997), *Employment Outlook 1997*, Paris: OECD.
OECD (2004), *Employment Outlook 2004*, Paris: OECD.
OECD (2015), *In It Together: Why Less Inequality Benefits All*, Paris: OECD.
Pillinger, J. (2016), *Feminising the Market: Women's Pay and Employment in the European Community*, e-book, 27 July, Palgrave, accessed 21 November 2017 at http://fetchbookgoods.com/gunysi.pdf.
Rowthorn, R.E. (1992), 'Centralisation, employment and wage dispersion', *Economic Journal*, **102** (412), 506–23.
Rubery, J. (2015), 'Closing the gender pay gap in the EU', *Intereconomics*, **50** (2), 62–3.
Rubery, J., D. Grimshaw and H. Figueiredo (2005), 'How to close the gender pay gap in Europe: towards the gender mainstreaming of pay policy', *Industrial Relations Journal*, **36** (3), 184–213.

Rubery, J., S. Horrel and B. Burchell (1994), 'Part-time work and gender inequality in the labour market', in A. MacEwan Scott (ed.), *Gender Segregation and Social Change*, Oxford: Oxford University Press, pp. 205–34.

Salverda, W. and K. Mayhew (2009), 'Capitalist economies and wage inequality', *Oxford Review of Economic Policy*, **25** (1), 126–54.

Teulings, C. and J. Hartog (1998), *Corporatism or Competition? Labour Contracts, Institutions and Wage Structures in International Comparison*, Cambridge: Cambridge University Press.

United Nations General Assembly (2015), 'Transforming our world: the 2030 Agenda for Sustainable Development', adopted at the seventieth session (Agenda items 15 and 116) of the General Assembly on 25 September 2015 (fourth plenary meeting), distributed on 21 October 2015 (A/RES/70/1), accessed 11 November 2017 at https://sustainabledevelopment.un.org/post2015/transformingourworld.

Van Gyes, G. (2012), 'Union protest against government's austerity package', accessed 17 November 2017 at http://www.eurofound.europa.eu/observatories/eurwork/arti cles/industrial-relations/union-protest-agsinst-governments-austerity-package.

Vaughan-Whitehead, D. (ed.) (2011), *Work Inequalities in the Crisis: Evidence from Europe*, Cheltenham, UK and Geneva: Edward Elgar and ILO.

Visser, J. (2015), *Data Base on Institutional Characteristics of Trade Unions, Wage Setting, State Intervention and Social Pacts, 1960–2014 (ICTWSS). Version 5.0*, Institute for Advanced Labour Studies AIAS, Amsterdam, October.

Visser, J. (2016), 'What happened to collective bargaining during the great recession', *IZA Journal of Labor Policy*, **5** (9).

Visser, J., S. Hayter and R. Gammarano (2015), 'Trends in collective bargaining: stability, erosion or decline?', Issue Brief No. 1, Labour and Collective Bargaining, October, ILO, Geneva.

Wallerstein, M. (1999), 'Wage-setting institutions and pay inequality in advanced industrial societies', *American Journal of Political Science*, **43** (3), 649–80.

Zimmermann Verdejo, M. and F.J. Pinilla García (2010), *Estudio de los sectores económicos en los que se recurre habitualmente a la contratación y subcontratación de obras y servicios*, Instituto Nacional de Seguridad e Higiene en el Trabajo (INSHT), Madrid.

APPENDIX

This Appendix shows similar estimates to those presented above, but using only eight countries: Belgium, Bulgaria, Cyprus, Estonia, Hungary, Latvia, Lithuania and the United Kingdom. The dynamics of 'types of collective' pay agreements in these countries is consistent with the information provided by the ICTWSS dataset. Therefore, a similar analysis can be completed as above, but distinguishing five categories of enterprise: those covered by (1) national pay agreements; (2) sectoral agreements; (3) enterprise agreements; and (4) other (but with some sort of agreement). There is also a category of enterprises that is 'not covered by any type of collective pay agreement'. Estimates for this latter are identical to those presented above for the so-called 'no CPA' category.

Table 1A.1 is based on Figures 1.1 and 1.2. It shows, for each type of CPA, the period-to-period percentage change in wage employees for each percentage change in enterprises.

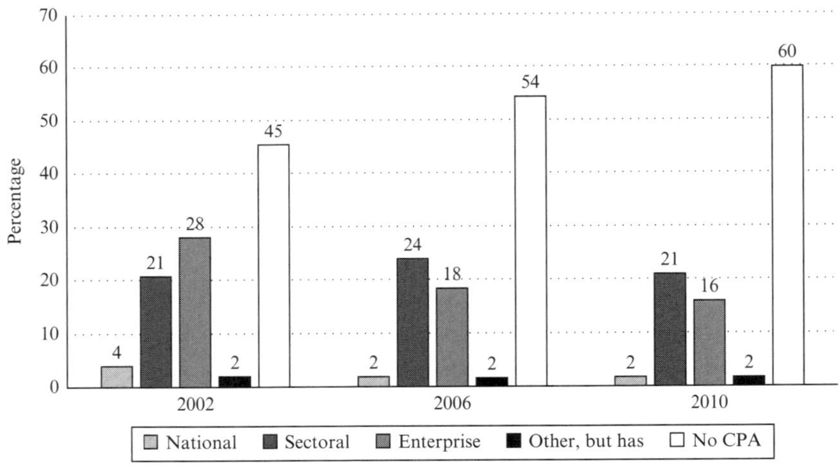

Figure 1A.1 Distribution of enterprises by types of collective pay agreements (CPA) (percentage)

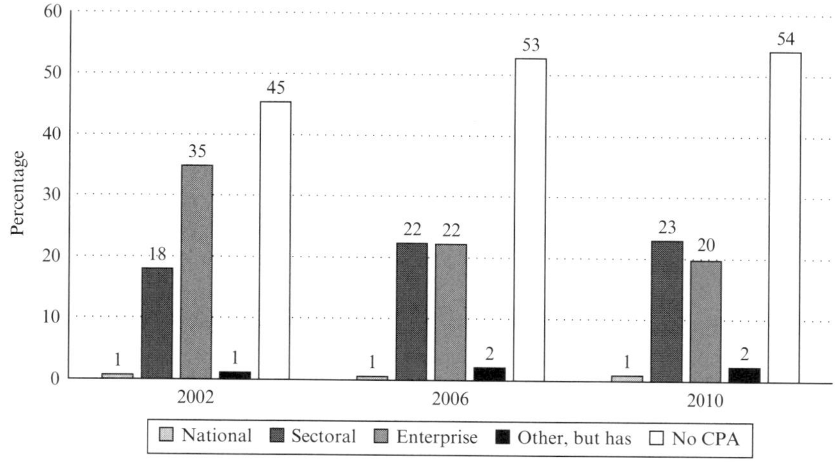

Figure 1A.2 *Distribution of individuals (wage employees) by type of CPA (percentage)*

Table 1A.1 *Period-to-period change in wage employees to changes in enterprises by type of collective pay agreement (percentage)*

	Elasticity 2002–06	Elasticity 2006–10
National level collective pay agreement	0.04 (decline)	–1.8 (increase)
Sectoral collective pay agreement	1.4 (increase)	–0.2 (increase)
Enterprise level collective pay agreement	1.3 (decline)	1.02 (decline)
Other type of collective pay agreement not mentioned (but has)	–2.4 (decline)	2.3 (increase)
Does not have any type of collective pay agreement	0.82 (increase)	0.24 (increase)

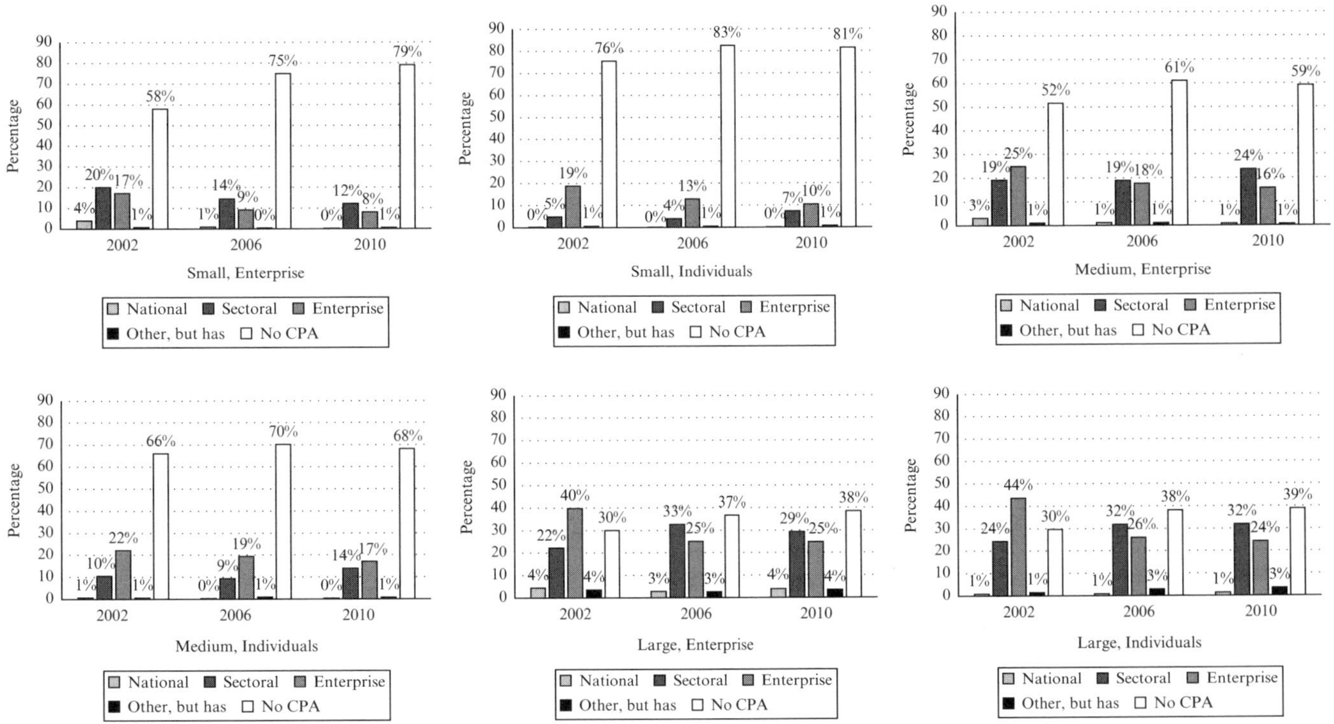

Source: ILO estimates based on the SES.

Figure 1A.3 Collective pay agreements and enterprise size, 2002–10 (percentage)

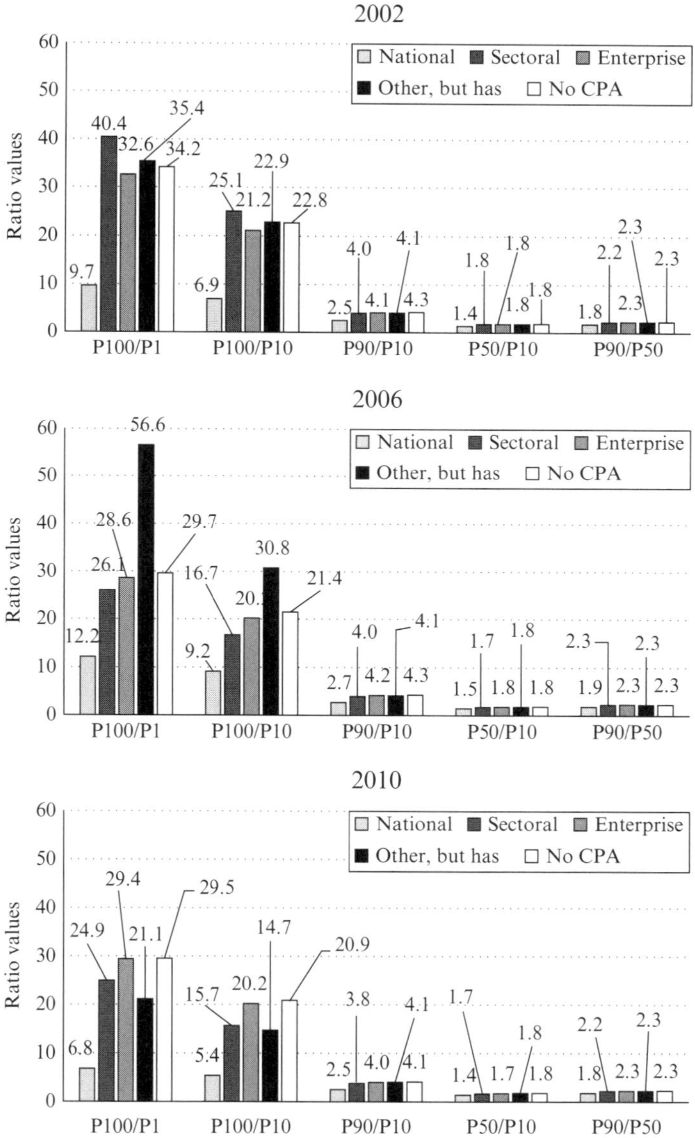

Note: Estimates are based on real hourly wages which includes contractual wages, overtime payment and non-regular bonus and benefits. All measures are based on real values with base year in 2010. We estimate the ratios on a country-by-country basis – for each of the 22 economies and for each of the three periods.

Figure 1A.4 Wage inequality and collective pay agreements, 2002–10 (percentage)

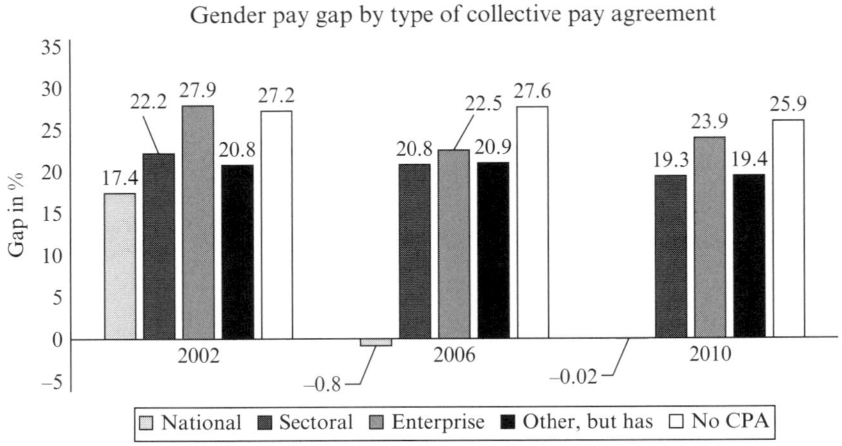

Figure 1A.5 Wage inequality and type of collective pay agreement, 2002–10

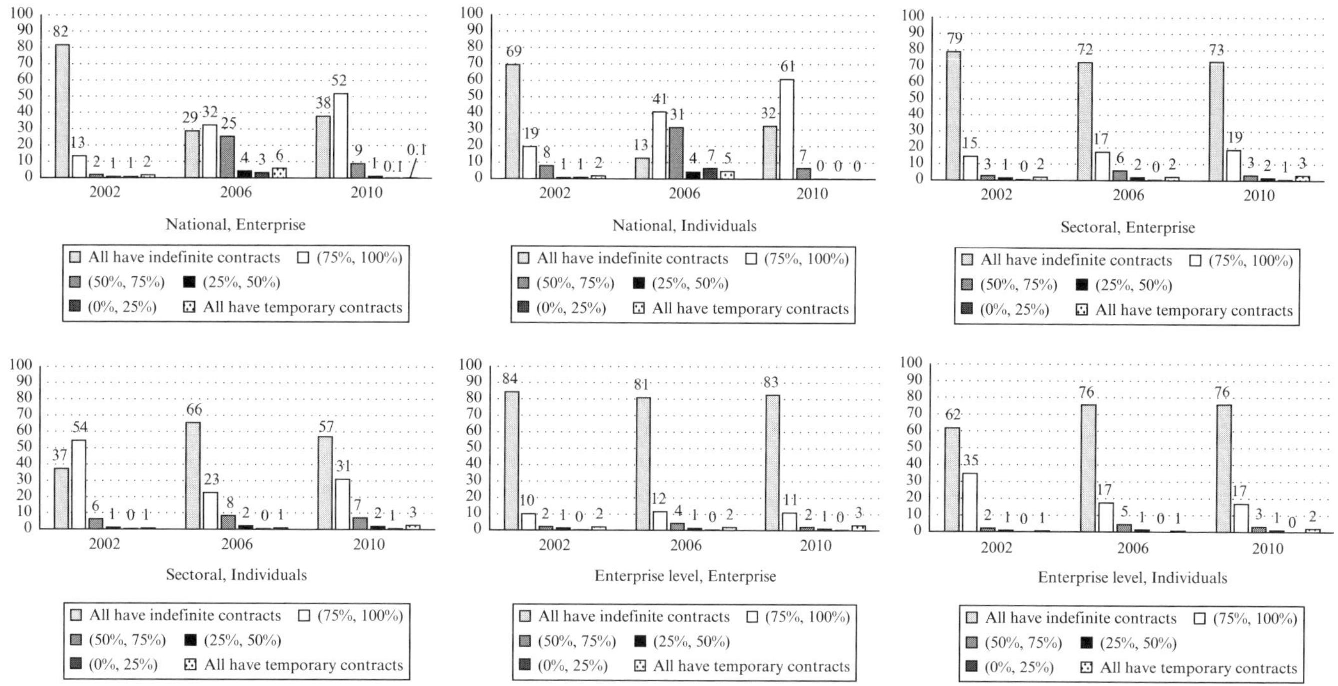

Figure 1A.6 Categories of contractual agreement by type of collective pay agreement, 2002–10 (percentage)

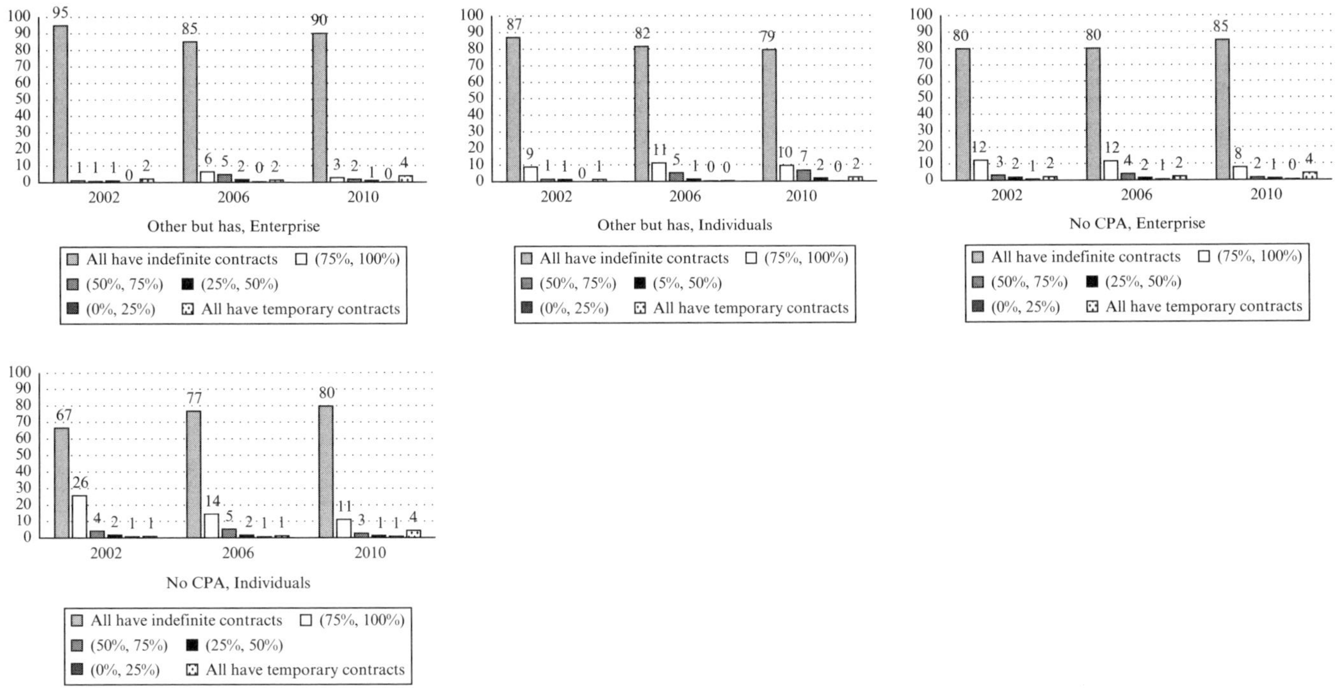

Figure 1A.6 (continued)

Table 1A.2 Hours worked and overtime (2010)

	All employees		Full-time employees		Part-time employees		Percentage of part-time wage employees
	Average hours worked per week	% of which are overtime	Average hours worked per week	% of which are overtime	Average hours worked per week	% of which are overtime	
By type of collective pay agreement:							
National	31.4	1.3	33.6	1.2	21.9	1.9	19
Sectoral	32.6	2.7	38.0	2.5	19.7	3.4	29
Enterprise	35.5	3.4	39.8	3.3	19.6	3.5	22
Other (but with some sort of agreement)	31.6	5.9	38.8	3.9	19.9	9.2	38
No CPA	34.5	2.2	39.7	2.0	18.2	3.0	24

Note: CPA = collective pay agreement.

2. Labour market inequalities in conditions of limited social dialogue: The case of the Baltic States

Jaan Masso, Maryna Tverdostup, Inta Mierina and Kerly Espenberg

1. INTRODUCTION

After regaining independence, social dialogue[1] has not been of key importance in the functioning of Baltic labour markets. For instance, it has been argued that social dialogue was not needed for the implementation of the neoliberal economic model of the Baltic States (Woolfson and Kallaste, 2011). However, it has also been considered that social dialogue is exportable to the new European Union (EU) member states (Woolfson and Kallaste, 2011). Workplace social dialogue has wider importance than the mere provision of a collective 'voice' for employees, as it harnesses the broader concept of pluralism in society by promoting solidarity (Guest, 1987). Thus, in addition to mapping the past and current situation and all the problems, it is important to study what could be the potential of social dialogue not only for resolving social issues such as inequalities, but also the competitiveness of these catching-up economies.

Although the Baltic countries are a fairly uniform group of countries in terms of economic development and the institutional setting of labour markets, there are differences concerning the development paths of unions and non-union forms of representation. In the Baltics, it is much easier to highlight problems related to the lack of social dialogue or the unheard voice of the social partners than to identify best practices. We discuss some of the latter, such as the relatively recent increase of the minimum wage in Estonia.

The rest of the chapter is structured as follows. Section 2 summarises existing studies and statistics on the trade unions, collective bargaining and worker representation in the Baltic States. Sections 3 and 4 study the linkages of these, first, with flexibility–security balance and, second, with inequalities. The two case studies try to shed further light on the effects of social dialogue by studying, first, the issue of inequalities in Estonian firm-level collective bargaining and, second, social dialogue in Latvia.

2. DYNAMIC EVALUATION OF INDUSTRIAL RELATIONS

2.1 Union Density and Collective Agreement Coverage

Table 2.1 presents information about union density and collective agreement coverage in the Baltic States. In the Baltic States as well as in the other central and eastern European countries (with the exception of Slovenia) the role of trade unions is less important in comparison to the old EU member states. Although the trend of union density has been downward in all European countries for some time (Van Gyes et al., 2006), the importance of trade unions, either in terms of union density or coverage, has decreased especially rapidly in all the Central and Eastern European (CEE) countries since the 1980s. While at the end of the 1980s the whole labour force were trade union members, by the mid-1990s the number had dropped to 30-60 per cent and by 2004 to 14.4 per cent of the labour force (Masso and Eamets, 2007). Nowhere has union density declined as steeply as in the Baltics (Kallaste and Woolfson, 2009), and trade union density in Baltic States has reached the lowest level in the EU27 (Van Gyes et al., 2006). The sharp decline in unionisation in the 1990s continued

Table 2.1 Trade union and employer organisational density, collective agreement coverage and extension practices, Baltic States (percentage of all employees)

	Union density			Employer organisational density		Coverage by collective agreements		Extension of (sectoral) collective agreements by law since:	Presence of trade union at the work-place
	1995	2005	2014	2005	2014	2005	2015		2002–03
Estonia	32.0	9.7	6.5	23.0	25.0	25.0	23.0	2000	25.0
Latvia	25.0	15.1	13.1	35.0	41.0	15.0	15.0	2002	27.0
Lithuania	15.0	9.6	9.0	20.0	14.4	10.6	9.9	2003	23.0

Source: Masso and Eamets (2007); Visser (2015).

later; according to Visser (2015) union density declined in Estonia during 2003–12 from 11.7 to 6 per cent, in Latvia from 20.2 to 13.1 per cent and in Lithuania from 13.6 to 9.0 per cent. Concerning later data from the Baltic Working Environment and Labour (BWEL) survey, the share of people working in unionised companies ranged from 10 per cent in Estonia to 23 per cent in Latvia, while the self-reported union density in the 2006 BWEL survey was 5 per cent in Lithuania, 15 per cent in Latvia and 4 per cent in Estonia (Kallaste and Woolfson, 2009). The higher numbers for Latvia are mainly owing to the higher unionisation rates in the public sector, for example, in 2002, 38 per cent in the public sector and 8 per cent in the private sector, a possible explanation being the survival of a single trade union confederation relative to their fragmentation in Estonia and Lithuania (Kallaste and Woolfson, 2009), which is discussed further below.

The fall in trade union membership in the CEE countries (including the Baltic States) has to some extent had different roots from the declining unionism in old EU member states. The reasons behind such downward unionisation dynamics include historical inheritance owing to ideological reasons and the particularities of the institutional set-up of post-transition industrial relations. The most important explanation for declining union membership, in the Baltic States, is the abolition of the obligatory union membership after the Soviet period (Järve et al. 2001; Espenberg et al., 2012). In the Soviet Union, trade unions had a completely different role than in a market economy, such as providing access to social benefits and goods, and, instead of being independent, they were the arm of the state at the workplace (Kallaste and Woolfson, 2009). The other reasons for declining union membership include globalisation (for example, a high share of foreign direct investment, FDI, in the economy), structural shifts in the economy (decline in the share of industries and increasing share of services, development of information and communication technologies), declining company size and increasing share of small and medium-sized enterprises, increase of atypical forms of employment and flexible forms of work. Among the Baltic States the decreases in industrial employment and increases in employment in services have been especially rapid (Eamets, 2001). The larger union decline in the Baltic States relative to the other CEE countries may also be due to the Soviet legacy, such as starting economic reforms from scratch and their integration in the union apparatus of the Soviet Union. Yet another argument was that the post-transition performance of unions and union leaders working with the elite to introduce reforms at the expense of the workers could be a factor behind the distrust towards unions. The Latvijas Darba Devēju Konfederācija (LDDK, 2014) mentions among the problems hindering unionisation and social dialogue: unwillingness of employees to join unions; membership fees; difficulty in finding volunteers who would be willing to lead a new non-governmental organisation (NGO); unwillingness of employers to talk about establishing employers' organisations within these companies and to sign collective agreements; a lack of understanding of the meaning and importance of social dialogue among some employers, employees and representatives of municipalities; and general pessimism and scepticism as regards the efficiency of social dialogue.

The observed decline is also self-reinforcing to a certain extent. While the low importance of unions is due to low membership, low union membership, in turn, prevents them from running a large union apparatus; it has also been causing the organisations financial problems and has led to a fragmented structure of union membership (especially in Estonia and Lithuania;, but less so in Latvia, see Table 2.2), thus further aggravating the problems. Finally, one of the most important reasons why the bargaining power of unions in the Baltic States and CEE countries has decreased is rising unemployment during the 1990s.

Even more important than the number of unionised workers is the

Table 2.2 Trade union structure in the Baltic States

Country	Confederations	Number of branch unions in the largest confederation	Members of the largest confederation		Main division between confederations
			Total number	% of all trade union members	
Estonia	EAKL, TALO	18	30 000 (2012, Visser 2015)	66 (Visser, 2015 for 2011)	Macro-sector/ status/ profession
Latvia	LBAS	20	98 000 (Visser, 2015 for 2012)	91 (Visser, 2015 for 2012)	
Lithuania	LPSK, Solidarumas, LDF	25	90 000 (Visser, 2015 for 2012)	45 (own calculations for 2012) to 75 (Visser, 2015 for 2008)	Political; religious

Source: Blažiene 2004; Karnite (2004); Masso and Eamets (2007) based on Van Gyes et al. (2006); Internet homepages of confederations, Visser (2015), own calculations.

coverage by collective agreements. While in Western European countries union coverage is usually much greater than the number of union members (with the extreme example of France and Spain where less than 20 per cent of employees belong to unions but about 80 per cent are covered by collective agreements), the surprising evidence from the Baltic States, as well as from the other transition economies, shows that coverage by collective agreements usually does not differ much from union membership. The result might be partly owing to the lack of data on collective agreements, because until recently they were not registered. The other reason for low collective agreement coverage is the small number of sectoral-level agreements. The right-most column in Table 2.1 indicates density of workplace representation; again, the Baltic States have the lowest figures in Europe.

Concerning other forms of representation, Kallaste et al. (2007) studied the role of non-unionised representatives.[2] Estonian law stipulates that there can be two kinds of representatives – union representatives and representatives selected by the general meeting of employees not belonging to the union. Kallaste et al. (2007) found that the roles of the two representatives do not differ much. The Estonian system is neither a single-channel system, as there are two kinds of representatives (one for unionised and the other for non-unionised workers), nor a dual channel system, as both representatives have the same role in the company. Although the non-unionised representatives have exactly the same rights as unions and similar functions (collective bargaining, information and consultation) – which is rare in Europe – the competition from the non-unionised representatives has not contributed to low union membership. The non-unionised representatives also have low representation and low effectiveness; also they have fewer opportunities in collective bargaining and, compared with union representatives, a less clear mandate. Although employers have sometimes initiated the creation of the non-unionised representatives, we are not dealing here with so-called 'yellow' trade unions (union initiated by the employer). There is also a mandatory health and safety workplace representation in all three Baltic countries offering another, though weaker, form of collective representation (Woolfson et al., 2008).

Antila and Ylöstalo (2003), based on surveying employees' attitudes towards collective bargaining in Baltic countries, concluded that some employees would prefer more collective forms of activity in the workplace relative to what they have. Kallaste and Woolfson (2009) analysed employees' attitudes towards trade unions or interest in joining a union using the BWEL 2006 survey to understand what the low level of union representation in the Baltics actually means; for example, whether it could be due to low demand for union membership or restricted access to union membership. They argued that contrary to expectations, frustrated demand is fairly low (for example, related to various restrictions on establishing a union) for union membership in comparison with the size of the representation gap in other countries. However, there is a rather large group of 'undecided' employees. These employees could be potential trade union members if they could see benefits from collective representation. Kallaste and Woolfson (2009) argued that this large undecided group specific to CEE countries corresponds with the representation gap in other countries. The attitudes of employees reveal that there is a shortage of knowledge regarding trade union activities in market economies and social networks with experience of trade unions in a market economy (Kallaste and Woolfson, 2009). In Estonia and Latvia 17 per cent and in Lithuania 22 per cent of working people without unions said they would prefer a union at their workplace, numbers lower than in Anglo-American countries (30–40 per cent). Among union members, from 55 per cent (Lithuania) to 62 per cent (Estonia) agreed that union membership brings benefits. However, unions have been unable to promote themselves.

There are some differences across the Baltic States regarding the structure of unions (Table 2.2). In Estonia, there are two central trade union organisations (confederations with overall membership varying over time by about 9 per cent; Kallaste et al., 2007) of employed persons. The Confederation of Estonian Trade Unions (Eesti Ametiühingute Keskliit, EAKL) organises both workers and salaried employees; it is a trade union of blue-collar workers. The EAKL was established in 1990 and is the largest of the confederations. In 2015 it comprised 18 branch unions with about 47 500 members. The Estonian Employees' Unions' Confederation (Teenistujate Ametiliitude Keskorganisatsioon, TALO), established in 1992, concentrates its organising efforts on salaried employees; it is the organisation of trade unions for white-collar employees and consists of seven branches with around 7500 members (in 2012, calculated using data from Visser, 2015). There are trade unions that are independent of the two large confederations (for example, the trade union of doctors) and around 8000–10 000 employees do not belong to central confederations (Eamets and Kallaste, 2005); according to Visser (2015) the combined share of the two confederations was around 73 per cent in 2012. There are more trade unions in the public sector. The largest unions are in manufacturing, the energy sector and transportation. There are some sectors where unions are missing, for example, some services industries. In Estonia, unions exist mostly in the sectors with a female workforce, which causes a larger number of women among union membership. Of the two confederations, EAKL has been the more active with a more prominent voice in policy-making.

In Latvia, in contrast to the other Baltic States, there is a single unified confederation, the Free Trade Union Confederation of Latvia (Latvijas

Brivo Arodbiedribu Savieniba, LBAS) that re-emerged in the post-Soviet era. It has been argued that the single confederation in Latvia, as compared with Estonia and Lithuania, may partly explain the higher union density in Latvia. In 2015, LBAS members represented around 15 per cent of all the employed in Latvia (according to the homepage of LBAS; LBAS, 2017) and around 90 per cent of all union members; with 20 branch organisations it probably had around 134 000 members in 2013, while Visser (2015) reports 98 000 for 2012. The LBAS has collective agreements in a number of industries, especially in the public sector where the education trade unions have been the strongest organised section of the labour force. The public sector's level of organising is higher than that of the private sector and 60 per cent of the organised labour force consists of women. The largest is the teachers' union, followed by two health-care unions. The other main sectors with trade union membership are transport, communication, public services, agriculture, food and fisheries, industry, energy and construction. The most active engagement of the social partners can be identified in the education and health-care sectors (even though with limited success for the employees of these sectors). In the private sector, the sectors in which employers are very active in the development of social dialogue include metalworking, the wood industry and food production, whereas the problematic sectors in which social dialogue should be promoted more include chemicals and related industries, the production of electrical and optical equipment, construction, transport and logistics. Concerning particular institutions of social dialogue in Latvia, the National Tripartite Co-operation Council – a national social dialogue institution involving delegated representatives of the Latvian government, the LDDK, and the LBAS – gets involved in signing agreements at the sectoral, municipal and state levels.[3] The voice of the LDDK is heard most loudly in the negotiations, while employees and employee organisations are less represented and the interests of employers sometimes contrast with the interests of other partners (LDDK, 2014). Situations when an agreement with the social partners is not respected and not followed are common in Latvia, thus the challenge is to move from a formal process of consulting, to an efficient involvement of the social partners in decision-making (Ozola, 2010). One successful example is the State Employment Agency (SEA) Advisory Board established in 2004 whose aim is to analyse problems and develop proposals to reduce unemployment and to support the unemployed, job seekers and people at risk of unemployment, in close cooperation with the representatives of employers, other sectoral bodies, local authorities and NGOs. Development of a strong and targeted cooperation with the employers, local authorities, associations and organisations is one of SEA's strategic orientations. One of the problems noted by the LDDK in their recent report on social dialogue is that while there is often an exchange of opinions, as well as identification of the problems of the parties, specific agreements and actions that would be acceptable to all parties are lacking (Ozola, 2010).

Lithuania has three central trade union organisations with a total membership of about 14 per cent of all employed persons; these organisations are the Lithuanian Trade Union Confederation (Lietuvos profesiniu sajungu konfederacija, LPSK), the Lithuanian Trade Union 'Solidarumas' (Lietuvos profesine sajunga Solidarumas, LPS Solidarumas) and the Lithuanian Labour Federation (Lietuvos darbo federacija, LDF). The largest among them is the LPSK, in 2008 uniting around 75 per cent of all unionised labour, with membership organised on a branch/sectoral basis (Visser, 2015) and having 25 affiliated branch trade unions (approximate membership of 120 000). The second confederation LPS Solidarumas unites basic trade union organisations at enterprise level grouped in county, city or town and regional territorial bodies and federations, currently having 20 affiliated territorial unions and 18 federations (LPS Solidarumas, 2017). A Christian-based trade union confederation, the LDF also exists with some limited enterprise agreements. In total, therefore, there were three separate trade union confederations representing 7.6 per cent of employed people in 2009. Independent trade unions are also active in Lithuania (Blažiene, 2004). In the past these confederations have not always been cooperative, have held different positions and even competed with each other (Paas et al., 2003, Blažiene, 2004). The main sectors in which trade unions are active are health care, transportation, construction, railways, agriculture, trade, education and the civil service.

Bipartite dialogue from below as compared with tripartite consultation from above has been more prevalent in the Baltics (Vatta, 2001). While in the absence of effective bipartite social dialogue tripartite social dialogue has been more important in setting national agendas, even the latter has sometimes been insufficient, with a lack of substantive content and unable to compensate for the dialogue deficit at the enterprise level (Jensen, 2003). Many writers have argued that the positive impacts of tripartite social dialogue on post-communist society have been minimal and that the emphasis on national-level tripartism may have proven to be detrimental for the development of workplace bargaining (Fenger, 2006). On the contrary, Woolfson and Kallaste (2011) argued that tripartite 'concertation' between labour, capital and government in eastern Europe has provided a key mechanism for resolving social tensions.

Some evidence on employee representation can also be inferred from Eurofoundation company surveys (Eurofound, 2015). As regards direct employee participation in organisational decision-making, Latvia and

Estonia had a fairly high share (around 65 per cent, not much lower than in Scandinavia) of companies with extensive and supported employee participation, and Lithuania around 60 per cent. Latent class analysis identifying three types of establishments based on the participation of employees showed that of the three identified classes that of limited employee participation ('low effort and little change' type of companies) was the least frequent in the Baltics, although the small differences across countries and possible composition effects from firm size may reduce the relevance of these numbers. Surprisingly, Estonia had a share of companies with official structures of employee representation close to the EU28 average (around 38 per cent), while Lithuania had one of the highest (58 per cent) and Latvia one of the smallest frequencies (8 per cent; Eurofound, 2015). Similarly, Latvia and Estonia were highlighted as countries where a high percentage of establishments with employee representation coincided with the 'trusting social dialogue establishment' type. The percentage of establishments that are members of employers' organisations is low anyway in all three Baltic States, at less than 10 per cent (Eurofound, 2015). In all three Baltic States both the trust of management in employee participation and the trust of employees' representative in management were at high levels compared with the other EU countries. All this evidence is at odds with the other evidence on the importance of social dialogue in Baltic State enterprises.

2.2 Wage Bargaining Levels

Information on wage bargaining centralisation is presented in Table 2.3. In the Baltic States the centralisation of wage bargaining[4] is among the lowest in Europe. The reason for this is that in the Baltic States, as well as in the other transition economies, collective wage bargaining has taken place mostly at individual level or national level (minimum wages), but has been much less developed in the sectoral and regional levels (Casale, 1999). The important role of national-level wage bargaining has probably been caused by the traditional coordinating role of the government. The larger scale of enterprise-level bargaining compared with that at the sectoral level is due to the less well organised employers. This is probably also one of the most important reasons for the low level of collective bargaining in the Baltic States where, as demonstrated by Visser (2005), across European countries the employers' rate of organisation has been shown to be closely correlated with collective bargaining coverage. The peculiarity of Baltic States in Europe is that the collective agreement coverage rate does not exceed the employer organisation rate owing to almost non-existent sectoral- or regional-level bargaining, but with some important exceptions, such as the teachers union in Latvia. The Baltic countries with decentralised industrial

Table 2.3 Indicators of collective bargaining centralisation, Baltic States

Country	Index of centralisation, average of 2005–14	Government intervention into wage-bargaining, average of 2005–14	Level of wage bargaining		
			National	Sector	Company
Estonia	0.33	2.0	*	*	***
Latvia	0.51	2.6	*	*	***
Lithuania	0.35	2.6	*	*	***

Notes:
*** = principal or dominant bargaining level; ** = important but not dominant level; * = existing level of bargaining.
Index of centralisation – the index combines the information on union concentration (the number of unions and confederations) with the measure of prevalent level of bargaining (national or sectoral). The index varies from 0 to 1, larger value indicates more centralised bargaining. The index is from Visser (2005).
Government intervention into wage bargaining – the index has 5 values: 1 = No role of government in wage-setting; 1.5 = Government only involved in minimum-wage setting; 2 = Government tries to influence wage bargaining by providing institutional framework for consultation or dialogue; 3 = Government determines wage-bargaining outcomes indirectly through minimum wage-setting tax-based income policies or threats of sanctions (positive or negative); 4 = Government participates directly in wage bargaining by providing norms or ceilings (social pacts); 5 = Government imposes private sector wage settlements or suspends bargaining (involuntary wage freeze).

Source: Van Gyes et al. (2006); Visser (2015).

relations frameworks are thus more similar to the Anglo-American countries than to continental European or Northern European countries (Kallaste and Woolfson, 2009). Similar to the low level of centralisation, coordination of wage bargaining has been practically non-existent, with some national coordination mainly on minimum wages in Latvia (Visser, 2005). With that, the Baltic States are clearly at the low end of wage bargaining coordination in the EU, where most countries do have some level of coordination (either implicit or explicit at national or sectoral level).

The Baltic States introduced national-level bargaining at the beginning of the transition process. National-level bargaining takes place in both tripartite and bipartite bodies. Other issues include reforms of labour market legislation, social reforms, pensions and taxations (at least in Latvia). One of the main tasks of national-level bargaining is to decide the level of the minimum wage, but in Estonia the government does not participate in minimum-wage negotiations, unlike in Latvia and Lithuania. The importance of unions even in national-level bargaining is marginal and the main function of tripartite bodies is consultative.

Regional-level bargaining is not developed in the Baltic States (with the exception of sectoral-level agreements concluded in the past in Ida-Viru county in Estonia, which has been characterised by a high unemployment rate and a high proportion of the workforce employed in large enterprises) (Arro et al., 2001). In general, the social partners in the Baltic States have a weak regional structure; in some cases there are no local organisations. One of the main reasons for the lack of regional-level bargaining in the Baltic States is the small geographical unit. At least in the case of Latvia, the disparities in economic activity and development between the regions can also be mentioned as a reason, as Riga is overwhelmingly the centre of economic activity with much less going on in the regions.

Sectoral-level bargaining has also been rare in the Baltic States (Due and Mailand, 2004) with the usual aim of providing minimum standards, for example, fixing the minimum wage in the sector. The main problem in sectoral-level bargaining is weak employer associations, and trade unions have been helping to establish employer federations at branch level to have a social partner in the negotiations. Both employers' and employees' organisations have expressed the need to strengthen collective bargaining at sectoral level. Most of the sectoral-level bargaining takes place in the public sector or sectors with large privatised enterprises. In Estonia sectoral-level agreements exist only in transport and health care; Latvia has sectoral agreements covering energy, nursing and health care, construction, education, culture, forestry, the food industry, trade and fishing, with a total of 30 sectoral agreements in 2004 (EIRO, 2005). Lithuanian industry-level agreements are the least developed in the Baltic States, with only a few such agreements, for example, the agreement in the telecommunications industry and transport (Due and Mailand, 2004; EIRO, 2005). In Latvia, workers in some sectors signed a general agreement that – depending on the sector – regulates the minimum wage or working conditions (length of working day, extra holidays and additional training).

One of the most common forms of cooperation with social partners at the sectoral level in Latvia is the advisory councils. For example, in the area of education there is an advisory council 'Education for all' as well as a youth advisory council, and in the area of health care there is a strategic council of the health sector, the State Employment Agency Advisory Board. In order to ensure an efficient social dialogue, some ministries have formed working groups in which they involve different representatives of the NGO sector. Entrepreneurs' advisory councils operate in several larger cities (Jelgava, Valmiera and Liepaja) advising municipalities on issues related to business development. A particularly successful example is the Liepaja city Tripartite Cooperation Council established in 2009. Its aim is to establish cooperation between Liepaja municipality, employers and the Liepaja labour union (five representatives of each of these three partners) in order to ensure coherent action, consistent with the interests of city problem-solving as regards social and economic issues that would raise the level of social stability and prosperity in the city and increase co-responsibility of the social partners for the decisions and their implementation (Ozola, 2010).

Besides national-level agreements, enterprise-level agreements are the most common in the Baltic States. The problem is that employers are not always interested in concluding collective agreements. Although employers are under a legal obligation to engage in negotiations about the conclusion of an agreement if the employees wish to do so, in practice there are often disputes where employers attempt to avoid signing agreements. Most enterprise-level agreements are concluded in the public sector, in large public sector enterprises or in privatised enterprises. Enterprise-level bargaining has been much less developed in foreign companies (Due and Mailand, 2004) although there is anecdotal evidence that Nordic companies have provided guidelines to their Estonian subsidiaries for the development of collective labour relations. Estimates about enterprise-level agreement coverage in the Baltic States vary. According to Visser (2015), in 2012 the proportion of employees covered by firm-level agreements was 18.5 per cent in Estonia and 8.9 per cent in Lithuania, with no data available for Latvia.

3. EFFECTS OF CHANGES IN INDUSTRIAL RELATIONS ON THE BALANCE BETWEEN FLEXIBILITY AND SECURITY

In the Baltic States the balance between flexibility and security has clearly been biased towards flexibility, so that in the typology of the varieties of capitalism they have been labelled 'flexible market economies' (Kuokštis, 2011). By clustering the countries based on a large number of indicators indicating labour market flexibility and security, Eamets et al. (2008) found that the Baltic countries were characterised by relatively high flexibility, but low levels of social protection. A later study by Eamets et al. (2015) on the mapping of countries on the flexibility and security dimensions indicated that during the crisis years between 2007 and 2011 the Estonian labour market became more flexible (related mainly to the decrease in the Employment Protection Legislation, EPL, index), was still characterised by low social security and experienced large relative changes in active labour policy measures.

As regards inequalities, despite the similar situation with social dialogue and labour market institutions, the inequality dynamics have been different in each of the three Baltic States: in Estonia the initial large increase in inequality (from a Gini index of 0.23 in 1990 to 0.389 in 1993) was followed from around 2000 by decreasing inequality (to 0.31 in 2000); in Latvia there was a continuous rise in inequalities (0.38 in 2010); and in Lithuania an initial increase was followed by a period of stability during 1994–2004 and a further increase to 0.36 by 2010 (Masso et al., 2014). Wage inequalities, similar to overall inequality, have not been stable, although their evolution has been shaped by the business cycle rather than by developments in social dialogue; in 2010 the ratio of the 9th to the 1st wage decile was relatively high, ranging from 4.6 in Latvia to 4.1 in Estonia (Masso et al., 2014). These development differences are thus probably unrelated to social dialogue, given its relatively limited role. Also, although Latvia seems to be the country with the strongest union movement, generally it seems that this has not given rise to more balanced labour market outcomes or inequalities.

One possible explanation of the developments described above is that the Baltic States, together with some other EU countries, have had inadequate social dialogue on flexicurity (from national experts' reports; Philips and Eamets, 2007). Also, policy-makers have sometimes misused the flexicurity concept by adopting only the flexibility part of the reform packages, as was the case in Estonia's 2009 reform of labour legislation, in which the state abandoned its earlier promises (Masso et al., 2015). Woolfson and Kallaste (2011) argued that the agreement reached on the new labour legislation in 2008 in Estonia proved to be a double-edged sword for the trade unions; although it was supposed to follow the principles of flexicurity, in the end only the flexibility part of the agreement was adopted. The government's steps simply overrode the social dialogue process and broke the tripartite principles in place since 2003 that required all employment policies to be subject to consultation with the social partners.

While there was some progress in social dialogue before the crisis in Estonia regarding, for example, minimum wage negotiations, agreement on general principles of consultation since 2003, agreement on a new labour law (Woolfson and Kallaste, 2011) and the crisis – 'Great Recession' – which was especially deep in the Baltics (Masso and Krillo, 2011) – also had negative consequences for the existing structures of social dialogue in the Baltic States. Woolfson and Kallaste (2011), when analysing the viability of social dialogue related to the Great Recession, argued that trade unions failed to influence government actions (austerity measures) despite the existence of neo-corporatist forms of social dialogue. In response to the crisis, the social partners in each of the Baltic States formulated their proposals for alternative policy responses (Masso and Krillo, 2011), but in order to achieve its fiscal goals (balancing the state budget) the Estonian government pushed through several austerity measures without any negative reaction from either employees or employers. There were demonstrations in Latvia and Lithuania in 2009, but not in Estonia. In Lithuania the tripartite negotiations were swept away as involving unacceptable delays for imposing the adjustment deemed necessary to cope with the crisis (Woolfson and Kallaste, 2011). In Latvia, the unions found themselves excluded from the agreement with the International Monetary Fund (IMF). The slightly higher residual strength in Latvia compared with Estonia may be related to a readiness to involve unions in discussions in 2010 (Woolfson and Kallaste, 2011). As a consequence of the crisis, Baltic representatives of organised labour were unable to mobilise a sustained broader opposition to government-imposed crisis measures, and now face their own crisis of credibility (Woolfson and Kallaste, 2011). Woolfson and Kallaste (2011) indicate that the response in Latvia and Lithuania and the lack of a response in Estonia indicate their different capabilities. Woolfson and Kallaste (2011) were critical about the partial reinstatement of social dialogue in the Baltics after the crisis, calling it 'Illusory corporatism "Mark 2"' as it may further undermine representational credibility and collective bargaining.

4. EFFECTS OF CHANGES IN INDUSTRIAL RELATIONS ON LABOUR MARKET INEQUALITIES

4.1 Effects of Minimum Wages on Inequalities

In this section we look at how in Estonia the minimum wage – which arises from social dialogue – has made it possible to decrease inequalities. However, although minimum wages are subject to social dialogue, average wages are relatively unaffected owing to low collective agreement coverage. In Estonia minimum wages have increased considerably during the past decade. Compared with 2005, the minimum wage was 150 per cent higher in 2016 (see Figure 2.1). During the pre-crisis boom years (2005–07) the minimum wage increased gradually. However, the minimum wage–average wage (MW/AW) ratio decreased, because the increase in average wages exceeded the minimum wage increase.

During the economic recession years (2008–09) and two years of recovery (2010–11) the minimum wage stayed at the same level. Since the average wage decreased during the recession, the MW/AW ratio increased in 2008–09, but after that decreased again during 2010–12. For more

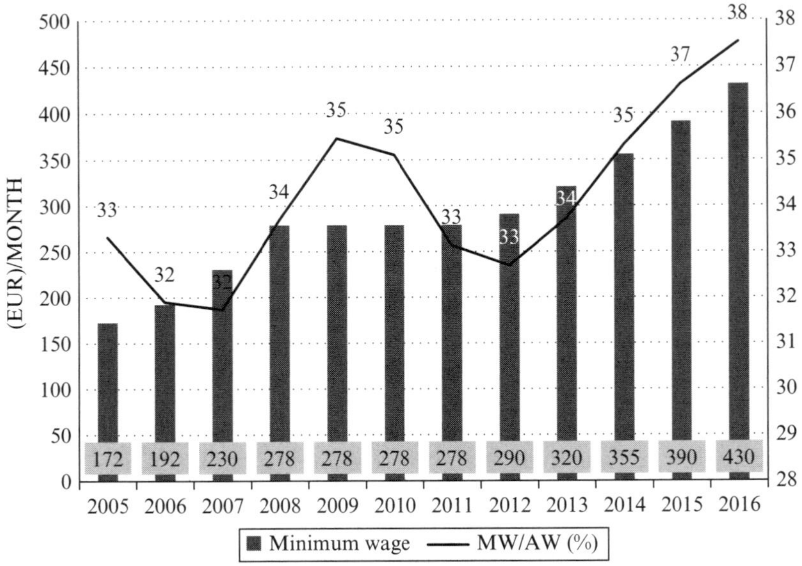

Figure 2.1 Minimum wages (primary axis) and MW/AW ratio (secondary axis) in Estonia

details about development in minimum wages before the recession, see Masso and Krillo (2010) and for adjustments during the recession, see Masso and Krillo (2011).

During the recovery the minimum wage increased quickly, driven by rapidly increasing average wages and an increasing labour shortage. Since the increase in minimum wages has exceeded the increase in average wages, the MW/AW (Kaitz index) ratio has increased (see Figure 2.1). That indicator had already increased in the past, from 18.9 per cent in 1995 to 31.9 per cent in 2007, although never reaching the target of 41 per cent set for 2008 in 2001 (Masso and Krillo, 2010).

The national minimum wage in Estonia is agreed in annual bipartite meetings between the Estonian Trade Union Confederation (employees' representative at national level, ETUC) and the Estonian Employers' Confederation (employers' representative at national level, EEC), and is given legal force by the government, which does not actively participate in negotiations. During the past decade, the national minimum wage negotiation process has been rather smooth. Employees' and employers' representatives have reached agreement about the minimum wage each year, even during difficult economic situations. As can be seen from the

MW/AW ratio, the relative bargaining power of the employers was higher than for employees' representatives. During the crisis years it was agreed that the minimum wage should stay at the same level. Both employers' and employees' representatives agreed that this was necessary to soften upward wage pressure and to avoid an increase in the shadow economy and redundancies.

The ETUC opened the minimum wage negotiations again in mid-2011 demanding a minimum-wage increase of 17 per cent to €325 in 2012 (at first the ETUC demanded that the minimum wage should be increased to this level in July 2011, but this was not accepted by the EEC). For the ETUC the main argument for a minimum-wage increase was the need to recover its purchasing power because of the rising cost of living and pensions. Although initially the employers' organisation declared that it could not accept an increase in the minimum wage until the economy had grown in four consecutive quarters, the minimum wage was increased by 4 per cent in December 2011. At that time the employers emphasised that the minimum-wage increase was necessary in the light of increasing pensions to avoid the situation in which people prefer to retire early.

During 2012–14 the minimum-wage negotiations saw no particular problems; each year the agreement was made between the ETUC and the EEC. In 2015 the negotiations for the 2016 minimum-wage level were very intense. The negotiations reached a deadlock because neither of the parties made concessions. The ETUC demanded that the minimum wage be increased to €488 in 2016 and €609 in 2017. Their main argument was the problem of in-work poverty, employees' expectations of a wage increase and promises made by the new government (in power since 2015) to increase the minimum wage to 45 per cent of the average wage in the next four years. The EEC proposed a minimum-wage level of €417 in 2016 and €448 in 2017. They reasoned that a wage increase that exceeded economic growth and a lower minimum wage in the other Baltic States endangers low-paid jobs. In June 2015 the ETUC declared that since the EEC had not made an acceptable proposal, they would turn to the official mediator. The ensuing process was intense, but finally, with the help of the official mediator, an agreement was made at the end of October 2015.

Minimum wages may have an impact on wage inequality depending on the extent of the spillover effects. One possible explanation for the increase in the observed MW/AW ratio could be that the lack of collective bargaining limits the minimum-wage spillover effect and thereby minimum wages may have reduced inequalities to the detriment of all other employees, so that the balance of flexibility–security does not reach all workers but only those at the bottom. While in a company survey in 2006 around 30 per cent of surveyed firms indicated the presence of minimum-wage spillover effects, in another, more recent, survey (Rõõm, 2015) only 16 per cent of employers participating in the study said that there were spillover effects; that is, they increased the wages of non-minimum-wage earners and 10 per cent of employees' wages were increased due to the increase in the minimum wage. Ferraro et al. (2016) analysed the effects of the statutory minimum wage on the wage distribution in Estonia during 2011–14. They found that there are substantial spillover effects from the minimum wage to the lower percentiles of the wage distribution, but the spillover effect declines markedly as the wage approaches the median wage. The computed marginal effect is positive and statistically significant for wages up to the 45th percentile; the effects are most substantial up to the 20th percentile and then decline quickly as the wage approaches the median. Therefore, the minimum wage appears to have contributed to lower wage inequality in Estonia. The estimated spillover effects imply for 2014 that an increase of €1 in the minimum wage is associated with an increase of €0.11 in the average wage of all full-time wage earners. A recent study analysed the economic effects of minimum wage increases based on a survey of companies (Rõõm, 2015). More specifically, the focus was on the 2014 minimum-wage increase. The study revealed that 0.7 per cent of employers had to lay off workers, 2.8 per cent of employers could not create new jobs and 1.6 per cent left vacant positions unfilled owing to the increase in the minimum wage. In total, generally owing to the increase in the minimum wage, the decrease in employment was 0.2 per cent.

Several fees and prices are linked to the minimum wage, therefore it also affects inequalities via this channel. For example, in several Estonian local governments (including Tallinn and Tartu, the two largest cities) kindergarten fees depend on the minimum wage, as do child vacation benefit, the minimum level of alimony, the minimum level of parental benefit and so on. However, since there are no studies, there is no information on how large the effects of minimum-wage increases are on inequalities.

4.2 Effect of Unionisation on Wages

One of the strongest channels through which unionisation affects labour market outcomes of employees is collective bargaining power. Previous empirical evidence (Nickell and Layard, 1999; Western and Rosenfeld, 2011) has shown that union bargaining power fosters higher wage rates among unionised workers and, hence, might generate more unemployment.

In this section we, first, analyse the effects of collective bargaining. That is, we focus on: (1) the average wage premium to workers in a union, relative to non-unionised employees; (2) the wage premium to unionisation across different wage-groups; and (3) the effects of unionisation on the gender pay gap. The analysis relies on the Estonian Labour Force Survey (EE-LFS) panel data for 2006–13. The survey is conducted on a quarterly basis among Estonia's working-age population (15–75 years of age). Union membership is explicitly asked about in the survey. Thus, the unionisation identifier was constructed as a dummy variable equal to 1 for those working at enterprises or organisations with unions representing employees' interests. The main outcome variable is net salary earned in the previous month (including bonuses). We limit our sample to full-time employed respondents with wages in the previous month. This limitation leaves us with a sample of 55 162 observations of whom 9921 are union members and 45 241 are non-members.

Descriptive profiles of unionised and non-unionised employees are presented in Table 2.4. This table reveals that there are systematic differences in individual and employment profiles of union and non-union members. Among non-union workers males constitute around 51 per cent, whereas among union workers the share of males is only about 38 per cent. Union employees are on average older than non-union employees (46 years compared with 42 years) and possess a better educational profile (37.7 per cent have a higher education compared with 21.7 per cent among non-union employees). Estonian is a native language for 65.8 per cent and 75.2 per cent of union and non-union workers, respectively. In terms of occupational characteristics, union members predominantly occupy high-level positions (48.4 per cent) and have longer employment tenure at their current workplace (around 12 years compared with about seven years among non-unionised employees). Remarkably, almost 9 per cent of unionised workers participated in on-the-job training over four weeks prior to the survey, while only around 4 per cent of non-unionised employees did so. As expected, union workers are dominant in the public sector (51.5 per cent), followed by the secondary sector (20.9 per cent) and transport (15 per cent). Non-union workers are mostly employed in the private sector (33.3 per cent). In terms of employer size, union workers are more often employed in larger enterprises: 17.8 per cent of union members work in organisations with 500 or more employees, compared with 3.3 per cent of non-union members.

Starting from 2007, the EE-LFS also asks which union confederation the employee's union belongs to. This allows us to disentangle respondents affiliated with the two central trade union organisations, highlighted in section 2.1, TALO and EAKL. As expected, members of TALO and EAKL are systematically different because they organise different types of workers. As stressed in section 2.1, TALO mainly represents white-collar workers, whereas EAKL represents blue-collar employees. Our descriptive

Table 2.4 Descriptive characteristics of unionised and non-unionised workers, Estonia

Variable	Non-union workers	Union workers
Male, %	50.9	37.9
Age	42	46
Basic education, %	21.1	14.2
Medium education, %	57.2	48.1
Higher education, %	21.7	37.7
Married, %	71.8	73.7
Single, %	18.7	13.7
Widowed, %	9.5	12.6
Estonian home language, %	75.2	65.8
Occupation level, %		
High occupation	33.4	48.4
Medium occupation	20.1	19.1
Low occupation	45.8	32.4
Work tenure, years	6.8	12.4
Hours usually worked	41	41
Written regular employment contact, %	91.7	93.1
Industry of employment, %		
Primary	6.5	3.5
Secondary sector	25.7	20.9
Energy	1.1	2.8
Construction	11.6	3.5
Sales and trade	33.3	.
Hotels	3.4	0.3
Transport	8.6	15.0
Finance	1.4	0.6
Other business services	5.5	1.4
Public services	20.4	51.5
Workplace size, %		
1–10	22.3	4.5
11–49	44.5	28.6
50–199	22.4	35.0
200–499	5.5	13.5
500 and more	3.3	17.8
Workplace location, %		
Northern Estonia	39.7	40.0
Central Estonia	14.1	10.6
North-eastern Estonia	6.5	16.2
Western Estonia	14.3	10.4
Southern Estonia	25.4	22.8
Training at work, %	3.9	8.8
Number of observations	45241	9921

Note: Estimates based on 2006–13 EE-LFS.

evidence supports this notion. That is, TALO members possess much better educational profiles (61 per cent have a university degree, whereas among EAKL union workers only 33 per cent have a university degree) and occupational characteristics (73 per cent of TALO members hold high-level occupations, compared with 43 per cent in EAKL). It is worth noting that average wages are almost identical across the two organisations, despite the better occupational and educational traits of TALO members. The latter can be explained to some extent by the larger share of state-owned enterprises affiliated with TALO (91 per cent) than with EAKL (61 per cent), yielding on average a lower wage level compared with the private sector.[5]

4.2.1 Effect of unionisation on average wages

To approximate the effect of union bargaining power in Estonia, we measure the wage difference of unionised workers over the non-unionised. We apply two methodological tools: ordinary least squares (OLS) regression with unionisation dummy variable and propensity score matching (PSM). Previous evidence showed that in Estonia union membership does not have a statistically significant wage effect when controlling for a wide set of socio-demographic and occupational characteristics of respondents (Eamets and Kallaste, 2005). We first estimate the wage OLS regression in order to evaluate how the unionisation coefficient changes with stepwise adding of individual regression controls. Second, we replicate the PSM estimation similar to Eamets and Kallaste (2005) using the same survey but a much longer panel (2006–13). Although PSM provides much more robust estimates of the union wage differential compared with OLS regression, the latter will better illustrate the variation in wage effects of unionisation when other factors are taken into account.

Table 2.5 presents the results of OLS regressions with five model specifications. All models regress individual monthly net earnings on the union status dummy and a set of additional controls, included stepwise. In the base specification (model 1) the set of controls includes socio-demographic characteristics (age, education, marital status and Estonian as native language). Model 2 additionally to the socio-demographic variables accounts for industry of employment and enterprise ownership. Model 3 adds enterprise size and location to the list of controls. In model 4, occupation level is added. The final, preferred, specification (model 5) adds to all previous variables additional employment characteristics – employment contract type, work tenure, usual work hours and overtime work.

The baseline model reported a statistically significant wage premium to union membership of 7.6 per cent. Including industry of employment and enterprise ownership, variables increased the union coefficient to 8.7

Table 2.5 OLS wage regression, Estonia

	Model 1	Model 2	Model 3	Model 4	Model 5
Union (1 = yes)	0.076 0.005***	0.087 0.005***	0.023 0.005***	0.02 0.005***	0.012 0.005**
Demographic characteristics	Yes	Yes	Yes	Yes	Yes
Industry of employment		Yes	Yes	Yes	Yes
State-owned enterprise (1 = yes)		Yes	Yes	Yes	Yes
Enterprise size			Yes	Yes	Yes
Location of the enterprise			Yes	Yes	Yes
Occupation level				Yes	Yes
Employment contract type					Yes
Work tenure (years)					Yes
Overtime work (1 = yes)					Yes
Hours worked					Yes
Yearly dummies	Yes	Yes	Yes	Yes	Yes
N	52 140	44 218	42 269	42 001	39 324
Adj. R^2	0.892	0.892	0.91	0.918	0.92

Notes:
***, ** and * indicate results significant at 1 per cent, 5 per cent and 10 per cent levels respectively.
Dependent variable is logarithm of monthly wage. Demographic characteristics comprise age, age squared, education, marital status and Estonian as native language. Industry variables include: primary and secondary sectors, energy, construction, transport, hotels, sales and trade, finance, other business services and public services. Enterprise size dummies: 1–10, 11–49, 50–199, 200–499 and 500 and more employees. Location of enterprise variables: Northern, Central, North-eastern, Western and Southern Estonia. Occupational level defined based on ISCO codes as follows: 0–3 corresponds to low-level occupations, 4–6 and 7–9 to medium and high level accordingly. Employment contract type dummies: regular, fixed-term, service, verbal and other type of contract. Estimated based on EE-LFS panel data for years 2006–13.

per cent. However, when accounting additionally for location and size of enterprise (model 3) the amount of the union wage premium decreased by a factor of four, to 2.3 per cent. Occupation-related characteristics included in models 4 and 5 appeared to further reduce the union pay premium, although marginally. The final specification (model 5) with the full set of characteristics accounted for a reported 1.2 per cent union membership effect. Thus, stepwise inclusion of regressors revealed that the major part of the initial union membership wage premium disappears when adding enterprise location and size variables. The latter is associated with high dependency of wage level on firm size – larger enterprises on average have higher pay rates – and substantial regional heterogeneity of pay rates (on average higher wages are payable by enterprises located in, for example, northern Estonia, where the capital city is located).

Matching-based techniques, including the PSM procedure, allow us to more precisely evaluate the true wage effects of union membership by constructing a counterfactual group of non-unionised workers (control group) with characteristics similar to unionised workers (treatment group). Thus, the pay gap between unionised workers paired with their counterfactual non-unionised counterparts is the wage differential of prime interest. Since the latter is evaluated on otherwise similar matched pairs of union and non-union employees it is believed to reflect the 'true' effect of unionisation. We control for the most extensive list of variables from model 5 in the PSM estimation (socio-demographic characteristics together with a full set of employment-related variables). The matching algorithm allows for a 0.002 maximal distance in probabilities (propensity scores) to be considered the same. We perform matching without replacement[6] (observations from control group are used once) and the probability of belonging to a union is estimated using a probit model.[7]

The results of PSM estimation, together with matched sample sizes are presented in Table 2.6. Unlike the OLS estimates of model 5, matching-based estimates reported an insignificant wage premium to union membership. The estimated difference in the average pay of unionised and non-unionised workers declines from 7.5 per cent in the unmatched sample to 1.8 per cent in the matched one. Hence, similar to Eamets and Kallaste (2005) our results show that the union pay differential originates almost entirely from the difference in individual characteristics across unionised and non-unionised groups of workers. As expected, the PSM procedure provides more robust estimates of union pay effect, as it estimates wage differential on the groups of fully comparable unionised and non-unionised workers, having identical likelihood to be in the union.

4.2.2 Effects of unionisation on wage inequality

Although the overall effect of unionisation on wage level is insignificant, some categories of workers may still benefit from union membership to a larger extent. To estimate a heterogeneous effect of unions on wages, returns to union membership have to be evaluated over a full wage distribution, but not only at mean earnings. For that we apply a conditional quantile regression, allowing us to estimate the effects of controls on

Table 2.6 Propensity score matching estimation, Estonia

Matching results (probit estimation of propensity scores, caliper 0.002, matching without replacement)

Sample	Treated	Controls	Difference	S.E.	T-stat
Unmatched	7.999	7.924	0.075	0.016	4.720
ATT	7.979	7.962	0.018	0.020	0.870

Treatment assignment	Common support		Total
	Off support	On support	
Untreated	31 488	6778	38 266
Treated	1612	6742	8354
Total	33 100	13 520	46 620

Note: Assignment to treatment variable is union membership dummy (1 = in union). Dependent variable is logarithm of monthly wage. Matching procedure controls for age, age squared, education, marital status, Estonian as native language, industry of employment, enterprise ownership, location and size, and occupational characteristics, including level of occupation, type of employment contract work tenure, hours usually worked and overtime work.

individual quantiles of the wage distribution. This approach was previously widely applied in the analysis of wage disparities (Christofides et al., 2013).

Table 2.7 presents a model of the same specification as model 5, but estimated over the entire wage distribution. The results reveal that the effects of union membership vary depending on workers' earnings' category. The most beneficial unions appear to be for low- and high-earning employees. In particular, a statistically significant, albeit small positive effect on earnings is observed for employees in the 10th and 90th quantiles of wage distribution (2.8 per cent and 2.6 per cent, respectively). Hence, at the lowest and highest ends of the wage distribution unions yield higher earnings for their members, compared with non-unionised employees. For median earners unions do not contribute significantly to the wage level. One potential reason for heterogeneous wage effects is a lack of union bargaining power, which impedes the extension of the positive wage impact to medium-category workers. Positive wage effects on the upper end of the earnings distribution may be partly explained by public sector high-level employees, who are mostly covered by collective agreements.

Table 2.7 Effect of union membership across wage quantiles, Estonia

Variable	OLS	Quantile regression				
		10th	25th	50th	75th	90th
Union member	0.012 (0.005)**	0.028 (0.02)**	0.022 (0.01)*	0.017 (0.01)	0.015 (0.02)	0.026 (0.01)**
Number of observations	39 324					

Notes:
***, ** and * indicate results significant at 1 per cent, 5 per cent and 10 per cent levels respectively.
Dependent variable is logarithm of monthly wage. The model additionally controls for age, age squared, education, marital status, Estonian as a home language, industry of employment, enterprise ownership, size and location, occupation level, contract type, work tenure, overtime work, usual hours worked during a week and year dummies. Estimated based on EE-LFS panel data for years 2006–13.

4.2.3 Effects of unionisation on gender pay gap

While aiming to support workers' rights and foster wage benefits, unions can contribute significantly to overcoming gender pay disparities in the labour market. Male–female pay inequality has remained a substantial issue in recent decades, despite women's continuously improving educational and employment possibilities, as well as active policy measures tackling gender inequality issues. The wage-bidding power of unions can be another mechanism for reducing the male–female pay gap. Given that in Estonia unions dominate in the industries with predominantly female employees (see Table 2.4), collective bargaining power is expected to positively affect women's wage rates, relative to non-unionised female workers.

To check this proposition, we perform parametric Oaxaca-Blinder decomposition (see Oaxaca, 1973, for technical details) of gender pay difference among unionised and non-unionised employees. Decomposition allows us to identify the extent to which the actual mean wage difference between men and women is explained by the observed difference in a set of their characteristics. Consequently, the remaining fraction, which cannot be attributed to differences in personal traits between the two groups, is commonly referred to as the unexplained part of a gap or discrimination. In order to account for all possible observable differences in male and female characteristics, we incorporated all controls specified in model 5 (Table 2.5) and grouped them in two categories: socio-demographic and employment traits.

The last row of Table 2.8 documents the fact that among non-unionised workers the male–female pay gap is 34 per cent, whereas among unionised

Table 2.8 Gender wage gap among unionised and non-unionised workers, Estonia

Factors	Union workers			Non-union workers		
	Gaps in ln(netwage)			Gaps in ln(netwage)		
	Explained	*Unexplained*	*Total*	*Explained*	*Unexplained*	*Total*
Socio-demographic	0.04***	–0.18	–0.14	0.03***	–0.14	–0.11
Employment related	–0.02*	0.61	0.59	–0.06***	–0.54***	–0.60
Total	0.04*	–0.24***	–0.20***	–0.09***	–0.25***	–0.34***

Notes:
***, ** and * indicate results significant at 1 per cent, 5 per cent and 10 per cent levels respectively.
Decomposition was performed using grouped control variables. Socio-demographic: age, education, marital status and native language. Employment related: industry, enterprise ownership and location, size of the enterprise, occupation held, type of employment contract, work tenure, overtime work and work hours. Decomposition procedure incorporates year effects. Estimated based on EE-LFS panel data for years 2006–13.

workers it is 20 per cent. Thus unionisation narrows the gender wage gap by 14 percentage points. Remarkably, the fraction of the explained wage differential for union members is positive (4 percentage points), whereas among the non-unionised the fraction is negative (–9 percentage points). This implies that unionised female employees are relatively stronger in their background and employment characteristics relative to non-unionised female employees, yielding their better wage returns and a smaller wage gap with their male counterparts. Otherwise, a relatively higher explained part could also favour the narrative that unions improve the position of females; for example, a smaller unexplained part means there are fewer differences with regard to how females' skills are valued – males and females get more equal returns for their skills. However, among men and women with a comparable set of characteristics, women are disfavoured among both unionised and non-unionised employees. The latter effect is absorbed by the unexplained fraction of the pay differential.

4.2.4 Relationship of unionisation to inequalities in other working conditions

Besides wages, unionisation and social dialogue may be related to other kinds of work-related inequalities. Table 2.9 presents means and standard deviations of indicators of working conditions available in the EE-LFS for unionised and non-unionised workers. For most of these – such as

Table 2.9 Working conditions among unionised and non-unionised workers, Estonia

Variable	Union workers		Non-union workers	
	Mean	Standard dev.	Mean	Standard dev.
Working hours	39.049	7.129	39.114	7.234
Satisfied with safety (dummy)	0.918	0.274	0.939	0.239
Satisfied with work intensity(dummy)	0.885	0.319	0.914	0.281
Satisfied with health checks (dummy)	0.852	0.355	0.844	0.363
Satisfied with design of workplace (dummy)	0.885	0.320	0.911	0.285
Training (dummy)	0.069	0.254	0.034	0.181
Training paid by employer (dummy)	0.049	0.215	0.024	0.154
Training hours	22.321	92.044	20.811	84.297
Unpaid overtime	0.023	0.149	0.014	0.117
Permanent contract	0.932	0.251	0.917	0.276
Temporary contract	0.035	0.183	0.032	0.177
Oral contract	0.000	0.014	0.012	0.107

Source: Own calculations by EE-LFS panel data for years 2006–13.

working hours, type of employment contract or satisfaction with working conditions – the differences are relatively small, but one result that is robust across different indicators is that union workers are clearly better off in terms of training.

4.3 Discussion

Overall, our results show that trade unions in Estonia lack bargaining power in wage negotiations. Workers employed in unionised enterprises earn, on average, higher wages compared with employees from non-unionised units, although this difference is almost fully attributed to individual profiles of workers and characteristics of enterprises. On average, union membership status exhibits no positive statistically significant effect on the wage level once all the other characteristics are taken into account. However, positive effects of union membership on wage rates may be relatively small owing to collective agreement legislation. Trade unions do not necessarily enforce collective agreements, although they foster the negotiation process.

However, the results provided some evidence of heterogeneous effects of unionisation, depending on wage category. While overall returns to unionisation are relatively insignificant, we documented that workers at the very low and high ends of the wage distribution benefit more from union membership. This result is particularly important in the context of low-earning individuals. Utilising wage-bidding power by supporting employees in the lowest wage categories is one channel of the union for reducing income inequality. Similarly, we found that females benefit from union membership relatively more than their male counterparts. This provides further evidence in favour of unionisation, as it contributes to the gender wage gap, an acute issue in Estonia.

5. CASE STUDIES

5.1 Addressing (In)equality Issues in Collective Agreements, Estonia

5.1.1 Introduction

Social dialogue takes place at three levels: state, sector and enterprise. In this case study the focus is on enterprise-level industrial relations. Because there are only a few sectoral collective agreements, we provide an extensive overview of the situation. We address the question of how (in)equality issues are addressed in the collective agreements signed at company level. This analysis is complemented with experience of two organisations – Eesti Energia and the Estonian Police and Border Guard Board – that recently addressed inequality issues due to the need to equalise the working conditions of workers of different units of the organisation.

5.1.2 Data

In the analysis, data from the database of collective agreements is used. This database includes all collective agreements signed in Estonia, because according to the Collective Agreements Act, section 41, collective agreements entered into force shall be registered in a database maintained by the Ministry of Social Affairs. The database contains data on the signatory parties, number of workers covered by the collective agreement, date of entry into force, term of validity, date of submission, which working and pay conditions are regulated in the agreement, and so on (Statutes of Estonian Collective Agreements Register, s. 3).

In the analysis we use data from the collective agreements signed. Although it would also be informative to give an overview of the number of collective agreements in force, it is not possible owing to lack of reliable data. The database of collective agreements includes information on date of expiry, but according to the Ministry of Social Affairs, this information is not correct for all contracts. For many agreements this information is missing, therefore it is also not possible to give an overview of how many employees are covered by the collective agreements.

The analysis covers 2005–16. The longer time period – more than a decade – enables us to see trends that could not be observed when analysing data for only a few years. Also, during this period rapid changes occurred in the Estonian economy: during 2005–07 there was rapid economic growth, followed by economic crisis and recovery.

In addition to the statistical analysis, interviews were completed with the human resource (HR) manager and trade union representative of Eesti Energia. This company has recently addressed inequality issues because of the need to harmonise the working conditions of different units. The experience of Eesti Energia provides useful information on challenges faced during this process and the importance of constructive social dialogue between employer and employees' representatives.

5.1.3 How equality issues are covered in collective agreements

In Estonia, the number of collective agreements signed has decreased considerably during the past decade (see Figure 2.2 which includes all collective agreements signed in Estonia, at enterprise level, sector level and

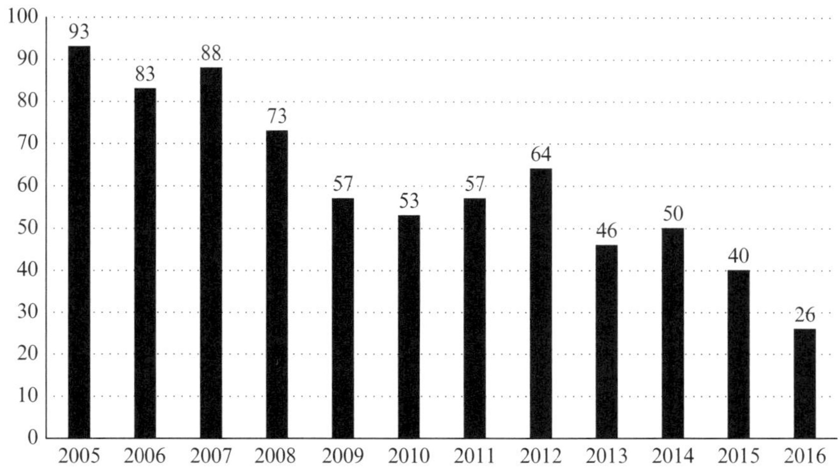

Note: * At 10 August 2016.

Source: Collective agreements database, Ministry of Social Affairs.

Figure 2.2 Number of collective agreements signed in Estonia

state level). While during the economic boom of 2005–07 about 90 collective agreements were signed each year, the activity decreased during the recession in 2008–10. During the economic recovery in 2011–15, however, the number of collective agreements signed was stable at between 40 and 50. For comparison, in 2014 there were more than 76 000 active enterprises in Estonia, compared with 44 000 in 2005 (Statistics Estonia database). The vast majority – more than 90 per cent – of collective agreements are signed by a single employer (from one company only, rather than a group of companies) in Estonia. The EEC signs statutory minimum wage agreements.

Only in a very limited number of individual company-level collective agreements are there provisions regulating the equal treatment of employees and avoiding discrimination. In Box 2.1, the exact wording of the

BOX 2.1 AGREEMENTS ON FOLLOWING AND PROMOTING EQUAL TREATMENT AND AVOIDING DISCRIMINATION IN COLLECTIVE AGREEMENTS SIGNED IN ESTONIA DURING 2010–16

- The employer shall treat all employees equally in job-related issues (collective agreement between Estonian Public Broadcasting and Estonian Union of Journalists, signed in 2010).
- The employer shall treat all employees equally in wage and job-related issues (collective agreement between Estonian Public Broadcasting and Estonian Union of Journalists, signed in 2012; collective agreement between Estonian Public Broadcasting and Television Creative Workers' Union, signed in 2012).
- With the collective agreement, the employer guarantees the protection of employees from discrimination, follows the principle' of equal treatment and promotes equal rights according to the Equal Treatment Act and the Gender Equality Act (collective agreement between Haapsalu city government, Lääne county central library and employees' trustee, signed in 2012, collective agreement signed by same parties in 2014 and 2015).
- The employer and the union confirm that all employees of the group shall be treated equally based on the principle of equal treatment and differences in treatment can be made only based on differences of work specifics and the tasks of the employee (collective agreement between Eesti Energia, Elektrilevi, Eesti Energia Võrguehitus, Estonian Federation of Trade Unions of Energy Workers, Independent Union of Miners and Energy Workers, signed in 2013; collective agreement between Eesti Energia Õlitööstus and Narva Energy Trade Union, signed in 2014; collective agreement between Elektrilevi and Estonian Federation of Trade Unions of Energy Workers, signed in 2015; Leonhard Weiss Energy and Southern-Estonian Electricity Trade Union, signed in 2015; collective agreement between Eesti Energia, Estonian Federation of Trade Unions of Energy Workers, Independent Union of Miners and Energy Workers, signed in 2015).

- The employer shall pay an annual bonus to workers on the same basis as other employees (collective agreement between Estonian Air Navigation Services and Estonian Air Traffic Controllers' Association, signed in 2013).
- Men and women shall be paid equally for equal work (collective agreement between Paide Taxi and workers' representative, signed in 2014; collective agreement between Rescue Board and Estonian Rescue Workers' Trade Union, signed in 2014 and 2015).
- When communicating, parties shall maintain mutual trust, honouring interests and equal treatment principles (collective agreement between G4S and Security Guards' Trade Union and trustee, signed in 2014).
- The employer must guarantee equal remuneration for equal and equivalent work for men and women (collective agreement between Collade and trustee, signed in 2015).
- Parties shall monitor that in the recruiting process and during the employment relationship persons are not treated unequally based on gender, nationality, union membership and so on. The employer shall guarantee to the trade union the access to data necessary to check compliance. The employer and the trade union shall cooperate to guarantee a working environment that takes into account the needs of different people without infringing the rights of others (collective agreement between Eesti Teed and Estonian Transport and Road Workers' Trade Union, signed in 2016).

collective agreement including such provision is provided. As can be seen, the provisions are rather general.

5.1.4 Experience of Eesti Energia

Eesti Energia, the first case study, is an international energy company that operates in the unified electricity market of the Baltic and Nordic countries. Its sole shareholder is the Republic of Estonia. With its approximately 6300 employees (in 2015), Eesti Energia is one of the largest employers in Estonia. Eesti Energia Group consists of a number of companies, as can be seen in Figure 2.3. The companies belonging to the Eesti Energia Group have their own collective agreements; there is no unified collective agreement for the group as a whole.

As can be seen from Box 2.1, all collective agreements of Eesti Energia and its different units include a declaration that all employees of the group shall be treated equally based on the principle of equal treatment, and differences in treatment can be made only based on differences of work specifics and specifics of the tasks of the employee. In the interview, the HR director of Eesti Energia said that in reality the situation is much more complicated. There are major changes in the energy sector and pressure for price reductions at the same time. These developments are forcing the organisation to change and modernise and this in turn has an influence on industrial relations.

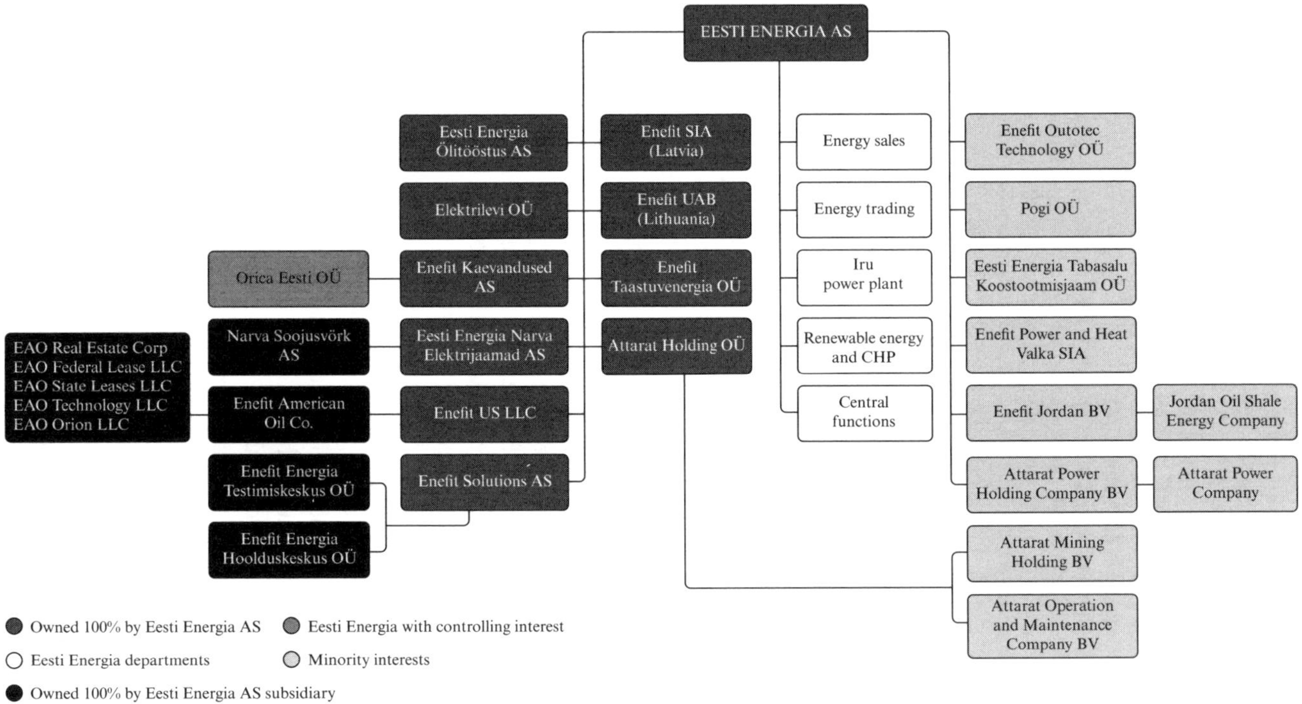

Figure 2.3 Structure of Eesti Energia Group (at July 2016)

The HR director admitted that although collective agreements include a clause declaring equal treatment, the collective agreements signed in the Eesti Energia Group are different and at the moment the situation is fairly unequal. The challenge is related to mergers of affiliates. According to Estonian law, when companies merge and both companies have signed a collective agreement, both collective agreements apply (only the more beneficial articles, of course) to the employees of the merging company. This situation lasts until the company signs a new collective agreement. Until then there may be a situation in which 'old' and 'new' employees are treated unequally. A solution could be either to apply more beneficial conditions to all employees or to sign a new collective agreement that includes conditions favourable to the employer. The first is not economically reasonable to the employer because it results in an increase of costs, the latter is likely to meet the resistance of the trade union.

The goal of the Eesti Energia Group is to move towards unified collective agreements, said the HR director. This, she said, would enable it to decrease the inequality between employees of different companies belonging to the group and be more competitive. The employer would like to move towards modernising collective agreements and make pay more dependent on work quality and economic results. However, this is complicated because the social partners want to hold on to the old fringe benefit system, including vacation benefit, Christmas benefit, additional benefit for working in the evenings, and so on. In her opinion this system is not suitable for employees working in a successful company and does not motivate employees to do their best in delivering high-quality products on time to the customer.

The representative of the Eesti Energia trade union also pointed out in the interview that for several years Eesti Energia has proposed that all collective agreements of the group should be equal. The representative of the trade unions admitted that trade unions do not oppose this idea per se, but he said that it is unlikely to succeed because the employer and employees' representatives cannot reach agreement on the terms of the unified collective agreement. He said that while the employer would like to minimise benefits, the trade unions would accept a solution in which the unified collective agreement consists of only the most beneficial clauses of the valid collective agreements.

It is thus highly likely that at least in the near future the situation will remain unchanged and the subunits of the group have their own collective agreements. This means that employees are treated equally within the subunit, but not in the group. The trade union representative also admitted that the most urgent problem for them at the moment is that in recent years attempts to organise new trade unions in the energy sector have failed. The attempts to start negotiations with the employers' federations in the energy sector have also not been successful. As the representative said, this means that trade unions have not been successful in decreasing social dumping by enterprises that do not have trade union and collective agreements.

5.1.5 Conclusion

In Estonia, the issue of equal treatment has been addressed only in a very limited number of collective agreements. The experience of Eesti Energia, one of Estonia's largest employers, illustrates the challenges involved in achieving equality for the employed. Eesti Energia is one of the few companies that has explicitly included the claim of equal treatment of employees in the collective agreements signed. The reality is more complex, however. In the Eesti Energia Group several companies have signed collective agreements with different trade unions. These collective agreements include different bonuses, creating inequality between employees in the Eesti Energia Group. While the employer would like to sign a unified collective agreement, the trade unions oppose the idea unless the unified collective agreement includes the most beneficial clauses of all collective agreements in force in the group. This, in turn, is not acceptable to the employer, who says that this would have a major impact on competitiveness. A solution has not yet been found. This case well illustrates the challenges related to equal treatment of employees and the importance of collective bargaining.

5.2 The Micro-enterprises Law and the Effects on Inequality

Amid the latest economic crisis, on 1 September 2010 a new law on micro-enterprises came into effect in Latvia. It introduced a new type of contract, that of micro-entrepreneurs (Law on Micro-enterprises 2016). At the core of it was a much reduced tax rate (9 per cent micro-enterprise tax) envisaged to facilitate entrepreneurship during the crisis. The law was a result of the social dialogue between the government of Latvia, the Confederation of Employers and the Free Trade Union Confederation (Martinsone, 2010). It was most strongly advocated by the Confederation of Employers as an effective means to increase entrepreneurship, decrease unemployment and help companies to survive the crisis and come out of the grey economy (Makarovs, 2016). Jānis Endziņš, the Chairman of the Board of the Latvian Chamber of Commerce and Industry, comments:

> At the epicentre of the economic crisis in Latvia the situation was very serious – unemployment was 17 per cent, and the prime minister asked the Latvian Chamber of Commerce and Industry: 'How can we resolve the situation?' Our

answer was – it is necessary to create a support system for micro companies, so that unemployed people can create jobs for themselves. (EURONEWS, 2014)

Besides a lower tax rate, tax calculations and tax accounting were simplified for micro-entrepreneurs (Leibus, 2014). Micro-enterprises could also receive expert advice on their business plans and even have access to micro-credits. While this law secured employment for some workers and profits through lower taxes during the crisis, it also increased flexibility in the labour market in terms of lowering social security contributions and reducing access for employees to social protection and pensions, thus contributing to growing inequalities.

A micro-enterprise can be (1) an individual merchant, individual enterprise, farm or fishing company, (2) a private individual registered in the State Revenue Agency as conducting a business activity, or (3) a limited liability company (LLC). Currently legal entities, mainly limited liability companies (Ltd), account for most micro-enterprise tax (MET) payers (Figure 2.4). Certain criteria must be met, though; for example, all employees must be board members, the income from economic activity or turnover in a calendar year may not exceed €100 000, the number of employees may not exceed five and employees' income may not exceed €720 per month.

The tax rate of micro-enterprises is 9 per cent of total turnover (up to €100 000). If the micro-enterprise turnover exceeds €100 000, the tax rate

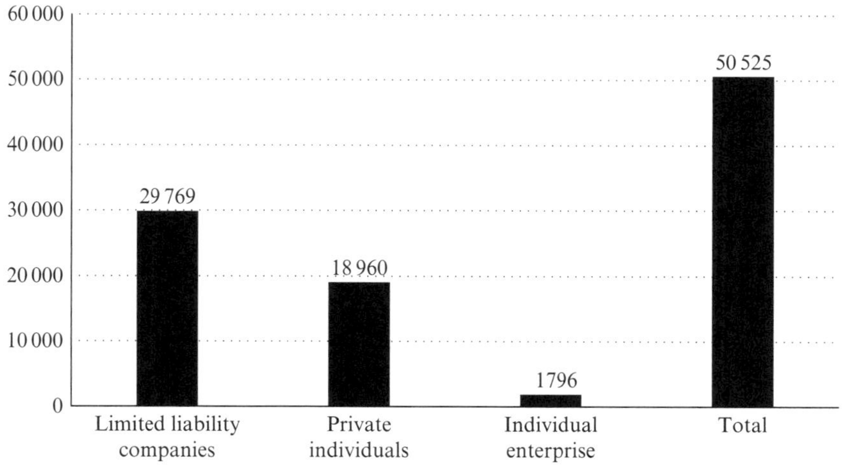

Source: Ķezbere and Žukova (2016).

Figure 2.4 Statistics on the status of micro-enterprises

Table 2.10 *Tax differences for a limited liability company paying taxes consistent with the general procedure or paying the MET under the minimum criteria of a micro-enterprise in 2014, Latvia (euros)*

Indicator	MET	General procedure
Turnover	100 000	100 000
Number of employees (excluding the owner)	5	5
Gross monthly income per one employee (owner)	720	1032
Net monthly income per one employee (owner)	720	720
Labour taxes (MSSIC and PIT) total for five employees, if the monthly tax-exempt minimum for each employee is €75	x	33 329
Paid to employees (net)	43 200	43 200
Other expenses, 20% of turnover	20 000	20 000
Income taxable by the CIT	x	3471
Corporate income tax, 15%	x	521
Micro-enterprise tax, 9%	9000	x
Taxes total	9000	33 850
Profit after taxes	27 800	2950
PIT 10% of the maximum amount of dividends	2780	295
Taxes total	11 780	34 145
Net profit (of an entrepreneur) after taxes	25 020	2655

Source: Leibus (2014) calculations, assuming equal net wages.

rises to 20 per cent on the exceeding part. If the number of employees of a micro-enterprise during a quarter is more than five, then 2 percentage points are added to the 9 per cent tax rate for each additional employee. The micro-enterprise taxpayer calculates and pays micro-enterprise tax, but does not separately pay personal income tax or corporate income tax, not to mention standard mandatory contributions (Table 2.10). Most importantly, an enterprise choosing to pay the MET has the possibility to save on labour taxes (Leibus, 2014). In sum, employees of micro-enterprises pay very little tax, even less than those who are self-employed. Almost two-thirds of the 9 per cent micro-enterprise tax goes to social insurance contributions and one-third to personal income tax, but it is still very little compared with the normal 34.9 per cent mandatory social security contribution rate in Latvia. Owing to low social contributions, the employees of micro-enterprises receive very few benefits in case of unemployment, sickness, or birth of a child, and save very little in the mandatory pension fund, reducing social security in the future (Leibus, 2014), unless they have made voluntary contributions into the state social security system (which very few do). This problem was acknowledged early on by the Ministry of Welfare. In 2013 the average social contributions for one employee of a micro-enterprise were 112.3 euros. To save the capital necessary for a minimum pension equal to someone who had worked 10–20 years but paid contributions using the regular scheme, an employee of a micro-enterprise would need to work 58 years; for a pension equal to those who worked 21–30 years, it would take 69 years and to match 31–40 years, they would have to work 79 years. Importantly, recent analysis by Hazans (2016) has shown that about 40 per cent of micro-enterprise employees do not have employee earnings under general regime, and in 2015 micro-enterprise earnings accounted, on average, for three-quarters of total labour income. In 2014, the Ministry of Welfare acknowledged 'At present, micro-enterprise employees' contributions are not sufficient to ensure the minimum old-age pension savings, thus taxpayers *who pay contributions using the general procedure will actually sustain the micro-enterprise employees when they reach retirement age*' (Ķezbere and Žukova, 2016, original emphasis).

The number of micro-enterprises in Latvia has been growing rapidly, and the number of people employed as 'micro-entrepreneurs' and paying the respective tax was about 50 000 at the end of 2016. By the end of 2013, the number of MET payers had reached 9.2 per cent of the total number of taxpayers (Leibus, 2014) and at the time of writing has reached almost 10 per cent (Hazans, 2016). It is an empirical question whether the MET allows employers to pay more competitive wages that would otherwise be lower, however, legitimate concerns have been raised by government officials that a whole class of citizens is being created who have little social protection today and face poverty in old age.

The share of MET revenues in the state budget also tends to grow, and the impact of the MET on the national economy of Latvia continues to increase every year (Leibus, 2012). State Revenue Service data show that each year, increasing taxes are collected from micro-enterprises (Figures 2.5 and 2.6).

The State Revenue Service statistics (Table 2.11) show that the micro-enterprise's status is most often used in the sector of individual services (12.3 per cent of companies), while the largest share of MET payers is observed in telecommunications (16.4 per cent), other individual services (12.3 per cent), medicine (11.7 per cent) and construction (11.4 per cent). More than 50 per cent of micro-enterprise employees work in highly skilled non-manual occupations (Hazans, 2016).

In late November 2012, the Parliamentary Budget and Finance (Taxation)

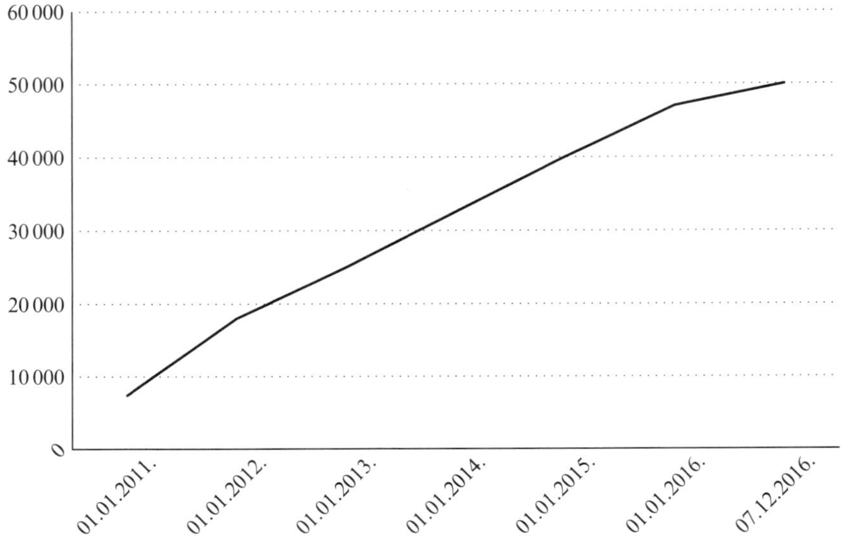

Source: Ķezbere and Žukova (2016).

Figure 2.5 The number of people paying micro-enterprises tax

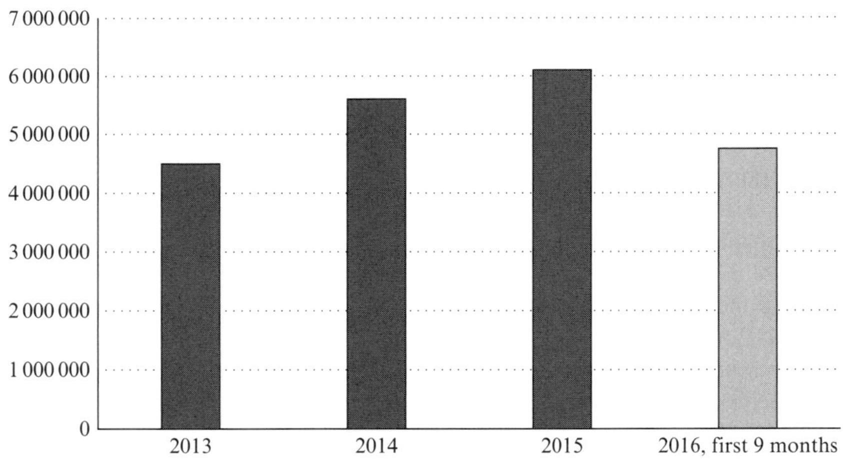

Source: Ķezbere and Žukova (2016).

Figure 2.6 Taxes collected from micro-enterprises (euros)

Table 2.11 *Ten sectors of the national economy with the largest number and share of micro-enterprise taxpayers as of 25 September 2013*

Sector	Number	%	Sector	Number	%
Other individual services	3759	12.3	Telecommunications	166	16.4
Trade	3062	5.8	Other individual services	3759	12.3
Construction	2627	11.4	Medicine	784	11.7
Forestry	1213	8.0	Construction	2627	11.4
Transport	1024	8.6	Tourism	136	10.3
Real estate transactions	946	3.4	Catering	478	9.6
Medicine	784	11.7	Furniture production	106	9.6
Catering	478	9.6	Transport	1024	8.6
Agriculture	332	0.8	Forestry	1213	8.0
Telecommunication	166	16.4	Trade	3062	5.8

Source: Leibus (2014) calculations based on the statistical data of the SRS of the Republic of Latvia.

Committee announced that the micro-enterprise tax had not reached the desired goal. A similar opinion was expressed by the Committee of Social Affairs and the Labour Commission. One of the major drawbacks of the scheme was that owing to the gaps in legislation it was applied not only by new entrepreneurs but also by existing companies to reduce their tax burden (Leibus, 2014). According to Makarovs (2016), contrary to Latvian government intentions, a positive effect on employment was not achieved with the Micro-enterprise Tax Law (MET, 2010), partly because the majority of micro-business owners were previously engaged in other businesses, rather than being unemployed. This is partially confirmed by Hazans' (2016) analysis. To obtain the MET's benefits, large companies deliberately split themselves into several micro-enterprises and separated their structural entities, especially those related to the provision of services. They required their employees to establish a 'micro-enterprise' to pay less tax (Leibus, 2014). One scandal involved the media company TV3, where a former employee exposed the fact that such a scheme was used there (PIETIEK, 2013). While moving to micro-enterprises leads to greater flexibility and allows savings on taxes, it is unknown – but unlikely – whether employees benefit from the scheme by earning higher wages. The employees are frequently the ones to suffer in such cases, because competitiveness is achieved mainly at the expense of employee social security (Leibus,

2012). 'The micro-enterprise tax was introduced during the crisis to help people start a business more easily. Later, in most cases it was transformed into a tax optimisation scheme,' commented the Minister of the Economy, Arvils Ašeradens. The recent World Bank draft report comes to a similar conclusion: 'The special tax treatment of micro-enterprises is a recipe for large-scale tax arbitrage in CIT and PIT inviting avoidance of labor taxes, social-security contributions and capital taxes' (World Bank, 2016: 103).

The parliament started discussing possible changes in the law, among them an increase in the tax rate, shortly after the law came into effect, driven mainly by concerns that the scheme was being used for tax evasion, not due to worries about workers' social security or trade union interest in the matter. From 2012 the opportunities to use micro-enterprises law to 'optimise taxes' were reduced, by prohibiting companies from buying services from their own employees, or 'bogus self-employment' (Leibus, 2014). The social dialogue while developing the MET law and the respective amendments was not very efficient, as the trade unions and employers' organisations were presented with proposals developed by policy-makers, rather than asking them to get involved in the process of designing the solutions and listening to their suggestions (LBAS, 2013).

On 6 November 2013 amendments to the micro-enterprise tax law were adopted by the Latvian parliament envisaging an increase in the tax rate from 1 January 2015 for all micro-enterprises with a turnover of more than €7000. According to the amendments, the tax rate will rise in three steps: (1) in 2015 to 11 per cent; (2) in 2016 to 13 per cent; and (3) in 2017 to 15 per cent. Thus, micro-enterprises would pay tax at the level of other economic forms and be integrated into the general tax regime. The changes in the tax rate were justified by the necessity to increase state social insurance (SSI) for the employees of micro-enterprises (Leibus, 2014). However, giving in to employers' organisations, the decision was cancelled. At the end of 2015 the parliament amended the budget so that the micro-enterprises would only pay 9 per cent for the first three years, and 12 per cent – starting from the fourth year, delaying further changes until 2017.

Several other possible amendments considered in 2013 were also dropped, mostly owing to the objections by employers' organisations. One suggestion by policy-makers to combat abuses of the tax regime has been to limit the branches of economy in which micro-enterprises could be established. The LDDK objected, arguing that it would make the administering of these taxes more complicated, compromising the initial goal of the micro-enterprises law (LETA, 2015). Another recommendation, aimed at preventing bogus self-employment (forcing employees to become a 'micro-entrepreneur' to save tax and benefit payments), is that micro-enterprises not be allowed to sell their services to companies.

The Latvian Chamber of Commerce (LTRK) strongly objected to the measure, arguing that it would destroy the small businesses, 'We are very shocked by the FM proposal that totally undermines the idea of micro and small business in general,' says the Chairman of LTRK, Janis Endziņš (DELFI, 2015). As a result, these amendments were abandoned. Other suggestions by experts included prescribing the maximum annual amount of dividends paid to the owners of capital companies–micro-enterprise taxpayers (Leibus, 2014), but such amendments have not been introduced. We can conclude that the resistance of employers' organisations has prevented a serious reorganisation of the micro-enterprises regime, which is detrimental to workers' rights to social security and their subsistence in old age. While employers value the increased flexibility and argue that the reduced taxes offered to micro-enterprises are necessary to secure not just competitiveness, but in many cases the very existence of small companies, the micro-enterprises regime contributes to economic inequality, as well as increases inequality in terms of health, access to training and job security, access to social benefits and pensions.

Despite recognising the drawbacks, the Employers' Confederation of Latvia (LEC) continues to strongly defend the micro-enterprise law, arguing that lowered tax related to the status of a micro-entrepreneur makes it possible to reduce unemployment and, for some companies, to come out of the 'shadow economy' (PIETIEK, 2013). Unfortunately, so far no academic studies have analysed the total effect of the MET on unemployment or tax revenue (considering the effect on other collected taxes), so its total economic and fiscal effect is currently unknown. The scheme has been praised by the European Enterprise Promotion Awards as 'the most creative and inspiring in Europe' (EURONEWS, 2014), yet the experts clearly failed to acknowledge the risks associated with the meagre social protection of micro-entrepreneurs. Considering the drawbacks of the scheme, the micro-enterprises regime was supposed to be phased out completely by 2019, and registration as a micro-enterprise would only be allowed until June 2017. However, on 23 November 2016 a protest was organised near the parliament against scrapping the micro-enterprises regime (TVNET, 2016b). Partially owing to the protests by NGOs, with the final amendments of the micro-enterprises law, the idea was abandoned and micro-enterprises will continue for now.

To ensure at least minimum state social insurance contributions for all micro-entrepreneurs, as well as those who earn less than the minimum wage (31.2 per cent of all socially insured persons), the 2015 'micro-enterprise tax law' amendments approved in parliament envisaged that from January 2017 the minimum state social insurance contributions would be required for all workers in the amount of at least 75 per cent of the minimum wage (34.9 per cent tax on the minimum wage of €380, that is, approximately €100 per month). Starting from 2018, full social contributions would be required from at least the minimum wage for all workers, even if they do not work full-time (Ķezbere and Žukova, 2016). Thus, it could happen that a person who earns, for example, €1000 for one particular job in summer months – for example, translation – over the year has to pay more than €1000 in taxes. In this case, the social insurance contribution tax would make it senseless to establish such a company (Makarovs, 2016; TVNET, 2016a). The costs would need to be covered by employers; it also means that micro-enterprises would need to cover at least the minimum social contributions for all employees. A snap survey organised by the Confederation of Employers found that for many companies the mandatory social contributions would be a reason to lay-off workers, reduce wages or close the company altogether (TVNET, 2016b). As noted by Zondlere (2015), the hope that everyone will simply change micro-enterprise status into other economic forms was naive and would have grave consequences. Non-governmental organisations started their fight against this law relatively late. The LTRK actively argued against these amendments, that would 'undermine the business environment', in the parliament and the government, threatening to take the case to the Constitutional Court. Other NGOs, such as the Latvian Chamber of Commerce, also objected to the law by arguing that it would lead to outward migration, growth of the shadow economy and resulting tensions for the social budget. Finally, the government gave in to the employers' pressure and, shortly after the budget approval, the Commission of Social and Labour Affairs 'opened' and amended the law again. At the end of 2016, parliament approved the final amendments in the micro-enterprises law and the law on state social security, which were very different from what was previously discussed. On 20 December 2016, after extensive discussions, parliament approved in the final reading amendments that imply the abandonment of minimum social security contributions.

The final agreement about the micro-enterprises tax rate was that in 2017 companies with a turnover lower than €7000 would pay 12 per cent tax and companies with a larger turnover 15 per cent. From 2018, all micro-enterprises will pay 15 per cent tax (Žukova, 2016). It did not go smoothly, though, as initially the law was sent back for review by the Latvian President, Vejonis. He argued that the regulation is incomplete and goes against previous decisions that the society and entrepreneurs were counting on. Several experts note the lack of economically adequate and substantiated analysis of the increase in the MET rate (Leibus, 2014). It is likely that the increase in the MET from 9 per cent to 15 per cent from 2015 might destroy a few hundred micro-enterprises that cannot afford higher taxes and will force some of them back into the shadow economy. However, the effect on enterprises would not be great, as it would only be paid if something is earned (Makarovs, 2016).

From the trade union perspective, the main aspects of the MET are its impact on employment and welfare (LBAS, 2013). However, up to now, the employees' organisation – the LBAS – has been relatively quiet. This can partly be explained by the fact that micro-enterprises are small and usually do not have a trade union – at best, there are individual union members in micro-enterprises. Nevertheless, the chairman of LBAS, Egils Baldzēns, acknowledges the need to strengthen the trade unions, particularly in the private sector. The low unionisation, especially in the private sector, limits the weight of the arguments of employees' organisations and their ability to influence policy development (TVNET, 2016a). 'It is clear that employers will always have a little more opportunity to influence government decisions, but trade unions with their membership and representation also may affect them', indicates Baldzēns (TVNET, 2016a). He continues: 'It is important to ensure that employers' and workers' interests are in balance. Currently they are biased towards employers.' The LBAS believes that the changes in taxation have been too rushed and chaotic. Work has to be done carefully and strategically on matters of remuneration and tax policy, and together – employers, employees and the government. One suggestion is to ask politicians, instead of achieving a compromise in the coalition first and then turning to the social partners (National Tripartite Council), to do it the other way around – first listen to the suggestions of the social partners and then discuss them in the coalition council.

5.3 Conclusions

The case study demonstrates that when we talk about social dialogue, it is important to consider the type of actors involved in it, as well as the core interests. In this case (as in many others in Latvia) the interests of employers' organisations, which are more influential, organised and motivated than the workers' organisations, have dominated the social dialogue. They have been prominent in blocking any of the proposed changes to the micro-enterprises law that might have alleviated some of the evident problems associated with this tax, including extremely weak social protection. A full-scale evaluation of the MET's effects on employment and total tax revenue has not been conducted yet (but see the World Bank draft report; Hazans, 2016), but the risks were clear very early on. While the law achieved some of its goals, it has also led to a weakening of social guarantees for workers, thereby increasing both current and future inequality (Hazans, 2016). The position of both the government and employees' organisations in this dialogue has been weak and indecisive, as they tried to find a compromise between the perceived needs of the economy and workers' social protection. Unfortunately, the opinion still often persists that it is better to have any job – even without social protection – than no job at all. The micro-enterprises law could be an example of 'social dumping' and flexibility at the expense of security, which too often is seen as necessary to reduce unemployment and acquire a competitive edge, especially during the recent financial crisis. In a situation in which the trade unions are weak and society – passive and social dialogue – poorly developed, these policies are much more likely to pass. As the case of the proposed mandatory social contributions demonstrates, awareness of the problem of a lack of social protection is rising, but the offered solutions have been far from optimal. Moreover, the chaotic process of decision-making has further diminished the confidence of potential investors, thus having an additional detrimental effect. It is necessary, as noted by several experts, to base decisions not just on the opinions of the social partners, but also on hard data and estimates of the effects of specific policies – something that in this case was missing. The solution achieved at the end of 2016 can be expected to improve the situation by increasing social contributions and making employment in micro-enterprises more similar to other forms of employment, but it will not undo the previous years of meagre accumulated social contributions for a significant number of workers.

6. CONCLUSIONS

The case of the Baltic States is hard to characterise as a good example of active and effective social dialogue in Europe. In summary, the trade unions' role in the Baltic States is limited in terms of union density and collective agreement coverage. Trade unions are the dominant form of workers' representation in the Baltic States; there are no other traditional forms of workers' representation, such as works councils. However, although in Estonia and Latvia employees' rights are expressed in principle by unions, the law provides a mechanism for employee representation in non-union firms (Visser, 2005). Collective agreements are more common at enterprise or national level. At industry or regional levels, the bargaining process is less developed. Coordination of wage negotiations is low. As most employees are not covered by collective agreements, the effect of labour unions on labour market flexibility is currently minimal.

To sum up, industrial relations are regulated by the minimum standards fixed by the state, social dialogue between the social partners at the national level and individual employment contracts or enterprise level collective agreements. The very low rates of unionisation and collective agreements mean that the labour market role of the unions is limited. Unions have to a certain extent been unable to overcome the Soviet legacy and reverse the downward trend in union density. The expectations regarding the growing importance of unions after the EU enlargement did not materialise and the initial sharp decline in union density in the 1990s continued, albeit at more moderate rates. Some still argue that perhaps the unions have some unused potential or some segment of the workforce exists that could provide union members. The low density and limited importance of unions at workplaces is coupled with their weak role in national social dialogue, which is one explanation why poor policies have been implemented. This seems to apply also to the balance between flexibility and security at the aggregate level, where unions or social dialogue more generally have not been able to shift the balance towards security, which is currently very much biased towards flexibility. The favourable inequality dynamics in Estonia during the past 15 years are also probably due to other reasons than the successful activities of unions and social dialogue.

On the positive side, we could still argue that the situation is not hopeless. Some anecdotal evidence suggests that the younger generation, free of Soviet experience, may have more realistic expectations of the role of unions in a market economy. As limited as the density of unions is, when they are present, we can find moderate evidence of their effects on inequalities and wages. The dynamics of minimum wages in Estonia in recent years are probably one of these positive cases.

NOTES

1. Eurofound has defined social dialogue as discussion, consultation, negotiation and joint actions involving recognised representatives of the two sides of industry (employers and workers) (Eurofound, 2012). The types of actors vary, as do their roles in the process of social dialogue.
2. It can be argued that social dialogue includes any representative voice (such as a works council or trade union), any direct voice and any combination of these (Eurofound, 2012).
3. For example, LDDK and LBAS were recently involved in negotiations about raising the minimum wage in Latvia, the indexation of pensions and, most recently, the 'solidarity tax' on the most wealthy employees, as well as the introduction of the differentiated untaxed minimum.
4. Wage bargaining centralisation is determined in two dimensions: first, the level at which bargaining takes place (national, sector or firm) and, secondly, by the organisational concentration (the number of confederations, unions or bargaining units) at each level (Visser, 2005).
5. Based on EE-LFS for 2006–13, average monthly wage rates in the public and private sectors were €548 and €578, respectively.
6. Alternative matching specifications were considered in the analysis. In particular,

matching with replacement of the control group reported similar estimation results, although treatment and matched-control groups were substantially different in their average observed characteristics, relative to matching without a replacement procedure.
7. For technical details see Rosenbaum and Rubin (1983).

REFERENCES

Antila, J. and P. Ylöstalo (2003), 'Working life barometer in the Baltic countries 2002', Labour Policy Studies 247, Ministry of Labour, Helsinki.

Arro, R., R. Eamets, J. Järve, E. Kallaste and K. Philips (2001), 'Labour market flexibility and employment security: Estonia', International Labour Office, Geneva.

Blažiene, I. (2004), 'Lithuania. Trade unions in focus', European Industrial Relations Observatory, Loughlinstown, Co. Dublin.

Casale, G. (1999), 'Tripartism and industrial relations in Central and Eastern European countries', in G. Casale (ed.), *Social Dialogue in Central and Eastern Europe*, Geneva: ILO, pp. 1–36.

Christofides, L.N., A. Polycarpou and K. Vrachimis (2013), 'Gender wage gaps, "sticky floors" and "glass ceilings" in Europe', *Labor Economics*, **21** (C), 86–102.

DELFI (2015), 'FM ieceres iznīcinās mikrouzņēmējus, paziņo LTRK', *DELFI*, 19 November, accessed 8 January 2017 at http://www.delfi.lv/bizness/biznesa_vide/fm-ieceres-iznicinas-mikrouznemejus-pazino-ltrk.d?id=46737227.

Due, J. and M. Mailand (2004), 'Social dialogue in Central and Eastern Europe: present state and future development', *European Journal of Industrial Relations*, **10** (2), 179–97.

Eamets, R. (2001), 'Reallocation of labour during transition. Disequilibrium and policy issues', The Case of Estonia, Dissertatsiones Rerum Oeconomicarum Universitatis Tartuensis (PhD thesis in economics), no. 5, Tartu University Press.

Eamets, R. and E. Kallaste (2005), 'The lack of wage setting power of Estonian trade unions?', *Baltic Journal of Economics*, **5** (1), 44–60.

Eamets, R., M. Beblavý, K. Bheemaiah, M. Finn, K. Humal, J. Leschke, et al. (2015), 'Mapping flexibility and security performance in the face of the crisis', STYLE Working Papers, WP10.1. CROME, University of Brighton, Brighton, accessed 2 November 2017 at http://www.style-research.eu/publications/working-papers/.

Eamets, R., K. Philips, J. Alloja and K. Krillo (2008), 'Benchmarking EU countries against Danish flexicurity model', West European Studies Working Paper, Indiana University, Bloomington, IN, accessed 3 November 2016 at https://euro.indiana.edu/docs/archive/working-papers/Eamets_Philips_flexicurity.pdf.

Espenberg, K., K. Jaakson, E. Kallaste and K. Nurmela (2012), 'Kollektiivlepingute roll Eesti töösuhetes', Discussion Paper Series, No 1, Ministry of Social Affairs.

Eurofound (2012), Workplace social dialogue in Europe: an analysis of the European Company Survey 2009, Eurofound, Dublin.

Eurofound (2015), 'Third European Company Survey – overview report: workplace practices – patterns, performance and well-being', Luxembourg, Publications Office of the European Union.

EURONEWS (2014), 'Micro-management. Why are small businesses flourishing in Latvia?', *EURONEWS*, 18 April, accessed 2 November 2017 at http://www.euronews.com/2014/04/18/micro-management-why-small-businesses-are-flourishing-in-latvia.

European Industrial Relations Observatory (EIRO) (2005), 'Changes in national collective bargaining systems since 1990', accessed 2 November 2017 at https://www.eurofound.europa.eu/observatories/eurwork/comparative-information/changes-in-national-collective-bargaining-systems-since-1990.

Fenger, M. (2006), 'Promoting or preventing reforms? Trade unions and social policy reforms in Central and Eastern Europe', *Society & Economy*, **28** (1), 1–26.

Ferraro, S., J. Meriküll and K. Staehr (2016), 'Minimum wages and the wage distribution in Estonia', Eesti Pank Working Paper No. 6/2016.

Guest, D. (1987), 'Human resource management and industrial relations', *Journal of Management Studies*, **24** (5), 503–21.

Hazans, M. (2016), 'Microenterprise tax regime in Latvia. Background paper for World Bank (2016)', Latvia Tax Review report.

Järve, J., E. Kallaste and R. Eamets (2001), 'Töösuhted Euroopa Liiduga liitumise taustal', report for Friedrich Ebert Foundation, mimeo.

Jensen, S. (2003), 'Baltic corporatist arrangements – a comparative analysis of tripartite arrangements in Estonia, Latvia and Lithuania', MA thesis, University of Bergen.

Kallaste, E. and C. Woolfson (2009), 'The paradox of post-communist trade unionism: "you can't want what you can't imagine"', *Economic and Labour Relations Review*, **20** (1), 93–110.

Kallaste, E., K. Jaakson and R. Eamets (2007), 'Two representatives but no representation: cases from Estonia', *Employee Relations*, **30** (1), 86–97.

Karnite, R. (2004), 'Latvia. The development and current situation of trade unions', European Industrial Relations Observatory.

Ķezbere, Z. and K. Žukova (2016), 'Mikronodoklis – no veiksmes stāsta līdz sociālai katastrofai: kas mainīsies nākamgad', *DELFI*, accessed 2 November 2017 at http://www.delfi.lv/bizness/budzets_un_nodokli/mikronodoklis-no-veiksmes-stasta-lidz-socialai-katastrofai-kas-mainisies-nakamgad.d?id=48328535.

Kuokštis, V. (2011), 'What type of capitalism do the Baltic countries belong to?', Employment and Economy in Central and Eastern Europe (EMECON), 1/2011, accessed 9 September 2014 at http://www.emecon.eu/archive/.

Latvijas Brivo Arodbiedribu Savieniba (Free Trade Union Confederation of Latvia) (LBAS) (2013), 'Ekspertīze Valsts atbalsta mikrouzņēmumiem ietekme uz nodarbinātību Latvijā', accessed 2 November 2017 at http://www.lbas.lv/upload/stuff/201311/valsts_atbalsta_mikrouznemumiem_ietekme_uz_nodarbinatibu_latvija.pdf.

Latvijas Brivo Arodbiedribu Savieniba (Free Trade Union Confederation of Latvia) (LBAS) (2017), LBAS website, accessed 21 January 2017 at http://www.lbas.lv/?locale=en.

Law on Micro-enterprises (2016), *Mikrouzņēmumu nodokļa likums*, accessed 2 November 2017 at http://likumi.lv/doc.php?id=215302.

Latvijas Darba Devēju Konfederācija (LDDK) (2014), 'Nozaru sociālā dialoga analīze', Rīga, accessed 2 November 2017 at http://providus.lv/article_files/2714/original/Nozaru-SD1.pdf?1414053732.

Leibus, I. (2012), 'Micro-enterprise tax as means of promoting entrepreneurship in Latvia', *Science and Studies of Accounting and Finance: Problems and Perspectives*, **8** (1), 116–20.

Leibus, I. (2014), 'Problematic aspects of micro-enterprise tax in Latvia', accessed 2 November 2017 at https://www.researchgate.net/publication/278683772_Problematic_Aspects_of_Micro-Enterprise_Tax_in_Latvia.

LETA (2015), 'LDDK: jaunais mikrouzņēmumu regulējums visu sarežģī', *DELFI*, 11 April, accessed 2 November 2017 at http://www.delfi.lv/bizness/biznesa_vide/lddk-jaunais-mikrouznemumu-regulejums-visu-sarezgi.d?id=45805963.

Lithuanian Professional Union (LPS) Solidarumas (2017), website, accessed 21 January 2017 at http://www.lps.lt/.

Makarovs, V. (2016), 'Latvian micro-enterprise tax law amendments: effect for social security', *The Baltic Course*, 29 January, accessed 2 November 2017 at http://www.baltic-course.com/eng/analytics/?doc=116014.

Martinsone, I. (2010), 'LDDK: Saeimai jāpieņem Mikrouzņēmuma nodokļa likums, kas kāpinās deklarēto nodarbinātību un uzņēmējdarbību', *DELFI*, accessed 2 November 2017 at http://www.delfi.lv/bizness/versijas/lddk-saeimai-japienem-mikrouznemuma-nodokla-likums-kas-kapinas-deklareto-nodarbinatibu-un-uznemejdarbibu.d?id=32850735.

Masso, J. and R. Eamets (2007), 'Macro-level labour market flexibility in the Baltic States', in T. Paas and R. Eamets (eds), *Labour Market Flexibility, Flexicurity and Employment: Lessons of the Baltic States*, New York: Nova Science, pp. 101–42.

Masso, J. and K. Krillo (2010), 'Estonia, Latvia and Lithuania: minimum wages in a context of migration and labour shortages', in D. Vaughan-Whitehead (ed.), *The Minimum Wage Revisited in the Enlarged EU*, Cheltenham, UK and Geneva: Edward Elgar and ILO, pp. 113–52.

Masso, J. and K. Krillo (2011), 'Mixed adjustment forms and inequality effects in Estonia, Latvia and Lithuania', in D. Vaughan-Whitehead (ed.), *Work Inequalities in the Crisis: Evidence from Europe*, Cheltenham, UK and Geneva: Edward Elgar and ILO, pp. 35–98.

Masso, J., K. Espenberg and I. Mierina (2015), 'The Baltic States: convergence with the European Social Model or further liberalization?', in D. Vaughan-Whitehead (ed.), *The European Social Model in Crisis: Is Europe Losing its Soul?*, Cheltenham, UK and Geneva: Edward Elgar and ILO, pp. 66–120.

Masso, J., K. Espenberg, A. Masso, I. Nierina and K. Philips (2014), 'Between economic growth and social justice: different inequality dynamics in the Baltic States', in. B. Nolan, W. Salverda, D. Checchi, I. Marx, A. McKnight, I.G. Toth, et al. (eds), *Changing Inequalities and Societal Impacts in Rich Countries. Thirty Countries' Experiences*, Oxford: Oxford University Press, pp. 96–125.

Micro-enterprise Tax Law (MET) (2010), *Mikrouznemumu nodokla likums: LR likums* (*Microenterprise Tax Law: Law of the Republic of Latvia*), accessed 20 December 2013 at http://www.likumi.lv.

Nickell, S. and R. Layard (1999), 'Labour market institutions and economic performance', in O. Ashenfeelter and D. Card (eds), *Handbook of Labour Economics*, vol. 3, pt C, Amsterdam: North Holland, pp. 3029–84.

Oaxaca, R. (1973), 'Male–female wage differentials in urban labor markets', *International Economic Review*, **14** (3), 693–709.

Ozola, Z. (2010), 'Sociālā partnerība Latvijas reģionos: piemēri, analīze, attīstība', Rīga, Latvijas Darba devēju konfederācija, accessed 2 November 2017 at http://www.sif.gov.lv/nodevumi/nodevumi/3419/Sociala_partneriba_Latvija.pdf.

Paas, T., R. Eamets, J. Masso and M. Rõõm (2003), 'Labour market flexibility and migration in the Baltic States: macro evidences', Faculty of Economics and Business Administration Working Paper Series, No. 16, University of Tartu.

Philips, K. and R. Eamets (2007), 'Approaches to flexicurity: EU models', European Foundation for the Improvement of Living and Working Conditions, Luxembourg.

PIETIEK (2013), 'Vēstule Saeimai atklāj mediju "virtuvi" un to darbinieku neapskaužamo stāvokli', PIETIEK.com, 12 February, accessed 18 February 2013 at http://www.pietiek.com/raksti/vestule_saeimai_atklaj_mediju__virtuvi__un_to_darbinieku_neapskauzamo_stavokli.

Rõõm, T. (2015), 'Ettevõtjate uuring: miinimumpalga tõus mõjutas hõivet vähe, kuid kergitas palku ja hindu', Eesti Pank, accessed 6 January 2017 at https://www.eestipank.ee/blogi/ettevotjate-uuring-miinimumpalga-tous-mojutas-hoivet-vahe-kuid-kergitas-palku-ja-hindu.

Rosenbaum, P. and D. Rubin (1983), 'The central role of the propensity score in observational studies for causal effects', *Biometrika*, **70** (1), 41–50.

TVNET (2016a), 'Baldzēns: Ir jādomā par vispusēji izsvērtu nodokļu politikas plānu', *TVNET*, 1 December, accessed 3 November 2017 at http://financenet.tvnet.lv/zinas/637081-baldzens_ir_jadoma_par_vispuseji_izsvertu_nodoklu_politikas_planu.

TVNET (2016b), 'Piketē pret mikrouzņēmumu nodokļa likvidēšanu', *TVNET*, 23 November.

Van Gyes, G., T. Vanderbrande, S. Lehndorff, G. Schilling, S. Schief and H. Kohl (2006), 'Industrial relations in the member states of the European Union. A basic comparison of 25 national systems', European Foundation for the Improvement of Living and Working Conditions, Loughlinstown, Co. Dublin.

Vatta, A. (2001), 'The enlargement of the European Union and social dialogue in Central and Eastern Europe', *Perspectives on European Politics and Society*, **2** (1), 127–46.

Visser, J. (2005), 'Patterns and variations in European industrial relations', in European Commission, *Industrial Relations in Europe 2004*, Luxembourg: European Commission, pp. 11–57.

Visser, J. (2015), ICTWSS Database. Version 5.0, Amsterdam Institute for Advanced Labour Studies AIAS.

Western, B. and J. Rosenfeld (2011), 'Unions, norms and the rise in U.S. wage inequality', *American Sociological Review*, **76** (4), 513–37.

Woolfson, C., D. Calite and E. Kallaste (2008), 'Employee "voice" and working environment in post-communist new member states: an empirical analysis of Estonia, Latvia and Lithuania', *Industrial Relations Journal*, **39** (4), 314–34.

Woolfson, C. and E. Kallaste (2011), 'Illusory corporatism "Mark 2' in the Baltic States', *Warsaw Forum of Economic Sociology*, **2** (3), 51–72.

World Bank (2016), *Latvia Tax Review*, accessed 3 November 2017 at http://documents.worldbank.org/curated/en/587291508511990249/pdf/120580-WP-P158470-PUBLIC-117p-WBLatviareportPOP.pdf.

Zondlere V. (2015), 'Likumprojekts "Grozījumi Mikrouzņēmumu nodokļa likumā"', 10 September, accessed 1 November 2017 at http://titania.saeima.lv/LIVS12/SaeimaLIVS12.nsf/.

Žukova, K. (2016), 'No 1. janvāra būs augstāka mikrouzņēmumu nodokļa likme, nolemj Saeima', *DELFI*, accessed 2 November 2017 at http://www.delfi.lv/bizness/budzets_un_nodokli/no-1-janvara-bus-augstaka-mikrouznemumu-nodokla-likme-nolemj-saeima.d?id=48325017.

3. Belgium: Is robust social concertation providing a buffer against growing inequality?

Ive Marx and Lien Van Cant

1. INTRODUCTION

Belgium's social concertation model is extraordinarily resilient. Union membership and collective bargaining coverage remain among the highest in the industrialised world. This goes together with a deep-rooted tradition of multi-tiered bargaining and consultation on all aspects of working conditions. Social dialogue is firmly embedded in an extensive institutional framework and the social partners continue to wield significant influence in shaping social and economic policy through their institutionalised advisory and co-governance roles, notably in the sphere of social security.

Belgium is an international outlier in another respect. First and foremost, households across the income spectrum have seen steady increases in their living standards, including during the recent crisis. Belgium is among the few Organisation for Economic Co-operation and Development (OECD) countries not to have seen growing income inequalities. Belgium maintains just about the most compressed wage distribution in the capitalist world – including one of the smallest gender pay gaps – and there is also little evidence of precarisation in the world of work.

This chapter argues that these observations are interrelated. The key argument is that extensive and robust social dialogue has helped to contain inequality. The Belgian experience provides a powerful antidote to views that growing inequalities are inevitable in advanced economies. However, while inequalities among workers are remarkably and sometimes exceptionally low by international standards, Belgium's labour market is not as inclusive as would be wished. This, too, has to be seen, at least in part, in the context of the institutional rigidities and insider biases inherent in an extensive social concertation model such as Belgium's.

The chapter is structured as followed: section 2 sets out the main features of social dialogue in Belgium and its key actors, notably the trade unions and employers' organisations. The same section identifies how the social dialogue model has changed over time, making a distinction between the period before and after the recession of 2008. Section 3 looks in more detail at equality outcomes in the sphere of income and work, and how these relate to social dialogue institutions and practices in Belgium. Before bringing together the main conclusions and highlighting some policy issues, two informative case studies, on the gender wage gap and the perceived work–life balance, are considered.

2. BELGIUM'S CONCERTATION MODEL

2.1 Social Dialogue

Belgium's complex multi-level political governance system firmly embeds trade unions and employers' organisations in the institutional framework. Social dialogue is institutionalised in a system of consultative, advisory and management institutions in which the social organisations act as authorised representatives (Cantillon i.c.w. Buysse, 2016). This fulfils three major functions: consultation, co-governance and bargaining.

There is bipartite dialogue between social partners, which can result in advice to the government. Two important national negotiation and consultative bodies are in place: the National Labour Council (NLC) and the Central Economic Council (CEC). One of their main competences is to advise the national authorities on labour and social security law and on general economic issues (for example, market conditions, expansion policy, taxation, inflation and competitiveness). Moreover, numerous other consulting socio-economic councils are in place at the sectoral (for example, joint committees), regional (for example, the Flanders Social and Economic Council, SERV) and firm levels (for example, works councils) (Vilrokx and Ranson, 2000; Cox and Verreyt, 2013; Cantillon i.c.w. Buysse, 2016).

The social partners are represented on the governing boards of social security institutions, vocational training (sectoral training funds) and labour market agencies. They sit also on the governance and supervisory boards of numerous other bodies, including the National Bank of Belgium to name just one example.

On matters on which the social partners have autonomy the dialogue is bipartite, resulting in collective agreements. This includes, for example, wages (formation and development), working time, non-discrimination and training opportunities. Bargaining on all these aspects of work occurs in a multi-tiered coordinated system. The traditional system of collective bargaining in Belgium is regulated by the 1968 Act on Collective Bargaining Agreements and Sectoral Joint Committees. Collective bargaining takes place at multiple levels, namely, national, sectoral and organisational, whereby for each level an institutionalised negotiating forum is established (Vandekerckhove and Van Geys, 2012; Cantillon i.c.w. Buysse, 2016).

Every two years, the Group of Ten social partners – representatives of the main employers' organisations and trade unions – attempt to reach a national interprofessional agreement (IPA). This intersectoral agreement functions as a general framework for further negotiations and covers issues such as wages, social contributions and replacement incomes.

Implementing the framework negotiated at the national level, social partners bargain over different aspects of working conditions (for example, pay levels, classification schemes, working-time arrangements and training) at the intermediate sectoral level, which is the most important level. Bargaining takes place in joint committees and subcommittees for specific sectors, resulting in collective agreements covering all the employers and employees assigned to the committees concerned (Van Gyes, 2009a; Humblet et al., 2014; Cantillon i.c.w. Buysse, 2016). Whereas numerous OECD countries have moved toward firm-level negotiations, the sectoral level remains the dominant bargaining level (OECD, 2004). The social partners enjoy considerable autonomy at this level and their influence in shaping the conditions in the world of work is substantial and even decisive.

It is not exceptional for employers and employees to have a third round of bargaining at the firm level. Three bodies are institutionalised at this level, namely, a works council, a committee for prevention and protection at the workplace, and a trade union delegation. The former has an advisory competence on financial, economic, technical and social matters, and has the authority to decide on issues in the social area, such as labour regulations, educational leave and dates for annual vacations. The committee for prevention and protection at the workplace oversees issues related to workers' health, safety and hygiene. Finally, in contrast to the works council, which has a mainly informative and consultative function, the trade union delegation negotiates directly on working conditions with the employer (Humblet et al., 2014; Perin and Ajzen, 2015; Cantillon i.c.w. Buysse, 2016).

Collective bargaining is hierarchical. The national cross-sectoral agreement provides a framework within which the social partners at sectoral level negotiate. Similarly, the sectoral collective agreements concluded in the joint committees set a framework for bargaining at the company level. That is, Belgian law does not allow collective agreements concluded at a lower level to deviate, for the worse, from the collective agreements set at a higher level (Perin and Ajzen, 2015; Cantillon i.c.w. Buysse, 2016).

As regards collective agreements negotiated within the enterprise, the law of 5 December 1968 guarantees the extension of the negotiated agreement to all employees, including non-unionised staff. Nearly all collective agreements are made generally binding, greatly extending their impact. Belgium therefore belongs among the leading countries as regards employees covered by collective agreements, with a coverage rate of approximately 96 per cent (Perin and Ajzen, 2015; Visser, 2016).

2.2 The Social Partners: Trade Unions and Employers' Organisations

2.2.1 Trade unions

Trade unions in Belgium are organised mainly by economic sector – some very large, some very small – rather than by occupation. The resulting confederations are historically organised in terms of the traditional ideological 'pillars' of Belgian society. The three main trade union confederations have clear political traditions: the two largest – the Confederation of Christian Trade Unions (ACV/CSC) and the Belgian General Federation of Labour (ABVV/FGTB) – are linked to the Christian and socialist movements, respectively, while the smaller Federation of Liberal Trade Unions of Belgium (ACLVB/CGSLB) is linked to the liberals.

As Figure 3.1 shows, union membership remains relatively high in

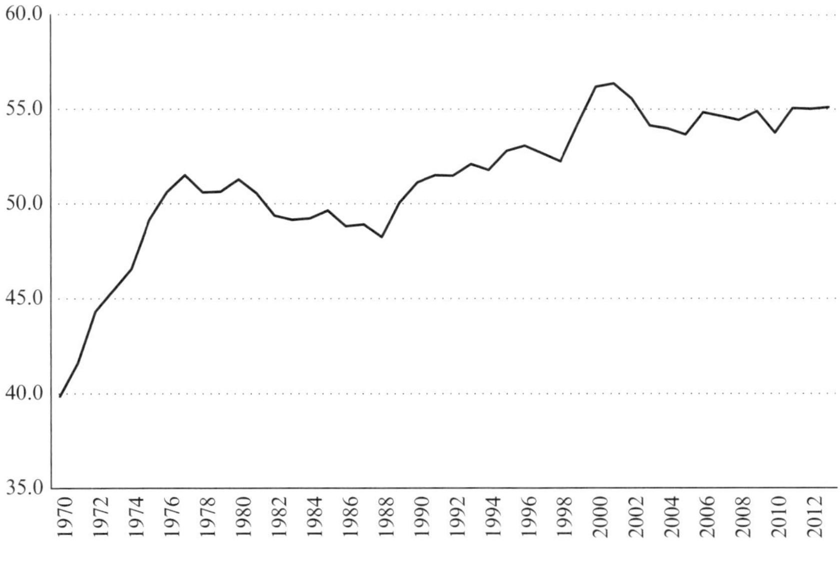

Source: Visser, ICTWSS database.

Figure 3.1 Trade union density, Belgium, 1970–2013

Belgium. Against the backdrop of a general decline in union membership in nearly all OECD and European Union (EU) member states, Belgium's divergent trajectory is remarkable. A number of employment and institutional features promote participation, which explains Belgium's high density rate. First, unionisation is very often positively related to public sector employment. A large share of countries with declining unionisation have cut back the public sector – known as a union stronghold – in the course of fiscal consolidation measures, whereas Belgium is still characterised by a large public workforce. Moreover, while other countries have seen a marked increase in fixed-term and temporary agency employment contracts – which discourage employees from becoming members of a trade union (Ebbinghaus et al., 2011) – this is not the case for Belgium (as is discussed later).

In addition, a society's institutional framework proves to be a fundamental determinant of unionisation (Ebbinghaus et al., 2011). In the case of Belgium, one institutional variable that has been found to strongly affect unionisation in most cross-national studies is the union-run unemployment insurance. The so-called Ghent system, which means that unemployment benefits are, as a rule, administered by union-affiliated institutions, has been shown to promote high and resilient union density rates. The system comes in two variants. In Denmark, Finland and Sweden the system takes the form of voluntary unemployment insurance funds, set up by the unions and heavily subsidised by the state. In this respect, Belgium features a partial Ghent system: while unemployment insurance is compulsory, trade unions retain a major role in the provision of benefits. Notwithstanding that union membership is not mandatory for those insured, the vital role of trade unions in the provision of unemployment benefits and the regular contact with union officials during spells of unemployment are said to strongly motivate workers to join unions. This way, the union-run insurance functions as a 'selective incentive' (Vandaele, 2009; Ebbinghaus et al., 2011; Van Rie et al., 2011; Schnabel, 2013). This is evident in the profile of union membership.

2.2.2 Employers' organisations

The Belgian landscape of industrial relations is characterised by a well-established and structured network of employers' organisations. The Belgian Federation of Employers (VBO-FEB) is the main cross-sector employers' organisation representing companies in all three regions of Belgium. At the regional level, the most important employer organisations are the Flemish Organisation for Independent Entrepreneurs and Small and Medium-Sized Enterprises (SMEs) (Unizo), the Flemish Network of Enterprises (VOKA), the French-speaking Union des Classes Moyennes

(UCM), the Walloon Union of Enterprises (UWE) and the Brussels Enterprises Commerce and Industry (BECI). Alongside these national and regional interprofessional organisations there are a number of SME confederations, interest groups (Federation of Farmers, BB), social profit confederations (Confederation of Social Profit Enterprises, UNISOC) and corporate social responsibility (CSR) networks or platforms of entrepreneurs.

As for the density rate of employers' organisations, a common trend seen in almost all countries is that such bodies have maintained their level of membership, when measured relative to their potential membership; that is, their organisational density has remained fairly constant, in contrast to union membership (Schnabel, 2013). With regard to Belgium, although no accurate data are available, employers' organisation density rates are high and stable (Visser, 2016).

2.3 Transformation of Industrial Relations

The year 1944 is a key milestone in the development of Belgium's concertation model. Created in the exceptional atmosphere of solidarity of the final war days, the 'Social Pact' marked a move towards more peaceful social relations. The institutions established then to foster social dialogue have since undergone change. In this section, we attempt to outline some important developments.

2.3.1 Period before the recession of 2008

Belgium's extensive social concertation model emerged gradually. The Social Pact of 1944 is regarded as a key moment in this process. Economic prosperity during the 1960s made it possible for the institutions established in the post-war period to develop further. The social partners concluded a social planning agreement on the joint bargaining rounds to take place every two years. These negotiations, on wages, working conditions and social benefits, would result in IPAs. On these issues social dialogue became bipartite instead of tripartite. The institutional edifice of the social dialogue was reinforced by the law of 1968 on collective agreements and joint committees. At the end of the 1960s, trade unions and employers' organisations obtained a high degree of autonomy and were able to negotiate on various labour market issues in a range of institutionalised bargaining bodies (Cassiers and Denayer, 2009).

The 'golden age' of the post-war years was followed by a drastic sea change. Belgium, as an early industrialiser, was extremely hard hit by the oil price shocks and the subsequent economic downturn of the 1970s and 1980s. Furthermore, the collapse in the demand for labour occurred precisely at a time when many youngsters (the sizeable post-war baby boom cohort) and women were entering the labour market. This change in workforce composition not only substantially increased unemployment rates; it also had a significant impact on trade union organisation as well. Traditionally, trade union members were a homogeneous group of male industrial full-time workers, whereas the changing labour market made this group more and more heterogeneous (Marx, 2009).

The changed socio-economic context strengthened the divergence in interests of trade unions and employers' organisations, resulting in a turbulent social climate in which agreements became harder to reach. Firms started to focus more on lowering production costs and increasing productivity, relying on a small (highly skilled) workforce. Employers' organisations called for the suspension of the automatic indexation of wages, wage moderation and the reduction of employers' social contributions. Not surprisingly, trade unions sought to protect the purchasing power of their members (Cassiers and Denayer, 2009). The demands of both sides of industry were often too divergent, resulting in an increased number of interventions by the government (Dryon and Krzeslo, 1997).

The law of 1989 sought to respond to intensifying international competition. This marked a turning point because this was the first government initiative to structurally limit the bargaining freedom of the social partners in an *ex ante* way (see below). As there was little room for manoeuvre as regards wages, social agreements increasingly focused on flexibility, education and training, innovation and the work–life balance. Pensions and public health care also became major topics (Cassiers and Denayer, 2009; Cox and Verreyt, 2013).

2.3.2 Period during and after the recession of 2008

The resilience of Belgium's social dialogue model was put to the test again during the crisis of 2008. Automatic stabilisers (for example, several unemployment insurance schemes) helped to mitigate the negative impact of the recession on output and employment. Apart from the fact that the public debt rate rose again for the first time since 1993, Belgium weathered the economic storms remarkably well because both its gross domestic product (GDP) and employment rate declined less than in most European member states (Vaughan-Whitehead, 2015b; Marx and Schuerman, 2016).

Nevertheless, the crisis restricted the room for compromise in collective bargaining. Tensions between the social partners rose to serious levels, making the IPA of 2009–10 extremely hard to reach. Consequently, the negotiations succeeded only due to government mediation (Ajzen and

Vermandere, 2013). The government unilaterally made the 'wage norm' mandatory by Royal Decree. This restricted the bargaining power of social partners at both the national and sectoral levels. The bargaining rounds for IPA 2011–12 did not go easily either. At the end of 2010, negotiations were blocked owing to conflicting opinions on whether or not to retain indexation and to increase wages. The discussion on the harmonisation of the employment status of blue-collar and white-collar workers proved to be a persistent stumbling block as well (Cox and Verreyt, 2013). In response to the stalled negotiations and rising social unrest, the Belgian government decided to unilaterally extend the anti-crisis measures it had taken in April 2009. These measures include, among other things, the decision to extend the short-time compensation scheme to white-collar workers and a special redundancy payment for dismissed blue-collar workers (Van Gyes, 2010). Moreover, the new government, which – after a record-breaking 541 days of political negotiations – was sworn in at the end of 2011, embarked on a reform programme. The pension reforms in particular, which made it harder to retire early, sparked reactions from unions, resulting in a 24-hour general strike. The unions criticised the lack of social dialogue on the issue and demanded changes to the reforms (Van Gyes, 2012).

To make matters worse, there were the numerous business closures and restructuring, leading to high job losses. October 2012 was even called 'the dark month' for employment in Belgium, because more than 6000 jobs were lost. While the trade unions called a number of strikes in response to planned restructurings, employers' organisations stressed the importance of keeping Belgian companies competitive. As a result, cross-industry partners again could not sign an agreement for the period 2013–14. This tense climate put pressure on the federal government, which was forced to reduce the public budget deficit to 2.15 per cent before the end of 2012. The government decided to retain the automatic wage indexation, although the composition of the index basket was altered to temper its effects. While aiming to reduce the labour cost gap with neighbouring countries and thereby strengthen competitiveness, the government also imposed a wage freeze in 2013–14 (Ajzen and Vermandere, 2013). It was a long time before the 'Group of Ten' got back on speaking terms as the government had limited the possibility of wage rises and, as a consequence, restricted the margin to negotiate. After turbulent negotiations, and under pressure from Prime Minister Di Rupo, a new IPA for 2013–14 was agreed upon in January 2013 (Cox and Verreyt, 2013).

Recovering from the economic crisis, the new federal government – elected in 2014 – decided in its coalition agreement to create a 'wage index jump' in 2015, which stopped the automatic pay increases based on the Health Index figures. Alongside other 'austerity measures', such as raising the pensionable age to 67 and reducing public sector spending, the coalition agreement provoked severe social unrest, resulting in successive national days of demonstrations and strike actions (Vermandere and Van Gyes, 2015). Social dialogue was clearly in disarray and its relevance was even questioned because these austerity measures were imposed without consulting the social partners. Nevertheless an IPA was reached for 2015–16, although without the signature of the socialist trade union.

Social unrest continues at the time of writing. The so-called Peeters Law (named after the minister for employment, Kris Peeters) has angered trade unions, leading to a tense social climate. The law provides, among other things, for a more flexible distribution of working time. Working time is to be calculated annually and no longer weekly, albeit with a working-time limit of nine hours a day and 45 hours per week (Peeters, 2016). Trade unions disagreed and claimed that, under the new rules, employers would be able to demand from workers that they work long days for multiple weeks in a row. They also believe that working conditions will worsen because stress at work may increase and finding an optimal work–life balance will become more difficult. The flexibility granted by this law seems to work particularly in favour of the employer and, to a much lesser extent, their employees (Peeters, 2016; Van Oycke, 2016).

In summary, the economic crisis has not been without consequences for social dialogue. Negotiations on interprofessional agreements have proved difficult throughout the crisis period. The government has frequently intervened in negotiations and become more involved in wage setting as compared with the pre-crisis years (Visser, 2016). Nevertheless, the institutionalised collective bargaining mechanisms remain firmly in place.

3. THE BELGIAN EXCEPTION: RISING LIVING STANDARDS, LOW AND STABLE INEQUALITY

We now turn to outcomes. Various sources and studies have shown Belgium to be among the few rich countries that has not seen growing income inequality over the past two decades (OECD, 2011, 2015; Van Rie and Marx, 2013; Kuypers and Marx, 2016). In addition, living standards have increased steadily (Table 3.1), including during the recent crisis period. Automatic stabilisers, such as extensive short-time compensation schemes, have proved instrumental in sheltering the Belgian population from its adverse impacts (Marx and Schuerman, 2016).

Table 3.1 Equivalent median income and inequality, Belgium 1996–2015

	Median income (€)	Gini coefficient
1996	14111	0.280
1997	14089	0.270
1998	14027	0.270
1999	14200	0.290
2000	14778	0.300
2001	15492	0.280
2003	15522	0.203
2004	15674	0.261
2005	16581	0.280
2006	17213	0.278
2007	17566	0.263
2008	17985	0.275
2009	19313	0.264
2010	19464	0.266
2011	20008	0.263
2012	20280	0.265
2013	21483	0.259
2014	21705	0.259
2015	21654	0.262

Source: Eurostat.

With just under 15 per cent of its population at risk of poverty (Figure 3.2), Belgium takes an average position, which stands at odds with its remarkably low overall level of income inequality (Figure 3.3). It is worth pointing out, however, that Belgium's in-work poverty rate ranks consistently among the lowest of the industrialised nations. In 2015, EU-SILC data indicates that only 4.6 per cent of employees live in a household with an equivalised disposable income less than 60 per cent of median household income, half the EU28 average rate. However, poverty rates for working-aged households with little or no labour income are far worse.

The overall level of income inequality is determined by a host of factors (Atkinson and Bourguignon, 2015; OECD, 2015), but decisive drivers are wages, taxes and benefits. Belgium stands out in having an exceptionally compressed wage distribution, in addition to a very large welfare state. In both these drivers of equality, Belgium's extensive social concertation model plays a key role, as we now discuss.

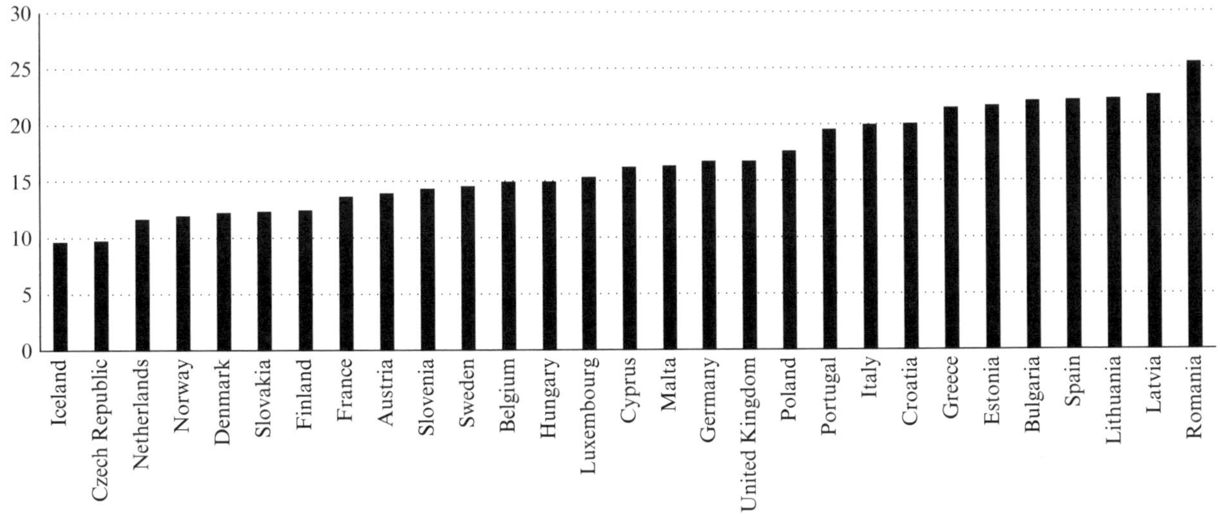

Source: Eurostat (2017).

Figure 3.2 At-risk-of-poverty rate, Belgium, 2015

Source: Eurostat (2017).

Figure 3.3 Evolution of the Gini-coefficient based on equivalent income, Belgium, 1995–2015

3.1 The Principal Equality Generator: Pervasive Collective Bargaining on Wages and Work Conditions

3.1.1 Extensive social dialogue mechanisms: the source of high and stable wage equality

Exceptional wage equality: brief evidence As the main income source for most households, wages play a key role in shaping the income distribution (Salverda and Checchi, 2014). Belgium's highly compressed wage structure is a major driver of low overall inequality.

Figures from the OECD indicate that Belgium has the smallest share – only 3.4 per cent – of workers earning less than two-thirds of median earnings. The incidence of high pay among full-time workers in Belgium is very low as well (see Figure 3.4). Three inter-decile ratios to measure wage inequality provide the same picture. As shown by Figure 3.5, Belgium belongs among the top three and top four performing countries in terms of overall wage equality (D9/D1) and the D9/D5 ratio, respectively. Nowhere is the lower half of the wage distribution (D5/D1) more compressed. The workers at the median of the earnings distribution earn only 1.34 times

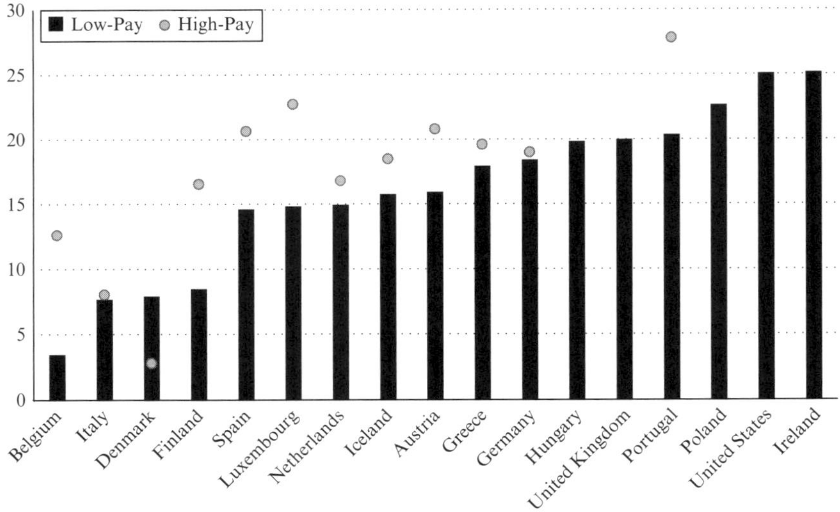

Source: OECD (2016a).

Figure 3.4 Incidence of high and low pay, Belgium, 2014

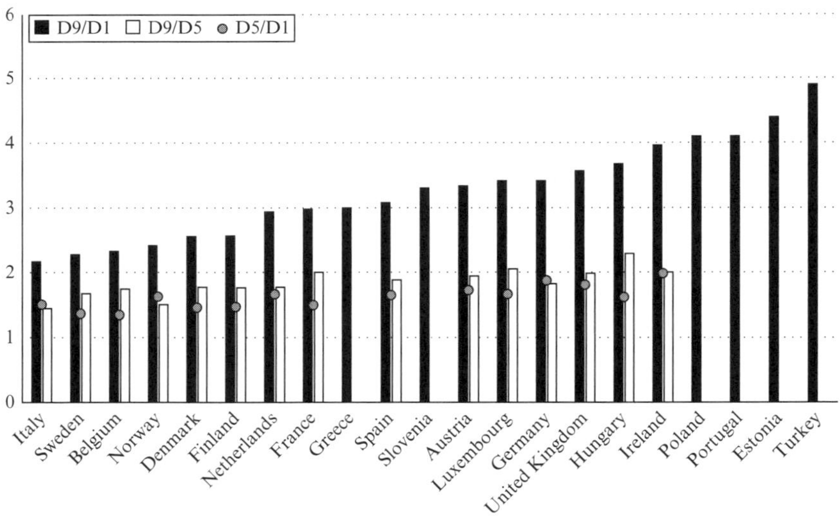

Source: OECD (2016a).

Figure 3.5 Earnings dispersion, Belgium, 2014

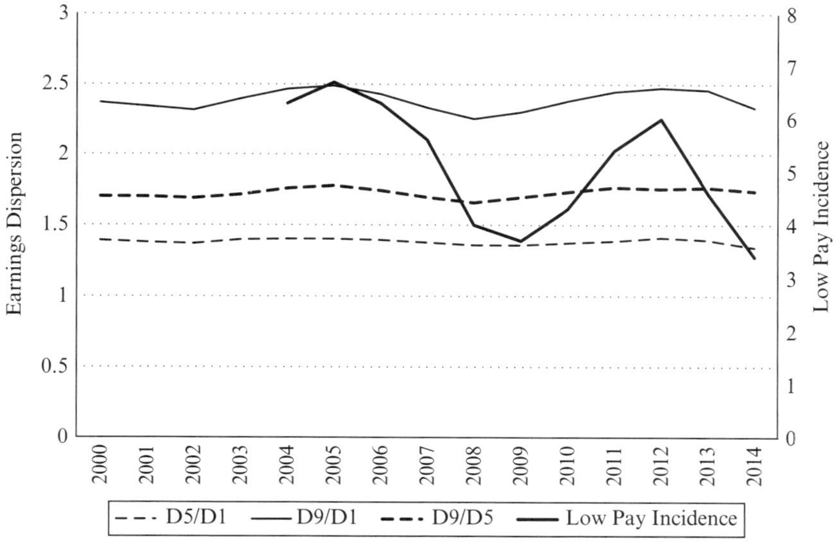

Source: OECD (2016a).

Figure 3.6 Change in earnings dispersion and low pay incidence, Belgium, 2000–2014

more than the 10 per cent lowest-paid workers, while on average this is 1.70 times more.

Moreover, in contrast to many other industrialised countries, there is no indication that wage dispersion increased substantially between the middle of the 1980s and the late 2000s (Horemans et al., 2011; OECD, 2011). This stability becomes even clearer when looking at Figure 3.6 as all three inter-decile ratios have remained virtually unchanged for the past 15 years. The incidence of jobs paying less than two-thirds of median earnings is now lower than in the early 2000s.

The gender wage gap in Belgium, while still significant, has narrowed considerably. The difference between men's and women's median wages was 13.6 per cent of men's median wage in 2000, down to 3.3 per cent in 2014 (Figure 3.7). The gap is widest among the oldest age categories and narrower among the youngest. From an international perspective, Belgium performs very well (see Figure 3.8). This trend in labour market inequality is further discussed as a case study in section 4.1 in this chapter.

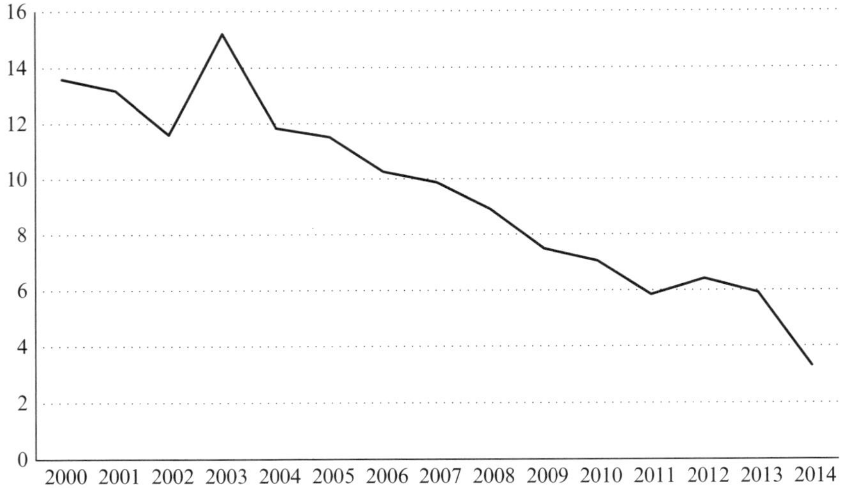

Note: The unadjusted gender wage gap is defined as the difference between median wages of men and women relative to the median wages of men.

Source: OECD (2016b).

Figure 3.7 Change in gender wage gap, Belgium, 2000–2014

3.1.2 Pervasive collective bargaining as a driving force: how it works

Belgium is characterised by comprehensive collective wage setting. Wage setting in Belgium is a matter in which unions and employers have a large degree of autonomy. While there was decentralisation of wage setting over the course of the 1980s, wage formation in Belgium remains comparatively centralised and coordinated (Plasman et al., 2007; Vaughan-Whitehead, 2015a). Wage bargaining occurs at all three interlinked levels. A first round of bargaining at the national level results in an overall agreement (IPA), which covers all companies in the private sector and sets out general principles and some essential parameters; for example, the scope for overall wage growth and minimum wage levels. Subsequently, agreements in the joint committees – which can vary considerably by sector – implement the national target at the (dominant) sectoral level. A third round of bargaining can take place at the firm level, but this is not always the case (especially in smaller firms). Firm-level agreements tend to focus on issues of working conditions rather than wages. Lower-level agreements must respect employees' rights laid down in higher-level agreements. Furthermore, strict regulations and procedures govern the bargaining process as agreements are made generally binding, covering

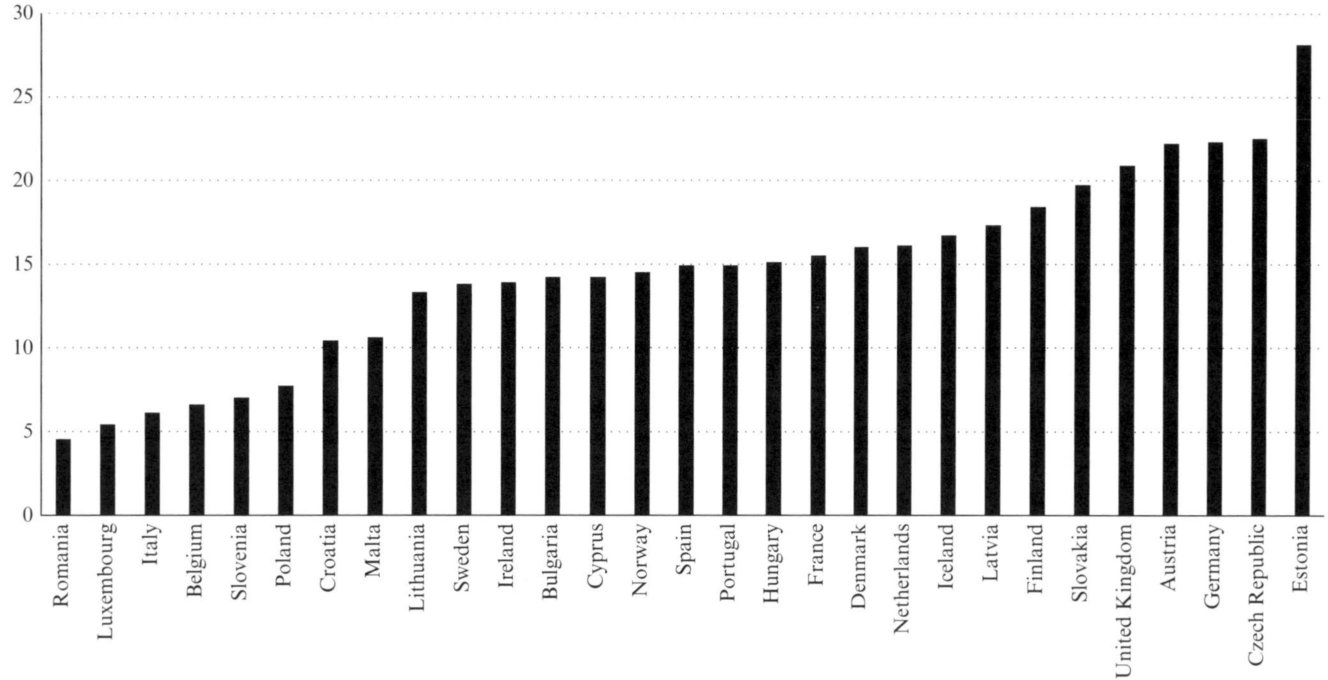

Note: The unadjusted gender wage gap is defined as the difference between average gross hourly earnings of male paid employees and of female paid employees as a percentage of average gross hourly earnings of male paid employees.

Source: Eurostat (2016b).

Figure 3.8 Gender wage gap, Belgium, 2014

the whole workforce concerned (Van Gyes, 2009a; Vandekerckhove and Van Gyes, 2014).

Indexation mechanism and wage norm Belgium is one of the few industrialised countries that has an automatic cost-of-living adaptation mechanism for wages and social benefits. This prevents downward tendencies in real living standards. However, concerns about 'competitiveness' have led consecutive governments to reform the indexation mechanism. This resulted in a series of indexation freezes in the mid-1980s and – as a crisis measure – in 2014–15, and in the adaptation of the basket of goods and services included in the index (Vandekerckhove and Van Gyes, 2012; Van Rie and Marx, 2013; Vermandere, 2014). Nevertheless, the system continues to play a key role in wage setting.

Second, the social partners are required to negotiate on upper limits of wage growth. The so-called Competitiveness Law of 1989 (which was extended in 1996 and modified in 2014) institutionalised government intervention in wage setting when wage developments are considered harmful to competitiveness. This way, the government tries to balance the automatic indexing of wages. A monitoring system was introduced, benchmarking Belgian wage developments against those in main trading competitors and neighbouring countries Germany, France and the Netherlands. The weighted average of pay developments in these countries is considered the upper margin for negotiations ('wage norm'), as wage increases beyond this limit trigger government intervention (Vandekerckhove and Van Gyes, 2012; Van Rie and Marx, 2013). It is set every two years in the IPA by the social partners, based on estimates provided by the CEC, in which the social partners are represented (Van Gyes, 2009a).

High minimum wage Belgium does not have a statutory legal minimum wage. Instead there is a minimum wage on which employers and trade unions agree at the national level. It applies to all workers (collective wage agreements are legally binding; they also cover non-unionised workers) and it sets sector-wide or even national-level thresholds and definitions of adequate pay. This minimum wage thus has more of a benchmark purpose than anything else – it constitutes the absolute base of the wage edifice. While this nation-wide minimum is at a comparatively high level (see Figure 3.9.), 'real' minimum wages (that is, pay scales for the youngest, least qualified and least experienced workers) are collectively negotiated at the industry level and tend to be considerably higher than the nationwide minimum wage as they cannot undercut the national minimum standard. Industries in which the lowest pay scales are 20 to 30 per cent higher than the nationwide minimum are not exceptional. In some sectors, the

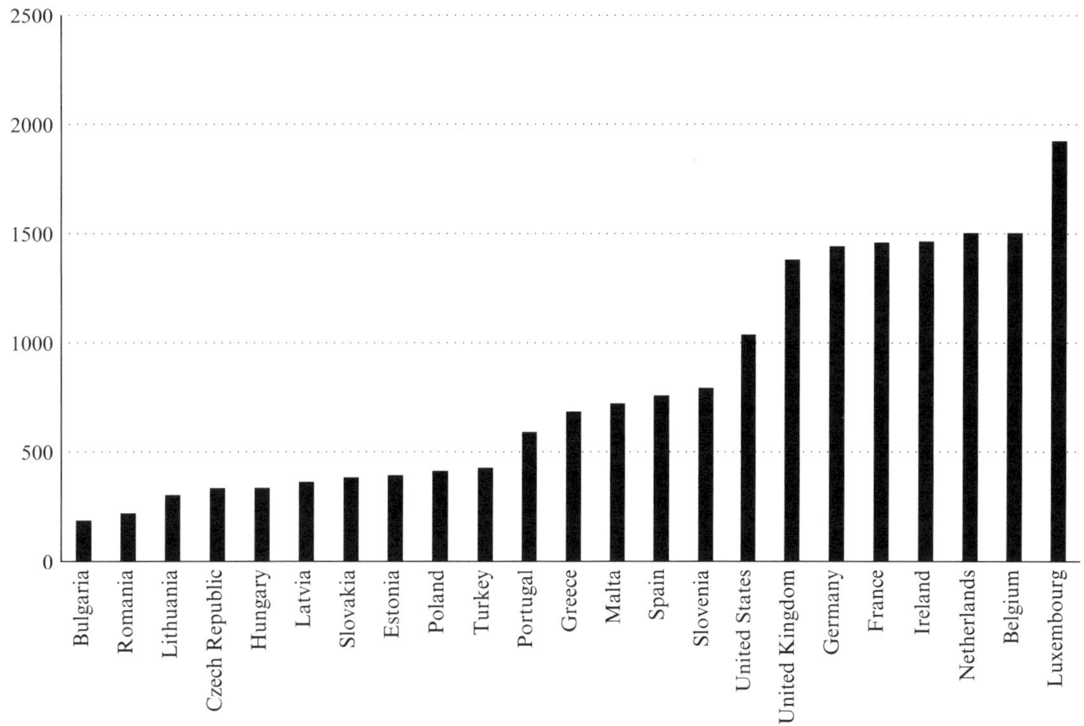

Source: Eurostat (2016c).

Figure 3.9 Monthly national minimum wages, Belgium, 2015 (euros)

lowest pay scales are almost twice as high as the nationwide minimum (Vandekerckhove and Van Gyes, 2014; Marx et al., 2012). In the services sector, minimum wages tend to deviate less from the nationwide minimum but it is difficult to make general statements as wages are set in dozens of separate collective agreements. All the available evidence suggests that very few people actually work – or can work – for the nationwide minimum. As a consequence, relatively low-paid work is considerably less prevalent in Belgium than in most other comparable countries, including the Netherlands and Germany (Van Rie and Marx, 2013).

Social partners have significant room to negotiate agreements at the sectoral level, leading to additional minimum wages for nearly all sectors. This leads to significant wage differentials across sectors. However, the minimum wage is reached at national level and the outcome of the negotiation there is reflective of overall union bargaining power. Agreements reached there are extended to the weakest sectors, thereby compressing the Belgian wage structure. Vandekerckhove et al. (2014) empirically confirmed this finding by using administrative data on sector and time variation in minimum wages for the period 1996–2006 in Belgium. The authors find that higher minimum wages reduce not only lower-tail but also overall wage dispersion.

Recent government reforms will lower the minimum wage for young workers. This has sparked a fierce reaction from the trade unions as, in previous years, agreements were reached to let the minimum wage system for young workers gradually catch up with the full minimum wage. On the other hand, since the index-jump of 2015 has come to an end, the minimum wage for employees over 21 is adjusted to the index again. Some sectors, however, have needed to wait until 2017 for their (minimum) wages to be adapted.

Extension mechanism Another equalising feature of the Belgian wage-setting system is the widespread use of extension mechanisms, resulting in near universal bargaining coverage. Over 90 per cent of wage and salary earners (including non-unionised workers) are covered by collective wage agreements, a share that has been constant since the middle of the 1980s (Van Ruysseveldt and Visser, 1995; Van Gyes, 2009a; Vaughan-Whitehead, 2015a). This way, social dialogue determines just about everybody's pay. This reduces inequality among workers as the standards set at national and sectoral levels are extended to employees with weaker bargaining power, particularly those working in small firms. As already highlighted, the pay scales negotiated by collective bargaining are generally higher than the minimum wage and, moreover, extend into the intermediate or even higher pay brackets. Extension mechanisms therefore not only protect the most vulnerable workers, through underpinning low earnings, but generate a compression effect on the overall earnings distribution as well (Bosch, 2015; Villanueva, 2015).

While these extension mechanisms reduce unequal treatment of unionised and non-unionised workers as regards wages and working conditions, it can hamper wage flexibility. A report by the European Commission (2016a) indicates that wages may not be able to fully adjust to differences in productivity across firms or geographical areas within the same sector when collective agreements are made binding for every worker in the sector. This may result in a misallocation of labour (Villanueva, 2015).

However, opt-outs from collective agreements are used, albeit exceptionally, at company level. Collective agreements negotiated on the lowest level can deviate from sectorally defined standards if the agreement explicitly allows for this. The minimum wage agreed at the interprofessional level must, however, always be respected (Perin and Ajzen, 2015; Visser, 2016).

Also worth noting is that some sectors, such as services, allow for greater wage flexibility compared with others (for example, manual sectors) (Vandekerckhove et al., 2010). However, Belgium is clearly characterised by rigid wage-setting institutions which – in face of asymmetric shocks — are often argued to hamper the functioning of the labour market (Vaughan-Whitehead, 2012; Fitzenberger et al., 2013).

3.2 Working Conditions: Negotiated Flexibility

3.2.1 Limited growth of non-standard work

The gradual growth of non-standard employment is one of the most fundamental structural labour market changes in western countries (Buelens and Pearson, 2012; ILO, 2016). Belgium appears to be one of the exceptions in this respect. Although a slight increase can be noted, there is not much evidence of dramatic growth in temporary or precarious work, not even during the recession of 2008. On several measures of 'atypical' employment, such as the incidence of fixed-term contracts, temporary work, night work and weekend work, Belgium is to be found at the lower end each time. This is arguably related to the continued strength of unions and collective bargaining. To the extent that there have been trends towards more flexibility in the sphere of contract type, working time and work organisation, these have been negotiated rather than politically imposed. We now discuss some trends in more detail.

Part-time work Part-time work, an important form of non-standard employment, as a share of total employment has risen substantially and steadily in Belgium, from less than one out of ten workers in the early

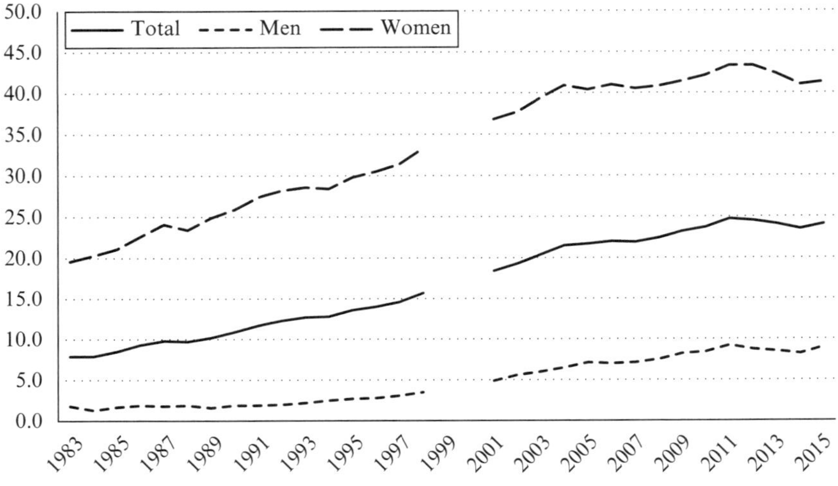

Source: Eurostat (2016d).

Figure 3.10 Part-time employment as share of total employment, Belgium, 1983–2015

1980s to nearly one out of four in the late 2000s. The number of part-time employees was not strongly affected by the recession of 2008, while in most other countries this was the case (Figure 3.10). Figure 3.10 furthermore indicates that women are clearly overrepresented among the part-time workers (41.4 per cent of working women in 2015, compared with 9.3 per cent of working men). While men have caught up, part-time work remains dominated by women as they combine work and caring activities. Moreover, for typically underrepresented groups in the labour market, such as young people and older workers, part-time jobs ease transitions in and out of the labour market (Horemans, 2016). The proliferation of part-time work in Belgium has not been associated with a rise in involuntary part-time work. On the contrary, Eurostat figures suggest a steady decline in the share of part-time workers that would prefer but cannot find full-time work, from approximately one-third in the mid-1980s to only 15 per cent in 2006 and 10 per cent in 2015. In contrast to many other countries, the recession did not increase the number of involuntary part-time workers.

The social partners have had a strong influence on the regulation of part-time employment. The regulatory framework prevents the working conditions of part-time workers from being less favourable than for full-time workers. The remuneration, for example, of part-time employees may, in proportion to hours worked, not be inferior to the remuneration of

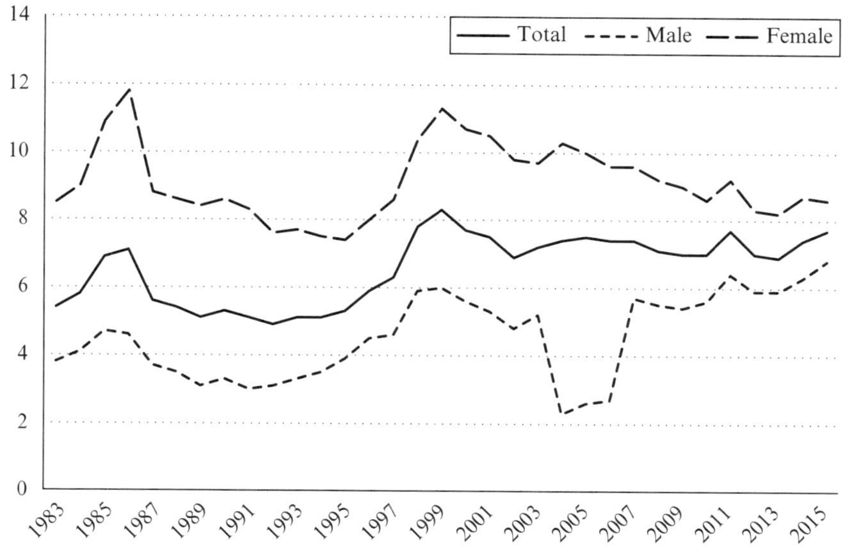

Source: Eurostat (2016d).

Figure 3.11 Temporary employment as share of employees, Belgium, 1983–2015

employees on a full-time contract. These principles are defined in Belgian labour law and were extended, in consultation with social partners, by collective agreement No. 35 (27 February 1981) on part-time employment, the Programme Act of 22 December 1989 and the Law on Non-discrimination regarding Part-time Employees of 5 March 2002.

Temporary employment As in most European countries, the share of employees with a temporary contract in Belgium is now higher than in the early 1980s, with some degree of fluctuation over time. Nonetheless, the share of temporary employment remains relatively low (Figure 3.11) compared with the European average (7.7 per cent in Belgium in 2015, compared with 11.9 per cent for the EU28). Just as for part-time work, women are overrepresented among temporary employees. However, their rates have converged with those of men as well (from two times the men's rate in the mid-1980s to 1.3 times in the late 2000s).

This rather low share of temporary contracts can be linked to the strict legislation regarding this type of contract. Belgium remains among the more strongly regulated OECD countries according to some comparative studies (OECD, 2013; European Commission, 2014). While the core provisions as regards temporary employment are codified in the law of 1987, more detailed rules are laid down in collective agreements reached by bargaining between trade unions and employers' organisations (for example, No. 108 on procedures and duration) (Pecinovsky and Van den Bergh, 2014).

The 1987 Law on Temporary Employment makes a distinction between regular fixed-term contracts and temporary-work-agency employment, the latter being more tightly regulated (OECD, 2013). The law requires equal pay and working conditions for regular workers in the user firm and temporary agency workers on assignment. Another feature that clearly indicates the important role of the social partners and collective bargaining regarding temporary employment contracts is the fact that the use of temporary work has traditionally been prohibited in some sectors, such as the transport sector (Pecinovsky and Van den Bergh, 2014).

Furthermore, when hiring an employee on a temporary contract, the employer is often required to ask prior permission from union delegates or worker representatives. However, since 2013 the use of temporary agency contracts as a recruitment channel, with the agency period serving as a prohibition period, has been included in the list of legitimate reasons for the use of this form of temporary contract. Employers are no longer required to ask for permission from union delegates in this case, thereby restricting union participation.

In addition, a new law enables temporary work agencies to conclude permanent contracts with the people they send out to their clients. Permanent temporary work contracts are only possible, however, if a collective bargaining agreement is concluded within the joint committee for temporary agency work (JC No. 322) and the wage between two assignments is guaranteed by the temporary work agency (Peeters, 2016).

3.2.2 Flexible working schemes

The growth of non-standard employment is often related to the shift towards a service-based economy, where employers have more flexible staffing needs in order to cope with irregular demand and flexible opening hours (Horemans, 2016). However, as indicated by Figures 3.12, 3.13, and 3.14, night, weekend and shift work remains less widespread in Belgium than elsewhere. While Sunday work has increased slightly, working in shifts and at night has decreased over the years. The figures for Belgium show a large gap with the EU28 average.

Nevertheless, negotiations between trade unions and employers' organisations have brought changes. Examples are the collective agreement on part-time employment of 1981, collective agreements No. 47, which contained provisions on temporary and agency work and collective agreement

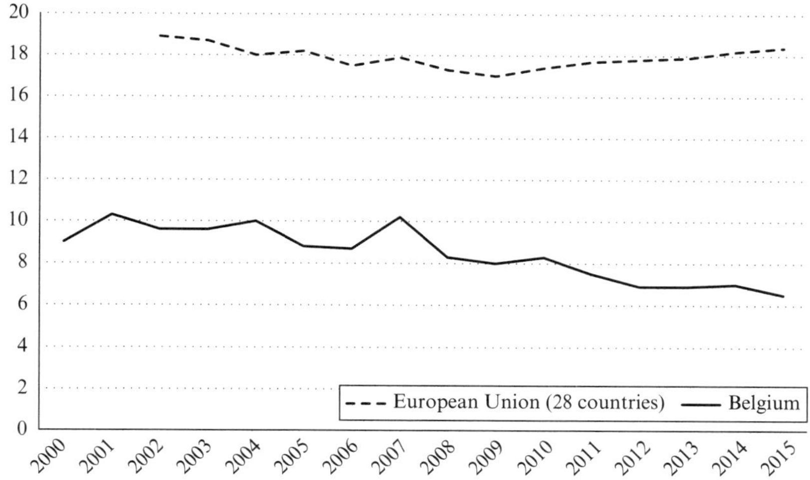

Source: Eurostat (2016e).

Figure 3.12 *Employees working shifts as a percentage of the total of employees, Belgium, 2000–2015*

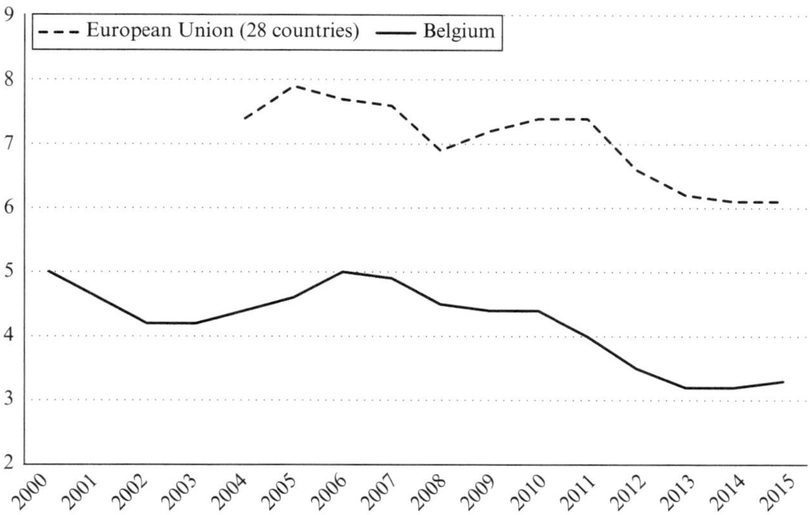

Source: Eurostat (2016f).

Figure 3.13 *Employed persons working at night (regularly) as a percentage of the total employment, Belgium, 2000–2015*

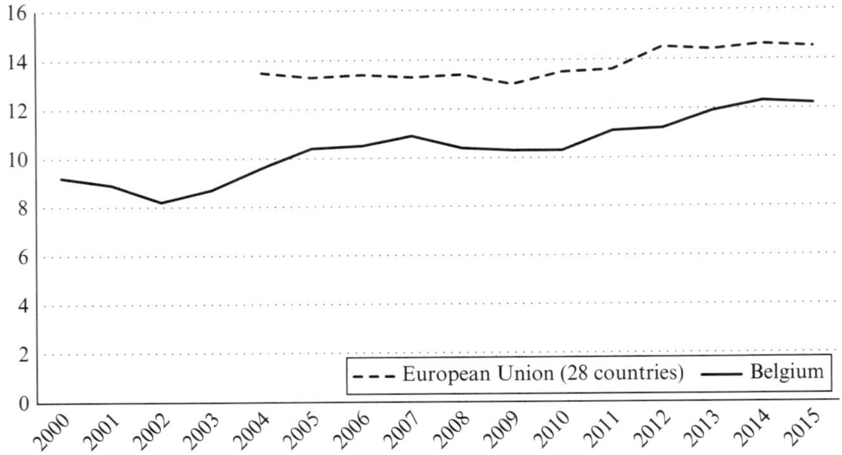

Source: Eurostat (2016g).

Figure 3.14 Employed persons working on Sundays (regularly) as a percentage of the total employment, Belgium, 2000–2015

No. 46 on shift and night work, both introduced in 1990, and the Act of 1997 on establishing the equality of women and men with respect to night work.

More recently, however, Belgium's centre-right coalition government unilaterally moved to increase working-time flexibility. Not surprisingly, the so-called Peeters Law encountered significant resistance.

The law contains several measures, such as the annualisation of working hours. This will make it possible for companies in internationally competitive sectors to develop customised work arrangements by spreading the calculation of the 38-hour week over several years (maximum six years). The concrete terms for application of the system need to be laid down in a sectoral collective agreement. The law also develops a new concept of 'voluntary overtime', whereby each worker has an allotment of 100 voluntary hours of overtime. Other measures supporting labour market flexibility include the administrative simplification of part-time work and reform of the employer grouping scheme.

The law, furthermore, enables workers themselves to increase flexibility as regards their working time and place. Important measures in this respect are the establishment of a legal framework for both occasional telework and flexible working hours during which the employee can determine the beginning and end of their working hours, within certain limits. Finally, legal opportunities to adapt working time over the life course, through various forms of (paid) leave (parental leave and medical assistance), are further extended and a system of 'career saving' is put in place. The latter makes it possible for employees to save up additional holidays.

Despite union protests, the law was approved by the government on 28 October 2016 and by the parliament on 23 February 2017. It was finally published in the Belgian official journal on 15 March 2017. However, the government allocated a key role to the social partners in implementing the law. While the law provides the legal framework for more working-time flexibility, its implementation is only possible through collective agreements to be negotiated by trade unions and employers at the sectoral and firm levels. Any moves towards more flexibility that may happen as a result will thus remain negotiated.

3.3 The Secondary Equality Generator: Co-governed Social Security

The remarkable stability of Belgium's income inequality is due in major part to exceptional wage equality and negotiated, rather than imposed, labour market flexibility – both an outcome of pervasive collective bargaining. Besides, through the above-mentioned mechanisms, the social partners affect income inequality through their influence on redistribution mechanisms as well. We turn to this now.

3.3.1 Belgium's social security system

Brief history Belgium's extensive social security system is both co-founded and co-governed by trade unions and employers' organisations. In order to understand the key role played by the social partners in the Belgian welfare system it is important to briefly sketch its history.

It was the same climate of social unrest that led Otto Von Bismarck to institute the first labour protection laws and social security provisions in Germany, which triggered the introduction of similar laws and provisions in Belgium. Social security arrangements had by then already emerged on a voluntary basis, usually in the context of mutual societies and organisations set up under the influence of the emerging trade unions. Out of a patchwork of arrangements, set up by the social partners, emerged a compulsory and increasingly universal system of social security and health care (Deleeck, 2001).

A long phase of incremental expansion of various, mostly occupationally segregated social security schemes culminated in the Social Pact of 1944 – agreed on by the social partners and the government. Born in the exceptional atmosphere of solidarity of the final war days, the pact marked a consolidation of the welfare system. The Social Pact, while extending compulsory social security coverage, confirmed the subsidiarity principle in the sense that non-government organisations (unions and mutual societies) remained responsible for the administration of benefits. In addition, national agencies were created for those not affiliated to such organisations. The role of the state remained, as before, mainly regulatory and complementary. A final safety net, guaranteeing minimum income protection to all, was ensured through three laws enacted around the late 1960s and early 1970s.

The economic downturn of the 1970s and 1980s, caused by the oil price shocks, profoundly challenged the social protection system. Confronted with a massive increase in dependency, the social security system was transformed from a system largely in the Bismarckian mould into one in which there is an overriding emphasis on minimum income protection.

3.3.2 Social spending in general

As shown by Figure 3.15, Belgium features one of the largest social expenditure budgets (relative to GDP), which also accounts for its stable and low overall household inequality and moderately low poverty rate (OECD, 2011, 2015; Nolan et al. 2014).

The Belgian system of social security features a wide range of income replacement benefits to compensate workers (and increasingly citizens) against income loss linked to a number of contingencies. Belgian social spending is strongly geared towards cash transfers, with unemployment benefits comprising an exceptionally large branch (Table 3.2). Compared with the EU28 average, Belgium spends twice as much on unemployment benefits. The social partners, and especially the unions, play a key role in this system. For this reason, we briefly elaborate on the unemployment insurance system.

3.3.3 Belgium's sprawling unemployment insurance system

Belgium's unemployment insurance system provides a wider range of benefits than is the case in most other countries, making the country an outlier in terms of spending on unemployment benefits. Apart from unemployment insurance proper, the unemployment insurance system also forms the basis of the principal early retirement scheme. Career interruption and worktime reduction benefits also fall within the system.

The system is financed mainly through social contributions (with some additional financing from earmarked value added tax, VAT, levies) and is co-governed by the social partners. The bulk of expenditure on unemployment insurance (unemployment benefits, early retirement benefits and administration costs) is distributed by the payment bodies of the three

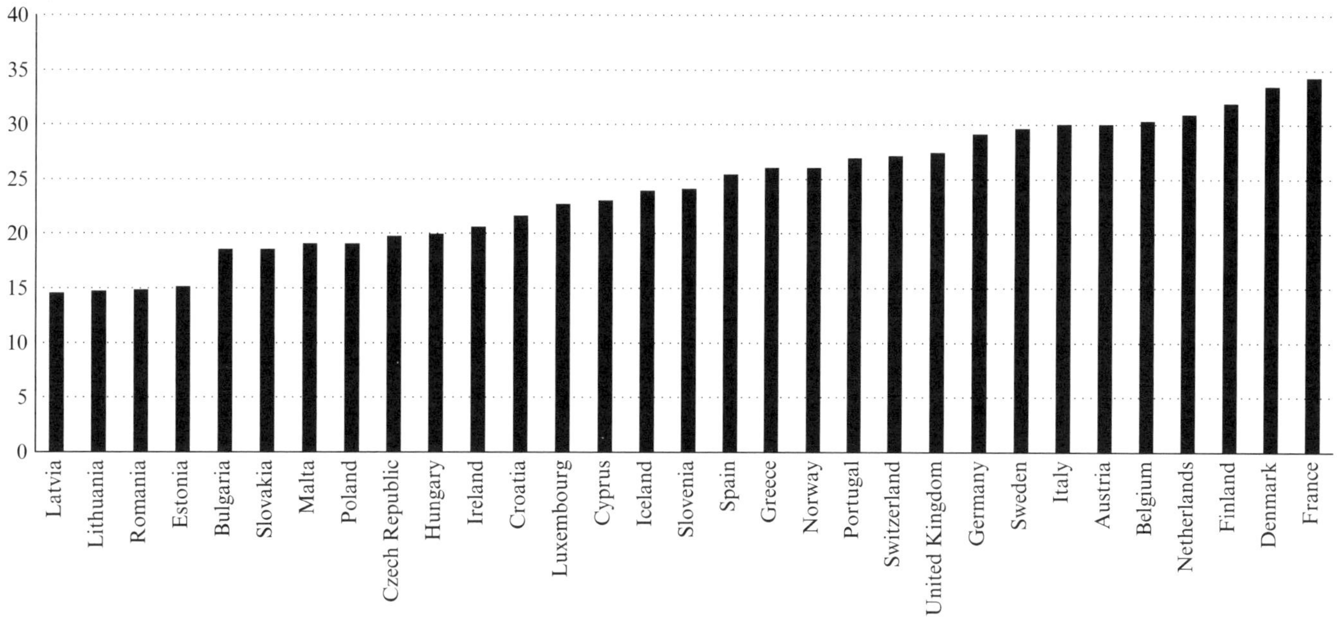

Source: Eurostat (2016h).

Figure 3.15 Social expenditure as a percentage of GDP, Belgium, 2014

Table 3.2 Social benefits by functions, Belgium and EU28, 2014 (percentage)

	Belgium	EU-28
Total expenditure	100.00	100.00
Sickness/health care	28.90	29.22
Disability	8.28	7.25
Old age	33.62	40.23
Family/children	7.53	8.54
Unemployment	11.64	5.13
Housing	0.86	2.05
Social exclusion	2.44	1.90

Source: Eurostat.

trade union confederations. The remaining expenditure is managed by a public non-union agency in which both trade unions and employers' organisations are represented (Vandaele, 2009; Van Rie et al., 2011).

Besides paying out unemployment benefits, trade union membership offers a lot of advantages, such as extra services in terms of personalised advice and administrative support (filling out forms, compiling dossiers), a union bonus (financed by employers) to partly reimburse membership fees and the right to be represented by a union representative during procedures and appeals in front of administrative bodies and labour courts (which deal with disputes relating to unemployment benefits) (Van Rie et al., 2011).

Belgium's unemployment insurance system has a number of particular characteristics. First, unemployment benefit entitlement in the main 'full-time unemployment' scheme is in principle unlimited in duration. However, controls on work search efforts have strongly intensified and the previous government made benefit amounts more strongly regressive over time. This accounts in part for Belgium's comparatively high spending on unemployment insurance. The reverse of this coin is that fewer of the unemployed than elsewhere deplete their insurance entitlement and end up in means-tested social assistance schemes. Second, unemployment benefits are differentiated by family situation: single persons and heads of household receive significantly more than people living together with others that have an income, especially after long spells of unemployment. Over time, benefit cuts have been mainly concentrated on the latter category, as these are assumed to be in lower need. Third, the unemployment insurance system comprises a very wide range of benefits. These include not only benefits to full-time unemployed jobseekers, but also to employees who reduce working hours, whether involuntarily (short-time working schemes or part-time unemployment) or voluntarily (a range of leave and career interruption systems). The system also comprises the main early retirement provision, which we discuss below.

Finally, the system provides unemployment benefits to workers who are forced to reduce their working time because of factors such as bad weather, technical failures, severe drops in demand and other factors theoretically beyond the control of the employer. The short-time working scheme was established well before these became prominent in other countries (Van Rie et al., 2011). Moreover, one of the measures taken during the crisis was to extend the system to white-collar workers; previously it had only been available to blue-collar workers. With demand being strongly cyclical or erratic in some sectors, this system is an important source of income stabilisation, which proved to be especially the case during the economic recession of 2008 (Marx and Schuerman, 2016).

As a consequence of the multiple functions the unemployment insurance system has taken on, a large number of people of working age receive some kind of unemployment benefit. At the peak of the recent economic crisis Figure 3.16 shows that more than 1.3 million people were receiving

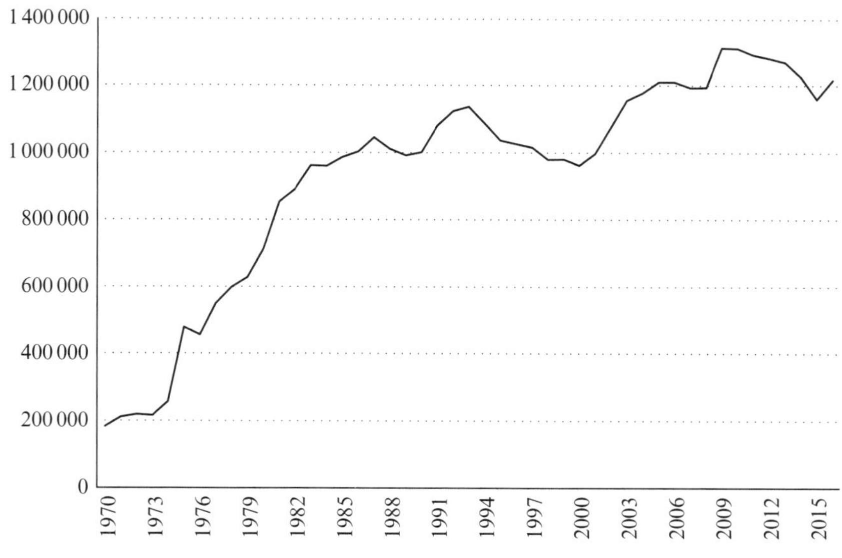

Source: Milquet et al. (2010), in which the statistics are supplemented with statistics (annual report) on the website of the RVA (see National Employment Office, 2016).

Figure 3.16 Unemployment insurance benefit receipt, Belgium, 1970–2016

unemployment benefit. This roughly equals one person receiving a benefit for every four persons working, although there is some overlap, as in the case for workers receiving short-time compensation benefits.

The massive rise in the number of people receiving some type of unemployment insurance benefit cannot be seen separately from the unions' role in the payment of unemployment benefits. The added services offered by the unions provide a clear and substantial incentive to become or remain a union member. Van Rie et al. (2011) show that the profile of union members closely matches such selective incentives. The unions have strongly resisted attempts to scale back unemployment benefit receipt, whether through the imposition of time limits or the tightening of age and other requirements for early retirement, while they have supported the proliferation of other functions the system has taken on. As demonstrated in this chapter, many of those functions have turned out to be beneficial, be it the stabilising role of the short-time compensation scheme during the crisis or the work–life balance improving impact of career interruption benefits. However, the continued rise in the number of people receiving benefits has come at a price in a context in which financial resources are not unlimited. As the number of beneficiaries rose, benefit levels became less generous and adequate in providing protection against poverty.

While still enjoying a comparatively low poverty rate, Belgium has been slipping down the tables during the past decade and does not seem to be managing to drive back poverty. At-risk-of-poverty rates of people living in jobless households, who are for that reason most reliant on the adequacy of transfer incomes, are extremely high (58 per cent in 2015). There is a growing income gap between those who receive income from work and those who rely mainly on income replacement benefits. While Belgium has a system (indexation) that is designed to safeguard the purchasing power of both benefits and wages, the latter have clearly outperformed the former. All social minima have been eroded relative to overall living standards. The reason is in part structural. As dual-earnership became the norm and drove up overall living standards, individuals or households having to rely on a single benefit (or wage for that matter) inevitably fell behind. There have been repeated beyond-cost-of-living increases but benefits often fall well short of poverty risk thresholds, as Figure 3.17 shows.

3.4 Activation

While Belgium's unemployment rate is below the EU15 average, its employment rate remains among the lowest of the northern continental European welfare systems. Employment growth has remained sluggish (Figure 13.8).

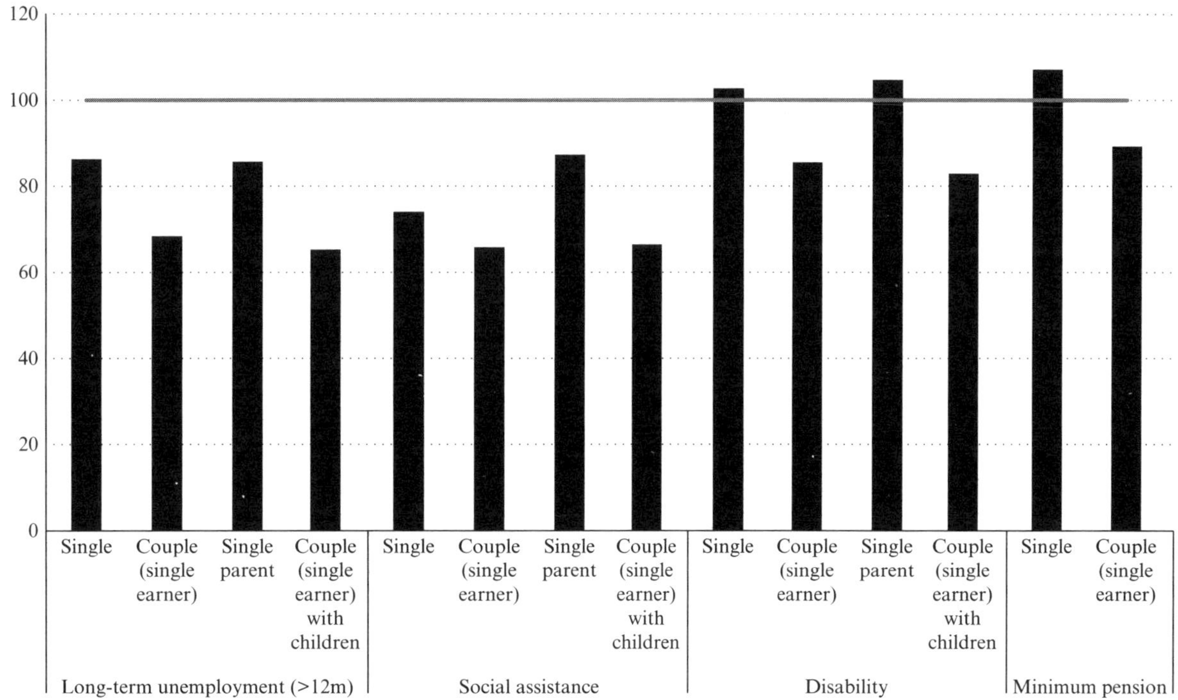

Source: Cantillon, B. i.c.w. Buysse, L. (2016: 442, fig. 8.13).

Figure 3.17 Minimum income packages of households in various situations relative to the poverty line, Belgium, 2014 (net disposable household income as a percentage of the poverty line)

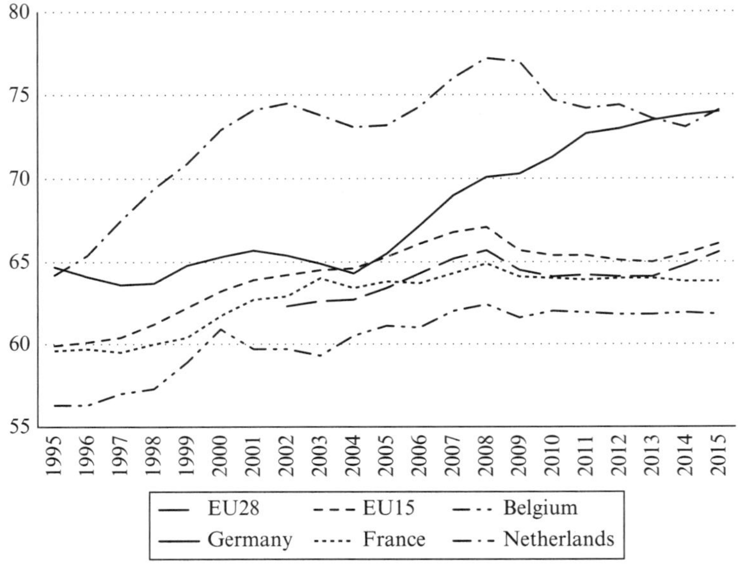

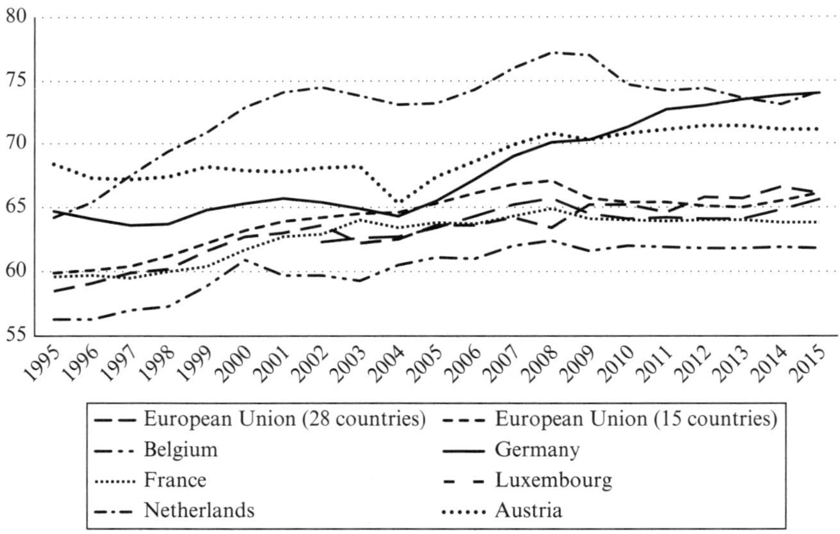

Source: Eurostat (2016i).

Figure 3.18 Change in employment rate, 15–64 years of age, Belgium, 1995–2015

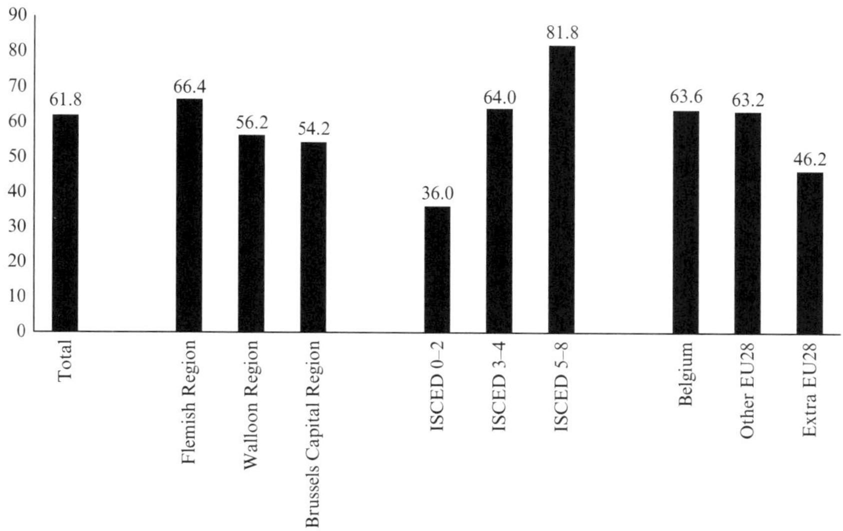

Source: Eurostat (2016i, 2016j, 2016k).

Figure 3.19 Employment rates for population aged 15–64 by region, educational attainment and country of birth, Belgium, 2015

One consequence is that a relatively large number of people of working age rely on some type of income support. Another consequence is that the share of the population paying taxes and social security contributions is relatively small, imposing heavy burdens on those who do pay.

3.4.1 Significant labour market exclusion

While unemployment is just below the EU average, there is significant long-term unemployment, especially among the less skilled. Belgium has the highest rate of household joblessness in the EU. The employment deficit among the less skilled (relative to the better skilled) is larger than in most other countries. Young people leaving school with no or few formal qualifications face dismal job prospects. The employment rate of immigrants in Belgium – particularly those born outside the EU – is also very low (about 46.2 per cent in 2015, as Figure 3.19 shows). The employment gap between migrants and natives is very high by international comparison (about 17 percentage points difference).

There are also vast regional and local differences in employment outcomes. No European country has such diverse labour market outcomes within such a confined geographical space. The main difference is between the Flemish- and the French-speaking parts of the country, but even within regions the differences are considerable.

All this may appear surprising because spending on active labour market programmes (training, job subsidies, social security contributions and public employment programmes), as well as on childcare, has increased substantially, putting Belgium in the league of the top spenders on such items. The social partners play an important role in many of these programmes, as (co-)funders or (co-)executors.

Vocational training, for example, falls under the authority of the three regions, whereby the social partners, at all levels (cross-industry, sectors and companies), play an important role in devising, organising and managing the training programmes. Training as part of active labour market policy (ALMP) measures, to foster reintegration into employment, is organised by regional public employment and training services (Walloon Community and Regional Vocational Training and Employment Service, FOREM, for the Walloon region; Flemish Office of Employment and Vocational Training, VDAB, in the Flemish region; Brussels Regional Office for Employment and Vocational Training, ORBEM/BGDA, in Brussels; and the Office for Employment and Vocational Training for the German Community, ADG, for the German-speaking community). The social partners develop specific training programmes and set up joint sectoral funds for vocational training. Intersectoral, and in a next step sectoral, collective agreements define objectives in terms of, among other things, mandatory financial contributions from the employers and minimal participation rates to training programmes. The interprofessional and sectoral levels therefore represent the most important bargaining levels with respect to vocational issues. However, training plans are often further discussed and negotiated within the company (Perin and Ajzen, 2015).

Despite many active labour market efforts, employment outcomes remain problematic. That is in part because Belgium's tradition of negotiated change through social dialogue is hampering some of the structural changes needed for activation efforts to have a real impact. In the next section we briefly set out the argument.

3.4.2 Belgium's reluctant turn to activation

As elsewhere in Europe, the 1990s mark a clear shift towards 'activation'. In Belgium, the dire state of public finances added further impetus. The introduction of the Competitiveness Law of 1989 and 1996 structurally limited the bargaining freedom of the social partners and institutionalised government intervention in wage setting (Van Ruysseveldt and Visser, 1995). There was a further expansion of active labour market programmes, making Belgium one of the biggest spenders on active labour market policies in the OECD, relative to GDP. Many of these efforts were focused on the demand side, mainly through employers' social security contribution reductions.

Efforts on the supply side were more hesitant, to the extent that when steps were taken, they happened mainly through non-intervention than through policy reforms specifically aimed at boosting work preparedness. Living on a benefit became less attractive from the late 1980s onwards because benefits were allowed to erode in value relative to wages and general living standards.

It has proved more difficult to introduce reforms in a more purposeful way. Unemployment insurance benefits remained unlimited in time, keeping Belgium a clear international outlier in this respect. During the 1990s, there was a wave of benefit terminations and suspensions on a variety of grounds. Nevertheless, average benefit duration in Belgium remained, and remains, higher than in most other comparable countries.

Belgium's relative incapacity to reform social security in order to improve work incentives is nowhere more evident than if we look at early retirement. There are few European countries where so few people work after the age of 55. The main scheme, colloquially known as a 'bridge pension', was conceived as a retirement scheme and not as an unemployment scheme, despite the fact that it formally is. It is now called 'unemployment benefit with company supplement'. It was implemented in the late 1970s to shelter the casualties of the economic downturn and industrial decline. It saw its biggest expansion during the 1980s.

The vast expansion of early retirement had a number of beneficial effects at the time (Marx, 2007). It provided adequate income protection to those who lost their jobs during a time when re-employment chances were extremely low, if not virtually non-existent. Job losses in Belgium's industrial sector were massive in the wake of the oil price shocks and many of the workers who lost their jobs were sole breadwinners with few formal qualifications or with very specific technical skills. In the Walloon region in particular, industrial employment was hit hard.

The co-funded nature of the principal early retirement scheme helped to contain the public sector cost of industrial restructuring, while dampening the social consequences. At the same time, the co-funded set-up facilitated industrial restructuring because it enabled employers to externalise a substantial part of the cost of laying-off redundant older workers. This allowed Belgium to pursue a high-productivity path. Moreover, early retirement also reduced competition for jobs. Employers who resorted to early retirement were principally required to hire a young person to replace the person taking early retirement. In practice, however, the replacement rule was never strictly adhered to. Still, unemployment rates for prime-age men – those still most likely to be the principal breadwinner – did remain comparatively low in Belgium, even when overall unemployment reached peak levels.

The attitude of employers' organisations towards this scheme has oscillated over recent decades. When confronted with labour shortages during economic upswings, they demanded the scaling back of the system. However, generally speaking, and despite an increasingly cooler stance towards early retirement taken by the representative organisations, individual employers have remained happy users of the bridge pension as a vehicle for facilitating restructuring. The attitude of trade unions towards the early retirement scheme was strongly driven by their members' expectations. Workers had come to expect to get what many of their former co-workers had got: the chance to leave the labour market early with a relatively attractive financial package. They had built up strong expectations regarding the possibility of early retirement.

Successive attempts by the government, and at times by employers' organisations, to scale back early retirement and to increase the effective age of retirement have encountered strong resistance from the trade unions (Marx and Schuerman, 2016). This became clear in the negotiations on the Generation Pact in 2005, from which a watered down version was adopted. A more recent pension reform, in which social partners were consulted less, led to the extension of the statutory retirement age and restricted the possibilities of retiring early. These – and other – unilateral actions of the government prompted industrial action. Reforms to the unemployment benefit system have sparked protest from trade unions as well. In November 2012, new unemployment benefit scales were implemented and benefit amounts were made more regressive over time. Trade unions have strongly criticised these reforms and have mounted protests. However, the current government aims to further reform unemployment benefits.

4. CASE STUDIES

4.1 Case Study 1: The Gender Pay Gap

The gap between male and female earnings remains significant across all EU member states despite equal pay legislation having been in place in the EU now for over 30 years (Smith, 2012). Women's gross hourly earnings are on average 16.7 per cent below those of men in the EU. Figure 3.8 has indicated the exceptional position of Belgium in international perspective since it has managed to narrow gender pay inequalities (see Figures 3.7 and 3.20). This can in part be attributed to Belgium's well-developed legislative

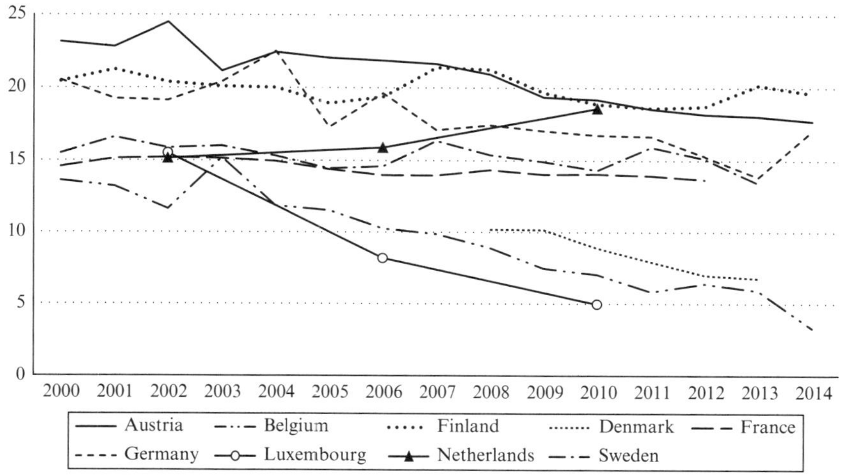

Note: Gender wage gap unadjusted and defined as the difference between median wages of men and women relative to the median wages of men.

Source: OECD (2016b).

Figure 3.20 Change in gender wage gap, Belgium and a selection of well-performing EU countries, 2000–2014

framework, which strongly enforces the principle of 'equal pay for equal work'. The Constitution contains the basic rules on which the principle of equal remuneration rests. Furthermore, a Royal Decree in 1987 requires companies to present an annual report on gender equality. A further development of this principle of non-discrimination was introduced in the Act on the equal treatment of men and women in the fields of wage determination, job evaluation and job classifications in 1999. Finally, a specific law was voted in 2012 (and revised in 2013) on the fight against wage inequalities between men and women. A number of European and international agreements guarantee standards of equal treatment as regards wage determination as well (Van Gyes, 2009a).

When focusing on the critical years of the Great Recession (see Figure 3.20), almost all countries have experienced a narrowing of the gender pay gap. This is explained by the levelling down of men's earnings during this period (Smith, 2012). For Belgium, the gap narrowed by nearly 3 per cent, while it was slightly on the rise just before the onset of the crisis. Again, Belgium is found to be one of the best performing countries as regards gender pay inequality.

When analysing the gender pay gap by sector, the majority of countries record a higher gap in gender earnings in the private compared with the public sector. The fact that, in most countries, employees in the public sector are strongly protected by collective pay agreements and other similar contracts, establishing pay could be one explanation for this finding (Eurostat, 2016a). However, for Belgium, a peculiar and even unique outcome is observed. In the public sector, women's gross hourly earnings are on average higher than those of men. This can partly be attributed to the possible higher educational level of women in public posts in comparison with men in this sector.

However, the high percentage gap between men's and women's earnings in the private sector needs a more nuanced approach as great disparities between private economic activities exist. According to Eurostat figures of 2016 (Eurostat, 2016l), the gender pay gap in the financial and insurance activities and electricity, gas, steam and air conditioning supply are considerably higher than in water supply, mining and construction activities (in which the gap is even negative). A clear link can be made with trade union representation because the manufacturing and construction sectors traditionally report higher trade union density. In these sectors, higher trade union presence may have a positive impact on the narrowing of the gap, as underlined by Smith (2012). On the sectoral level we do find some collective agreements which have a positive impact on narrowing the gender pay gap. The joint committee for metal construction (JC 111), for example, ensures equal access for men and women to all functions and all hierarchical levels. The Collective Agreement of 23 April 2001 even introduced a permanent workgroup based on parity, which is responsible for drawing up constructive proposals with regard to increasing the opportunities for women in the sector (Liagre et al., 2010). However, another explanation could be that these 'gender equal' sectors are male dominated and the small number of women are either equally paid owing to non-discriminating collective agreements or are better educated. Female-dominated sectors are, on the contrary, generally characterised by lower rates of unionisation (with the exception of the public sector) (Smith, 2012), which may explain the wide gender pay gap in, for example, the information and communication sector.

4.1.1 Social partners as equalising actors

The promotion of better working conditions and equal pay for women has long been an important theme for the social partners. Belgium was the first country to introduce an 'Equal pay day', on the initiative of the social partners.

An important framework is set by the law on the fight against the gender pay gap (revised in 2013) (Van Hove, 2013). The law involves the social partners in actions in the field of wage formation and makes gender discrimination a permanent theme in social dialogue. The law, furthermore, induced measures at the three hierarchical levels. At the interprofessional level, the technical report of the CEC, which prescribes the maximum margins for wage development, needs to include data about the gender pay gap. This information needs to be available for social partners while negotiating wages at sectoral level. Moreover, the social partners in the Group of Ten are obliged to enter into dialogue on policies to combat the unequal treatment of men and women in the labour market. The social partners are required to negotiate on such measures in joint committees as well. These sectoral measures are supposed to address the gender pay gap and to take into account gender-neutral measures in job-grading systems. Of note is the collective agreement No. 25 ter – in effect since 9 July 2008 and made generally binding by Royal Decree – which requires sectors and companies to test job and pay classification systems for gender neutrality. The law of 2012 took further steps in this respect as it required monitoring of the joint committees for gender neutrality. Finally, companies have an obligation to submit a report on their wage structure to the works council on their efforts towards gender equality (Van Hove, 2013; Perin and Ajzen, 2015).

Besides the above-mentioned general legislative measures, more specific initiatives on sectoral level are worth mentioning. Most of the Belgian joint committees have introduced non-discrimination of women as a clause in their collective agreements, whereby 'equal pay for equal work' is their most important concern (JCs 111, 124, 130). The joint committee for hairdressing and beauty care (JC 314) includes a general clause on 'preventing and combating any form of discrimination based on sex' in all the collective agreements concluded. The joint committee representing the banking sector (JC 310) refers to a 'Charter of Diversity in the banking sector'. Furthermore, almost all joint committees target the equal treatment of career breaks (maternity leave, paternity leave and time credit schemes).

Social partners thus play a key role in combating the unequal treatment of men and women. Nevertheless, there is clearly scope for improvement. The Institute for the Equality of Women and Men and the Federal Public Service for Employment, Labour and Social Dialogue have made a number of recommendations in their report on gender pay inequality. These include discouraging stereotypical study choices, improving work–life reconciliation and further measures to break the 'glass ceiling' (for example, quotas on a minimal presence of women in boards of directors) (Van Hove, 2013).

4.2 Case Study 2: Work–Life Balance

With regard to the quality of jobs and equality of outcomes in the world of work, the balance between work and personal life is a key consideration.

Belgium performs comparatively well when it comes to the perceived work–life balance of its workforce. In 2015, more than four workers in five (85 per cent) reported a good fit between their work and family or social commitments, with just 15 per cent reporting that the fit was poor. This is a favourable outcome judged by international standards since on average, in the EU, 81 per cent report having a good and 19 per cent a poor work–life balance. Figure 3.21 highlights Belgium's position at the higher end.

The sources of conflict between working and non-working time commitments are numerous. On the one hand, the characteristics of the household affect the pattern of time use. A couple with young children, for example, will report more conflicts in their work–life balance compared with a young single earner living with parents. The reported tension between work and private life is even worse for single parents. In general, the younger the children, the poorer the fit (Raymo and Sweeney, 2006; Delecta, 2011; Eurofound, 2016). Policies need to guarantee that personal circumstances and needs, in relation to such issues as care, are accommodated for the whole workforce, and for vulnerable groups in particular, hence enabling them to continue working over the life course (Eurofound, 2016). In this regard, work and working conditions play a key role, as well as the social infrastructure and social protection provisions.

4.2.1 Influence of the social partners

At European level, several directives address issues that are directly relevant for the work–life balance, such as minimum standards for parental leave and maternity leave. The social partners have special prerogatives in the social policy field, including in relation to working conditions. Important parts of the legislative framework in the area of work–life balance – notably the Parental Leave Directive (2010/18/EU), the Pregnant Workers (Maternity Leave) Directive (92/85/EEC) and the Directive on Part-Time Work (97/81/EC) – are based on social partner agreements and set out the basic rights in the EU (European Commission, 2016b). Relevant EU legislation also exists in the area of equal treatment between women and men in employment and occupation, the Gender Equality Recast Directive (2006/54/EC), a commitment of the European social partners, contained 'supporting work–life balance' as one of its priorities (Smith, 2012). In summer 2016, a second-stage consultation of the social partners at European level took place on possible legislative action in the area of work–life balance, which aimed to address the problem of women's underrepresentation in the labour market owing to the lack of effective possibilities to balance caring responsibilities with the demands of their working life. However, while the trade unions are favourable to new

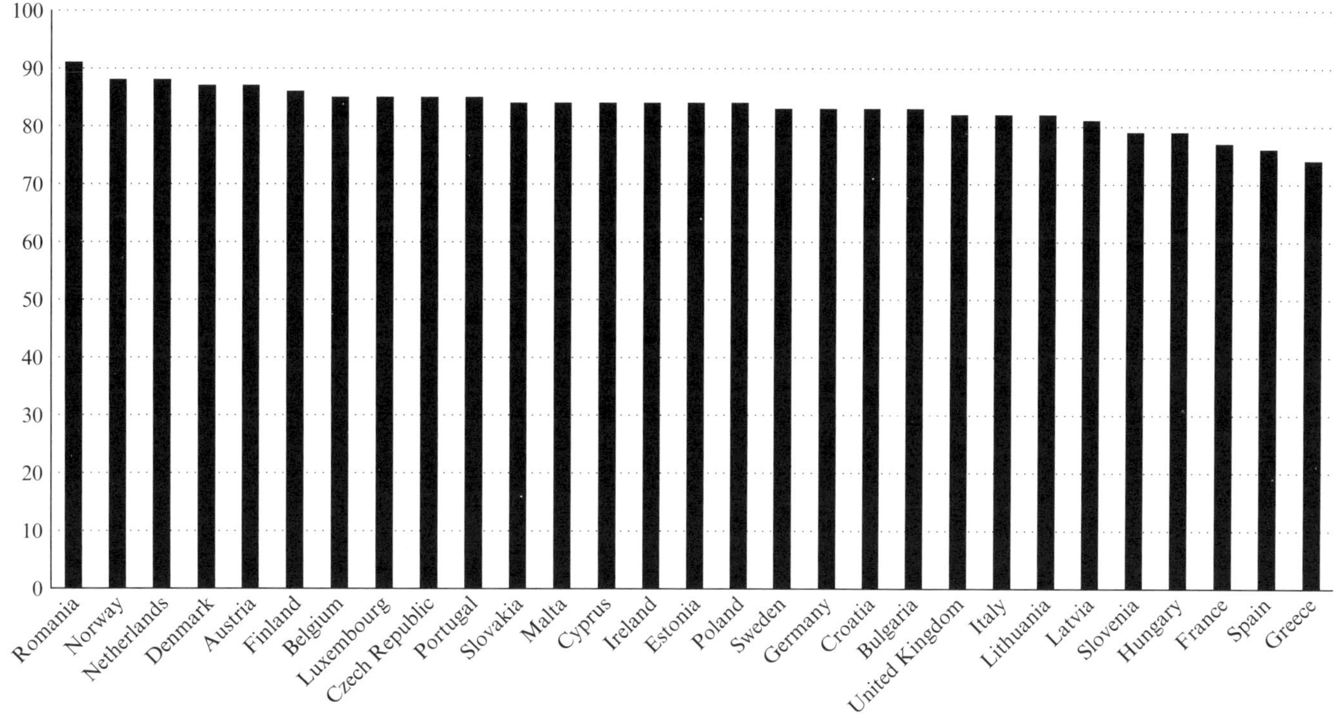

Source: Eurofound (2015: 114, fig. 109).

Figure 3.21 Share of workers indicating a good fit between work and commitments outside work, Belgium, 2015

measures in this field, employers' organisations declared they were against further action (European Commission, 2016b).

Besides the legal instruments set out above, the EU has been addressing work–life balance issues through complementary support measures. These include work–life balance guidelines for member states' employment policies, country-specific recommendations in the European Semester, financial support, analytical support, awareness-raising activities and quantitative targets to improve the provision of childcare (the Barcelona Targets) (European Commission, 2016b).

Working-time arrangements represent a key concern in Belgium. Belgium has comparatively strict working-time regulation, but collective bargaining at the sectoral level leaves a lot of room for alternative agreements (Van Gyes, 2009b). In the intersectoral agreement of 2001–02 the social partners agreed on a reduction of the statutory working week from 39 hours to 38 hours in an attempt to promote both employment growth and better reconciliation of work and private life (Delbar, 2000). The recent Peeters Law reforms the working-time regulation. Important measures in this regard are the 'plus minus account' and the annualisation of working time. By no longer calculating working time on a weekly basis, workers may perform more hours during peak periods and offset this 'surplus' during quieter periods throughout the year. The working-time limit will be nine hours a day and 45 hours a week (Peeters, 2016). Although the Minister of Work, Kris Peeters, asserts that there is no question of abolishing the 38-hour week, the reform has triggered protests from the unions, who see it as a threat to the work–life balance of employees.

In encouraging a better work–life balance, the career break and time credit scheme –also important measures in the context of working-time regulations– were introduced and regulated by the social partners in the IPA of 2000. Later, this framework was complemented by several collective agreements (77, 77bis, 103, 103bis). Trade unions have always been great supporters of these schemes, because they facilitate the combination of work and family life (Van Gyes, 2009b). The tightening of the time credit scheme, an important measure in combating early labour market exit, has thus resulted in trade union protests (Ajzen, 2015).

According to the labour force survey data, non-standard working arrangements, such as night work and weekend work, are less frequently applied in Belgium than in many other countries. This can in part be linked to the negative attitude of trade unions towards this kind of working-time flexibility (Van Gyes, 2009b). The government pledged, at the start of its term, however, to provide more flexibility on working time related to 'market needs' (in favour of employers), as well as work–life balance needs (in favour of employees). The Peeters Law sets a legal framework for both occasional telework and flexible working hours, within certain limits. In addition, a system of 'career saving' is put in place which enables workers to save up time in order to 'fund' a career break at a later date. As to employer-orientated flexibility, the law offers, among other things, the expansion and simplifying of rules regarding the use of overtime and the introduction of permanent temporary work contracts (Peeters, 2016). These measures, which might hamper a good balance between work and private life, have led to trade union actions.

As regards the specific impact of social partners the collective cross-sectoral labour agreement No. 85 of 9/11/2005 is worth noting. This agreement covered the implementation of telework, a vital flexibility tool used by employees. Another important collective agreement – No. 46 and extensions – establishes a cross-sectoral framework for night work. This agreement lays down conditions on the use of night work (compulsory consultation of trade union delegation, remuneration, time schedule), which seek to protect employees because working shifts at night might cause work–life balance conflicts. Other cross-sectoral labour agreements in the context of achieving a better work–life balance are agreements No. 35 on part-time work, No. 36 on temporary agency work and No. 45 on leave for compelling reasons (Nationale Arbeidsraad, 2016). These sector-wide agreements are complemented by collective agreements at industry and, eventually, firm level. In particular employee-orientated flexitime is a working condition chiefly agreed on between the employer and employees at firm level.

Other policies facilitating the reconciliation of work and private life formally set up by the federal or regional Belgian government, but subject to great influence from the social partners, include extensive childcare provisions for working parents. Provisions come both in the form of institutionalised day-care centres and private but subsidised 'care mothers'. Gross fees are strongly income related, as well as partially tax deductible, rendering childcare close to costless for those with the lowest incomes. Furthermore, parental, maternity and paternity leave and legal absenteeism for medical assistance are strictly framed by law and further determined by collective agreements. The Peeters Law, moreover, extended these legal opportunities by adding an additional three months of time credit for health-care reasons and one additional month of time credit for palliative care (Peeters, 2016).

Moreover, the Belgian Service Voucher Scheme, in place since January 2004, has proved to be tremendously popular in relieving reconciliation pressure. Because service vouchers can be used for such activities as cleaning and ironing, consumers are partially freed from some daily chores. This opens up more time for leisure and childcare or workers are able to put in more paid hours than they would otherwise (Marx and Vandelannoote, 2015).

Finally, it is worth highlighting the link between this case study and the previous one. Because women experience particularly strong balancing difficulties, measures taken by the social partners to combat work–life balance conflicts improve their career opportunities. More equal career opportunities are conducive to more equal pay. This way, the impact of social dialogue on both aspects – equal pay and the work–life balance – may well be mutually reinforcing.

5. CONCLUSION

In maintaining a strong social concertation model Belgium goes against international trends. Trade unions and employers' organisations – the social partners – remain institutionally strongly embedded. Bargaining on all aspects of working conditions, including wages, occurs in a multi-tiered bargaining system, and legal extension of collective agreements ensures close to full coverage. Although the role of the state has increased over recent years, the social partners continue to enjoy considerable autonomy in this respect, especially at the sectoral level. The social partners also continue to play an important and stabilising role in social and economic policy through their advisory and (co-)governing capacities in various institutions of the welfare state.

This chapter has highlighted that the Belgian social concertation model has many positive, even exemplary, aspects and outcomes. It has brought stability even in the most turbulent of times. That was very much in evidence when Belgium broke the record of the longest government formation period in modern history, and this during times of unprecedented economic and monetary turmoil. However, living standards increased in Belgium throughout this episode, while they were dropping or stagnating elsewhere in Europe.

We have highlighted other outcomes. Belgium is among the few rich countries not to have seen growing income inequality over the course of the past two decades, while living standards have risen steadily. Belgium's exceptionally compressed wage structure is a major driver of its low overall inequality. Belgium has the lowest incidence of low-paid work in the industrialised world. As far as we know there have been no increases in low-paid work or in wage inequality. The gender pay gap has decreased significantly to one of the lowest levels found anywhere. All this is directly related to Belgium's comprehensive wage bargaining system and the fact that nearly all workers are covered by collective agreements.

Those favourable outcomes extend beyond wages. There is little evidence of precarisation in the world of work. There has been little state-imposed deregulation and various forms of non-standard work remain less widespread in Belgium than elsewhere. To the extent that there have been moves towards more flexibility, these have been mostly negotiated. Many Belgian workers express relatively high levels of satisfaction with their work–life balance.

In brief, on such dimensions as wage equality, job stability, atypical employment or gender equality, Belgium does relatively well for reasons that can be directly related to its social concertation model, especially the fact that rules are set through negotiations at various levels rather than by decrees from above.

However, this does not mean that there are no inequalities to worry about. Job growth has been weak and there is particularly strong stratification in labour market participation and unemployment rates in such dimensions as education level, migration background or region. Despite low overall income inequality, Belgium's labour market is not as inclusive as it needs to be, and this is, arguably, at least in part a consequence of institutional rigidities and insider biases inherent in such an extensive social concertation model as Belgium's. Furthermore, for a country with a comparatively low level of income inequality and a comparatively high level of social spending, most of it channelled through social insurance systems co-governed by workers and employers, Belgium is confronted with a comparatively high level of relative income poverty.

Belgium's social model has thus not shown itself sufficiently capable of dealing with the root problems of sluggish job growth, unemployment and poverty among those of active age. In addition, there are further pressures for change.

External pressures derive from Belgium's economy being about as internationally orientated as is possible. Few countries in the world import and export a higher percentage of their GDP. That exposure requires constant adaptation to international demands and practices, such as just-in-time production and delivery. This competitive pressure for flexibility in responding to demand fluctuations can be at odds with work conditions agreed in countless collective agreements, often the product of extensive and long negotiations. To deal with these pressures, employers are demanding more flexibility in addition to perennial demands for lower wage costs.

Internally, political changes are challenging the status quo. Until recently Belgian governments were dominated by parties with very strong links to the labour movement, whether of the Christian Democrat, Socialist or Liberal variety. For the first time in modern history the government is dominated by a political party that does not have such links and that even sees its independence from the labour movement as one of its defining features.

Because of these and other external and internal pressures, Belgium's social dialogue model will need to adapt. Unfortunately, Belgium's institutional context is not conducive to rapid change in the directions needed. For all the stability on the surface, Belgian governance is characterised by a particularly complex and tense equilibrium, where the next (redistributive) conflict is always on the horizon. A legacy of decades of inter-linguistic group conflict is a complex federal system in which competencies are allocated in a way that almost inevitably precludes a high degree of policy consistency. The field of industrial relations is just as fractured; there are multiple and, in effect, competing trade unions and employers' organisations. All this makes for a context in which coherent and purposeful change is difficult to implement.

While demanding profound adaptations, the Belgian system features an institutional context that makes major changes extremely difficult to bring about. Belgium is often considered a prime example of an 'immovable object' meeting 'irresistible forces'. Yet, in concluding, it bears stressing that Belgium's social concertation system has often proved more adaptive than it may appear from the outside. Change tends to occur incrementally, in ways barely noticeable to outsiders, through numerous small changes. The pace of change may appear glacial at times, but there have been many demonstrable functional adaptations over past decades, arguably in some respects more successful than 'big reform' changes elsewhere. Still, this mode of adaptation poses issues in terms of consistency, timeliness and thus ultimately sustainability.

REFERENCES

Ajzen, M. (2015), 'Belgium: turbulent industrial relations follow new government agreement', accessed 27 October 2016 at http://www.eurofound.europa.eu/observatories/eurwork/articles/industrial-relations/belgium-turbulent-industrial-relations-follow-new-government-agreement.

Ajzen, M. and C. Vermandere (2013), 'Economic crisis puts social dialogue in disarray', accessed 27 October 2016 at http://www.eurofound.europa.eu/observatories/eurwork/articles/industrial-relations/economic-crisis-puts-social-dialogue-in-disarray.

Atkinson, A.B. and F. Bourguignon (2015), *Handbook of Income Distribution*, Amsterdam: Elsevier.

Bosch, G. (2015), 'Shrinking collective bargaining coverage, increasing income inequality: a comparison of five EU countries', *International Labour Review*, **154** (1), 57–66.

Buelens, J. and J.A. Pearson (2012), *Standard Work: An Anachronism?* Antwerp: Intersentia.
Cantillon, B. i.c.w. L. Buysse (2016), *De staat van de welvaartsstaat*, Leuven: Acco.
Cassiers, I. and L. Denayer (2009), 'Sociaal overleg en sociaal-economische veranderingen in België van 1944 tot heden', Discussion Paper 2009-42, Institut de Recherches Economiques et Sociales van de Université catholique de Louvain UCL.
Cox, G. and I. Verreyt (2013), *Ondernemingsraadzakboekje: sociaal overleg*, Mechelen: Kluwer.
Delbar, C. (2000), 'Minister launches debate on working time reduction', accessed 27 October 2016 at http://www.eurofound.europa.eu/observatories/eurwork/articles/minister-launches-debate-on-working-time-reduction.
Delecta, P. (2011), 'Review article work–life balance', *International Journal of Current Research*, **3** (4), 186–9.
Deleeck, H. (2001), *De architectuur van de welvaartsstaat opnieuw bekeken*, Leuven: Acco.
Dryon, P. and E. Krzeslo (1997), 'Apparent breakdown of Belgian central bargaining', accessed 23 October 2016 at https://www.eurofound.europa.eu/nl/observatories/eurwork/articles/industrial-relations-labour-market/apparent-breakdown-of-belgian-central-bargaining.
Ebbinghaus, B., C. Göbel and S. Koos (2011), 'Social capital, "Ghent" and workplace contexts matter: comparing union membership in Europe', *European Journal of Industrial Relations*, **17** (2), 107–24.
Eurofound (2015), *Sixth European Working Conditions Survey*, Luxembourg: Publications Office of the European Union.
Eurofound (2016), *Sixth European Working Conditions Survey*, Luxembourg: Publications Office of the European Union.
European Commission (2014), *Industrial Relations in Europe 2014*, Luxembourg: Publications Office of the European Union.
European Commission (2016a), *European Semester Thematic Fiche Wage Developments and Wage Setting Systems*, Luxembourg: Publications Office of the European Union.
European Commission (2016b), *Second-stage Consultation of the Social Partners at European Level under Article 154 TFEU on Possible Action Addressing the Challenges of Work–Life Balance Faced by Working Parents and Caregivers*, Brussels: European Commission.
Eurostat (2016a), *Gender Pay Gap Statistics*, accessed 27 October 2016 at http://ec.europa.eu/eurostat/statistics-explained/index.php/Gender_pay_gap_statistics.
Eurostat (2016b), *Gender Pay Gap in Unadjusted Form % [tsdsc340]*, The structure of Earnings Survey (SES), accessed 21 November 2016 at tsdsc340.
Eurostat (2016c), *Minimum Wages – EUR/Month [tps00155]*, accessed 24 November 2016 at tps00155.
Eurostat (2016d), *Part-time Employment and Temporary Contracts – Annual Data [lfsi_pt_a]*, Labour Force Survey, accessed 14 November 2016 at lfsi_pt_a.
Eurostat (2016e), *Employees Working Shifts as a Percentage of the Total of Employees, by Sex and Age (%) [lfsa_ewpshi]*, Labour Force Survey, accessed 7 November 2016 at lfsa_ewpshi.
Eurostat (2016f), *Employed Persons Working at Nights as a Percentage of the Total Employment, by Sex, Age and Professional Status (%) [lfsa_ewpnig]*, Labour Force Survey, accessed 7 November 2016 at lfsa_ewpnig.

Eurostat (2016g), *Employed Persons Working on Sundays as a Percentage of the Total Employment, by Sex, Age and Professional Status (%) [lfsa_ewpsun]*, Labour Force Survey, accessed 7 November 2016 at lfsa_ewpsun.

Eurostat (2016h), *Expenditure on Social Protection (% of GDP) [tps00098]*, accessed 11 October 2016 at tps00098.

Eurostat (2016i), *Employment Rates by Sex, Age and Educational Attainment Level (%) [lfsa_ergaed]*, Labour Force Survey, accessed on 13 October 2016 at lfsa_ergaed.

Eurostat (2016j), *Employment Rates by Sex, Age and NUTS 2 Regions (%) [lfst_r_lfe2emprt]*, Labour Force Survey, accessed on 13 October 2016 at lfst_r_lfe2emprt.

Eurostat (2016k), *Employment Rates by Sex, Age and Country Of Birth (%) [lfsa_ergacob]*, Labour Force Survey, accessed on 13 October 2016 at lfsa_ergacob.

Eurostat (2016l), *The Unadjusted Gender Pay Gap by Economic Activity (%) [earn_gr_gpgr2]*, Structure of Earnings Survey, accessed 4 November 2016 at earn_gr_gpgr2.

Eurostat (2017), *Gini Coefficient of Equivalised Disposable Income*, EU-SILC survey, accessed 24 January 2017 at ilc_di12.

Fitzenberger, B., K. Kohn and A. Lembcke (2013), 'Union density and varieties of coverage: the anatomy of union wage effects in Germany', *ILR Review*, **66** (1), 169–97.

Horemans, J., O. Pintelon and P. Vandenbroucke (2011), 'Inkomens en inkomensverdeling op basis van Belgische enquêtegegevens: 1985–2007', Centrum voor Sociaal Beleid Herman Deleeck, University of Antwerp.

Horemans, J. (2016), 'Half a job, twice as poor: empirical investigations into the role of earnings, family composition, and institutions as factors underlying. The poverty risk of part-timers across Europe', PhD thesis, Faculty of Social Sciences, University of Antwerp.

Humblet, P., M. Rigaux, R. Janvier, J. Peeters, W. Rauws, K. Van den Langenbergh, et al. (2014), *Synopsis van het Belgische arbeidsrecht*, Antwerp and Cambridge: Intersentia.

ILO (2016), *Non-standard Employment around the World: Understanding Challenges, Shaping Prospects*, Geneva: ILO.

Kuypers, S. and Marx, I. (2016), 'Social concertation and middle class stability in Belgium', in D. Vaughan-Whitehead (ed.), *Europe's Disappearing Middle Class? Evidence from the World of Work*, Cheltenham, UK and Geneva: Edward Elgar and ILO, pp. 112–59.

Liagre, P., L. Damhuis, G. Van Gyes, G. Valenduc and M. Lamberts (2010), 'Het genderperspectief in het sociale overleg op sectorniveau: Een analyse van en voor het ACV-optreden', research report, HIVA-KU Leuven and FTU Namur.

Marx, I. (2007), *A New Social Question? On Minimum Income Protection in the Postindustrial Era*, Amsterdam: Amsterdam University Press.

Marx, I. (2009), 'Belgium: a post-Bismarckian welfare state looking for legitimacy, sustainability and a way out of "welfare without work"', in K. Schubert, S. Hegelich and U. Bazant (eds), *European Welfare Systems*, New York: Routledge, pp. 49–64.

Marx, I. and N. Schuerman (2016), 'Belgium, or how inertia can have unexpected benefits in times of crisis', in Schubert et al. (eds), *Challenges to European Welfare Systems*, Basel: Springer International, pp. 37–57.

Marx, I., and D. Vandelannoote (2015), 'Matthew runs amok: the Belgian service

voucher scheme', in C. Carbonnier and N. Morel (eds), *The Political Economy of Household Services in Europe*, Basingstoke: Palgrave-Macmillan, pp. 197–220.
Marx, I., J. Vanhille and G. Verbist (2012), 'Combating in-work poverty in continental Europe: an investigation using the Belgian case', *Journal of Social Policy*, **41** (1), 19–41.
Milquet, J., X. Verboven and G. Carlens (2010), *75 jaar RVA: Een blik op verleden, heden en toekomst*, Tournai: Lesaffre.
National Employment Office (2016), *Jaarverslag 2016: Volume 2: Indicatoren van de arbeidsmarkt en evolutie van de uitkeringen*, accessed 8 November 2016 at http://www.rva.be/sites/default/files/assets/pu blications/Rap port_Annuel/2016/Ra pport_annuel_NL_Vol2.pdf.
Nationale Arbeidsraad (2016), *Cao's per thema*, accessed 12 December 2016 at http://www.cnt-nar.be/Cao-thema.htm.
Nolan, B., W. Salverda, D. Checchi, I. Marx, A. McKnight, I. Tóth, et al. (eds) (2014), *Changing Inequalities and Societal Impacts in Rich Countries: Thirty Countries' Experiences*, Oxford: Oxford University Press.
OECD (2004), *Employment Outlook 2004: Wage-setting Institutions and Outcomes*, Paris: OECD.
OECD (2011), *Divided We Stand: Why Inequality Keeps Rising*, Paris: OECD.
OECD (2013), *Employment Outlook 2013: Protecting Jobs, Enhancing Flexibility: A New Look at Employment Protection Legislation in OECD*, Paris: OECD.
OECD (2015), *In It Together: Why Less Inequality Benefits All*, Paris: OECD.
OECD (2016a), *OECD.Stat*, Employment Database, accessed 12 October 2016 at OECD.Stat.
OECD (2016b), *OECD.Stat: Gender Wage Gap*, Employment Database, accessed 6 December 2016 at OECD.Stat.
Pecinovsky, P. and P. Van den Bergh (2014), 'Comparative labour law dossier: temporary employment contracts in Belgium', Institute of Labour Law, KU Leuven.
Peeters, K. (2016), 'Werkbaar wendbaar werk "mijlpaal voor de belgische arbeidsmarkt"', legislative proposal by the Minister of Labour, Brussels.
Perin, E. and M. Ajzen (2015), *Belgium: Working Life Country Profile*, accessed 27 October 2016 at http://www.eurofound.europa.eu/observatories/eurwork/com parative-information/national-contributions/belgium/belgium-working-life-count ry-profile.
Plasman, R., M. Rusinek and F. Rycx (2007), 'Wages and the bargaining regime under multi-level bargaining: Belgium, Denmark and Spain', *European Journal of Industrial Relations*, **13** (2), 161–80.
Raymo, J.M. and M.M. Sweeney (2006), 'Work–family conflict and retirement preferences', *Journal of Gerontology: Social Sciences*, **61** (3), 161–96.
Salverda, W. and D. Checchi (2014), 'Labour-market institutions and the dispersion of wage earnings', IZA Discussion Paper Series 8220, Institute of Labour Economics, Bonn.
Schnabel, C. (2013), 'Union membership and density: some (not so) stylized facts and challenges', *European Journal of Industrial Relations*, **19** (3), 255–72.
Smith, M. (2012), 'Social regulation of the gender pay gap in the EU', *European Journal of Industrial Relations*, **18** (4), 365–80.
Van Gyes, G. (2009a), 'Belgium: wage formation', accessed 23 October 2016 at http://www.eurofound.europa.eu/observatories/eurwork/comparative-information/natio nal-contributions/belgium/belgium-wage-formation.
Van Gyes, G. (2009b), 'Working time in the European Union: Belgium', accessed

23 October 2016 at http://www.eurofound.europa.eu/observatories/eurwork/comparative-information/national-contributions/belgium/working-time-in-the-european-union-belgium.
Van Gyes, G. (2010), 'Crisis in social dialogue due to anti-crisis measures', accessed 23 October 2016 at http://www.eurofound.europa.eu/observatories/eurwork/articles/industrial-relations/crisis-in-social-dialogue-due-to-anti-crisis-measures.
Van Gyes, G. (2012), 'Union protest again government's austerity package', accessed 23 October 2016 at http://www.eurofound.europa.eu/observatories/eurwork/articles/industrial-relations/union-protest-against-governments-austerity-package.
Van Hove, H. (2013), *The Gender Pay Gap in Belgium Report 2013*, Brussels: Institute for the Equality of Women and Men.
Van Oycke, J. (2016), 'Belgium: latest working life developments – Q3 2016', accessed 27 October 2016 at http://www.eurofound.europa.eu/observatories/eurwork/articles/working-conditions-industrial-relations/belgium-latest-working-life-developments-q3-2016.
Van Rie, T. and I. Marx (2013), 'Growing Inequalities' Impacts (GINI): country report on Belgium', Centrum voor Sociaal Beleid Herman Deleeck, University of Antwerp.
Van Rie, T. and I. Marx (2014), 'Belgium: when growing background inequalities meet resilient institutions', in B. Nolan (ed.), *Changing Inequalities and Societal Impacts in Rich Countries: Thirty Countries' Experiences*, Oxford: Oxford University Press, pp. 126–51.
Van Rie, T., I. Marx and J. Horemans (2011), 'Ghent revisited: unemployment insurance and union membership in Belgium and the Nordic countries', *European Journal of Industrial Relations*, **17** (2), 125–39.
Van Ruysseveldt, J. and J. Visser (1995), 'Weak corporatisms going different ways? Industrial relations in the Netherlands and Belgium', in J. Van Ruysseveldt and J. Visser (eds), *Industrial Relations in Europe: Traditions and Transitions*, London: Sage, pp. 205–64.
Vandaele, K. (2009), 'The Ghent system, temporary unemployment and the Belgian trade unions since the economic downturn', *Transfer*, **16** (3–4), 589–96.
Vandekerckhove, S. and G. Van Gyes (2012), *Collective Agreed Wages in Belgium: Indicators And Trends*, Leuven: HIVA – Research Institute for Work and Society.
Vandekerckhove, S. and G. Van Gyes (2014), *Minimum Wages in Belgium: A Maze, or Amazing?* Brussels: European Commission.
Vandekerckhove, S., C. Vermandere and G. Van Gyes (2010), 'Loondrift en loonflexibiliteit: de grillen van de loonvorming bij sociaal overleg', *Over-werk: Tijdschrift van het Steunpunt WSE*, **2**, 119–24.
Vandekerckhove, S., M. Goos and G. Van Gyes (2014), *Reassessing the impact of minimum wages on wage dispersion and employment: evidence from an institutionalized wage bargaining system*, paper presented at the PEAC Conference, Brussels, 5–7 March.
Vaughan-Whitehead, D. (2012), *Work Inequalities in the Crisis: Evidence from Europe*, Cheltenham, UK and Geneva: ILO.
Vaughan-Whitehead, D. (2015a), *The Minimum Wage Revisited in the Enlarged EU*, Cheltenham, UK and Geneva: Edward Elgar and ILO.
Vaughan-Whitehead, D. (2015b), *The European Social Model in Crisis: Is Europe Losing Its Soul?*, Cheltenham, UK and Geneva: Edward Elgar and ILO.
Vermandere, C. (2014), 'Belgium: changes to wage-setting mechanisms in the context of the crisis and the EU's new economic governance regime', accessed 23

October 2016 at http://www.eurofound.europa.eu/ observatories/eurwork/comparative-information/national-contributions/belgium/belgium-changes-to-wage-setting-mechanisms-in-the-context-of-the-crisis-and-the-eus-new-economic.
Vermandere, C. and G. Van Gyes (2015), 'Belgium: effects of the economic crisis on wage indexation', accessed 23 October 2016 at http://www.eurofound.europa.eu/nl/observatories/eurwork/articles/working-conditions-labour-market-industrial-relations/belgium-effects-of-the-economic-crisis-on-wage-indexation.
Villanueva, E. (2015), 'Employment and wage effects of extending collective bargaining agreements', *IZA Worlds of Labor*, **136** (1), 1–10, doi:10.15185/izawol.136.
Vilrokx, J. and D. Ranson (2000), 'The National Labour Council in 1999: an overview', accessed 16 October 2016 at http://www.eurofound.europa.eu/observatories/eurwork/articles/social-policies/the-national-labour-council-in-1999-an-overview.
Visser, J., ICTWSS Data base, version 5.1, September 2016, Amsterdam Institute for Advanced Labour Studies (AIAS), University of Amsterdam.
Visser, J. (2016), 'What happened to collective bargaining during the great recession?', *Journal of Labor Policy*, **5** (9).

4. Social dialogue in France under pressure: Can worker security be achieved in a context of increasing job flexibility?

Pierre Courtioux and Christine Erhel

1. INTRODUCTION

The French industrial relations system dates back to the end of the nineteenth century and to the development of the welfare state after the Second World War. It is characterised by important protections and rights for trade unions, strong involvement on the part of the state (setting the minimum wage, but also legal rules for working time) and an important role for sectoral bargaining (as in other continental European countries). This system succeeded in achieving high coverage rates for workers and making important social progress, including a decrease in working time – weekly and annual holidays for all – and a good level of social protection. Over a long period, inequalities also tended to decrease.

This model has been under pressure since the end of the Fordist era and the rise in unemployment (in the 1970s), facing substantial criticisms concerning its lack of flexibility at the firm level, the attitude of trade unions – which appear to favour insiders at the expense of the unemployed and young people – and the liability of the state in rising labour costs that impair competitiveness (increase in minimum wage and high levels of social contributions). As in other countries, some structural factors are also in play, such as the decline in industrial employment and the rise of services, or the change in the composition of employment in terms of qualifications (a decrease in blue-collar and low-qualified employment, and the rise of jobs requiring higher qualifications). Furthermore, internationalisation has resulted in more frequent comparisons with other countries (the Nordic model and the economic liberal decentralised model as two opposite benchmarks in the political debate), as well as the increased influence of international organisations (especially the Organisation for

Economic Co-operation and Development and its 'Jobs Strategy' and the European Union's European Employment Strategy and more recently its 'flexicurity' goals).

In this context, the French model of social dialogue has undergone several reforms, accelerating over recent years (since the 2008 crisis). Decentralisation has increased with a stronger role for company-level agreements, social dialogue has been encouraged in smaller firms, and tripartism has been developed to achieve some national agreements, trading more flexibility against measures that are supposed to ensure more security in labour market transitions for workers. Although the reality of the so-called 'modernisation'[1] of social dialogue cannot be called into question, its impact on the labour market and on inequalities cannot be estimated quantitatively. Indeed, aggregate level analysis in this field suffers from important biases, and even using firm-level data it appears very difficult to disentangle different factors explaining wage (level or inequalities) or employment trends (Ferracci and Guyot, 2015). Therefore, the ambition of the present chapter is more limited. We identify the recent trends in French social dialogue and analyse (in a descriptive way) its links with labour market inequalities, wages but also employment inequalities.

Section 2 describes the evolution of French social dialogue towards more decentralisation and the inclusion of some flexicurity components; section 3 explores the new balance obtained at the end of that process for three different levels (national, sector and firm); and section 4 describes the various dimensions of inequality on the labour market before exploring the links between social dialogue and some indicators of labour market inequalities. Section 5 focuses on two case studies that highlight the links between social dialogue and inequality from a world of work perspective.

2. THE TRADITIONAL FRENCH SOCIAL DIALOGUE SYSTEM AND ITS EVOLUTION TOWARDS MORE DECENTRALISATION SINCE THE 1980S

Historically, the French industrial relations system has been characterised by strong involvement of the state and the law in a conflictual social relations context. Its foundations date back to the end of the nineteenth century (freedom of association in 1884, the first collective agreement in the mining sector in 1891 and coverage of work accidents in 1898) and to the post-Second World War context that established the sector (*branche*) as the main level for bargaining, together with principles of generalisation and extended coverage (1950 Act).

In practice, the functioning of French labour law (*Code du travail*) regulating social dialogue has traditionally been based on two key principles: a hierarchy between standards[2] and the principle of the most favourable rule – that is, core workplace guarantees (*ordre public social*) – which implies that a lower-ranking rule can take precedence over a higher-ranking rule only if it is more beneficial to the employee. That traditional system also involves a definite number of social partners: five trade unions enjoying a presumption of representativeness since 1966 (the CGT, the CGT–FO, the CFDT, the CFTC and the CFE–CGC; see the glossary to this chapter for a description of each social partner abbreviation) and three employers' organisations (the MEDEF, the CGPME and the UPA). These social partners have also been involved in the institutions of the social security system that were built after the Second World War, based on tripartism (state, trade unions and employers' organisations). Finally, the state plays a crucial role in industrial relations: the government sets the minimum wage and the Ministry of Labour extends almost all collective agreements.

However, since the Auroux Acts in 1982, there have been a number of reforms of company/workplace-level collective bargaining and the rules governing representativeness and workplace-level employee representation have been transformed.[3]

The first step towards decentralisation of collective bargaining in France was the Auroux Acts in 1982 that established an obligation to negotiate wages and working time annually. Initially, this company-level negotiation had to comply fully with the favourability principle (unless the law expressly authorises deviations). However, more recent acts have undermined that rule. Since 2004 lower-ranking contractual provisions need not comply with higher-ranking provisions, apart from those dealing with legal or conventional minimum wages and collective job guarantees (training and welfare).[4] Since 2008 company-level agreements concerning working hours need not comply with sector agreements and the latter are unable to forbid such deviation. However, company agreements must comply with legal rules concerning overtime hours (paid 25 per cent more than normal hours). Finally, the highly contested 'El Khomri Act' (July 2016) reforms the hierarchy between standards in the cases of working time and employment maintenance agreements, establishing the pre-eminence of company agreements on these issues. Employment maintenance agreements have taken precedence even over individual labour contracts, including wages (the monthly wage is still guaranteed but flexible pay and premiums can be adjusted) and working time. If an employee refuses to accept the new rules, they can be dismissed. However, facing the resistance of trade unions and public opinion, the government finally established that a number of important topics constitute 'fundamental issues' in relation to which company agreements cannot undercut sectoral agreements: minimum wages, occupational classifications, private social protection, vocational training, gender equality and hard/dangerous working conditions (*pénibilité*).

The growing importance of company-level bargaining made it necessary to modernise the rules governing social partners' representativeness and employee representation at the workplace or company level.

Since 2008, union representativeness has been based on a minimum percentage of the votes in staff elections (10 per cent at company level and 8 per cent at sectoral or national multi-sectoral level). Elections were organised in 2013, and the five 'traditional' unions maintained their position at the national multi-sectoral level, even though they did not always obtain the minimum requirement at the sectoral level. Two smaller unions (UNSA and Solidaire) have been enabled to set up shop in some sectors thus promoting multiple union representation at sectoral level.

As regards employers' federations, an Act of 2014 introduced a rule for measuring representativeness on the basis of membership, which will become effective in 2017: at least 8 per cent of companies must be members of a federation to allow it to be considered representative.

In parallel, the rules of validity for collective bargaining agreements (at company and sectoral levels) also changed in 2008 and 2016 and now make reference to election results to increase their legitimacy. Since the July 2016 Labour Act, to be valid a company-level agreement must be signed by union representatives representing one or more organisations accounting for at least 50 per cent of the votes[5] and by at least one employers' federation recognised as representative. If trade unions do not reach the majority threshold they have the right to demand a referendum.

A recent Act (2015) also modified the rules for employees' representation at the company level to simplify the existing framework in medium and large firms, and to better cover employees in small firms. In France, employees' representation is governed by legal thresholds, so that the number of representative types and the number of works councils grows with the size of the firm (Table 4.1).

Another important reform that is being implemented is sectoral reorganisation. Collective bargaining at the sectoral level in France appears highly fragmented, with sectors covering a particular job function (for instance, journalists), or a geographical area or socio-professional category. In 2012 there were 710 sector-level collective agreements (excluding the agricultural sector), with significant variations in size. In October 2015, the government announced its goal of reducing the number of sectors to 100 in the long run, with intermediate targets of 400 by the end of 2016 and 200 by the end of 2017. That reform is aimed at reducing fragmentation and clarifying labour standards.

Table 4.1 Staff representation in France up to 2017

Number of employees	11–49	50–299	> 300
Staff representative bodies	Staff rep.	Staff representatives Works council Health and Safety Committee Option of appointing a single employee representative body	Option of merging via majority agreement
Union representation		Union delegate Local union delegate	Union delegate Local union representative Works council representative

Source: Direction Générale du Trésor (2016). These rules were modified in September 2017.

Apart from these rule changes, which tend to favour the development of decentralised social dialogue and to simplify the organisation of the French industrial relations system, there has been an increase in the social partners' commitment to negotiate at the firm level on wages and other topics, such as working time, work organisation, collective health insurance, gender equality and so on,[6] and more recently a trend to oblige companies to reach agreement on some issues. In case of failure to reach an agreement at the company level, an action plan has to be implemented: that principle applies to gender equality (2006) and to seniors' employment at companies employing 50 or more people (2008).

Tripartite social dialogue has also been developing in recent years.[7] The social partners are still heavily involved in the management of social security, especially public health insurance and unemployment benefits, and participate in the design and delivery of vocational training. Furthermore, the 2007 Act on modernisation of social dialogue makes it compulsory for the government to consult national trade unions and employers' organisations when proposing reforms of industrial relations, employment and vocational training. Several important reforms have been carried out on the basis of collective bargaining and national agreements that were then transposed into law.

Despite this stronger involvement of social partners in labour market reforms, the state has kept control of determining the minimum wage, although the process was reformed in 2008. Since then,[8] an independent expert group has been created, which gives its advice every year on the evolution of the minimum wage, but the group is composed of academic researchers and representatives from economic and statistical administrations, and does not include social partners, in contrast to the British case, for instance. Social partners are only advised of the different analyses and of the government's decision through the Commission Nationale de la Négociation Collective (CNNC).

Several recent reforms based on national-level collective bargaining can be considered implementations of a 'flexicurity' perspective, providing more security for workers in exchange for increased labour market flexibility. In 2008 the increase in labour contract flexibility (through a mutual agreement for the termination of indefinite contracts, *rupture conventionnelle*) was 'compensated' by a right for workers – in the case of lay-offs – to retain their health coverage and training entitlements. In 2013, the obligation for employers to provide health insurance and a minimum duration for part-time employment (24 hours) was obtained in return for deregulation with regard to economic redundancies and potential wage cuts in case of economic difficulties. Vocational training was also reformed on the basis of a national agreement and a law enacted in 2015, which creates an individual training account (accessible via an online service) that will follow the employee for all their working life.[9] The same reform changes the calculation of employers' vocational training contributions (single contribution of 1 per cent of payroll for all firms with more than ten employees[10] and 0.55 per cent for firms with fewer than ten employees).

The 'El Khomri Act' (July 2016) was also intended to develop 'flexicurity' in France (the final title of the Act was 'Rules relating to labour, social dialogue modernisation and secure occupational trajectories'[11]), by reforming social dialogue, as well as some rules concerning economic redundancies and providing more security for workers through a new personal training account (*Compte Personnel d'Activité*, CPA). It also includes the extension of the 'Youth Guarantee' offering low-income and low-qualified young people (under 28 years of age) intensive job search assistance and a one-year allowance (€461 a month). However, the bill was not based on social dialogue and was strongly rejected by trade unions (except the CFDT), public opinion (with several public demonstrations) and political parties (even among socialist representatives, resulting in the use of a special procedure to have the bill passed into law at the National Assembly[12]).

Social partners are directly involved in the management and design of unemployment insurance, but their participation in active labour market policy is rather limited, although cooperation between social partners and the government has been relaunched in the context of the crisis, with two social summits in 2008 and 2009, and some specific inter-sectoral agreements about short-time working and some reintegration schemes for workers – Contrat de Reclassement Professionnel (CRP), and Contrat de Transition Professionnelle (CTP).

To conclude this section, after 15 years of intensive reforms, the French industrial relations system has evolved in two main directions: first, a trend towards higher decentralisation of social dialogue, accompanied by some changes in rules for representativeness of agreement validity; and second, higher participation on the part of the social partners in labour market reforms, especially in the recent crisis, involving some trends towards 'flexicurity'. These trends have been driven by several factors, including the need for greater flexibility in the service sector, but also the influence of several general policy trends observed in most Organisation for Economic Co-operation and Development (OECD) and European Union (EU) countries (trends towards flexibilisation of the labour market, flexicurity and so on). However, the recent debate around the 'El Khomri' bill may have altered that second trend and provoked a new increase in social conflicts.

The potential consequences of these trends in terms of inequalities are not straightforward: the development of firm-level agreements may increase inequalities among employees, but at least until 2016 the importance of national and sectoral level wage determination mechanisms was maintained.

3. UNOBTAINABLE SECURITY IN A FLEXIBILISING LABOUR MARKET?

What have been the consequences of these reforms for the general balance between flexibility and security? How does the frequent reference to flexicurity principles translate into practice? Given the existence of strong regulations on the French labour market, we could expect relatively strong bargaining power for trade unions, resulting in the development of fairly good security options for workers, even at a more decentralised level. However, unionisation rates are very low, inducing some representativeness problems and weakening trade unions, and the functioning of the industrial relations system is quite diverse in practice (by sector, firm size and so on). High unemployment rates (for more than 30 years) have also reduced labour bargaining power. Also, the culture of conflict remains strong in France and makes it more difficult to reach agreement. As a result, labour market trends seem generally unbalanced and favour flexibility. Given the existence of three bargaining levels in the French industrial relations system, we successively consider national (macroeconomic) trends in social dialogue, before analysing the sectoral and firm levels.

3.1 Global Trends: Higher Labour Market Flexibility, with Some Additional Protections for Workers

As in other OECD economies the main trend in the French labour market since the 1980s has been the increase in labour flexibility, through the development of fixed-term contracts, temporary agency work and part-time work (Courtioux and Erhel, 2016).

That trend has accelerated from the mid-2000s to the very recent and contested Labour Act of July 2016. Indeed, the development of low-income independent employment was favoured by a new scheme (*auto-entrepreneurs*, 2009) introducing simpler administrative procedures under a certain turnover threshold. The growth of short-duration contracts (less than a month) that was enabled by law has been spectacular since 2004 and has not been stopped by the crisis or by the introduction of an additional contribution in 2013. In parallel, conditions for economic redundancies were simplified (in 2013 and 2016) and in 2008 the law introduced the possibility of breaking indefinite contracts by mutual agreement.

The initiative for these reforms came from the state. However, to a certain extent, social dialogue has accompanied flexibility. For instance, in the field of unemployment insurance, tripartite dialogue has led to a better coverage of fixed-term workers through a decrease in the minimum number of months to obtain entitlement (four months since 2008) and the recent creation of cumulative rights (*droits rechargeables*) in 2015. At the same time the increase in the number of very short duration contracts also put pressure on the financing of unemployment insurance and led the social partners and the state to introduce an additional contribution for these contracts in 2013. In a more specific area, reform of the unemployment insurance regime for artists (*intermittents*) occurred in 2016 after a year of consultation and bargaining, and is generally considered a success, providing better coverage for workers in exchange for some measures to reduce expenditure (especially the limitation of possibilities to cumulate wages and unemployment insurance allowances).[13]

At the national level, most 'flexicurity' measures were also developed in law on the basis of social dialogue, generally transposing some national agreements into law (several Acts in 2008, 2013 and 2015). Better transferability of social rights for workers, compulsory private social protection schemes or the 24-hour threshold for part-time work were 'traded' against increased flexibility in standard labour contracts. The recent Labour Act appears to be an exception, as it was based on a unilateral decision of the French government – but some bargaining took place after the first presentation of the project, in the face of strikes and social contestation.

All these flexicurity Acts have been criticised for being unbalanced, increasing flexibility immediately whereas the outputs in terms of security remain uncertain. For instance, the 24-hour threshold concerning part-time work has been adapted by branch-level collective bargaining – as authorised by the 2013 Act: in general, these sector agreements (covering 44 per cent of employees in 2015) set a minimum part-time duration below the 24-hour threshold, either for all employees, or according to occupation or type of firm. In practice the 24-hour threshold for part-time duration, which was supposed to increase job quality and income security for workers, appears largely virtual.

Furthermore, there has been no consensus among the trade unions about flexicurity: the most reformist trade unions (the CFDT, the CFE–CGC and the CFTC) were in favour of these agreements and Acts after bargaining on some issues (such as the additional contribution for fixed-term contracts in 2013, or the conditions concerning dismissals and the contents of personal activity accounts in 2016), whereas the CGT–FO maintained their opposition. Apart from 'flexicurity' the introduction of new topics for social dialogue (gender equality, hard working conditions and so on) was mainly driven by the state, although the trade unions participated in the process.

3.2 Sectoral Level: High Coverage Rates but Fragmented Collective Bargaining, with Substantial Heterogeneity of Sectoral Characteristics

As previously mentioned, the share of employees covered by sectoral agreements stands at a very high level in France and has even been increasing over the past 20 years. However, the relevant sectors appear diverse, in terms of both the socio-demographic characteristics of the workers covered and the outcomes and contents of social dialogue. First, we present the diversity of sectoral agreement coverage; then we present the results of sectoral wage negotiations on a number of wage agreements.

Since the mid-1990s, the percentage of workers covered by sectoral collective agreements has increased (Combault, 2006). In 1997, 93.7 per cent of private sector workers (excluding the agricultural sector) were covered by such an agreement; the coverage rate reached 97.7 per cent in 2004 and has remained stable. This extension is due mainly to the 'hotel-café-restaurants' agreement in December 1997: it led to a substantial increase in small-firm coverage (fewer than ten workers); most other firms were already covered by this kind of agreement (Combault, 2006).

The socio-demographic profiles of the covered workers differ widely by occupation, gender and age across sectoral agreements (Boudjemaa, 2015, 2016). This large diversity in terms of characteristics of employees covered by sectoral agreements suggests (even in a context of agreement extension by the state to all firms) that the impact of the bargaining process and of new agreements (on wages, gender equity and working conditions) has to be interpreted in line with the main characteristics of the industrial sector and the jobs covered.

The main outcome of sectoral collective bargaining is agreements defining occupational and wage grids. For each level, a minimum sectoral wage is defined. Annual negotiations on wages at the sectoral level are mandatory, but they do not have to lead to an agreement between social partners.

A first way of looking at the evolution of social dialogue at that level is to identify the trends in the number of annual wage agreements actually signed at the sectoral agreement level.[14] That number increased during 2003 to 2006 and then remained almost stable until 2008 (80 per cent of agreements signed). After the crisis, there was a slight decrease of signed sectoral wage agreements, but it was followed during 2010 to 2012 by an increase. The level reached in 2012 corresponds to 92 per cent of sectoral agreements. However, the number of agreements signed in 2013 declined again, by 20 per cent (Naouas and Combault, 2015). There are several elements to explain such a dynamic. The increase of signed agreements during 2003–06 is partly technical and may be explained by the convergence of the different minimum wages[15] during the period; convergence needs the signature of specific agreements on wages at the sectoral level. More generally the change in minimum wages (Salaire Minimum Interprofessionnel de Croissance, SMIC) decided by the state may explain the high level of agreements signed, because social partners at the sectoral level want to maintain a difference between the national minimum wage and the sectoral minimum wages or adapt the hierarchy of their wage grid to the new SMIC. According to Naouas and Combault (2015), this may explain the high level of agreements in 2011 and 2012; during this period the SMIC was raised twice a year. By contrast, in 2013, which corresponds to a decrease in the number of sectors that actually signed a wage agreement, the SMIC was raised only once a year.

Therefore wage bargaining at the sectoral level appears very much related to the dynamics of the minimum wage and therefore to government decisions. However, the impact of sectoral wage bargaining on wage dynamics was important during the crisis and maintained some real wage growth until 2010 (Askénazy et al., 2013).

3.3 Workplace/Firm Heterogeneity of Social Relations in France and Recent Trends in Decentralised Bargaining

In France, negotiations at the firm level are related to legal obligations, but they also depend on firms' social climate. To describe the trend of decentralised bargaining at the firm level, first we focus on the presence of unions at the firm level; and second, we specify the relative place of unions in the different institutions of employee representation at the workplace and then present the characteristics of French collective bargaining at the workplace.

3.3.1 Unionisation and trade union presence

France is characterised by a low unionisation rate (8 per cent for the whole economy in 2005, including the public sector[16]). The rate is higher in the public (15 per cent) than in the private sector. In terms of employees' characteristics, unionisation increases with education and occupational levels: the unionisation rate of managers amounts to 14.9 per cent (for the whole economy, 7.7 per cent in the private sector), compared with 5.9 per cent for blue-collar workers (4.6 per cent in the private sector). In the context of increasing labour contract flexibility, it is important to note that employees on temporary contracts are less unionised: during 2001–04, only 3 per cent of those on fixed-term contracts and 0.9 per cent of temporary agency workers were members of a union (6.5 per cent of full-time permanent contracts employees). This contributes to the weakening of unionisation for lower-qualified/blue-collar workers and clerks, and may reinforce some insider/outsider mechanisms as flexible workers are under-represented within unions.

Despite low unionisation rates, France is characterised by a high union presence within firms, a notable feature from a comparative perspective (Wolff, 2008). This is related to the maintenance of an important role for trade unions in social dialogue (as explained in section 2), which is guaranteed by law. However, it appears heterogeneous by firm size and sector. In 2005, 41 per cent of employees declared that at least one trade union was present at their workplace and 56 per cent in their firm or administration (private or public sector). Union presence is higher in the public sector than in the private sector[17] and increases with establishment size. It is also stronger in the manufacturing sector, as well as in banking and insurance, whereas it is low in hotels, cafés, restaurants and household services.

3.3.2 Dynamics of firm-level collective bargaining

In relation to the trend towards decentralisation of collective bargaining, firm-level bargaining has been intensifying over the 2000s: the number of firm-level agreements signed after bargaining increased from 20000 in 2003 to 40000 in 2013. However, the literature on industrial relations, based on firm case studies, generally finds that this increase was partly formal, following obligations or incentives introduced in recent laws, but without substantial deliberation between employers and trade unions at the firm level (Béthoux et al., 2015). Also, heterogeneity remains high across firms.

Several data sources can be used to obtain information about firm-level collective bargaining: the REPONSE survey (using samples of private workplaces with at least 11 employees in 2011, 20 employees in 1999 and 2005), as well as the Activité et Conditions d'Emploi de la Main d'Œuvre (ACEMO-DSE) database, including a representative sample of firms with over ten employees in the business sector (excluding agriculture) and an administrative database including information about all agreements signed at the company level (registration of agreements is compulsory in France).

Employee representation (staff representatives, union delegates and work councils) is related to workplace size, following the legal framework presented in section 2, with a strong gap between workplaces of fewer than 50 employees and workplaces over that threshold. According to REPONSE wage negotiation or discussion at the workplace, firm or group level concerned 44 per cent of workplaces and 66 per cent of employees in 2010 (at workplaces with 11 or more employees). That share is higher when union delegates are present, and grows with establishment and firm size. It is higher in manufacturing (81 per cent of employees covered) than in trade or services (42 per cent) or in construction (45 per cent).[18] Other topics have also been the object of discussions or negotiations: between 2008 and 2010, 55 per cent of workplaces negotiated or discussed about working conditions, 33 per cent about working time, 39 per cent about employment, 62 per cent about vocational training, 31 per cent about gender equality and 46 per cent about private social protection.

A specific survey (ACEMO *Très Petites Entreprises*) of very small firms (two to nine employees) shows that the majority of decisions in such firms are taken by management without any consultation: this is so for 92 per cent of decisions concerning wages, 87 per cent of those on employment, 79 per cent of those on concerning working time and 68 per cent of those on working conditions.

The ACEMO survey also provides information about firm-level conflicts and strikes. Cross-referencing the two types of information brings interesting results, showing that in France negotiation and conflicts are interrelated. Other things being equal, firms at which conflicts have taken place are those at which the probability of having collective bargaining is highest (Desange and Rosankis, 2015).

In terms of negotiation topics, both ACEMO and administrative databases on company-level agreements confirm the variety of topics for collective bargaining at the firm level. These topics are strongly influenced by obligations laid down at national level through national tripartite agreements or the law. Apart from wages and working time, firms frequently negotiated about hard working conditions and gender equality in 2011–12, and about employment in 2013. These themes are directly related to specific obligations or measures, for instance in 2013 the creation of the 'generation contract', a job subsidy that is conditional on having signed an agreement about youth and senior employment. However, some measures are less popular than others; for instance, employment maintenance agreements (involving wage and/or working time flexibility to maintain jobs) did not meet any success (only ten agreements were signed between 2013 and 2015) and the opportunity to negotiate about employment programmes in case of economic redundancies (Plan de Sauvegarde de l'Emploi) was used by fewer than 100 firms in 2013. In practice flexicurity arrangements designed at the national level had limited success at the firm level, which may be explained by several reasons. First, these arrangements do not necessarily correspond to the needs of companies, which more often use 'traditional' internal flexibility agreements when they bargain on employment maintenance and hours' flexibility or wage moderation. In that respect, coordination between the different levels of collective bargaining appears low in France. For instance, some important agreements were reached in 2013 in the car industry (for example by Renault and Peugeot) avoiding lay-offs in exchange for increased working time flexibility and wage freezes or wage moderation.[19] In 2016 Peugeot signed a new agreement involving 1000 new hires, 2000 hires of young people using the subsidised 'generation contract', and introducing new forms of flexibility (eight working days over the year may be adapted to existing demand, functional flexibility will be developed and tele-working will be developed for 4000 employees). However, despite some interesting examples of flexicurity-orientated company-level bargaining, the majority of French firms are still using external flexibility to adjust to the economic cycle.

Recent analyses of firms' reactions to the crisis confirm that flexicurity arrangements and internal flexibility were not the main types of adjustment in France. According to Amossé et al. (2016), using REPONSE, most French firms hit by the recession have cut employment rather than wages. Union presence at the firm level, and even the existence of negotiations, appear correlated with these employment cuts and thus did not seem to encourage internal flexibility.

Firm-level case studies confirm that internal flexibility was generally not the first way chosen to adjust to the crisis: according to Perez et al. (2015), firms mostly started by reducing the volume of temporary and fixed-term employment, before considering adjustments in working hours, and as a very last resort cuts in permanent employment. Wage moderation or cuts were envisaged only in a second step when other types of adjustment were impossible. Contrary to the discourse on flexicurity and the importance of further training for workers' transitions (inside and outside the firm), Bethoux et al. (2015) also observe that training was not considered as a tool to face the crisis. Although firm-level bargaining about vocational training has been developing in recent years, its content has remained largely formal (without real bargaining on the goals and contents of that training) and set by management. Among permanent workers, firms generally preserved managers and professionals, as well as the higher qualified. Job losses affected particularly blue-collar workers and seniors, especially through 'voluntary departure' programmes (Perez et al., 2015).

The development of firm-level collective bargaining did not prevent firms from implementing strategies that preserve the core workers (permanent and higher qualified, median age) at the expense of those at the 'periphery' (temporary and fixed-term employees, lower qualified, seniors). Trade unions and workers' representatives did not oppose these adjustments, which generally took place in a non-conflictual manner.

These results of company-level collective bargaining converge on the importance of the legal rules in the French system; decentralised collective bargaining is clearly influenced by regulations concerning employee representation and by the content of labour market policy and social dialogue at the national level (including the definition of topics for decentralised collective bargaining). 'Flexicurity' does not appear to be the main concern at firm level despite a few examples of agreements, even in the context of the crisis. To conclude this section, our three-level analysis of recent trends in social dialogue leads to two main results. First, the rising concern for 'flexicurity' that can be found at the national level (mainly driven by the state and some unions, such as CFDT) does not seem to translate directly into firms, where external flexibility focusing on non-permanent employment remains the more frequent type of adjustment to the economic cycle. Second, in terms of inequalities among workers, the heterogeneity of collective bargaining conditions across sectors and even more across firms may induce or reinforce specific inequalities on the French labour market (despite well-developed social rights and high coverage rates at the sectoral level). Firm-level adjustments to the 2008 crisis also imply a risk of rising inequalities between core and peripheral workers.

4. SOCIAL DIALOGUE AND INEQUALITIES: A DEBATED ISSUE BUT LIMITED EMPIRICAL EVIDENCE

It is very difficult to disentangle the effects of such multi-level social dialogue on inequalities in the world of work. In addition to some data limitations, the question raises important methodological problems. Inequalities are the result of a large set of individual and economic factors and may themselves influence the propensity of firms or sectors to engage in collective bargaining. In this section, we first review the available results on inequality at different levels (national, sectoral and firm). Then, on the basis of available data, we explore the correlation between the intensity of social dialogue and the level of inequality according to various dimensions.

To provide an overview of inequalities on the French labour market and relate them to social dialogue, we proceed in three steps, corresponding to the three-level bargaining system. First, we focus on the national level and the main differences with other EU and OECD countries. Then we review the results available for the sectoral level to highlight some effects of branch-level collective bargaining (especially in terms of wages). Finally, we investigate some links between collective bargaining at the workplace level – which recent reforms were intended to develop – and labour market outcomes.

4.1 Overview of Inequalities on the French Labour Market: Dualisation or Segmentation?

At first sight, France is characterised by an average level of labour market inequalities, in comparison with the rest of the EU15 or the OECD in general. Wage inequalities are lower than in 'Anglo-Saxon' and southern countries, but higher than in the Nordics (Table 4.2) and have remained relatively stable over time,[20] whereas inequalities by social groups in terms of unemployment rates appear very close to the EU15 level (Table 4.3). Unemployment affects particularly young people and the lower qualified (Table 4.4). However, looking at employment rates reveals a gap with the EU average, especially for young people, seniors and the lower qualified. Employment in France appears concentrated in the mid-life period (25–54 years of age), with an important gap between the low and high qualified, which has been growing since the crisis. The gender pay gap is medium compared with other OECD countries (Figure 4.1) and has slightly declined since the early 2000s. This is confirmed by more detailed analyses of the French Labour Force Survey, showing a reduction in activity and unemployment gaps by gender (Bruneau et al., 2016). However, according

Table 4.2 Wage inequalities in France and selected OECD countries 1995 and 2009–10

	Gini coefficient		Earnings dispersion among employees (Decile 9/Decile 1)	
	1995	2010	1995	2009
Belgium		24.5		2.8
Denmark	20.0	26.9		2.7
Finland	19.1	20.2	2.2	2.3
France	29.0	29.8	3.1	2.9
Germany	29.0	29.3	2.9	3.3
Greece	35.0	32.9		
Italy	33.0	31.2	2.3	
Portugal	34.5		4.0	3.8
Spain		33.4		3.9
Sweden		24.1		2.0
United Kingdom	32.0	33.0		7.3
United States			4.6	5

Source: ILO Global Wage Database, ILOSTAT (accessed 2 September 2016).

to this analysis, wage differences remain important for given occupations and women do not easily access higher-paid jobs. That study also highlights the persistence of inequalities (according to several indicators: the probability of being in employment, in a permanent full-time job and in the top 10 per cent of the wage distribution, as well as wage inequalities) according to origin (for second-generation immigrants) or place of residence (for those in disadvantaged areas). These inequalities remain when controlling for observable characteristics.

In addition to these inequalities by age, gender, education or origin, the French labour market also displays important inequalities by labour market status, which has led several authors to develop the hypothesis of a dual labour market (Palier and Thelen, 2012). This is especially true when considering a dynamic perspective on the labour market and looking at transitions. Indeed, according to the OECD, France is characterised by one of the lowest transition rates from temporary to permanent jobs in a medium-term perspective; only 20 per cent of fixed-term contract employees in 2008 accessed a full-time permanent job in 2011, whereas that proportion is almost 50 per cent in the United Kingdom or in Finland. Also, the annual probability of transition from a fixed-term to a permanent job has decreased over time, from 40 per cent at the end of the 1990s to less than 25 per cent in 2014. These transition probabilities partly

Table 4.3 Unemployment rates by social groups in France and in the EU15 in 2015

	Global 15–64	Youth 15–24	Medium age group 25–54	Seniors 55–64	Low qualified (ISCED 0–2)	Medium qualified (ISCED 3–4)	Higher qualified (ISECD 5–6)	Men 15–64	Women 15–64
EU15	9.9	20.3	9.1	7.2	18.0	8.9	6.0	9.9	10.0
France	10.4	24.7	9.2	7.4	17.8	10.9	6.3	10.9	9.9

Source: Eurostat, LFS, lfsa_urgaed (accessed 2 September 2016).

Table 4.4 Employment rates by social groups in France and in the EU15 in 2015

	Global 15–64	Young people 15–24	Medium age group 25–54	Seniors 55–64	Low qualified (ISCED 0–2)	Medium qualified (ISCED 3–4)	Higher qualified (ISCED 5–6)	Men 15–64	Women 15–64
France	63.8	27.8	79.4	48.6	39.7	65.9	81.4	67.1	60.6
EU15	66.1	35.0	77.7	55.3	45.8	70.0	82.4	71.1	61.2

Source: Eurostat, LFS, lfsa_ergaed (accessed 2 September 2016).

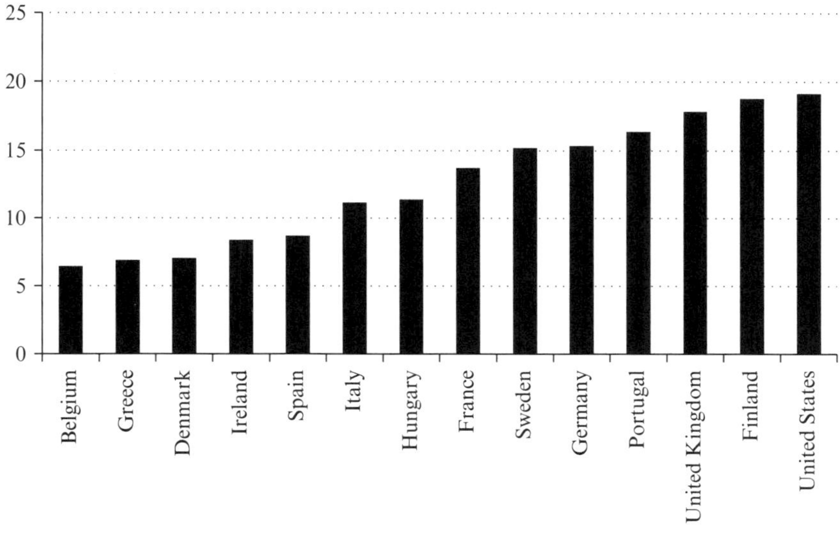

Source: OECD statistics database.

Figure 4.1 Gender pay gap in France and selected OECD countries, 2012

reflect the individual characteristics of fixed-term employees, but the gap between fixed-term and permanent employees is still high when correcting for observed and unobserved heterogeneity: according to Givord and Vilner (2009), fixed-term employees are only three times more likely to be employed on a permanent contract after one quarter than the unemployed, whereas permanent employees are 18 times more likely to remain in permanent employment over the same period.

In relation to labour market trajectories and transitions, data on further training also reveal important inequalities by labour market status: in 2012, the access rate was 40 per cent for fixed-term contracts and 33 per cent for the self-employed, against 53 per cent for permanent employees. These differences are observed in a context in which access to training is generally unequal: important training inequalities also affect occupation (68 per cent of managers and professionals were trained in 2012, compared with 37 per cent of blue-collar workers), or to initial education levels.[21]

Apart from segmentation by labour market status and by type of contract, the French labour market is also segmented by industry and firm size. For instance, firm size matters for further training access; 34 per cent of employees in small firms (fewer than ten employees) were trained in 2012, against two-thirds of employees in bigger companies (more than 250 employees).[22]

To conclude, although inequalities in France generally remain at the European or OECD average, with relative stability of wage inequalities, the French labour market shows some signs of segmentation by labour contract and firm size. In the policy debate, this is frequently related to the characteristics of social dialogue; as mentioned earlier, unionisation rates of fixed-term employees are low, which could lead the unions to favour permanent employees, and the relative absence of unions and collective bargaining in smaller firms would disadvantage their employees.

4.2 Sectoral Bargaining and Wages

As described in section 3, the branch or sectoral level plays an important role in wage setting, complementing the minimum wage. To analyse its contribution to inequalities we focus first on existing studies analysing the impact of sectoral agreements on wage rises independently of the minimum wage effect. Then we describe the difference in wage inequality across sectors and comment on some results on gender inequality at sectoral level.

As explained in section 3, most sectoral wage agreements are linked to changes in the national minimum wage (SMIC) and may only be adaptations. In this view it is difficult to identify the impact of collective bargaining on wages independently of rises in the national minimum wage. However, Naouas and Combault (2015) propose an estimation of such an effect[23] and show the positive contribution of sectoral wage bargaining.

The average wage increased from 2.6 per cent in 2003 to 3.4 per cent in 2005. For the sectors that signed an agreement, sectoral wages increased from 1.5 per cent in 2003 to 3.3 per cent in 2005. When controlling for the influence of the national minimum wage, the impact of social dialogue on wages remains significant: from 1.2 per cent in 2003 to 2.8 per cent in 2005. After the economic crisis, there was a decrease in the wage growth rate that is partly explained by falling growth rate of the national minimum wage.[24] However, the impact of sectoral wage agreements (independently of that) also fell by 0.4 percentage points. Despite a high level of wage negotiation, the period is characterised by wage moderation at sectoral level.

To analyse its contribution to inequalities, the impact of collective bargaining on wages has to be disaggregated by social groups.

Following Naouas and Combault (2015), it seems that managers and intermediary occupations have preserved most of their wage increases in sectoral wage bargaining after the crisis, contrary to blue-collar workers: they lost between 0.2 and 0.3 of a percentage point of average annual wage increases between the two periods, whereas the rate for workers as a whole decreased by 0.4 of a percentage point. Such differences, although not huge, could reflect their bargaining power, which should be higher given their relatively high unionisation rates and the low unemployment rates for these occupations.

The level of wage inequalities by occupations varies across sectoral agreements. For instance, considering managers and professionals, wage inequality ranges from 1.7 (pharmaceuticals) to more than 3.7 (professional accountants). Moreover, the level of the ninth decile (D9) for managers differs strongly across sectoral agreements: it rises above €9000 in some sectors (such as banks).

Apart from wages, sectoral collective agreements have concerned topics such as further training and apprenticeship (232 agreements in 2015 according to the Labour Ministry), private retirement plans (232 agreements), gender equality (166 agreements), individual wage premiums (142 agreements), working conditions (264 agreements) and working time (60 agreements). The importance of further training or private retirement plans is related to the national agreements and Acts involving these dimensions as part of worker security. However, the impact of these agreements on workers (for instance, on access to further training) cannot be evaluated yet.

4.3 Workplace Collective Bargaining and Inequality: An Exploration

In this section we explore the correlations between indicators of collective bargaining at the workplace level and indicators of employment, as well as of inequalities at the firm level. We use the available employment and wage data at the sectoral level (*branche*) computed and disseminated by French Labour Administration (coming from administrative data, Déclarations Annuelles de Données Sociales – DADS) and the results of a survey on social dialogue at the workplace launched in 2010 (REPONSE 2010 survey). The two datasets are merged at the sectoral level for 13 sectors.[25] We use information about social dialogue from REPONSE (questions about firm-level wage bargaining coverage, but also about the existence of other topics of negotiation, working conditions, working time, qualifications, employment, innovation, training and gender equality) and for employment we consider the structure of employment in the firms (by qualifications, type of contract, age and gender) and information about wages (inequalities measured by decile ratio, gender wage gap by qualifications, percentage of low and high wages and so on).[26]

To study the links between collective bargaining indicators and employment characteristics (including inequalities) we use data analysis techniques, starting with a principal component analysis to identify correlations, followed by a typology (obtained through ascending hierarchical classification techniques). Our purpose is descriptive, as we cannot identify any causality between collective bargaining indicators and employment characteristics.

The classification identifies three clusters of sectors on the basis of firm-level collective bargaining indicators and employment and wage characteristics. These clusters group sectors that are close in terms of firm-level collective bargaining and employment conditions, whose average characteristics are displayed in Table 4.5.

The first cluster includes two industrial sectors (chemicals and pharmaceuticals, and metal industry), as well as banking and insurance and culture and communications. It is characterised by very dynamic firm-level collective bargaining, a highly qualified workforce (with a share of managers and professionals of 32 per cent, twice the average) and limited atypical contracts (part-time or short-term contracts). Wage inequalities are above average (and the highest of the three clusters), but the share of low wages is limited and inequalities seem to be driven by the proportion of higher wages.

The second cluster includes transport, food industry, construction and commercial services. It exhibits the lowest coverage rates by firm-level wage bargaining, but higher than average firm-level collective bargaining about working conditions, working time, training, employment and voice. Firms in these industries seem to have reacted to incentives to engage in company-level bargaining, even if they tend to have limited dialogue on wages. The proportion of managers and professionals is the lowest of the three clusters, although the share of white-collar workers is 54 per cent (average 34 per cent). Part-time employment is very frequent and short-term contracts also stand at a high level. Wage inequalities are the lowest of the three clusters, but the proportion of low wages is the highest.

The third cluster groups hotels and restaurants, retail, cleaning and security services, health and social services. Firm-level collective bargaining concentrates on wages, but is below average for all indicators included in the analysis. This cluster has the highest share of small firms. The share of blue-collar workers is very high (40 per cent – the average is 29 per cent) and the proportion of women is the lowest in the three clusters (38 per cent). Atypical jobs are average, as are inequalities.

That typology shows that collective bargaining goes together with better job quality (first cluster). However, it does not prevent wage inequalities, partly because the sectors in which firm-level collective bargaining is traditionally strong have higher wages and a higher share of managers and professionals who tend to receive more flexible and dispersed pay. In other clusters firm-level collective bargaining lags behind, especially in the third cluster involving a higher proportion of small firms and composed of service industries. Interestingly, the second cluster combines employment

Table 4.5 Characteristics of sectors (averages by clusters) for some key variables, France

	Cluster 1	Cluster 2	Cluster 3	Sample mean
	Chemicals and pharmaceuticals, metal and steel industries, banking and insurance sector, culture and communication	Transport, food industry, construction, company services	Hotels and restaurants, retail, cleaning and security services, health and social services	
Share of workplaces covered	63.0	39.8	43.8	48.5
Share of employees covered	85.8	55.3	62.4	67.4
Share of workplaces negotiating on working conditions	61.0	61.8	48.4	56.4
Share of workplaces negotiating on working time	36.0	34.3	24.8	31.2
Share of workplaces negotiating on professional skills	36.0	33.8	28.4	32.4
Share of workplaces negotiating on employment	49.8	41.8	31.4	40.2
Share of workplaces negotiating on technological and organizational change	57.8	46.5	45.8	49.7
Share of workplaces negotiating on vocational training	69.0	64.5	56.4	62.8
Share of workplaces negotiating on union rights and communication	31.3	37.3	24.8	30.6
Share of workplaces negotiating on gender equality	47.0	36.0	23.6	34.6
Share of workplaces negotiating on saving plans (*épargne salariale*)	51.5	28.3	28.6	35.5
Share of workplaces negotiating on private social protection	55.3	45.8	41.2	46.9
Share of managers (cadre)	32.1	6.4	12.2	16.5

Table 4.5 (continued)

	Cluster 1	Cluster 2	Cluster 3	Sample mean
	Chemicals and pharmaceuticals, metal and steel industries, banking and insurance sector, culture and communication	Transport, food industry, construction, company services	Hotels and restaurants, retail, cleaning and security services, health and social services	
Share of foremen and supervisors	27.0	13.1	17.2	18.9
Share of white-collars	19.7	54.8	30.3	34.6
Share of blue-collars	21.1	25.8	40.3	30.0
Share of women	45.9	56.8	38.9	46.5
Share of youth (less than 30 years)	17.9	26.0	23.2	22.4
Share of fixed-term contracts	5.3	10.5	7.5	7.8
Share of part-time	16.9	36.1	19.1	23.7
Share of very small firms (less than 10 employees)	12.9	13.7	31.5	20.3
Gender wage gap for managers (cadre) in percentage points	–23.1	–20.2	–23.6	–22.4
Share of low wages (between 1 and 1.05 minimum wage)	2.8	11.9	7.1	7.2
Share of high wages (more than 3 minimum wages)	23.7	3.8	10.3	12.4
Wage decile ratio D9/D1	3.3	2.1	2.7	2.7

Source: Data from DADS 2013 (in Boudjemaa, 2016) and the REPONSE 2010 survey (DARES, 2015), authors' calculations.

status inequalities (high share of part-time and temporary contracts) with a high proportion of firms involved in collective bargaining about specific topics (including working conditions). This may be a sign of a trade union strategy focusing on the working conditions of core workers in a context in which they cannot prevent the rise of atypical employment and the use of external flexibility (Bethoux et al., 2015).

In any case this exploration at the industry level suggests that firm-level collective bargaining contributes to better job quality, but that it cannot prevent inequalities, either concerning wages or in terms of employment status.

5. CASE STUDIES

5.1 Inequality in Private Social Protection at the Workplace

Social protection helps to reduce inequality among households. However, the various dimensions of social risk coverage are not measured homogeneously. Generally, the inequality measurement focuses on disposable income, which includes unemployment insurance, compulsory retirement pension schemes and some family-oriented social policies (Courtioux and Erhel, 2016). However, this measurement does not include the potential redistributive impact of public health insurance and private social protection. Including these dimensions is crucial to assess the issue of inequality and the world of work.

In the French context, workers have access to compulsory state pensions and compulsory complementary pension schemes; however, the so-called Fillon pension reform of 2003 introduced the possibility to contribute to private pension schemes, some of them available at the company level. These schemes benefit from tax rebates and could lead to various contributions from the employers to their employees' plans. Moreover some changes are directly linked to the French decentralisation trend of industrial relations and are one of the security outputs of the bargaining of flexibility principles (see *supra*, section 3). In France, workers have statutory health insurance which covers a high share of current health expenditure, although it decreased slightly from 78.2 to 77.4 per cent between 2006 and 2013 (Franc and Pierre, 2015). The remainder is not out-of-pocket individual health expenditure: actual access to health care is dependent on whether or not an individual possesses complementary private health insurance (Jusot and Pierre, 2015). Workers could have access to complementary private health insurance through their company (with company-run schemes) or on an individual basis. Following the National

Interprofessional Agreement (Accord National Interprofessionnel, ANI) of 2013 it has become compulsory since 2016 for a private sector employer to provide a sponsored health insurance contract. Moreover, coverage portability has been extended to 12 months following the end of the work contract for previous employees.[27] The various levels of contribution of individuals and their employers to these private complementary health and retirement schemes may induce some kind of hidden inequality across firms, which we assess in what follows.

In 2014, around 3 million people had a private individual retirement plan. But only half of them made a deposit in 2016 (Drees, 2016a). The number of employers' sponsored private retirement plans is not known precisely. It comprises at least 8.3–8.5 million plans. Among them, about 18 per cent concern schemes for the self-employed who are not well covered by the French compulsory retirement system. For these workplace pension plans, around 52 per cent received a deposit in 2016. This share is higher for self-employed (64 per cent) and lower for wage earners (49 per cent).

At a macro level the share of these private pension plans remains marginal. In 2014 it corresponded to 4.2 per cent of contributions and 2.1 per cent of pensions paid. But it is interesting to focus also on a more micro-level. For instance, the *plan d'épargne pour la retraite collectif* (PERCO) is a collective retirement contract type launched by the Fillon reform in 2003 and has been a success. In 2013, 20.8 per cent of workers were covered by such a plan (Drees, 2016b). However, the coverage rate increases with firm size. For very small firms (fewer than ten employees) the coverage rate is only 2.4 per cent, whereas it reaches 51.7 per cent for firms with more than 1000 employees. In terms of industrial sector, manufacturing tends to have higher coverage (32 per cent) than services and construction (23 and 24 per cent, respectively), but among services the banking and insurance sector is better covered (59 per cent).

We have to keep in mind that being covered does not necessarily mean actually contributing in the current year to this pension plan. Moreover, this contribution could have several sources. It could stem from wage-earner decision (16 per cent of the current contribution amount) to make a contribution and/or a complementary contribution from the firm (27 per cent), from some contribution linked to a profit-sharing agreement (*participation and intéressement schemes*) or, more marginally, from time balance agreements (*compte épargne temps*).[28]

On average, the share of plans receiving a contribution (of any amount) is lower than the coverage rate, at 6.9 per cent. Here, too, the share of actual contribution is linked to the firm's size; only the employees in big firms (with more than 500 employees) are above this average. However, very small firms, which are less covered than small firms (2.7 compared with 3.9 per cent) tend to have a higher share of actual contributions (1.0 compared with 0.6 per cent). In terms of industrial sectors, the hierarchy previously mentioned for coverage is still valid here; the share of actual contributions for industry (13 per cent) is higher than the share for services (7 per cent) and construction (5 per cent), but among services the rate for banking and insurance sector is higher (22 per cent). In 2013, the average contribution was €1350.

Finally, when looking at the sectoral level, it appears that the construction sector has a relatively low coverage rate, a low actual contribution rate and low contributions (€670 in 2013). Manufacturing industry and banking have relatively high average contributions (€1470 and €1450, respectively) that go with high coverage rates and a relatively high probability of actual contributions.

In terms of inequality, this means that there is a risk of developing inter-sector inequalities among workers in terms of pension level on retirement (for instance, between workers in construction and in banking), but also intra-sector inequalities (within sectors characterised by a low coverage rate and a high amount of actual contributions for those who are covered).

As in the case of private retirement schemes, complementary private health insurance is divided into collective and individual contracts. The collective contracts cover the workers and their family. In 2012, only 5 per cent of individuals were not covered by a complementary private scheme (Célan et al., 2014). Among those covered, 34 per cent are covered by at least one collective contract, 53 per cent are only covered by individual contracts and 6 per cent are covered by a complementary insurance financed by the state and targeted at the beneficiaries of minimum income (*Couverture Maladie Universelle Complémentaire*, CMU-C). Among private sector employees, the share of coverage by collective contracts is higher (63.7 per cent), whereas the share of persons only covered by individual contracts is lower (28.4 per cent). This distinction is interesting because generally these two types of contract do not provide the same level of reimbursement. Workers in the private sector with collective contracts are more satisfied, on average, with their reimbursement level for different types of health consumption that are not well covered by social security (glasses, dentists, specialists) than private sector workers with individual contracts (Célan et al., 2014). These higher levels of satisfaction may be linked to the fact that such health insurance contracts are generally sponsored by the employers.

Jusot and Pierre (2015) propose some simulations to evaluate the impact of the ANI 2013.[29] They estimate that this agreement should decrease the share of people not covered by complementary health insurance from 5 to 3.7 per cent. The mid-term impact of such a reform seems good for private workers who will benefit from collective contracts, which are generally more attractive than individual contracts. However, it may increase the gap between them and other workers (civil servants and self-employed) or other categories (retirees, long-term unemployed persons and students). Moreover, as mentioned by Franc and Pierre (2015), it may have adverse consequences for people with individual contracts, as insurers who have mainly individual contracts will have to adjust their premiums consecutively to the loss of employees in their risk-pool.

In France, compulsory social protection is managed mainly by the social partners; for instance, unemployment insurance (cf. the next case study, in section 5.2) and compulsory complementary pension schemes. However, private social protection historically has not been managed by for-profit insurance companies. Some funds dedicated to private social protection are directly run by employers for their own workers. This corresponds to almost €13 billion out of the €689 billion of public and private welfare benefits distributed in 2014. Some welfare benefits are managed by non-profit companies (Régimes de la Mutualité et de la Prévoyance). This corresponds to almost €27 billion of welfare benefit distributed in 2014.[30] There are some differences between these non-profit companies that are operating in the social protection market. First, the *Mutuelles* are non-profit insurance companies that operate under a special law; historically they have specialised in individual health contracts. As already mentioned, the ANI 2013 reform is likely to increase the share of high health risks (retirees and so on) in their risk-pool, which may lead to problems of adverse selection and an increase in premiums. Second, the Instituts de prévoyance (IPs) are non-profit companies managed by social partners under social security law; historically they have specialised in collective contracts (at the company or branch levels) and traditionally cover more diverse social risks: health insurance, accidents in the workplace, some family-oriented benefits.

In 2015, 82 per cent of private sector workers declared that they were covered by at least one guarantee of social risk coverage (Bigot et al., 2015); 72 per cent by an agreement complementing the covering of social security in case of sick days off work, 54 per cent by life insurance and 52 per cent by special benefits in case of invalidity. For more than 50 per cent of all cases this social protection guarantee is obtained through collective bargaining and a sectoral agreement (*accord de branche* or *convention collective*) (Bigot et al., 2015).

More generally, workers have little knowledge of the governance and management of workplace social protection. For instance, the specificities of IP governance are not well known; only a quarter of workers and one-third of employers know that they are managed by social partners (Bigot et al., 2015). Among the employers that use IPs' services this knowledge is higher (52 per cent), but remains relatively low. When IPs' services become known workers tend to express a favourable opinion (two-thirds of workers and just over half of employers). When the company uses IP services, 66 per cent of employers have a favourable opinion of the governance principle. For employers and employees who have a favourable opinion the main reason put forward is that it better takes into account employees' needs (19 per cent for the employer and 24 per cent for the employee). The non-profit legal status of IPs seems not to count much in this favourable opinion (8 per cent for employers and 4 per cent of employees).

The recent developments in flexicurity should lead to an increase in the number of workers covered by complementary private social protection. That trend contributes to a better security of access to private social protection within the world of work, but includes some risks of inequalities related to the heterogeneity of private arrangements. Moreover, these good general trends for the workers may also increase social risk coverage inequalities between employees and other worker and inactive statuses (self-employed and retiree). The existing challenges suggest that it will be difficult for decentralised social dialogue institutions to tackle this new inequality issue alone.

5.2 Collective Bargaining in the Cultural Sector: A Success in 2016 Based on an Innovative Process?

In France, as in other European countries, employment in the culture sector has been rising over the past 20 years, representing 1.7 per cent of total employment in 2009 (in line with the EU average).[31] In comparison with total employment it is characterised by a higher proportion of (very) short-term contracts, a higher share of employees holding more than one job and a bigger proportion of self-employment (Eurostat, 2011). In a context of labour market deregulation and job fragmentation, cultural employment may therefore be considered a forerunner of tomorrow's employment, making the debates around contractual regulation or unemployment insurance coverage in these activities particularly up to date.

In France, an important number of employees in the cultural sector (and a majority in the show business sector) are employed on a specific labour contract called a *contrat à durée déterminée d'usage* (CDDU), which offers employers the possibility to hire workers for very short periods with no additional costs.[32] If they have worked at least 507 hours over the past 12 months,[33] these employees are covered by specific rules in the framework of unemployment insurance (called '*annexes 8 et 10*', appendices 8 and 10) that provide them with some benefits when they are out of employment. Appendix 8 concerns blue-collar workers, technicians and engineers working in audio, video, movie production, in the media (television, radio and so on) or show business, whereas appendix 10 concerns artists in show business (musicians, comedians and dancers). In practice these workers alternate between periods of employment and periods where they receive unemployment benefits, and are usually called '*intermittents*'.[34]

After more than ten years of intensive conflicts around the rules for appendices 8 and 10, an agreement was signed in April 2016, despite the very tense social context (strikes and social conflicts against the 'El Khomri' law). The aim of this case study is to understand the logic of social dialogue that stands behind this (unexpected) historical agreement and which helped to reach a balanced outcome.

5.2.1 Dynamics of cultural employment: important growth, but increased fragmentation and substantial income inequalities

Cultural employment has been dynamic over the past 20 years in France; employees in cultural occupations as a main job numbered 381 000 in 1991 and 573 000 in 2011, according to the Labour Force Survey (an increase of over 50 per cent, compared with the 16 per cent growth of total employment over the same period). A majority of these workers have a permanent contract in the private or public sector, but the fixed-term employment rate in these occupations is higher than average (30 per cent in 2011).[35]

To identify *intermittents* properly one has to use other (administrative) sources. According to the employment service (Pôle Emploi) 253 000 employees were affected by a fixed-term contract in the creative arts and entertainment or in the audio-video/television sector in 2015. However, only 114 000 persons received unemployment insurance benefits related to appendices 8 and 10. The others may be occasionally employed on a fixed-term contract in the sector, either because they hold another position in the sector (permanent job) or in other sectors, or may also not be eligible because they have not worked enough hours (the 507 cumulated hours described previously) in the occupations concerned by appendices 8 and 10.

Whatever the source, the trend in the number of *intermittents* and in the number of contracts signed in the sector is clearly positive. As shown by Figure 4.2 employees on fixed-term contracts who have declared at least one contract during the year in occupations concerned by appendix 8 and 10 more than doubled between 1990 and 2007, more rapidly than the total number of employees in the cultural sector.

However, the trend in average annual wages has been slightly decreasing since 1990, and the average number of contracts per person has increased strongly, from six a year in 1990 to 16 a year in 2007. This trend reveals the growing fragmentation of employment for *intermittents* that has to be related to shorter contract duration.

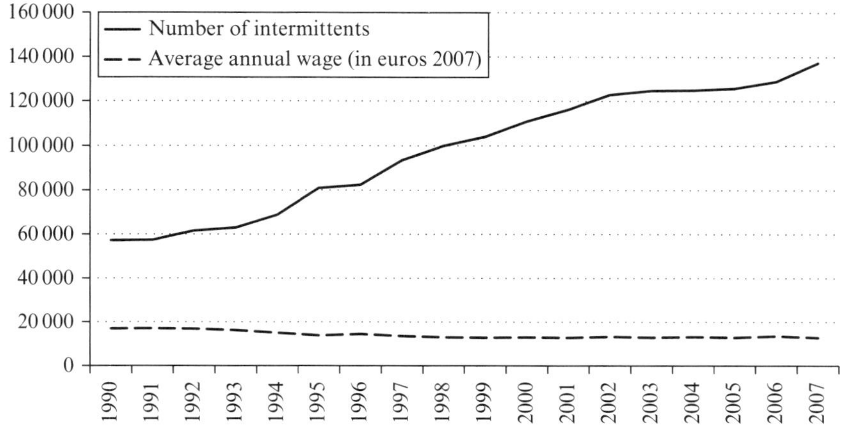

Source: Caisse des congés spectacles/CESPRA/DEPS, in Gilles (2013).

Figure 4.2 Employees on fixed-term contracts who declared at least one contract in the occupations affected by appendices 8 and 10

Income inequalities appear to be a structural characteristic of artistic and cultural employment, with an interdecile ratio of 7.4 on average, reaching 9 and over for some occupations (visual arts for instance) compared with 4.7 for employment in the national economy.[36] Surveys focusing on *intermittents* also highlight a high level of wage inequalities, depending on occupations (technicians and engineers covered by appendix 10 have higher wages on average than artists), but also on gender. Low wages are very frequent; more than half of *intermittents* earn less than the monthly minimum wage.[37]

In that context, unemployment insurance plays an important role in two directions: covering periods of non-employment in a context in which employment fragmentation has been increasing, and redistributing income towards the lower wage levels.

5.2.2 A history of conflicts[38]

In France unemployment insurance is managed by the social partners inside UNEDIC, which was created in 1958. Unemployment insurance is supposed to cover all employees, whatever their occupation, labour contract type or sector, and is based on an inter-sectoral solidarity principle.

Appendices 8 and 10, which contain specific rules for cultural occupations, were introduced in 1964 and 1967, but became effective to cover the discontinuous employment of cultural workers in 1979, when the threshold for benefits was reduced from 1000 to 520 hours (over the previous 12 months). That reform changed the nature of the system, which initially covered the unemployment risk of a 'happy few' and was made open to a substantial number of discontinuous workers. Despite the fact that these specific rules of appendices 8 and 10 were introduced by the social partners in the bargaining process around unemployment insurance, there has never been a consensus about them and conflict has been almost permanent since 1986 and especially strong since 2003 and between 2014 and 2016.

From the beginning, employers' organisations directly involved in UNEDIC management (Centre National du Patronat Français, CNPF, replaced by the MEDEF, after 1998) have claimed that unemployment insurance for the cultural sector should be financed by cultural employers and workers themselves, and not by general unemployment and intersectoral solidarity. Indeed, appendices 8 and 10 are characterised by expenditure that persistently exceed contributions. On the other side, the unions (including *CGT spectacles*), associations representing *intermittents* and employers in the show business sector defend the existence of specific rules and the principle of financing through the general unemployment insurance budget. Such rules are supposed to be justified by the nature of employment in the artistic sector, entailing flexibility and the aim of sustaining artists' and technicians' incomes, as well as reducing inequalities. The state has also been constantly in favour of maintaining specific rules, both as a support to the cultural sector and as a policy to compensate precarious employment.

Even though conflicts have been present from the start, they have intensified since the 2003 reform that introduced important restrictions to unemployment insurance for *intermittents*, following the position of the MEDEF. The most important and contested restriction was the shortening of the period over which workers had to reach a minimum number of 507 hours worked (ten months instead of 12 months between 1979 and 2003). The strengthening of this eligibility criterion resulted in a short-term decrease in the number of *intermittents* covered by unemployment insurance. However, that decrease was only temporary and the upward trend resumed as early as 2006. These developments can be explained by the behaviour of *intermittents* and actors in the show business or audio/video/television sectors, who progressively adapted to the new rules in order to be covered by unemployment insurance. On the workers' side, the *Fédération Spectacle* CGT and the coordination for *intermittents* and precarious workers never accepted that reform and have demanded a return to the 12-month eligibility period.

5.2.3 The 2016 agreement and the role of expertise[39]

The conflict accelerated between 2014 and 2016, in the context of renewed negotiations over the unemployment insurance regime.

In February 2014, owing to an increasing unemployment insurance deficit (following rising unemployment after the 2008 crisis) the MEDEF opened unemployment insurance collective bargaining by proposing to remove appendices 8 and 10, which resulted in numerous strikes or demonstrations by *intermittents* as well as political reactions. The final agreement on the new unemployment insurance convention in 2014 maintained the appendices but introduced a delay for receiving the benefits, which hit the most precarious *intermittents*. That decision led immediately to new strikes and actions by artists, cultural institutions and so on and forced the state to intervene by compensating for the effects of the delay through a special fund and by launching a consultation process to reach new proposals for reforming appendices 8 and 10.

This consultation process represented an innovation in the field of unemployment insurance social dialogue, as it forced the UNEDIC to discuss matters in the presence of politicians, unions and employers' representatives, as well as independent experts. That process was generally considered a success and resulted in a report published in January 2015, analysing three alternative scenarios proposed by those in the sector.

In the same spirit the Rebsamen law of July 2015 introduced two procedural 'innovations', in addition to the recognition of appendices 8 and 10 in the law. First, the decision-making process about *intermittents*' unemployment insurance was placed in the hands of people in the sector (the inter-sectoral level can only impose financial targets but not the rules for benefits); second, the consultation method was extended through the creation of an independent experts' group.

These innovations have been implemented within the framework of the 2016 unemployment insurance bargaining. That bargaining started in a very conflictual way as the MEDEF and three unions (the CFDT, the CFTC and the CFE–CGC) signed a letter setting targets for the sectoral bargaining process that included a strict goal of deficit cuts and some proposals for regulation, and which was perceived as a provocation. However, as the sectoral bargaining went on, including the budgetary goal, and finally led to an agreement that satisfied the most important demands of the *intermittents* and was supposed to reduce the deficit of appendices 8 and 10: the 507 hours worked will be calculated again over 12 months, the possibility to accumulate unemployment insurance allowances and wages will be limited in order to ensure some redistribution and employers' contributions will be increased. This sectoral agreement was signed by employers' representatives and unions despite the opposition of the national organisations (the MEDEF, but also the CFDT). Given the failure of global unemployment insurance negotiations, the government was able to directly introduce the agreement on appendices

8 and 10 in the unemployment insurance convention, without conceding the financial contribution that was demanded by the MEDEF and the CFDT.

In a very conflictual social conflict (following the 'El Khomri' law) these events were a success for the *intermittents* and social demands in France. The new rules are intended to ensure better coverage of artists and cultural employees working on fixed-term contracts and a reduction in income inequalities, especially owing to problems of access to unemployment insurance for those who had difficulties in accumulating the number of hours required to get unemployment benefits. From a social dialogue point of view, the process (since 2014) seems to have given greater importance to expertise and to public debate about the consequences of different reform scenarios. This appears new in the French context in which social dialogue is rarely based on detailed and contradictory scenarios – even outside the field of culture – and may lead to similar initiatives in the future in the cultural sector or in other sectors.

The bargaining process around unemployment insurance for *intermittents* displays some traditional features of the French social dialogue model; inequalities tend to be reduced through fairly voluntarist policy schemes that are supported by trade unions and by the state. However, recent developments in this field show the role of some new tools and resources for social dialogue, especially the role of experts in building different policy scenarios and improving the quality of information for the social partners, thus introducing new types of actor in industrial relations (Heery and Frege, 2006).

6. CONCLUSION

The traditional French industrial relations system based on three levels of bargaining and a strong involvement of the state has contributed to the reduction of inequalities in the world of work, through the combination of minimum wage and wage bargaining at the sectoral level, the role of labour law in setting common rules (for working time, further training and so on) and the extension of collective agreements by the Ministry of Labour. The fairly generous social protection system, which is managed by the social partners and the state, also contributes to a good level of security for French workers, in the case of unemployment or illness. However, the French industrial relations system has also been criticised for generating inequalities by types of employment contracts, protecting the social rights of 'insiders', while young people or low-qualified workers are affected by flexible contracts and more difficult access to training. These new types of inequalities put the model under pressure: how to increase security for all workers in a context of more flexible employment?

In this context, social dialogue has evolved in two main directions: first, more decentralisation and changes in bargaining rules to settle an agreement, and second, increased participation of the social partners in social dialogue, notably in the trend towards more 'flexicurity'. However, the autonomy of social dialogue is still an issue. For instance, the sectoral level of wage bargaining appears very much related to the dynamics of the minimum wage and therefore to government's decision-making. The results of company-level dialogue also converge on the importance of legal rules in the French system; decentralised collective bargaining is clearly influenced by regulations on employee representation and by the content of labour market policy and social dialogue at the national level. Besides, 'flexicurity' does not appear to be the main concern at the firm level and external flexibility has remained predominant in employment adjustments since the 'Great Recession'.

The consequences of these developments for inequalities are uncertain. Firm-level collective bargaining seems to be associated with better job quality, and some examples of innovative agreements developing internal flexibility are found in some firms. However, firm-level collective bargaining does not seem to prevent wage inequalities and the heterogeneity of labour power in different contexts may result in higher inequalities in terms of working time or effective access to training. In that context it seems ever more important to provide workers new rights to favour good transitions and better security over the life course; new policies such as individual training accounts or individual activity accounts represent first steps in that direction, and their implementation seems crucial for the success of any flexicurity strategy in France.

NOTES

1. As formulated in the Labour Act of July 2016.
2. Legislation and regulation prevail over agreements; national multi-sectoral agreements prevail over sectoral agreements, which in turn prevail over company level agreements.
3. These developments with regard to reforms are based on DG Trésor (2016) and Eurofound (2015). This chapter was written in 2016 and does not include the reforms introduced by September 2017 Labour ordinances, which emphasised the trend towards social dialogue decentralisation.
4. Unless otherwise stipulated in the higher-ranking agreement.
5. The rate was 30 per cent between 2008 and 2016.
6. On an annual basis on wages, working time, organisation of work and collective health insurance; on a multi-annual basis on gender equality and employment of disabled workers.
7. For a more detailed analysis of this trend and its limits, see Freyssinet (2010).

8. Act of 3 December 2008.
9. Every employee receives 20 hours per year worked on a full-time basis during the first six years, then ten hours during the next three years (maximum of 150 hours over nine years).
10. Before the reform the contribution was 1.6 per cent of payroll costs for firms with 20 employees or more and 1.09 per cent for firms with between ten and 19 employees.
11. *Loi relative au travail, à la modernisation du dialogue social et à la sécurisation des parcours professionnels.*
12. The procedure relates to Article 49-3 of the French Constitution.
13. See below for a detailed analysis of this reform.
14. To identify the number of annual sectoral negotiations that led to an agreement, DARES uses a panel of sectoral agreement over 2003–13 based on 247 sectoral agreements, each of them covering more than 5000 workers (Naouas and Combault, 2015).
15. Following the time reduction Acts, there were several minimum wages depending on the date the firm enforced the working time reduction.
16. *Source* (for the whole paragraph): 'Enquêtes permanentes sur les Conditions de Vie des Ménages', INSEE, in Wolff (2008).
17. As the public sector is characterised by better employment security (especially for civil servants) and fewer inequalities (voluntary part-time schemes and compressed wage grids) union presence correlates with better security, but it is not possible to establish any causal link.
18. *Source:* REPONSE survey, table 'Proportion d'établissements et de salariés couverts par une discussion ou une négociation salariale en 2010', in DARES (2015).
19. Other examples are mentioned by Freyssinet (2013).
20. Although a slight increase in the Gini coefficient has been observed since the crisis (Courtioux and Erhel, 2016).
21. Insee – Données 2012, Observatoire des inégalités, population des 18-64 ans, accessed 31 October 2017 at https://www.inegalites.fr/Les-inegalites-d-acces-a-la-formation-professionnelle.
22. Insee – Données 2012, Observatoire des inégalités, population des 18-64 ans, accessed 31 October 2017 at https://www.inegalites.fr/Les-inegalites-d-acces-a-la-formation-professionnelle.
23. This estimate is based on the matching of a sub-sample of sectoral wage agreements and the ACEMO survey (DARES) which follows wages for firms with more than ten workers (agricultural sector excluded).
24. The increase in the SMIC is also mechanically linked to a rising inflation rate; after the crisis the inflation rate was particularly low.
25. Matching at the workplace or firm level is technically possible but requires specific access and financing, which is beyond the scope of the present study.
26. The variables used for the analysis are listed in the Appendix to this chapter.
27. Portability means that even after a redundancy the former employee has access to company health insurance with the same conditions as current employees.
28. Drees (2016b).
29. That is, employer-mandated compulsory private complementary health insurance and coverage portability are for the short-term unemployed.
30. Drees (2016a).
31. Employment in the cultural sector includes five 'cultural' Nomenclature statistique des Activités économiques dans la Communauté Européenne (NACE) divisions at two-digit level: NACE 58 – Publishing activities; NACE 59 – Motion picture, video and television programme production, sound recording and music publishing activities; NACE 60 – Programming and broadcasting activities; NACE 90 – Creative arts and entertainment activities; NACE 91 – Libraries, archives, museums and other cultural activities.
32. Contrary to other fixed-term contracts there is no precarity premium in the case of CDDU.
33. Ten months between 2003 and 2016.

34. Casual workers; as the word '*intermittent*' refers to a specific category of casual workers – in the show business sector – we will keep the French word throughout this case study.
35. Gouyon and Patureau (2014).
36. *Source:* ERF, INSEE/DEPS, Ministère de la Culture et de la Communication, in Gouyon (2015).
37. See, for instance, Corsani and Lazzarato (2008), appendix 3.
38. This section is mainly based on Grégoire (2009), who presents a detailed history of unemployment insurance for show business workers.
39. This section is based on an interview with Mathieu Grégoire, who participated as an independent expert in the consultation process during 2014–15 and the expert group in 2015. The interview was conducted in December 2016.

REFERENCES

Amossé, T., P. Askénazy, M. Chevalier, C. Erhel, H. Petit and A. Reberioux (2016), 'Relations sociales et ajustements à la crise: une analyse micro-statistique comparative franco-britannique', Document de Travail du CEE, June, Centre d'Etudes de l'Emploi, Noisy-le-Grand.

Askénazy P., A. Bozio and C. García-Peñalosa (2013), 'Dynamique des salaires en temps de crise', La note du CAE, no. 5, April, Conseil d'Analyse Economique, Paris.

Bethoux, E., A. Mias, G. Blache, C. Dupuy, A. Jobert, J.L. Renoux, et al. (2015), 'Dialoguer plus, mais sur quoi? Les régulations d'entreprise en matière d'emploi, de formation et de conditions de travail en temps de crise', *Revue de l'IRES*, **1** (84), 91–123.

Bigot, R., S. Hobian, P. Jauneau and S. Lautié (2015), 'Synthèse des principaux résultats du 11ème baromètre de la prévoyance', Centre Technique des Institutions de Prévoyance/Centre de Recherche pour l'Étude et l'Observation des Conditions de Vie (CTIP/CREDOC), research report, CREDOC, Paris.

Boudjemaa, F. (2015), 'Portrait statistique des principales conventions collectives de branche en 2012', DARES Analyses, no. 097, March, Ministry of Labour, Paris.

Boudjemaa, F. (2016), 'Portrait statistique des principales conventions collectives de branche', DARES Résultats No. 016, March, Ministry of Labour, Paris.

Bruneau, C., C. Dherbécourt, J. Flamand and C. Gilles (2016), 'Marché du travail: un long chemin vers l'égalité', La note d'analyse de France Stratégie, no. 42, France Stratégie, Paris.

Célan, N., S. Guillaume and T, Rochereau (2014), 'Enquête sur la santé et la protection sociale 2012', Les rapports de l'Irdes, no. 556, Institut de Recherche et Documentation en Economie de la Santé (Irdes), Paris.

Combault, P. (2006), 'La couverture conventionnelle a fortement progressée entre 1997 et 2004', Premières informations, Premières synthèses, no. 46.2, November, Ministry of Labour, Paris.

Corsani, A. and M. Lazzarato (2008), *Intermittents et précaires*, Paris: Editions Amsterdam.

Courtioux, P. and C. Erhel (2016), 'Transformation in the world of work and the middle class: the French experience', in D. Vaughan-Whitehead (ed.), *Europe's Disappearing Middle Class? Evidence from the World of Work*, Cheltenham, UK and Northampton, MA, USA: Edward Elgar, pp. 160–97.

DARES (2015), 'Les thèmes de négociation dans les établissements et les entreprises, selon la présence d'institutions représentatives du personnel (IRP)', xls data, accessed at http://dares.travail-emploi.gouv.fr/dares-etudes-et-statistiques/statistiques-de-a-a-z/article/les-institutions-representatives-du-personnel.
Desange, G. and E. Rosankis (2015), 'Des négociations collectives plus orientées vers l'emploi en 2013', DARES Analyses No. 94, Ministry of Labour, Paris.
Direction de la Recherche des Etudes et de l'Evaluation et des Statistiques (Drees) (2016a), 'La protection sociale en France et en Europe en 2014', Collection Etudes et Statistiques, Drees.
Direction de la Recherche des Etudes et de l'Evaluation et des Statistiques (Drees) (2016b), 'Les retraités et la retraite', Panorama de la Drees, Drees.
Direction Générale du Trésor (2016), '30 years of modernising social relations in France', *Tresor Economics*, no. 160.
Eurofound (2015), 'France: working life country profile', accessed 31 October 2017 at https://www.eurofound.europa.eu/country/france.
Eurostat (2011), *Cultural Statistics*, Luxembourg: Publications Office of the European Union.
Ferracci, M. and F. Guyot (2015), *Dialogue social et performance économique*, coll. 'Sécuriser l'emploi', Paris: Presses de Sciences Po.
Franc, C. and A. Pierre (2015), 'Compulsory complementary health insurance offered by employers in France: Implications and current debate', *Health Policy*, **119** (2), 11–116.
Freyssinet, J. (2010), 'Les réponses tripartites à la crise économique dans les principaux pays d'Europe occidentale', Document de travail no. 12, Département des relations professionnelles et des relations d'emploi, International Labour Organization, Geneva.
Freyssinet, J. (2013), 'L'emploi au cœur de la négociation d'entreprise: quel impact de l'accord du 11 janvier 2013?', *La Revue de l'Ires*, **2** (77), 3–38.
Gilles, J.-P. (2013), 'Rapport d'information en conclusion des travaux de la mission sur les conditions d'emploi dans les métiers artistiques', Assemblée Nationale, rapport no. 941.
Givord, P. and L. Wilner (2009), 'Les contrats temporaires: trappe ou marchepied vers l'emploi stable?', Documents de travail INSEE, G2009/4, Institut national de la statistique et des études économiques (INSEE), Paris.
Gouyon, M. (2015), 'Revenus d'activité et niveaux de vie des professionnels de la culture', Culture Chiffres No. 2015-1, Ministry of Culture, Paris.
Gouyon, M. and F. Patureau (2014), 'Vingt ans d'évolution de l'emploi dans les professions culturelles', Culture Chiffres No. 2014-6, Ministry of Culture, Paris.
Grégoire, M. (2009), 'Un siècle d'intermittence et de salariat', thesis, Université Paris X – Nanterre.
Heery, E. and Frege, C. (2006), 'New actors in industrial relations', *British Journal of Industrial Relations*, **44** (4), 601–4.
Jusot, F. and A. Pierre (2015), 'How will employer-mandated complementary health insurance impact insurance coverage in France? A simulation based on the 2012 Health, Health Care and Insurance survey (EPS)', Questions d'économie de la Santé, no. 209, Institut de Recherche et Documentation en Economie de la Santé (Irdes), Paris.
Naouas, A. and P. Combault (2015), 'L'impact des relèvements salariaux de branche sur la dynamique des salaires de base, accentué pendant la crise, reste modéré', DARES analyses, no. 33, May, Ministry of Labour, Paris.

OECD (2016), 'Gender wage gap (indicator)', doi:10.1787/7cee77aa-en.
Palier, B. and K. Thelen (2012), 'Dualisation and institutional complementarities: industrial relations, labor market and welfare state changes in France and Germany', in P. Emmenegger, S. Häusermann, B. Palier and M. Seeleib-Kaiser (eds), *The Age of Dualisation*, Oxford University Press, pp. 201–24.
Perez, C., N. Thèvenot, N. Berta, D. Brochard, N. Delahaie, S. Jallais et al. (2015), 'Modes d'ajustement par le travail en temps de crise: des relations professionnelles sous tension', *Revue de l'IRES*, 1 (**84**), 61–90.
Wolff, L. (2008), 'Le paradoxe du syndicalisme français', Premières Informations et Premières Synthèses, no.16.1, Ministry of Labour, Paris.

GLOSSARY OF SOCIAL PARTNER ABBREVIATIONS

CFDT, Confédération française démocratique du travail, French Democratic Federation of Labour
CFE–CGC, Confédération française de l'encadrement – confédération générale des cadres, French Confederation of Professional and Managerial Staff-General Confederation of Professional and Managerial Staff
CFTC, Confédération française des travailleurs chrétiens, French Christian Workers' Confederation
CGPME, Confédération générale du Patronat des Petites et Moyennes Entreprises, Confederation of small and medium-sized enterprises
CGT, Confédération générale du travail, General Confederation of Labour.
CGT–FO, Confédération générale du travail – Force Ouvrière, General Confederation of Labour – Force ouvrière
MEDEF, Mouvement des Entreprises Françaises, Movement of French Enterprises
UNEDIC, Union nationale interprofessionnelle pour l'emploi dans l'industrie et le commerce, National Inter-professional Union for Employment in Industry and Commerce
UNSA, Union Nationale des Syndicats Autonomes, National Union of Autonomous Trade Unions
UPA, Union Professionnelle Artisanale, Craftwork Employers' Association

APPENDIX: VARIABLES USED FOR PRINCIPAL COMPONENT ANALYSIS AND CLUSTERING (SECTION 3.3)

Source: REPONSE DARES (DARES, 2015).
(All indicators at the sectoral level)

- share of workplaces covered by firm-level wage bargaining
- share of employees covered by firm-level wage bargaining
- share of workplaces negotiating on working conditions
- share of workplaces negotiating on working time
- share of workplaces negotiating on professional skills
- share of workplaces negotiating on employment
- share of workplaces negotiating on technological and organisational change
- share of workplaces negotiating on vocational training
- share of workplaces negotiating on union rights and communication
- share of workplaces negotiating on gender equality
- share of workplaces negotiating on saving plans (*épargne salariale*)
- share of workplaces negotiating on private social protection

Source: DADS, DARES (DARES Résultats no. 16 2016)
(All indicators at the sectoral level)

- share of managers and professionals
- share of foremen and supervisors
- share of white-collar workers
- share of blue-collar workers
- share of women
- share of young people (below 30 years of age)
- share of seniors (50 years of age or above)
- share of fixed-term contracts
- share of part-time
- share of very small firms (fewer than 10 employees)
- gender wage gap for managers (*cadre*) in percentage points
- gender wage gap for foremen and supervisors in percentage points
- gender wage gap for white-collar workers in percentage points
- gender wage gap for blue-collar workers in percentage points
- share of low wages (between 1 and 1.05 minimum wage)
- share of high wages (more than 3 minimum wages)
- wage decile ratio D9/D1

5. Social dialogue in Germany: Innovation or erosion?

Gerhard Bosch

1. INTRODUCTION

Research has shown that the level of inclusiveness of the wage-setting system is the main factor in explaining inequality of market incomes for dependent employees, over and above the median wage level. By contrast, inclusive systems allow workplace negotiations to be managed collectively by employees with varying degrees of bargaining power. The agreed terms are then made universal for all employees working in that particular company or industry or for the overall economy. If these agreements are to achieve macroeconomic distributional effects, they have to be implemented at an industry-wide or national level. In exclusive wage-setting systems, employees with strong bargaining power negotiate only the terms of their own wages and social security benefits, which means that the outcomes of their negotiations have no bearing on the wages and benefits of those employees with fewer bargaining powers, thus fuelling the social divide between well-paid and poorly paid employees (Bosch et al., 2010). However, micro-solidarity at the departmental or company level has only limited aggregate impact. It is therefore unsurprising that the only systems that actually reduce income inequality are centralised and coordinated wage-setting systems with a higher prevalence of collective agreements and therefore highly effective macro-solidarity, something that has been confirmed repeatedly over the years (see Salverda and Mayhew, 2009; Sniekers, 2011).

Germany is unquestionably an excellent example to take as a basis for investigating this link between primary income distribution and industrial relations. Income inequality in Germany has increased dramatically owing to the erosion of its wage-setting system, which followed the inclusive model until the mid-1990s. This increase was particularly noticeable in those industries and companies in which workers were neither covered by a collective agreement nor represented by a works council. They therefore found themselves in wage negotiations without the protection of the two main institutions that constitute the German model of industrial relations. Coverage by collective agreement also remained high in certain sectors of the economy, particularly in those with greater trade union density and strong works councils. Even less-skilled workers continued to be paid well as a result. However, the reach of this organised wage solidarity was increasingly confined to certain firms and industries, because the other sectors were not able to adhere to the good wage agreements as they had in the past. This is described in the literature as a transition from an employment system with low income inequality to a dualised job market with extremely heterogeneous terms of employment (Carlin and Soskice, 2009; Palier and Thelen, 2010).

The correlation between industrial relations and secondary distribution – that is, disposable household income – is less apparent, as the majority of social security benefits in developed European welfare states are guaranteed by the state and, unlike in the United States, not collectively agreed.[1] However, the state can adjust the primary distribution through tax and social security in order to favour lower-paid workers. Unlike the primary distribution, the social partners can influence this politicised distribution process, if only by indirect means. They participate to an extent in an advisory capacity, engaging in social dialogue with the state, although they attempt to exert influence over distribution decisions through other political processes.

The social partners' influence on the distribution process depends on their strategic capacities, their power resources (Korpi, 2006) and their ability to use them strategically and effectively (Lèvesque and Murray, 2010). These power resources result from the social partners' organisational and institutional powers. The term 'organisational power' denotes the specific power resources that can be mobilised during distribution disputes, examples of which include level of membership, financial reserves and the narrative resources available to persuade large sections of the company that the central demands of the negotiation are beneficial. The power resources that are guaranteed by law are also embedded in the employment system's central institutions, which emerged from historical compromises between labour and capital. The German sociologist Theodor Geiger described this development as the 'institutionalisation of the class struggle'. Its function was to turn the aspects of the struggle that threatened the system into procedures that could be controlled, thereby depoliticising the process (Geiger, 1949).

The change in power relations is again calling these historically won compromises into question and may set in motion a process of institutional erosion. The different ways in which institutions can be eroded and revitalised are the object of new theories on employment system transformation (Crouch and Farrell, 2002). Trade unions' organisational power is the primary power resource that created the institutions as secondary power resources. When the primary power resources decline, the secondary resources come under political pressure as well.

The rest of the chapter is structured as follows. In section 2, the most important actors in the German industrial relations system, the trade unions and employers, with their organisational power, are analysed, together with the two central institutions of the German wage system, namely, free collective bargaining and codetermination. This is followed by an investigation of the erosion of the German wage system and its consequences for income distribution, putting particular emphasis on the decentralisation of bargaining and its consequences (section 3). The systematic failure of so-called 'mini-jobs' to comply with social standards will then be examined. Mini-jobs are a type of marginal part-time employment found in Germany and are a prime example of how companies are able to withdraw from the collective bargaining system (section 4). The next section focuses on innovative agreements, whether at industry or company level, that help to strike a balance between employers' flexibility requirements and employees' social protection (section 5). Two contrasting case studies then follow. The first describes the introduction of the statutory minimum wages, in which social dialogue played a major role despite all the controversies. The second case study reports on an exemplary company agreement concluded at ThyssenKruppSteel Europe on the socially responsible management of subcontractors (section 6).

2. ACTORS AND INSTITUTIONS IN INDUSTRIAL RELATIONS

2.1 Trade Unions

With a total of 6.1 million members, over three-quarters of all trade union members in Germany are organised by the Confederation of German Trade Unions (Deutscher Gewerkschaftsbund, DGB). The German Civil Service Association (Deutscher Beamtenbund, DBB) is the second biggest umbrella organisation with 1.3 million members, 915000 of whom are public officials with lifelong tenure (*Beamte*). Some trade unions within the German Civil Service Association, such as the German Train Drivers' Union (Gewerkschaft Deutscher Lokomotivführer, GDL), have grown in importance owing to the privatisation of some formerly public services. Newly employed train drivers, for example, were no longer given *Beamte* status following privatisation, thereby giving them the right to strike like any other employees – a privilege that they now make full use of. A third umbrella organisation is the Christian Trade Union Confederation (Christliche Gewerkschaftsbund Deutschlands, CGB), which claims to have 280000 members, although this figure is highly contested. The trade unions affiliated with this organisation are well known for entering into accommodating collective agreements with companies in poorly unionised industries, the principal aim of which is to undercut the better terms agreed by DGB unions. Their reputation as 'company unions' is indisputable. There are also other trade unions that do not belong to any umbrella organisation, the biggest of which is the Union of Salaried Medical Doctors (Marburger Bund, MB), which is a union for employed doctors, with a membership of around 118000 (see Table 5.1).

The German unions' umbrella organisations have relatively little power. They do not organise employees and do not have their own income from members' dues, so they are dependent on subsidies from the individual trade unions. Collective bargaining and strikes are always organised by the industry-level trade unions, which thereby occupy the most important sphere of trade union action and embody the real centre of power in the trade union movement. However, the DGB has an important role to play in politics, coordinating with its members to exercise its political influence. It is especially important when it comes to labour legislation, social policies and other central political activities, such as vocational training initiatives.

This coordinated, policy-making role was considerably more powerful 20 years ago at the start of the 1990s, when the DGB still had 16 affiliated unions. Owing to the reduction in members, the unions decided to pool their resources and, in doing so, halved the number of affiliated unions. The two biggest unions, the German Metal Workers' Union (IG Metall) and the United Services Union (ver.di), have more than 2 million members each and account for around 70 per cent of all DGB union members (Table 5.1). They are less reliant on the DGB than the small unions and are increasingly representing themselves at political level – a shift in power that is weakening the DGB.

Even at the height of their power, the German trade unions were organising little more than a third of workers and consequently did not enjoy anywhere near the same degree of organisational power as the Scandinavian trade unions, for example. At the end of the 1970s, trade union density in the former West Germany reached its zenith at 35.5 per cent (in 1978). This then began to drop in the 1980s. Following reunification, trade union density quickly increased to 36 per cent (in 1991) owing to the merger with the well-organised East German unions which existed until the old industrial combines were broken up; however, this figure has continued to fall ever since, reaching just 17.7 per cent in 2013 (Visser,

Table 5.1 Trade union members in Germany: 2001, 2008 and 2015

	2001	2008	2015	2001–08	2008–15
Deutscher Gewerkschaftsbund (DGB) (Confederation of German Trade Unions)	7 899 000	6 322 000	6 096 000	–20.7%	–2.7%
DGB affiliates:					
Industriegewerkschaft Metall (IG Metall) (German Metalworkers' Union)	2 710 000	2 301 000	2 274 000	–15.1%	–1.2%
Vereinte Dienstleistungsgewerkschaft (ver.di) (United Services Union)	2 807 000	2 138 000	2 039 000	–23.8%	–4.6%
Industriegewerkschaft Bergbau, Chemie, Energie (IG BCE) (Mining, Chemicals and Energy Industrial Union)	862 000	701 000	651 000	–18.7%	–7.1%
Industriegewerkschaft Bauen-Agrar-Umwelt (IG BAU) (Building, Agriculture and Environment Workers' Union)	510 000	336 000	273 000	–34.1%	–18.8%
Gewerkschaft Erziehung und Wissenschaft (GEW) (German Union of Education)	268 000	252 000	281 000	–6.0%	+11.5%
Gewerkschaft Nahrung-Genuss-Gaststätten (NGG) (Food, Tobacco, Hotel and Allied Workers Union)	251 000	206 000	204 000	–17.9%	–1.0%
Eisenbahn- und Verkehrsgewerkschaft (EVG) (Railway and Transport Union)	306 000	219 000	197 000	–28.4%	–10.0%
Gewerkschaft der Polizei (GdP) (German Police Union)	185 000	169 000	177 000	–8.6%	+4.7%
Deutscher Beamtembund (DBB) (German Civil Service Association)	1 211 000	1 280 000	1 294 000	+5.7%	+0.2%
Christlicher Gewerkschaftsbund (CGB) (Christian Trade Union Confederation)	not available	275 000	280 000		+1.8%
Non-affiliated unions*	220 000	255 000	270 000	+15.9%	+5.9%
Among them: Marburger Bund (MB) (Union of Salaried Medical Doctors)	70 000	106 000	119 000	+51.4%	+11.3%
In total	9 330 000	8 132 000	7 940 000	–13.5%	–1.8%
Net union density	23.7%	19.1%	17.7%**		

Note: * Estimation by WSI; ** 2013.

Source: Driebbusch et al. (2017: 200) (data based on information from the respective trade unions; union density: ICTWSS Database Version 5.0).

2015). In particular, the unions have not succeeded in making good the members they have lost in the bastions of the manufacturing sector, whose share in total employment has shrunk as a result of structural change, by organising workers in the growing private service sector, especially the increasing numbers of women employed there. Unlike in Denmark or Sweden, the German unions did not succeed in offsetting the loss of male members with a rising trade union density among women. Trade union density among women even decreased between 1980 and 2008, from 21.4 per cent to 12.9 per cent, which was almost as fast a decline as among men (reduction from 50.2 per cent to 24.7 per cent over the same period).

The situation appears more favourable, however, if we look at union coverage. This key figure measures the number of employees in workplaces or establishments covered by unions or works councils as a proportion of all wage and salary earners in employment This indicator is inherently higher than trade union density because in most cases not all employees are organised, and representation through works councils is also included in the figure. Union coverage was 42 per cent in 2011, although this was considerably lower than 30 years previously, when it was still 63.2 per cent (Visser, 2015).

Trade union density in large manufacturing companies and sections of the public services can occasionally be as high as 90 per cent (in the steel industry, for example). In many service industries and small to medium-sized enterprises, however, unions scarcely have a presence. In these types of companies, the unions are unable to assert themselves sufficiently to force employers by their own efforts to conclude collective agreements. The same is true even in some new areas of manufacturing industry, such as wind turbine production. In this and other industries, the German trade unions are trying to build a critical mass of members through organising campaigns in order, first, to institutionalise works councils before attempting to secure coverage by collective agreement (Wetzel, 2013). Successes have been achieved through organising campaigns and the targeted representation of certain groups, such as kindergarten teachers or airport security employees. Small unions that represent only specific occupational groups with considerable strike leverage, such as the Train Drivers Union (GDL), have been considerably more successful in this than the large trade unions, which always have to balance the interests of different professions.

Reforms of internal union activities have been just as important as the organising campaigns. In the 1990s, member recruitment was not at the forefront of daily union activities; instead, it was left to works councils to organise. The trade unions did not perceive this as a problem as long as companies did not take advantage of the unions' weakness. However, when increasing numbers of companies began to withdraw from the employers' associations in order to avoid implementing collective agreements, and when they refused to continue negotiating industry-wide collective agreements, the unions experienced a loss of primary power resources, the negative consequences of which were obvious. The former chairman of IG Metall, Detlef Wetzel, wrote: 'The depressing thing about it was that it made it clear to us that in truth we had never had the power to enforce collective agreements in the event of a dispute' (Wetzel, 2012: 156). Furthermore, the loss of members led to a considerable loss of revenue, which meant that the unions had to reduce their staff numbers. At the same time, their workloads in their core activity of collective bargaining increased several times over owing to the fragmentation of the bargaining system. As a consequence, important areas of activity such as vocational and further training or social policy are no longer worked on as intensely as in the past. As a matter of survival, the industry trade unions have made member recruitment a focus of their activities owing to the loss of organisational power. The work of union officials is increasingly being evaluated on their success in attracting and retaining members, so tasks are prioritised according to the impact on members.

2.2 Employers' Associations

Historically, the trade unions were the midwives of employers' associations, which were formed primarily as counterweights to the unions, above all as anti-strike associations, initially. The fact that unions are the primary and employers' associations the secondary organisations is still evident today, even if the latter now have a considerably wider range of activities than in their start-up phase. These include many advice services specialising in employment law and social policy. It is where unions are strong, such as in the German metalworking and engineering industry, that by far the strongest employers' association, Gesamtmetall, is to be found; conversely, where they have become weaker, such as in the meat processing industry, the employers' associations play only a marginal role.

The associations responsible for private sector industrial relations are organised as part of the Confederation of German Employers' Associations (Bundesvereinigung der Deutschen Arbeitgeberverbände, BDA). The membership of the BDA consists of 52 sectoral federations representing individual industries, 24 of which represent manufacturing industries. In addition, there are 14 cross-sectoral federations at *Land* level whose membership consists of the various industry associations at that level.

The industry associations conduct negotiations at national or regional level. Similar to the DGB, the BDA does not itself conclude agreements, although it does coordinate collective bargaining to a considerably greater extent than the DGB. In its so-called 'Catalogue of wage and collective bargaining issues to be centrally coordinated', which has been revised at intervals, the BDA sets out binding limits on collective bargaining; these are in effect red lines that individual employers' associations must not cross without prior consultation with and the agreement of the BDA. This is popularly known as the 'taboo list'. In the past, common lines of defence were established with regard to holiday entitlement and weekly working time. Now, however, it is not publicly known whether there is still an official taboo list or whether it has been replaced by an unofficial one. This argument is supported by the absolute block the central collective bargaining committee places on all applications for the general extension of wage agreements.

While unions as mass organisations are relatively transparent, employers' organisations do not release much information regarding the evolution of their membership, let alone their finances. This makes it difficult to assess their organisational power. Visser estimates that employer density was 63 per cent in 2002 and 58 per cent in 2011 (Visser, 2015). These figures suggest that the employers' associations are also being eroded, as a number of individual studies have clearly demonstrated. The weakening of the unions has allowed many companies to leave employers' associations and renegotiate wages at company level without fear of labour disputes. This started to happen in East Germany and then increasingly in West Germany as well. Employer density in the metalworking and engineering industry, as reflected in membership of Gesamtmetall, the largest employers' association in Germany, fell in West Germany from 77.4 per cent in 1985 to 56.5 per cent in 2006, a drop of more than 20 per cent. In East Germany, membership fell from approximately 65 per cent in 1992 to less than 20 per cent in 2006 (Haipeter, 2011), with members citing dissatisfaction with working time regulations as their main reason for resigning. As well as the resignations, the fact that many newly established companies did not join the association is another important factor in the erosion of employers' associations (Schroeder and Ruppert, 1996). A survey of managing directors in employers' associations showed that the fall in membership numbers seems to have stopped since 2005 (Nicklich and Helfen, 2013).

Similar to the unions, companies now regard their most important task to be that of gaining and retaining members, which they seek to achieve by improving their advice services (Nicklich and Helfen, 2013). Since the 1990s, employers' associations have tried to retain members increasingly by offering membership without the obligation to comply with collective agreements (so-called OT – *ohne Tarifbindung* – membership). In this way, members have continued to benefit from the advice services but are excluded from shaping collective bargaining policies and receiving financial assistance from strike funds. By offering this category of membership, the associations were seeking, on the one hand, to retain members and, on the other, to put pressure on the unions, which now increasingly have to consider the stability of employers' associations when negotiating collective agreements.

In some associations, such as Gesamtmetall, this seems to have staunched the loss of members. Its membership increased from 5861 companies in 2005 to 6565 in 2011, while the number of member companies bound by collective agreements decreased from 4429 to 3652 (Behrens, 2013: 477). This type of OT membership is held mainly by small and medium-sized enterprises. Behrens (2013: 479) states that: 'Figures collected by Gesamtmetall in 2010 showed that 42 per cent of all member companies in affiliated *Land* and regional federations used OT membership; however, these companies accounted for only 17 per cent of all employees in member companies'. However, the destabilising effect of OT membership for employers' associations over the long term can be seen in the fate of smaller associations that are no longer able to conclude industry-level collective agreements. Some leading employers' representatives have now been heard to say, secretly, that allowing OT membership was a major error.

The situation is completely different for the public sector, almost 100 per cent of whose employers are organised. Local authorities are a part of their local employers' associations together with their member companies, and these local associations are in turn a part of the Federation of Local Authority Employers' Associations (*Vereinigung der Kommunalen Arbeitgeberverbände*, KAV). At *Land* level, the organisation is more loosely structured. The 16 *Länder* have special departments with experts on collective bargaining and are less dependent on the expertise of an employers' organisation. They coordinate their collective bargaining in a working partnership (*Tarifgemeinschaft deutscher Länder*, TDL) with minimum staff. The *Länder* are represented in the TDL by their ministers of finance. At national level, there is no employers' organisation. The minister of internal affairs, together with the minister of finance coordinates collective bargaining for the federal government. The constitution of the KAV and the TDL requires all its members not only to follow the collective agreements but also not to improve on the agreed standards, which is usually allowed by employers' organisations in the private sector. Consequently, there is no wage drift at establishment level, as there is in the private sector (Bosch, 2013).

2.3 Collective Bargaining Policies

Following bad experiences with state-enforced settlements during the Weimar Republic, the Federal Republic of Germany refrained from direct intervention in collective bargaining. One of the basic rights enshrined in the German Constitution is the freedom of coalition. The freedom enjoyed by the social partners to engage in collective bargaining on behalf of their members without state intervention is one of the most important concrete manifestations of this basic right. It was therefore expected that there would be no need for state intervention in wage setting in order to guarantee minimum working and employment conditions, such as a statutory minimum wage. The German collective bargaining system can therefore be characterised as an autonomous wage-setting system in which the state delegates wage bargaining to the social partners and provides a legal framework for that purpose.

The legal regulations governing collective bargaining are deliberately few in number, their main objective being to strengthen the negotiating privileges of trade unions and employers' associations and to establish collective agreements as binding. The basic legal instrument is the Collective Bargaining Act of 1949. The main points of the legislation are as follows:

- Only unions and employers or employers' associations can conclude a collective agreement.
- The agreed standards are binding on union members and members of employers' organisations.
- The social partners have certain obligations, such as refraining from industrial action while the agreement is in force and enforcing the agreement by informing their members of it.
- The agreed standards cannot be undercut but only improved at plant level (the so-called 'favourability principle'); however, the negotiating partners can agree to allow downward deviations.
- The state can declare collective agreements as generally binding if an agreement already covers 50 per cent of the employees in the industry in question and if the majority of the central collective bargaining committee with its six members, three from the employers' federation and three from the unions, agrees.
- If a company leaves the employers' association, the validity of the agreement is extended until a new agreement has been concluded. This extended validity makes it difficult for companies to opt out of industry-wide collective agreements. However, this extended validity does not apply to newly employed personnel.

The legislature has forgone any attempt to define more precisely what constitutes a trade union, such as specifying criteria for representation (for example, a minimum membership threshold, minimum level of representation in different regions or the recognition of certain representative unions). However, in order to exclude bogus, employer-funded unions, independence from the employer, enforced by prohibiting company funding and union 'powerfulness' (the ability to initiate disputes or a minimum number of members in the bargaining unit) have been established in case law as criteria for defining a trade union. Some bogus collective agreements negotiated by the Christian trade unions have been declared null and void by the courts on the grounds of inadequate union 'powerfulness'.

The basic principle of collective agreement unity, according to which only one collective agreement can be applied in any one company, was also firmly established in case law. This basic principle obliged competing trade unions to negotiate together in collective bargaining groups. In 2010, the German Federal Labour Court abandoned this principle, however, and allowed the existence of competing collective agreements in one company. Several occupational trade unions (train drivers, doctors, cabin crews and pilots) left the collective bargaining groups and took industrial action for better work conditions for their own members. The Collective Agreement Unity Act (Gesetz zur Tarifeinheit) has been in force since July 2015. The legislation was enacted mainly owing to pressure from the employers' associations, which wanted to prevent disputes from being scattered across different trade unions. The large industrial trade unions also pushed for the law because they wanted to stop the smaller, powerful occupational unions from selecting those most beneficial to them. The law stipulates that, in the event of conflicting agreements, the only legal norms that shall apply are those laid down in the collective agreement concluded by the trade union that had the most members in the company at the time when the most recent collective agreement was signed. This Act has become the object of several constitutional challenges, which have a good chance of being successful in court.

German collective bargaining law is open to collective agreements made at different levels. It permits collective agreements to be concluded at national or regional level, or even at industry, company or establishment level. Because of the trade union structure, the industry level has emerged as the dominant bargaining level. There have never been national collective agreements in Germany akin to those in France, for example, where they have become an important instrument in the national social dialogue and laid the groundwork for changes in legislation. Except for the attempts to establish a productivity-based wages policy through so-called 'concerted action' (Konzertierte Aktion) (1967–77) and the Schröder government's 'Alliance for Work' (Bündnis für Arbeit) (1998–2003), the national social dialogue in Germany is not institutionalised but rather organised on a case-by-case basis, as evidenced, for example, by the informal agreements between the government and the collective bargaining partners during the financial crisis in order to avoid redundancies (see section 3.2) and the regular national agreements on vocational training for young people.

As the trade unions weakened, conservative politicians increased their efforts to forcibly decentralise collective bargaining and weaken industry-wide labour standards by abolishing the favourability principle and trade union privilege in negotiating collective agreements. If works councils had been granted these rights, however, it would have been necessary to grant them the right to strike, which is enshrined in the constitution. Consequently, some employers' associations warned against such a move, as they feared pay disputes could be played out at establishment level, thereby jeopardising the largely cooperative industrial relations at that level. Nevertheless, the Sozialdemokratische Partei Deutschland (SPD) and Green coalition government at that time threatened the unions that, as part of the 2003 Hartz reforms, they would also abolish the favourability principle and grant works councils their own negotiating rights if the unions did not voluntarily accept the inclusion of derogation clauses in collective agreements. The so-called 'Pforzheim Agreement' of February 2004 allowed companies in the metalworking and engineering industry to derogate temporarily from the provisions of collective agreements, although the derogations had to be negotiated by the social partners and not by the works councils (section 3.2).

2.4 Codetermination at Establishment and Company Level

In the post-war years, the unions demanded institutionalised codetermination at establishment and company levels. This was controversial, but it came at a time when trade unions were in a position to mobilise effectively their membership around the issue. The disputes ended with the adoption of the 1952 Works Constitution Act (Betriebsverfassungsgesetz, BetrVG), which provided for a weak form of codetermination at company level (one-third parity on supervisory boards). Works councils' rights of codetermination were improved in several amendments to the Act. The right to equal participation on the supervisory board was introduced in 1976 in companies with more than 2000 employees. The arrangement places an executive member of staff among the employee representatives, while the chairman, who has double voting rights, is appointed from among the management's representatives.

According to the Works Constitution Act, works councils are elected by all the employees in an establishment. They offer employees a legally well protected and resourced system of interest representation. In contrast to the Scandinavian system, works councils are not organs of the trade unions but have nevertheless emerged as the biggest source of trade union power at company or establishment level. The most important provisions in the 1952 Works Constitution Act, which have since been improved several times, can be summarised as follows:

- Works councillors may be dismissed only under extraordinary circumstances (for example, theft). A special type of dismissal protection also applies to the members of the electoral board when works councils are being set up. Since 2001, a simplified election procedure has been in place for small and middle-sized businesses in order to protect the works councillors. They can be elected at a workplace assembly and there is only one week between the first proposal to set up a works council and the meeting to elect its members.
- Works councillors have to be released from work as required in order to carry out their duties. In companies with 200 or more employees (300 before 2001), one works councillor is released completely from work. The number released from all work duties rises with the number of employees, reaching 12 in companies with 10 000 or more employees.
- They have the right to the resources they require in order to carry out their duties. Such resources include offices and secretarial assistance and, in large companies, specialist staff and access to professional advice. Companies must also release works councillors for further training relevant to their duties.
- They have strong rights to codetermination on social and personnel issues. For example, overtime can be scheduled only if they agree. They have the right to oppose redundancies or new appointments under certain circumstances, for example, if a redundancy could be avoided by transferring the employee or providing them with further training.
- They have strong rights to access information on economic issues via their own economic committee, which can view the relevant company documents.
- It is expressly stipulated in the Works Constitution Act that one of the works council's central tasks is to monitor the company's compliance with labour laws and collective agreements.
- In contrast to trade unions, the principle of trustworthy cooperation applies to works councillors. They must not call for industrial action but in the event of disputes over codetermination issues they can call on an arbitration committee whose decisions are binding.
- Works councils can conclude agreements with company management pertaining to various working and employment conditions that fall outside the competence of the parties to collective bargaining.

> The favourability principle applies here as it does for all collective agreements, meaning that individual employment contracts cannot undercut the working and employment conditions set out in company agreements.

Similarly structured staff councils also exist in the public sector. Works councils' rights to codetermination have given rise to a body of collective labour law in addition to standard labour law. However, employees benefit from this only if a works council has been elected. In many industries, company agreements have in practice become the main standard-setting instrument on many important issues, such as the organisation of working time.

Many studies have demonstrated that companies with works councils are more likely to comply with collective agreements and legislation than those without. However, not all employees benefit from this. In the public service, nearly all employees are represented by staff councils. However, in 2014 only 43 per cent of all employees in the western German private sector were represented compared with 33 per cent in eastern Germany. Representation through works councils is very much dependent on size of company. Works councils have been elected in almost all large companies, but their share decreases with size of company. Only in 38 per cent of companies with 50–100 employees have works councils been elected and in smaller companies the share is considerably lower (Hans-Böckler-Stiftung, 2016). This also explains the pronounced differences between industries. In well-established sectors dominated by large companies – such as energy, financial services and manufacturing – the majority of employees are represented by works councils. In industries with small and newly founded companies, however, works councils are the exception (see Figure 5.1). In small and medium-sized enterprises particularly, there are widespread attempts by companies to hinder the formation of works councils by employing a range of methods to threaten and pressure employees, even going so far as dismissing employees (Behrens and Driebbusch, 2014). These are similar tactics to those used for 'trade union busting' in the United States. This led to the introduction of the aforementioned simplified election procedures for small and middle-sized businesses in 2001.

In 2010, approximately 174 000 German works councillors were elected on a voter turnout of almost 80 per cent. Of these, about 8400 are released from all work and about 1000 from some of their work duties in order that they can perform their council duties. They are mostly trained at trade union training centres at their employers' cost. More than two-thirds of works councillors and the majority of those released from work are members of a DGB trade union (Greifenstein et al., 2011). This is several times

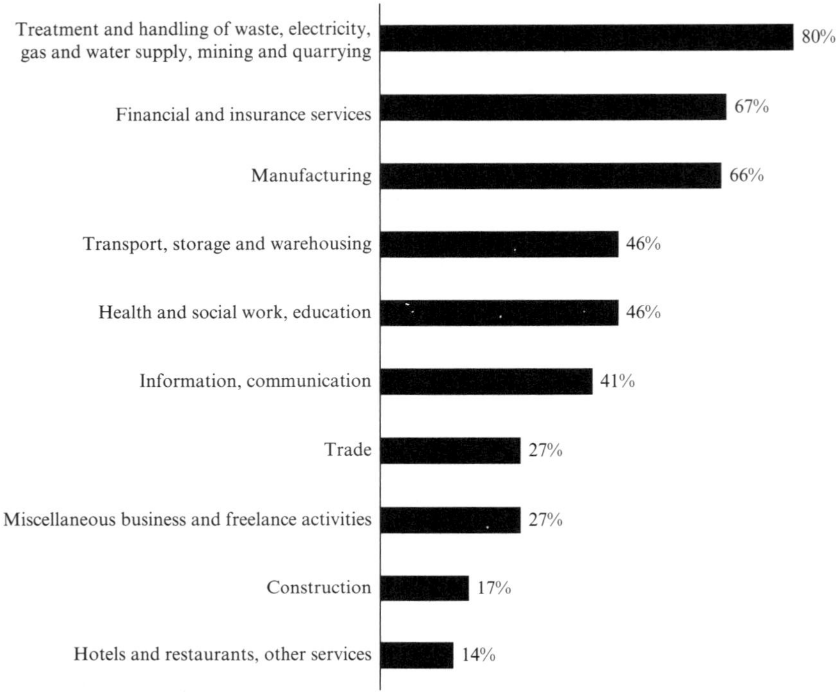

Note: * Basis for inclusion: companies with at least five employees.

Source: Hans-Böckler-Stiftung (2016: 5).

*Figure 5.1 The number of employees represented by a works council in Germany by industry**

the number of full-time workers employed by the German trade unions. Works councils are now the main actors in union recruitment. In only a few big companies do trade union shop stewards still operate alongside works councils.

In addition, in 2016, employee representatives were elected to the supervisory board in 641 larger companies with codetermination on a parity basis (HBS, 2017). Employee representatives in these companies account for half of the supervisory board mandates. Codetermination rights in the steel and mining industries are more extensive. The human resources director is appointed on the recommendation of the employee representatives in the supervisory board. In a further 1500 companies with fewer than 2000 but more than 500 employees, one-third of the supervisory board is made up of employee representatives (one-third parity).

By virtue of their access to resources and their professionalisation, works councillors constitute the main trade union power base. Even in a number of sectors in which the membership base is weak, such as the financial sector, trade unions manage to exert influence via active works councils. Union recruitment largely takes place through the works councils, which are also the most important bodies monitoring compliance with legislation and collective agreements. Employee representation on supervisory boards is most effective when it is coordinated with the activities of works councils.

Approximately 800 000 employees in large companies are denied codetermination on the basis of parity on supervisory boards through legal manoeuvring. This is the case, for example, in large independent enterprises, such as Aldi or Lidl, which are controlled by 'foundations' that do not have to comply with codetermination legislation. Other expanding companies are converted into European companies (SEs), in which the existing German codetermination policies are frozen before they reach the thresholds of 500 or 2000 employees, at which improved codetermination regulations come into force (Böckler-Impuls, 2016: 2–3).

In western Germany, the two major institutions addressing distribution issues – collective agreements and works councils – still cover two-thirds of employees in private sector companies with more than five employees; the share in eastern Germany is scarcely more than half. Since 2000, both shares have decreased by approximately 10 per cent (Ellguth and Kohaut, 2015). Even smaller is the share of employees that benefit from both institutions (Figure 5.2).

3. WEAKENING OF THE INCLUSIVE WAGE-SETTING SYSTEM SINCE 1995

Autonomous collective bargaining systems come with a lot of preconditions, including a reliance on strong social partners who are able effectively to set their own and binding standards. These preconditions are increasingly unlikely to be fulfilled owing to the erosion of the membership base in trade unions and employers' associations. However, when collective agreements can no longer establish binding standards, then wages become a competitive factor again. In a bid to undercut competitors' rates, wages come under pressure and collective agreements start to be eroded. The following section examines the causes behind the decrease in collective agreement coverage and its effects on income distribution (section 3.1). The different forms of collective bargaining policy decentralisation are then described (section 3.2). This decentralisation ranges from a unilateral

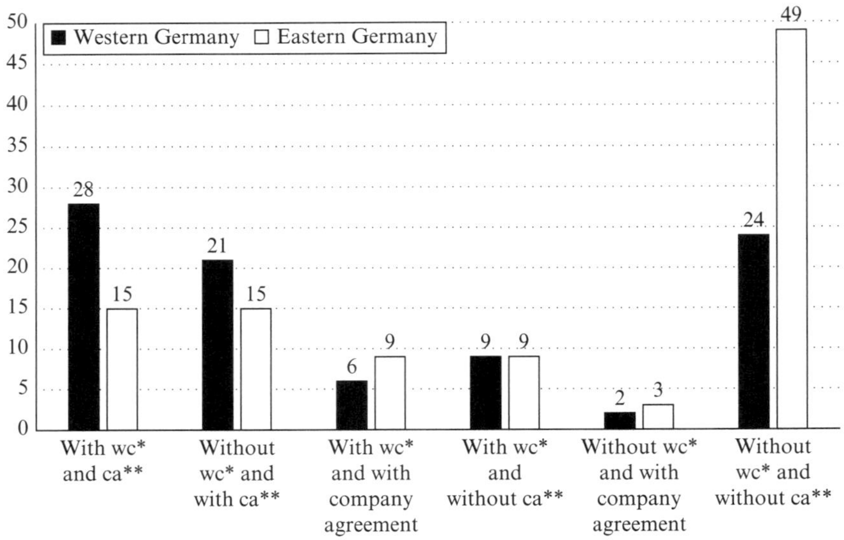

Notes: * Works councils; ** collective agreement.

Source: Ellguth and Kohaut (2015).

Figure 5.2 Works councils and collective agreements in private sector companies with more than five employees in 2014, Germany

undercutting of collective agreement standards by employers through to compromises on the organisation of working time negotiated on an equal footing by the social partners. This distinction is important for the future of collective bargaining, because undercutting without negotiation is a form of erosion, while the negotiated implementation of collective agreements at company level or even of temporary derogations may be a necessary adjustment to a more complex world of work and, by complementing the agreements, may even serve to strengthen the collective bargaining process.

3.1 Decrease in Collective Agreement Coverage

Until the start of the 1990s, Germany was renowned for its low income disparity (OECD, 1996). Until German reunification, in fact, collective agreement coverage was around 85 per cent (Visser, 2015); this was several times greater than trade union density, as the majority of companies belonged to an employers' association. Even businesses that were not covered by collective agreements mostly decided to pay the collectively agreed rates. In particular, the agreed terms in well-organised industries –

especially those in the metal industry – functioned as pattern agreements, which were adopted by the less-organised sectors. This caused wages to rise in lockstep throughout the economy, which in turn safeguarded the type of macro-solidarity beyond individual companies and industries characteristic of inclusive wage-setting systems.

The high levels of corporate compliance with collective agreements can be attributed, first, to the low unemployment rates in the former West Germany. This strengthened employees' bargaining power and made unilateral wage settings without the protection of employers' associations in the event of disputes unattractive to employers. Secondly, the associations and chambers in the old German corporatist system, with its closely interconnected companies that took a long-term view of business, were able to exert moral pressure in order to ensure fair wage competition (Tullius and Wolf, 2012).

From the mid-1990s onwards, compliance with collective agreements began to crumble. Collective agreement coverage declined to 60 per cent and 47 per cent in western and eastern Germany, respectively (WSI Tarifarchiv, 2015). Since 1995, the considerable reduction in collective agreement coverage has led to a rise in the share of low-paid workers, which is now above average by international standards. Furthermore, because of the absence of a statutory minimum wage, wage levels collapsed to such an extent that by 2010 the gap between the average pay of low-wage workers and the low-wage threshold was greater in Germany than in any other European country (Figure 5.3).[2]

Alongside areas that continued to be well organised, there were now large swathes of the labour market in which wages were no longer negotiated collectively but set unilaterally by employers. The good wage settlements no longer acted as pattern agreements for other industries, so settlements were becoming increasingly differentiated depending on trade union bargaining powers. This development is also reflected in the wage drift that has occurred in most years since 2000. Collectively agreed wage rates have usually risen faster than actual wages because only a decreasing share of employees benefit from collective bargaining (Figure 5.4).

In 2010, with controls for different individual and company variables, the 'collective bargaining premium' for industry-level agreements was 5.6 per cent and for company agreements 8.2 per cent per hour worked. Without controls, the average premium was 22.2 per cent and in firms with a company collective agreement it was 29.3 per cent. The variables taken into account included size of firm, industry affiliation, age, gender, hours worked, job tenure and type of contract (permanent/temporary) (Amlinger, 2014). The 'collective bargaining premium' could, however, be higher than calculated in the regression analysis, first, because companies

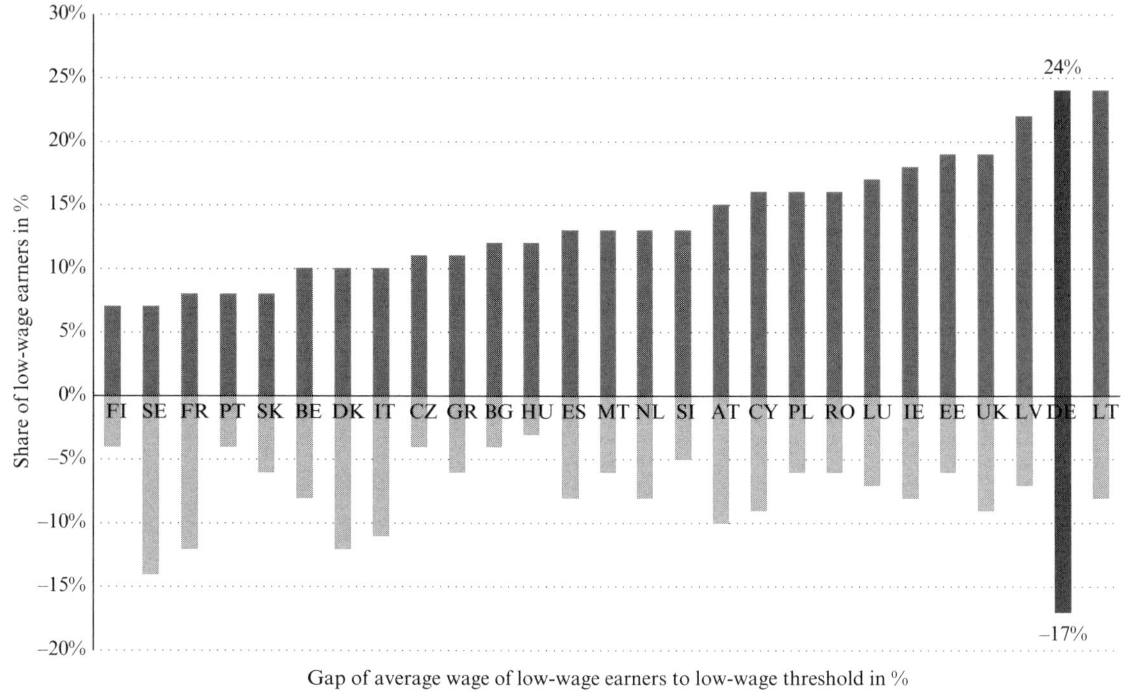

Source: Fernández-Macías and Vacas-Soriano (2013); author's illustration.

Figure 5.3 Proportion of low-paid workers and the difference between their average wage and the low-wage threshold (under 60 per cent of the median wage) in the EU in 2010

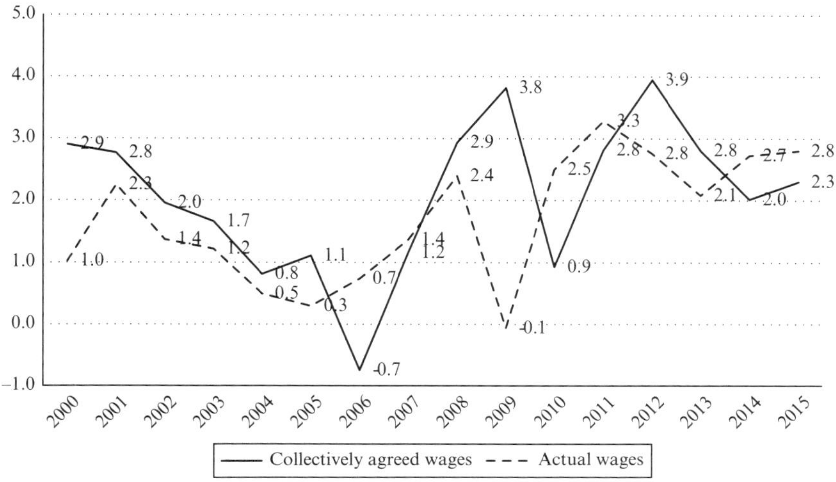

Source: Bispinck (2017, table 2.1); author's presentation.

Figure 5.4 Increases by collectively agreed and actual wages per hour, Germany, 2000–2015

with fewer than ten employees are not included in the German earnings structure survey and, secondly, because some of the variables controlled for are 'endogenous'. In the past few years companies have systematically outsourced jobs to low-wage industries or small businesses because of the differences in wage rates. They have also increased the number of temp agency employees. In 2010, for example, collective agreement coverage in companies with 10–19 employees was only 23.3 per cent, compared with 86.8 per cent in companies with more than 500 employees (Amlinger and Bispinck, 2013: 5). However, the 'collective bargaining premium' can also be reduced by the 'legacy effect' of collective agreements that remain in force in companies that have withdrawn from the employers' association and as a result of the guiding role that collective agreements continue to play in areas where there is no collective bargaining. About half of the companies without collective agreements have stated that they use collective agreements as a guide in setting wage rates. Their rates are higher than in companies not bound by collective agreements, although they are lower than the collectively agreed level, because compliance with non-monetary stipulations is greater than with monetary stipulations (Addison et al., 2014). The logical extension of this, however, is that industry-wide wage rates in an economy in which more than half of employees' wages are still set by collective agreement play a significantly greater guiding role, particularly for skilled workers with considerable bargaining power, than in countries – such as the United States and the United Kingdom – in which industry-wide rates of pay in the private sector have largely disappeared.

The substantial growth in low wages indicates that wages have returned to being a competitive factor, with bad standards squeezing out good standards over the long run. The major reasons for this development can be summarised as:

- *The high rate of unemployment since 1991.* With the collapse of the eastern German economy and the end of the post-reunification boom, unemployment in the whole of unified Germany increased from 1.9 million in 1990 to 4.9 million in 2003. The increase in mass unemployment weakened job seekers' ability to negotiate as they increasingly had to accept low wages.
- *The eastern Germany productivity deficiency.* The rapid transfer of western German employment conditions to eastern Germany failed to serve many of the companies that were established just after reunification, since their productivity level was too low to benefit from the conditions. This led to the large-scale abandonment of collective agreements, which in turn led to companies withdrawing from the employers' associations (or newly established companies refusing to join).
- *Corporate strategy change.* The growing number of areas in eastern Germany that were not covered by collective agreements showed companies that, in view of the mass unemployment, it was possible to get out of the collective bargaining system without having to fear sanctions from the weakened trade unions. As previously mentioned, the employers' associations encouraged this behaviour by offering membership to companies that did not have collective agreements in place (OT). At the same time, they repeatedly blocked the collective bargaining committee from extending collective agreements, which could have contained the mass withdrawal from collective agreements. In industries such as meat processing or motor trade and repairs, companies refused to renegotiate industry-level agreements.
- *Product market deregulation.* It was mainly the effect of EU directives that opened up former public services to private suppliers. New suppliers that were not covered by collective agreements were able to undercut the old public suppliers with low wages and prices. Subsequently, collective agreement coverage decreased in industries that had been previously at 100 per cent, such as the railways, postal services, telecommunications, public transport and waste management services. In addition to this, trade unions had to agree

to further wage reductions and increases in working time through concession bargaining in order to safeguard the survival of the old suppliers.

- *Fragmentation of companies.* The growing wage differences induced companies and the state to outsource many jobs in order to save on wage costs. As a result, poorly paid workers employed as 'subcontractors' have ended up working alongside well-paid members of the core workforce. Owing to this fragmentation of companies, trade unions find it significantly harder to organise solidarity among workers. In order to prevent job outsourcing from domestic and non-domestic companies and to safeguard companies' ability to compete, trade unions had to accept more and more collective agreements with derogation clauses (section 3.2).
- *Labour market deregulation.* There was increased pressure on the unemployed to accept low-paid jobs owing to the 2003 Hartz laws, which had lowered unemployment benefit entitlements and introduced a harsher definition of a reasonable job offer. At the same time, tax-free mini-jobs with a maximum monthly salary of €450 were further deregulated along with temporary work and both were developed as alternatives to well-paid jobs. During one of the largest economic upturns of the past decade, between 2004 and 2008, the Hartz laws ensured that the number of low earners increased further.
- *Women's employment as a built-in deregulator.* Owing to changing expectations of gender roles, the number of women in employment has increased substantially in Germany, as it has in other European countries. Many women worked in mini-jobs for several reasons. First, owing to the lack of childcare and the half school days that are customary in Germany, they would have to work marginal hours in order to be available at the appropriate times to look after their children. Secondly, there was the benefit of mini-jobs being tax-free. Finally, they were not dependent on the mini-jobs for health insurance or as a main source of income as this came from their partners' employment. The majority of companies use mini-jobs as a way of circumventing collective agreements and the German social security system (Section 4).
- *Public service downsizing and privatisation.* The number of public sector employees decreased from 6.74 million in 1991 to 4.65 million in 2014 due to the outsourcing of formerly public jobs to the private sector and the downsizing of public services (Destatis, 2014). This led to the loss of many well-paid jobs, because all public employees are still covered by collective agreements or have *Beamte* status with relatively good salaries (Bosch, 2013).

3.2 Decentralisation of Collective Bargaining Policies: Deviations and Differentiation

The decentralisation of collective bargaining began with the working time reductions below the 40-hour mark that were negotiated in 1983. As a quid pro quo for the cuts in working time, companies were able to push through a more flexible distribution of working time over a year or more. The negotiation of working time was devolved to company level; by the mid-1980s, more than 3000 company agreements modifying the scheduling of working time had been concluded in the metalworking industry alone (Bosch et al., 1988). The second wave of decentralisation began in eastern Germany following reunification and then spread to western Germany. The objective was no longer to differentiate working time but to reduce wages below the collectively agreed, industry-wide standards or to increase working time. Furthermore, clauses were added to collective agreements providing for temporary reductions in collectively agreed working time in order to safeguard jobs. However, there were often no agreed procedural arrangements for using these derogation clauses, particularly in western Germany. In contrast to the implementation of working time reductions, which was mainly based on compromises that were accepted on both sides and well coordinated by the trade unions, this process was much more chaotic, with the unions not prepared to coordinate it and conditions often being dictated by the employers.

The third wave of decentralisation came in 2003 when, as previously mentioned, the Social Democrat Schröder government demanded that derogation clauses be used in order to undercut collectively agreed standards, its principal target being the export-orientated metalworking and engineering industry. In the 2004 'Pforzheim Agreement', so called after the place at which the negotiations took place, IG Metall drew lessons from the bad experiences of uncontrolled decentralisation in the 1990s and used this as the basis for its decisions. It was stipulated that deviations from the collective agreements should serve to safeguard employment, be used by companies only in emergency situations and be negotiated by the parties to collective bargaining rather than works councils. In addition, the unions were given further rights to information, which would enable them to appraise the emergency situation.

An evaluation of some 800 collective agreements in the metalworking and engineering industry and company case studies has shown that IG Metall not only made concessions but also received some quid pro quos, such as dismissal protection for a number of years and agreements that plants would remain open, with guarantees of investment or enhanced initial and further training. At the same time, the works councils and the workforces were involved in the negotiations, the results of which in many companies were presented to the union membership for voting. The stronger coordination of divergences from the collective agreements, the laying down of exact procedures and the inclusion of the workforce in the negotiations even helped strengthen union organisation (Haipeter and Lehndorff, 2009; Haipeter, 2011).

Thus the term 'derogation clause' and the associated decentralisation of agreements conceal very different realities. On the one hand, it denotes the concrete implementation at firm level of general, collectively agreed standards, while on the other hand other collectively agreed standards, such as pay, working time or other arrangements can be temporarily undercut. Nearly all collective agreements now contain derogation clauses permitting negotiations at company level.

Table 5.2 shows that 47 per cent of the companies surveyed said that there were derogation clauses in their bargaining area, 75 per cent of which were used in practice. Derogation clauses are utilised more frequently in large companies than in small ones. The reasons for this may be that these companies are better informed about them, that they have fewer opportunities for informal agreements and that their professionalised human resources (HR) policies enable them to sound out and make use of the

Table 5.2 Distribution and use of derogation clauses by company size, Germany, 2011 (percentage share of companies; extrapolated results)*

Derogation clause of any kind		
Available[a]	% used[b]	Share of all companies using derogation clauses
25	73	19
42	72	30
54	76	41
62	73	45
28	73	20
47	75	35

Notes:
* Base: private sector companies with more than five employees and covered by collective agreements, excluding agriculture and non-profit organisations.
[a] Share of all private sector companies with more than five employees and covered by collective agreements.
[b] Share of companies that have derogation clauses in their collective agreements.

Source: Ellguth and Kohaut (2014: 442).

available room for manoeuvre more systematically than smaller firms can. The survey also shows that derogation clauses tend to be used mainly to negotiate company agreements on working time and pay. The multivariate analysis reveals that companies with economic problems are more likely to use opening clauses for wage negotiations in order to temporarily lower their wage costs. However, clauses on flexible working times are not used for economic reasons but instead are more likely to be a part of companies' pre-emptive flexibility strategies. Thus Berthold et al. (2003) rightly differentiate between 'crisis' and 'innovation pacts', which characterise relatively well the two aspects of the decentralisation of collective bargaining. In crisis pacts, the aim is to reduce wage costs quickly, whereas innovation pacts are intended to achieve 'a quick and flexible adjustment to ever-changing market conditions' (Berthold et al., 2003: 8). Addison et al. (2015) show that company employment pacts established with modernisation in mind usually have positive effects on wages, productivity and innovation. Besides the purely employer-orientated perspective in Berthold's differentiation, it is also worth noting that decentralised agreements are necessary to safeguard workers' interests (such as the organisation of working time). Similarly, good compromises can be reached between employees' and employers' interests in respect of flexibility if there is strong company-level employee representation.

Thus the architecture of the overall system has changed. The German collective bargaining system now has multi-level bargaining, in which the industry level still takes priority but derogations can increasingly be negotiated at company level. The social partners are increasingly legitimising their agreements, particularly vis-à-vis companies, by including derogation clauses in them in order to stabilise the membership of employers' associations. Derogations can also have a symbolic function, such as allowing late payment of an agreed wage increase on the grounds of economic difficulties. However, the monitoring and coordination of these derogations has become an ever-present task for the unions if they wish to maintain the supremacy of the industry level.

4. MINI-JOBS AS AN EXIT OPTION FOR COMPANIES

Mini-jobs are a form of marginal employment offering a maximum monthly salary of €450. They are a particular form of dependent employment characterised by exemption from social security contributions and income tax; however, employers have to pay a flat-rate charge of approximately 30 per cent on top of the €450. Because the same labour legislation applies to mini-jobs as to all other paid employment (such as dismissal protection, paid holiday, sick pay and so on), they are technically more expensive per hour than socially insured part-time employment, for which the employers' contributions are around 20 per cent.

This special status was originally justified by the supposed limited labour market attachment of married women, whose role in the traditional German family model was at best that of supplementary income earner. In order to prevent excessively low wages, working time was limited to a maximum of 15 hours per week. Labour market policy considerations were to the fore in 2003, when it became legal to take a mini-job as a second job and the limit on weekly working time was abolished. The intention behind the deregulation of atypical employment was to create a springboard into regular employment.

Since mid-2003, the number of mini-jobs has increased by 1.7 million to 7.3 million (mid-2015), which represents a rise of 30.3 per cent. This increase is due primarily to a sharp rise in the number of mini-jobs taken as second jobs (up almost 1.6 million or 159.4 per cent). Mini-jobs are particularly common in the service sector. In December 2015, the retail industry, with more than 1.2 million mini-jobbers, had the most employees on marginal pay. Various business services, which include temporary agency work and security and cleaning services came in second place, followed by the hospitality industry with 819 000 mini-jobs and then health and social services with around 703 000. Over 60 per cent of mini-jobbers are women, with pensioners and school and university students making up the next biggest group.

Hanau describes mini-jobs as a puzzle. 'In actual fact, it's rather a puzzle what might induce employers to hire workers for whom the non-wage costs are significantly higher' (Hanau, 2006: 809). The puzzle can be solved only by close examination of mini-jobbers' working and employment conditions. Extensive research has clearly shown that, in practice, mini-job employees are treated unequally. Their hourly wage is often less than the equivalent wage for socially insured workers. They are also generally paid only for the hours actually worked and do not receive the holiday or sick pay to which they are entitled. The most up-to-date data were gathered in an Institut für Arbeitsmarkt- und Berufsforschung (IAB) survey of employees and companies carried out in 2015. This revealed that the average hourly wage for mini-job employees was only €9.30, in contrast to an average of €16.70 for socially insured part-time employees, €18.30 for full-time temporary employees and €21.00 for full-time permanent employees. Furthermore, over half of mini-jobbers earned less than €8.50 (Fischer et al., 2015: 56 f.) and no fewer than 68.6 per cent of them are low paid, the highest share of any employment form (Kalina and Weinkopf, 2014).

The IAB employment survey also revealed high levels of non-compliance with the law. According to the mini-jobbers:

- only 49.6 per cent of respondents received holiday pay. It remained unclear whether they were able to take their full holiday entitlement (Fischer et al., 2015: 100);
- only around 50 per cent of mini-jobbers continued to receive their regular wage when sick (Fischer et al., 2015: 129);
- only around 45 per cent of mini-jobbers were paid for public holidays (Fischer et al., 2015: 131).

Among socially insured full- and part-time employees, in contrast, the comparable figures were 97 per cent for paid holidays, 95 per cent for sick pay and over 87 per cent for paid public holidays. When asked about the lack of pay for sick leave or public holidays, companies responded with reasons that are deemed illegal (see Table 5.3).

This unequal treatment means that mini-jobs are, in practice, considerably cheaper for employers than socially insured jobs. In some sectors, such as retail or hospitality, this has led to socially insured part-time jobs being converted into mini-jobs. For some employees, mini-jobs are often

Table 5.3 Reasons why mini-jobbers did not receive sick pay or public holiday pay, descriptive results, Germany (by companies)

Reasons why mini-job employees did not receive pay for:	Percentage of respondents answering 'Applies' (95% – CI)	
	Sick leave	Public holidays
Company cannot afford to pay it	17.2 (9.5–29.1)	13.2 (6.8–24.1)
Mini-jobbers are only employed on a temporary basis	73.7 (60.5–83.7)	67.5 (55.1–77.9)
Mini-jobbers have only been employed at the company for less than four weeks	16.8 (9.0–29.3)	*
They do not work on public holidays	*	64.2 (51.8–74.9)
They only work a small number of hours	76.3 (63.3–85.7)	74.3 (63.2–83.0)
Mini-jobbers are not entitled to sick pay	41.3 (28.9–55.0)	30.4 (20.1–43.0)
Other reason given	11.0 (5.8–19.8)	9.6 (4.8–18.2)

Notes:
Extrapolated results, CI = confidence interval.
* This reason for failure to pay was not offered to respondents as a possible answer for the entitlement in question.

Source: Fischer et al. (2015: 152).

an attractive option because the lower wages are partly offset by lower taxes and contributions; for second jobs, the tax and social security bill is lower than for overtime in a socially insured job. Married mini-jobbers benefit from their partner's health insurance and can earn up to €5400 per year (12 × €450) tax-free without endangering the family's tax benefits of the German income splitting tax system. School and university students, finally, are covered by their families' insurance and the student health insurance scheme.

Mini-jobs offer strong financial incentives for both employees and employers to stick with marginal part-time employment, because the marginal costs of a changeover to socially insured jobs can be very high. It is hardly surprising, therefore, that the transfer rates from mini-jobs into regular employment are low, particularly for married women. In contrast, the transfer rate for school and university students is naturally very high: for them, mini-jobs are only a temporary option.

Research shows that those employed solely and permanently in marginal part-time jobs are at particularly high risk of long-term scarring effects, for several reasons. First, mini-jobbers are often employed to perform simple tasks that do not match their formal qualifications and are often excluded from companies' further training provision, which hampers their transition into better paid jobs and occupational career paths. Secondly, they are not independently covered by social security and acquire only minimal pension entitlements in their own right. Because by no means all mini-jobbers have derived entitlements from a partner and relationships are not in any case necessarily stable, mini-jobbers are more likely than average to claim social assistance and the poverty rate among them has risen particularly sharply in recent years. Employee surveys on working time preferences show that many marginal part-timers would like significantly longer weekly working times (6.5 hours more per week on average) (IAB, 2012). However, the artificial income barrier created by mini-jobs prevents a gradual transition to longer working times and hence into more stable and lucrative employment.

For these reasons, a disparate alliance of actors ranging from the Council of Economic Experts via the Women's Council to the Expert Commission on the Compilation of the German Federal Republic's First Gender Equality Report (SEEGB, 2011) were unable to find any justification for subsidising this employment form. Thus the Expert Commission, for example, declared that 'It must be our aim . . . to make all employment relationships liable for social insurance contributions' (SEEGB, 2011: 135). The recommended reforms range from proposals for the complete abolition of mini-jobs to permitting them only up to a derisory limit of €100 or €200. The introduction of the minimum wage has re-established an upper limit on weekly working time of around 12 hours. However, the problems with implementation of the minimum wage are particularly challenging in the case of mini-jobs (section 6.1).

The technical proposals are certain not to be implemented because of the strong political resistance from both employees and employers. The political parties try to avoid the topic altogether, deeming it 'maximum trouble, minimum gain'. For this reason, it was proposed that existing mini-jobs should be protected in order to keep the number of losers low while slowly rolling out better protected employment forms with new recruitments (Bosch and Weinkopf, 2016).

5. INNOVATIVE COLLECTIVE AND COMPANY AGREEMENTS

The range of topics covered by collective agreements has expanded significantly in recent years. The differences between blue- and white-collar workers have been blurred as a result of corporate restructurings; in the major manufacturing industries (for example, chemicals, metalworking and engineering) and in the public services, unified pay scales have been introduced in which all employees covered by collective agreements are graded by the same criteria. Increasing inter-firm mobility and ageing workforces have led seniority pay, which was once commonplace, to be critically assessed. For example, in the public sector 12 seniority levels were replaced by six experience levels. Such major reforms, which have an impact on several million workers and have both winners and losers, had to be introduced over an extended time period and with guaranteed protection for those who stood to lose out. These reforms would have been unthinkable without solid mutual trust.

The reforms also address several new requirements for companies, brought about by technological change, a changing labour supply and the transformation of social values, such as gender equality, work–life balance, the avoidance of discrimination and the promotion of lifelong learning. In some cases, companies have to react to new legislation that they have to implement within a given time frame, such as the quotas for women on supervisory boards or the provisions of the Anti-Discrimination Act. Legal norms are implemented and many new norms created by collective and company agreements. By balancing social security and flexibility, these norms contribute to economic and social modernisation, although declining coverage by collective agreement means they do not apply to all employees. The following sections describe two examples of social modernisation brought about by collective agreements.

5.1 Further Training and Collective Agreements

Because trade unions consider support for further training to be the key element in safeguarding workers' employability, they have long sought to regulate this area at both company and industry level. In contrast to pay claims, however, it is difficult to mobilise union members around demands for further training, so that the unions are unable to reach consensus on this question. As with all net investments, the aim in promoting further training is to grow the pie. This being so, Ok and Tergeist (2003) see opportunities for integrative bargaining, in contrast to pay bargaining, which tends to be conflictual and which they characterise as 'distributive bargaining'. Since distribution disputes have been avoided, for example by establishing rights to funded further training, these further training arrangements can be characterised as 'soft law' (Bahnmüller and Hoppe, 2012).

There is a long tradition of negotiating training agreements. In the 1960s and 1970s, for example, further training measures were agreed in conjunction with social plans and agreements on employment protection during rationalisation processes. However, further training remained a mere appendage to all of these agreements. They were agreed in response to specific situations and consequently further training was only temporarily an object of negotiation.

It is only since the early 2000s that primary collective agreements on further training have been concluded. The collective agreements on further training in the metalworking and electrical engineering industry (2001) and the public service (2005) strengthened employees' individual rights to have an annual training needs meeting convened by employees themselves. It was hoped that this would bring about an expansion and systematisation of company staff development programmes. Only in Baden-Württemberg, where a joint body for the promotion of further training was set up, did the social partners agree to put in place a joint support organisation. The extensive empirical research that accompanied these two further training agreements (Bahnmüller and Hoppe, 2012) showed that the main effect of these collective agreements was to reinforce the trend in companies that were already prepared to provide further training. However, companies' training activities were not correlated with trade union density; rather, they were driven by active works councillors and HR managers, whose views on this topic were not a given even in the trade union representative bodies. Thus the collective agreements also had an activating function within the unions' own organisation.

At company level, a similar shift from event-driven to primary agreements can be observed. An analysis of 146 company agreements on further training shows that they give priority to process over content, that is, on aspects such as participation in the planning of training needs, discussions with employees, equality of access to training, support for particular groups of employees and the establishment of bipartite training committees with rights over the planning and implementation of further training measures and dispute resolution (Busse and Seifert, 2009). Only 33 per cent of the agreements provided for extensive participation on the part of works councils. With regard to funding, a distinction was frequently made between training measures required by the company, which were paid for by the company itself, and further training undertaken on the initiative of individuals, which had to be paid for by the employees themselves. Some companies also made certain financial commitments, by agreeing training budgets or paid leave (Busse and Seifert, 2009: 68 ff.). In many cases, reimbursement clauses were agreed in the event of early departure from the company in order to reduce the company's investment risks (Busse and Seifert, 2009: 77 ff.).

In a survey of 350 private sector manufacturing and service companies with more than 50 employees, Cantner et al. (2014) established a connection between the existence of works councils and further training activities. This suggests that the collective and works council agreements were both being used but they required active support from works councils. Companies with works councils invest significantly more in further training and are generally more innovative than those without (Figure 5.5).

In the 2014 bargaining round, IG Metall attempted to fortify its collective training agreements with stricter regulations, although it only managed to implement them in part, owing to a lack of support from members. Nevertheless, employees in this industry are now entitled to a training agreement with a maximum time horizon of seven years, which even allows

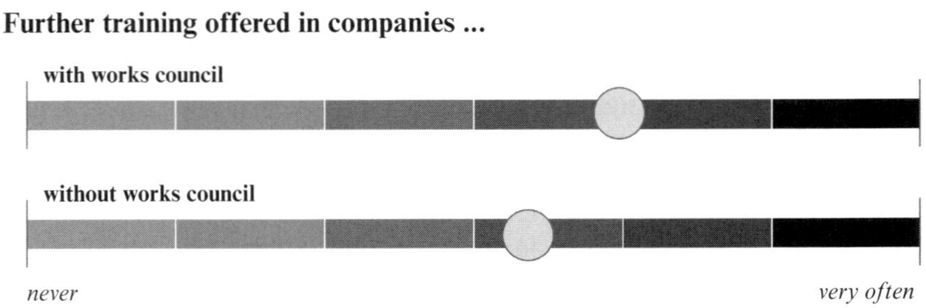

Source: Cantner et al. (2014).

Figure 5.5 Further training in companies with and without works councils, Germany

them to study for a degree. During this time, they can work part-time, take a period of leave with the right to return afterwards and save up certain elements of their pay in a training account to cover the period of absence. IG Metall has agreed a quota of 4 per cent of the workforce for the employer-subsidised partial retirement scheme, which can also be used to support employees involved in further training if the quota is not fully used up.

Together with many other agreements on flexible working times over the working life or the reconciliation of work and family life, this marks the negotiating parties' first venture into a collective bargaining and personnel policy that seeks to take into account the various phases of the life course. Its effects will become apparent only over the long term.

5.2 Dealing with the 2009 Financial Crisis

German manufacturing industry was particularly affected by the financial crisis, as it mainly produces long-lasting consumption goods (such as cars) and capital goods, the purchase of which can be easily postponed during a period of recession. With a reduction of 4.9 per cent in 2009, Germany's gross domestic product (GDP) declined more significantly than that of the United States or the United Kingdom. That said, employment and unemployment rates remained stable, as companies reduced hours, not employees.

Trade unions, employers and politicians worked together in a type of informal Coalition for Work set up in the Federal Chancellery in order to prevent job cuts. This employment miracle was made possible by a package of working time measures ranging from the depletion of accumulated working time credits, via reductions in overtime and temporary reductions in agreed weekly working times to short-time working. In the course of what were at the time very heated debates over the past 20 years, the parties to collective bargaining had developed socially acceptable models for working time flexibilisation, which paid off during the financial crisis. Additionally, they had agreed on the possibility of temporarily reducing agreed working time within a certain corridor – a measure that was reserved for times of crisis. The chemical industry had agreed a working time corridor of between 40 and 35 hours with a collectively agreed working time of 37.5 hours. In the metal industry, it was possible to temporarily reduce working time from 35 to 30 hours. Also, the introduction of short-time working became the most important state policy instrument in safeguarding industrial capacities without breaching EU aid regulations.

Even in Germany, short-time working had not been used anywhere near as intensively in earlier crises, such as the end of the dotcom bubble in the year 2000 or the 2003–04 crisis, as it was in the financial crisis. The main reason why companies changed their approach in 2009 was the negative experiences they had had in the previous two crises, which were marked by severe job cuts. At that time, the companies had become victims of their own declarations on the future of German manufacturing industry. They no longer believed that Germany had a future as a major manufacturing economy and felt they had to be significantly reduced in size. They then found that they lacked the skilled workforce to capitalise on the lengthy economic upswing between 2004 and 2008. Another factor was the strong trade unions and works councils, who wanted to negotiate alternatives to redundancies and were no longer able to use early retirement schemes as they had in the past.

Other countries, such as France, Austria, Belgium and the Netherlands, also expanded their short-time working arrangements, although they were not used anywhere near as intensively as in Germany (Figure 5.6). For example, the hierarchical nature of the French productive system probably explains why French companies used the similarly generous short-time work regulations less than German companies. French management (*cadres*) regard production workers, most of whom are semi-skilled, as largely interchangeable, so they can be let go during crises without the

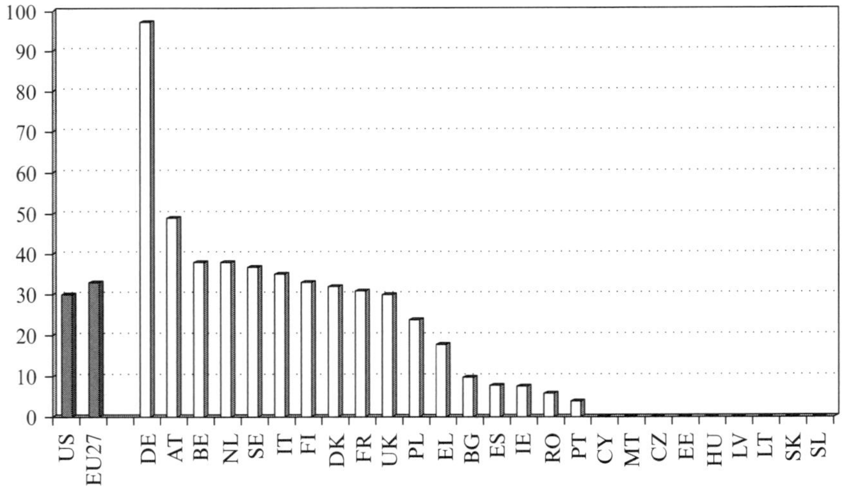

Source: Eurostat (2010).

Figure 5.6 Share of working time reductions in the reduction in the total volume of work in the EU in 2008–09

company suffering any long-term negative effects. Moreover, the trade unions and politicians did not campaign so actively to safeguard jobs but relied on early retirement, which in Germany had become too costly for companies, following several pension reforms.

The second aspect of the employment miracle – the prevention of high youth unemployment – has been completely forgotten by the public and ignored in the literature. Most European companies reacted to the crisis by freezing recruitment. Labour market outsiders were affected by this, particularly young people, among whom unemployment rates increased more than average, so that high youth unemployment became a central problem in many European countries. In Germany, by contrast, 566000 new trainees were recruited in 2009, the year of the crash (albeit this was 50000 less than the number in the previous year) (Bosch, 2011: 261 ff.). However, a complete collapse of firm-based vocational training was averted through the work of many training alliances between the social partners at the national, regional and company levels. It turned out that considering apprentices as insiders was a central advantage of the dual vocational training system. As a result, the recruitment of trainees was almost as much a priority for trade unions and works councils as safeguarding the jobs of older workers. Temporary reductions in working hours, such as those during the financial crisis, make it possible to combine both objectives even in difficult times. In many companies, apprentice recruitment was even facilitated by an increase in the share of workers on short time.

The successful management of the financial crisis has become etched in the memory of the social partners and policy-makers as a fortunate example of joint crisis management based on the mobilisation and coordination of all bargaining levels (national, industry, region and company) and may be used as a model in future crises. In any event, support for cooperative relations between the social partners among officials in the employers' associations increased considerably over 2005–06. A repeat survey of employers' association managers showed that this change is particularly pronounced in the chemical and metalworking industries, two sectors particularly affected by the financial crisis. Besides the favourable economic situation in 2012, this change can also certainly be explained by the high levels of flexibility that collective agreements now permit and the joint approach to managing the crisis (Table 5.4).

Table 5.4 Support for social partnership among employers associations' officials by trade union area, Germany (results given in percentage and absolute numbers)

Union area	2005/06			2012		
	Disagreement* in %	Agreement in %	*n*	Disagreement in %	Agreement in %	*n*
with the statement: The German social partnership is an advantage in international competition:						
IG Metall	78.4	21.6	37	25.0	75.0	24
ver.di	82.9	17.1	41	41.2	58.8	34
IG BCE	47.4	52.6	19	18.2	81.8	11
IG BAU	72.1	27.9	43	47.8	52.2	23
Other	86.7	13.3	30	22.7	77.3	22
Total	75.9	24.1	170	33.3	66.7	114
	Pearson χ^2 (4) 11 925***			Pearson χ^2 (4) 6111		

Note: * Including 'fence-sitters' who did not express a clear preference.

Source: Helfen (2013: 484).

6. CASE STUDIES

Arguably the most important innovation in the German wage-setting system has been the introduction of the statutory minimum wage, making it the obvious choice for a case study (section 6.1). The second case study focuses on an exemplary company agreement at ThyssenKruppSteel Europe on the socially responsible management of subcontractors (section 6.2).

6.1 Introduction of a Minimum Wage

In January 2015, following more than ten years of heated debate, Germany introduced a national statutory minimum wage for the first time in its history, set at €8.50 per hour. The new minimum wage was not a 'planned child' but rather was born out of necessity. For almost a decade, virtually nobody took any notice of the rapid increase in low wages and the sharp downward extension of the wage spread because all the actors concerned – including the trade unions – feared the obvious conclusion that the traditional German wage system was no longer future-proof and needed reform. Trade unions on their own were no longer powerful enough to enforce effective low-wage thresholds in many sectors. This first became clear when the government used the 2003 Hartz Acts to further expand the German low-wage sector, which at that point was already too large by international standards. The minimum wage debates then started to move beyond expert circles and became a national issue. Attempts between 2005 and 2013 to make a statutory minimum wage redundant by agreeing industry-specific minimum wages failed. This was because the employers' associations in the largest low-wage sectors were no longer able or willing to negotiate industry-specific minimum wages with the trade unions.

A joint campaign involving all trade unions for the introduction of a statutory minimum wage was deemed impossible by many observers because of the dualisation of the labour market and the irreconcilable differences between insiders and outsiders. Palier and Thelen (2010: 139) even claimed to be witnessing the emergence of 'a new (less egalitarian but possibly quite robust) equilibrium'. As proof, they cited the disputes over the minimum wage within the German trade unions, writing: 'The stronger unions are joined in their opposition to a statutory minimum wage by the main employers' federations' (Palier and Thelen, 2010: 125). Adducing the emergence of stable new power configurations as evidence, they argued that the process of change had stalled, leaving the current level of dualisation 'frozen in'. Well-protected core workforces were unaffected by labour market deregulation. They would now confine themselves to defending their own interests and were no longer in a position 'to perform the leadership functions they once did, providing collective goods for all' (Palier and Thelen, 2010: 120). Hassel was still endorsing this analysis in 2014, when all German trade unions had long been supporting the demand for a minimum wage, when she wrote: 'The capacity of service unions . . . to protect and raise wages by campaigning for a national minimum wage . . . is severely limited by the opposition of manufacturing unions' (Hassel, 2014: 72).

Undoubtedly there are tensions between the interests of labour market insiders and outsiders. However, the alleged new equilibrium has never materialised. Neither companies nor trade unions have accepted this dualism, which is more accurately characterised as a state of uncertainty in which distribution and power disputes remain unresolved. Companies attempted to capitalise on the power they had gained and attack the core workforce as well. In neoliberal insider–outsider models, their good working and employment conditions are regarded as 'unjustified privileges' that act as 'barriers' to outsiders and 'obstacles' to 'full employment'. Many core jobs were outsourced to less regulated segments of the labour market and the trade unions were forced by the threat of outsourcing into concession bargaining, with cumulative consequences for other firms. However, the negative experiences of many members of the core workforce helped actors in the strong industrial unions to build on their still extant tradition of solidarity politics and support the service unions' demand for a statutory minimum wage. The joint unions' strength then became an essential power resource in implementing the minimum wage. It was further enhanced by research as another type of resource. The recent research on minimum wages conducted in the United States and the United Kingdom, as well as in Germany, showed that minimum wages do not harm employment. This disrupted the neoliberal political narrative according to which the only choice is that between more inequality or more unemployment. A coalition of trade unions and SPD politicians succeeded in combining forces to construct a new narrative whose main theme was the fight against precarious employment and social inequality. This created the link that had hitherto been missing between the service unions' demand for a statutory minimum wage and the manufacturing unions' drive for a re-regulation of temporary agency work and the prevention of outsourcing.

For a decade, the employers' associations had fought bitterly against the introduction of a statutory minimum wage. The new minimum wage was not to mark a break with the German system of free collective bargaining but to be introduced in such a way as to maintain path dependency as far as possible. Despite all their other differences of opinion, politicians, trade unions and employers' associations were as one on this point at least. When it became clear in 2014 that employers were not able to dissuade the coalition government from moving ahead with their plans, they sought an alliance with trade unions at the last moment in order to shape the minimum wage together.

The philosophy behind the industry minimum wages – namely, to strengthen the role of the social partners and to revitalise collective bargaining – also underpinned the new minimum wage legislation. Owing to pressure from the trade unions, the Minimum Wage Act became part of a legislative package entitled the 'Act on the Strengthening of Free Collective Bargaining' (*Tarifautonomiestärkungsgesetz*) which, as well as introducing the minimum wage, is also intended to expand collective agreement coverage once more and to facilitate declarations of general enforceability. The Minimum Wage Act provided for the establishment of a minimum wage commission, which was originally to be modelled on the British example. However, the two industrial unions IG Metall and IGBCE wanted to minimise political influence on the minimum wage as far as possible and were successful in doing so. In a departure from the British model, the three representatives of each side of the social partnership are nominated by their respective organisations and are not selected as individuals by the government. The two academics on the commission are proposed by the social partners, but they do not have voting rights, unlike in the United Kingdom. The government appoints an independent chairman proposed by the social partners. The commission proposes increases in the minimum wage to government, which enacts them through statutory order but cannot alter them. Derogations from the minimum wage are possible through collective agreements that are declared generally binding.

Two important amendments were made to the legislation at the last moment as a result of a joint employer and trade union initiative. In the government's bill, the level of the minimum wage was originally to be frozen until the end of 2017. In order to prevent the minimum wage rising too sharply in 2018 and possibly causing a shock after three years of stagnation, the social partners' first amendment stipulated that the minimum wage should be increased every two years. The second amendment ensured that the benchmark for any increase in the minimum wage would be the average increases in collectively agreed rates of pay. The social partners wanted to make it clear that it should be collective bargaining that sets the pace for increases in the minimum wage. The social partners adopted this approach also in order to avoid energy-sapping disputes and votes, in which the chair ultimately casts the deciding vote. In addition to this, the commission is expected to evaluate the minimum wage and present a report to the government every two years. An office was set up in order to facilitate this process.

The minimum wage commission has further strengthened the use of average increases in collectively agreed wage rates as a benchmark in a unanimously agreed amendment to its standing orders. It was decided that a two-thirds majority vote would be required before any deviations from this formula would be permitted. As a result, the minimum wage has been virtually index linked. The first increase in the minimum wage to €8.84, which came into force on 1 January 2017, was decided unanimously in June 2016. As expected, any disputes were confined to establishing the index of agreed hourly earnings.

The minimum wage commission's first report showed that the new minimum wage regulations have led to significant wage increases in the low-paid sectors (Figure 5.7). In some cases, there have been double-digit increases for low-skilled workers in typical low-paid sectors, such as hospitality or in eastern Germany, without the reductions in employment that were forecast by many economic research institutes. The report also showed that, in April 2015, 1.36 million workers were still earning less than €8.50 per hour, half of them in mini-jobs and a further quarter in socially insured part-time work (Mindestlohnkommission, 2016). This high figure cannot be explained by the legal (workers under 18 years old and newspaper deliverers) or collectively agreed exceptions (for example, in the meat

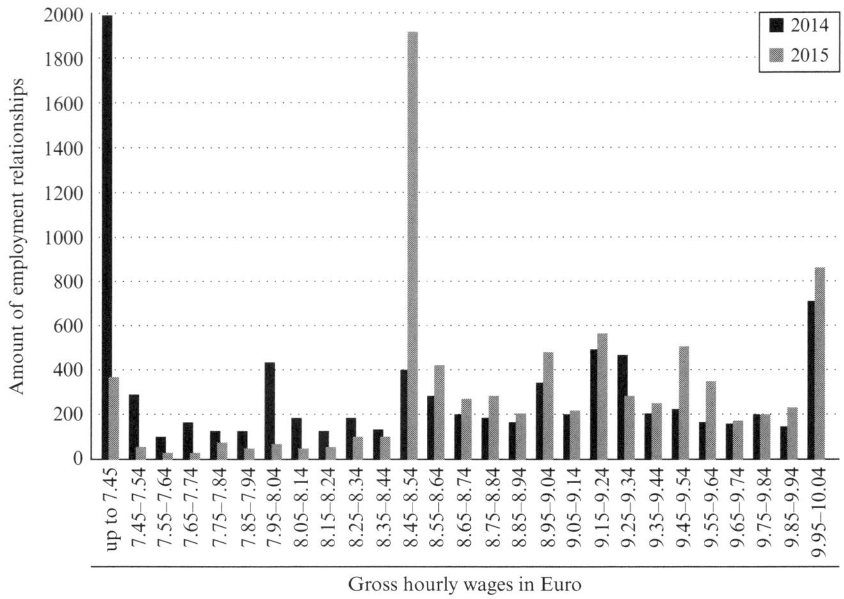

Source: Mindestlohnkommission (2016: 51).

Figure 5.7 Distribution of employment relations by hourly wage, Germany, April 2014 and 2015

processing industry and several other sectors), but suggests there are still problems with monitoring and enforcement, particularly in mini-jobs.

6.2 Socially Responsible Management of Subcontractors in the Steel Industry

One of the most important reasons for the increase in the number of badly paid workers in Germany is the outsourcing of work from firms bound by collective agreements with strong employee representation bodies to subcontractors that offer significantly worse conditions of employment. Because few collective pay agreements are declared generally binding in Germany, the German wage system is particularly susceptible to such undercutting competition.

IG Metall's 'Work – Safe and Fair' campaign has for some years been focused on improving the working and employment conditions of subcontractors' employees. 'Campaign' means that resources are made available that were released for new priority issues and campaigns at union headquarters by staffing cutbacks in the years prior to the launch of the campaign. This campaign is organised on a national basis, with the local union branches giving prominence to different issues. Union headquarters provide information material and action guidelines. Examples of activities in this campaign include the very successful organisation of subcontractors in the Leipzig automotive cluster (IG Metall, n.d.).

Another example is the steel industry, in which the trade unions are highly organised. It is the only industry in which the unions have succeeded in negotiating a collective agreement, signed in 2010, providing for equal pay for equal work for all temporary agency workers. In 2014, standards governing the working and employment conditions of all agency workers were agreed. It was settled that existing collective agreements and legislation, on minimum wages, health and safety and working time, among other things, should be observed. In addition, work councils were given a greater voice in decision-making. Employees of subcontractor companies have a right of complaint to the works councils of the steel companies that awarded the contract. Moreover, before a contract is awarded, checks have to be carried out and the works council consulted in order to ascertain whether it would be technically and economically feasible for the work to be carried out by the company's own workforce.

The employers' willingness to agree to this collective agreement was also strengthened by the legislation that had already been enacted which established the principle of general contractors' liability in the event of failure to pay the industry minimum wages that had been in force since 2007, notably in the cleaning and security industries and various construction trades. It was also foreseeable that this liability would be extended to the national minimum wage which at the time was going through the consultation process in the German Parliament.

A collective agreement of this kind cannot be given substance unless it is systematically incorporated into company procedures and the decision-making processes in the various departments that deal with subcontractors, and unless subcontractors' compliance with standards is monitored and any infringements are sanctionable (Jaehrling et al., 2016).

This was investigated by taking the example of ThyssenKrupp Stelle AG Europe (TKSE), which employs 20 000 people, most of them at seven locations in North Rhine-Westphalia.[3] On average, the company issues contracts for between 300 000 and 400 000 hours' work each month and has between 1500 and 5000 subcontractors' employees working at its various sites. The figure varies because the number naturally rises sharply when major repairs are being carried out. Monitoring of the subcontractors' working and employment conditions did not begin with the signing of the collective agreement, because regular negotiations with

Table 5.5 Accident rate at ThyssenKruppSteel Europe (TKSE) and its subcontractors*

	2012–13	2013–14	2014–15	2015–16
TKSE	7.1	5.4	6.0	5.8
Subcontractors	20.3	13.6	9.4	8.8

Note: * 1 – *n* days lost per million hours worked.

Source: Statistics supplied by TKSE, 2016.

the works council on the use of outside contractors had been going on since 2001.

Responsibility for dealing with this issue at company level lies with the HR director who, as provided for in the Act on Codetermination in the Iron, Steel and Coal Industry (Montanmitbestimmungsgesetz), is elected on the suggestion of the employee representatives on the supervisory board. The HR director in this case was eager to call attention to the extraordinarily high accident rate among the outside companies (see Table 5.5), to the new liability risks and also to the possible reputational damage the company might suffer because of the scandalous treatment of subcontractor labour on TKSE's premises. In doing so, he was able to obtain the support of the entire supervisory board and the board of directors for a change of direction in subcontractor management. The unanimous commitment of the entire board of directors was a precondition for the implementation of fair labour standards in the departments managed by other board members, particularly in the purchasing department.

In 2014, a new organisational unit with the title of 'Responsible Subcontractor Management' was set up in one of the HR director's departments; its staff of four work together with the health and safety and works security departments to implement social standards in subcontractor companies. Since then, subcontractor companies have been known as 'partner firms', the intention being that standards should be discussed and implemented jointly with them. The most important elements of the new subcontractor management system can be summarised as follows:

- The compilation of a code of conduct for partner firms, in which it is stipulated that safety regulations and the relevant legislation and collective agreements must be adhered to. Furthermore, TKSE has the right to carry out spot checks on-site at any time. The code of conduct has now become a binding contractual element in the commissioning process.

- The incorporation of social standards into purchasing procedures. The various purchasing departments are given advice when invitations to tender are being issued and contracts are awarded. Some bids that are clearly incompatible with compliance with the law are rejected in the preliminary stages.
- Training; some 1000 managers have received training in this area to date. The training focuses on the code of conduct and its implementation in the company's daily routines, as well as on contract-compliant behaviour on the part of managers. Thus they are not allowed to give agency workers any instructions, because those workers could otherwise institute a claim as TKSE employees. The training sessions also provide an opportunity to exchange information about possible abuses.
- Information and advice for partner firms. A so-called 'partners' day' is held each year, which is attended by some 300 people. Staff from the health and safety, responsible subcontractor management and works security departments explain the compliance rules and offer advice to subcontractors.
- The right of complaint for subcontractors' employees. These workers are kept informed of their rights by means of a 'Fair Play' poster campaign and have a hotline at their disposal for making complaints. Up until now, it has in practice been mainly TKSE employees who have brought abuses to management's attention.
- On-site checks. Complaints are followed up and subcontractors must provide explanations where necessary. Spot checks are also carried out, as well as further inspections by health and safety, subcontractor management and works security staff.
- Sanctions; there are escalation procedures in the event of infringements. A yellow card issued by health and safety staff constitutes a warning to cease the behaviour for which the subcontractor has been reprimanded. A red card leads to termination of the contractual relationship. The purchasing department has similar procedures in place.

In practice, a cultural change has been under way since 2014. Subcontractor management is no longer simply the preserve of the personnel department but part of the entire company's compliance policy. The initial resistance from the sales departments, which were used to accepting the lowest bids without checking social standards, has been replaced by close cooperation with the subcontractor management unit. Most infringements are remedied following consultation and advice. Four companies have been given a red card, as have individual subcontractor employees for infringements such as driving too fast on the factory premises. In the case of violations of the law, such as not paying the statutory minimum wage, the company cooperates with external agencies such as the German customs authorities, who are responsible for enforcing the minimum wage legislation.

Parallel efforts by IG Metall to organise subcontractor employees and to negotiate collective agreements in the subcontractor companies are also of significance; at the Duisburg plant, a project secretary has even been appointed. One of the subcontractors systematically blocked the election of a works council and was asked to file a report to TKSE because that constituted a violation of the Works Constitution Act. In the end, a works council was elected.

Subcontractors' accident figures have been reduced significantly. When they recently rose again temporarily as a result of several falls, the board of directors decided to toughen the escalation procedures for health and safety violations. Subcontractors that do not install guardrails or safety barriers now receive a red card immediately. It has now become clear that the subcontractor management unit is understaffed; its heavy workload means its staff have virtually no time for on-site checks. Staffing levels in the unit are to be increased in the foreseeable future.

Besides the positive results, the case study also reveals the limits of this approach. First, the outsourcing of jobs has reached such a pitch that only a certain proportion of the infringements can be stopped with this system of subcontractor management. Secondly, in many sectors in Germany – this applies particularly to the outsourced activities – there are now few companies bound by collective agreements, so that, in practice, only compliance with the minimum wage but not with collective agreements can be monitored. This could be changed only by making collective agreements generally binding.

However, because large firms, with their cost-driven outsourcing of good jobs, are one of the most important creators of bad work, a change in the behaviour of the large commissioning companies is a crucial lever in improving working and employment conditions. In particular, employees and trade unions can make use of their position in large companies, which remains strong, in order to 'lend power' to weaker employers in subcontractor companies and improve their employment conditions. It is important to note that this is in their own interest as well, because it will help to slow down the outsourcing of good jobs. The state can be interested only in binding compliance arrangements in this area, because the retrospective monitoring it carries out in respect of the minimum wage, for example, means it is not in a position to monitor compliance with labour laws. By exposing commissioning firms to liability risks, the state can increase firms' willingness to commit themselves to a greater degree of social responsibility in the value-added chain. However, such a commitment cannot be put into practice unless there is a change of culture in the relevant companies, with all departments taking joint responsibility for socially sustainable subcontractor management, which is in permanent conflict with corporate cost-reduction targets.

7. CONCLUSION

The development of the German wage-setting system since 1990 demonstrates that income inequality increases rapidly as an inclusive wage-setting system is eroded – a lesson that has already been learned in other countries. Germany's autonomous wage-setting system has been particularly vulnerable to these developments because in many sectors the high level of coverage by collective agreement was not a result of primary trade union power, that is, high trade union density. In many industries and companies, it was based solely on high employer association density rates, without the trade unions having the power to enforce coverage by collective agreement.

Membership of employers' associations began to crumble in the changed social and economic environment following German reunification, which was actively promoted by policy-makers through product and labour market deregulation. Political pressure on the most important institutions of the German industrial relations – the collective bargaining and codetermination systems – also increased. Trade unions had to accept derogation clauses in their collective agreements, but then increased their influence in those sectors with high density rates by involving members in company-level bargaining.

Collective agreements and works councils were now disappearing from broad swathes of the economy and, as a result, income inequality increased rapidly. The share of low wage workers grew to the highest level in the EU and, since there was no minimum wage to put a floor under pay levels, the wage spread in Germany plunged downwards to a greater extent than in any other EU member state.

Nevertheless, social dialogue continued to play a central role in Germany and in recent years has revived. Trade unions remained strong in many industries and companies, and they were able to negotiate innovative collective agreements dealing with fundamental social and economic issues. These agreements now play a guiding role for some non-union organised industries and companies. It was possible to reach good compromises between the interests of employers and employees on standard issues in the European flexicurity dialogue. Particularly worth mentioning in this regard are company working time models that give companies more flexibility, while at the same time giving employees greater freedom of choice over the course of their working lives, thereby making it easier to reconcile career and family life. Also worth noting are agreements on support for individual further training and employability. The joint management of the financial crisis by means of innovative working time systems and the recruitment of more than 540 000 trainees in the midst of the crisis, in order to prevent youth unemployment from rising, marked a milestone in the revitalisation of social dialogue. This crisis management through dialogue at every level (national, industrial, regional and company) etched itself on the memory of the social partners, who were all proud of this success. In any event, it certainly improved the employers' associations' attitudes towards social partnership and the social partners, and is perhaps the blueprint to follow in the next crisis.

The introduction of the statutory minimum wage was very controversial for a long time, even among some trade unions who did not want state intervention in wage setting, which they saw as their domain. The new minimum wage was then implemented, following a joint campaign by all trade unions and some political parties, against the will of the employers. However, when it could no longer be prevented, the employers' associations joined forces with the trade unions to help shape the legislation. The minimum wage has therefore been placed in the hands of the social partners to a much greater extent than in almost all other European countries – with the exception of Belgium and pre-2012 Greece.

However, the strengthening of social dialogue in recent years should not blind us to the fact that wages have increasingly become a competitive factor owing to the decrease in collective agreement coverage, with bad wages squeezing out good wages and even worse wages squeezing out bad wages. The growth of mini-jobs – the least regulated, most precarious form of employment – is a good example of the enormous energy companies constantly put into seeking out gaps in the wage system for the purpose of 'institutional avoidance' (Jaehrling and Mehaut 2013). The new minimum wage only sets a floor on this wage competition and cannot by itself prevent the undercutting of more generous collective agreements. This can only be prevented by restricting certain forms of precarious work, such as mini-jobs, and increasing collective agreement coverage.

NOTES

1. Unlike in the United States, laws such as those in the EU determine the level of sick pay, the length of paid holidays or payment for time off during public holidays. The minimum legal standards are improved in collective agreements in some cases, such as the length

of paid holidays, which is six weeks in the majority of German industry-level collective bargaining agreements – two weeks more than the legal minimum entitlement.
2. The authors have not used the standard low-wage threshold of two-thirds of the median wage here, as they wanted to calculate the effects of a European minimum wage, which is set at 60 per cent of the median wage.
3. For the purposes of the case study, interviews were conducted with the industrial relations director, works councillors and employees in the 'subcontractor management' unit, founded in 2014.

REFERENCES

Addison, J., P. Teixeira, K. Evers and L. Bellmann (2014), 'Indicative and updated estimates of the collective bargaining premium in Germany', *Industrial Relations*, **53** (1), 125–56.
Addison, J.T., P. Teixeira, K. Evers and L. Bellmann (2015), 'Pacts for employment and competitiveness as a role model? Their effects on firm performance', IZA Discussion Paper No. 9323, Institute of Labor Economics, Bonn.
Amlinger, M. (2014), 'Bestimmungsfaktoren der individuellen Verdiensthöhe', WSI Report No. 20, Düsseldorf.
Amlinger, M. and R. Bispinck (2013), 'Tarifbindung in Deutschland Ergebnisse der Verdienststrukturerhebung (VSE)', WSI Arbeitspapier 1/2013, Düsseldorf.
Bahnmüller, R. and M. Hoppe (2012), 'Von den Mühen der Ebenen: Wirkungen tarifvertraglicher Weiterbildungsregelungen im öffentlichen Dienst und in der Metall- und Elektroindustrie im Vergleich', *Industrielle Beziehungen*, **19** (1), 7–30.
Behrens, M. (2013), 'Arbeitgeberverbände – auf dem Weg in den Dualismus?', *WSI Mitteilungen*, **66** (7), 473–81.
Behrens, M. and H. Driebbusch (2014), 'Angriffe auf die betriebliche Mitbestimmung', *WSI Mitteilungen*, **67** (2), 140–48.
Berthold, N., M. Brischke and O. Stettes (2003), 'Betriebliche Bündnisse für Arbeit – Gratwanderung zwischen Tarifbruch und Tariftreue, Wirtschaftswissenschaftliche', Working Paper 64, Beiträge des Lehrstuhls für Volkswirtschaftslehre, Wirtschaftsordnung und Sozialpolitik, University of Würzburg.
Bispinck, R. (2017), 'WSI-Tarifarchiv 2016', Statistisches Taschenbuch, Tarifpolitik, Düsseldorf.
Böckler-Impuls (2016), 'Wie Firmen die Mitbestimmung aushebeln', *Böckler-Impuls*, 6/2016.
Bosch, G. (2011), 'The German labour market after the financial crisis: miracle or just a good policy mix?', in D. Vaughan-Whitehead (ed.), *Work Inequalities in the Crisis: Evidence from Europe*, Cheltenham, UK and Geneva: Edward Elgar and ILO, pp. 243–77.
Bosch, G. (2013), 'Public sector adjustments in Germany: from cooperative to competitive federalism', in D. Vaughan-Whitehead (ed.), *Public Sector Shock: The Impact of Policy Retrenchment in Europe*, Cheltenham, UK and Geneva: Edward Elgar and ILO, pp. 214–58.
Bosch, G.,N., Engelhardt, K. Hermann, I. Kurz-Scherf and H. Seifert (1988), *Arbeitszeitverkürzung im Betrieb. Die Umsetzung der 38,5-Stunden Woche in der Metall-, Druck- und Holzindustrie sowie im Einzelhandel*, Cologne: Bund-Verlag.
Bosch, G. and C. Weinkopf (2016), 'Minijobs. Eine Expertise für die Sachverständ

igenkommission Zweiter Gleichstellungsbericht', Institute for Work, Skills and Training, Duisburg.
Bosch, G., K. Mayhew and J. Gautié (2010), 'Industrial relations, legal regulations, and wage setting', in J. Gautié and J. Schmitt (eds), *Low-Wage Work in the Wealthy World*, New York: Russell Sage, pp. 147–82.
Busse, G. and H. Seifert (2009), 'Tarifliche und betriebliche Regelungen zur beruflichen Weiterbildung. Eine explorative Studie – Gutachten für das Bundesministerium für Bildung und Forschung', Edition Hans-Böckler-Stiftung No. 233, Düsseldorf.
Cantner, U., W. Gerstlberger and R. Ipsita (2014), 'Works councils, training activities and innovation: a study of German firms', Jena Economic Research Paper No. 6.
Carlin, W. and D. Soskice (2009), 'German economic performance: disentangling the role of supply-side reforms, macroeconomic policy and coordinated economy institutions', *Socio-Economic Review*, **7** (1), 67–99.
Crouch, C. and H. Farrell (2002), 'Breaking the path of institutional development? Alternatives to the new determinism', EUI Working Paper SPS No. 2002/4, European University Institute, Florence.
Destatis (2014), *Finanzen und Steuern. Personal des öffentlichen Dienstes*, specialist series 14, vol. 6.
Driebbusch, H., S. Lehndorff and T. Schulten (2017), 'Two worlds of unionism? German manufacturing and service unions', in H. Driebbusch, S. Lehndorff and T. Schulten (eds), *Rough Waters: European Trade Unions in a Time Of Crises*, Brussels: European Trade Union Institute.
Ellguth, P. and S. Kohaut (2014), 'Öffnungsklauseln – Instrument zur Krisenbewältigung oder Steigerung der Wettbewerbsfähigkeit?', *WSI Mitteilungen*, **67** (6), 439–49.
Ellguth, P. and S. Kohaut (2015), 'Tarifbindung und betriebliche Interessenvertretung: Ergebnisse aus dem IAB-Betriebspanel 2014', *WSI Mitteilungen*, **68** (4), 290–97.
Eurostat (2010), *National Accounts*, Luxembourg: Eurostat.
Fernández-Macías, E. and Vacas-Soriano, C. (2013), *A Coordinated EU Minimum Wage Policy?* Dublin: Eurofound.
Fischer, G., S. Gundert, S. Kawalec, F. Sowa, J. Stegmaier, K. Tesching, et al. (2015), 'Situation atypisch Beschäftigter und Arbeitszeitwünsche von Teilzeitbeschäftigten – Quantitative und qualitative Erhebung sowie begleitende Forschung IAB', Forschungsprojekt im Auftrag des Bundesministeriums für Arbeit und Soziales, Nuremberg.
Geiger, T. (1949), *Die Klassengesellschaft in Schmelztiegel*, Cologne: Kiepenheuer.
Greifenstein, R., L. Kißler and H. Lange (2011), *Trendreport Betriebsratswahlen 2010*, Hans-Böckler-Stiftung Arbeitspapier 231, Düsseldorf.
Haipeter, T. (2011), 'Unbound employers' associations and derogations: erosion and renewal of collective bargaining in the German metalworking industry', *Industrial Relations*, **42** (2), 174–94.
Haipeter, T. and S. Lehndorff (2009), 'Collective bargaining on employment', Dialogue Working Paper No. 3, International Labour Office, Industrial and Employment Relations Department, Geneva.
Hanau, P. (2006), 'Das Rätsel Minijob', *Neue Zeitschrift für Arbeitsrecht, Zweiwochenschrift für die betriebliche Praxis*, **15**, 809–11.
Hans-Böckler-Stiftung (HBS) (2017), 'Grafik zur Entwicklung der Anzahl der mitbestimmten Unternehmen seit 1981', Düsseldorf, accessed 9 November 2017 at https://www.boeckler.de/66942.htm.

Hans-Böckler-Stiftung (HBS) (2016), 'Zahlen und Fakten Betriebsräte in Deutsch land', Düsseldorf, accessed 10 August 2016 at http://www.boeckler.de/5306.htm.
Hassel, A. (2014), 'The paradox of liberalization – understanding dualism and the recovery of the German political economy', *British Journal of Industrial Relations*, **52** (1), 57–81.
Helfen, M. (2013), 'Sozialpartnerschaft bei Arbeitgeberverbänden: "Schnee von gestern" oder vor der Renaissance?', *WSI Mitteilungen*, **66** (7), 482–90.
Institut für Arbeitsmarkt- und Berufsforschung (IAB) (2012), 'Arbeitszeitwünsche', accessed on 18 August 2016 at http://doku.iab.de/arbeitsmarktdaten/arbeitszeit wuensche.pdf.
IG Metall (n.d.), 'Zur Lage der Beschäftigten bei industriellen Dienstleistern. Wege zu einem gemeinsamen tariflichen Ordnungsrahmen', Sozialreport Automobilcluster Leipzig, accessed 2 December 2016 at http://www.fokus-werkvertraege.de/w/files/igm031/studien/sozialreport_automobilcluster_leipzig.pdf.
Jaehrling, K. and P. Méhaut (2013), 'Varieties of institutional avoidance: employers' strategies in low-waged service sector occupations in France and Germany', *Socio-Economic Review*, **11** (4), 687–710.
Jaehrling, K., I. Wagner and C. Weinkopf (2016), 'Reducing precarious work in Europe through social dialogue: the case of Germany', report produced for the EC project 'Reducing precarious work in Europe through social dialogue', DG Employment, Social Affairs and Equal Opportunities Project VP/2014/004 (Industrial Relations and Social Dialogue), with the support of T. Kalina and G. Bosch, European Commission, Employment, Social Affairs and Inclusion DG V, Brussels.
Kalina, T. and C. Weinkopf (2014), 'Niedriglohnbeschäftigung 2012 und was ein gesetzlicher Mindestlohn von 8,50 € verändern könnte', IAQ Report 2014-02, Institute for Work, Skills and Training, Duisburg.
Korpi, W. (2006), 'Power resources and employer-centered approaches in explanations of welfare states and varieties of capitalism: protagonists, consenters, and antagonists', *World Politics*, **58** (2), 167–206.
Lèvesque, C. and G. Murray (2010), 'Understanding union power: resources and capabilities for renewing union capacity', *European Review of Labour and Research*, **16** (3), 333–50.
Mindestlohnkommission (2016), 'Erster Bericht zu den Auswirkungen des gesetzlichen Mindestlohns', Berlin, accessed 16 August 2016 at http://www.mindestlohn-kommission.de/DE/Bericht/pdf/Bericht2016.html?nn=7081728.
Nicklich, M. and M. Helfen (2013), *Wirtschaftsverbände in Deutschland: Mitgliedergewinnung und -bindung als zentrale Herausforderung*, Kurzstudie des Lehrstuhls für Unternehmenskooperation im Management-Department der Freien Universität Berlin. accessed 18 August 2016 at http://www.wiwiss.fuberlin.de/fachbereich/bwl/management/sydow/media/pdf/Wirtschaftsverbaende-2013_Nicklich_Helfen.pdf.
Ok, W. and P. Tergeist (2003), 'Improving worker's skills: analytical evidence and the role of the social partners', OECD Social, Employment and Migration Working Paper No. 10, Paris.
OECD (1996), *Employment Outlook*, Paris: OECD.
Palier, B. and K. Thelen (2010), 'Institutionalizing dualism: complementarities and change in France and Germany', *Politics & Society*, **38** (1), 119–48.
Sachverständigenkommission zur Erstellung des Ersten Gleichstellungsberichtes der Bundesregierung (SEEGB) (2011), 'Neue Wege – Gleiche Chancen.

Gleichstellung von Frauen und Männern im Lebensverlauf, Gutachten der Sachverständigenkommission an das Bundesministerium für Familie, Senioren, Frauen und Jugend für den Ersten Gleichstellungsbericht der Bundesregierung', Essen and Munich.

Salverda, W. and K. Mayhew (2009), 'Capitalist economies and wage inequality', *Oxford Review of Economic Policy*, **25** (1), 126–54.

Schroeder, W. and B. Ruppert (1996), *Austritte aus Arbeitgeberverbänden. Eine Gefahr für das deutsche Modell?* Marburg: Schüren.

Sniekers, F. (2011), *The Changing Impact of Labour Market Institutions on Earnings Inequality, a Study of the Effects of Trade Unions and the Minimum Wage in Advanced Industrial Countries since the 1980s*, Amsterdam: Tinbergen Institute.

Tullius, K, and H. Wolf (2012), 'Legitimationsprobleme im System industrieller Beziehungen: Krise oder Revitalisierung des sozialpartnerschaftlichen Geistes?', *Industrielle Beziehungen*, **19** (4), 367–410.

Visser, J. (2015), *Institutional Characteristics of Trade Unions, Wage Setting, State Intervention and Social Pacts (ICTWSS). An International Database*, Amsterdam: Amsterdam Institute for Advanced Labour Studies.

Wetzel, D. (2012), *Mehr Gerechtigkeit wagen. Der Weg eines Gewerkschafters*, Hamburg: Hoffmann & Campe.

Wetzel, D. (ed.) (2013), *Organizing. Die Veränderung der gewerkschaftlichen Praxis durch das Prinzip Beteiligung*, Hamburg: VSA.

WSI Tarifarchiv (2015), *Statistik Tarifbindung*, Düsseldorf, accessed 16 August 2016 at http://www.boeckler.de/wsi-tarifarchiv_2257.htm.

6. Industrial relations, imposed flexibility and inequality during the Greek Great Depression

Maria Karamessini and Stefanos Giakoumatos

1. INTRODUCTION

Inequalities in the world of work have both structural and institutional determinants. Tenure in the public sector, higher market power and productivity in big private firms or higher profits in dynamic rather than in declining sectors have always been a favourable ground on which unionism has developed and obtained higher earnings and better working conditions for employees. However, the particular type of industrial relations and social dialogue – that is, the forms of collective organisation and action, as well as the distinctive roles and interaction of the state and social partners in wage determination and employment regulation – constitutes an independent determinant factor with regard to inequalities in earnings, employment and working conditions among employees.

In this chapter we study the effects of industrial relations and social dialogue on inequality among employees in Greece, a country in which state intervention was the dominant feature of post-war industrial relations, diminished after the fall of the Colonels' Dictatorship in 1974 but remained important until the end of the 1980s. In the 1990s and 2000s national-level bargaining on the minimum wage, as well as on sectoral or occupational wage grids was the main level of a multi-layered and articulated collective bargaining system that allowed for real wage increases in line with productivity, but also widening earnings differentials. Given the failed attempts to develop an effective tripartite social dialogue, trade unions have successfully resisted several policy measures promoting labour market flexibility and maintained security in the formal labour market. Industrial relations were radically transformed within the recent prolonged crisis, leading to wage devaluation and a decrease in labour costs in the business sector of the economy and fiscal consolidation in the public sector.

In Greece, as in many other Southern European countries, public/

private and formal/informal sectors, along with large/small firms have been the three main divides along which labour market segmentation was constructed in the post-war years and was maintained until recently. The current crisis has blurred these demarcation lines because of the collapse of the traditional industrial relations system. While in the past the latter had, in different phases or at the same time, reduced and augmented inequalities in the world of work, its recent dismantling also has contradictory effects on inequalities, for instance, by narrowing wage differentials across pre-existing divides while reinforcing the public/private sector divide with regard to employment security and precariousness. The process of reshaping inequalities in the new context of industrial relations is ongoing, and the direction of change is shifting according to the second-order effects of radical institutional change. At the same time, the final form of the collective bargaining system is under negotiation between the Greek government on the one hand and the European institutions and the International Monetary Fund (IMF) on the other, under the third Economic Adjustment Programme of Greece.

In this chapter we examine the role of industrial relations in Greece – namely, those of key institutions, such as collective bargaining and tripartite social dialogue, and actors – in determining the extent and forms of labour market flexibility and security, and in generating inequalities in employment and working conditions between different groups of workers. The chapter is divided into five sections, including the introduction. In section 2 we study how the industrial relations system before the recent economic crisis and the rupture in this system that occurred during the ongoing Greek Great Depression from 2008 onwards have impacted upon and shaped the long-term trend in wage inequalities. Section 3 is dedicated to an analysis of the trends in flexibility, security and non-wage inequalities in connection with the changes in industrial relations described in the previous section. The two case studies in section 4 enrich the analysis of the national triangular relationship of 'industrial relations – labour market flexibility/security – inequalities in the world of work' by extending it to an intermediate level. The first case study, in section 4.1, focuses on the first of the main labour market segmentation dividing lines, namely, the public/private sector divide. The second case study, in section 4.2, deals with the youth/non-youth divide which was brought to the fore with the establishment of a special minimum wage for employees under 25 years of age in 2012. Both case studies are preoccupied with the effects of radical institutional change on hollowing out or blurring the boundaries of the labour market segments during the prolonged and structural economic crisis the country has been enduring since 2008. Section 5 concludes and discusses relevant policy issues.

2. INDUSTRIAL RELATIONS, SOCIAL DIALOGUE AND WAGE INEQUALITIES BEFORE AND AFTER THE GREEK GREAT DEPRESSION

In this section we study the interrelationship between industrial relations and wage inequality before and after 2008, the year the ongoing structural economic crisis in Greece erupted. There is no previous research on this issue. Given that tripartite social dialogue has never gained ground in determining employment and working conditions in the country, our analysis is necessarily limited to the impact of the collective bargaining system on wage inequality trends first in the 1990s and 2000s and then from 2008 until today. In so doing, we will try to deal with issues such as how industrial relations are aiming to address wage inequalities, as well as how trade unions have contributed to this issue and what they have achieved in this respect. The Greek Great Depression and radical change in industrial relations during 2010–13 have triggered contradictory forces that at first resulted in compressing wage inequalities, whereas now they are pushing towards their expansion.

2.1 Industrial Relations in the 1990s and 2000s: What Contribution to Wage Inequality?

Strong state intervention was a dominant feature of the post-war industrial relations system established in 1955. Labour law regulated employment and working conditions, while state intervention in wage determination consisted of the control of wage increases and the extension of collective agreements by the Minister of Labour and of compulsory arbitration whose outcomes were determined by the board members nominated by the state. After the fall of the Colonels' Dictatorship (1967–1974) state intervention was relaxed but remained strong until the late 1980s, a period characterised by extremely adversarial and highly politicised industrial relations and a lack of social dialogue institutions. State-controlled compulsory arbitration and the extension mechanism were maintained and a system of automatic indexation of wages to inflation was put in place in 1982.

The 1990s and 2000s saw an overhaul of the system of collective bargaining, the restriction of state intervention in wage-setting to the extension of collective agreements, a decrease in strike activity and union density, a move towards more consensual industrial relations and attempts to introduce tripartite social dialogue.

2.1.1 From adversarial to more consensual industrial relations but weak tripartite social dialogue

As also happened in Spain and Portugal in the mid-1970s, the fall of the Colonels' Dictatorship in Greece opened up a period of rising unionism and intensive industrial action. From 1974 through to the 1980s industrial relations were extremely adversarial. Although highly politicised and internally divided into factions, Greek unions remained unitary, unlike their counterparts in Italy, Spain and Portugal. The 1990s and 2000s saw a decrease in strike activity, while union density fell from 37.6 per cent in 1992 to 23.5 per cent in 2008.[1]

The recession of 1990–93, the ideological impact of the collapse of the communist bloc on the union factions of the left and the accession to power of a liberal government that remained in office during 1990–93 contributed to a turn by the majority of trade unionists towards a social-partnership approach to industrial relations. European Union (EU) integration has been an additional determinant of the gradual decline in industrial relations conflict. Its influence has been exerted through the establishment of social dialogue institutions and the achievement of social consensus on the country's entry into the Economic and Monetary Union (EMU), which persuaded trade unions to make moderate wage claims (Kouzis, 2002). The Economic and Social Committee (OKE) was founded in 1994 as a tripartite body whose mission is not only to conduct social dialogue on economic and social policy issues, but also to give the government an opinion on bills and legislative proposals referred to it. However, social dialogue has culminated in only one social pact since the creation of OKE.

2.1.2 Wage determination through multi-layered and articulated collective bargaining

Wage determination in Greece was the joint outcome of collective bargaining and state intervention from the mid-1950s until recently. National-level negotiations over the National General Collective Agreement (NGCA) between the General Confederation of Greek Labour (GSEE) and peak employer organisations have been the core element of the collective bargaining system. This is because the NGCA set the floor not only for wages (national minimum wage), but also for all the other employment and working conditions and rights (working time, leaves, rights of part-timers, apprentices, student workers, equal treatment, funding of training, severance pay and so on) of employees working under private-law labour contracts in the economy as a whole. National-level collective bargaining on sectoral or occupational minima was the second most important feature of the wage-setting system, while company-level bargaining was added to this level after 1974 and company-level agreements always improved over sectoral and occupational minima. Collective bargaining on wages only excluded civil servants, whose wages have always been determined directly by the government.

State intervention is the second basic feature of the wage determination system. Until the end of the 1980s its role was to make collective bargaining outcomes compatible with the income policy targets, either through direct control of wages or through state-controlled compulsory arbitration, which was established in 1955. Also, in 1982 a system of automatic indexation of wages to inflation was put in place but abolished in 1990. In the same year, a law on 'free' collective bargaining replaced compulsory arbitration by independent third-party mediation and arbitration and introduced the favourability clause for company versus sectoral collective agreements. However, the Ministry of Labour kept its prerogative to extend collective agreements to non-unionised employees and employers, limiting state intervention to this particular form.

As a result of its above-described features, the Greek wage determination system of the 1990s and 2000s combined high coverage of employees by collective agreements, which reached 83 per cent in 2008 (ILO, 2015), with a system of multi-layered articulated collective bargaining that reinforced employees' bargaining power.

As in Spain during the 1990s and much of the 2000s, the national minimum wage operated in 'distant coexistence' with the basic wage rates negotiated in collective agreements (Grimshaw and Bosch, 2013: 59) and its coverage in the official labour market was very low. Less than 1 per cent of employees in firms with ten or more employees were paid up to 105 per cent of the minimum wage in 2010 (OECD, 2015: 44, fig. 1.13) and this rate would remain low even if employees from small firms were included. However, national bargaining on the national minimum wage was extremely important in two respects (Karamessini and Grimshaw, 2017). First and foremost, minimum wage increases functioned as a minimum standard for national sector- and occupation-level bargaining. In practice, bargaining rounds were articulated, with those over the NGCA and collective agreements in public utilities and the banking sector taking the lead. Depending on their bargaining power and the particular conditions in their industry or occupation, unions customarily set their target increases somewhere in between minimum wage increases and those achieved by the most powerful public utilities and banking federations. They were assisted in their claims by the Mediation and Arbitration Agency, which intervened in case of industrial conflict and when called upon by weak unions. In the late 1990s, the bargaining rounds between management and the strong unions in public utilities and banking were decoupled from the bipartite fixing of the national minimum wage. A basic mechanism of articulated bargaining and wage drift was thus broken (Ioannou, 2000). However, public utilities and banking remained in the 2000s – as in the 1980s and 1990s – the strongholds of the union movement and dominated the leadership of the GSEE. General strikes supported by these unions were often used to reinforce the GSEE's bargaining power during negotiations on the national minimum wage. A second reason for the importance of the national minimum wage during the 1990s and 2000s was that it constituted a reference point for individual bargaining on pay in the relatively large informal labour market, similar to evidence in other countries of the 'lighthouse effect' of minimum wages (Boeri et al., 2010). Informality is a structural feature of the Greek labour market but the massive inflow of migrants after the collapse of the communist regimes in Eastern Europe and the Balkans further expanded informal work from the beginning of the 1990s to the onset of the current crisis. However, the rapid growth of the economy through 1994–2008, the pressures of competition in the European Single Market and the lack of low-skilled labour in certain sectors have constituted important pull factors of immigration.

Alongside constant and robust productivity growth, the above-described wage determination system combining multi-layered and articulated collective bargaining with governmental wage policy in public administration allowed for a steady increase in real compensation per employee between 1993 and 2009, amounting to 55 per cent in cumulative terms.

2.1.3 The wage determination system and trends in wage inequalities, 1993–2008

Our elaboration of European Community Household Panel (ECHP) and European Union Statistics on Income and Living Conditions (EU-SILC) microdata on net annual earnings of employees shows a substantial increase in overall individual wage inequality measured by the decile 9-to-decile 1 ratio between 1993 and 2008, but with a decline from 2006 and a parallel but smoother trend in wage inequality among full-time employees (Figure 6.1).

The wage determination system has greatly influenced the trend in wage inequality among full-time employees which, first and foremost, has followed closely the uninterrupted fall in the Kaitz index until 2004 and, with some delay, the rise in the Kaitz index afterwards (Figure 6.2). As minimum wage increases were taken by private sector unions as the floor in their negotiations with employers on basic wage rates in different sectors and occupations, the collective bargaining system has contributed to growing wage dispersion in the bottom half of the wage distribution and to the fall in the Kaitz index until 2004. The rise in the Kaitz index after 2004 has been due to the large increases in the minimum wage achieved by the GSEE

Source: Authors' elaboration of ECHP microdata (years 1993 and 1999) and EU-SILC microdata (years 2002–14).

Figure 6.1 Wage inequality, Greece, 1993–2014 (interdecile ratios of net annual earnings)

through negotiations with employer organisations on the NGCA coupled with lower increases in basic wages obtained by sector and occupational unions. We can thus deduce that the large relative increases in the minimum wage between 2004 and 2008 reduced inequalities in the bottom half of the wage distribution, thus contributing to a compression of the wage scale.

Minimum relative-to-average wage increases reflected by the Kaitz index have not been the only determinant of the trend in wage inequality among full-time employees in the period under consideration. Our analysis of ECHP and EU-SILC data shows that this has also been determined by other wage developments and structural changes, namely, a rising ratio of net annual earnings of full-timers in the public in contrast to the private sector (see Table 6.2 in section 4), the deepening of wage differentials between large/medium and small private firms (Figure 6.3) and the increasing share of private sector employees working in large/medium

Notes:
* Minimum wage: annual average, assuming paid for 14 months.
** Median wage: calculations based on gross annual earnings.

Source: OECD Statistics online (accessed 2 January 2017).

Figure 6.2 Kaitz index, Greece, 1990–2015

firms (Figure 6.4) who are better paid on average than their counterparts working in small firms. Rising public–private sector differences in the average wages of full-time employees have been determined by the large bargaining power discrepancies of unions in the two sectors while increasing wage differentials between large/medium and small firms have been the outcome of successful bargaining over wage premiums by enterprise unions in large firms. According to Greek law, such unions can be formed only in firms with 20 or more employees.

In summary, the collective bargaining system which set both the minimum wage and basic wages in sectors and occupations produced growing

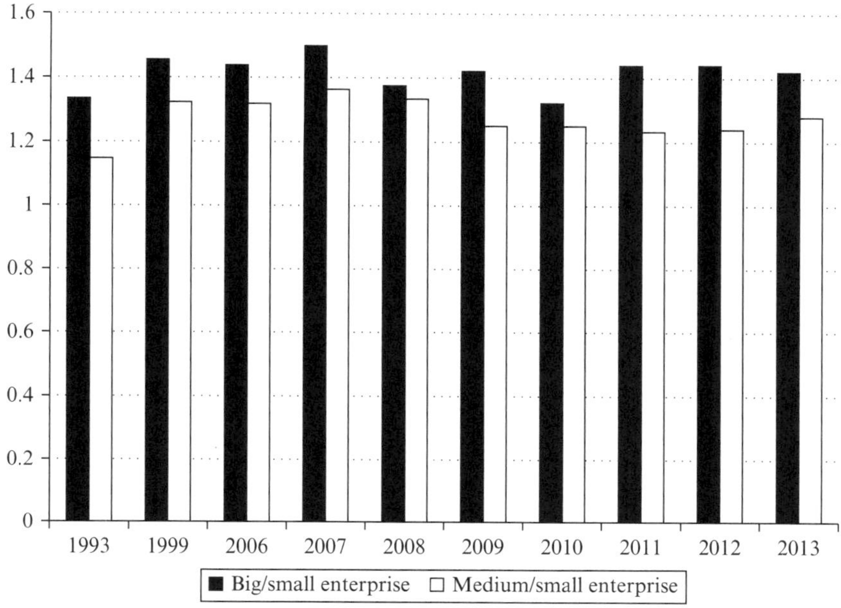

Source: Authors' elaboration of ECHP (years 1993 and 1999) and EU-SILC microdata (years 2006–14).

Figure 6.3 Wage differentials between big/medium and small enterprises, Greece, 1993–2013 (ratio of annual average wages)

wage inequalities among full-time employees between 1993 and 2008, which were considerably dampened by the offsetting effect of the falling share of public sector employees (35 per cent in 2008 compared with 40 per cent in 1993) who are better paid on average than their private-sector counterparts (see case study in section 4.1).

Inequality in annual earnings increased much more among employees as a whole than among full-time employees in the 1990s and 2000s, until the 2008 crisis. This is mainly accounted for by the increasing share of part-time and temporary workers among all employees (Figure 6.5).[2] The vast expansion of informal labour due to mass immigration has certainly also contributed to the rise in overall wage inequality, but official statistics are unable to capture informality and its impact on inequality.

As a result of the particular features of the wage determination system and structural changes in the employment system, at the onset of the current crisis overall individual wage inequality in Greece was medium compared with the rest of Organisation for Economic Co-operation and Development

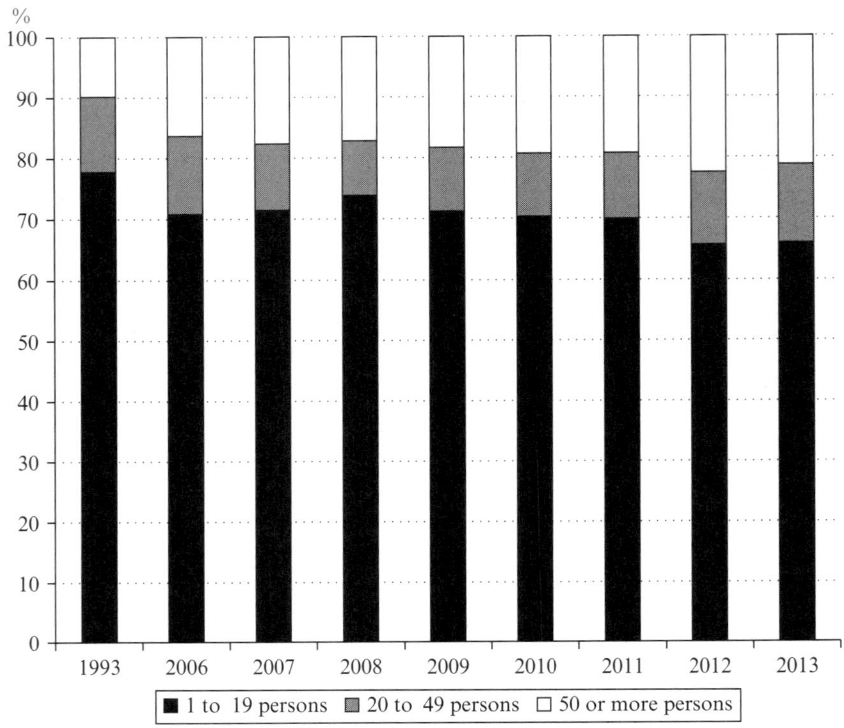

Source: Authors' elaboration of ECHP (year 1993) and EU-SILC microdata (years 2006–14).

Figure 6.4 Distribution of employees by size of firm, Greece, 1993–2013 (%)

(OECD) member states, while top-centre wage inequality was medium-to-high and centre-bottom wage inequality medium-to-low. Indeed, in 2008, Greece ranked seventeenth among 29 OECD countries as regards the value of the decile 9-to-decile 1 ratio, ninth as regards that of the decile 9-to-decile 5 ratio and nineteenth as regards that of the decile 5-to-decile 1 ratio.[3]

2.2 Dismantling Wage-setting Institutions and Undermining Social Dialogue during the Economic Crisis and Austerity: Contradictory Effects on Wage Inequality

The global financial crisis triggered a deep structural crisis of the Greek socio-economic growth model in the context of the EMU. The macro-

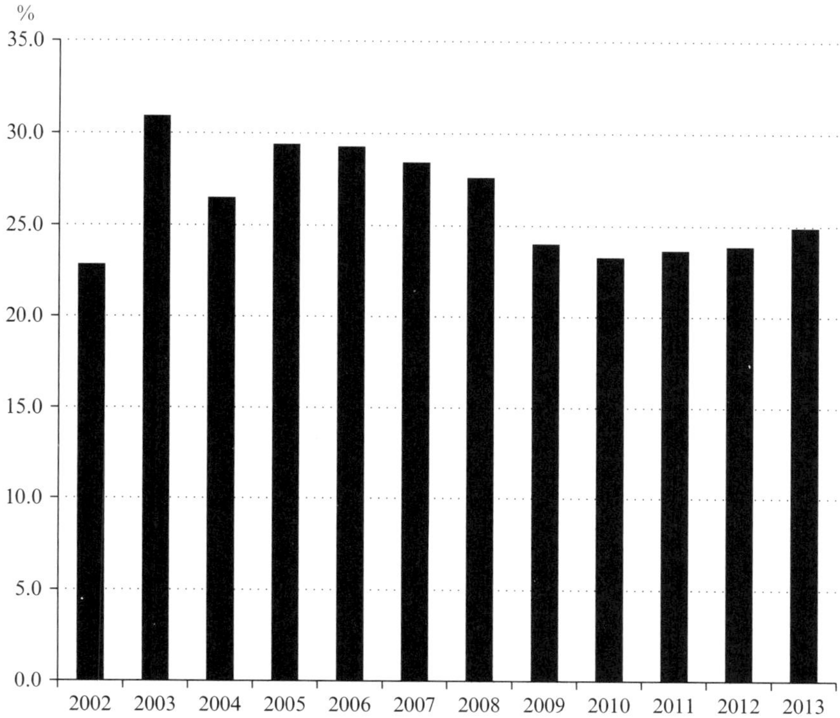

Source: Authors' elaboration EU-SILC microdata (years 2002–14).

Figure 6.5 Part-time and temporary workers, Greece, 2002–13

economic management of the economy during the first two years of the crisis (2008–09) exacerbated pre-existing fiscal imbalances and led to the sovereign debt crisis at the end of 2009 and the call for financial assistance of the Greek economy by eurozone partners and the IMF. The loans granted by the creditors have been made conditional on the strict implementation by Greek governments of three successive Economic Adjustment Programmes (EAPs) which were adopted in 2010, 2012 and 2015, respectively, and are due to end in mid-2018. The implementation of the first two EAPs was set under the supervision of the European Commission, the European Central Bank and the IMF (Troika); these three institutions were joined by the European Stability Mechanism in the supervision of the third EAP (Quartet).

Financial stability, fiscal consolidation and internal devaluation through reduced labour costs were the main goals of the EAP. Fiscal consolidation and substantial wage reductions in the private sector produced a shock to the economy, which incurred a 26 per cent loss in gross domestic product (GDP), a 24 per cent decline in employment and an explosion of unemployment reaching a peak of 29 per cent in 2013. This is what we call the Greek Great Depression, which has been entirely state-led since 2010. Besides public expenditure cuts and tax hikes in order to reduce public deficit, the first two EAPs included a series of structural labour market reforms, including those in the industrial relations system, meant to reduce labour costs, enhance the competitiveness of domestic production and redress current account imbalances (internal devaluation mechanism). These 'reforms' have actually dismantled the wage-setting institutions and mechanisms in place, abolished social dialogue, individualised industrial relations, and increased flexibility in employment and working conditions (dismissals, atypical contracts, working hours and so on). At the same time, fiscal consolidation entailed a drastic reduction in the public sector wage bill.

In this section we examine the effects of the deregulation of the wage determination system on wage inequalities, after having discussed the radical nature of reforms in this system under the first and second EAPs. The effects have been contradictory, narrowing inequalities in the first place and instigating them in the second.

2.2.1 Deregulation of the wage determination system and abolition of social dialogue

Reducing labour costs in the business sector of the economy, to be achieved by 'structural labour market reforms', was one of the key goals of the first EAP and became an explicit and quantified target under the second (15 per cent reduction). To achieve this goal, the wage-setting system has seen unprecedented changes since mid-2010, meant to bring about substantial wage reductions for employees working in both private firms and public companies and agencies in which wages were set at the firm level through collective bargaining (Ioannou, 2012; Dedoussopoulos et al., 2013; Karamessini, 2015; Koukiadaki and Kokkinou, 2016). The most important changes took place in industrial relations institutions (the dismantling of collective bargaining in the public sector, and the removal of extension mechanisms, decentralisation and difficulties of collective agreement renewal in the private sector), but also in the determination of wage floors (state-imposed minimum wages).

One of the first aims of the reforms under the first EAP was to end collective bargaining on wages for public sector employees – outside public administration and excluding civil servants – where union power has been concentrated for decades. Collective bargaining on wages was suspended in all public utilities, agencies and undertakings where cuts in nominal wages were imposed by law in 2010 and 2011. In February 2012 a law imposed the civil servants' wage grid on the employees of all private-law legal entities that belong to or are subsidised by central and local government. This fundamental pillar of the pre-crisis wage-setting system was thus neutralised. A second aim of the reforms was the weakening of sectoral and occupational collective bargaining and the decentralisation of the latter at the firm level. First, the 'favourability clause' in case of overlapping provisions of collective agreements was suspended, allowing firm-level agreements to prevail over occupational and sectoral agreements. Second, firm-level agreements were allowed to be negotiated in firms with at least five and fewer than 50 employees by workers' associations representing at least three-fifths of the workforce (in addition to trade unions), thus potentially bypassing the trade union through possible employer manipulation. Third, the extension of nationwide occupational and sectoral collective agreements to non-signatory firms by the Minister of Labour was suspended. This last measure operated as a strong incentive for firms to quit employers' organisations in order to have more freedom to determine employment and working conditions.

However, the pace of wage reductions was slow between May 2010 and February 2012, while the provisions of the NGCA signed in July 2010 for minimum wage increases in 2011 and 2012 equal to eurozone average inflation, were judged by the Troika and the Greek government as contradicting the goal of labour cost reduction (Kanellopoulos, 2015). After an increase of 1.6 per cent was applied to the minimum wage in July 2011, the government launched a tripartite dialogue to discuss national minimum wage developments. The results of this dialogue were considered by the Troika to be unsatisfactory because they did not ensure 'the quick responsiveness of wages to the fall in economic activity' (European Commission, 2012: 38).

> During the discussions, the employers' associations opposed the reduction of the minimum wage but were in favour of a three-year freeze in wage and maturity increases and the reduction on social insurance contributions. On the other hand, GSEE rejected any change in relation to wage costs and stated that the discussion should focus only on non-wage costs. (Koukiadaki and Kokkinou, 2016: 145)

The stalemate led the Troika and the Greek government to decide in February 2012 on a series of measures building on two pillars: an immediate and drastic adjustment of wage floors and the completion of the project of radically recasting the pre-existing wage-setting system initiated in the previous phase. The measures can be grouped as follows:

- a legislative reduction of the minimum wage by 22 per cent and then its freezing until the end of 2016;
- the introduction of a lower minimum wage for young people aged below 25 years at 87.2 per cent of the reduced minimum wage and then freezing it until the end of 2016;
- a further dismantling of the collective bargaining system through the reduction from six to three months of the after-effects of collective agreements and freedom to negotiate individual contracts thereafter; the restriction of the after-effects to only the basic wage and four allowances (seniority, children, education and hazardous work), the elimination of unilateral recourse to arbitration and its restriction to ruling only the basic wage, the freezing of all seniority bonuses provided by law or collective agreements and the removal of 'tenure' from all existing labour contracts;
- an invitation to social partners to simplify the NGCA by establishing a single-rate statutory minimum wage and abolishing the different minimum wages according to type of work, education, marital status and seniority. The failure of the National Committee for Social Dialogue set up in September 2012 to conclude on the indicated reform led to the establishment of a state-determined (after consultation) national minimum wage from 1 January 2017.

The above-described reforms under the first two EAPs have not only deregulated the previous wage-setting system based on collective bargaining at the national level by promoting and stimulating a decentralised and individualised system of industrial relations. They have equally had destructive effects on unions and social dialogue. By shrinking or abolishing the role of unions in wage determination, which is crucial for collective action, they have undermined collective organisation in a period in which the unions are also losing members and bargaining power because of dismissals and mass unemployment. Union density retreated from 23.5 per cent in 2008 to 21.5 per cent in 2013,[4] but these figures mainly reflect public sector membership. Social dialogue which has traditionally been bipartite and identified with collective bargaining received a terrible blow. The number of sector and occupational collective agreements fell from 101 in 2009 to 23 in 2015[5] while that of collective agreements at firm level evolved from 227 in 2009 to 409 in 2013 and back to 263 in 2015. The coverage of employees by collective agreements fell from 83 per cent in 2008 to 40 per cent in 2013 (ILO, 2015), while the coverage rate of private sector employees was estimated at 10 per cent in 2014 (ILO, 2014: 16).

Most importantly, the dismantling of wage-setting institutions, the drastic reduction of wage floors and the introduction of a lower minimum wage for young people under 25 have caused a 26 per cent decrease in the nominal compensation per employee.

Under the third EAP (2015–18) the Greek government has negotiated with the Quartet on the revival of collective bargaining and the architecture of the new system. It was recently agreed that the favourability principle and the extension mechanism of collective agreements will be reinstated on 1 September 2018, immediately after the end of this third programme.

2.2.2 Wage inequalities during the economic crisis and austerity: the impact of wage deregulation

The trends in wage inequality during the Great Depression, measured in terms of net annual earnings, are depicted in Figures 6.1 and 6.6. Overall wage inequality saw a steep fall equal to 25.2 per cent from 2008 to 2010 and a significant rise of 30.3 per cent from 2010 to 2014. The fall was jointly determined by a moderate decrease in wage inequality among full-timers, measured by the decile 9-to-decile 1 average wage ratio, and a substantial decline in the share of part-time or temporary workers in all employees (24 per cent in 2010 against 28.4 per cent in 2008) because these were the groups of employees who suffered proportionally more from losing their jobs than full-timers at the beginning of the crisis.

Inequality among full-timers shrank by 17.7 per cent between 2008 and 2011 and followed a steady increase in 2012–14. The main reason behind retreat in 2008–11 is the large wage reductions in the public sector that were much greater in cumulative terms than those in the private sector over the same period, leading to lower public/private disparities (see the case study in section 4.1). It is also worth noting that the reduction in wage inequality among full-timers was more important at the bottom than in the upper half of the wage distribution, measured by decile 5-to-decile 1 and decile 9-to-decile 1 average wage ratios respectively (Figure 6.6).

The shrinking of inequality at the bottom half of the wage distribution is due to the rise in the minimum along with a fall in the median wage. The minimum wage increased by 5.7 per cent in 2009, 1.7 per cent in 2010 and 0.9 per cent in 2011 (Bank of Greece, 2015: 106, table V.10). The median wage rose by 3.1 per cent in 2009 and dropped by 5.7 per cent between 2009 and 2011 with the important cuts imposed on public sector employees under the first EAP and the erosion of employee pay in the private sector owing to the downward adjustment of working time as a reaction of firms to the retreat in turnover and economic activity. As a result, the Kaitz index mounted from 48 per cent in 2008 to 52.4 per cent in 2011 (Figure 6.2).

The year 2011 is pivotal for earnings inequality among full-timers; the downward trend, which in the first two years of the EAP was mainly determined by wage cuts in the public sector, was reversed immediately

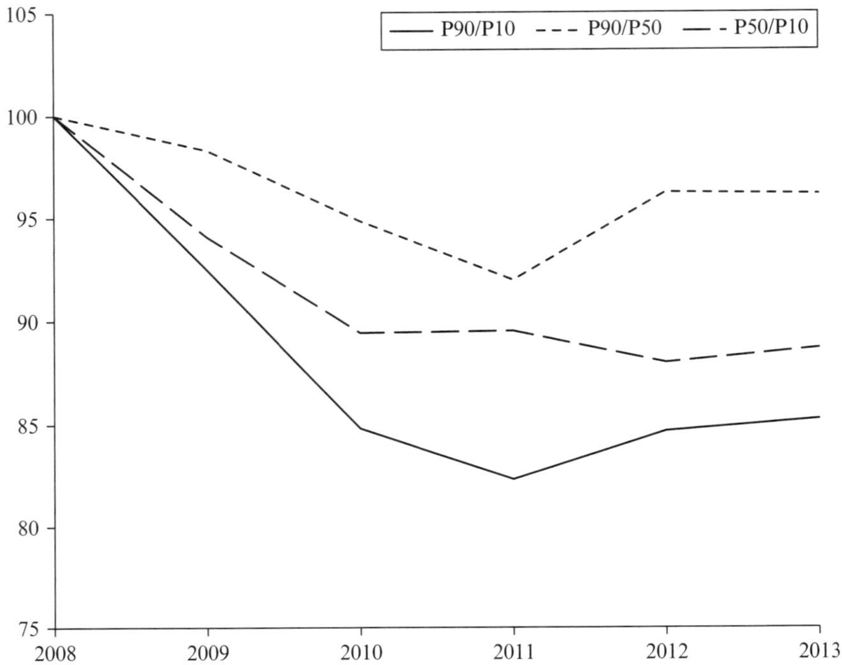

Source: Authors' elaboration EU-SILC microdata (years 2008–13).

Figure 6.6 Trends in wage inequality among full-time employees during the Great Depression, net annual earnings, Greece, 2008–13 (interdecile ratios, 2008 = 100)

afterwards. From 2012 onwards the crisis hit wages in the private sector with great severity because of the deepening of the recessionary spiral, the completion of reforms in industrial relations and collective bargaining, the legislated reduction in the minimum wage and the establishment of a subminimum wage for young workers under 25 years of age. Apart from allowing a substantial reduction in nominal wages through the whole wage distribution without any obstruction from a high wage floor, the reduction in the national minimum wage and the establishment of a special minimum wage for young people aged below 25 years were also explicitly meant by the authors of the second EAP to reverse the trend of narrowing wage inequalities at the bottom end of the wage distribution, thought to be pricing out of employment low-skilled and inexperienced workers who would be paid at or above the minimum wage (European Commission, 2012: 38). In 2012, the huge fall in the minimum wage pulled the Kaitz index down to 43.8 per cent, from 52.4 per cent in 2011. As the nominal value of the minimum wage has remained the same ever since and the median wage has continued to decline, the Kaitz index rose and reached 47.4 per cent in 2015.

Over the same period, wage inequality was further fuelled by the rising incidence of part-time and temporary employment (Figure 6.3) as a result of labour market reforms under the EAP that eased the use of flexible forms of work by firms in need of flexibility because of depressed demand. A countervailing factor contributing to the narrowing of wage inequalities was the closure of thousands of small firms, which increased the share of private sector employees working in firms with 20 or more employees between 2011 and 2014 (Figure 6.5).

In summary, the dismantling of collective bargaining, the drastic reduction of wage floors and the introduction of a lower minimum wage for young people under 25 have not only caused a huge decrease in the nominal compensation per employee in the business sector but, from 2012 onwards, also an increase in wage inequalities around a lower median wage.

3. FLEXIBILITY, SECURITY AND INEQUALITIES IN EMPLOYMENT AND WORKING CONDITIONS: FROM 'FLEXIBILITY AT THE MARGINS' TO 'IMPOSED FLEXIBILITY'

In this section we summarise developments in non-wage inequalities in the 1990s and 2000s and during the current crisis and we analyse the effects of industrial relations and their changes on the balance between flexibility and security in employment and working conditions. We maintain that before the Great Depression flexibilisation in the formal labour market was limited and concentrated at the 'margins' of the labour force (young people, women and migrants), while 'informal flexibility' was extended and produced large inequalities not captured by official statistics. During the Great Depression and under austerity, flexibility in the regulation of employment was imposed by the EAP through the list of 'structural labour market reforms' without any compensation of security inside or outside the labour market for employees. Flexibilisation has led to reduced inequalities in employment and working conditions in recent years.

3.1 Flexibilisation with Security, Extended Informal Flexibility and Rising Inequalities in the 1990s and 2000s

In the early 1990s, Greece's labour market and institutional arrangements had many similarities in common with Italy, Spain and Portugal, often considered typical of a south European employment model (Karamessini, 2008). As regards structural labour market features, Greece at that time had the highest self-employment rate in the EU and informal work was widespread. It also had among the lowest rates of female and part-time employment, very high unemployment rates among young people and women, very low unemployment rates among prime-age men and older workers, and pronounced labour market segmentation along various lines (public/private, large/small firms and formal/underground economy), as well as by age, sex and ethnic origin/nationality.

The divide between the public and private sectors is a very important source of inequality not only because the public sector has always paid employees higher wages than the private sector, on average, but also because it has offered and is still offering them tenure and good working conditions. The important fall in the share of public sector employees between 1993 and 2008 reduced the impact of the public–private divide on inequalities, although it would have been better if the latter had been reduced by a private sector catching-up process.

The regulation of employment and working conditions in the private sector has traditionally been primarily the competence of the Ministry of Labour; the vast majority of conditions are still set by law. Second in importance is the NGCA whose provisions on employment and working conditions apply to all employees who work in the private sector. Negotiations over the NGCA have traditionally represented the upper level of social dialogue, because the Economic and Social Committee in which social partners are represented operated only as consulting body to the government, issuing opinions. Sectoral or occupational bargaining at the national level did not engage much with the regulation of employment and working conditions, and when this was the case the issues were limited in scope and importance. It follows that the Greek system of industrial relations and social dialogue was highly centralised with regard to employment regulation and thus contributed to a relative homogeneity of employee rights in the private sector, including those of atypical workers.

The core elements of the traditional Greek employment regime were strong protection against the dismissal of formally employed permanent employees, especially white-collar, and extensive informal/irregular work. The former element remained intact during the 20 years before the current crisis; the only exception was a 2005 law that abolished for persons newly hired in public utilities the stronger protection against dismissal compared with that in private firms. As for informal work, this expanded in the 1990s and 2000s, mainly owing to mass illegal immigration and the irregular situation of large numbers of migrants staying and working in Greece.

Efforts have been made by several governments to introduce employment and working-time flexibility in the Greek labour market in the 1990s and 2000s but they faced strong opposition from the unions. Union opposition tempered the degree of flexibility actually introduced and succeeded in ensuring relatively good protection for employees involved in some forms of atypical work, such as part-timers and temporary agency workers. In 2007, Greece had the lowest rate of part-time employment and incidence of flexible working-time arrangements in the former EU15, while the rate of fixed-term contracts among employees was below the EU27 average. However, at the same time, project/service contracts among dependent workers, uninsured employment and informal/irregular work thrived but, by their very nature, remained unrecorded. Consequently, although the Greek labour market could be objectively characterised as flexible enough for firms to cater to their needs over the period under study, lack of flexibility in formal employment and working-time arrangements amplified demand for and use of informal forms of flexibility by firms and concentration of insecurity in particular labour force groups.

Slowly increasing formal flexibility and rapidly escalating informal flexibility were concentrated at the so-called 'margins' of the labour force, that is, among young people, women and migrants considered as inexperienced, and secondary and/or exploitable workers. The spread of informal flexibility in the 1990s and 2000s has generated marked inequalities between migrants and nationals and deepened labour market segmentation along the long-lived formal/informal work divide. In the case of pre-existing labour market inequalities based on sex and age, these have been reinforced or weakened by growing flexibility, depending on the type of inequality (Table 6.1). Gender inequalities in employment, which were very large by

Table 6.1 Employment inequalities and distribution of flexible employment, by sex and age, Greece

	1993	2008	2015
Male employment rate (%) 25–64 years of age	81.6	83.8	67.4
Female employment rate (%) 25–64 years of age	40.6	54.7	48.2
Youth employment rate (%) 15–24 years of age	27.5	23.5	13.0
Part time workers (% of all employees)	7.8	8.7	13.4
Female share	*59.4*	*67.7*	*63.4*
Youth share	*10.3*	*9.6*	*7.6*
Temporary workers (% of all employees)	10.4	11.6	12.0
Female share	*38.6*	*50.4*	*48.4*
Youth share	*29.6*	*19.2*	*12.8*

Source: European Labour Force Survey, Eurostat data online (accessed 2 January 2017). For figures on part-time employees OECD statistics online (accessed 2 January 2017).

European comparison at the beginning of the 1990s, have been reduced, but women increased their share of part-time dependent workers from 59.4 per cent to 67.7 per cent and their share of temporary employees from 38.6 per cent to 50.4 per cent between 1993 and 2008; the respective youth shares decreased across the same period. It follows that women and migrants were the main labour force groups to have been mobilised by employers as a flexible labour force in the 1990s and 2000s.

3.2 Imposed Flexibility without Security during the Great Depression: Muddling Segmentation in the Private Sector and Reinforcing the Public–Private Divide

The first and second EAPs included a host of measures that were unilaterally imposed by Greek governments and aimed at recasting the pre-crisis employment regime by significantly increasing employment and working-time flexibility in the formal labour market. The most important of them were those meant to ease dismissals. Private sector employees experienced a reduction in the notice period for individual dismissals from a maximum of 24 to a maximum of four months and in the level of severance pay from 2–24 months to 1–6 months (with prior notice) or 2–12 (without prior notice), and an increase in the minimum threshold for collective dismissals from 2–3 per cent to 5 per cent. The employees of public enterprises saw the abolition of all clauses on tenure provided for by collective agreements and their labour contracts transformed into open-ended agreements. Finally, in public administration, labour reserve and mobility schemes were created in order to receive personnel made redundant, some of whom were dismissed. The above measures entailed the dismantling of a core feature of the Greek employment regime, namely strong employment protection of permanent employees.

Another group of measures was intended to make it easier for employers to use atypical contracts, make the latter more flexible by reducing protection of atypical employees, reduce the cost of overtime work and adapt working time to the needs of firms. These measures include: the extension of the probation period for new hires from two months to one year; the extension of the cumulative maximum duration of fixed-term contracts from two to three years; the easing of the conditions for derogations; the extension of maximum duration of spells of employment for temporary agency workers from 18 to 36 months; and the extension of the maximum duration of rotating work at a given firm from six to nine months per year in case of financial difficulties – it can now be applied by the employer unilaterally after consultation. Furthermore, the employer can now decide unilaterally on layoffs of up to three months in firms with up to 5000 employees; part-time work is now allowed in public utilities; the employer is now allowed to transform the labour contract from full- to part-time with only the consent of the employee; the 7.5 per cent wage premium for short part-time working and of the 10 per cent premium for each working hour of part-timers over the agreed daily time have been abolished; overtime pay has been reduced by 20 per cent; flexible working-time arrangements have been eased; the number of maximum workdays per week has been increased from five to six; and the minimum daily rest has been reduced from 12 to 11 hours.

The joint outcome of these measures is the generalisation of precariousness in the private sector, which entails the muddling of segmentation lines between permanent and atypical employees, on the one hand, and atypical and informal employment on the other. For instance, the share of part-time or rotating work contracts in new hires increased from 21 per cent in 2009 to 55 per cent in 2015[6] and the part-time work rate among all employees rose from 8.7 per cent in 2008 to 13.1 per cent in 2015; conversely, the incidence of temporary work remained stable over the same period (Table 6.1). Both part-time work and temporary employment have become less feminised, while the participation share of young people has fallen during the economic crisis and austerity. Uninsured work and unpaid overtime have also expanded as a result of firms' financial difficulties, as well as the readiness of employees to accept such work owing to mass unemployment, the retreat of unions and their presence at the workplace, and the incapacity of the Labour Inspectorate to effectively supervise the enforcement of labour law owing to staff shortages. Given the erosion of employee rights and the dramatic deterioration of employment and working conditions in the private sector, segmentation along the public–private divide has become much more pronounced than before. Deterioration in working conditions in the public sector mainly took place by an increase in the standard working time from 37.5 to 40 hours a week.

In summary, segmentation of employment and working conditions has weakened among private sector employees, while the public–private divide has been reinforced.

As previously mentioned, the EAP measures promoting employment and working-time flexibility were unilaterally imposed by Greek governments without prior consultation with social partners, with the exception of the first bill regulating industrial relations which was submitted to the Economic and Social Committee for its opinion on 25 June 2010.[7] Had consultation taken place, the measures would undoubtedly have been much more balanced not only because they would have taken into account unions' opposition but also because employer organisations were officially unfavourable to measures promoting extreme flexibility both at the beginning and in the course of the austerity period. This is true in spite of differences in positions on particular issues between employer organisations representing small businesses and SEV, the federation representing big firms. However, many changes brought by the EAP were among the proposals of a document published by SEV in 1993–94, while certain individual employers, especially large enterprises that were members of SEV, were able to access directly the Troika and lobby for the adoption of specific reforms (Koukiadaki and Kokkinou, 2016: 144).

4. CASE STUDIES

In this section we focus on two case studies in order to analyse in more detail the impact of radical change in industrial relations and the abolition of social dialogue during the current economic crisis on labour market flexibility/security and inequalities in the world of work. The first study demonstrates how 'structural labour market reforms' under the EAPs have affected public/private sector and within-sector inequalities and how these trends are related to the trend in overall wage inequality during the ongoing crisis. The second study examines whether recent institutional changes, such as the easing of part-time and temporary contracts and the special minimum wage for young people under 25 years of age, have exacerbated or attenuated pre-crisis youth/non-youth labour market inequalities. Both case studies are preoccupied with the effects of radical institutional change since 2010, including the hollowing out or blurring of the boundaries of labour market segments.

4.1 The Public–Private Sector Divide and its Contribution to Wage Inequality Trends

Industrial relations and wage determination differ largely between the private sector, where collective bargaining applies, and the public sector. The latter is divided between public administration, in which wages and other employment conditions of civil servants have always been and are still determined by law (incomes policy), and public agencies and companies, in which, until recently, collective bargaining at the enterprise level dominated and through which unions had imposed tenure clauses for the employees, which formed a firm basis of union strength. Differences in industrial relations between and within the public and private sectors have been the cause of large differentials in wages and employee rights.

There is no research on the contribution of public–private sector differences in industrial relations and wage determination to the trends in overall wage inequality. To explore this topic, we examine the effect on overall wage inequality of the evolution of public–private wage differentials and the changing shares of the public and private sectors in all employees and link changes in industrial relations with the analysis of trends.

4.1.1 Trends in public–private sector wage differentials

Since the post-war years civil servants have enjoyed higher wages, on average, than private sector employees. As invariably a greater share of public than private sector employees are highly educated, higher relative wages in the public sector cannot be regarded *a priori* as an indication of 'unjustified' inequalities to be reduced in order to promote pay equity. To estimate the wage premium – that is, the part of wage differentials whose reduction would be desirable – we control for differences in observable characteristics that justify wage rewards.

There is a rich literature on public–private sector wage differentials in Greece before the 2008 crisis. Kioulafas et al. (1991) found a 20–25 per cent pay gap in favour of the public sector between 1975 and 1985 and proved that the public sector paid education and experience more than the private sector, while Kanellopoulos (1997) reported a difference in average wages of 19 per cent for men and 42 per cent for women in 1988, but attributed the observed pay advantage of male public sector employees entirely to their higher qualifications and part of the pay advantage of female public sector employees to the same reason. Similarly, in a more recent article, Papapetrou (2006) established that 59.6 per cent of wage differentials between the two sectors in 1999 were accounted for by differences in education, experience and occupation. In the latest study available, Christopoulou and Monastiriotis (2014) estimated the net public sector premium (after controlling for observable characteristics) in 2005 at 11.3 per cent for monthly and 15.2 per cent for hourly wages and found that it amounts to about 35–40 per cent of the public-private wage differential observed in the raw data.

Existing research has not made any distinction between public administration, on the one hand, and public agencies and companies, on the other, despite the fundamental differences in wage determination between the two subsectors and the relatively higher wages that the employees of the latter have always enjoyed (24 per cent higher on average in 2009 just before the austerity phase of the crisis commenced – see Table 6.2). Moreover, there is no available study on how and why public–private wage differentials evolved before and during the crisis.

Public–private sector wage differentials increased over the 15-year period before the current economic crisis. In 1993 wages in the public sector were on average 22 per cent higher than in the private sector while in 2008 they were 37 per cent higher (Table 6.2). Wage differentials between public administra-

Table 6.2 Public/private sector wage differentials among full-time employees, Greece, 1993–2014 (ratio of average net annual earnings)

	Public/private sector	Public enterprises/ private sector	Public administration/ private sector	Public enterprises/public administration
1993	1.22	–	–	–
1994	1.20	–	–	–
1999	1.35	–	–	–
2006	1.38	1.54	1.35	1.15
2007	1.34	1.53	1.31	1.17
2008	1.37	1.60	1.33	1.20
2009	1.36	1.63	1.31	1.24
2010	1.24	1.49	1.20	1.24
2011	1.20	1.38	1.17	1.17
2012	1.14	1.31	1.12	1.18
2013	1.14	1.32	1.12	1.17
2014	1.19	1.39	1.17	1.19

Source: Authors' elaboration of ECHP microdata (years 1993, 1994 and 1999) and EU-SILC microdata (years 2002–14).

tion and the private sector reached their peak in 2006 (35 per cent) while those between public enterprises and the private sector in 2009 (63 per cent).

The first and second EAPs imposed a severe reduction in the wage bill of the public sector through cuts in wages, bonuses and personnel. Between May 2010 and May 2011 nominal wages in the civil service were reduced by 15 per cent and those in public utilities, agencies and undertakings by 30 per cent, on average, by eliminating or imposing caps on bonuses and wages. A new salary grid was introduced subsequently in the public administration, taking effect on 1 November 2011, which brought about a further reduction in civil servants' nominal wages by 17 per cent per cent on average (IMF estimates, cited in Tzannatos and Monogios, 2012). Wage cuts of similar magnitude in public utilities and undertakings took effect on the same date. Finally, a reform of the special wage regimes (judges, diplomats, doctors, university professors and so on) took effect on 1 August 2012, resulting in 20–30 per cent wage reductions, on average. Outside public administration, except for the suspension in 2010 and 2011 of collective bargaining on wages in all public utilities, agencies and undertakings, in 2012 the civil servants' wage grid was imposed by law on the employees of all private-law legal entities belonging to or receiving subsidies from the central and local state. All wage cuts imposed in the public sector were more substantial the higher the level of pay and thus contributed to a narrowing of within-(public)sector wage inequalities.

Over the whole austerity period (2009–14), public–private sector wage differentials declined by 56 per cent; they narrowed by 61 per cent between 2009 and 2012 and increased by 41 per cent between 2012 and 2014. In 2014, average wages were 19.3 per cent higher in the public than in the private sector; 17 per cent higher in public administration and 39.4 per cent in public enterprises. The differential between public administration and private sector employees is small and may well reflect relatively higher average qualifications of the former employees rather than wage premiums, after controlling for education, experience, occupation and other characteristics.

4.1.2 The relative size of the public sector and wage inequality

The relative size of the public sector is a significant determinant of wage inequalities, especially when public–private sector wage differentials are important, which was the case in Greece in the 2000s. Since public sector wages tend to be more concentrated than private sector wages at the top deciles of the wage distribution, an increasing share of public sector in all employees instigates wage inequality while this diminishes when the share shrinks.

Between 1993 and 2008, the number of private sector employees increased by 58.9 per cent and that of public sector employees by 28.2 per cent. As a result, the share of public sector in all employees dropped from 40 per cent to 35 per cent, thus contributing to a narrowing of wage inequality. This has represented a countervailing factor against growing public–private sector wage differentials over the period which have pushed towards a widening of overall wage inequality. Over the crisis period 2008–16, wage employment retreated more in the public than in the private sector, namely, 23.4 per cent compared with 10.2 per cent. The ensuing decrease in the share of public sector employees from 35 per cent in 2008 to 33 per cent 2016 has contributed to the narrowing of wage inequalities. However, we can distinguish two phases. During the first phase (2008–13), the private sector shed labour more than the public sector, and during the second (2013–16) there was a net rise in the number of private sector employees while the number of public sector employees continued to fall. The important decline in wage employment in both sectors was the joint outcome of a decrease in hires and an increase in firings and quits. As regards the public sector, the strict hiring rules since 2010 (currently one hire for five exits) have created great labour shortages in many crucial services of the state. Besides, these have not only stalled the access of women, especially the highly educated, to good jobs but also the intergenerational reproduction of the middle classes and the upward social mobility of the lower classes through employment in the sector (Karamessini and Giakoumatos 2016).

4.1.3 How to assess the reduction in the public–private wage gap?

The public sector was more affected by wage cuts during the crisis and this may have helped to reduce the wage gap that existed between the public and private sectors and overall wage inequality, but this was brought about by levelling down wages in both sectors. In order to assess the contribution of public sector wage developments in reducing inequality, it is important to understand the linkage between wage developments in the two sectors and the policy goals that have been promoted by wage cuts in the public sector under the EAP.

While reducing public sector wages and employment was an explicit goal of the first two EAPs in order to cut public expenditure and the primary deficit of general government and achieve fiscal consolidation, compressing public/private sector wage differentials has been an implicit goal in order to cut labour costs and bring about internal devaluation. This can be understood by the role played by unions and collective bargaining in public utilities and companies for the determination of wages in the private sector through the 1990s and 2000s. They reinforced the bargaining power of the GSEE to negotiate the NGCA and the wage increases they achieved represented the upper limit for the claims of private sector unions and for the rulings of the Mediation and Arbitration Body on collective labour disputes (see section 2). Moreover, large wage differentials between the private and the public sector as a whole indirectly exerted pressure on employers in the private sector for wage concessions by creating competition in the recruitment of employees with the same skills.

It is consequently obvious that challenging union power in public utilities and companies by suspending collective bargaining and levelling down wages in the public sector has been a key policy instrument for deactivating unions and levelling down wages also in the private sector. More generally, by pushing the public sector to fall toward private sector wages and the private sector to reduce wages, the Troika and Greek governments have succeeded in producing poorer employment conditions in both sectors and cutting labour costs.

If in the first place relative wage cuts in the two sectors have led to a reduction in public–private wage differentials, the dismantling of collective bargaining – if not reversed – eventually will lead to greater relative wage reductions or lesser relative wage increases, thus expanding public–private wage differentials once more. Moreover, the narrowing of the public–private wage gap and the diminishing role of the public sector as employer are doomed to increase gender inequalities in pay, employment and working conditions, given that the public sector represented a place for highly educated women to find jobs of higher quality.

4.2 Youth–Non-youth Wage and Employment Inequalities: The Role of the Special Minimum Wage and Flexibility Measures

Young people's problems with regard to access to employment and their long transition periods from education to work were well-known phenomena of the Greek labour market in the 1990s and 2000s. In 2008, the unemployment rate of young people aged 15–24 (21.9 per cent) was the second highest and their employment rate the third lowest (23.5 per cent) in the EU, while those working part-time or having a temporary job represented a low share of all employed youth: 14.3 per cent and 28.8 per cent respectively, against 26 per cent and 40.2 per cent in the EU. Young people were entitled to the same minimum wage as older workers, while youth/non-youth wage differentials had remained relatively stable from 1993 to 2008 with the ratio of average net annual earnings fluctuating around 49 per cent and that of average monthly earnings around 59 per cent (Figure 6.7).

A direct consequence of the abolition of social dialogue at the upper level in early 2012 was not only the legislated reduction of the wage floor by

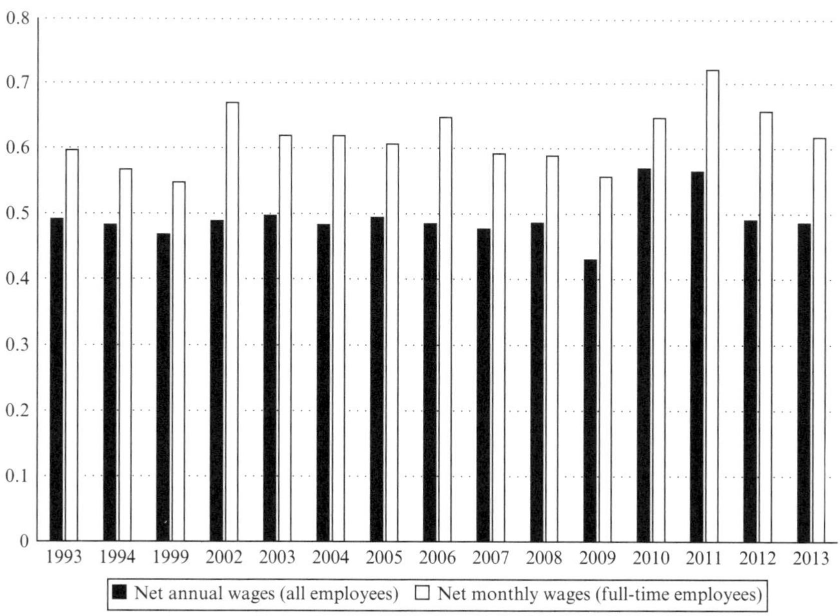

Source: Authors' elaboration of ECHP (years 1993, 1994 and 1999) and EU-SILC microdata (years 2002–13).

Figure 6.7 Youth/non-youth earnings differentials, Greece, 1993–2013 (ratio of net annual and monthly average earnings)

22 per cent in February 2012, but also the establishment by law of a special minimum wage for young people aged below 25 years whose rate was set at 87.2 per cent of the new reduced wage floor, which was below the poverty line of that year for an individual person living alone (€540). The action was justified in the second EAP by 'the downward rigidities in wage-setting systems, which have prevented the adjustment of private sector wages and contributed to the sharp increase in unemployment, in particular among the low-skilled and youth' (European Commission, 2012: 38). It was thus promoted by the authors of the second EAP as a means to combat youth unemployment, which had risen sharply in the first years of the economic crisis. However, the main reason for the explosion of youth unemployment was recession itself because firms in Greece – as everywhere – first reacted to the economic downturn by not renewing temporary contracts and by reducing hires of permanent or temporary personnel, thus disproportionally affecting young people.

The depressing effect on the wages of young people of lowering the wage floor for those aged below 25 years was immediate. Young people are typically offered entry-level wages close to the minimum wage. The dramatic deficiency of job opportunities for young people and the concomitant risk of unemployment as well as the deregulation of the wage-setting system (minimum wage and collective bargaining), which was intensifying at that time, made this phenomenon even more widespread in 2012 and 2013. Figure 6.7, based on ECHP and EU-SILC data, shows that the trend of youth/non-youth earnings differentials during the crisis years followed the upswing of the Kaitz index in 2010 and 2011 and dropped in 2012 and 2013, after the establishment of the subminimum wage for young people.

The impact of the Greek subminimum wage on youth employment has not yet been evaluated. However, its introduction has not prevented young people from losing jobs disproportionally in 2012–13 (Table 6.3). Jobs for 15–19-year-olds and 20–24-year-olds fell by 40.3 per cent and 36.2

Table 6.3 Employment changes by age group, Greece, 2006–15 (base to end year; change)

	15–74	15–19	20–24	25–29	30–44	45–55	55+
2006–08	1.8	–8.7	–8	–1.6	2.8	3.7	4.1
2008–11	–12.1	–52.1	–34.3	–25.2	–9.9	–5.4	–6.8
2011–13	–14.5	–40.3	–36.2	–31.7	–12.4	–7.3	–11.6
2013–15	2.7	–4.1	7.7	4.2	1.1	6.1	0.0

Source: European Labour Force Survey, Eurostat data online (accessed 1 September 2016).

per cent, respectively, while those for 25–29-year-olds fell by 31.7 per cent despite a higher minimum wage. This means that a high minimum wage is not among the determinants of the mass reduction in jobs offered to young people in 2012–13. The same is true for the higher job growth among 20–24-year-olds between 2013 and 2015, which should be attributed to the strong employment performance of sectors traditionally hiring young people, such as tourism and retail, rather than the subminimum wage. Despite a higher minimum wage applying to them, employment growth in the 25–29 and 45–55 age groups has been weaker but, nevertheless, quite strong. This means that the higher flexibility that was requested in terms of wages for young workers did not bring the expected additional security for young workers to have more jobs and to keep them, thus leading to an imbalance in terms of flexicurity owing to this reform. A proper evaluation of the measure is needed to provide firmer evidence.

The flexibility in employment and working conditions brought about by the EAP measures has not disproportionally affected young people, apart – probably – from the extension of the length of the probation period of new hires from two months to one year. The share of young people in part-time employment fell from 9.6 per cent in 2008 to 7.1 per cent in 2014, while the respective share in temporary employment fell from 19.2 to 11.7 per cent over the same period (Table 6.1). However, the incidence of temporary work among young employees mounted from 28.8 to 33.3 per cent while the part-time work rate among employed young people passed from 13.2 to 23.1 per cent. It follows that young workers were forced to assume a heavy burden in terms of involuntary part-time and have also suffered in terms of distribution of working time. Precariousness and underemployment have significantly increased among young people, although recession and austerity have attenuated rather than reinforced the youth–non-youth divide in employment and working conditions.

The age threshold for the Greek subminimum wage is higher than in any other EU country (Eurofound, 2016). Only the United Kingdom has introduced – in April 2016 – a lower living wage for young people between 21 and 24 years old since this age group was excluded from the recent increase in the minimum wage. However, this subminimum stands at 93 per cent of the standard rate. The obvious risk of a high age threshold is that employers will exploit young employees who have comparable levels of work experience and productivity to those of adults.

Under the third EAP (2015–18) the majority of the members of the commission of high-level international experts which was formed in March 2016 to make independent recommendations on industrial relations and collective bargaining reforms has proposed the replacement of the special minimum wage for youth by experience-based subminimum wages for a maximum of two years (Hellenic Republic, Ministry of Labour, Social Security and Social Solidarity, 2016: 39). It has challenged the subminimum wage for young people on age discrimination grounds, following a ruling by the European Court of Justice on a similar case, and for not guaranteeing a decent wage, in accordance with the Opinion of the European Committee of Social Rights of the Council of Europe in October 2012. The Quartet has refused any changes on the issue in the negotiations with the Greek government.

In summary, the establishment of a subminimum wage for young people, the lack of collective bargaining and the adoption without social dialogue of tough reforms relaxing employment protection legislation and easing the use of non-standard employment contracts have significantly increased part-time work and temporary employment among young people, attenuated the divide between younger and older workers as regards employment and working conditions, and widened the wage gap between youth and non-youth.

5. CONCLUDING REMARKS AND POLICY ISSUES

It is difficult to disentangle the impact of institutions and agency from the structural determinants of inequalities in the world of work and hard to gauge the contribution of institutional in contrast to compositional factors in shaping inequality trends. However, in this chapter we have analysed the institutions, actors and changes in industrial relations, wage determination and regulation of employment in Greece and made the link with the forms of flexibility and security and the different kinds, degrees and trends in observed wage and non-wage inequalities.

We have shown that, in the 1990s and 2000s, the multi-layered and articulated system of collective bargaining, the extension process of collective agreements and the activity of the mediation and arbitration body ensured high coverage of employees by collective agreements, an uninterrupted increase in average real compensation per employee along with productivity but also important wage inequalities, especially between public and private companies in the business sector of the economy. Strong unions in public agencies/enterprises and banking were the leading actors in collective bargaining. Apart from obtaining high wage increases for the employees they represented, by dominating the leadership of the GSEE these unions achieved a constant rise in the national minimum wage in real terms and set the ceiling for the wage claims of private sector unions, thus contributing to the rise in the living standards of the rest of the employees with low(er) bargaining power. With regard to employment regulation, the centrality of law and the NGCA in the determination of employment and working conditions ensured a high degree of homogeneity in employee rights. At the same time, the informal labour market expanded with mass immigration and became a powerful determinant of wage and non-wage inequality, while the unions' successful resistance to the expansion of formal employment and working-time flexibility limited the proportion of employees working officially under flexible employment forms and confined the latter to migrants and women, who saw their share of part-time and temporary employees greatly increase.

Wage inequality thus increased during the fifteen-year period that preceded the 2008 crisis taken as a whole, the trend reflecting growing public–private sector and large–small firm wage differentials, the rising incidence of part-time and temporary employment and the expansion of informal labour. The Greek labour market in the 1990s and 2000s has been characterised by relatively limited formal flexibility, accompanied by security for employees and a deep formal/informal labour divide. Lack of 'negotiated flexibility' seems to have directed firms towards informal flexibility as a means of adjusting labour costs downwards in the absence of any serious inspection mechanism of employment and working conditions.

During the Great Depression, the EAP infused large doses of flexibility without security through 'structural labour market reforms' easing the recourse of employers to flexible employment forms and flexible working-time arrangements, while mass dismissals, closures of firms and explosive unemployment generalised precariousness. This was an 'unnegotiated flexibility' imposed by the Troika, which has blurred the segmentation lines of standard/non-standard employment and formal/informal labour. However, imposed employment and working-time flexibility has reinforced segmentation in employment and working conditions between the public and private sectors. While these conditions have dramatically deteriorated in the private sector, they have been largely maintained in the public sector in which employees incurred an increase in standard working time by 2.5 hours per week but have preserved intact all the other working conditions together with employment security.

The economic crisis and austerity first compressed wage inequalities and then widened them. Compression of wage inequalities until 2011 was mainly due to shrinking public–private sector wage differentials and to the fall in the share of temporary workers who were the first victims of numerical flexibility strategy adopted by firms and the state as a means of adapting to depressed demand. The shrinking of public–private sector wage differentials was the outcome of larger wage cuts in the public than in the private sector. The widening of wage inequalities from 2012 onwards is primarily accounted for by radical changes in the wage determination system in the business sector; the rise in the incidence of part-time employment resulting from the promotion of flexible employment under the EAPs has also contributed.

Social dialogue has fallen victim to 'structural labour market reforms' since the government adopted all of them with little or no consultation with social partners. Those concerning the wage determination system intended to bring down wages and reduce labour costs in the business sector of the economy. This was achieved by suspending collective bargaining on wages in public agencies/companies, decentralising bargaining at the firm level in the private sector and reducing wage floors to allow the whole wage scale to adapt downwards.

Suspension of collective bargaining in public agencies/companies has been a key policy instrument for challenging union power starting from its main strongholds. It has contributed to the reduction in public–private wage differentials until 2013 when the trend was reversed. Decentralisation of collective bargaining was meant to promote wage flexibility at the firm level, that is, the adjustment of wages to firms' economic situation. However, after an initial increase under the first EAP, the number of enterprise agreements dropped considerably under the second EAP with the suspension of the extension of collective agreements.

> This was likely to have resulted from the fact that fewer sectoral-occupational agreements were in force, which allowed companies to follow basic working conditions established by law and the NGCA directly, without the need to negotiate an enterprise agreement. Indeed, in the Greek business environment, with micro and small enterprises in a significant majority, incentives for collective bargaining at the enterprise level seem to be few. (ILO, 2014: 16)

The end results of all reforms in collective bargaining and the abolition of social dialogue were the destabilisation and erosion of collective bargaining, the dramatic fall in the coverage rate of employees by collective agreements, a great reduction in wages and the expansion in the share of employees enduring in-work poverty. Our analysis has illustrated that by promoting flexibility and diminishing security these reforms have also played a crucial role in amplifying wage inequalities from 2012 onwards, including those between young and older workers.

Restoring collective bargaining and social dialogue is the aim of the Greek government, which recently agreed with the Quartet that the favourability principle and the administrative extension of collective agreements will be reinstated after the end of the third Economic Adjustment Programme (2015–18). Collective bargaining is a fundamental right in democratic societies and a prerequisite for decent work and social cohesion. At the same time,

> collective agreements with a high coverage or applicability create a level playing field for companies that can invest in skills and retain experienced employees by paying decent wages without being undercut by competitors who are not covered by a collective agreement. They direct competition between companies from wage reductions to improvements of the work organisation and quality of the products and services. (Hellenic Republic, Ministry of Labour, Social Security and Social Solidarity, 2016: 31)

This means that collective agreements are a prerequisite for both sustainable and equitable growth.

After nine years of recession and seven years of austerity, it has become evident that wage devaluation is not a viable way out of the Greek Great Depression and that sustainable growth requires a new institutional set-up that promotes productivity growth and investment in product and services quality. A multi-level social dialogue framework is part of this institutional set-up. Apart from producing better outcomes in terms of flexibility/security it could also safeguard against growing inequalities produced by a deregulated labour market.

NOTES

1. According to OECD data (online database).
2. There are no available data from the ECHP on temporary workers for 1994–2000.
3. OECD.Stat online, 'Decile ratios of gross earnings', accessed 2 January 2017 at http://stats.oecd.org/Index.aspx?DataSetCode=IDD.
4. Data from OECD.Stat, accessed 7 January 2017 at stats.oecd.org.
5. Unpublished data by the Ministry of Labour.
6. ERGANI (Ministry of Labour database) http://www.ypakp.gr (accessed 2 January 2017).
7. The bill raised the thresholds for collective dismissals from 2 to 5 per cent, reduced the notice period for individual dismissals, introduced a subminimum wage for youth and so on. The reaction of employer organisations' representatives to the changes proposed by the bill exemplifies their 'flexibility with security' approach at that time (OKE, 2010).

REFERENCES

Bank of Greece (2015), 'Annual Report of the Governor for 2014', Bank of Greece, Athens.

Boeri, T., P. Garibaldi and M. Ribeiro (2010), 'Behind the lighthouse effect', IZA DP No. 4890, April, Bonn: Institute of Labour Economics.

Christopoulou R. and V. Monastiriotis (2014), 'The Greek public sector wage premium before the crisis: size, selection and relative valuation of characteristics', *British Journal of Industrial Relations*, **52** (3), 579–602.

Dedoussopoulos, A., V. Aranitou, F. Koutentakis and M. Maropoulou (2013), 'Assessing the impact of the memoranda on Greek labour market and labour relations', Governance Working Paper No. 53, Geneva: ILO.

Eurofound (2016), *Statutory Minimum Wages in the EU 2016*, European Observatory of Working Life, accessed 19 September 2016 at http://www.eurofound.europa.eu/observatories/eurwork/articles/working-conditions-industrial-relations/statutory-minimum-wages-in-the-eu-2016.

European Commission (2012), *The Second Economic Adjustment Programme for Greece*, European Economy Occasional Papers No. 94, Directorate-General for Economic and Financial Affairs Publications, Brussels, accessed 1 September 2016 at ec.europa.eu/economy_finance/publications/occasional_paper/2012/pdf/ocp94_en.pdf.

Grimshaw, D. and G. Bosch (2013), 'The intersections between minimum wage and collective bargaining institutions', in D. Grimshaw (ed.), *Minimum Wages, Pay Equity and Comparative Industrial Relations*, New York and London: Routledge, pp. 50–80.

Hellenic Republic, Ministry of Labour, Social Security and Social Solidarity (2016), Extract from the recommendations of the Commission of Independent Experts, as summarised by its President, Professor Jan van Ours, press release, 30 September, Athens, accessed 15 October 2016 at www.ypakp.gr/uploads/docs/9946.pdf.

ILO (2014), *Greece: Productive Jobs for Greece*, Geneva: ILO.

ILO (2015), 'Trends in collective bargaining coverage: stability, erosion or decline?', Labour Relations and Collective Bargaining Policy Brief No. 1, accessed 15 September 2016 at www.ilo.org/global/topics/collective-bargaining-labour-relations/publications/WCMS_409422/lang--en/index.htm.

Ioannou, C. (2000), 'Social pacts in Hellenic industrial relations: Odysseus or Sisyphus?', in G. Fajertag and P. Pochet (eds), *Social Pacts in Europe – New Dynamics*, 2nd edn, Brussels: ETUI, pp. 219–36.

Ioannou, C. (2012), 'Recasting Greek industrial relations: internal devaluation in light of the economic crisis and European integration', *Industrial Relations*, **28** (2), 199–222.

Kanellopoulos, C.N. (1997), 'Public–private wage differentials in Greece', *Applied Economics*, **29** (8), 1023–32.

Kanellopoulos, K. (2015), 'The effects of minimum wages on wages and employment', *Economic Bulletin*, **41**, 7–30, Bank of Greece, Athens (in Greek).

Karamessini, M. (2008), 'Still a distinctive southern European employment model?', *Industrial Relations Journal*, **39** (6), 510–31.

Karamessini, M. (2015), 'The Greek social model: towards a deregulated labour market and residual social protection', in D. Vaughan-Whitehead (ed.), *The European Social Model in Crisis. Is Europe Losing its Soul?*, Cheltenham, UK and Geneva: Edward Elgar and ILO, pp. 230–88.

Karamessini, M. and S. Giakoumatos (2016), 'Public sector and the middle classes in bad times: factor or erosion or resilience during the Greek Great Depression?', *Economia e Lavoro*, (2), 59–69.

Karamessini, M. and D. Grimshaw (2017), 'Minimum wages and the remaking of the wage-setting systems in Greece and the UK', in D. Grimshaw, C. Fagan, G. Hebson and I. Tavora (eds), *Making Work More Equal: Understanding The International, Societal and Systemic Effects on the Organisation of Employment*, Manchester: Manchester University Press, pp. 330–55.

Kioulafas, K., G. Donatos and G. Michailidis (1991), 'Public and private sector wage differentials in Greece', *International Journal of Manpower*, **12** (3), 9–14.

Koukiadaki, A. and C. Kokkinou (2016), 'The Greek system of collective bargaining in (the), crisis', in A. Koukiadaki, I. Tavora and M. Martinez Lucio (eds),

Joint Regulation and Labour Market Policy in Europe during the Crisis, Brussels: ETUI.

Kouzis, Y. (2002), 'The changes in labour relations in Greece', in P. Getimis, A. Dedousopoulos, X. Petrinioti, S. Robolis, Y. Kouzis (eds), *Yearbook of Labour 2002*, Athens: Institute of Human Resources and Urban Environment, Panteion University.

Organisation for Economic Co-operation and Development (OECD) (2015), 'Recent labour market developments with a focus on minimum wages', in OECD, *Employment Outlook 2015*, Paris: OECD.

OKE (2010), *OKE Opinion on the Bill 'New Insurance System and related provisions. Rulings on Industrial relations'*, Opinion No. 241, accessed 30 July 2016 at http://www.oke.gr/opinion/op_241.pdf.

Papapetrou, E. (2006), 'The public–private sector pay differential in Greece', *Public Finance Review*, **34** (4), 450–73.

Tzannatos, Z. and Y. Monogios (2012), 'Public sector adjustment amidst structural adjustment in Greece: subordinate, spasmodic and sporadic', in D. Vaughan-Whitehead (ed.), *Public Sector Shock: The Impact of Policy Retrenchment in Europe*, Cheltenham, UK and Geneva: Edward Elgar and ILO, pp. 259–99.

7. Social dialogue and inequality: Ireland

Brian Nolan

1. INTRODUCTION

This chapter is concerned with the way social dialogue and inequality have evolved and interacted over recent decades in Ireland. This represents an interesting country study in that over this period Ireland has seen major changes in industrial relations and broader social dialogue structures and processes, dramatic swings in average income levels, substantial fluctuations in wage dispersion, but overall fairly stable levels of income inequality. As a country conventionally categorised as having an 'Anglo-Saxon' or 'liberal' welfare regime and mode of capitalism, highly flexible in terms of employment protection and with a common institutional heritage with the United Kingdom, the extent to which social dialogue processes and inequality trends have differed from the United Kingdom is of particular note.

Here we, first, examine through the lens of inequalities how social dialogue structures evolved in the decades up to and through the crisis and 'Great Recession'. This includes industrial relations institutions, the trends in union membership that are an important part of the context in which those institutions and broader social dialogue processes operate, and the role of the legislative and regulatory setting in terms of flexibility and security in the labour market. We then turn to the outcomes of social dialogue and how these were related to flexibility and security and inequalities, including in particular how wage dispersion evolved. This brings out the crucial role of the minimum wage, which can be seen to some extent as a product of social dialogue, with other linkages between social dialogue and inequality less easy to pin down empirically. We then consider two informative case studies. The first focuses on the relationship between social dialogue/wage-setting processes and public sector pay, which is distinctive, has major implications for inequality and is a key issue on the current Irish policy agenda. The second deals with social dialogue structures themselves and the inability of the high-level social partnership structures that operated in Ireland over two decades to survive the onset of the crisis, with lasting consequences. Finally, we bring together the main conclusions and policy implications from the Irish case and highlight some open questions for the future.

2. INEQUALITIES AND SOCIAL DIALOGUE STRUCTURES

A key feature of the context in which social dialogue institutions operate and evolve is the extent of unionisation and how that changes over time. The institutional setting itself is potentially a major influence on union membership, so it is important first to sketch out the background. As in the majority of European Union (EU) countries, union density in Ireland has been falling during recent decades, though it remains above the Organisation for Economic Co-operation and Development (OECD) average. The proportion of workers in unions fell markedly from the late 1970s and this decline continued through the boom, with much of the growth in employment in non-union or weakly unionised firms. Union density is now down to about one-third of Irish workers, a major decline from close to 60 per cent of Irish workers three decades ago. As in many other countries, public sector workers have increasingly come to dominate union membership. Walsh (2015), focusing on the past decade or so, spanning both growth and recession, states that union density in the private sector declined from 27 per cent in 2004 to 17 per cent in 2014 (although Sweeney (2015) suggests the decline may not have been that marked), and the percentage of union members accounted for by public sector workers rose from 40 per cent to 55 per cent.

Studies suggest that, as elsewhere, shifts in the sectoral composition of employment and changing work practices have played a major part in the decline in union density since its peak in the 1980s. Membership is strongly structured by sector, with older, more traditional sectors having higher rates, and during the economic boom unions faced particular challenges in organising the new migrant workforce. Changes in the legislative framework for union recognition and operation in Ireland may have made some contribution (notably the Industrial Relations Amendment Act 2001, see D'Art and Turner, 2006), but this was much less important than in Britain, where the changing legal context of industrial relations has been seen as central to the sharp fall in union coverage during the Thatcher years (see, for example, Freeman and Pelletier, 1990; Ebbinghaus and Visser, 1999). The role of multinational companies is particularly important in the Irish case, given the centrality of foreign direct investment in the country's growth strategy, and the fact that this sector became much more resistant to unionised workplaces over the period seems to have been a significant contributor to declining union density.

The development of industrial relations structures in Ireland has also been deeply influenced by the macroeconomic context, which has fluctuated dramatically. A centralised structure for social dialogue emerged as a response to the prolonged recession of the early to mid-1980s and, as we shall see, that structure disintegrated in the face of the strains produced by the onset of the financial and economic crisis in 2008–09. Centralised wage bargaining at the national level was adopted in 1987 in response to the economic stagnation experienced through the 1980s. A widespread consensus emerged that a new approach was needed to reverse that economic decline. The 'social partnership' process had government, employers and unions conclude agreements on wage levels in both private and public sectors, together with a wide range of economic and social policies. Successive multi-year agreements were negotiated, each exceeding the previous agreement in its ambition and scope. The range of objectives extended far beyond the basic goal of promoting industrial peace and keeping the economy competitive to include such objectives as promoting an entrepreneurial culture, but also clearly encompassed inequalities broadly conceived, as captured by the aim of bringing about a fairer and more inclusive Ireland.

As Begg (2016) notes, social partnership followed immediately the institutionalisation of social dialogue as part of the Single Market, as a social policy counterbalance to the negative aspects of integration, concerned with the threats to social inclusion and equality posed by the opening up of markets and capital flows. What was distinctive in the Irish context was its broad scope and reach across the range of public policy and administrative activity, and its inclusiveness in terms of the number of social actors engaged. From 1987 to 2009 seven social pacts were agreed, with both participants and commentators tending to highlight its 'pragmatic' and 'non-ideological' nature (Hastings et al., 2007) as opposed to a deeply rooted commitment to neo-corporatism. From a trade union perspective, wage moderation was agreed in return for boosting the social wage by a combination of tax cuts and increased public spending, reflecting a broad focus on promoting living standards (and employment) rather than simply negotiating over pay. The collectively agreed wage increases at national level generally set a floor, with more profitable firms – particularly, but not only, in the multinational sector – often giving higher increases, while strike activity stayed well below what had been seen in previous eras (as discussed in more detail below). As Regan (2012) notes, employers welcomed the industrial peace and the saving of time and energy at the level of the firm achieved by the centralisation and coordination of wage bargaining, with many multinational firms comfortable with the corporatist approach at the national level while having a union-free workplace.

The remarkable growth in gross domestic product (GDP), employment and incomes seen in Ireland over the 'Celtic Tiger' period from the mid-1990s and up to the crisis meant that support for structured social dialogue was maintained among the key social actors. The average annual increase in real gross national product (GNP) was 7 per cent from 1994 to 2000 and continued at 4–6 per cent up to 2007, while the numbers employed rose from 1.2 million to over 2 million and unemployment fell from 16 per cent to 4 per cent by 2000, where it remained until 2008. As discussed in more detail in one of the case studies in section 4, public sector workers benefited particularly from the partnership approach in the latter part of the boom, receiving substantial additional increases via a 'benchmarking' process aimed at preventing public sector workers from falling behind rapidly rising private sector wages. Because public sector unions played a very important role in the trade union movement, this also underpinned support for the process. With public finances boosted by rising tax receipts, government finances were in surplus and public debt was only 25 per cent of national output by 2008.

Ireland then saw the most precipitous decline in national output of any OECD country on the immediate onset of the Great Recession, so that by 2010 GNP per head in real terms was back to levels last seen a decade earlier. This occurred together with a bursting of the property bubble, a collapse in asset values, a banking crisis of unprecedented proportions and a ballooning fiscal deficit and debt to GDP ratio. The scale of the crisis was seen in the fact that by 2010, despite substantial increases in taxation and expenditure cuts, the Irish government was no longer able to borrow on international financial markets at acceptable rates and had to avail itself of a 'bail-out' by the EU and the International Monetary Fund (IMF). The social partnership process that had come to define Irish industrial relations over the two previous decades could not cope with the profound strains associated with the onset of this financial and economic crisis, its impact on employment and the public finances, and the fiscal correction required. In the absence of tripartite agreement on the appropriate response, reductions in public service salaries were imposed and social partnership structures became inoperable. While an agreement was then reached between government and public sector unions to avoid further cuts in pay and involuntary redundancies in the public sector, wage bargaining in the private sector reverted to company level (but with employers and unions centrally agreeing protocols around that). This remained the situation through the deep recession and the recovery from 2013, with as yet little sign of enthusiasm for the revival of social partnership institutions from government, employers or unions. The inability of what had seemed to be reasonably robust social dialogue structures to survive that macroeconomic shock, much less contribute to framing the policy response, is a striking feature of the Irish experience, which we elaborate on in the second of the case studies presented in section 4.

In terms of regulation of pay and working conditions, the most important institutional innovation over the social partnership period, with major implications from an inequalities perspective, as we shall see, concerns the minimum wage. A national minimum wage was introduced in Ireland for the first time in 2000; rather than being a direct product of partnership per se or a core demand of trade unions, this was very much influenced by the establishment of the UK minimum wage in 1999. The extent to which this should be seen as a direct product of partnership per se can be debated. The notion of a minimum wage had certainly featured in social partnership discussions, with the agreement for the early 1990s (the Programme for Economic and Social Progress), for example, noting that the Irish Congress of Trade Unions proposed in the course of discussion that there should be a statutory national minimum wage, but the employer organisations opposed it. This and the following agreement emphasised the enforcement of the minimum pay rates set by Employment Regulation Orders for certain occupations/sectors.

The introduction of the minimum wage featured in the agreement covering 2000–2002 (the Programme for Prosperity and Fairness), including both the initial rate set and the increases to be implemented in 2001 and 2002. However, the impetus to do so came primarily from the election manifesto commitment of the Fianna Fáil party in the 1997 general election, which brought it back into government after a period in opposition, to introduce a minimum wage. That commitment noted that this would be following 'similar moves in Britain' (with the decision to introduce a national minimum wage there having already been announced at that stage). The partnership structures and the ongoing dialogue they underpinned can, however, be seen as helpful to the smooth introduction and functioning of the minimum wage, and more broadly as framing this within an overarching context of shared perspectives on competitiveness and the broad developmental model.

The minimum wage introduced was structured as an hourly minimum rate of pay to be set by the relevant minister for all employees aged 18 or over, with reduced rates payable for younger and inexperienced workers. Until 2014 the relevant government minister changed the level of the minimum wage at irregular intervals, with input from employers and trade unions serving only as an information function unless they could agree a joint position on what the change should be. More recently, the independent Low Pay Commission was established, starting its work in 2014, and was put on a statutory basis by the National Minimum Wage (Low Pay Commission) Bill 2015. Its role, similar to the corresponding body in the United Kingdom, is to recommend annually to government the appropriate rate of the National Minimum Wage, taking an evidence-based approach; it may also examine other issues related to the National Minimum Wage if the Cabinet agrees.

For many years before the national minimum wage was introduced, Ireland, similar to the United Kingdom, had a system under which minimum rates of pay and conditions were agreed for certain industries or occupations, mainly in low-paid sectors such as hotels, catering, cleaning and retail. Agreements between employers and trade unions in those sectors, adopted by the relevant Joint Labour Committee (JLC), were given force of law, binding on all workers and employers in the affected sectors. This was subject to successful legal challenge in 2011–12, but the Industrial Relations (Amendment) Act 2015 reintroduced a means of registering employer–union agreements on pay and conditions in certain sectors, now binding only on the parties who agree them and not others within the sector. However, the Labour Court can also start a review of pay, sick pay and pension entitlements of workers in a particular sector and make a recommendation to the minister, who can make a Sectoral Employment Order which would be legally binding and enforceable.

The 2015 Industrial Relations (Amendment) Act 2 also impacts on the industrial relations framework for non-unionised employers and employees. This was a (delayed) response to a decision by the Supreme Court in 2007 which found that an employer engaged in negotiations with staff groups (rather than traditional collective bargaining with unions) should be exempt from the provisions of the Industrial Relations Acts, severely restricting the scope for such workers to appeal to the Labour Court. The Act stops short of imposing mandatory collective bargaining (for which trade unions campaigned), consistent with the voluntary nature of the Irish industrial relations system. However, it provides for a mechanism for workers where collective bargaining is not recognised by the employer to bring claims for improved pay and conditions and have these claims determined by the Labour Court based on comparisons with similar workplaces.

The responsibility for enforcing employment rights and dealing with industrial disputes was distributed across a range of bodies throughout the boom years, with significant institutional change only more recently. The Labour Court, originally established under the Industrial Relations Act 1946, played a key role as an industrial relations tribunal, hearing both sides in a case and then issuing recommendations which, although not binding on the parties concerned, were often followed. In 1990, early in the period of social partnership agreements, the conciliation service of the Labour Court was hived off into a new body, the Labour Relations Commission (LRC), which was also charged with the promotion of good industrial relations through its Advisory Service. The LRC also assumed responsibility for the administration of the Rights Commissioner Service, established in 1970 to handle disputes involving individuals or small groups. The provisions of the national social partnership agreements between 1987 and 2009 copper-fastened the role of the LRC and the Labour Court in collective dispute resolution. Referral to conciliation and adjudication was a mandatory feature of dispute resolution for all issues covered in these agreements; from 2003 Labour Court recommendations on pay-related disputes and disputes over normal ongoing change became binding on parties to national agreements (see Teague et al., 2015a).

Another development in the field of dispute resolution arising from partnership was the establishment in 2000 of the National Implementation Body (NIB), reflecting increasing concern with pay drift and threats of industrial disruption during the height of the economic boom. The NIB, comprising senior officers of the Irish Congress of Trade Unions and the Irish Business and Employers' Confederation and senior public servants, formalised earlier ad hoc joint conflict resolution initiatives. Its role was to use the influence and networks of its members to head-off, resolve or refer disputes that threatened social partnership pay agreements or that had caused or might cause disruption to essential services. The NIB was party to the resolution of a number of high-profile disputes and also worked to prevent pay drift in buoyant sectors from spreading across the economy and undermining national pay agreements (Higgins and Roche, 2013).

As a consequence of the crisis, major changes in this industrial relations landscape have taken place. The NIB was disbanded in 2010 following the collapse of social partnership; while provision for a tripartite body to perform some of its functions was contained in the protocol for collective bargaining and dispute resolution agreed between employers and unions following the return to firm-level bargaining, this body has largely remained dormant. Under the Workplace Relations Act 2015 a new Workplace Relations Commission (WRC) was established from October 2015 as an independent, statutory body responsible for employment rights issues. It assumes the roles and functions previously carried out by the National Employment Rights Authority, Equality Tribunal, LRC, Rights Commissioners Service, and the first-instance complaints and referrals functions of the Employment Appeals Tribunal. It is thus now the body to which all industrial relations, employment law and employment equality disputes and complaints are referred. It has responsibility for the maintenance and promotion of good workplace relations and compliance with relevant enactments, and its core services include the inspection of employment rights compliance and the provision of mediation, conciliation, facilitation and advisory services. The Labour Court retains its autonomy but now operates as the body to which appeals are made.

3. INDUSTRIAL RELATIONS, FLEXIBILITY AND SECURITY, AND INEQUALITIES

Structured social dialogue through the social partnership process described in the previous section was central to the operation of industrial relations and was an important input into policy formation across a broad span in Ireland over the period from 1987 up to the economic crisis. Its impact on employment and living standards and on the attainment of social goals – including addressing poverty, inequality and insecurity – has been hotly debated (see, for example, O'Donnell and O'Riordan, 2000; Baccaro and Simoni, 2002; O'Donnell, 2008; O'Riain, 2008; Sweeney, 2008). Baccaro and Simoni (2002) argued that centralised wage bargaining contributed to growth and employment by linking wage increases in the dynamic multinational sector to wage and productivity increases in the domestic sector. Honohan and Walsh (2004) note that while the factors underpinning wage developments have proved resistant to an agreed econometric explanation, most observers regard the coincidence of timing of the reversal of the deteriorating trend in competitiveness with the new approach to pay bargaining as suggesting that the latter did pay dividends. Wage restraint contributed to enhanced competitiveness as the Celtic Tiger boom accelerated, and while there was considerable drift in private sector wage rates above what was agreed in the national agreements in the late-1990s and early 2000s, the weakness of the euro between 1999 and 2002 helped to keep Irish labour competitive. Later analysis by Kelly et al. (2009b) also supports the notion that centralised wage bargaining generated restraint and improved competitiveness in unit labour cost terms for much of the boom period.

A key feature of the agreements was the lowering of income tax on employees, which was crucial to the moderation of nominal wage claims. Along with rapidly falling top marginal tax rates, income tax thresholds were raised sharply in real terms, taking increasingly more of the lower paid out of the income tax net. Towards the latter part of the growth period competitiveness was eroded, but the vulnerabilities that emerged were much broader. Domestic demand became the main driver of economic growth, with the construction sector growing very rapidly, fuelled by a very rapid increase in levels of household debt and accompanied by a property price surge. The tax base became dependent on property-related revenue, and thus especially vulnerable to a downturn in property prices, while this was even truer of the banks as they lent heavily for real estate purchases. Critics have argued that social partnership contributed to the failings in fiscal policy and regulation that exacerbated the impact of the global financial crisis on Ireland; whether these failings would have been addressed more effectively in a different institutional setting is difficult to judge.

What is not disputed is the positive impact of the social partnership agreements on the industrial relations climate. FitzGerald (1999), for example, argued that the main contribution of social partnership to Ireland's economic turnaround was in bringing about industrial peace and hence improving the country's competitiveness. The strike rate fell to a much lower level after the new wage bargaining system was launched in 1987, and for the next two decades strikes ceased to be a general problem, with only occasional upticks in the number of strike days lost per year, mostly due to public sector activity by, for example, teachers and nurses. As Teague et al. (2015b) put it, the period from the 1990s involved less collective workplace conflict than at any other time in Ireland's history since independence (in 1922). In assessing the influence of social partnership, they point out that working days lost owing to strikes also fell sharply from the 1980s in other developed economies with a variety of bargaining levels and configurations. The rate of decline was relatively high for Ireland, though, moving it from the middle range closer to low-conflict countries, suggesting that the partnership agreements helped – especially in reducing conflict over pay (rather than redundancies and reorganisation). Employers welcomed industrial peace and the saving of time and energy achieved by the centralisation and coordination of wage bargaining. Most multinational corporations had previously accepted the presence of unions in their Irish operations as a matter of course, but pressure to do so eased during the 1980s slump, and they were subsequently happy to combine the corporatist approach to wage bargaining at the national level with a union-free workplace. In 2007 the total number of days lost to strike activity was only 6038, a remarkably low figure in any circumstances but especially in a very tight labour market with unemployment at only about 4 per cent.

This underpinned the remarkable rise in employment over the boom period, which, as previously noted, went from 1.2 million to over 2 million. These jobs were created in a labour market characterised in comparative studies as very flexible (see, for example, Andranik, 2008). This view is supported by the OECD (2013) review of Employment Protection Legislation for 43 countries, showing that employment protection in Ireland is low across a range of dimensions, including procedural inconvenience, notice, severance pay and difficulty of dismissal. Based on a composite measure of these factors, only six of the 43 countries analysed (the United States, Canada, the United Kingdom, New Zealand, Hungary and Switzerland) have weaker employment protection legislation. Employment protection was enhanced over the period of the boom and strengthening employee rights and the enforcement of these rights featured in many of the partnership discussions and agreements. For example, the agreement intended to cover the period from 2006 to 2015, concluded at the height of the boom, devoted considerable attention to the creation of a new Office of Director for Employment Rights Compliance, to an agreed approach to attaining compliance and to strengthening penalties and redress.

While such institutional change, promoted via social dialogue, will have been important, so clearly was the fact that full-time work was available to most of those seeking it, and the strength of labour demand also empowered workers in bargaining in terms of contract type and working conditions. The numbers in part-time employment rose alongside full-time jobs, predominantly held by women as female labour force participation rose, in a context where childcare was particularly costly compared with other countries. Temporary contracts also became more common, but again their implications in terms of precarity should be seen in the context of strong labour demand. Zero-hours contracts and related contract types with variable and uncertain hours do not appear to have increased in the boom period: the in-depth study by O'Sullivan et al. (2015), for example, notes that labour force survey data show that the proportion of workers with constantly variable part-time hours fell slightly in the period 1998 to 2007.

The increase in employment during the boom was accompanied by strong growth in earnings across the distribution. Combining data from the European Community Household Panel (ECHP) and European Union Statistics on Income and Living Standards (EU-SULC), Maître et al. (2010) found that both mean and median hourly earnings rose by one-third in real terms between 1994 and 2007. Focusing on the dispersion of wages among employees, a number of cross-country studies have suggested that coordinated wage bargaining may limit growth in earnings inequality. Here the evidence for Ireland is mixed. Barrett et al. (2002) found that there was large growth in earnings dispersion in Ireland between the commencement of the social partnership arrangements in 1987 and 1994, and concluded that centralised wage setting was not sufficient to limit the growth in earnings inequality. This is despite the fact that the structuring of the wage agreements will have played some role in constraining earnings dispersion in the private sector, with some underpinning percentage increases in wages by floors for the absolute increase in wages to be awarded, benefiting low-paid workers. Further analysis by Barrett et al. (2002) demonstrated that wage inequality stabilised in the mid-1990s, a result they attributed in part to a marked increase in high-skilled inward migration. McGuinness et al. (2009) found that wage inequality fell for Irish men between 1994 and 2001, and for women between 1997 and 2001, the latter in particular being partly attributed to the introduction of the minimum wage in 2000 noted earlier. Initially set at IR£4.40 per hour for experienced adult employees in April 2000, equivalent to €5.58, it was increased over time at irregular intervals broadly in line with median earnings up to the onset of the economic crisis, at which point it had reached €8.65.

Voitchovsky et al. (2012) also found that dispersion in hourly wages fell sharply from 1994 to 2000, before increasing during the period to 2007. The latter increase in dispersion appears to have been primarily driven by rising returns to skill rather than changing composition; the latter contributed to wage growth throughout the distribution, but the magnitudes of these changes were small compared with the impact of rising returns. Centrally bargained wage increases generally acted as a floor in the private sector over this period of strong economic performance, with more profitable firms awarding larger increases, especially in the multinational sector. Once again the structuring of the centrally agreed wage increases in the partnership programmes over this period will have contributed to limiting or even compressing earnings inequality towards the bottom, for example, with some again providing minimum absolute increases for the low paid. The minimum wage was clearly also important in ensuring that the bottom of the distribution kept pace with the middle of the distribution, as reflected in the close correlation between the evolution of the bottom decile cut-off and the median shown in Voitchovsky et al. (2012) and other studies. Broader forces affecting the demand and supply of labour with different education and skill levels will have been the main drivers of the way earnings across the rest of the distribution developed. However, the fact that wage negotiations at both central and firm levels were framed within an agreed overall perspective on the importance of competitiveness may have been particularly important in limiting the growth in dispersion in the first part of the boom. The central role the partnership structures played in influencing wages in the public sector and the differentials between public and private sectors may have been particularly important in the latter part of the boom, as discussed in more detail in section 4.

The trend in earnings inequality changed dramatically with the onset of the crisis in 2008. The pattern of wage changes up to 2013 resulted in a significant fall in inequality, with real wages falling across most of the distribution but the bottom faring relatively well. Real wages fell despite substantial improvements in the skills of the workforce, which in more normal circumstances would have been expected to go with substantial wage gains. The fact that wages for the lowest paid workers held up reflects the protective impact of the national minimum wage. One of the government's responses to the crisis was to reduce the national minimum wage by €1 in early 2011, but this cut was reversed in mid-2011 after a change of government and an election promise to do so. The level of the minimum wage was close to the tenth percentile of the wage distribution in both 2008 and 2013, and wage growth at the tenth percentile closely tracked growth in the minimum wage throughout the entire period from its introduction. With inflation running at an exceptionally low level its value in real terms was largely sustained, providing an effective floor for the bottom of the wage distribution.

Firms responded to the crisis in part by adjusting hours of work, but Walsh (2012) found from employer surveys that 23 per cent of establishments also reported cuts in average hourly earnings between 2008 and 2009, rising to 31 per cent between 2009 and 2010. Doris et al. (2015) used administrative longitudinal data to follow individual annual earnings for employees between 2005 and 2013, concentrating on employees who stayed in the same employment. They found a substantial degree of downward nominal wage flexibility in the pre-crisis period, supporting the view that the Irish labour market is flexible. The proportion of workers receiving earnings cuts then increased more than threefold during the crisis, whereas after the peak of the crisis pay freezes became more common. Using data from EU-SILC they found that the initial impact of the crisis was a 1 per cent decline in median annual earnings in 2008–09 and 2009–10, with 55 per cent seeing an annual wage fall. In the period from 2010–11 to 2012–13, the median annual change was close to zero, while about one-third registered a wage fall, still well above pre-crisis levels. The earnings cuts during the crisis were highly progressive, though with the median pay change for those in the bottom one-third in 2008 who were in the same jobs in 2013 being positive, whereas for the middle third it was −0.5 per cent and for the upper third it was −5 per cent. This mostly reflected what happened to pay in the public sector during the crisis, as discussed in more detail in section 4.

While patterns of earnings change for those who kept their jobs are important, it is also worth highlighting that low-paid workers lost their jobs in relatively large numbers during the Great Recession. The serious impact of the crisis on highly educated workers such as architects and engineers, owing to the dramatic cutbacks in construction activity, were the subject of considerable media attention. However, Nolan and Voitchovsky's (2016) analysis of EU-SILC data shows that those with lower levels of qualifications and those in low-wage employment at the onset of the crisis had the highest risk of losing their job and being unemployed a year later.

The dramatic increase in unemployment was accompanied by a growth in precarious work. In the crisis, part-time employment became more important and the proportion saying they were involuntarily in that position rose significantly. Some other forms of precarious employment also became more prevalent. Temporary employment rose in the private sector to 2011 but then fell back, and rates of temporary employment were still low by international standards, at about 7 per cent of workers (some in high-skilled sectors such as information and communication technology – ICT – and finance). O'Sullivan et al. (2015) show that the proportion of workers with constantly variable part-time hours almost doubled between 2007 and 2014, rising from 1.4 to 2.6 per cent. The number of self-employed without employees, sometimes also seen as potentially precarious, had been rising up to the crisis but then fell back up to 2012, only now returning to pre-crisis levels. There is some evidence of 'bogus' self-employment, encouraged by the structure of the tax system, while flexibility in terms of working hours is also more commonly imposed by employers in the hospitality sector, construction, and finance and ICT (Bobek and Wickham, 2016).

Subjective job insecurity rose very rapidly in the recession: in 2010, over one-quarter of Irish workers feared that they would lose their jobs in the next six months, very high by international standards (Russell and McGinnity, 2014, 2015). Subjective insecurity was highly structured by sector and was higher among men, partly because it was lower in the public sector where women are more heavily represented. There is also evidence that work pressure increased for those remaining in employment, associated with staff reductions and company reorganisation; in this case public sector workers experienced higher work pressure and lower job control than their private sector counterparts, with average levels of job control in the public sector falling and work pressure rising between 2003 and 2009.

At the same time, both social protection levels for those experiencing unemployment and universal child benefit were cut as part of the fiscal adjustment strategy (whereas pensions were not). This reduced security in terms of the safety net provided by the social protection system, as well as incomes of families more broadly. The growth of insecure employment and a trend for employees to be converted into self-employed contract workers also became a serious source of concern. This has to be seen in a broader context in which the limited level and coverage of social security for the self-employed has been a particular focus, as their incomes were sometimes particularly seriously hit by recession.

In response the government has investigated ways of strengthening social protection for the self-employed, and introduced measures to ensure minimum pay for workers on zero-hours contracts, so that they must be compensated for 25 per cent or 15 hours of the time they had to make themselves available. It also commissioned an independent report on the prevalence of zero-hours contracts (O'Sullivan et al., 2015). This report concluded that zero-hours contracts as defined within current Irish employment rights legislation are not extensively used. There is, however, evidence of so-called 'if and when' contracts, where (unlike zero-hours contracts proper) workers are not contractually required to make themselves available for work, raising questions over the extent to which they are protected by employment legislation.

There have also been recent institutional changes with respect to the minimum wage, as noted previously, with the establishment of an independent Low Pay Commission to advise on the rate to be set. The commission's first report, in 2015 (LPC, 2015), recommended that the national minimum wage should go up by 50 cents per hour, a 5.8 per cent increase, with no change in the sub-minimum rates for young people and certain trainees, and this was implemented by the government from the beginning of 2016. In its second report, issued in mid-2016 (LPC, 2016), the commission recommended a marginal further increase of 0.10 cent per hour, with three of the nine members publicly disagreeing with that majority recommendation and arguing for a larger increase.

As far as industrial peace is concerned, strike activity remained very low through the recession, despite the collapse of the social partnership structure (with the exception of a one-day strike by public sector workers in late 2009, which boosted the total for that year). The total number of strikes reached a record low of just five in 2012. The very high level of unemployment brought on by the recession would be expected to have a dampening effect on dispute activity, but the role of state-led dispute resolution agencies was also important, with the LRC having an increased role (Regan, 2012). As economic activity and employment began to pick up and unemployment turned down from 2013, strike activity continued to be rare until recently, with industrial action by teachers accounting for most of the limited upturn in days lost up to 2016. However, recent months have seen strikes in public transport and industrial action in the broader public sector, as pressure mounts for the reversal of pay cuts imposed during the crisis. Prospects for industrial peace are highly uncertain, as discussed in the next section.

Focusing, finally, on overall inequality and social inclusion, the economic boom brought about a large reduction in absolute income poverty and in non-monetary measures of deprivation, which then rose markedly in the recession, but there has been no clear trend in income inequality (or relative income poverty) in Ireland over the past three decades. Indeed, standard measures of income inequality remained within a relatively narrow range throughout the period despite the dramatic macroeconomic fluctuations from recession to the fastest rates of growth in the OECD and then one of the most severe declines in income per head in the crisis. The Gini coefficient derived from household survey data, for example, was rarely outside the 0.30–0.32 range (for detailed discussion, see Callan et al., 2015; Maître and Nolan, 2016), though the share of total gross income going to the very top is seen from income tax data to have risen substantially over these years.

This stability in overall income inequality is a very different trajectory to the substantial increases in inequality seen in many rich countries, including Ireland's nearest neighbour the United Kingdom with which it has much in common in terms of institutional setting and broader 'liberal' model/welfare regime. The strong role which social dialogue played via the social partnership process is certainly a striking difference between Ireland and the United Kingdom, where centralised bargaining was absent and the unions had little or no direct input into the framing of economic and social policy. The social partnership process in Ireland clearly provided a mechanism through which policies could be discussed and agreed by the social partners going well beyond wages to incorporate most importantly tax and social transfers, which played a major role in the way income inequality evolved. The impact of direct redistribution via the tax-transfer system on different parts of the income distribution over different periods has been analysed using the SWITCH tax-benefit simulation model developed by Tim Callan at the Economic and Social Research Institute. This focuses on the effects of discretionary changes in the structure and parameters of the system, compared with a 'distributionally neutral' benchmark that would index those parameters (such as welfare rates) to the change actually observed in average wages. These analyses show that budgetary changes in direct taxes and transfers had distributive effects that varied considerably across different sub-periods when the partnership process was in place, including from programme to programme – not least because the underlying macroeconomic environment varied greatly.

Under the initial Programme for National Recovery from 1987, for example, budgetary packages produced very substantial gains for the bottom quintile, because welfare increases focused on raising the lowest rates of social welfare payment (in line with the recommendations of an official commission that had just reported). The top quintile also experienced above-average gains, though, reflecting the fact that the top rate of income tax was cut from 58 to 53 per cent, while the standard rate was cut from 35 to 30 per cent. With the next agreement, the Programme for Economic and Social Progress to 1994, gains were greatest for the top quintile. From then through to about 2000, bottom quintiles saw below-average gains or even losses from budgetary changes in the tax-transfer system as the economy grew rapidly, mainly because social transfers lagged behind wages, whereas policy led to substantial gains for middle and upper income groups (see Callan et al., 2002). In marked contrast, budgets over the next five or six years produced substantial percentage gains for those at the bottom of the distribution and very limited gains towards the top of the distribution (see, for example, Callan et al., 2006). No summary simulation analysis of the overall impact of tax-transfer changes over the entire social partnership period is available, but such an exercise would be of limited value in light of the profound changes in the underlying structure of employment that was seen over those two decades.

In the crisis, tax-transfer policy was a major instrument in the government's effort to close the yawning fiscal deficit that emerged. Savage et al. (2015) show that while inequality in market incomes rose sharply, the redistributive impact of the tax and transfer systems taken together also rose substantially, reflecting both discrete policy choices, but also the 'automatic stabilisers' which operate through taxes and transfers as household incomes from the market fall. The distributional impact of the measures adopted varied considerably from one budget or year to the next, as revealed by similar simulation-based studies, and depend on whether the analysis is extended beyond direct taxes and cash transfers to include other policy responses, such as raising indirect taxes and reducing public sector pay. In broad terms the packages implemented were more progressively structured in the early years of the crisis than during the later part and the emerging recovery. The overall impact of the broad set of discretionary tax-transfer and public pay measures introduced in exchequer budgets for 2009 to 2015 was to produce substantial income losses at all income levels. Callan et al. (2015) report broadly similar percentage losses of 10–11 per cent over much of the income range, but higher percentage losses for the lowest income group (close to 13 per cent) and the highest income group (about 14 per cent). In interpreting these estimates of impact on various deciles, it must be stressed that these will not contain the same people from one year to the next; especially in such a deep recession, there was significant income mobility for households from year to year. Savage et al. (2015) show that the above-average fall in average income for the bottom decile was driven by the incomes of those dropping into the bottom 10 per cent, including, for example, self-employed suffering major declines in income and falling through the social security safety-net rather than those who were at the bottom of the distribution as the crisis struck.

The role of social partnership, in the years in which it operated, was not confined to concern with inequality in household incomes. A great deal of attention was paid in the various partnership programmes to 'social progress', in particular public services and the 'social wage', to labour market interventions directed towards the unemployed before unemployment plummeted, and to equality and fairness construed in broad terms and encompassing gender, disability and discrimination. The development of greater social rights within health, education, social welfare and housing services was a prominent theme throughout. The 2003 programme 'Sustaining Progress', for example, had 'Delivering a fair and inclusive society' as a core aim, to be promoted by addressing poverty, health inequalities, and discrimination and improving access to quality public services. The final programme agreed, 'Towards 2016', set out a framework within which the key social challenges facing individuals at each stage of life would be tackled, focusing on the needs of children, young adults, people of working age, older people and people with disabilities. The scope of the partnership agreements in policy terms, especially the later ones, was very wide, bringing together strategies and specific government actions across policy domains ranging from health and education to transport, housing, regional and rural development, tourism, energy, enterprise and sustainability. Social partnership was seen by some key actors as settling the distributional questions, leaving the government free to concentrate on growing the economy (see, for example, Begg, 2016). It is difficult to know how policies across such a broad span would have evolved in the absence of the social partnership mechanism, much less to evaluate their combined effects on inequality broadly conceived over two decades. Irish politics and the electoral system are generally characterised as limiting ideological debate and promoting a 'something for everyone' approach in good times, which may be seen as applying across the years of the Celtic Tiger boom.

While the social partnership process disintegrated in the crisis, we could arguably see the policies adopted then as also 'sharing the pain' of adjustment even in the absence of structured social dialogue, although views differ markedly as to how fairly that burden was spread (see, for example, Callan et al., 2015, Whelan and Nolan, 2016; Whelan et al., 2016). The capacity of the social protection system to provide an effective safety net was severely tested, but the extent to which enhanced redistribution via transfers and direct taxes served to counteract the increase in inequality in market income in the Irish case has been remarked on in comparative studies. The reduction in the numbers working in the public sector and the broader cuts in expenditure on public services entailed by 'fiscal correction' will have impacted on the quality of services provided across the healthcare and education systems in particular, which account for much of the expenditure, but in ways that are very difficult to capture empirically and to assess. The collapse in property values at the time of the crash, following on the explosion in borrowing during the latter part of the boom, also affected households across the income distribution. The limited supply of social housing has meant that more low-income families have been pushed into the private rented sector, where rent levels have been increasing as economic recovery set in, and a marked increase in homelessness has brought that centre-stage as a pressing societal problem.

4. CASE STUDIES

We now go on to consider in more depth two topics that represent interesting case studies with respect to social dialogue, each flagged up in our earlier discussion as of critical importance in the Irish case. The first of these focuses on inequality, social dialogue and public sector wages and employment, while the second is concerned with inequality, social dialogue and macroeconomic shocks. These are interlinked, with the inability of social dialogue to arrive at an agreed response to the economic crisis, in particular with respect to public sector pay and conditions, central to both.

4.1 Inequality, Social Dialogue and Public Sector Pay

While Ireland's social partnership arrangements provided a mechanism for the consideration of government policy across a very wide span, as well as for wage bargaining, the latter was of central importance, and within that, the determination of pay and conditions for public sector employees was a core element. In the early part of the economic boom, wages in the private sector accelerated alongside the number in employment as national output grew at the fastest rate in the OECD and wage awards in profitable companies exceeded the floors agreed through the collective bargaining component of the partnership agreements. Public sector pay then rose particularly rapidly in the latter part of the boom, owing to a combination of the national pay agreements negotiated under the social partnership process, together with special 'benchmarking' and associated awards to public servants. The key Public Service Benchmarking Body Report (2002) recommended such increases on the basis that pay for public sector employees had lagged behind their private sector counterparts, although it did not produce compelling evidence that this was the case. Academic studies suggested that public sector workers already enjoyed a wage premium at that point (Boyle et al., 2004), while comparisons of recent trends in public versus private sector pay were constrained by the data available and varied with the base date chosen.

Subsequently, studies that appeared just as the economic and financial crisis struck, by Kelly et al. (2009a, 2009b), were particularly influential in suggesting that the public sector premium for all employees rose sharply as a consequence of these increases. They estimated the increase in this premium from 2003 to 2006 at 12 percentage points on average (from between 10 and 14 per cent to between 22 and 26 per cent, depending on the precise definition of public sector and specification of the statistical model employed). Quantile regression indicated that this advantage was greatest for public sector employees at the lower end of the earnings distribution and also varied widely across sub-sectors and occupations, being lowest in the central Civil Service and local authorities and highest in education and for police and prison officers. Such public sector premia are high compared with those estimated for other countries, as presented in, for example, Lucifora and Meurs (2006) and Bargain and Melly (2008). There was some argument over the data and methodology employed, focused on the appropriateness of including controls for organisational size and trade union membership and the difficulty of finding appropriate comparators (see, for example, Central Statistics Office, 2009; Geary and Murphy, 2009), but the notion that pay in the public sector was 'out of line' – particularly in light of their pension arrangements – was widely advanced.

This had a significant effect on how debates on how best to respond to the economic crisis were framed. With wages and salaries one of the most important elements in public expenditure, the scale of the deterioration in the public finances left the government with little choice but to reduce the public sector wage bill. Public sector trade unions ended up reluctantly accepting this and the argument that it would be preferable to achieve those reductions through cuts in pay rather than numbers employed. However, agreement between government and unions could not be reached on how this could be achieved, and as a consequence the government imposed a set of pay cuts, described as 'Financial Emergency Measures in the Public Interest', as part of its broader package of spending cuts and tax increases. A public sector pension levy was introduced in 2009, from which the first €15 000 of earnings were exempt, but with 5 per cent charged on the next €5000 of earnings, 10 per cent on earnings between €20 000 and €60 000 and 10.5 per cent on earnings above €60 000. The Budget for 2010 then cut public service salaries by 5 per cent on the first €30 000 of pay, 7.5 per cent on the next €40 000 and 10 per cent on the next €55 000; salaries above €125 000 were reduced by proportionately more.

These cuts in public sector pay made a significant contribution to the fiscal adjustment achieved by the Irish government, under the oversight of the 'Troika' following the 'bail-out' by the EU, the European Central Bank (ECB) and the IMF from 2010. Research has shown that these cuts were progressive in terms of where their impact was felt across the income distribution (Callan et al., 2014a, 2014b). With few public servants in the bottom 40 per cent of the household disposable income distribution, income losses ranged from 6–8 per cent in deciles 5 to 9 to over 9 per cent in the top decile. This progressive impact reflected the fact that public sector workers had higher pay (partly reflecting their higher education and skill levels) than private sector workers, on average, and that both the pension levy and pay cuts were structured to affect higher-paid employees more in proportionate terms than lower-paid employees.

An agreement was subsequently made between the government and public sector unions (the so-called 'Haddington Rd Agreement') that there would be no further reductions in pay and that cuts in employee numbers would be through voluntary redundancy or retirement, in return for staff engagement with efficiency-enhancing measures, including increasing hours of work. A further such agreement (the 'Lansdowne Rd Agreement') was subsequently made covering 2013–16. While these succeeded in maintaining industrial peace through the period of deep recession and extremely painful fiscal 'correction', this is now under serious threat in the recovery as industrial action has been taken or threatened by a variety of public sector workers, including nurses, teachers and transport workers. The government has established a non-statutory Public Service Pay Commission with a former chairman of the Labour Court (with a trade union background) as chair. This is to be advisory in nature, its role being to provide evidence-based objective analysis on pay matters to assist officials in negotiating with the unions on behalf of the government. It has been asked to provide an initial report in the second quarter of 2017, to include input on how the unwinding of the Financial Emergency Measures in the Public Interest legislation should proceed. However, in the face of unprecedented threats of industrial action from the police (who are not a party to the pay agreement), a settlement was recently agreed with them for pay increases that may set a headline for other public sector employees. The appropriate pay levels for these employees, in a context in which workers more generally are seeking tax cuts and there is widespread demand for improved public services, is perhaps the most challenging issue facing the current (minority) government.

4.2 Inequality, Social Dialogue and Macroeconomic Shocks

As we have seen, 'social partnership' was an innovative institutional structure for social dialogue in Ireland, introduced in response to the prolonged recession of the 1980s. While its contribution to underpinning the economic boom from the mid-1990s is debated, as was discussed in some detail in section 2, our focus here is on the 'bust' and the disintegration of these arrangements in the face of another, even more severe, economic shock in 2008. The inability of these social dialogue structures to survive and prove helpful in addressing the crisis merits careful consideration, with implications beyond the Irish case.

Owing to the crisis, the Irish government looked to cut public sector pay and job numbers as a central plank of fiscal adjustment, as outlined in the first case study, in the face of union opposition. The government stated its intention to seek a coordinated response and discussions were held through the National Economic and Social Council (which includes representatives of business and employers' organisations, trade unions, farming organisations, community and voluntary organisations, heads of government departments and independent experts, and played a key role in the social partnership process), as well as directly with the trade unions. However, agreement could not be reached, the public sector pension levy and subsequent reductions in public service salaries were implemented and the partnership process disintegrated, as described earlier. The sectoral agreement made with public sector unions in 2010 and its successor from 2013 succeeded in maintaining industrial peace through the period of fiscal adjustment, but social dialogue made little or no direct contribution to how that adjustment was implemented. Trade unions became increasingly vocal in their opposition to the pace of adjustment or 'austerity', the balance between tax increases and public expenditure reductions and particular cuts in services.

The Irish Business and Employers Confederation (IBEC) formally walked away from the final partnership agreement in December 2009 and few private sector companies implemented its terms. There was no collective negotiation to minimise lay-offs in the private sector in return for wage and/or working time concessions, as occurred in some other countries with strong social dialogue. It could be argued that the much greater scale of the collapse in economic activity in Ireland than in most other EU countries, not least because of the openness of the economy, the scale of the property and construction collapse and the bank 'bail-out', militated against such an outcome. However, the way social partnership evolved, operated in the 'good times' and was perceived also played a role.

Regan (2012, 2013) argues that a social pact could not be negotiated in Ireland to frame the response to the crisis because Irish trade unions lacked sufficient deterrent power in the labour market and the voluntarist nature of the process (with no legal requirement to implement collectively negotiated wage increases or extend them to non-union employees) enabled employers and government to walk away from social partnership with limited repercussions. Others regard the collapse of partnership as more contingent and something that might have been avoided, with the media representation of union proposals for short-time working in the public sector as 'extra paid holidays' being particularly unhelpful (Roche, 2013). It is clear, though, that by the time the crisis struck, partnership was already the subject of serious criticism. Some critics saw social partnership as contributing to the increase in public spending and tax cuts, as well as lax regulation, which fuelled domestic demand, borrowing and the property and construction boom that left Ireland particularly vulnerable when the global financial crisis hit. Some in the trade union movement had always been critical of involvement in the social partnership process, arguing that wage bargaining at national level helped to undermine the legitimacy of organised labour in influencing practices at the workplace level and weakened unions at that level (see, for example, Allen, 2010). Others criticised the corporatist nature of the social partnership arrangements, seeing them as reducing the role of elected members of parliament; furthermore, the breadth of representation in the partnership process beyond the traditional 'core' of government, employers and trade unions was seen by some as a strength but by others as diluting its effectiveness.

As a consequence of the collapse of the social partnership process, the government continues to negotiate public sector pay and conditions directly with the relevant unions in the manner described in the previous case study, while collective bargaining in the private sector decentralised to company level. Roche (2011) regards this as a relatively orderly decentralisation of collective bargaining, with private sector employers and unions agreeing 'Protocols' on mechanisms for the orderly conduct of collective bargaining at firm level. While Regan (2012) argues that the breakdown of social partnership at national level has gone hand in hand with a lack of effective trade union activity at sectoral and company level, others argue that trade unions and employers adapted to the very different economic environment and implemented strategies for local bargaining negotiations (Eurofound, 2014). As the economic recovery gathers pace and the labour market tightens, the absence of centralised structures for wage bargaining and social dialogue may come to be seen as a more significant gap, but there is little evidence of support for a restoration of social partnership-type structures. As one academic commentator put it, 'the predominant face of Irish trade unionism continues to be one of restrained mobilisation and of attempts to preserve [its] cooperative orientation and to portray itself as a vehicle for the achievement of social cohesion' (Geary, 2016). The emerging demand for wage rises in the private sector and the competing pressures for the 'restoration' of pay in the public sector, improved public services and tax cuts will be very difficult to manage. These key societal choices, with potentially critical implications for inequality, will not be informed by structured high-level social dialogue.

5. CONCLUSIONS AND KEY POLICY ISSUES

This chapter has described how a highly structured social dialogue or 'partnership' process operated over the two decades up to the economic crisis in Ireland. Over this period Ireland remained towards the flexible end of the spectrum in terms of employment protection and provided a social security safety net that, although not particularly generous, was regarded as robust in terms of coverage, with few gaps. While union density continued to decline and public sector employees became more important in that regard, industrial relations institutions and the broader social partnership process combined to maintain industrial peace before the crisis and this is widely regarded as having underpinned rapid economic growth. The benefits of that growth were widely dispersed across the income distribution and social partnership may also have played a role there, most obviously in the way tax and income support policies operated to redistribute income. The extent of the increase in employment during the boom years and the pattern of wage rate increases also meant that gains in market income were seen across much of the income distribution. Both the collectively bargained pattern of wage increases and the underpinning of employment growth via an overall strategy agreed through social partnership are likely to have made some significant contribution in that respect, although the centrality or otherwise of that contribution is not easy to pin down empirically.

We then saw how the high-level social partnership process disintegrated in the face of the economic and financial crisis, which affected Ireland particularly badly. The dramatic increase in unemployment and job insecurity meant there was little strike activity through the recession, despite the breakdown of social partnership, and involuntary part-time working and precarious employment also increased, although extreme forms of precarity, such as zero-hours contracts, were still not widespread. The severity of the Great Recession also revealed some gaps in the coverage of the social safety net that had not been evident previously, notably for the self-employed. The crucial role of the minimum wage in underpinning low earnings through the recession is clear and its smooth introduction could be seen as a product of social dialogue, at least to some extent.

As a form of deliberative governance, social dialogue in its Irish variant did not seem fit for purpose when it came to hard decision-making in the crisis, as we have discussed in the course of the chapter and in detail as one of the case studies. Some have argued that governmental unilateralism was always likely to take the upper hand in such times, whereas others have seen the demise of social partnership as more contingent and potentially avoidable (see Eurofound, 2014; Regan, 2012; Farrelly et al., 2013; Roche, 2013). The sheer depth of the crisis and recession, which were especially severe in the Irish case in terms of the scale of the decline in incomes and the bank bail-out required, the fall in property prices and private debt overhang, and the increase in the fiscal deficit and public debt, militated against the survival of the social partnership structures. Opinions also differ as to the likelihood of some such centralised form of high-level social dialogue re-emerging now that economic growth has returned and unemployment has come down substantially, but there is no evidence as yet of it doing so.

Public service pay and public services were a central focus for social partnership when it operated and reductions in pay for public sector employees and restrictions on their numbers played a central role in the response to the economic crisis, as detailed in our other case study. The scale of the public sector pay increases awarded at the height of the boom under social partnership would now be seen by many as a key argument against reinstating such high-level social dialogue structures. However, the emergence of industrial unrest across the public sector is now challenging industrial relations institutions, which have themselves been recently re-configured, in its absence. The scale of the overhang from the crisis, with high public debt and pent-up demand for higher wages, lower taxes and improved public services, means that very substantial challenges face government, employers and unions whatever mechanisms for dialogue are adopted.

REFERENCES

Allen, K. (2010), 'The trade unions: from partnership to crisis', *Irish Journal of Sociology*, **18** (2), 22–37.

Andranik, T. (2008), 'On the European readiness for flexicurity: empirical evidence', Discussion Paper No. 160, Institute of Economic and Social Research (WSI), Hans-Böckler-Foundation, Dusseldorf.

Baccaro, L. and M. Simoni (2002), 'Centralized wage bargaining and the "Celtic Tiger" phenomenon', *Industrial Relations*, **46** (3), 426–55.

Bargain, O. and B. Melly (2008), 'Public sector pay gap in France: new evidence using panel data', IZA Discussion Paper No. 3427, Institute for Labour Economics, Bonn.

Barrett, A., J. FitzGerald and B. Nolan (2002), 'Earnings inequality, returns to education and immigration into Ireland', *Labour Economics*, **9** (5), 665–80.

Begg, D. (2016), *Ireland, Small Open Economies and European Integration: Lost in Transition*, Basingstoke, UK: Palgrave Macmillan.

Bobek, A. and J. Wickham (2016), *Enforced Flexibility? Working in Ireland Today*, Dublin: Tasc.
Boyle, G., R. McElligot and J. O'Leary (2004), 'Public–private wage differentials in Ireland, 1994–2001', *Quarterly Economic Commentary*, (2), 1–23.
Callan, T., K. Coleman and J.R. Walsh (2006), 'Budget 2006: impact on income distribution and relative income poverty', *Quarterly Economic Commentary*, Winter, Economic and Social Research Institute, Dublin.
Callan, T., B. Colgan, C. Logue, M. Savage and J.R. Walsh (2015), 'Distributional impact of tax, welfare and public service pay policies: Budget 2016 and Budgets 2009–2016', *Quarterly Economic Commentary*, special article, Winter.
Callan, T., C. Keane, M. Savage, J.R. Walsh and B. Colgan (2014a), 'Ireland's economic adjustment: from crisis to recovery', *Intereconomics*, **49** (6), 318–22.
Callan, T., M. Keeney and J.R. Walsh (2002), 'The distributive impact of budgetary policy: a medium-term view', in T. Callan, D. McCoy and D. Madden (eds), *Budget Perspectives*, Dublin: Economic and Social Research Institute, pp. 33–40.
Callan, T., B. Nolan, C. Keane, M. Savage and J.R. Walsh (2014b), 'Crisis, response and distributional impact: the case of Ireland', *IZA Journal of European Labor Studies*, **3** (9), 3–9.
Central Statistics Office (2009), 'Specific analysis of the public/private sector pay differential for National Employment Survey 2009 & 2010 data', research paper, Central Statistics Office, Dublin.
D'Art, D. and T. Turner (2006), 'Workers and the demand for trade unions in Europe: still a relevant social force?', *Economic and Industrial Democracy*, **29** (2), 165–91.
Doris, A., D. O'Neill and O. Sweetman (2015), 'Wage flexibility and the great recession: the response of the Irish labour market', *IZA Journal of Labour Studies*, **4** (1), 1–24.
Ebbinghaus, B. and J. Visser (1999), 'When institutions matter: union growth and decline in Western Europe, 1950–1995.' *European Sociological Review*, **15** (2), 135–58.
Eurofound (2014), *Impact of the Crisis on Industrial Relations and Working Conditions in Europe*, Dublin: Eurofound.
Farrelly, R., C. Higgins, A. Prendergast and A. Sheehan (2013), 'The impact of the crisis on industrial relations in Ireland', paper for the ILERA 2013 Eurofound symposium 'The impact of the crisis on industrial relations,' Amsterdam, 22 June, IRN, Dublin.
FitzGerald, J. (1999), 'Wage formation and the labour market', in F. Barry (ed.), *Understanding Ireland's Economic Growth*, Basingstoke, UK: Palgrave Macmillan, pp. 137–66.
Freeman, R. and J. Pelletier (1990), 'The impact of industrial relations legislation on British union density,' *British Journal of Industrial Relations*, **28** (2), 141–64.
Geary, J. (2016), 'Public sector pay talks are a matter of urgency', *Irish Times*, 21 November, accessed 21 November 2017 at https://www.irishtimes.com/opinion/john-geary-public-sector-pay-talks-are-a-matter-of-urgency-1.2875479.
Geary, J. and A. Murphy (2009), 'Cutting public sector pay: an alternative view', *Industrial Relations News*, 4 November.
Hastings, T., B. Sheehan and P. Yeates (2007), *Saving the Future: How Social Partnership Shaped Ireland's Economic Success*, Dublin: Blackhall.
Higgins, C. and W.K. Roche (2013), 'Networked pay coordination and the con-

tainment of second-tier pay bargaining: social partnership at the height of the economic boom', *Economic and Industrial Democracy*, **35** (4), 667–93.
Honohan, P. and B.M. Walsh (2004), 'Catching up with the leaders: the Irish hare', *Brookings Papers on Economic Activity*, **1,** 1–57.
Kelly, E., S. McGuinness and P. O'Connell (2009a), 'Benchmarking, social partnership and higher remuneration: wage settling institutions and the public–private sector wage gap in Ireland', *Economic and Social Review*, **40** (3), 339–70.
Kelly, E., S. McGuinness and P.J. O'Connell (2009b), 'The impact of wage bargaining regime on firm level competitiveness and wage inequality: the case of Ireland', *Industrial Relations*, **49** (4), 593–615.
Low Pay Commission (2015), *Recommendations of the Low Pay Commission for the National Minimum Wage 2015*, Dublin: Low Pay Commission.
Low Pay Commission (2016), *Recommendations of the Low Pay Commission for the National Minimum Wage 2016*, Dublin: Low Pay Commission.
Lucifora, C. and D. Meurs (2006), 'The public sector pay gap in France, Great Britain and Italy', *Review of Income and Wealth*, **52** (1), 43–59.
Maître, B. and B. Nolan (2016), 'Middle incomes in boom and bust: the Irish experience', in D. Vaughan-Whitehead (ed.), *Europe's Disappearing Middle Class? Evidence from the World of Work*, Cheltenham, UK and Geneva: Edward Elgar and ILO.
Maître, B., B. Nolan and S. Voitchovsky (2010), 'Earnings inequality, institutions and the macroeconomy: what can we learn from Ireland's boom years?', Working Paper, Geary Institute, Dublin: UCD.
McGuinness, S., F. McGinnity and P. O'Connell (2009), 'Changing returns to education during a boom? The case of Ireland', *Labour Economics*, **23** (S1), 197–221.
Nolan, B. and S. Voitchovsky (2016), 'Job loss by wage level: lessons from the Great Recession in Ireland', *IZA Journal of European Labor Studies*, **5** (1), 1–29.
O'Donnell, R. (2008), 'The partnership state: building the ship at sea', in M. Adshead, P. Kirby and M. Millar (eds), *Contesting the State: Lessons from the Irish Case.* Manchester: Manchester University Press, pp. 73–99.
O'Donnell, R. and C. O'Riordan (2000), 'Social partnership in Ireland's economic transformation', in G. Fajertag and P. Pochet (eds), *Social Pacts in Europe — New Dynamics*, Brussels: ETUI, pp. 237–57.
O'Riain, S. (2008), 'Competing state projects in the contemporary Irish political economy', in M. Adshead, P. Kirby and M. Millar (eds), *Contesting the State: Lessons from the Irish Case*, Manchester: Manchester University Press, pp. 165–85.
O'Sullivan, M., T. Turner, J. McMahon, L. Ryan, J. Lavelle, C. Murphy, et al. (2015), *A Study on the Prevalence of Zero Hours Contracts among Irish Employers and their Impact on Employees*, Limerick: Kemmy Business School, University of Limerick.
OECD (2013), 'Detailed description of employment protection legislation, 2012–2013 OECD countries', accessed 21 November 2017 at http://www.oecd.org/els/emp/All.pdf.
Public Service Benchmarking Body (2002), *Report of the Public Service Benchmarking Body*, Dublin: Stationery Office.
Regan, A. (2012), 'The political economy of social pacts in the EMU: Irish Liberal Market Corporatism in Crisis', *New Political Economy*, **17** (4), 465–91.
Regan, A. (2013), 'The impact of the eurozone crisis on Irish social partnership: a political economy analysis', Dialogue Working Paper 49, ILO, Geneva.

Roche, W. (2013), 'Social partnership: From Lemass to Cowen', *Economic and Social Review*, **40** (2), 183–205.
Roche, W.K. (2011), 'The breakdown of social partnership', *Administration*, **59** (1), 23–37.
Russell, H. and F. McGinnity (2014), 'Under pressure. The impact of recession on employees in Ireland', *British Journal of Industrial Relations*, **52** (2), 286–307.
Russell, H. and F. McGinnity (2015), 'Work–life balance, working conditions and the Great Recession', in S. Ó Riain, F. Behling, R. Ciccia, E. Flaherty (eds), *The Changing Worlds and Workplaces of Capitalism*, Basingstoke, UK: Palgrave Macmillan, pp. 201–20.
Savage, M., Callan, T., Nolan, B. and Colgan, B. (2015), Crisis, Austerity, Recovery: Income Distribution through the Great Recession in Ireland, Working Paper No. 499, Dublin: Economic and Social Research Institute.
Sweeney, P. (2008), *Ireland's Economic Success: Reasons and Lessons*, Dublin: New Island Press.
Sweeney, P. (2015), 'Discussion of F. Walsh, "Union membership in Ireland since 2003"', *Journal of the Statistical and Social Inquiry Statistical Society of Ireland*, **44**, 100–102.
Teague, P., W.K. Roche, T. Gormley and D. Currie (2015a), *The Development of Conflict Resolution Practices in Ireland*, Dublin: Labour Relations Commission.
Teague, P., W.K. Roche, T. Gormley and D. Currie (2015b), *The Changing Pattern of Workplace Conflict in Ireland*, Dublin: Labour Relations Commission.
Voitchovsky, S., B. Maître and B. Nolan (2012), 'Wage inequality in Ireland's "Celtic Tiger" boom', *Economic and Social Review*, **43** (1), 98–9.
Walsh, F. (2015), 'Union membership in Ireland since 2003', *Journal of the Statistical and Social Inquiry Statistical Society of Ireland*, **44**, 86–98.
Walsh, K. (2012), 'Wage bill change in Ireland during recession: how have employers reacted to the downturn', *Journal of the Statistical and Social Inquiry Society of Ireland*, **41** 39–70.
Whelan, C.T. and B. Nolan (2016), 'Austerity and inequality in Ireland', in E. Heffernan, N. Moore-Cherry and J. McHale (eds), *Debating Austerity in Ireland*, Dublin: Royal Irish Academy, pp. 100–114.
Whelan, C.T., H. Russell and B. Maître (2016), 'Economic stress and the Great Recession in Ireland: polarization, individualization or "Middle Class Squeeze"?', *Social Indicators Research*, **126** (2), 503–26.

8. Italy: Industrial relations and social dialogue in a recessionary environment

Annamaria Simonazzi and Giuseppe Fiorani

1. INTRODUCTION

Industrial relations are concerned with the relationship between capital and labour in the organisation of work. Their distinctive feature is to strike a balance between making work more humane, stable, professional, democratic and efficient. The latter is promoted by well-paid, reasonably safe, good quality jobs. Industrial relations depend on the principles that shape labour legislation and labour policy, on the pattern of production, the role of the social partners and the state. According to a recent classification of industrial relations regimes (Eurofound, 2014: 8), Italy falls within the category of 'polarised pluralism', together with Spain, Portugal, France and Greece. The role of the social partners is described as 'more irregular and highly politicised'.[1]

In Italy, industrial relations and social dialogue reflect various factors: the difficult economic and employment conditions, the approach of government, relations within the trade unions and the urgency imposed by the financial and economic crisis. Long labelled 'confrontational', since the early 1990s the Italian industrial relations system has come to be described as an example of the 'neo-corporatist revival' (Crouch, 1998). In this period, important agreements and reforms were implemented with the participation of the social partners. Since the financial crisis, the European social *acquis*, rooted in social dialogue and public systems of social protection has been in retreat everywhere. In Italy, with the deepening of the crisis and with the European Union (EU) governing bodies turning from moral suasion to conditionality, labour legislation turned from negotiated to unilateral (Eurofound, 2014). In the name of urgency, national governments have increasingly resorted to legislation by decree, sidestepping the social partners and national parliaments to pass reforms in the fields of labour, welfare and industrial relations. According to Hyman (2015), a 'toxic austeritarism' 'has left little or no margin for domestic democratic institutions and social actors, downgraded from political to executive subjects' (Leonardi, 2017: 83).

The industrial relations landscape has changed profoundly, because of the long crisis and the policies that have been implemented in response. In the following sections, we describe the evolution of industrial relations and social dialogue in Italy, highlighting their effort to achieve a balance between flexibility and security, lessen the negative impact of welfare reforms and support growth-enhancing policies. The analysis illustrates the difficulty of achieving these goals in a macroeconomic setting characterised by low growth and enduring fiscal retrenchment, and the costs that derive from relying exclusively on labour market reforms to rekindle employment and growth. Section 2 describes the changing fortunes of social dialogue in recent decades in Italy. Industrial relations have been based on the acceptance of the idea that negotiated flexibility, required to respond to the changing realities of the world of work, could guarantee well-functioning and fair labour markets and welfare systems. Section 3 provides an overview of labour market reforms and discusses their effects on labour market segmentation and growth. It is contended that, contrary to the common assumption postulating a positive relationship between flexibility and employment creation, the deregulation of the labour market has resulted in an increasingly polarised labour market, with no enduring effects on employment. The section closes with a brief assessment of the view that collective bargaining and social dialogue are a prerequisite for a different, more viable model for addressing the challenges of technological change in a globalised and competitive environment. With the crisis, governments intervened hurriedly and often without proper consultation with the social partners (Pedersini and Regini, 2014). Labour market reforms were accompanied by structural reforms in the areas of taxation, pensions and welfare, while budget constraints left little room for compensatory, active or passive labour policies or social spending. Section 4 illustrates how the interaction of these reforms with austerity policies has affected precariousness, inequality and poverty. It demonstrates that, in a recessionary macroeconomic context, no degree of flexibility can counteract the massive unemployment created by the crisis and by the subsequent austerity policies. It is argued that a revitalisation of social dialogue and a turn from austerity to the implementation of an effective industrial policy can provide a better recipe to weather the current difficult economic and social situation. Two case studies have been selected to exemplify the role that social dialogue and good industrial relations can play in supporting labour policies and enabling a growth-friendly environment. The first case study (section 5) compares the organisation of the employment services in

Lombardy and Marche. It shows how social dialogue at the regional level can be effective in supervising and directing the implementation of active employment policies, while allowing for different strategies concerning the public/private partnership. The second case study (section 6) analyses two models of industrial relations at the plant level: the Ferrari model, based on a corporatisation model of bargaining,[2] and the Lamborghini model of firm bargaining, enshrined in national collective bargaining. We address the question of whether one system can perform better in safeguarding job quality and the company's competitiveness goals. Section 7 concludes.

2. INDUSTRIAL RELATIONS IN ITALY

2.1 General Framework

Italy shares with other Mediterranean countries a model of industrial relations characterised by a traditionally high degree of central coordination in collective bargaining. The system of industrial relations is not regulated by law: key issues such as workers' representation, collective bargaining, minimum wages and strikes are regulated by tripartite and/or bilateral agreements; the only exception is the Workers' Charter of Rights (Statuto dei lavoratori), passed in 1970 (Law 300/1970).

Although declining, union density in Italy is still one of the highest in the world: it was 41 per cent in 1980 and it is now estimated at 33.4 per cent. The data include retired workers, but exclude workers affiliated to unions other than the three major ones – Confederazione Generale Italiana del Lavoro (CGIL), Confederazione Italiana Sindacati Lavoratori (CISL) and Unione Italiana del Lavoro (UIL).[3] Over time, there has been a huge reshuffling of membership composition, with an increasing proportion of pensioners – from 20 per cent in 1981 to 50 per cent in 2001 – and a decline in manufacturing in favour of the public sector and private services. However, in the latter, the rate of unionisation is still the lowest (17 per cent). Female and migrant participation is also low, but increasing. The weakest area continues to be the under-30s, where atypical workers are more concentrated: this age group is the least unionised (15 per cent), with a gap of 30 percentage points with respect to workers aged 45–60 (Leonardi, 2017).

Although collective bargaining, based on tripartite concertation, formally has no legal effect *erga omnes*, its enforceability, entrusted to the courts, results in a very high collective bargaining coverage. Similarly, there is no legal minimum wage, but the minimum pay laid down in sectoral agreements is commonly extended to all workers. The concept of fair pay is based on the Constitution (Article 36).[4] As in the case of the extension of collective agreements, traditionally, Italian judges have taken national contracts as a reference for defining what a fair wage is, de facto extending the coverage rate. With the constitutional minimum wage being enforced by law or administrative acts, the unions oppose any proposals of a legal minimum wage, because they fear that it may weaken their role and bargaining power. The absence of a legal minimum wage has left non-standard forms of employment without an anchor in wage setting.

According to a comparative study covering 27 EU member countries (Eurofound, 2014), Italy has one of the lowest levels of workers' participation (D'Amuri and Giorgiantonio, 2015). This result is confirmed by the Bank of Italy's survey of firms with more than 50 employees. Half of the companies observe only the forms of consultation contained in the collective agreement, and a quarter (the largest enterprises, foreign groups and firms where there is union representation) envisage other methods of participation. There is a positive correlation between employees' involvement and the share of compensation not determined by the national contract, and with innovation.

Although Article 36 of the Constitution envisages workers' participation in corporate governance, Italy lacked a unified strategy to encourage their direct participation. Most actions were undertaken only to comply with European legislation. Legislative Decree 25 of 6 February 2007 strengthened the rights to information and consultation on the company's economic situation, the possible risks for employment levels, changes in work organisation and labour agreements (outsourcing), which are included in collective bargaining. However, in Italy the focus has been mostly on employees' financial involvement in the company. To employers, participation means the introduction of forms of wage flexibility linked to firm performance in the context of decentralised bargaining. Conversely, in Europe, the perspective has been extended to include workers' involvement in education, training, lifelong learning and empowerment.

The pervasiveness of the national agreement in setting pay levels and work organisation, the limited diffusion of second-level bargaining and relations between the social partners that are historically less cooperative than in other countries explain the low level of workers' participation in Italy. What is needed is a unified strategy defining the fundamental aspects of participation by law, leaving its concrete implementation to individual collective agreements. The issue is intertwined with the reform of industrial relations, especially with the unitary trade union representation (RSU) in the enterprise. In fact, despite the agreement between unions and firms on representation in 2014, many uncertainties still remain on the discipline of workplace representation.

2.2 The Evolution of Industrial Relations and the Fiat Model

The evolution of industrial relations in Italy is going in the direction of greater decentralisation, bypassing consultation between the social partners. The last financial law provided incentives for firm-level bargaining, reducing to 10 per cent the tax rate on the variable wage up to €4000. Globalisation and increasing uncertainty, requiring greater capital and labour flexibility, and the demand for customised, high-quality products, calling for high production standards, motivation and commitment on the part of the workforce, are among the underlying factors. Greater involvement of employees in the definition of production processes and business strategies is considered a key part of personnel management systems. It ensures a positive effect in terms of productivity and innovation, and favours a cooperative climate between management and labour, with positive effects on the dissemination of information and responsibility. However, disintermediation increases the risk of dualism between successful and unsuccessful firms, north and south, insiders and outsiders in the labour market, especially if austerity measures limit welfare and industrial policies. Moreover, at the social level, it affects politics, intermediate bodies and the forms of representation.

The Fiat example – breaking away from national representation and from the national contract (CCNL) and activating a new contract (CCSL) with only the signatory trade unions[5] – constitutes a watershed, and is an option seriously being considered by other companies. The long-lasting tension between the two contractual levels was resolved by Article 8 Law 148/2011 in favour of the possibility for the second level to derogate from the collective agreement, binding only for the members of the signatory organisations.[6] Because disagreement between unions gave a veto power to the dissenter, even in the case of minority organisations (De Luca Tamajo, 2016), Fiat abandoned the CCNL, constituted a new company not associated with Confindustria (General Confederation of Italian Industry) and signed a first-level contract (CCSL) on 13 December 2011;[7] the terms of this agreement, no longer exceptions to a CCNL, apply to all employees, regardless of their union affiliation.

The new Fiat model of corporatisation intervenes in a situation of poorly cohesive, fragmented industrial relations and conflicts between unions. It is supposed to better adjust wage costs to global competition, given the delay of the CCNL in adjusting to the speed of innovation. It is based on the principle that protection of employment levels is possible only at the enterprise level. Compared with the CCNL (defended by the Federazione Impiegati Operai Metallurgici – Confederazione Generale Italiana del Lavoro, FIOM-CGIL), the Fiat Chrysler Automobiles's (FCA's) CCSL introduces flexibility on issues related to performance, overwork, excessive absenteeism and enforceability of the agreements.

According to De Luca Tamajo (2016) the Fiat case highlights a dysfunction of industrial relations in the event of conflicts between unions or separate agreements, which clearer rules on democracy and the effectiveness of the contract could avoid.[8]

Firm-level contracts can now derogate from collective agreements, except for the pay structure. Representation is being pulverised: within each firm, there are workers with dozens of different contracts. The main trade unions are divided on which level of bargaining to privilege: the CGIL supports the national contract, while the CISL and the UIL are in favour of the firm level. The situation calls for the implementation of Article 39 of the Constitution on union representation to regulate representation at the two levels of bargaining.

The priorities of the firm shape the trend of industrial relations. Global competition and the rapid obsolescence of skills are impossible to manage with rigid contractual arrangements (Bavaro, 2012). The trade union, too, acknowledges that, in these conditions, this is the only way to regulate the exchange between employment and productivity, to encourage investment and promote the well-being of the company. The social and economic implications of this trend deserve a deeper analysis, which cannot be provided here (we refer to Bavaro, 2012).

2.3 Social Dialogue: A New Start?

Social dialogue has trodden a rough path. The neo-corporatist phase was interrupted by attempts on the part of conservative governments to weaken the trade unions by isolating the CGIL, the main left-wing trade union confederation.[9] The difficult economic conditions have weakened the trade unions. Under pressure from the crisis, and emboldened by the EU stance in favour of structural reforms, employers pushed for a reduction in the role of the national contract in favour of firm-level agreements. The Fiat model and Article 8 of the June 2011 agreement, allowing derogations from collective bargaining, risk a disordered fragmentation of decentralised bargaining. The trade unions' weakness can be gauged also by other indicators. The fraction of workers waiting for contract renewal and the average delay for renewal – two indicators of the difficulty of reaching agreement on renewal of national contracts – have peaked in recent years, while unions' request for compensation for the delays were not accepted. Over the past two decades the nationwide Contractual Wages Index has grown on average next to zero in real terms, and real wage growth between 2010 and 2016 was negative (Figure 8.1). There was no redistribution of

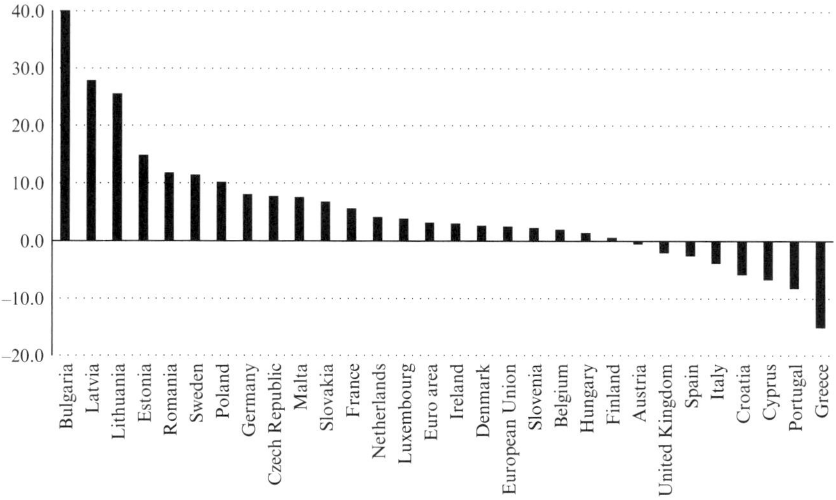

Source: European Commission, Economic and Financial Affairs, AMECO, Macroeconomic database, Consumer Price deflator, accessed 6 May 2017 at http://ec.europa.eu/economy_finance/ameco/user/serie/SelectSerie.cfm.

Figure 8.1 Development of real wages, Italy, 2010–16 (cumulative percentage change)

productivity (where and when productivity increased), while fiscal drag cuts deep into take-home pay.

Governments, too, have played a role in delegitimising the trade unions, reducing the role of social dialogue institutions, bypassing the procedures governing industrial relations, adopting major labour laws without previous consultation with the social partners (as in the case of the Fornero Reform and the Jobs Act and other labour laws passed by decree), or interfering with the wage bargaining process, as in the case of the €80 bestowed by the government on all employees, which came unsolicited by the trade unions, engaged in wearisome negotiations over pay and compensation for fiscal drag.

Modest outcomes in terms of working conditions (wages, employment, occupational safety, welfare and inequalities), limited representation among atypical workers and internal divisions have elicited criticism of trade unions as being either 'the harbingers of a worn-out notion of representation, concentrated in safeguarding the interests of the last bastions of the protected workforce, increasingly out of touch with the newer generations and jobs' or 'too accommodating and substantially unable to block the long-lasting erosion of wages, job security, labour rights, welfare protections and youth prospects' (Leonardi, 2017).

With trade union unity somehow reinstated, the unions are trying to resume their role in the policy arena. In 2015 the CGIL launched a proposal for a new Charter of Rights. According to some (Romagnoli, 2016), the reference target is still the worker at the big firms of the industrial era in the twentieth century, and leaves out the new jobs, new occupations, new services professions and, more generally, the de-structured/irregular workers and the 'Uber economy'. It is nonetheless a first step towards a relaunch of social dialogue. Initially ignored by the government, it seems to be commanding more attention, with the prospect of more consensual policy-making in matters of labour and welfare.

Further progress in the application of social dialogue can be seen in the development of bilateral funds. These are public entities managed jointly by firms and workers' unions. Firms pay contributions to the fund and can draw from it for specific labour purposes (for example, apprenticeship and unemployment insurance[10]) and welfare (social enterprise). Once again, opinions diverge: critics see risks to the trade unions of departing from the traditional functions of representation; others see bilaterality as the new frontier of trade union action in the field of services and cooperation with firms, especially needed in an increasingly flexible and fragmented labour market. The UIL and the CISL side decidedly with the latter opinion, while the CGIL has a more cautious attitude (Lai and Trovò, 2015).

3. LABOUR POLICIES, EMPLOYMENT AND GROWTH

3.1 Evolution of Labour Market Legislation

We can distinguish three phases of labour market legislation. In the first, in the early 1990s, agreements were targeted mainly at achieving wage flexibility; in the second, from 1997 to 2003, legislation aimed at increasing flexibility in the labour market through the liberalisation of a wide range of atypical contracts; since then, and especially since 2011, legislation has targeted dualism in the labour market.

In the 1980s, the persistence of inflation and the difficulties faced by the Italian economy were blamed on the labour market: namely, wage indexation and labour market regulation. In the early 1990s, a period of cooperative industrial relations (so-called *concertazione*) brought wage moderation and disinflation. While industrial unrest declined, tripartite social agreements were signed on practically all principal social issues (income policies, collective bargaining, workers' representation in the workplace, pension systems, economic development and competitiveness).

The two inter-confederal tripartite agreements, signed in 1992 and 1993 in a context of emergency conditions in the Italian economy, abolished the *scala mobile* (this mechanism of wage indexation had already been drastically reformed in 1984) to break the wage-price spiral, and reformed the bargaining system by setting two levels of bargaining: the national level – devoted to preserving the purchasing power of wages, by agreeing on a 'planned inflation rate'[11] – and the firm (or territorial) level, to distribute productivity gains. The two bargaining levels are coordinated hierarchically: the national level sets common, general minimum rights and standards; the second level integrates the first in various areas, ranging from functional flexibility to pay and working conditions. Its aim is to respond more closely to firms' needs for flexibility and competitiveness, by linking pay more closely to outcomes (productivity, profitability, quality, efficiency)[12] (Simonazzi, 2015).

Thanks to the wage freeze, by 1997 – the crucial year for Italy to qualify for European monetary union (EMU) – the inflation rate was brought down to 2 per cent. However, since the target inflation systematically underestimated actual inflation, and the second level of bargaining, which should have linked pay increases to productivity, was implemented only to a very limited extent and only in medium to large firms, the result was a decrease in the real wage (–2.9 per cent between 1992 and 2004). Moreover, by drastically flattening the progression of pay with seniority, reform of the bargaining system introduced a new element of inequality between those who were employed before the agreements, who had already accumulated significant seniority pay, and those entering after the agreements, whose wage profiles remained flat at the lower entry wages. In 1992 the Gini inequality index jumped upwards and has remained there ever since.

The first relevant step in the process of labour market liberalisation took place in 1997 with the so-called Pacchetto Treu (Law 196/1997). This law provided a new contractual framework, legalised temporary work agencies, regulated collaboration contracts and liberalised apprenticeships and fixed-term contracts, although providing a detailed list of circumstances under which they could be used. In 2001, the list was abolished, replaced by more general reasons of a technical, organisational, production or replacement nature, thereby extending the possibility and the terms for the use of temporary contracts. The 2003 Legge Biagi (Law 30/2003) facilitated the use of staff leasing contracts, part-time work and non-standard forms of employment relationships and reformed the apprenticeship contract.

In this first period, reforms were implemented with the participation of the social partners. The tripartite protocol signed in 1993, which established the framework rules for collective bargaining, workplace representation and labour policies, epitomises this phase in Italy's industrial relations, during which other important agreements were signed, heralding reforms on pensions, labour flexibility and welfare. This neo-corporatist approach began to ebb already before the crisis. With the deepening of the crisis and with the EU governing bodies turning from moral suasion to conditionality, labour legislation turned from negotiated to unilateral.

On 5 August 2011, European Central Bank (ECB) President Jean-Claude Trichet and Bank of Italy governor Mario Draghi sent a confidential letter to the Italian prime minister, demanding fiscal tightening and sweeping reforms before the ECB stepped into the market to ease mounting pressure on Italian bonds. In unusually clear and explicit language, Trichet and Draghi urged Prime Minister Silvio Berlusconi to make deep reforms, including opening up public services, toughening deficit cuts (for example, reducing the number of public employees and cutting their wages), overhauling rules on the collective bargaining system, fostering and prioritising company-level agreements, and reforming hiring and firing rules. Finally, they urged the adoption of these reforms by decree. Berlusconi duly complied: on 13 August he passed a decree that sidestepped a freshly signed agreement between the social partners regulating the conditions for derogation (see section 2.2), raised taxes and introduced a wage freeze in the public sector (initially for 2011 and then extended for three additional years).

Since then, labour policies have moved in somewhat conflicting ways. They aimed at reducing the dualism in the labour market by reducing the firing costs of open-ended contracts, while trying both to regulate and promote non-standard forms of employment.[13] A wide-ranging enabling law (the so-called Jobs Act, Law 183/2014) involved the regulation governing dismissals, simplification of contracts and labour law procedures, reformed unemployment benefits and active and passive labour market policies (see the case study in section 5), and improved reconciliation between work and family life. The Jobs Act abolished workers' reinstatement rights in case of dismissal[14] (except for discriminatory reasons), replacing it with monetary compensation amounting to two months' pay per year of work, reduced to half for firms with fewer than 15 employees. It introduced a new standard open-ended contract for new hires, which reduces the level and uncertainty of firing costs for all new permanent contracts in firms with at least 15 employees (the *contratto a tutele crescenti*, or graded security contract). Finally, while eliminating some forms of atypical contracts, such as project work contracts, it increased (from €5000 to €7000 per year) the maximum amount of income that can be received in vouchers.[15] Initially created to cover occasional work (for example, domestic work and gardening), the use of vouchers has mushroomed across the whole economy – growing from less than 1 million in 2008 to 115 million in 2015 – setting off an animated debate on how to interpret their growth; emergence of irregular work or transformation of regular contracts into occasional work? This law has been deeply divisive within the trade unions, with CGIL promoting a referendum for the abolition of the articles relating to vouchers and Article 18.

The Jobs Act was complemented by a measure, passed in the 2015 Budget Law, which provides a sizeable temporary rebate of non-wage labour costs (up to €8060 per year for three years) to new permanent hiring of workers who, in the previous semester, did not hold an open-ended position. These incentives are not targeted at specific groups of workers, nor are they contingent upon firm-level net job creation; that is, firms can use the subsidy to convert a temporary contract into a permanent contract.

Assessment of the success of the new law is necessarily still preliminary. Using microdata for the Veneto region, Sestito and Viviano (2016) conclude that the two measures contributed to double the monthly rate of conversion of fixed-term jobs into permanent positions. However, about 40 per cent of the new total gross hires with open-ended contracts occurred because of the incentives, whereas only 5 per cent can be attributed to the new firing regulations. Fana et al. (2016) also find that the increase in permanent contracts was due mostly to the conversion of temporary contracts into permanent ones. Excluding transformations, new permanent contracts (net of dismissals) were only 20 per cent of the total contracts activated during the first nine months of 2015, with a high share of involuntary part-time contracts. A dominant effect of fiscal incentives, especially for big firms, is also detected by the analysis of the Central Statistical Office (Istat, 2016a: 190–93). If the new firing rules made firms less reluctant to offer permanent job positions to as yet untested workers, the opportunity of benefiting from the incentives in case of a conversion certainly boosted temporary hiring, which came to be concentrated at the very end of the period set for claiming the subsidy. The high rate of subsidised conversions also raises the issue of the size of the deadweight loss implicit in these subsidies.

3.2 Development of a Dualistic Market

Flexibility policies were first advocated as the necessary response to the low job creation of the 1980s. In those years, jobless growth and 'Eurosclerosis' were imputed to the rigidity of the labour market. Deregulation, it was argued, would lead to a net creation of jobs. Until the outbreak of the crisis, labour market reforms in Italy had mostly targeted new hirings (so-called flexibility at the margin), while the firing rules for regular contracts had been left substantially untouched. This policy was originally

Table 8.1 Hiring and firing by type of contract, Italy, 2012

	Hiring		Firing	
	Number	%	Number	%
Permanent contracts	1 788 830	20.9	2 202 341	25.3
Temporary contracts	5 011 019	58.4	4 664 905	53.6
Apprenticeship	277 496	3.2	211 828	2.4
Collaboration contract	756 582	8.8	832 111	9.6
Other	745 247	8.7	791 384	9.1
Total	8 579 174	100.0	8 702 569	100.0

Note: 'Other' included agency contracts and job on call also in the public sector.

Source: ILO (2015).

justified as a means of promoting the participation of young people and others hard-to-employ in the labour market (Rubery and Piasna, 2016). Between 1995 and 2007, despite a mediocre rate of gross domestic product (GDP) growth, more than 3 million jobs were created (what has been called growth-less job creation), with flexible employment, characterised by fixed-term contracts, involuntary part-time, and bogus self-employed, accounting for most of it. On top of and often intermingled with them, a great number of informal workers were in the shadow economy. New hiring took place mostly through temporary work contracts. These workers are the first to be made redundant in a slowdown (Table 8.1). Their high turnover means that, while permanent contracts still account for the vast bulk of employment in Italy, young people are employed mostly with temporary contracts (Figure 8.2).

A lively debate on the employment effects of employment protection legislation (EPL) accompanied the labour reforms and growth-less job creation of that period. While the 1994 OECD Jobs Study (OECD, 1994) maintained that job creation relies on so-called efficient markets, free from institutional constraints, ten years later the 2004 Organisation for Economic Co-operation and Development (OECD) *Employment Outlook* drew more cautious conclusions, stating that employment cannot increase without economic growth, but differences in the strictness of EPL for regular and temporary jobs, respectively, may aggravate labour market duality and negatively affect the careers and productivity of those trapped in temporary jobs.

With dualism actually worsening, the debate about increasing inequalities in the labour market intensified. Various arguments, ranging from insider–outsider to inter-generational conflict, converged on attributing

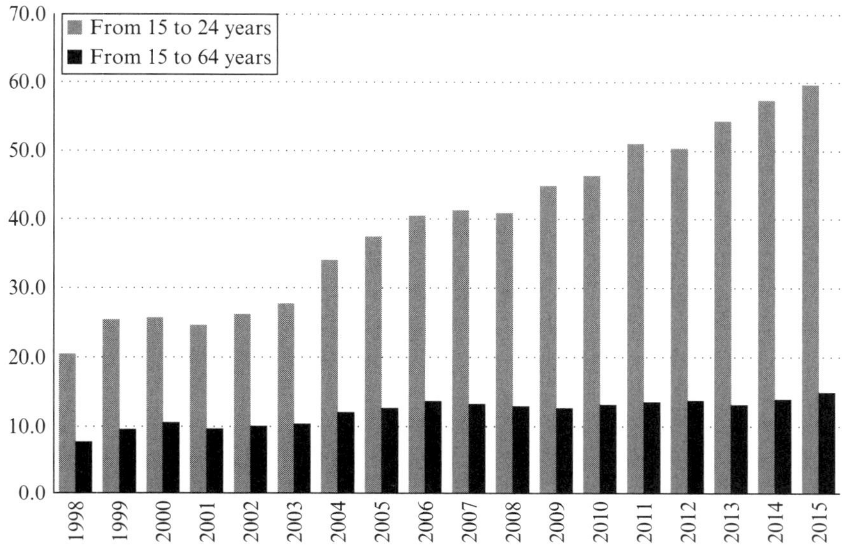

Source: Fana et al. (2016).

Figure 8.2 Share of temporary employment in total Italian employment by age group, Italy, 1998–2015

the precariousness of the outsiders to the protection of the insiders and contributed in orienting policies towards the reduction of protection. After decades of policies aimed at reducing the supposed rigidity of the labour market, compounded by austerity measures implemented in the crisis, the increasing precariousness of ever greater segments of the workforce produced by these policies has been instrumental in arguments for the need to eliminate the excessive protection of insiders that unfairly discriminates against outsiders.

This approach has been questioned on two grounds. First, was the Italian labour market as rigid as is commonly maintained? Second, does flexibility favour growth? We address these two questions in turn.

Despite wide differences in labour market institutions, firm and job turnovers are very similar across OECD countries. Empirical research on the Italian labour market demonstrated that a very high index of turnover coexisted with a high share of job positions with long tenure. Contini and Trivellato (2005) argued that this apparently contradictory evidence could be explained by the dichotomy between two different models of employment – extremely mobile and extremely stable workers – that were combined in the index. While young people account for most of the turnover, there are also plenty of workers in other age brackets in perennial flux (as still evidenced in the first case study). They include women, low-educated people, employees in small firms, or in low-technology segments of the value chain, or in the traditional reservoirs of irregular work (agriculture, commerce, construction and services). These workers experience long spells of unemployment, often longer than the periods spent in employment. Conversely, core workers' protection has to do more with professional skills, experience and firm-specific capabilities that make them valuable to the firm, than with EPL. As labour market segmentation theory has long made clear, multiple factors lead to the differentiation of employment conditions and rewards and it is worker–capital divisions, rather than employment regulation, which are the main source of inequalities in the labour market (Rubery and Piasna, 2016).

With increasing competition from low-cost countries in mature products and the swift path of technological change, even core male workers employed in sectors no longer protected from competition have come to be increasingly exposed to the risk of dismissal and unemployment. Meanwhile, the protection of regular employment has been gradually eroded. A (rough) indication of the decreasing degree of rigidity of the labour market is provided by the OECD index of EPL (OECD, 2017). The index for Italy fell from 3.82 in 1990 to 2.26 in 2013, and compares not too unfavourably with an index of 2 for Germany and 3 for France (Table 8.2). Firing obstacles, which have a great weight in the indicator, were further reduced in 2015 (as argued in section 3.1). Thanks to a policy approach of levelling-down equalisation, in 2013 the index no longer indicated the existence of dualism in the Italian labour market (Table 8.3). While there are good reasons to handle the indicator with care, the striking difference with Germany documents the difference in labour policies implemented in the two countries. The difference may indicate both the reduced protection of regular employment in Italy and the great increase in the precariousness of the secondary labour market in Germany.

Table 8.2 Employment protection legislation, selected countries, 1990, 1999, 2007 and 2013

	Italy	France	Germany	Spain	Portugal	Greece
1990	3.82	2.70	2.92	3.65	4.10	3.62
1999	3.19	2.98	2.34	2.80	3.70	3.62
2007	2.38	3.05	1.93	2.68	3.49	2.62
2013	2.26	3.00	2.00	2.31	2.50	2.07

Source: OECD (2017).

Table 8.3 Index of protection for open-ended contracts (EPRC) and ratio of temporary contracts (EPT) over EPRC, selected countries, 2013

	Italy	France	Germany	Spain	Portugal	Greece
EPRC	2.79	2.82	2.98	2.28	2.69	2.41
EPT/EPRC	0.97	1.33	0.59	1.39	0.87	1.21

Source: OECD (2017).

3.3 Flexibility, Productivity and Growth

Structural reforms have their roots in mainstream economic theory, which makes efficiency and productivity dependent on the market mechanism. According to this view, the problem with crisis countries is a lack of cost competitiveness due to excessive wage and labour protection. In 2004, however, the OECD *Employment Outlook* (OECD, 2004: 63) argued that a reasonable degree of EPL 'may foster long-term employment relationships, thus promoting workers' effort, cooperation and willingness to be trained, which is positive for aggregate employment and economic efficiency'. However, the 2016 OECD *Employment Outlook* (OECD, 2016a) turned this argument on its head: well-designed structural reforms of product and labour markets may entail costly adjustments in the short run, but in the long run the greater productivity of a more efficient allocation of labour will prevail again,[16] so that the high employment and wage losses associated with greater flexibility in regulation governing the dismissal of workers on regular (open-ended) contracts would be reversed in a few years. The short-run costs would be smaller if reforms were implemented in the upswing, though it is in a depression that they are politically more enforceable (OECD, 2016a). This view has legitimised the inclusion of structural reforms as a pre-condition in any agreements between the European Commission and programme or crisis member countries.

The results of these studies have not gone unchallenged. The short-run costs have been reassessed and found to be neither small nor transitory even for flexible labour markets such as the American labour market (Autor et al., 2016). The analysis of the long-term effects of labour reforms on productivity and growth has been challenged on two grounds. First, the model is based on the hypothesis of a smooth and efficient reallocation of labour. The assumption of a (full) employment equilibrium pre-empts any serious consideration of the costs of adjustment. Second, a truly dynamic analysis must consider the effects of employment relations on the factors determining innovation and competition. Specifically, competition increasingly relies on the quality and complexity of products, rather than on their price (Simonazzi et al., 2013). To be successful, firms must innovate their products, processes and organisation. To this end, as argued in section 2.2, a skilled and cooperative workforce is as essential as the firm's commitment to invest in its labour force. If arm's length labour relations can make cost competitiveness profitable in the short run, this strategy may not pay in the long run.

The extensive empirical literature indicates that EPL can have different effects in different macroeconomic and institutional contexts,[17] in the short and in the long runs (see Boeri and Garibaldi 2007 for a survey of the empirical literature). These results stress the strong complementarity between the national legislation concerning labour protection, the kind of industrial relations and overall employment policies. They also confirm one tenet of labour market segmentation theory, that flexibility is much more easily achieved by policies that support growth, when job opportunities are plenty and workers move between jobs. Data on gross labour turnover (hiring and firing) in Italy confirm this proposition (Checchi and Leonardi, 2015). Labour turnover was high at the beginning of the last decade before the reforms that tackled insiders' protection, but fell during the crisis when turnover mostly involved dismissals. Once dismissed, adult workers face greater difficulties re-entering the labour market (Simonazzi and Villa, 2007). The absence of effective re-training and activation policies makes these workers subject to the loss of human and social capital, increasing the risk of long-term unemployment: in 2015, 68.4 per cent of total adult unemployed and 55.5 per cent of unemployed young people were unemployed for more than 12 months (Istat, 2016a: 133).

The Italian experience provides support for the view that labour market institutions that favour cooperation between workers and firms prove essential in sustaining growth and innovation, even if on the negative side. Concern for excessive regulation of the labour market has diverted attention from the structural problems at the origins of the stagnation of the Italian economy. Labour market deregulation has been preferred to an alternative strategy based on investing in people in combination with an industrial policy aimed at strengthening and upgrading the industrial structure (Simonazzi et al., 2013). Social dialogue has been weakened and industrial relations have become more adversarial. The result has been slow growth and stagnant productivity, a segmented labour market and an impoverished workforce.

Deregulation and austerity policies in Italy have affected macroeconomic performance also via their effects on income inequality. The unions' weakened bargaining power has resulted in low or negative real wages.

More decentralised and individualised wage settings have increased wage dispersion and polarisation. Together, these factors have affected the rate of growth of domestic demand (consumption and investment). With the fiscal compact barring public expenditures, only exports have been left to counter the recession. By sustaining the share of wages and reducing inequality, industrial relations targeting a more equal society might have contributed to economic sustainability, thereby sustaining growth.

4. INEQUALITIES, UNEMPLOYMENT, PRECARIOUSNESS AND POVERTY

Since the crisis, labour market reforms have been accompanied by structural reforms in the areas of taxation, pensions and welfare. As argued above, the economic and financial urgency of initiatives such as the pension and labour market reforms have prevailed over the objective of finding an agreement with the social partners on the content of these reforms, while budget constraints left little room for compensatory, active or passive labour policies and social spending. Flexibility without security, together with the massive unemployment created by the crisis and by the subsequent austerity policies have had dramatic effects on job quality, inequality and poverty.

4.1 Job Quality

The deep and prolonged economic crisis has taken a toll on the labour market, with falling employment rates and dramatic increases in unemployment and its duration. Between 2007 and 2014 unemployment doubled, from 6 to 13 per cent, only partly mitigated by a massive use of short-time working schemes and wage redundancy funds. Employment and inactivity rates are now among the worst in the EU. Employment conditions have worsened especially for young people, but deterioration is common to all age groups. The unemployment rate, which has increased across all age groups, has reached a peak of 35.5 per cent in the 15–24 age bracket and is 9.7 per cent for the traditional male breadwinner category (35–49 years of age) (Table 8.4). The number of those not in education, employment, or training (NEETs) is especially worrying: 2.3 million aged 15–29 in 2015, 96 per cent of whom are in the age bracket 18–29. Their share increased from 17.7 per cent in 2008 to 25 per cent in 2013 (down to 22.3 per cent in the second quarter of 2016) (Istat, 2016b: 115).

The crisis has also affected those who remained in employment, substantially worsening the quality of existing jobs, the level of pay, and inequalities

Table 8.4 Employment and unemployment rates by sex, area, age, citizenship and education, Italy, 2016

	Employment rate (%)			Unemployment rate (%)		
	Total	Male	Female	Total	Male	Female
Total	57.7	66.9	48.5	11.5	10.6	12.8
Area:						
North	66.3	73.8	58.8	7.4	6.5	8.6
Centre	62.3	70.6	54.3	10.4	9.4	11.6
South	44.0	56.1	32.1	19.3	17.6	22.1
Age:						
15–34	40.6	46.3	34.7	21.4	20.2	22.9
15–24	17.2	19.5	14.7	35.5	35.1	36.1
25–34	61.0	70.2	51.7	16.9	15.4	18.9
35–49	72.8	83.7	62.1	9.7	8.3	11.5
50–64	58.3	70.0	47.2	6.2	6.2	6.2
Citizenship:						
Italian	57.5	66.5	48.4	11.1	10.4	12.2
Foreign	59.5	71.1	49.3	15.0	13.0	17.4
Education:						
Primary	43.1	55.3	29.7	15.8	14.4	18.5
Diploma	64.6	73.9	55.4	10.8	9.4	12.5
Graduate	78.6	83.6	74.8	6.2	5.0	7.2

Source: Istat (2016b).

across socio-economic groups.[18] The worst off are young people and low-skilled workers. Not only do they have the poorest performance in terms of employment and unemployment rates, but they also have the worst outcomes with respect to job quality, that is, lower earnings quality, considerably higher labour market insecurity and higher job strain.

The dynamics of wage inequality depicted in the OECD Job Quality index have to be seen against a context of falling average earnings. In addition, most of the jobs lost during the crisis were predominantly low-paid (Istat, 2015: 157). These two factors result in a deceptive increase in earnings quality. In effect, like all other crisis countries (but also the United Kingdom; see Blundell et al., 2014), between 2010 and 2016 Italy suffered a reduction in real wages (Figure 8.1). Another important factor is the increasing low levels of entry wages for newly hired young workers, due to the diffusion of atypical and apprenticeship contracts for first-job seekers (Figure 8.3). There is a persistent wage penalty, of the order of 11 per cent, associated with working under a temporary contract. Checchi

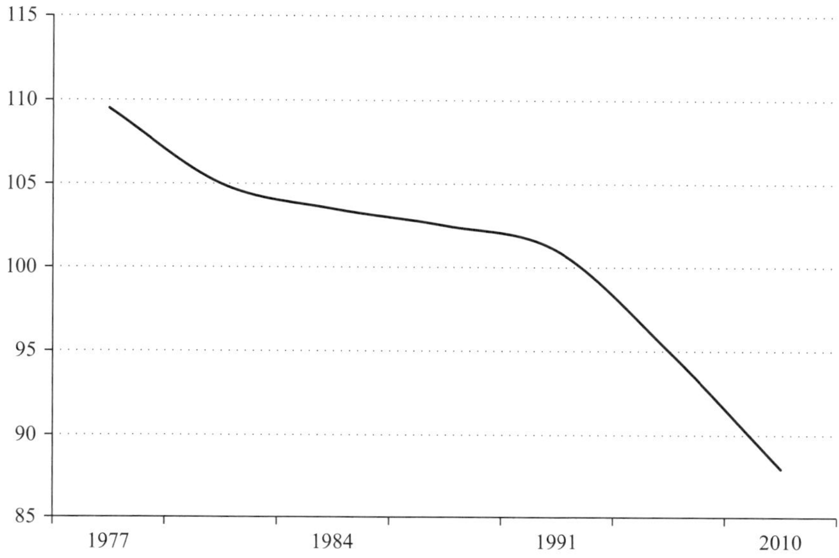

Source: Checchi and Leonardi (2015).

Figure 8.3 Relative wage of 30-year-olds to average wage, Italy, 1977–2010

and Leonardi (2015) have estimated that it mostly affects workers in the two bottom quintiles, while workers in the top quintile are less penalised. Moreover, this penalty is halved when individual fixed effects are included, suggesting that labour market flexibility increases wage differentials partly by sorting individuals according to their unobservable characteristics and partly by changing the wage for less qualified occupations. This indicates that there are at least two types of temporary workers: the professionals, who take advantage of temporary contracts to increase their market power by enlarging the set of potential employers; and the precarious, who do not succeed in achieving a permanent job because they do not have the abilities demanded in the labour market. This same difference determines the probability of moving out of a temporary contract into an open-ended contract. Checchi and Leonardi (2015) conclude that whenever a legislative reform expands the share of workers under temporary contracts then, other things being constant, an increase in earnings inequality should be expected.

4.2 Active Labour Market Policies Before and After the Jobs Act

Deregulation of the labour market (flexibility at the margin) has been accompanied by partial reform of the so-called shock-absorber systems. The Jobs Act further revised the unemployment insurance system, setting new conditions for the renamed unemployment benefit (NASPI), a new provision (ASDI) to cover unemployed workers in distressed economic conditions who had exhausted the period (up to 18 months) of normal unemployment benefit and a special benefit covering atypical workers (DIS-COLL). Moreover, from 2017, the NASPI also replaces the redundancy pay scheme for workers subject to collective dismissal by medium-large restructuring or closing firms (*mobilità*) (Arachi and Baldini, 2016). Despite several reforms, a truly universal unemployment benefit and income support schemes are still in the making in Italy.

Flexibility and security require services capable of implementing active labour market policies (ALMPs), although, as the International Labour Organization (ILO, 2015) report rightly emphasises, no ALMP, no matter how efficient, can work if the economy is not growing. As stressed by Martin (2015), in a depressed labour market, ALMPs may merely reshuffle the queue of the unemployed. Active labour market policies have had a secondary role in Italy. Traditionally, Italy prioritised hiring incentives, which are easy to implement, although subjected to significant deadweight losses. Consequently, most ALMPs consisted in introducing and/or modifying the eligibility requirements for employment subsidies, according to what were deemed the categories of worker most in need of employment opportunities at that time. Budget constraints aggravated the notorious inefficiency of the Public Employment Services (PES) in reallocating labour towards scarce job opportunities.

In the 1990s, labour reforms marked the end of the public monopoly of employment agencies and the devolution of their governance to the regions. The intermediation between labour demand and supply was overhauled: promoting activation to prevent long-term unemployment, favouring innovation, decentralisation and monitoring of public agencies, and opening up to private agencies for intermediation and training to overcome financial constraints (Gilli and Landi, 2009). Several institutional and political vicissitudes followed. The creation of Regional Agencies was followed by their demise and their competence with regard to the Centri per l'impiego (employment office, CpI) was assigned to the provinces, to respond more closely to local labour market needs. The passage from the national bureaucratic structure to the PES had been generously financed by the ESF, but the regional and provincial administrations had to build the new PES system from scratch, with no effective support from the centre in providing technical assistance or ensuring coordination between the various actors. The lack of an information system still represents one of the greatest weaknesses of the Italian employment system. Following a process of administrative simplification, the provinces were formally eliminated, but the constitutional revision that was to have confirmed their elimination was voted down in the December 2016 Referendum. Meanwhile, in 2015 the legislative decree implementing the Jobs Act created the National Agency for Active Labour Policies (Agenzia Nazionale per le Politiche Attive del Lavoro, ANPAL), which has the function of coordinating labour policies to assist job seekers and unemployed people benefiting from the various unemployment benefits. Thus the newly created agency in charge of ALMPs will coexist with the reinstated regional agencies, without a clear definition of functions and with the risk of leaving the PES isolated and unemployed workers lost in a multiplicity of agencies (Ministry of Labour, ANPAL, Istituto Nazionale Previdenza Sociale – INPS, Italia lavoro, Istituto per lo Sviluppo della Formazione Professionale dei Lavoratori – ISFOL, Consiglio Nazionale dell'Economia e del Lavoro – CNEL, private agencies and the Regions), training courses and red tape.

Among ANPAL's initial activities is experimentation with the re-employment agreement (*contratto di ricollocamento*) concerning workers unemployed for more than four months and receiving unemployment benefit (NASPI). It provides the unemployed with an amount intended to pay for a package of integrated services for job search, conditional on a commitment to seek employment, to be proved through meetings with staff. The amount of the voucher varies with the degree of employability and can be spent with a CpI or any other actor with accreditation for the provision of services in the field of ALMPs. To be effective, the system needs specific skills and capabilities in the analysis of competences, an efficient national information system, standardisation of the basic rules guiding the provision of active and passive labour policies and good coordination with firms and agencies in charge of professional training.

After 20 years of reforms and reorganisations, the structures that should have accompanied the increased flexibility in the labour market are still inadequate to meet the demand for their services. Insufficient financial and human resources prevent the efficient functioning of the PES, resulting in long waiting times, fragmented information spread over different agencies and limited capacity to offer solutions. According to the ISFOL Plus 2014 Survey (Landi et al., 2016), in the 12 months before the survey about 4.6 million people had called on the employment services, both CpIs and other labour agencies (APLs).[19] It is estimated that they can sign a commitment agreement for about 3 million people per year, and successfully meet the needs of 60 per cent of them.

In 2015, the Lombardy region estimated at 163 hours per person the amount of work required to ensure the full range of services[20] to every unemployed person (Olivieri, 2015). This maximum amount can be reduced to an average of 50 hours, given that the services will not be provided to everyone to the maximum level. If each unemployed (3.1 million in total) received 50 hours of services, it would be necessary to ensure a total of 155 million hours, equal to 90 116 full-time employees. At present, the staff of the CpIs is a mere 7000 employees, with a total budget of €700 million, and can provide only 350 000 hours of services. (By comparison, in Germany there are more than 100 000 PES employees, with a budget of approximately €9 billion.) Aware of the severe shortage of staff (and possibly of competences), Legislative Decree 150/2015 envisages the possibility of guaranteeing only the acceptance and granting of the re-employment allowance in-house, while outsourcing the package of hours of intensive care to authorised or accredited agencies and organisations. The remaining 154.6 million hours, outsourced at the cost of €30 per hour (estimated by Regione Lombardia) would require €4.64 billion, more than six times what is currently being spent on ALMPs in Italy (and half of what is spent in Germany).

The argument advanced by Ichino (2014) that the efficient organisation of CpIs would be self-financing (thanks to the savings on unemployment benefits) calls for two qualifications: (1) the economic cycle affects the chances of finding or losing a job, no matter how effective the CpI; and (2) 50 per cent of those out of work are unemployed for more than 12 months and are more difficult to employ even in favourable economic conditions. The less educated, less employable, long-term or female unemployed generally turn to the public agency. In order to reduce the obvious risk of adverse selection, the CpI should be able to rely on a good nationwide information system, an ability to profile the unemployed according to an index of disadvantage, a system of ranking of the credited agencies and a good administrative system. Finally, although the rate of user satisfaction is generally good – except with regard to their capacity to actually provide a job – waiting times are long: only 42 per cent of APLs and 33 per cent of CpIs provide a solution within four months.

To conclude, the heterogeneity across agencies, users and providers is high, calling for greater coordination among actors and greater public–private cooperation. Investment in infrastructure and personnel is totally inadequate. We analyse the issue of ALMPs, specifically the working of PES, in the first case study. Social dialogue at the regional level supervises and directs implementation of the services, in accordance with the different strategies chosen by the social partners. The comparative assessment of the different organisation of CpIs in two regions, Lombardia and

Marche, shows that Italy's difficulty in implementing ALMPs is not due only to their institutional design (centralisation versus decentralisation, public versus private), although that is important, but to the historical marginality of these services – in terms of financial and human resources – relative to other public administrations. This marginality can be partially explained by the lack of interest of social partners, owing to (excessive) reliance on their self-organisation and self-sufficiency, or even to a concern for competition.

4.3 Pension Reform

At the peak of the crisis, the Monti government implemented a pension reform that increased the minimum retirement age to 66 years, eliminating all forms of flexibility. Having fixed the calculation of pension benefits strictly according to contributions paid, it introduced an unnecessary rigidity with regard to retirement age. Precipitously and rigidly applied to respond to the urgent need to reduce spending and appease the financial markets (and the EU and German authorities), this reform left several short-term and long-term problems open. If, according to international assessments (the International Monetary Fund and the World Bank) after the Fornero-Monti reform the Italian pension system had become the most rigorous of EU systems, it was also the least adequate in terms of pension level and the most ineffectual with respect to the broader objectives of productivity, growth and employment. Two main trade-offs, which derive from the interrelation between the pension system, the labour market and the welfare state, threaten its long-term sustainability. First, by increasing the retirement age among older workers, the reform had a negative effect on youth unemployment. By slowing down the substitution between workers of different ages (Figure 8.4), this might have had an impact also on productivity, if young workers are more attuned to new technologies. Second, by allowing atypical workers with low pay and fragmented work careers to be inadequately covered, the new contribution-based system has set in motion a pension 'time bomb' set to explode when these people reach retirement age. This problem is especially severe for women, who are more exposed to the risk of career fragmentation because of a still incomplete reconciliation policy (Simonazzi, 2015). Under strong pressure from the social partners, subsequent laws attempted to respond to these problems by gradually extending coverage to larger sections of atypical workers and reintroducing some flexibility in retirement age.

The interaction between the crisis and the labour and pension reforms has produced conflicting effects on the female employment rate. While occupational segregation sheltered women (relative to men) from the first

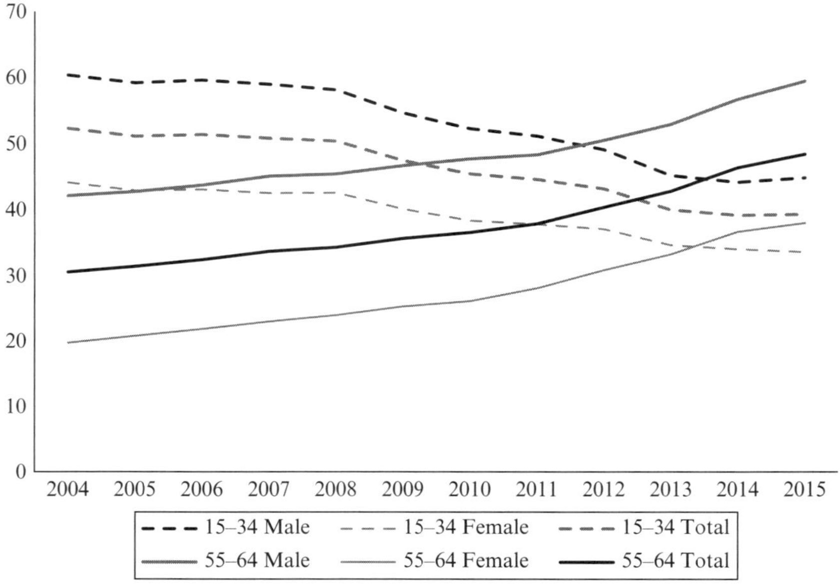

Source: Istat (2016a: 132).

Figure 8.4 Employment rate by age and gender, Italy, 2004–15

effects of the crisis, subsequently female employment has suffered the effects of the fiscal crisis because of their overrepresentation in public sector employment. While the pension reform forcibly sustained the employment rate of older women, overall the crisis has brought the slowly increasing long-term trend of the female participation rate (which is still far behind the European average) to a halt.

4.4 Poverty

The ongoing economic recession, which followed a long stagnation, has hit Italian families especially hard. Since the start of the crisis, all indicators of vulnerability, deprivation, and poverty have increased dramatically.[21] In 2015, 1.6 million families (6.1 per cent of total households) were in absolute poverty.[22] The incidence of absolute poverty is higher among households with four or more members, in particular couples with two or more children. This is why the incidence of poverty is even higher among individuals: 4.6 million (7.6 per cent of total population), an increase of 141 per cent since 2005 (3.3 per cent) (Figure 8.5). Absolute poverty is also high among households with all non-national members (28.3 per cent),

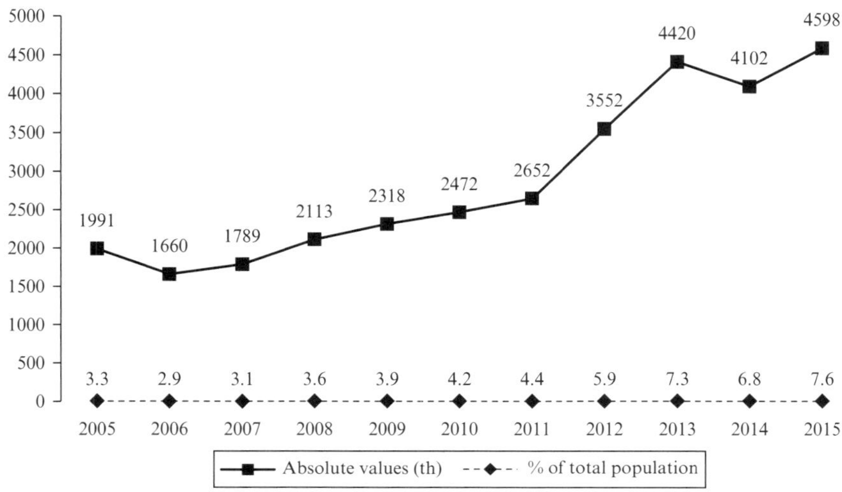

Source: Open Polis (2016).

Figure 8.5 Individuals in absolute poverty, absolute values and percentage of total population, Italy, 2005–15

especially among those living in the north of Italy (32.1 per cent). With only one-third of the population, the south accounts for almost half of the population in absolute poverty (45 per cent), but poverty has increased substantially in the whole country: it has nearly tripled in industrial northern areas (from 588 000 in 2005 to 1.8 million in 2015, from 31 to 40 per cent of the total population in poverty).

Between 2005 and 2015, the share of the population in relative poverty[23] increased from 11.1 to 13.7 per cent (8.3 million people), while 28.7 per cent of the population was at risk of poverty or social exclusion in 2015. It is mainly households of young people that are bearing the brunt of this long crisis, of the labour market reforms, of precarious employment or unemployment. Relative poverty incidence decreased only in households with reference person aged 65 and over (8.0 per cent in 2015), or retired from work (7.7 per cent), the only group enjoying the privilege of a reliable flow of income.

While unemployed, under-employed, unskilled workers and young people have the highest shares of absolute and relative poverty, having a job is no guarantee against poverty. In 2015, 10.9 per cent of households headed by an employee and 18.1 per cent of workers were relatively poor. The share of working poor – employed workers in absolute poverty – has almost tripled in ten years; up to 11.7 per cent in 2015 from only 3.9 per

Country	2005	2015	Difference
EU*	8.2	9.6	1.4
Belgium	3.9	4.8	0.9
Bulgaria	5.4	9.2	3.8
Czech Republic	3.5	3.6	0.1
Denmark	4.8	4.9	0.1
Germany	4.8	9.9	5.1
Estonia	7.5	11.8	4.3
Ireland	5.5	6	0.5
Greece	12.9	13.3	0.4
Spain	10.6	12.2	1.6
France	6.1	8	1.9
Croatia			0
Italy	8.7	11	2.3
Cyprus	6.5	7.8	1.3
Latvia	8.1	9	0.9
Lithuania	8.3	10	1.7
Luxembourg	9.8	11.1	1.3
Hungary	6.7	8.7	2
Malta	4.3	5.7	1.4
Netherlands	5.3	5.8	0.5
Austria	6.8	7.2	0.4
Poland	10.6	13.8	3.2
Portugal	10.7	11.9	1.2
Romania	17.4	19.6	2.2
Slovenia	4.6	6.4	1.8
Slovakia	5.7	8.9	3.2
Finland	3.7	3.7	0
Sweden	5.5	7.8	2.3
United Kingdom	8.2	8.7	0.5

Source: Open Polis (2016).

Figure 8.6 Employed workers at risk of poverty, percentage of total and rate of increase, EU28, 2005–15

cent in 2006. Italy is among the EU countries in which the increase in workers at risk of poverty has increased the most in the crisis; with 2.3 percentage points it comes second only to Germany (5.1) and a few Eastern European countries (Figure 8.6).

Compared with the rest of the EU28, in Italy social transfers are less effective in reducing poverty. This poor result is due as much to scant resources as to their inefficient use. Lacking a barely adequate social protection system, worsening economic conditions and fiscal austerity measures call for a reinforced role for the family as income shock absorber. With entry wages declining, real wages of standard employees stalling and unemployment and precarious work spreading, the capacity of the family to defend its living standards has come to rely increasingly more on the pooling of multiple earnings: pensions, even if low become the most reliable source of income, and previously inactive women may be shoved into the labour market to supplement or make up for the loss of the male's income. However, the declining average size and changing composition of households – declining marriage and increasing divorce rates, increased number of single-parent families and the decline in fertility – might have decreased the family's redistributive capabilities. Even so, with the welfare state in retreat, familism is likely to remain Italian families' last resort. In so far as income redistribution takes place inside the family, it is likely to lead to increasing inequality and decreasing intergenerational mobility. Because families' main resource to absorb external shocks (unemployment, disability and early retirement) are savings, which are very unequally distributed, reliance on families as insurers against social risk tends to reinforce social inequality (Simonazzi, 2015).

To conclude, since the crisis growth has eluded expectations and unemployment has grown, as have precariousness and insecurity. Income inequality and poverty have increased. Social expenditure and social investment (education, research and development, health and care, training and active labour market policies) have all been drastically curtailed because of the fiscal compact. While real earnings have stalled and mobility among income classes may not have decreased substantially, intergenerational mobility – measured across occupational groups (Simonazzi and Barbieri, 2016) and income groups (Franzini and Raitano, 2013) – has definitely decreased. Faced with the severity of the socio-economic conditions, social dialogue has focused on the creation of safety-nets, such as promoting the search for and experimentation with basic or minimum income policies, negotiating reductions of the fiscal drag on lower incomes, supporting proposals for an extension of care services provisions.

5. CASE STUDY: TWO DIFFERENT STRATEGIES IN THE ORGANISATION OF PUBLIC EMPLOYMENT SERVICES IN ITALY

5.1 Introduction

We compare the experiences of two regions that differ not only in size, but also by type of governance of Servizi per l'impiego (employment services, SPIs). Lombardy has anticipated the contract of re-employment devised by the Jobs Act through the system of so-called Dote Unica Lavoro (Dul, or Single Dowry for work), in force for many years: the entitled unemployed person can spend such a dowry in kind, namely, on services provided by public or private employment centres. Conversely, the Marche region has invested heavily in a capillary network of public employment centres (CpI), which represent a case of good public management.

5.2 Lombardy

The contract of re-employment is one of the main innovations of the Jobs Act: a redundant worker who receives unemployment benefits begins a path of reintegration into the labour market, through a programme coordinated by the region, choosing the structure from which they intend to be assisted. The structure – public or private – should be accredited. A tutor will check compliance with the path of relocation and their willingness to accept any reasonable offers.

This principle is already operating in Lombardy with the 'Single payment for work' (Dul).[24] Assessing the impact of Dul in the job market can be useful to gauge the effectiveness of the new employment policies. It should be noted that Lombardy has the strongest economy in the country, with more than 4 million people in work and about 380 000 unemployed.

Arifl (2015) tried to assess whether Dul improves the chances of its recipients' finding a job. It used compulsory notifications[25] to verify employment status six to 12 months after the signing of the commitment agreement with the CpI. A control group has been created, with the same characteristics as the 20 000 recipients: gender, age, level of education, nationality, period of unemployment and province. Data on the percentage of new hirings seem to indicate that Dul increases employment chances by at least 30 percentage points. However, the experience of Dul Lombardia suggests that the practical application of the re-employment agreement will take a long time; the policy started in Lombardy in 2007 and has undergone several corrections to reduce opportunism. There are also areas for improvement, for instance to take greater responsibility for the most disadvantaged.

The experience of Lombardy is definitely relevant. However, there are reasons to believe that the chances of employment and the potential savings have been overestimated. First, the counterfactual estimation cannot take into account individual skills or attitudes, so that the possibility that those endowed with the dowry were the most skilled or enterprising cannot be ruled out. Second, it excluded from the exercise the long-term unemployed, who are more difficult to re-employ. Finally, as for the potential savings to be reinvested in the CpI, it must be considered that those benefiting from the dowry are only 6 per cent of the unemployed in Lombardy. The extension of the service cannot avoid the necessary investments. The real challenge is the phase of signing the commitment agreement, because in a model based on competition, the private sector will tend to cream off those easier to employ. In Lombardy, the public institutions exert control on the accredited actors to prevent problems of adverse selection.

5.3 Marche

The employment centres of the Marche region are among the most efficient and well organised, although hard hit by the crisis, and historically considered by the region as the primary tool of active policies.

An extensive survey among people who turned to the CpIs between September 2014 and July 2015 provides an assessment of their working. The questionnaire, administered to a sample of 4839 people stratified by province, age, gender, citizenship, represents a population of more than 152 000 users of the services of CpIs in the region. The user's characteristics reflect the national data. Current job status (employed, searching, or neither employed nor searching) is related to motives for turning to the CpIs, assessment of their effectiveness and satisfaction with the service received.

Among the reasons for the termination of the last job, ranking first is a crisis at or closure of the firm, followed by the end of fixed-term contracts, seasonal work, internships, substitutions (most relevant in services and the most common reason for women), finally dismissals, followed by a smaller share of resignations.

At the time of the interview 33 per cent were working, 53 per cent not working and searching, 5 per cent were searching for the first time and 9 per cent not working or searching. Women, foreigners, adults, the less educated and the long-term unemployed are over-represented in the main group of those who were not working but searching. Young people, mostly with higher education, are among those seeking work for the first time. There are good reasons for estimating that more than half of the last group (neither working nor searching) belongs to the potential labour force.

A total of 81 per cent of those who found a job were in paid employment, 37 per cent with a permanent contract. Given the high percentage of fixed-term work (seasonal, periodical or flexible) for the remaining 63 per cent there are continuous cycles.[26] The average weekly working time is 32 hours, the median is 36. Acquaintances and friends remain the main channel to a job (nearly 46 per cent of respondents), personal initiative is the second channel (18.1 per cent), followed by the response to vacancies available in print or online (11.6 per cent). The percentage of those who found a job through the CpI (5 per cent) is slightly higher than the number of those who did so with private recruitment agencies and equal to that of the temporary employment agencies.

Almost everyone is willing to accept any kind of work, even part-time, precarious or underqualified, the only constraint being distance, especially for women and for those who have children. This makes for an extremely low reservation wage. The average wage is €952 and the median around €1000, but variation is very high and reflects the traditional segmentation of the labour market. Being a woman entails a wage penalty of €100 and being a foreigner €60. Wages increase with age; older people earn €130–150 more than young people. The wage is not related to education, with the exception of vocational education and training; firm-specific competences rather than general skills are more appreciated. Type of contract, size of the firm and profession affect the level of pay. Those who found a job through personal networks command the highest wages, those who found a job through a CpI the lowest.[27]

There is a strong correlation between the pay structure, the rating of job satisfaction and the rate of satisfaction with the services of CpIs. The latter is usually high for the services in general, but it drops to 19 per cent for the capacity to provide a job. The help in finding a job is the main reason to contact a CpI (90 per cent). Over the year under consideration, 10 per cent of all people who had signed a commitment agreement received a job offer from the CPI, and 42 per cent of these accepted. At the time of the interview, 35 per cent of the latter were still in employment. By comparison, 14 per cent of those addressing a private agency received a job offer and 61 per cent accepted. The comparison is ambiguous; it may signal a greater ability of private agencies to offer more targeted solutions, but it may also reflect their power to select the more employable workers (creaming), a possibility which is obviously not open to the CpIs.

The analysis shows that, even in a region with a widespread presence of CpIs and good organisational skills, the supply of ALMPs is far below demand.

5.4 Conclusion

Over the past 20 years, there have been several attempts to reorganise employment services, but it cannot be said that the operational and administrative structure of ALMPs is working well and is up to the task. Lack of investment, precariousness of the personnel and understaffing, lack of adequate management and information systems continue to weigh on their efficiency. All this frustrates the accomplishment of the social dialogue objectives.

The design of the Jobs Act attempts to change the industrial relations by offering less regulation in exchange for greater universal access to services in support of employment. However, the absence of a solution to the problems of the operating structure that is supposed to ensure that accessibility is likely to undermine a crucial pillar, necessary to accompany the development of good industrial relations between the social partners.

It must be emphasised that many temporary or economically fragile workers require services not dissimilar to those for the unemployed. More than half of unemployment is long term. For many people, job search is a continuous task, so that orientation, training and other services are also available to those who work. The regional level remains a key platform on which to implement solutions and the role of social dialogue is still crucial in this.

6. CASE STUDY: TWO MODELS OF LABOUR RELATIONS IN PRACTICE – FERRARI AND LAMBORGHINI

6.1 Introduction

As argued in section 2, the evolution of industrial relations in Italy is going in the direction of greater decentralisation. Although greater involvement of employees in the definition of production processes and business strategies is considered a key part of personnel management systems, since it ensures a positive effect in terms of productivity and innovation, the trend towards disintermediation increases the risk of dualism between firms and workers.

The Fiat example – breaking away from national representation and from the CCNL and activating a CCSL with only the signatory trade unions – constitutes a watershed and is being seriously considered by other companies. We compare two models of industrial relations within the same product niche to assess the existence of different effects on job quality and firm performance.

6.2 Case Study: Ferrari and Lamborghini

Ferrari and Lamborghini are two well-known worldwide supercar companies belonging to two multinational corporations. They are quite similar in terms of product, local culture and human capital, and they are geographically close, but have different models of industrial relations. Ferrari applies the corporatisation model of bargaining (FCA's CCSL); there is only one level of bargaining for the group, which applies to all production sites, although at Ferrari there is also factory-level bargaining. A protocol regulates the relations between the management and the specific trade union representation at factory level (RSAs), limited to the signatory representatives. Conversely, at Lamborghini, the firm-level bargaining is within the national sectoral contract system. The relations between the unitary trade union representation at factory level (RSU) and the management cover a wide range of organisational and strategic issues, in close relationship with the workers' assemblies. We compare the two companies to test whether, from the point of view of workers' conditions (wages, incentives, time, health and benefits), the model of industrial relations matters also in companies producing high-quality products, where the management has an interest in getting the maximum commitment out of the workforce.

The comparison is based on an analysis of the companies' contracts, integrated with interviews with experts and trade union representatives – the RSA in the case of Ferrari and the RSU in the case of Lamborghini – on several issues,[28] supplemented with informal interviews with union leaders and workers at the two companies.[29] We also used the recent literature on the topic and the information available on the companies' websites. The aim is to shed light on the influence of industrial relations on the quality of the product, the company climate and dignity at work.

Some caveats are in order. First, these are two companies of excellence, both known worldwide and leaders in technological innovation, product quality, up-to-date plants, attention to safety and ergonomics, as well as staff training. The respective codes of conduct are exemplary for corporate social responsibility. They have high profit margins and are not representative of the average firm in the sector or industry. Workers are eager to work at these companies because of professional status and access to company benefits.

Second, the two companies are similar, but not identical. Ferrari is much bigger, has a wider range of products and keeps in house the entire cycle of production, except for some special components, such as brakes, automatic transmission, computers and car body. The racing department is also unique. Lamborghini has a narrower range of production in house; it has a patented carbon-fibre car body, while the engines come from the Volkswagen (VW) group. Although a few kilometres apart, history and corporate culture are very different. Both are growing rapidly in their respective markets. These differences give rise to a different company climate, which is not attributable solely to labour relations.

Third, the number of respondents cannot be considered representative of the reference community, while lack of time prevented us from interviewing management. Thus the present assessment concerns essentially the workers' side and cannot aim to establish a ranking between two realities 'so close, so far away' – to paraphrase a famous Wim Wenders film – but, more modestly, to give a partial account of two types of labour relations. Thus, the study does not conclude with a verdict on the best industrial relations; its aim is to look at the main variables that a comparative assessment must consider and highlight their interactions with factors such as management style and organisational constraints.

6.3 A Preliminary Assessment

We can draw a preliminary scheme to analyse the differences between these two types of industrial relations, keeping in mind the three caveats. There are two levels, one relating to the company and one more general.

As noted, these are two companies of excellence, belonging to large corporations with a global vision and ethical codes of conduct. They are located in the same geographic area, from which they draw culture and human capital; the product is similar, but made with a different proportion between internal and external production. The cycle of assembly is different, shorter at Ferrari (about 16–17 minutes), longer at Lamborghini (over 30 minutes). In short, two high-end companies, whose interest is to ensure good treatment of employees in order to get a top-quality product.

6.3.1 Similarities and differences between the two cases examined

1. *Participation*. In both cases, there are bilateral committees for major issues of common interest. Their work corresponds to different procedures. As part of the FCA group, Ferrari applies the CCSL, with the chargeability (responsibility) principle and the cooling mechanism in the event of conflicts. Because of the lack of between-union cooperation, information provided by the company is received and disseminated passively among the workers; there seems to be no feedback mechanisms and confrontation appears asymmetrical. At Lamborghini, there is mutual recognition of the parties, the union has an autonomous vision – not necessarily conflictual – and information is open to bargaining on potential occupational or organisational repercussions, not only for direct employees but also for the whole chain of supply and subcontractors.
2. *Ergonomics and safety*. Great attention is paid by companies and unions to reduce risk. The firms' investment in safety and ergonomics call for equal care paid by workers not to adopt risky behaviours. The working facilities are good, and Ferrari has received numerous international awards in this field.

3. *Pay*. At Ferrari pay is linked to profitability, quality and physical presence; the latter can entail penalties of up to 30 per cent of the company bonus. On top of that, there is also a bonus bestowed discretionally, which is not guaranteed every year. All things considered, the pay is about €10 000 euros higher than the basic. At Lamborghini, company bargaining ensures pay higher than the basic level and affects all the components of remuneration; that is, about €6000 euros in corporate indemnities and pre-agreement on basic pay, the 14-month salary and performance bonus. The working hours are shorter and there is a premium for on-call working and an occupational allowance.
4. *Hours and shifts*. At Ferrari, shifts are 7 hours 30 minutes, at Lamborghini 7 hours with a break. At Ferrari overtime is a tool for making up for unplanned variances in production. They are not subject to negotiation, but they are appreciated by most workers as a way to increase pay. At Lamborghini overtime is lower, not systematic, and voluntary, and it is not used to maintain production volumes.
5. *Professional skills and training*. At both companies, training is an ongoing activity and involves almost all the staff. At Lamborghini task or job classification is on average higher and achieved through a shared, less discretionary track. Training is provided at the individual level, both inside and outside the company, and is provided to temporary staff.
6. *Work organisation*. The plants have different levels of complexity. Ferrari keeps the complete production cycle in house, while Lamborghini does not produce engines, which are provided by the group, but does produce the carbon car body. Cycles are more intense at Ferrari, where there seems to be a higher level of variance or imperfections, which often cause the exit of the car from the chain or reworking. These problems are coped with by extended use of overtime, promotion of presence at work, discipline and compliance with the rules. At Lamborghini, given the slower cycle, overtime is not necessary in order to cope with production variances. With the exclusion of the racing department, at Ferrari overtime seems to be a symptom of organisational problems.
7. *Company climate*. At Ferrari, horizontal and vertical working relationships seem to be more competitive, not only in the racing department. The attention to ensure the result at all costs involves tensions between the departments, between production and testing, and a continuous tension to protect oneself to avoid becoming the scapegoat for what goes wrong. There seems to be the idea that problems do not depend on the organisation, but on insufficient dedication. This pressure, and the stress that comes especially for middle management, has not

emerged at Lamborghini, where, possibly thanks to slower cycles, the problems are addressed in a constructive way, also through the RSU's direct intervention. Another important difference is the direct solidarity with outside workers, which does not exist at Ferrari. The climate in Lamborghini can be defined as more inclusive, that at Ferrari as more competitive.

8. *Industrial relations*. The cohesion among trade unions is key to their ability to influence the organisation of work. Ferrari's competitive climate is transmitted to the signatory trade unions, which cannot or will not form a common position, thereby accentuating the asymmetry of power between management and labour. The fact that a significant proportion of workers – if only because of their trade union's choice – are virtually excluded from participating only makes things worse.

We cannot say that the differences in industrial relations affect technological innovation at the two companies,[30] which must adopt the most sophisticated technologies to compete. In both companies industrial relations accompany the adoption of new technologies; they contribute to reducing uncertainty in order to ensure the level of commitment needed to match the heavy investments that are required. At Ferrari this is obtained by stressing attendance and chargeability, together with a massive recourse to internal training. At Lamborghini, hours of training are an individual right, as is the perspective of lifelong learning. The union that we defined as fair (Lamborghini) takes care of the firm's viability, competitiveness and profitability as much as the so-called reformist model (Ferrari). The former also acts on the basis of a principle of general protection and solidarity, caring for temporary and external workers. The latter appears to be more passive, less concerned about an autonomous and shared vision to address working conditions. This denotes a greater pragmatism about contingent problems or micro-adjustment, without interfering with the organisation or with the management's choices.

At Lamborghini, there seems to be more balance between management and labour; individual rights seem more transparent and less dependent on unilateral decisions. It seems to work more according to a criterion of mutual adaptation, rather than mere hierarchical authority. However, at Ferrari the non-signatory union does not participate in the social dialogue, while representing, directly and indirectly, a substantial share of workers (as evidenced in the election of the safety representatives), but overall there is greater union pluralism, which also encompasses clerical staff. For historical reasons, at Lamborghini union cohesion is achieved without pluralism (one union, FIOM, covers 96 per cent of members), and white-collar staff do not seem to get involved in collective participation, a phenomenon that is not specifically Italian.

6.4 Conclusion

Further research is required on these issues. At this stage, we can say that these two cases seem to represent well the models differentiating the two multinationals, the Anglo-Saxon model, largely focused on finances and efficiency, and the northern European model, more inclusive and concerned to adapt to local cultures.

However, there is a second trend related to what we have called corporatisation. On the one hand, the national labour contract allows derogation, albeit within a framework. On the other hand, there is the Fiat system, based on corporate autonomy in the production and management of the rules governing work; there is only one bargaining at the group level, so that the solidarity with the rest of the workers in the industry is lost.

There are social costs of corporatisation that should not be overlooked. First, power relations are asymmetrical and favour the firm. Far from fostering collaboration and dialogue, decentralised bargaining weakens the bargaining power of labour and becomes ancillary to the company's objectives. Second, it weakens the solidarity between workers, which is the real purpose of labour market regulation; the trend towards corporate and individual contracts increases the competition between workers, whose personal well-being comes to be identified with the firm's economic objectives. Moreover, the growing amount of benefits, such as company benefits, increases dependence and loyalty, rather than professionalism; these institutions are not transferable in the event of mobility, widening the gap between insiders and outsiders. Finally, company-level bargaining is present in a small percentage of firms; the vast majority of companies are small and without the presence of a union.

The question is whether one system is better than the other in safeguarding the company's competitiveness goals. If both produce the same results, there is no a priori reason to move in the direction of corporatisation. A system based on the national collective bargaining agreement, while leaving increasing freedom to company specificities, seems to fit better a productive system in which a small group of large and medium enterprises are surrounded by small and micro enterprises.

No model of industrial relations will provide the necessary balance between capital and labour unless unions are capable of cohesive action and backed by democratic representation. Thus, trade unions should devote at least an equal effort to devising how to be effective in practice as they do to trying to define their identity. In this perspective, a positive note is provided by the recent Metalworking and Mechanical Engineering Industry Collective Agreement, signed by FIOM, Federazione italiana metalmeccanici (FIM), Unione Italiana Lavoratori Metalmeccanici (UILM) and Federmeccanica. Its conclusion is important both because it is once again unitarian (the previous agreement was signed separately by the trade unions) and because it confirms the role of the CCNL as the pivot of industrial relations. The Fiat model, announced as an example for future industrial relations, does not seem to have any followers, for now.

7. CONCLUSIONS

The analysis in this chapter started from the premise that the labour market is a social institution. Industrial relations and social dialogue reflect the social, economic and legal environment and interact with economic, labour and welfare policies in determining the path and quality of growth. As in many other EU countries, the Italian labour market has gone through a process of deregulation, based on the idea of the self-regulating market. Since the crisis, within the EMU framework, austerity measures and structural reforms (labour and wage flexibility) have been the only instruments used to address macroeconomic imbalances. Drastic cuts in social investment and internal devaluations have magnified the dualism in the labour market and increased inequality and poverty.

We argue that the Italian experience does not support the view that, if sufficiently flexible, labour markets adjust quickly to shocks, so that, in the long run, the benefits of flexibility outweigh the short-run adjustment costs. No degree of labour flexibility can provide an adequate response to the multiple challenges represented by technological, organisational and social changes. These changes call for coordinated responses in the production, employment and social spheres. The diverse experiences of European countries over recent decades highlight the role of social policy as a productive factor. In Sweden, technological change has been tackled within a cooperative climate in industrial relations; new forms of work organisation and generous policies favouring the upgrading of skills and the improvement in the quality of work have turned the challenge of technical change into an opportunity (Anxo, 2016). Conversely, Germany seems to have co-opted only one part of the labour force, leaving behind a large proportion of low-skilled or vulnerable workers. However, as argued by Lehndorff (2015: 170–71), Germany's comparatively positive economic development is not to be attributed to 'Agenda 2010', but rather to the first attempts at limiting the damage caused by it. The growing trade union influence over wage development has played an important role here.[31] In southern

European countries, the structural reforms implemented in the crisis have eroded labour rights and weakened labour unions, reinforcing a 'low road' of wage cuts and precarious work that has priced out any alternative attempt at benefiting from technological innovation. Wage moderation and low wages could not counter the effects of the productivity decline; on the contrary, they are at the root of the productivity problem.

We conclude that there is increasing theoretical and empirical evidence in favour of the hypothesis that social dialogue and good industrial relations can be good for innovation and growth. Their effects work through two channels: (1) a cooperative environment within firms that encourages on-the-job skills upgrading, workers' cooperation and the adoption of new technologies and innovations; and (2) a more equal income distribution – and higher wages – that sustain domestic demand. In this light, labour market policies supporting less adversarial social relations and strengthening unions' bargaining position may represent a key element within an overall industrial policy directed to achieving a long-term sustainable growth. Cooperation between unions and firms can interact with the government in devising a long-term industrial policy capable of fostering organisational changes and patterns of innovation that better respond to the social model of the country. The comparative analysis of industrial relations in Ferrari and Lamborghini, two firms producing top-quality cars, but with different models of industrial relations, sheds light on the influence of industrial relations on various factors, such as product quality, internal climate and the dignity of work. While we could not find clear evidence of the superiority of one system in terms of firm performance, we can conclude that no model of industrial relations will provide the necessary balance between capital and labour unless unions are capable of cohesive action and backed by democratic representation.

The chapter concludes that there is evidence in favour of a different model in which unions, firms and the state can interact to devise a long-term industrial policy capable of fostering organisational changes and patterns of innovation that better respond to a shared social model. This calls for a complete reboot of the European and national approaches to macroeconomic, labour and social policies.

NOTES

1. 'The involvement of the social partners essentially takes place on an ad hoc basis at the initiative of the government and the relevant ministries according to the various policy areas. Another important contact with the policy-making process takes place through hearings in parliamentary committees, which are part of the more general advocacy initiatives carried out by interest organisations' (Eurofound, 2014: 25).

2. See note 5 for a definition.
3. Besides the three main unions, there is also a plethora of smaller unions. The Constitution guarantees trade union freedom and therefore pluralism.
4. The Constitution mandates a fair wage, proportional to effort and sufficient for a dignified quality of life for workers and their family.
5. There are two levels of bargaining in collective agreements: the national or industry level and the firm level (CCNL, Contratto Collettivo Nazionale di Lavoro) defines the national collective bargaining. We define corporatisation as a process of decentralisation of collective bargaining from industry to firms, which may no longer refer to a national agreement – as in the case of the CCSL (Contratto Collettivo Specifico di Lavoro) of Fiat Chrysler Automobiles (FCA) – or where the CCNL does not provide that very general framework.
6. In June 2011 an inter-confederal agreement, regulating the conditions for derogation from the national contract and settling the issue of representation, was signed by the three main trade union confederations. Although fiercely contested from within the CGIL, this agreement paved the way to end the CGIL's isolation.
7 The bargaining for the new rules took place in emergency conditions and under threat of relocation (to Poland and Serbia). The agreement was not signed by CGIL.
8. For instance, there is the anomaly of two types of representation – RSU (unitary trade union representation at factory level) and RSA (specific trade union representation at factory level) – while the 2014 Accordo Interconfederale stated the majority principle in the election of the RSU, it should be up to the law to choose between the two models of representation.
9. In 2009, two separate framework agreements were signed between two of the three main trade union confederations (with the exclusion of FIOM-CGIL) and Confindustria, with the backing of the government.
10. The extension of the Cassa integrazione (Wages Guarantee Fund) has been organised through bilateral funds rather than through INPS (a public institution) to relieve the public system of a new burden (Checchi and Leonardi, 2015). It covers only small and medium-sized firms and trade (besides construction).
11. Between 1993 and 2009, the planned inflation rate was agreed in regular tripartite sessions between government and social partners twice a year. Differences between this consensus inflation rate and the real rate were to be recovered after two years, in a new round of sector negotiations convened with the purpose of fixing the new increases for the next two years (Leonardi, 2017).
12. The second-level bargaining is now the prerogative of the unitary union representative body (RSU) whose members are elected by members and non-members in firms with more than 15 employees (Leonardi, 2017).
13. The Legge Fornero (Law 92/2012) aimed to address labour market dualism by acting on the firing and hiring costs of different types of contracts. On the one hand, it reduced the cost of individual dismissal, weakening the effectiveness of art 18 of Law 300/1970; on the other hand, it tried to limit employers' use of bogus self-employment and collaboration contracts and to create incentives for the greater use of apprenticeship contracts. It also reformed the system of unemployment benefits, extending the coverage to some forms of precarious contracts.
14. Article 18 of Law 300/1970, which regulates firing conditions on open-ended contracts. This law protected workers from invalid lay-offs, requiring reinstatement in a number of cases. Law 92/2012 (Legge Fornero) weakened this protection but did not completely abolish it (see note 13).
15. Vouchers are hourly tickets used to compensate workers for side jobs and represent the Italian version of the German mini-jobs. The net hourly pay amounts to €7.50, but workers under this kind of job relationship pay only a minimal social security contribution. Bettio and Mazzon (2017) call attention to the extremely low average amount of per-capita income earned from vouchers. Siding decidedly with the view that the labour market has undergone further precarisation, the CGIL has called for a referendum on

their abolition. In 2017, the government decided to abolish the voucher to avoid the referendum, but left open the question of how to regulate occasional work.

16. See Boeri et al. (2015) for a survey of the empirical research. By increasing firms' costs of dismissal, employment protection has a negative impact on productivity at the firm level: it lowers workers' effort (poor work performance or absenteeism) because there is less threat of lay-off, and it discourages firms from experimenting with new technologies with higher mean returns but also higher variance.
17. It is argued that in the United States skills are mostly scouted in the market, while in Europe they are chiefly nurtured within the firm. This difference may explain why the empirical literature has found that firms' innovative dynamics are associated with centralised bargaining systems in European economies (Addison, 2016) and with decentralised bargaining mechanisms and flexible labour markets in the United States (Menezes-Filho and Van Reenen, 2003). (See Fana et al., 2016 for a review.)
18. The OECD has developed a framework to assess the quality of jobs, structured around three main dimensions: earnings quality, labour market security and quality of the working environment. It is no wonder that all programme or crisis countries – Estonia, Greece, Hungary, Italy, Poland, Portugal, the Slovak Republic and Spain – do relatively badly in two or all of the three dimensions of job quality, and none performs well in at least one of these dimensions (OECD, 2016b). Conversely, Germany and the Nordic countries are among the best performers (at least two out of three dimensions).
19. Following ISFOL, we use SpIs (Servizi per l'impiego) to define the employment agencies, which include both the public employment agencies CpIs (Centri per l'impiego) and the private employment agencies (APLs), that is, private recruitment agencies, temporary agencies, employers' and trade unions' institutions, university job centres and so on.
20. The services to be provided by CpIs include: the profiling of competences and job search; stipulation of a service agreement that defines the tasks and intensity of job search assistance; specialist guidance; training; and job or internship offers.
21. The figures in this section are from Istat (2016) and Open Polis (2016).
22. Those in absolute poverty are defined as a family or group of individuals who are unable to obtain a monthly income which prevents them from obtaining necessary products and services needed to survive.
23. The relative poverty line depends year by year on variations both of consumer prices and of the mean of consumption expenditure.
24. See: Giubileo and Montaletti (2015); Arifl (the Regional Agency for Education, Training and Labour of Lombardy), accessed 6 May 2017 at http://www.arifl.regione.lombardia.it/cs/Satellite?c=Page&childpagename=Regione/MILayout&cid=1213305264818&pagename=RGNWrapper\&packedargs=ptype%3DRicerca%26TemplateDestinazione%3DRicercaPage%26assetid%3D1194454694556%26assettype%3DPage.
25. The law requires compulsory notification of any new hiring or firing by firms to the national insurance institute (INPS).
26. Data on mandatory communications show that, over a period of five years, the duration of contracts in the Marche region is as follows: 25 per cent of contracts up to two months, 25 per cent between two and five months, 25 per cent between five and 13 months, and only 25 per cent over 13 months.
27. See Regione Marche (2016a, 2016b) for a detailed analysis.
28. A description of the two company agreements is provided in the Appendix to this chapter. The following variables were considered: bargaining, pay, the system of bonus and incentives, corporate welfare; schedules, shifts and overtime; qualifications and professionalism, advancements and training opportunities; problems in product quality; internal flexibility, economic status and rights of external workers on different employment contracts (logistics, maintenance, information and communication technology, and services). Attention was paid also to the quality of industrial relations, the formal (contractual) and informal (implemented in practice) procedures to acquire and disseminate information (for example, on the group's investment decisions); whether the

management adapts to local traditions (history, culture) or acts to change them; the collaborative or hierarchical attitude of the management; the flow of information and the quality of work: the team's autonomy in coping with flaws and the use of overtime; finally, whether the company climate is collaborative or competitive.

29. Special thanks to the members RSA FIOM, RSU Lamborghini; UILM unionists, FIOM and workers who have told us about their experience. For the FIM and CISL we consulted the opinion of Bentivogli on the agreement FCA, cited in the bibliography. The authors have adapted the text from the interviews and are responsible for any inaccuracy or partiality. We intend to broaden the range of the interviews to complete the picture.
30. See the Bank of Italy's surveys on the influence of industrial relations on innovation (Visco, 2008).
31. Pointing to the discontinuity in the German labour policy, Lehndorff (2015) observes the paradoxical situation whereby the employment success at home served as a political platform for the German government to push for a policy of internal devaluation in other countries, the opposite of the policies underlying the German positive development.

REFERENCES

Addison, J.T. (2016), 'Collective bargaining systems and macroeconomic and microeconomic flexibility: the quest for appropriate institutional forms in advanced economies', *IZA Journal of Labor Policy*, **5** (1) 1–53.

Anxo, D. (2016), 'Upskilling to avoid jobs' polarisation and growing income inequalities: the Swedish experience', *Economia & Lavoro*, **50** (2), 13–24.

Arachi, G. and M. Baldini (2016), *La Finanza Pubblica Italiana*, Rapporto 2016. Bologna: Il Mulino.

Autor, D.H., D. Dorn and G.H. Hanson (2016), 'The China shock: learning from labour market adjustment to large changes in trade', NBER Working Paper No. 21906, January, National Bureau of Economic Research, Cambridge, MA.

Bavaro, V. (2012), *Azienda, contratto, sindacato*, Bari: Cacucci.

Bettio, F. and A. Mazzon (2017), 'Subsidiary employment in Italy: can commodification of labour be self-limiting?', in D. Grimshaw, C. Fagan, G. Hebson and I. Tavora (eds), *Making Work More Equal: A New Labour Market Segmentation Approach*, Manchester: Manchester University Press, pp. 150–67.

Blundell, R., C. Crawford and W. Jin (2014), 'What can wages and employment tell us about the UK's productivity puzzle?', *Economic Journal*, **124** (May), 377–407.

Boeri, T., P. Cahuc and A. Zylberberg (2015), 'The costs of flexibility-enhancing structural reforms: a literature review', OECD Economics Department Working Paper No. 1264, OECD, Paris.

Boeri, T. and P. Garibaldi (2007), 'Two tier reforms of employment protection: a honeymoon effect?', *Economic Journal*, **117** (521), 357–85.

Checchi, D. and M. Leonardi (2015), *Labour Market Measures in Italy 2008–13: The Crisis and Beyond*, Geneva: ILO.

Contini, B. and U. Trivellato (2005), 'Dinamiche e persistenze nel mercato del lavoro italiano: una sintesi', in B. Contini and U. Tivellato (eds), *Eppur si muove*, Bologna: Il Mulino, pp. 13–84.

Crouch, C. (1998), 'Non amato ma inevitabile il ritorno al neocorporatismo', *Giornale di Diritto del Lavoro e di Relazioni Industriali*, **77**, 55–80.

D'Amuri, F. and C. Giorgiantonio (2015), 'La partecipazione dei lavoratori in Italia', *Economia & Lavoro*, **49** (3), 67–78.
De Luca Tamajo, R. (2016), 'Postfazione', in P. Rebaudengo (ed.), *Nuove regole in fabbrica*, Bologna: Il Mulino, pp., 99–110.
Eurofound (2014), 'Role of social dialogue in industrial policies', Eurofound, Dublin.
Falco, P., A. Garnero and S. Scarpetta (2016), 'Il lavoro senza qualità', accessed 6 May 2017 at www.lavoce.info/archives/40406/il-lavoro-senza-qualita/.
Fana, M., D. Guarascio and V. Cirillo (2016), 'Did Italy need more labour flexibility? The consequences of the jobs act', *Intereconomics*, **51** (2), 79–86.
Ferrari spa (2016), 'Accordo Premio di Competitività', 22 June, accessed at https://www.sindacatometalmeccanici.it.
Franzini, M. and M. Raitano (2013), 'Economic inequality and its impact on intergenerational mobility', *Intereconomics*, **48** (6), 328–35.
Gilli, D. and R. Landi (2009), 'Il Sistema dei SPI', in M. Cantalupi and M. Demurtas (eds), *Politiche Attive Lavoro*, Bologna: Il Mulino, pp. 181–213.
Giubileo, F. and G. Montaletti (2015), 'Una dote da imitare', accessed 6 May 2017 at http://www.lavoce.info/archives/37375/una-dote-da-imitare-per-il-contratto-di-ricollocazione/.
Hyman, R. (2015),'L''austeritarismo' e l'Europa: quali vie per resistergli', *Quaderni Rassegna Sindacale*, **3** (July–September), 65–110.
Ichino, P. (2014), 'Che cos'è il contratto di ricollocazione e come funziona?', 6 May 2017 accessed at http://www.pietroichino.it/?p=29681.
ILO (2015), *Inventory of Labour Market Policy Measures in the EU 2008–13: The Crisis and Beyond. Synthesis Report*, Geneva: ILO.
Istat (2015), 'Rapporto annuale 2015', Istat, Rome.
Istat (2016a), 'Poverty in Italy 2015', 14 July, accessed 6 May 2017 at http://www.istat.it/en/files/2016/07/Poverty_in_Italy_2015.pdf?title=Poverty+in+Italy+-+14+Jul+2016+-+Poverty_in_Italy_2015.pdf.
Istat (2016b), 'Il mercato del lavoro', 12 September, accessed 6 May 2017 at http://www.istat.it/it/files/2016/09/Mercato-del-lavoro-II-trim_2016.pdf?title=Il+mercato+del+lavoro+-+12%2Fset%2F2016+-+Testo+integrale+e+nota+metodologica.pdf.
Lai, M. and A. Trovò (2015), *Bilateralità e lavoro*, Rome: Edizioni Lavoro.
Lamborghini spa. (2015), 'Contratto Integrativo Aziendale 2015–2017', accessed 13 November 2017 at www.bollettinoadapt.it.
Landi, R., E. Mandrone, M. Marocco and D. Radicchia (2016), 'Servizi per il lavoro, cosa fanno e cosa dovrebbero fare', *lavoce.info*, 12 July.
Lehndorff, S. (2015), 'Model or liability? The new career of the "German model"', in S. Lehndorff (ed.), *Divisive Integration. The Triumph of Failed Ideas in Europe – Revisited*, Brussels: ETUI, pp. 149–78.
Leonardi, S. (2017), 'Trade unions and collective bargaining in Italy in the years of the crisis', in S. Lehndorff, H. Dribbusch and T. Schulten (eds), *Rough Waters: European Trade Unions in a Time of Crisis*, Brussels: ETUI, pp. 83–107.
Martin, J.P. (2015) 'Activation and active labour market policies in OECD countries: stylised facts and evidence on their effectiveness', *IZA Journal of Labor Policy*, **4** (1), 4.
Menezes-Filho, N. and J. van Reenen (2003), 'Unions and innovation: a survey of the theory and empirical evidence', in J.T. Addison and C. Schnabel (eds),

International Handbook of Trade Unions, Cheltenham, UK and Northampton, MA, USA: Edward Elgar, pp. 293–334.
Oliveri, L. (2015), 'Il libro dei sogni dei servizi ai disoccupati', *lavoce.info*, 15 December, accessed 6 May 2017 at http://www.lavoce.info/archives/38955/il-libro-dei-sogni-dei-servizi-ai-disoccupati/.
Open Polis (2016), Poveri noi, Minidossier, no. 11, December, accessed 6 May 2017 at http://minidossier.openpolis.it/2016/11/Poveri_noi.pdf.
OECD (1994), *The OECD Jobs Study. Facts, Analysis, Strategies*, Paris: OECD.
OECD (2004), *Employment Outlook*, OECD, Paris, accessed 6 May 2017 at http://www.oecd.org/els/emp/34846856.pdf.
OECD (2016a), *Employment Outlook 2016*, OECD, Paris, accessed 6 May 2017 at http://www.keepeek.com/Digital-Asset-Management/oecd/employment/oecd-employment-outlook-2016_empl_outlook-2016-en#.WgGFZoWcHmQ.
OECD (2016b), 'How good is your job? Measuring and assessing job quality', February, accessed 6 May 2017 at http://www.oecd.org/std/labour-stats/Job-quality-OECD.pdf.
OECD (2017), 'Time series data on the OECD indicators of employment protection', accessed 6 May 2017 at http://www.oecd.org/employment/emp/oecdindicatorsofemploymentprotection.htm.
Pedersini, R. and M. Regini (2014), 'Coping with the crisis in Italy: employment relations and social dialogue amid recession', in K. Papadakis and Y. Ghellab (eds), *The Governance of Policy Reforms in Southern Europe and Ireland: Social Dialogue Actors and Institutions in Times of Crisis*, Geneva: ILO, pp. 109–26.
Regione Marche (2016a), 'Rapporto sul grado di soddisfazione degli utenti dei Centri per l'Impiego nelle Marche', accessed 6 May 2017 at http://luglio2016.europa.marche.it/FSE/AttuazioneeSorveglianzaFSE/RapportiannualidiesecuzioneevalutazioneFSE.aspx.
Regione Marche (2016b), 'Elementi per la sperimentazione di una analisi costi-benefici di alcune misure di politica attiva del lavoro cofinanziate da POR-FSE Marche 2007–13', accessed 6 May 2017 at http://luglio2016.europa.marche.it/FSE/AttuazioneeSorveglianzaFSE/RapportiannualidiesecuzioneevalutazioneFSE.aspx.
Romagnoli, U. (2016), 'Cgil, il nuovo Statuto non è per il nuovo mondo', *Eguaglianza e Libertà*, 2 March, accessed 6 May 2017 at http://www.eguaglianzaeliberta.it/web/content/cgil-il-nuovo-statuto-non-%C3%A8-il-nuovo-mondo.
Rubery, J. and A. Piasna (2016), 'Labour market segmentation and the EU reform agenda: developing alternatives to the mainstream', ETUI Working Paper 2016.10, European Trade Union Institute, Brussels.
Sestito, P. and E. Viviano (2016), 'Hiring incentives and/or firing cost reduction? Evaluating the impact of the 2015 policies on the Italian labour market', *Questioni di Economia e Finanza*, **325** (March).
Simonazzi, A. (2015), 'Italy: continuity and change in welfare state retrenchment', in D. Vaughan-Whitehead (ed.), *The European Social Model in Crisis: Is Europe Losing its Soul?*, Cheltenham, UK and Geneva: Edward Elgar and ILO, pp. 339–85.
Simonazzi, A. and T. Barbieri (2016), 'The middle class in Italy: reshuffling, erosion, polarisation', in D. Vaughan-Whitehead (ed.), *Europe's Disappearing Middle Class? Evidence from the World of Work*, Cheltenham, UK and Northampton, MA, USA and Geneva: Edward Elgar and ILO, pp. 360–95.
Simonazzi, A. and P. Villa (2007), 'Le stagioni della vita lavorativa e il tramonto del

"sogno americano" delle famiglie italiane', in P. Villa (ed.), *Generazioni flessibili*, Rome: Carocci Editore, pp. 25–51.
Simonazzi, A., A. Ginzburg and G. Nocella (2013), 'Economic relations between Germany and Southern Europe', *Cambridge Journal of Economics*, **37** (3), 653–75.
Visco, I. (2008), 'Indagine conoscitiva sull'assetto delle relazioni industriali e sulle prospettive di riforma della contrattazione collettiva', Camera dei Deputati, 25 November, accessed 6 May 2017 at https://www.bancaditalia.it/pubblicazioni/interventi-direttorio/int-dir-2008/Visco_25_11_08.pdf.

APPENDIX

Ferrari: Supplementary Agreement, Trade Union Relations, Company Climate

In 2016, FCA Ferrari produced 7900 cars, in a range of eight models; net revenues were US$3 billion and earnings before interest, tax, depreciation and amortisation (EBITDA) were more than 800 million. There is a complete cycle, from foundry, through car body, paint, machine tools manufacturing and assembly to finishing, plus the racing department. The firm employs approximately 2850 employees: 1600 blue-collar and 1250 white-collar workers. With the external personnel (canteen, maintenance, information and communication technology, technical drawing, cleaning, security, supply lines, shipping), the total number is 3500 people. The external workers do not enjoy company benefits, however.

Ferrari's company agreement, 22 June 2016

The agreement focuses on participation, which is prized as a useful tool to prevent conflicts, respond to market fluctuations, ensure full utilisation of the plant, reduce fixed costs and create the conditions for investment. The FCA Agreement enhances the direct participation of workers through the establishment of joint committees; the higher degree of labour utilisation is accompanied by a joint committee for the conciliation of disputes at the national level and a committee on organisation and production systems at the plant level (De Luca Tamajo, 2016). The FCA CCSL envisages four committees. The health and safety committee deals with health and well-being; it must ensure that risks are kept at a minimum, through compliance with the rules and programmes aimed at their reduction. The organisation committee examines the employment impact in any technological area and manages organisation, shifts and peaks of activity. The corporate services committee deals with social themes, such as catering, transport and employees' families. The absenteeism committee takes care of how to reduce absences. An additional committee on training and skills, not present in the FCA group, was established at Ferrari, since the excellence of the product depends on individual skills; this committee is responsible for training programmes and professional career advancement. Every year, a corporate observer examines the business forecasts, the development of the product range and of the sales network, and their effects on employment. Both parties prize stable relations, constructive dialogue and smooth resolution of conflicts. The number of hours for union activities has been increased for the signatory unions.

The competitiveness bonus is based on three indicators: production (number of cars delivered), profitability (EBITDA) and quality (50 per cent for internal verification initial customer perception, that is, car demerit points for finishing and aesthetics; 50 per cent for R100, that is, external audits on a sample of technical anomalies and reliability). The first two indicators provide economic value: the current volume of 7900 cars delivered corresponds to a value of €2150 per person. The value for the current level of EBITDA, €1 billion in 2017, is €2350. The third indicator is a multiplier of the previous two addenda. This multiplier varies by 10 per cent if quality deviates by 10 per cent from the target (a value between 90 and 110 per cent of the target is considered normal). In addition, because the premium must encourage individual productivity, it takes account of presence at work. So, if the hours of absence are more than 65 per year, the bonus is decreased by 15 per cent, and by a further 5 per cent for every 30 more hours, up to a maximum 30 per cent for those who exceed 170 hours (excluded from the calculation are holidays, paid leave, accidents, trade union leave, L.104, maternity, bereavement, marriage and blood donation). There is an additional cut of 7 per cent if the number of events that generate the absence is equal to or greater than seven (excluding hospitalisation). Finally, there is the award of a unilateral bonus of €5000 from Ferrari's president, a gift decided each year on the basis of business performance.

The signatory trade unions underline that this kind of industrial relations is favourable to workers, since it allows more degrees of freedom than in the FCA group, especially better recognition of professionalism and training. Production efficiency is critical; workers are very careful to avoid absences and prefer to use permits or leaves in order not to be penalised, although this does not mean that people work when sick, or that the frailest workers are discriminated against. The conflict cooling process must be respected. The climate among the signatory trade unions is one of competition, rather than collaboration. The signatory trade unions never convene before the meetings with the management, and proceed in open order.

The non-signatory trade unions, conversely, believe that the new system is unfavourable to workers: the management is dominant and workers' participation in the firm's decisions is null. In this kind of industrial relations, everything outside the firm seems subordinate, everything happens at the group level, there is no real enterprise bargaining. There are no shared rules for promotion or training. Only presence and commitment are really prized. The many hours of overtime are an indicator of quality problems upstream (except for the racing department). Many people work 50 hours a week, an indication that something prevents production from being accomplished within the 40-hour week.

Both signatory and non-signatory trade unions seem to agree on the following points. (1) The company climate can be described as strict and severe. The discipline is stricter than in other firms in the area. The stress is greater for the intermediate than the higher levels of management. Results are all that matters: that is why commitment is so important. Those who do not cooperate are frowned on. Because a large part of production is internal, there is even greater confrontation between the different departments. (2) The competition between trade unions gives more power to management. (3) The work setting is unique; all are in uniform, the site is spotless, the time of the chain is slow, company benefits are generous, the rates of absenteeism and accidents are lower than average.

Lamborghini: Supplementary Agreement, Trade Union Relations, Company Climate

Lamborghini Cars has been part of the VW Audi group since 1999. In 1985, the number of employees was 232, 70 per cent of them blue collar. In 2003, production jumped from 900 to 1800 cars a year and in 2006 the employees numbered 650 (60 per cent blue collar). Finally, after the 2009–10 slump, the workforce reached the current number of 1400 (40 per cent blue collar). Six hundred of them are directly responsible for the cars' cost; the remaining 800 include quality control and maintenance workers, as well as forklift truck drivers. The external workers (help desk, cleaning and logistics) number about 200, and temporary workers on the assembly line number about 60. The company produces about 3500 cars, with a turnover of approximately €1 billion. A new SUV model will join the current three-model range, plant size will double and the workforce is expected to increase.

The Aventador carbon frame is produced in-house. The carbon-fibre must be laminated and stretched by hand on the mould. The car consists of three templates (front absorption, the main cabin, engine box 12 cylinders) and two 'tanks', above and below; the one below is a Lamborghini patent. For the Aventador model the frame is made internally (Carbon Faserverstärkte Kunststoffe, CFK; that is, carbon fibre-enhanced plastics); painting is outsourced; motor is assembled and tested in-house; upholstering is internal; the assembly car is internal; test and finishing touch is internal. The daily production is 5.5 Aventadors and 11 Huracans. Workers assembling Aventadors have a 90-minute cycle, the Huracan takes 35 minutes.

Company contract

The labour and industrial relations, inspired by the VW Charter, are based on the principle of workers' cooperation and participation and are endorsed by the European and World Works Council. The objective is the competitiveness and profitability of the group, as levers to improve professional skills, working conditions and employment.

There are bilateral technical committees on performance bonuses, organisation, method and times; professionalism and skills; and safety. When no meetings are planned, a meeting can be convened at the request of at least two members of the committee.

The company agreement commits the company to a code of conduct for external contracts, suppliers or consultants. These contracts too must comply with the national collective agreements and the best economic and contractual conditions. The company provides the RSU with information on contracts, subcontracts and companies that are part of the supply chain, enabling the RSU to have direct contact with their workers. The company is open to discuss the re-internalisation of external strategic processes.

It is agreed that, when possible, in case of recruitment, preference should be given to the transformation of temporary contracts into permanent ones. If this proves impossible, the employee receives a non-confirmation allowance of €220 for every month of work (for those who have more than four months of seniority). In any case, fixed-term contracts must be an opportunity for professional growth, including at least one month of training. They shall not exceed 10 per cent of total employment, have a maximum cumulative period of 16 months and cannot be used to cope with production peaks or for starting a new process.

There is a seven-hour shift, with eight hours paid, with a pause of 19 minutes. The time in excess of normal hours can be accumulated over a three month period, to allow for work–life reconciliation. In the summer, it is possible to redistribute working hours.

Individual rights are given particular importance. The INPS's allowance for parental leave is increased by 30 per cent. In case of child sickness, the company pays the first two days of annual leave and recognises six more days of unpaid leave. In the case of medical tests the travel time is paid. The company pays for the supplementary health care and has increased its contribution to supplementary pension funds from 2 per cent to 2.2 per cent. There is the possibility to shift to part-time for a maximum of six months, in case of urgency, and a committee is working on the feasibility of tele-working (home office). The right to training consists of 250 hours of paid leave. There is an agreement with the municipality for summer camps. Lamborghini will adopt Audi VW's early retirement agreement to make way for youth employment.

Individual hours for training have been increased to 40 hours a year. There are specific initiatives for workers employed in quality, aesthetic and functional reworking of the car, as well as for the enhancement of managerial and relational soft skills, supervisors and team leaders. The committee is in charge of testing new career development paths.

Coming to the economic part, the main items include the additional monthly allowance of €89, €60 per month for professional skills, a €100–120 monthly increase of the basic allowance for availability, drivers, test drivers, coordination, specialisation and so on. The folder allowance has been increased to €40 a month. The annual performance bonus is now €2500.

The RSU FIOM notes that unionisation, high among blue-collar workers, is declining owing to the increase of technical employees, who are less likely to join a union. They tend to be passive even in the case of collective initiatives designed to protect them. The career system is negotiated. In case of problems, a worker can call the RSU representative, who can leave their work to go where the call came from, look at the workbook folder containing information about the relevant tasks, study the problem and, if failing to find a solution, pass on the problem to the technical committee. To understand why this model works, note that the RSU intervention also benefits the company. An RSU with more power is also more responsible and takes care of management issues, while trying to develop independent solutions with the workers' consent. Sometimes, middle management feels bypassed by union intervention. The supervisor's sensitivity is important; meetings between RSU, management and team leaders are planned to strengthen the cooperative goal of higher quality, without tension. The principles of the VW Charter are also important, as they have boosted a type of union participation that was already part of the local culture. Like collective bargaining and codes of conduct, the Charter is a set of formal principles that need to be translated into practice. It is important to find a balance between organisational needs that require coordination and protection of individual interests.

9. The Netherlands: Is the polder model behind the curve with regard to growing household income inequality?

Wiemer Salverda

1. INTRODUCTION

Social dialogue has been a hallmark of the Netherlands since 1945 (Salverda, 2008; SER, 2015), involving three parties – employer associations, union federations and government – and stretching beyond affairs directly concerning employers and employees. The dialogue extends to such matters as people out of work for economic reasons or personal reasons of disability or inability to perform or obtain paid work – including old age, for which the world's most extensive capital-funded occupational pension system has been built. The social partners view wage formation in a broad framework encompassing the effects on incomes and the (un)employment chances of workers, together with the incomes of other dependent members of society. The dialogue was institutionalised in two main bodies at the national level during the immediate post-war period: the Labour Foundation and the Social and Economic Council (Sociaal-Economische Raad, SER). Formally, achieving a 'reasonable distribution of incomes' is one of the latter's three main goals. Detailed institutions – not always embodied, for example, the statutory minimum wage – have been added (and sometimes removed again, such as obligatory disability insurance for the self-employed).

The whole apparatus has continued until this day and has become known as the polder model.[1] Social dialogue pervades it and is its main *raison d'être*. It brings the two countervailing powers of employees and employers together with each other, and with the government as a third power. However, there are no obvious independent checks and balances on the functioning of the whole. Nor is there a guarantee of equal power for the three actors, and outcomes may be skewed as a result. In addition, to keep up appearances, a party may sometimes trade off a change in its behaviour, however obvious the need may be in itself, against changes to be made by the other parties. Note that the set-up is particularly important for Dutch unions as they have comparatively little presence at the workplace and union density is declining and far below the organisational coverage of employer associations.[2] The model has become known for its secular wage moderation on the social partners' side, and the annual preoccupation on the government's side to consider in detail the possible effects of the new budget on income inequality.

Because of its long, 70-year existence the polder model demonstrates that institutions should not be taken at face value. Within the given framework the behaviour of the actors and their mutual interactions may change due to the actors' own evolution or that of the wider context, economic and institutional, within which it operates. Indeed, the parties themselves have changed over time. The employers' associations have become more concentrated organisationally, leaving less room for the different views of, for example, small employers. The trade union federations have also become more concentrated, but at the same time they sometimes seem more divided and mutually competitive. Also, since the liberalisation of international capital movements, employers have increased their power vis-à-vis the other two partners, that is, unions and government, and since European monetary union the government has been facing increasing constraints on policy-making. The rapid increase in (female) labour supply has added to the pressure on unions. Such effects are all the more important as, after all, the institutions are a *ménage à trois*, which creates a possibility that two parties may side against the third. Alternatively, if the social partners do not reach agreement between one another, the government may pick one opinion or go its own way.

The institutions impose a format on the parties' interactions but they are not deterministic of the contents and results of the interactions. The very format generates a positive social dialogue on low inequality, but it also assumes that this in itself assures its success. However, in examining success we cannot escape looking at the actual behaviour and outcomes. Clearly, inequalities have been growing, in the labour market and beyond, albeit not all at the same speed. Amid such widespread trends and underlying forces that may work from the labour market and the economy and from outside the country, the equal sharing among the population of the prosperity that economic growth can bring is a tall order, even for such a closely knit system of social dialogue as the polder model. Nonetheless it is important to consider whether and how such sharing was tried and what may have been the contributions of either the model or its actors which the other actors were unable to undo.

The challenge for the rest of the chapter is to consider how the inequalities hang together, and how they are related, or not, to the workings of the polder model. This is especially the case as we want to consider the effects on household income inequality – central to the public debate – which are found at arm's length from the traditional machinery of individual wage formation; individual wages and individual hours worked combine into individual annual earnings which, in turn, combine into household incomes. We need to take the long view as both institutions and distributions change slowly, and current policy-making builds on what went before. Therefore, I look back over the past 25 years.[3] As an important health warning I should mention that the focus is entirely on national developments. So, even if inequalities appear to have increased and the polder model is shown to have something to do with this, either stimulating or not (sufficiently) counteracting, the increase and/or the levels of inequality may still look moderate in international comparison. In addition, the Dutch economy combines a very strong focus on exports, with semi-permanent and record-high trade surpluses,[4] with a labour market holding the world championship for part-time employment (more than half of all jobs now) that rests on a very rapid rise of adult female employment from one of the lowest levels internationally in the 1970s to one of the highest recently.

The chapter proceeds in five steps. In section 2 I discuss the potential relationships between inequalities and the polder model, and the attention paid to inequalities in the social dialogue. Section 3 examines the actual effects on individuals in the labour market, while section 4 explores the subsequent effects on households. Section 5 adds two interesting case studies: the current process of changing the very low Dutch youth minimum wage, which involves the polder model *tout court*, and the strong deviation of pay in the banking sector from the general outcomes of the polder model. Finally, section 6 discusses the results and concludes.

2. DUTCH INSTITUTIONS AND INEQUALITIES

This section, first, briefly sketches the polder model and its main instruments and policies that may affect inequality, either positively or negatively, and, second, discusses the social dialogue concerning inequality since 1990. The effects are the subject of the subsequent sections.

2.1 Possible Effects on Inequality

Figure 9.1 shows the relevant interlinkages to inequality. It distinguishes between institutions, policies, main instruments and effects, and indicates

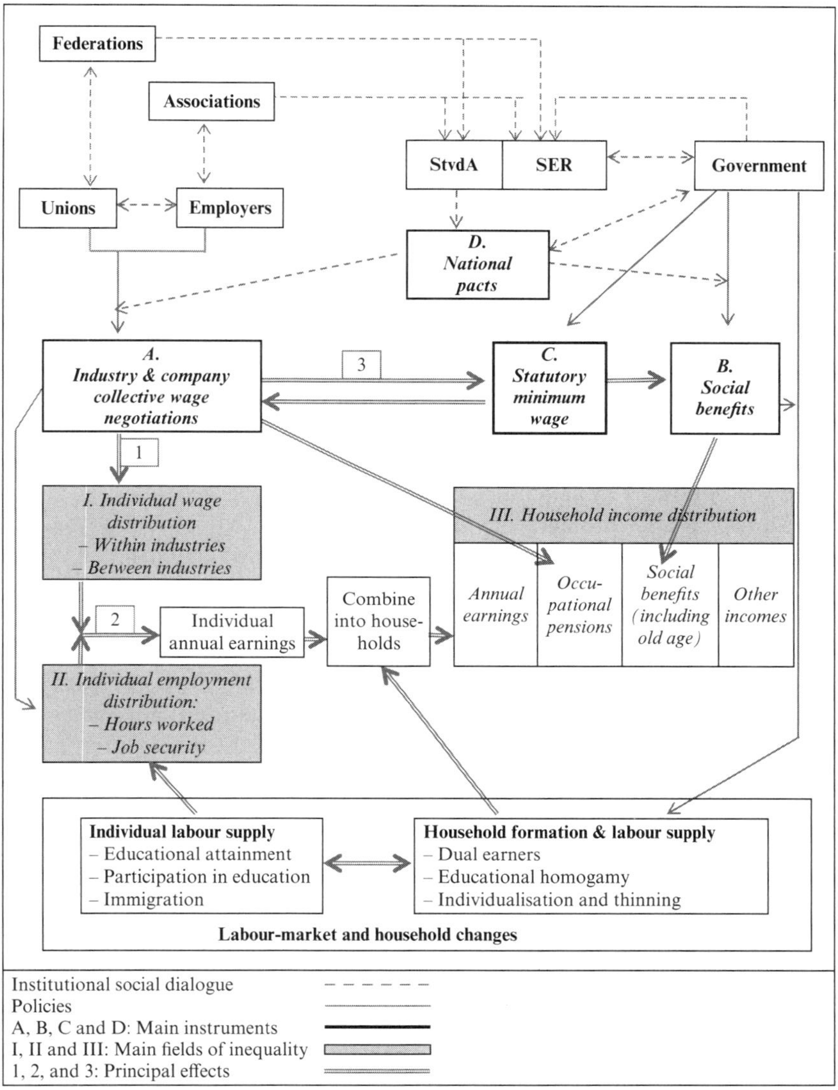

Figure 9.1 The polder model's institutional and policy links, main instruments and effects on inequality

the three main fields that together make up income inequality in the country. The upper part of the figure specifies the key actors: union federations, employer associations and government at the national level. It points out their mutual relationships and the two main platforms for the social dialogue: the bipartite Labour Foundation (Stichting van de Arbeid, StvdA) of union federations and employer associations, and the tripartite SER, the government's most important independent advisory body,[5] which brings together social-partner representatives (largely identical to StvdA delegations) with government-appointed experts, including the directors of the central bank De Nederlandsche Bank (DNB) and the Central Planning Bureau (CPB, the government's own main economic advisory body). The two platforms are complemented by occasional pacts resulting from direct negotiations either between the social partners in the StvdA or between the StvdA as a whole and the government. These bodies, and pacts, advise the unions and employers at industry and company level, who are the parties legally permitted to take measures on wages and other aspects of employment in their collective agreements, and on occupational pensions. They also may advise the government which acts on social benefits and taxation that, taken together, govern the redistribution of incomes and affect the supply of labour. The ensuing actions are indicated as policies.

Figure 9.1 also presents the main instruments that potentially affect inequality: collective labour agreements for unions and employers (A) and social benefits (B) for the government. Both are hard and legally binding instruments. Collective agreements have been the core instrument for unions and employers to influence labour market outcomes since their legal introduction in 1927. The possibility to declare industry-level collective agreements generally binding also for non-organised employers and employees was introduced in 1937; the declaration is the formal prerogative of the Minister of Social Affairs and Employment. Collective agreements are increasingly allowed to stipulate (modest) deviations from general rules. Almost 700 agreements provide a very large and stable coverage of the employee population and over time they have extended their reach beyond money wages to include non-monetary conditions of work and measures aimed at enhancing individual employment participation (the 'good causes'). The government extensively monitors some of the stipulations of collective agreements. Commonly the agreements specify the wages to be paid at different job levels, which is important for job mobility, in internal as well as external labour markets. The regular increases of collective agreement wages at renewal affect the evolution of all earnings, but they are the single factor for those who stay on the job and have passed all seniority levels, if any, of their wage scale. In addition, equally hard agreements form the basis of the extensive system of occupational pensions. Since the mid-1970s collective agreements and social benefits have been intricately linked by the statutory minimum wage (C), the workhorse for the (in)equality of wages and (minimum) benefits, including public old-age pensions. The minimum wage is the prerogative of the government but its uprating is legally linked to the average outcome of collective wage negotiations. The minimum wage is of pivotal importance as it puts a floor in wage negotiations and is key to the evolution of social security as a whole, which determines a large part of government spending. Thus collective agreements work in two directions and assume a crucial role affecting (the distribution of) incomes of the vast majority of the population from wage earnings and social benefits. Finally, pacts (D) constitute an irregularly used platform of social dialogue and formally comprise advice to industry and company actors and/or the government; however, de facto they play such an important role in subsequent policy-making that they can be considered instruments in their own right. Normally they trade off the interests of the three parties, exchanging, for example, wage moderation or other job measures for the level of social benefits, tax measures or macroeconomic policy-making. Nonetheless, they are legally weaker than the other instruments.

These instruments potentially affect the inequalities of wages and jobs, which make up individual annual earnings. The latter combine, or not, into household incomes, in interaction with individual (but largely household-determined) labour supply. These incomes depend also on occupational pensions and social benefits. The direct effects of the model's actions are fourfold. Collective agreements affect the distribution of individual wages (1) and of individual employment (2). At the same time the aggregate evolution of collective agreements wages determines the uprating of the minimum wage (3) and therewith of minimum social benefits. Conversely, the minimum wage increasingly affects the structure of individual collective agreements (4) as part of the social dialogue.

2.2 Social Dialogue on Wages, Employment and Labour Contracts

The long institutionalisation of the polder model offers the advantage that the contents of the social dialogue are available entirely in writing: StvdA agreements, SER advice and pacts (often including parties' detailed positions). I subsequently consider three issues of dialogue: wage formation, employment participation and employment contracts. I focus on inequality and the period since 1990 – all three issues figure from the beginning to the end. Note that in practice the issues may overlap. The first issue influences money incomes most directly, including the minimum wage. Secondly, the participation dialogue aims to enhance labour-market participation in general and broaden the basis of the economy; this is enacted in legal measures and collective agreement provisions of equal treatment of part-time jobs and non-discrimination by working hours, and reflected in explosive part-time growth. In addition, it targets specific groups such as non-employed or unemployed, low skilled, handicapped, older, or long-term unemployed persons, aimed at furthering their labour-market integration by means of collective agreements and government measures. Third, pacts, law-making and collective agreements address the flexibility and security of labour contracts, that is, employment protection and unemployment insurance. There is no room to discuss these issues in great detail, and important other issues have to be left out, such as retirement age or occupational pensions, which have preoccupied the social dialogue in recent years.

2.2.1 Wage formation

Four effects concerning collective agreement wages can be discerned: on actual wage formation, on the uprating of the minimum wage and therewith social benefits, and, conversely, from the level of the minimum wage to collective agreement wage formation and, finally, the inequality of wages within and/or across collective agreements and its possible widening.

Although collective agreement wages provide a highly significant input for actual wage earnings, the two can and do differ. The divergence is a recurrent subject of debate as there is no generally shared view on its measurement in relation to collective agreement wage growth (SER, 2006: 39–51; Salverda, 2009). Knowledge about the evolution of collective agreement wages is very limited; information on the spread of individual workers over the wage scales is non-existent. Statistically, collective agreement wage developments are measured solely by means of an index number of the average wage increase. It aims to mirror actual changes in wages, unaffected by the effects of a changing composition of the economy, by employing a fixed structure of the economy and the corresponding collective agreements.[6] The use of the statistic for the uprating of the minimum wage explains this situation. It contrasts with the available statistic on actual earnings which is not an index number but a running average incorporating compositional effects. In section 4 I examine the divergence, taking it at face value without going into detail.

The second and third effects warrant a discussion of the statutory minimum wage and its uprating in particular. This consists of two parts: a regular bi-annual uprating and an optional four-year uprating aimed at bridging the gap that the regular uprating may leave to the evolution of actual earnings. The mechanism of the former and the ad hoc decisions for the latter have been the subject of many SER discussions. The current mechanism was codified by the government in 1992, together with rules that would block its application if either the pace of wage growth supposedly affected employment negatively or the use of social security implied a sizeable increase in social contributions or tax rates. On this basis the SER agreed in 1993 to the government proposal for a nominal freeze of the minimum wage in 1994 and 1995, requesting compensation via income taxation from the government for households on low incomes. Increasingly, the road of an 'effective combination' of lowering the gross level of the minimum wage (and social benefits) and enhancing the net outcome by lowering taxation has been chosen. This was most clearly expressed the last time the four-year uprating was discussed by the social partners, in 1999. They jointly decided against a special adjustment because of expected negative employment effects and did not repair the freeze of 1993–95 (SER, 1999: 5–6). They were fully aware that uprating by means of the index number of collective agreement wages was insufficient to capture prosperity growth and actual earnings growth of households, because of the expansion of and employment and income improvements made by two-earner households. Instead, they pleaded for some additional income support measures for long-term poor families with children. This stance has two important implications: first, they definitively dropped their post-war agreement that a minimum wage should be sufficient for a family to live on and, second, they no longer considered the significance of the minimum wage as a floor to fair wage formation. The minimum wage was frozen another time, 2004–05, based on an agreement of the government with the StvdA, which from its side advised zero wage growth for collective agreement negotiations. Since then the regular uprating has become automatic, not receiving much further attention. Surprisingly, no freeze was imposed during the financial crisis. This led to the longest period of undisturbed uprating, 12 years from 2006 to 2017 at the time of writing, since the enactment of the minimum wage in 1969. Thus De Beer et al. (2017: 73) conclude that: 'there is generally low awareness among negotiators about the level of the statutory minimum wage'. Negotiators tend to regard it as irrelevant as long as the level of the lowest wage scale lies above the statutory minimum and as a given fact in those cases where the lowest wage scale is close or equal to the statutory minimum. The authors single out the cleaning sector as the exception, attributing this to strong industrial action in recent years.

The fourth effect of wage formation runs via the inequality of the edifice of collective agreement wage scales itself, within and across individual collective agreements. Unfortunately, very little systematic information is available on the range of wage scales that collective agreements actually offer.[7] However, there has been a clear drive since the early 1990s, stimulated by the then Minister of Social Affairs and Employment and supported by the social partners to introduce new scales or lower the existing ones. The aim is to bridge the gap with the minimum wage as a means of enabling the employment integration of worker categories with a weak labour market position (for example, StvdA, 1992: 3). This tends to invert

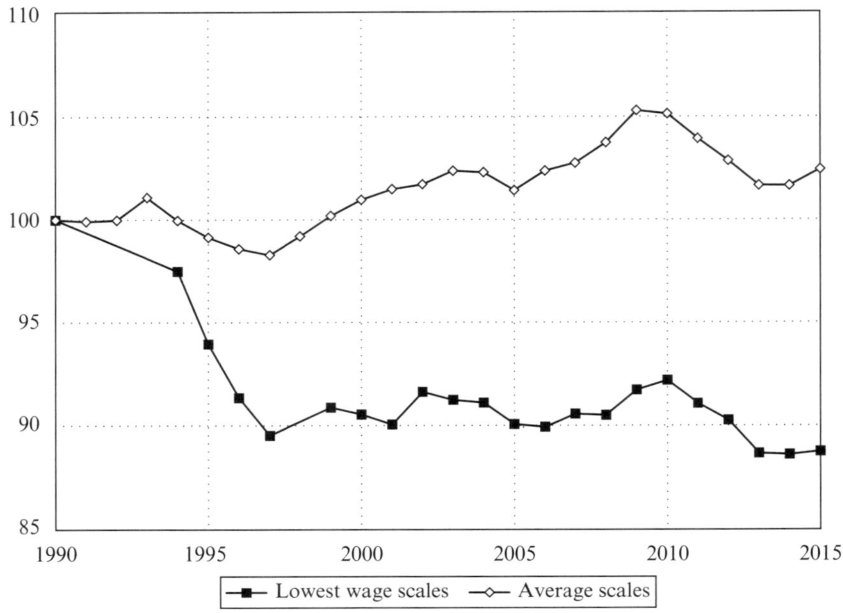

Source: De Beer et al. (2017); cf. Salverda (2010, fig. 10.14).

Figure 9.2 Average of lowest collective agreement scales compared with average collective agreement wage trend, Netherlands

the relationship between the minimum wage and collective agreement wages. The drive has been quite successful, as Figure 9.2 demonstrates. The average level of the lowest scale in the monitoring sample of collective agreements of the ministry has clearly declined, falling by more than 10 per cent, and has diverged downward from the average trend of collective agreement wages. *Ceteris paribus* this means that the edifice of collective agreement wages has become more unequal. In section 3 I consider whether the lowest scales are actually used.

2.2.2 Employment participation

Improving job access for people with a weak position in the job competition and promoting the employment participation of the population in general are the two main elements of the second type of social dialogue. The former may conflict with the latter. Tackling the former issue seems to have been conceived primarily in financial terms as we saw when discussing the gross–net trade-off around the minimum wage and the insertion of lower wage scales; it also motivated wage moderation (StvdA, 1992:

2). This is a recurrent theme. The poverty trap, an obvious effect of the gross–net trade-off, was added to the discussion ten years later, which ended in disagreement between employers who opposed introducing an earned income tax credit type of scheme while the union federations and independent experts supported this (SER, 2002: 107–14). Next came an almost identical dialogue in 2007 on adding 200 000 jobs in 2010 for those with a weak labour-market position; it ended in pious wishes that social partners and local authorities would consider how to solve the problems (StvdA, 2007). Fast-forward to 2013 when the same dialogue returns; this time it agrees on a target of 100 000 additional jobs in the private sector up to the year 2026 (StvdA, 2013; SZW, 2013). However, the most concrete outcomes are an expansion of wage subsidies for employers and the phasing out by the government of sheltered workplaces (Wet Sociale Werkvoorziening, WSW), which successfully provide 100 000 actual jobs for the same category and have done so for decades. The problems remain as real and the solutions as ineffectual as before.

'Jobs, jobs, jobs'[8] can characterise the other face of the participation dialogue, maximising general employment. It has helped the Netherlands to triumph as world champion of part-time jobs. Two main issues have dominated the social dialogue on part-time work: the growth of employment participation and the alignment of working hours with other activities (work–life balance). Part-time job growth started to increase rapidly in the early 1970s when individual taxation of labour incomes was introduced for household partners. Employers remained reluctant well into the 1980s, however, to hire on a part-time basis and the government explicitly advocated this several times (Salverda and Beukema, 1996). In 1993 the legal exemption of small jobs (less than 13 working hours per week) from the statutory minimum wage was abolished, against the opinion of employers (SER, 1990: 31). In 1996 any discrimination of pay and labour conditions by working hours was legally prohibited and equal treatment imposed instead. In 2000, individual employees were finally entitled to ask the employer for a change of working hours while remaining in the same job, subject to some conditions – against the unanimous initial wishes of the social partners (StvdA, 1993). To support the work–life balance this was further specified in 2016 by a new law, which, however, allows collective agreements to deviate. Income taxation has become more beneficial to dual earners with the important tax reform of 2001 that introduced individual tax credits for earnings from work and created options for tax optimisation over individual earnings at the household level. All this has made part-time work an essential part of individual working life. Its very success may help us to understand the failure of promoting the employment integration of weak groups, who depend on full-time earnings. However, the effects on the operation of the labour market receive little or no attention in the polder model.

2.2.3 Flexible labour contracts

Initially the issue of flexibility affected working hours, but from the mid-1990s this shifted towards contract flexibility and the trade-off with (job and income) security. The first result of the social dialogue on flexicurity was the Flexicurity Pact of 1996 between employers and unions. It aimed to improve the contractual position of temporary workers in exchange for shortened dismissal procedures and it coincided with the conclusion of an agreement between unions and the agencies supplying temporary workers to introduce a collective agreement for temporary workers. The pact incited the enactment of a corresponding law by the government, in 1999, which especially limited the possible number of consecutive temporary contracts but also allowed collective agreements to modestly deviate (Houwing, 2010). The rapid growth of flexible contracts that ensued has caused unease about the law. In the Social Pact of April 2013 the Labour Foundation insisted on improvements of the entitlements and protection of flexible workers (StvdA, 2013: 20). On the basis of this pact the 1999 law was recently replaced with the new Law on Work and Security (Wet Werk en Zekerheid, WWZ). It reinforced the legal entitlements with regard to work, sickness benefit, and dismissal for workers on various types of flexible contracts, including payroll workers, and reduced the possible number of consecutive temporary contracts (SZW, 2013). Measures explicitly exempted young workers up to the age of 18. Again collective agreements are allowed to introduce deviating provisions. The effects of the new law await evaluation and are politically important as feelings that flexibility has gone too far, for labour contracts as well as small, socially uninsured self-employment, are now widely shared (CPB, 2016). Flexible workers' access to training at the company was also discussed in the pact; evaluations two and three years later of measures taken by employers and industry-level training funds mentioned little tangible progress (StvdA, 2015a, 2015b, 2016).

In summary, collective agreements have added lower wage scales and likely offer a wider, more unequal range of wage scales nowadays. Wage moderation is the order of the day and the minimum wage is no longer uprated to general wage developments. Instead, the social partners leave it to the government to turn the gross minimum wage into a net living wage via income taxation, social contributions and special income support. The social dialogue has come back regularly since 1990 to the job problems at the lower end of the labour market and flexible contracts without finding an enduring solution.

Generally, the individual is the subject of the dialogue, not only in wage formation, participation and flexibilisation, but also in income taxation and social security. However, the great majority of individual workers operate from a (changing) household context. Therefore I look next at the effects on individuals (section 3) and then turn to how these come together in households (section 4).

3. INDIVIDUAL EFFECTS

I discuss the effects, first, on wage formation and the distribution of individual wages (section 3.1), and, second, on the nature of jobs and their distribution over individuals (section 3.2). Wages are the common target of collective agreements, the conclusion and general application of which is the central and legally strong instrument at the disposal of unions and employer associations. However, collective agreements can also act as an instrument for influencing the nature of employment, albeit often with legally weaker stipulations. Here I focus on working-time arrangements and flexible contracts. Both have grown exponentially and also show an important overlap.

3.1 Collective Wage Negotiations: Lagging Minimum Wage and Growing Wage Inequality

I discuss, first, the evolution of collective agreement wages, second how they compare with actual wage outcomes, and third with the evolution of actual wage inequality.

Union–employer negotiations regarding the pay that individuals receive in exchange for their work efforts are institutionalised in collective labour agreements. These specify different wage scales with longer or shorter trajectories of seniority, depending on the job and often based on a mutually employers–unions agreed job classification scheme. Industry-level agreements can be and commonly are declared binding for all enterprises and jobs operating in the corresponding industry by the Minister of Social Affairs and Employment at the request of the contracting parties on the condition that they represent a substantial majority (60 per cent) of all employees concerned. That condition is mostly fulfilled by the high level of employer associations, which cover 80 per cent of all employees, while union density is only about 20 per cent. This potentially weakens the influence of unions on the collective agreement result. Taken together, the collective agreements make up an impressive structure of pay determination. Unfortunately, little or no systematic information is available on the inside of that structure, namely, the distribution of the specified wages. We cannot say whether in general the range of scales has widened and enabled the potential growth of inequality, apart from the downward extension of the lowest wage scales that was mentioned previously and to which I will return. At the general level only the average increase of negotiated wages is known by means of an index number.[9] After integration with some (undisclosed) information about specific changes in low wage scales close to the minimum wage, this index number is used for the half-yearly uprating of the minimum wage (see De Beer et al., 2017, for more detail).

Wage moderation has characterised wage negotiations ever since the well-known Wassenaar Accord that was concluded in 1982. Figure 9.3(a) depicts the evolution of the average result since 1990, deflated by consumer prices to show its significance as an income for employees. This

(a) Real average hourly negotiated wage, including and excluding annual bonuses, 1990 = 100

Note: Industry collective agreements (Figure 9.3b) are shown up to the year 2012 to warrant a consistent classification of industries (SBI93).

Source: Centraal Bureau voor de Statistiek (CBS)/Statline (http://statline.cbs.nl/statweb/), CAO-lonen 1972–2014 (2000 = 100) chained with CAO lonen (2010 = 100); CBS (1994, 1996); CBS, *Sociaal-economische Maandstatistiek* (various issues); and tables of employee jobs by weekly hours and earnings made available to the author by CBS.

Figure 9.3 Negotiated wages, Netherlands, 1990–2013/16

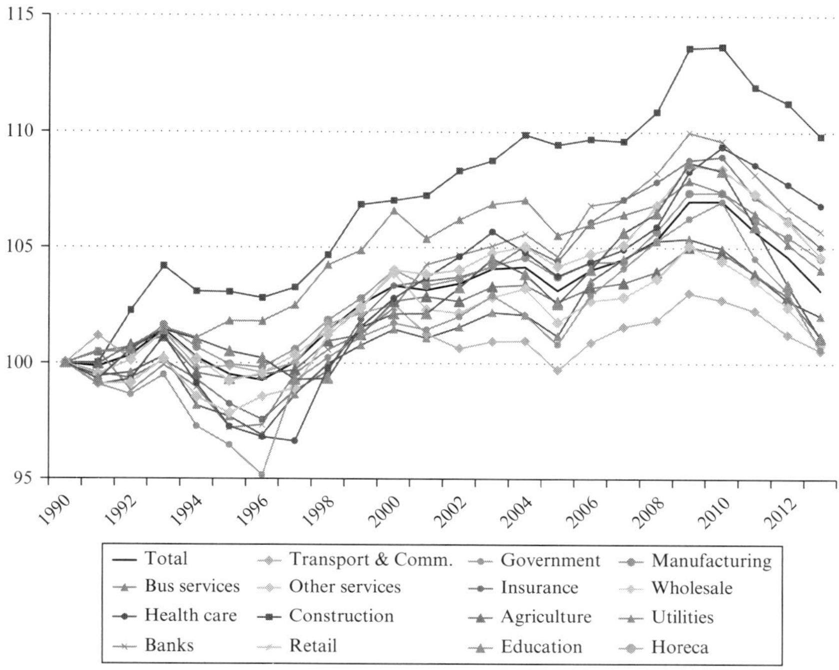

(b) Real average hourly negotiated wages including bonuses by 15 industries, 1990 = 100

Figure 9.3 (continued)

is presented in two ways: excluding and including annual payments, which encompass any additional disbursements, such as holiday allowance, thirteenth or fourteenth month, health-care insurance compensation (Zorgverzekeringswet, ZVW); and incidental payments. Both series are on an hourly basis[10] and they exclude employer contributions to social security and occupational pensions that top up gross wages received by the employees and that are exempt from income taxation. Figure 9.3 clearly indicates that negotiated wages excluding annual payments have stagnated and lagged behind those including such payments. In real terms over the 25-year period the former ended up, in 2014, with a purchasing power at a level 1 per cent below the starting level of 1990, while the latter increased by 6 per cent.

The stronger growth of annual payments seems to imply a potential own contribution of collective agreements to rising wage inequality because, first, they are generally more important at higher wage levels and, second, that association has grown stronger over time. Another potential contribution of collective agreements to inequality might be found in a divergence of collective agreement trends between (major) industries, which is shown in Figure 9.3(b) – again deflated for consumer prices. Although moving largely in tandem when it comes to cyclical patterns, the evolution between 1990 and 2013 has diverged between industries, ranging from zero hourly wage growth on balance for hotels and catering (Horeca) to a 10 per cent increase in construction.[11] Evidently, the effects on aggregate wage disparity will depend on the actual wage levels and the employment shares of the individual industries. Unfortunately, the collective agreement figure for the total economy is unable to show such effects given that it is an index number based on a fixed underlying structure of employment. However, scrutinising these growth disparities across industries shows them not to be correlated with the initial wage levels actually earned in 1990. Therefore they may not have contributed in their own right to growth in between-industry inequalities.[12]

However, at the same time, collective agreement wages have significantly lagged behind average actually earned wages as well as productivity growth, which ultimately offers the best metric for the growth of economic prosperity. Figure 9.4(a) elaborates on how negotiated wages and their trailing purchasing power fit the economy. It starts at the bottom of the figure with the negotiated hourly wages including bonuses of Figure 9.3(a): a 4 per cent increase. Then it, first, adds employer contributions to social insurance and occupational pensions, also at constant consumer prices.[13] These contributions have gradually grown in importance and they lift the increase of negotiated wages until 2014 from 4 to 10 per cent. As a second step, the deflation of the negotiated wages is changed from consumer prices to (basic) gross domestic product (GDP) prices to reflect the labour costs to the employers given their sales and production prices. This transformation lifts collective agreement wage growth to 22 per cent. The substantial effect between the two types of prices is especially important over the financial crisis as Dutch GDP prices stalled while consumer prices continued to rise. In particular, the prices of exported goods and services have lagged behind comparable European countries and the United States since 2008, while consumer prices evolved similarly to other countries. Still, the 22 per cent growth lags significantly behind productivity growth (32 per cent). Initially, both went up equally during the 1990s, but between 2000 and 2007 the deviation was particularly pronounced: negotiated wages remained largely unchanged while productivity grew quickly. Only over the past few years has collective agreement growth paralleled productivity growth again.

This 22 per cent growth of negotiated wages contrasts with the growth of actually earned hourly wages by 32 per cent, similarly measured including

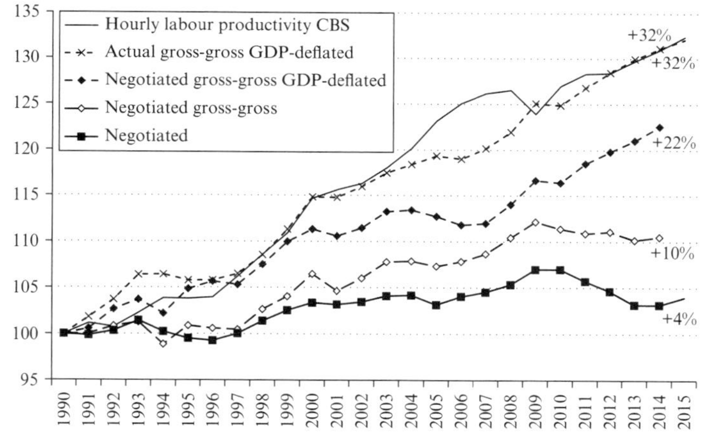

(a) Hourly wages, negotiated and actual, and productivity, 1990–2014

(b) Wage share (percentage) in GDP, 1990–2015

Note: Gross-gross means including employer contributions. Productivity is defined as GDP per hour worked (including self-employed). Imputed employer contributions to social security (for example, continued pay to sick employees) are considered here part of wages. Corrected for shift to employers of contributions to disability insurance in exchange for adaptation of gross wages.

Sources: CBS: Statline (http://statline.cbs.nl/statweb/): CAO-lonen 1972–2014 (2000 = 100) chained with CAO-lonen (2010 = 100), National Account, Labour Accounts and Consumentenprijzen; prijsindex 1900 = 100.

Figure 9.4 Negotiated wages and the economy, Netherlands, 1990–2015

employer contributions and deflated at GDP prices. This 9 percentage-points higher outcome came about in two different stages, in the early 1990s and over the 2000s, up to the start of the financial crisis and it has remained unchanged since. The gap suggests that the share of wages that is outside the grasp of collective negotiations has grown significantly – we ignore how substantial it was at the start. A deeper analysis is not possible here, but the case study on the banking industry below may provide some insights.

The evolution of these actual wages fluctuates around that of hourly labour productivity, which is measured as GDP growth per hour worked, including those of the self-employed. Wages lag productivity growth over 2004–06 but return to parity in 2009 (when productivity fell), but without making up for the lagging that preceded it. These oscillations are mirrored in the evolution of the share in GDP of wages including employer contributions that is presented in Figure 9.4(b). It shows a clear decline from 53 per cent in 1993 to 47 per cent of GDP in 2008,[14] which is followed by a slower decrease up to 2014 than has occurred after the previous downturns of 1993–97 and 2003–06.[15] The dashed line adds the returns to occupational pension savings, which in due course accrue to labour – however, even then the decline of the wage share remains. In addition, Figure 9.4(b) shows a larger decline for the wage share excluding employer contributions, down to a level of only 40 per cent of GDP in 2015.[16] However, the decline seems stronger than the oscillations of Figure 9.4(a) would suggest. It implies that the growth of labour productivity among employees only, excluding the self-employed, might be underestimated.[17] Conversely, although actual earnings have largely followed the evolution of productivity, the latter may have been reduced as a consequence of wage moderation (Vergeer and Kleinknecht, 2014).

Figure 9.5 elaborates on the changes in wage inequality on an hourly basis. These will be combined with hours worked to arrive at individual earnings on an annual basis at the end of this section, before the step towards annual household earnings in the next section.

Figure 9.5(a) presents the most direct effect of collective agreement wage developments: the evolution of the statutory adult minimum wage whose uprating depends entirely on the index of average collective agreement wages (excluding bonuses). Figure 9.5(a) shows how the level of the real minimum wage fell from €11.70 to €10.88, a 7 per cent decline. It lags behind the index number of real collective agreement wages, which still showed some increase, due to government interventions in the uprating that twice kept the nominal minimum wage frozen for five years out of the 25-year period (July 1992–December 1995, July 2003–December 2005). The relative position of the minimum wage in the wage distribution,

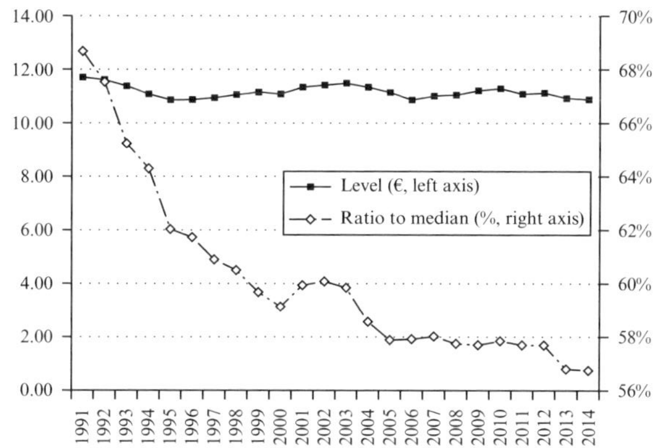

(a) Real hourly adult minimum wage level (€, 2014) and ratio to median wage (FTE)

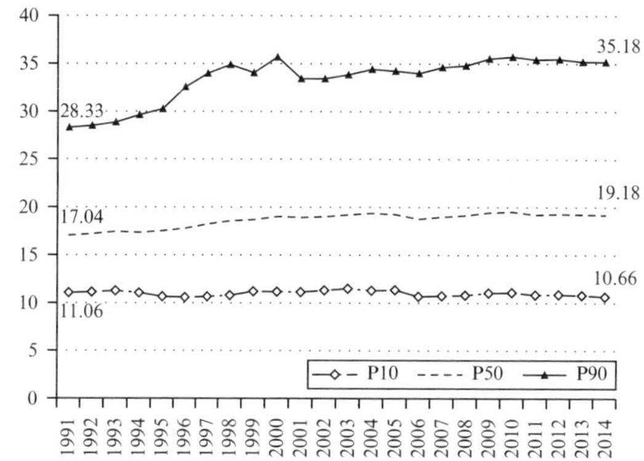

(b) Disparity of real actual hourly earnings (€, 2014) and low-pay incidence (percentage of FTE)

Notes:
Minimum-wage ratio to full-time equivalent (FTE) median wage (Figure 9.5(a)), actual earnings cut-offs (Figure 9.5(b)), and low- and high-pay incidence and employment incidence of the minimum wage (Figure 9.5(c)) are estimated using linear interpolation in tabulated classes of hourly wages, which are social-security defined and include the 8 per cent annual holiday allowance. These data show two important series breaks in 1995 and 2006 resulting from improved statistical observation of employment and pay, especially low pay.
Minimum wage per hour is approximated over full-time annual hours worked consistent with the data and it includes the statutory holiday allowance. Full-time equivalent is defined as 35 hours per week. Low pay is defined as being below two-thirds of the hourly median wage (FTE), high pay as above 1.5 times the median.

Source: Centraal Bureau voor de Statistiek (CBS)/Statline (http://statline.cbs.nl/statweb/), CAO-lonen 1972–2014 (2000 = 100) chained with CAO lonen (2010 = 100); CBS (1994, 1996); CBS, *Sociaal-economische Maandstatistiek* (various issues); and tables of employee jobs by weekly hours and earnings made available to the author by CBS; Ministry of Social Affairs and Employment (Ministerie van Sociale Zaken en Werkgelegenheid, SZW) for minimum wage levels and lowest wage scales (see De Beer et al., 2017).

Figure 9.5 Hourly wage inequalities, Netherlands, 1991/1995–2014

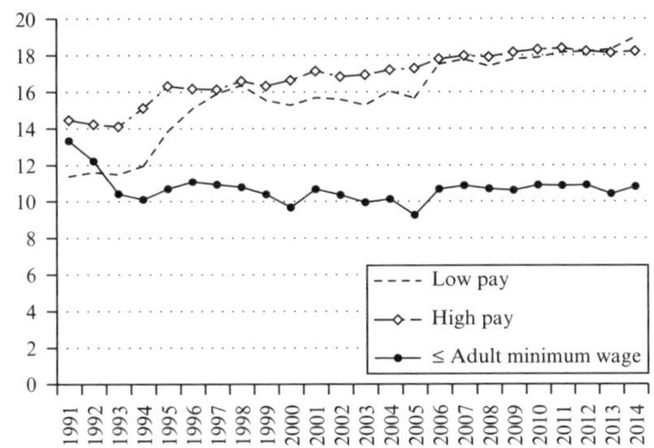

(c) FTE incidence (percentage) of hourly low and high pay and the minimum wage

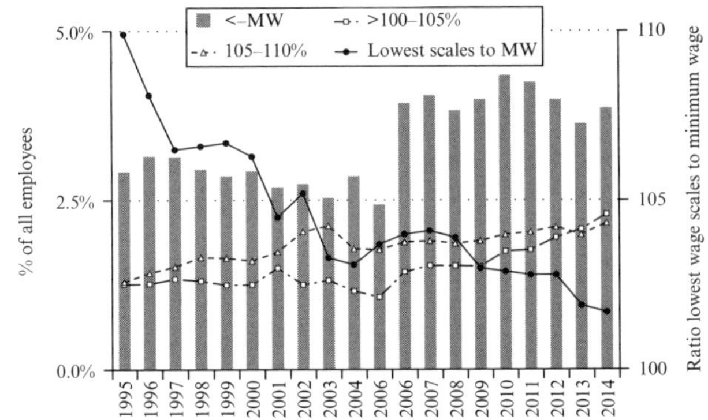

(d) Ratio lowest wage scales to minimum wage and jobs % in same range, 1990–2014

Figure 9.5 (continued)

indicated by a comparison with the median wage, taken on an FTE basis to include part-time workers, worsens substantially. The ratio falls continuously, with the exceptions of 2001–03 and 2005–12, by almost 10 percentage points in total.[18]

Figure 9.5(b) adds a stylised picture of how actual hourly wage inequality, after consumer-price deflation, has developed using the three common percentile cut-offs: the top of the first decile (P10), the median (P50) and the bottom of the tenth decile (P90). The distribution has clearly widened as P90 (+25 per cent) and P50 (+12 per cent) grew away from P10 (+6 per cent).[19] The level and trend of P10 are almost identical to the stagnating minimum wage.[20]

For an additional take on wage inequality Figure 9.5(c) shows how the incidence of low-wage employment and high-wage employment have increased, both measured in terms of FTE. The former grew by 4 percentage points, the latter by 2.[21] The tails of the hourly wage distribution apparently grew at the expense of a 6 percentage-point decline of the middle. Thus the lower paid are increasingly being put at a distance below the median – naturally, the decline in the ratio of the minimum wage to the median (Figure 9.5(a)) applies equally to its ratio to the low-pay threshold which is defined as two-thirds of that median. At the same time the employment incidence of the minimum wage has remained largely unchanged after an initial decline. Thus the range of low pay widened and the low-pay gap – the ratio of average low pay to the low-pay threshold – as an analogue of the poverty gap will have increased.

This increased density at the bottom of the wage distribution may partly reflect the pressure that subsequent governments have exerted since the mid-1990s on unions and employers to lower existing wage scales in collective agreements or introduce new scales closer to the minimum wage (De Beer et al., 2017). Union federations have fallen in with the narrative that this would help the less skilled and handicapped to find employment. Figure 9.5(d) shows how this has worked out in terms of scales, as a complement to Figure 9.2. The average level of the lowest scales has moved down from 10 per cent above the minimum wage first to 5 per cent in the early 2000s and to less than 2 per cent now. *Ceteris paribus*, the range of collective agreement scales has widened and become more unequal as a result. Figure 9.5(d) shows – for adults only to prevent mixing up with the much lower youth minimum wages – that the decline to 5 per cent above the minimum wage first, and to 2 per cent later, is reflected in the percentage of jobs found between 105 and 110 per cent of the minimum wage first and 100 and 105 per cent later. Movements are small (+0.8 per cent each) however, and the virtually unchanged employment incidence of minimum wage (grey bars) in spite of its strong relative decline, casts doubt on the causality. In addition, the simultaneous decline after 2008 in employment numbers further above the level of the minimum wage indicates that the growth just above the minimum wage has not been additional and may well have substituted for better paid jobs.

High wages, too, have grown away from the median. Note, however, that the level of low wages is constrained by the minimum wage below and the low-pay threshold above, which limits its share in total wages. This contrasts with high pay which is unconstrained above the lower boundary of 1.5 times the median. This can be illustrated (on an annual basis) by average board pay for the 100 largest Exchange-quoted companies: it increases over the 1990s from 33 times the minimum wage to around 55 times, where it has remained from 1999 to 2012 with some volatility and a very strong short-lived surge to 91 times in 2007 and 68 times in 2008.[22] Consequently, the high paid can attain a much higher share in total wages than their employment incidence would suggest. It also implies that the P90 cut-off is insufficient for measuring wage inequality, as the literature on top incomes has demonstrated for income inequality.

Apparently, the secular moderation of contractual wages has affected strongly the low end of the wage distribution and at the same time left ample room for increasing earnings at higher levels. Part of that rise cannot be attributed to collective negotiations, however, as pay at the top of private enterprises is often outside its scope.[23] That is, collective agreements have seen their grip on wage formation as a whole diminish. Nonetheless, the structure of wage scales that they impose may still be limiting within-firm inequalities.

3.2 Fragmentation and Flexibilisation of Jobs[24]

The number of part-time jobs has risen relentlessly since the 1970s and they now comprise a majority of all jobs. Flexible jobs have similarly expanded since the early 1990s up to about one quarter of all jobs, as shown below. These are very drastic changes in the structure and contractual nature of employment which merit examination for their role vis-à-vis rising inequality and their treatment by the polder model. I discuss part-time employment first and then turn my attention to flexible jobs.

3.2.1 Fragmentation of working hours

Over recent decades, the Netherlands has become the world champion of part-time employment. Figure 9.6 shows how dependent employment and the split between full-time and part-time jobs have evolved since 1991, together with the total FTE volume of hours worked on those jobs. The number of those in part-time employment almost trebled from 1.45 million

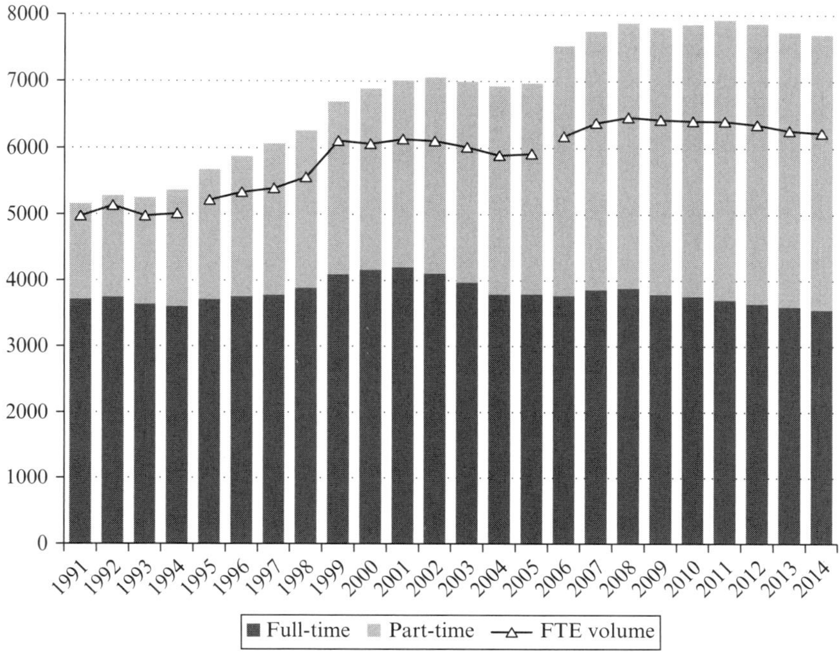

Note: Full-time/part-time distinction at 35 hours per week.

Source: Centraal Bureau voor de Statistiek (CBS)/Statline (http://statline.cbs.nl/statweb/), CAO-lonen 1972–2014 (2000 = 100) chained with CAO lonen (2010 = 100); CBS (1994, 1996); CBS, *Sociaal-economische Maandstatistiek* (various issues); and tables of employee jobs by weekly hours and earnings made available to the author by CBS.

Figure 9.6 Full-time and part-time jobs (× 1000) and FTE total (× 1 000 000), Netherlands, 1991–2014

to 4.15 million, exceeding total job growth (2.55 million) and implying some decline in full-time jobs (–0.15 million).[25] Thus the share of part-time jobs in the total has almost doubled from 28 to 54 per cent. The shift away from full-time to part-time employment has been reinforced by the recent crisis and its end is not in sight. The main growth was during the 1990s when both part-time and full-time jobs grew. Since then full-time numbers have stagnated and ultimately declined while part-time jobs still grew. The FTE volume of employment has lagged behind and stagnated, pointing to a redistribution of hours over more jobs. Although most people are satisfied with their part-time hours, an increasing proportion are not. They are concentrated among employees with flexible contracts working in more substantial part-time jobs of 12 to 34 hours per week (Figure 9.7). More than one-third of

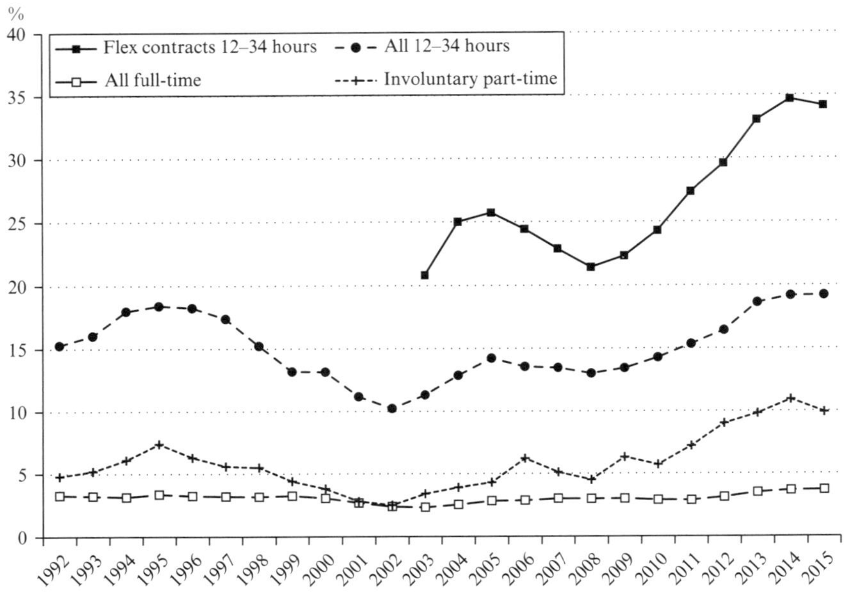

Note: Full-time/part-time distinction at 35 hours per week. Data for 1992–2013 extrapolated to 2015 with current, virtually identical series.

Source: CBS: Statline (http://statline.cbs.nl/StatWeb/publication/?DM=SLNL&PA=71948ned) and (http://statline.cbs.nl/Statweb/selection/?DM=SLNL&PA=82917NED&VW=T); Eurostat:)http://ec.europa.eu/eurostat/data/database?node_code=lfsa_eppgai).

Figure 9.7 Share of full-time and part-time employees preferring to work more hours (percentage) and involuntary part-time employment, Netherlands, 1992–2015

them would now prefer to work longer hours,[26] but not necessarily full time, as demanded by Eurostat for its statistic on involuntary part-time employment. Nonetheless, the latter has been rising as well and currently stands at 10 per cent, for all part-time workers. Surprisingly, full-time workers also sometimes express a wish to work longer hours and recently their preferences have been rising in tandem with part-time workers. The incidence of these preferences seems to rise and fall with the economic cycle, pointing to a problem of underemployment that, unfortunately, carries little weight in the Dutch debates on unemployment. Levels are particularly high for single parents, mostly women, and higher for women in general than for men (albeit not radically). In recent years they have risen along all dimensions of age (except below 18 and over 65), gender, educational attainment, household position, type of contract and hours worked.

Part-time jobs cover a much broader range of working hours (1–34 per week) than do full-time jobs, which start at 35 hours and have a strong peak close to 40 hours per week. Part-time employment has changed significantly over time, which is clearly linked to the dispersion of wages, and has fragmented jobs differentially, particularly at low levels of pay and occupations. I consider how both have evolved.

The within-distribution of part-time jobs across five bands of weekly working hours shows only minor changes, implying that all five categories have increased their shares in total employment roughly in line with the general rise in part-time jobs.[27] However, hourly pay levels appear to be very different between the bands, as Figure 9.8(a) indicates for the most recent year available. The spread over the wage distribution is skewed strongly to the right for full-time jobs, while the part-time categories concentrate mostly towards low pay at the left. The vertical line in the panel indicates the level of the low-pay threshold (LPT) at €11.94; a similar line drawn for the adult minimum wage (about €10.88) would be found slightly to the left. Figure 9.8(b) presents the low-paid shares within the separate hours bands to the left of that LPT. The incidence among the smallest two hours bands is much higher and also grows substantially over time: from 40 per cent to more than 50 per cent for less than 12 hours, and from 20 per cent to 30 per cent for between 12 and 20 hours. This contrasts with the larger part-time jobs which show a fluctuating, much lower incidence of between 14 and 17 per cent. However, it is still higher than for full-time jobs, whose incidence has been creeping up very slowly to 11 per cent. Figure 9.8(c) spells out the consequences for the evolution of low-wage employment as a whole, including full-time workers. Its total expands from 650 000 to 1.6 million employees. The share of full-time employees among the low paid almost halves from 48 to 25 per cent, though their absolute number expands from 308 000 to 407 000. Conversely, the part-time share expands to 75 per cent. Among them the role of the smallest jobs, with less than 12 working hours, grows very substantially (165 000 to 640 000) and their share in the low-pay total increases from 26 to 40 per cent. As a result low-wage jobs are now massively part-time, many of them very small part-time.[28] As mentioned previously, most people are explicitly satisfied with their number of working hours. It reflects a politically strong model of combining paid work with other activities, such as participation in education or home care, which may often be skewed towards higher-income households (Salverda, 2015b).

The spread of part-time jobs over the population and the economy is equally skewed. I leave the former aside, apart from the brief observation that part-time jobs in general are very strongly tilted towards women – some 75 per cent of female employees have a part-time job compared with 25 per cent for men – while within part-time employment the smallest

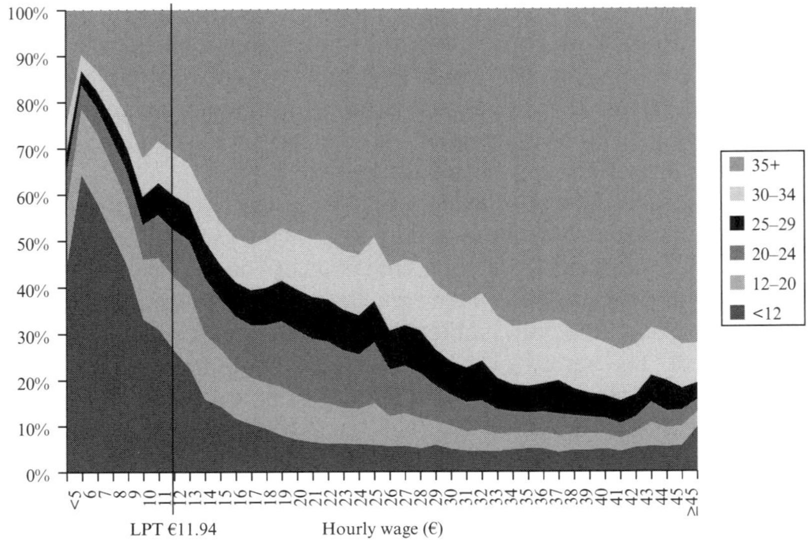

(a) Distribution of hourly wages by hours bands, 2014

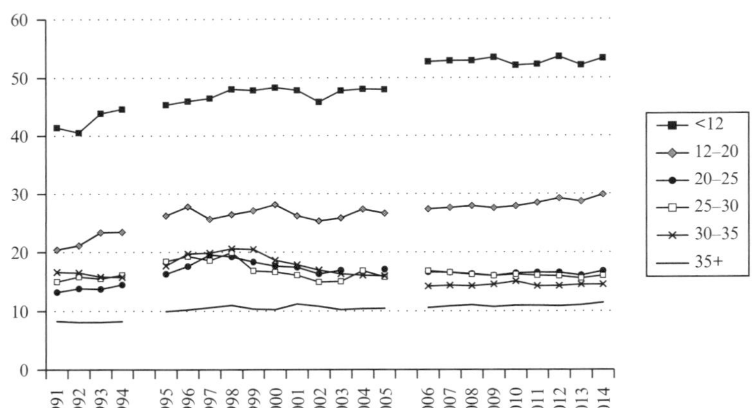

(b) Incidence of low pay by hours bands (percentage of part-time jobs within bands)

Note: Full-time is defined as 35 or more hours.

Source: Centraal Bureau voor de Statistiek (CBS)/Statline (http://statline.cbs.nl/statweb/), CAO-lonen 1972–2014 (2000 = 100) chained with CAO lonen (2010 = 100); CBS (1994, 1996); CBS, *Sociaal-economische Maandstatistiek* (various issues); and tables of employee jobs by weekly hours and earnings made available to the author by CBS.

Figure 9.8 Part-time hours and low pay, Netherlands, 1991–2014

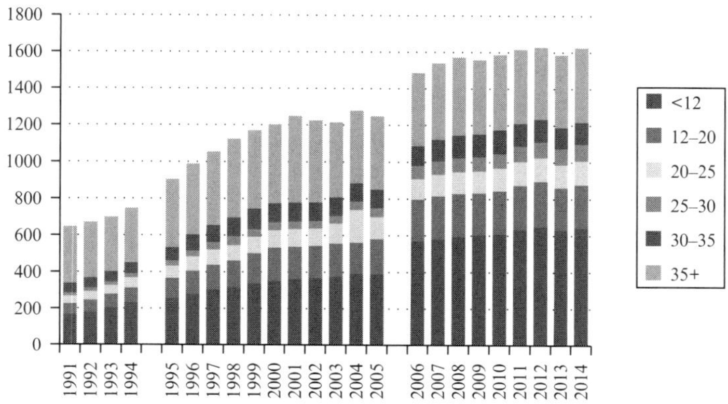

(c) Composition of low-wage jobs by hours bands, × 1000, 1991–2014

Figure 9.8 (continued)

jobs are tilted towards young people. Most of the incidence in Figure 9.8(a) to the left of the adult minimum wage (not shown) concerns young people, who may be paid well below the adult minimum wage because of their much lower youth minimum wages (see section 5.2). For the spread over the economy it is important to realise that part-time jobs in private enterprises are smaller and particularly low paid in contrast with the public sector (Berkhout and Salverda, 2012). Female part-time employees are spread over both sectors, while young people are concentrated in the private sector, largely in retail trade and hotels and catering. Consequently, smaller part-time jobs are also skewed towards low-skill occupations. At the lowest job level (number 1 in Figure 9.9(a)) only 30 per cent of all jobs are still full-time, and the share continues to decline. At that job level, the underutilisation of the educational attainment of the actual occupants of the jobs is massive and still rising; more than three-quarters of all jobs are occupied by employees with a higher level of education (Figure 9.9(b)). Part-time workers play a very important and also still growing role in this process: underutilisation is rife in the smallest jobs (Figure 9.9(c)). However, this is primarily because of their frequency distribution over occupational levels and less because they are more underutilised compared with full-time workers in the same type of job (not shown).

Clearly, the bottom end of the labour market – low pay and low occupational levels – is strongly affected by the growth of part-time jobs leading to a splintering of job opportunities in that segment. The declining hours, low hourly wages and increasing educational attainment make earning a living wage very difficult for people with the lowest educational attainment.

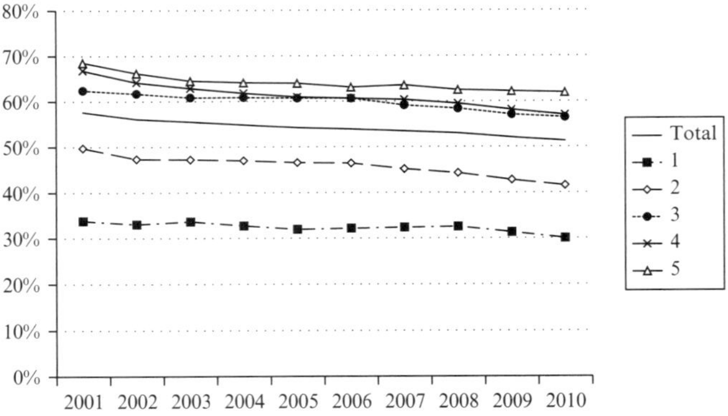

(a) Full-time jobs at five occupational levels

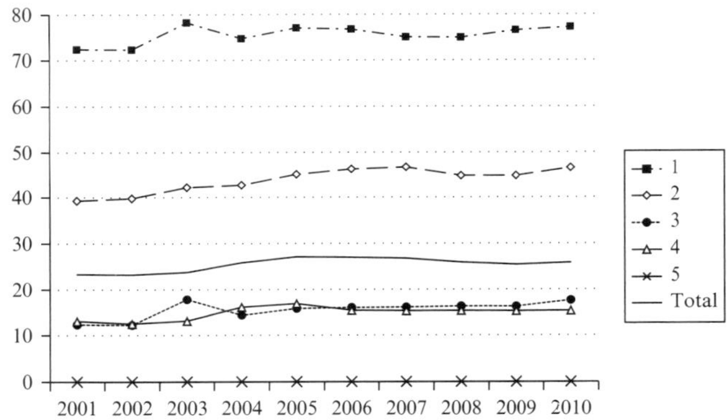

(b) Underutilisation at five occupational levels

Note: Full-time/part-time defined around 35 hours per week. Occupational levels from the Dutch classification, Standaard Beroepenclassificatie (SBC) 1992, levels corresponding directly with five levels of educational attainment: basic, low, middle, higher and scientific. (The classification stopped in 2011; data before 2001 do not cover jobs of less than 12 hours per week. Those less detailed data show similar trends of full-time decline and underutilisation. A declining full-time share at the lowest occupational level, 2003–15: 32 per cent > 25 per cent is shown also in new data using the Researchcentrum voor Onderwijs en Arbeidsmarkt (ROA) reclassification of International Standard Classification of Occupations (ISCO)-08 for European Labour Force Surveys, ELFS, data.) Underutilisation measured as educational attainment over and above occupational level (cf. Salverda and Brals, 2016).

Source: Authors' analysis of tabulated data made available by CBS from the Labour Force Survey (Enquête Beroepsbevolking) – LFS (EBB).

Figure 9.9 Working hours, occupational levels and educational attainment, Netherlands, 2001–11

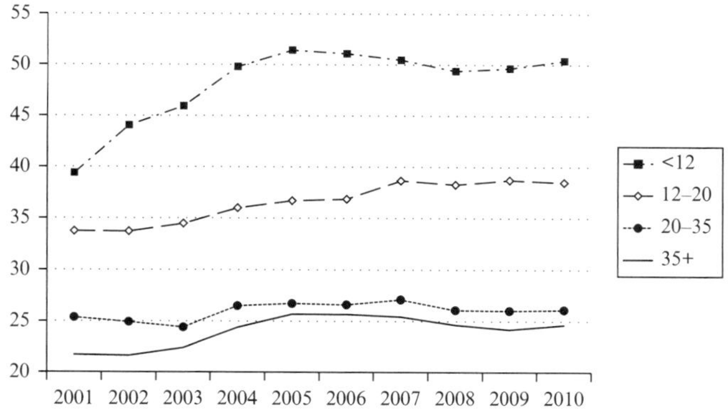

(c) Underutilisation by working hours

Figure 9.9 (continued)

Unsurprisingly, some 16 per cent of all small jobs of less than 12 hours are second jobs, while among adult employees (25–64 years of age) 9 per cent of those with small jobs combine it with a second job and 3 per cent of those with larger jobs (CBS, 2013). Thus the explosive growth of part-time jobs has added working time as a major new dimension to labour market inequalities, which was unknown to the world of the full-time breadwinner. I explore in section 4 how this works out for household income inequality.

3.2.2 The rise of flexible jobs

Contractual flexibility can pose an important problem of employment-and-income insecurity. With the help of Figure 9.10, I review the effectiveness of the social dialogue and policy interventions aimed at keeping this in check. The incidence of flexible jobs has grown relentlessly, from 8 per cent in 1990 to 21 per cent on the definitions of Eurostat's LFS (Figure 9.10(a)). Statistics Netherlands (Centraal Bureau voor de Statistiek, CBS) definitions put the level even higher and reached 25 per cent of all employees in 2015.[29] Data from CBS allow a further breakdown showing, first, an important overlap with small jobs ((Figure 9.10(b)). A steady one-third of all flexible jobs count less than 12 hours per week, larger jobs comprise the rest. Within the category of small jobs the incidence of flexible contracts is a stunning 71 per cent in 2015, compared with 50 per cent in 2003; among the larger jobs the incidence grows from 12 to 20 per cent. Second, these data indicate a 10 per cent decline in the number of permanent jobs and a 62 per cent increase in flexible jobs, implying a 9 per cent shift among all employees from the former to the latter ((Figure 9.10(c)). The data also

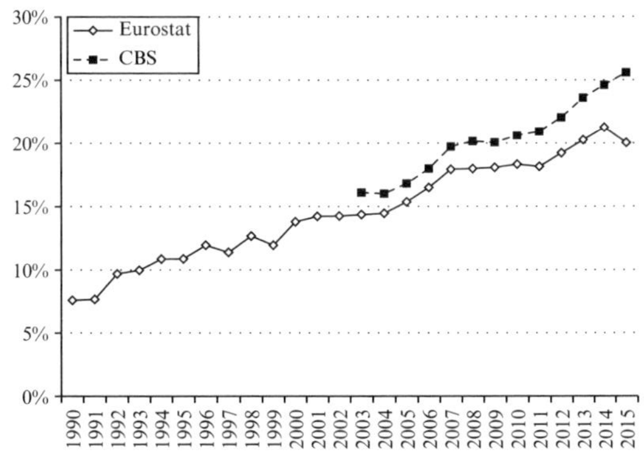

(a) Percentage of employees with flexible contracts and/or flexible hours, 1990–2015

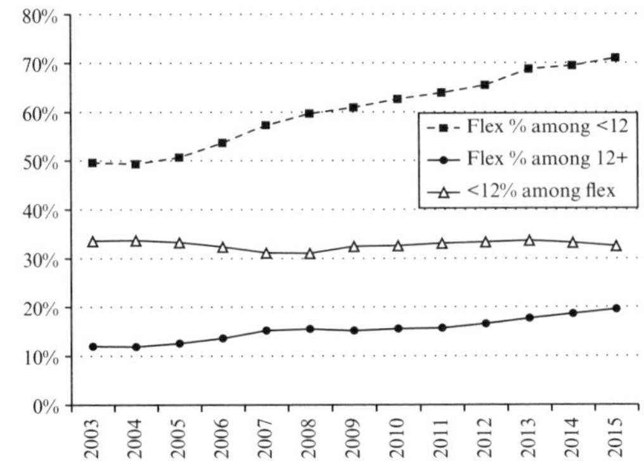

(b) Flexible contracts and working hours per week

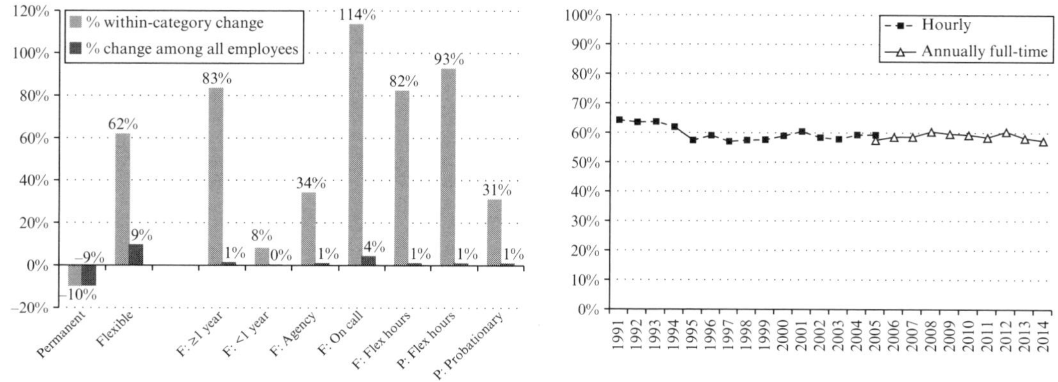

(c) Employee changes 2003–15 by type of contract

(d) Flexible pay, percentage of permanent pay, 1991–2015

Source: CBS: Statline: Banen van werknemers, lonen, arbeidsduur, SBI93 1995–2005 (http://statline.cbs.nl/Statweb/publication/?DM=SLNL&PA=37169ewl&D1=0&D2=0&D3=0&D4=0&D5=0&D6=(l-11)-l&VW=T) and Werkzame beroepsbevolking, gemiddeld inkomen (http://statline.cbs.nl/Statweb/selection/?DM=SLNL&PA=83686NED&VW=T); CBS (1994, 1996); CBS, *Sociaal-Economische Maandstatistiek*, 1994, no. 3.

Figure 9.10 Rise of flexible and small jobs, Netherlands, 1990–2015

show a clear shift among flexible jobs towards the most flexible types of contract. The number of on-call contracts expands by 114 per cent and is responsible for 4 percentage points out of the 9 per cent shift. These are followed by permanent and fixed-term contracts without fixed hours (P: Flex hours: +93 per cent, F: Flex hours +82 per cent), but here total numbers are still low. The most traditional type, temporary agency work, which characterised the early stages of growing flexibility and which was the prime subject of the Flexicurity Pact 1996, grows by one-third. The incidence of flexible contracts is rising across all relevant characteristics but shows large differences by age (young people and less than 12 hours correlate strongly) and surprisingly small differences by level of education and also by sex (that is, many part-time working women do have a permanent contract). Up to a point, the working-time differences and contract types correlate with employee preferences (CBS, 2016b). Half of all adults on on-call contracts and 41 per cent of adults in flexible small jobs appreciate the flexibility. However, these are small groups that contrast with only 7 per cent of adult full-time flexible workers who like the situation. Among all flexible employees taken together, 80 per cent are involuntary, while the remaining 20 per cent prefer the flexibility.

Data on the hourly pay of flexible jobs are erratic and incomplete as definitions of flexible work, as well as observations of pay have changed over time (Figure 9.10(d)). Up to 2005 data on hourly pay are available; the average level revolves around 60 per cent of permanent pay. From 2005 onward only annual earnings are available, which evidently are strongly affected by working hours. Focusing on full-time workers only, on the assumption that their working hours are reasonably uniform, the ratio of flexible pay to permanent pay is surprisingly similar to the preceding hourly ratio, and stable at close to 60 per cent.[30] However, there is also substantial variation between the different types of flexible work, ranging from 20 per cent or less for on-call contracts to more than 100 per cent for permanent contracts with indeterminate hours.[31] These differences show no relationship to the growing numbers of Figure 9.10(c).

3.3 Annual Individual Earnings

We conclude this section by combining the hours of work and hourly pay over the year as together these give us annual earnings, which are actually the individual incomes that people's activities in the labour market generate. The distributions of hours and work each have an inequality of their own, which their interaction may reinforce or mitigate. As far as wage labour is concerned these incomes are the basis of household incomes, which I discuss in section 4.

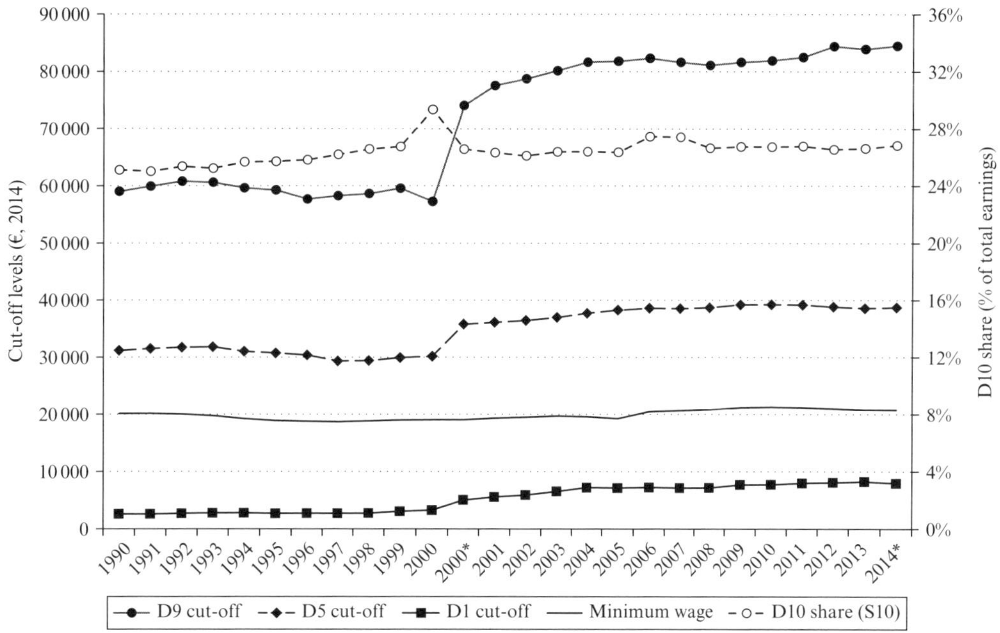

Note: Deflated by consumer prices. Linear interpolations in bands of income. wages: excluding employer contributions; primary incomes: <2000*: excluding employee pension contributions including employer contributions except pension contributions, including income from wealth attributed to highest income in household; 2000*>: including all pension contributions; excluding all incomes from wealth.

Source: CBS/Statline, Personal income statistics.

Figure 9.11 Individual annual earnings and employee primary income, decile cut-offs, Netherlands 1991–2014 (€, 2014)

Figure 9.11 presents rough approximations of the commonly used first, fifth and ninth decile (D1, D5 and D19, respectively) cut-off levels of annual earnings, together with the share of the tenth decile in total earnings. The data concern personal primary incomes of employees, which may comprise some other primary incomes, such as bank account interest, in addition to wage earnings. The series has an important break as more employer contributions, especially for occupational pensions are included after 2000. All three cut-off levels show stability over the 1990s and a slight increase after 2000. The D9:D1 decile ratio falls in each of the two periods, due to a decline in the D5:D1 ratio, while the D9:D5 ratio is largely unchanged (not shown).[32] The share of the tenth decile also seems to be fairly stable. Compared with the increased hourly wage inequality discussed previously (Figure 9.5(b)), the stable outcomes seem more benign, implying that people may have made up for that increase by putting in more hours over the year.

Figure 9.11 also presents the annual level of the adult minimum wage (AMW). It remains virtually stable and exceeds the first decile significantly. The important implication is that on an annual basis a very substantial proportion of between one-quarter and one-third of individual earners remain at or below the adult minimum wage.[33] This incidence is much higher than for the minimum wage as received on an hourly basis, which is one-tenth (Figure 9.5(c)). People earn more than the minimum wage hourly but stay below this annually because of lower working hours during the week and over the year.

Summarising this section, we can say that as a result of the way the polder model has been functioning in a situation of massively increased part-time labour, collective agreements have lagged far behind productivity growth, and their grip on wage formation has loosened. Effectively, they have mainly kept the minimum wage low and expanded the low end of the wage distribution, while actual wage formation at higher levels proceeded independently and faster but, nonetheless, barely matched productivity growth. This is the case in terms of general (GDP) prices, while in terms of consumer purchasing power they lagged productivity growth significantly too. At the same time the fragmentation of jobs – low-skill jobs in particular – and the flexibilisation of contracts have run out of control. However, the combined effects of hourly wage formation and annual hours worked by employees on the level of inequality of individual annual earnings seem to have been modest.

4. EFFECTS ON HOUSEHOLD INEQUALITIES

Household incomes are at the core of the public debate on inequality, fed by fears that top incomes are running away and middle incomes are falling. How did the Dutch economy fare in this respect and how is that related to the labour market outcomes discussed above?

As far as the earnings from labour are concerned the household income distribution builds on annual earnings, which combine annual hours with hourly earnings. Therefore I consider the combination of employment into households first, followed by the distribution of incomes.

Individual employment has grown significantly, primarily through part-time jobs (Figure 9.6). As a result the individual employment-to-population ratio shows a remarkable growth over the 1990s, followed by fluctuations because of bust-boom-bust which end in 2014 at about the same level as 2001 (Figure 9.12). This pattern is largely driven by those employees who are members of two-earner households. Initially, extensive growth increases the share of dual earners among all employees from 49 to 55 per cent over the 1990s, while subsequently that share fluctuates between 54 and 57 per cent. The evolution rests on two opposite movements: a significant decline in the formation of couples going hand in hand with a rise of single-person households, especially after 2000, and a growing rate of dual earning among the remaining couples (Salverda and Brals, 2016). However, at the same time the formation of couples increases among the highly educated and their share among adult (25–64) couples grows from 11 to 32 per cent, while the lowest two educational levels witness a share declining from a half to one-fifth.

Combining with the rise of part-time jobs, the distribution of employment and working hours over households has become an essential new dimension of inequality. In contrast with individual employment growth, there has been little change in the household employment rate, apart from some cyclical volatility. Job growth has kept the expanding number of single households in employment at the same rate as before and for the rest has fed into households that already had a job, thus enhancing dual earning. Although the phenomenon may be outside the reach of collective wage negotiations per se the broad, inclusive objectives of the polder model – witness the goal of a 'reasonable income distribution' – should not overlook this.

Next to this, Figure 9.13 presents the evolution of the household gross-income distribution after deflation for consumer prices. The focus is on average incomes in the ten deciles of the distribution. Averages enable the inclusion of changes in the top decile, which can make a huge difference to inequality – a lesson learned from the now famous literature on top-

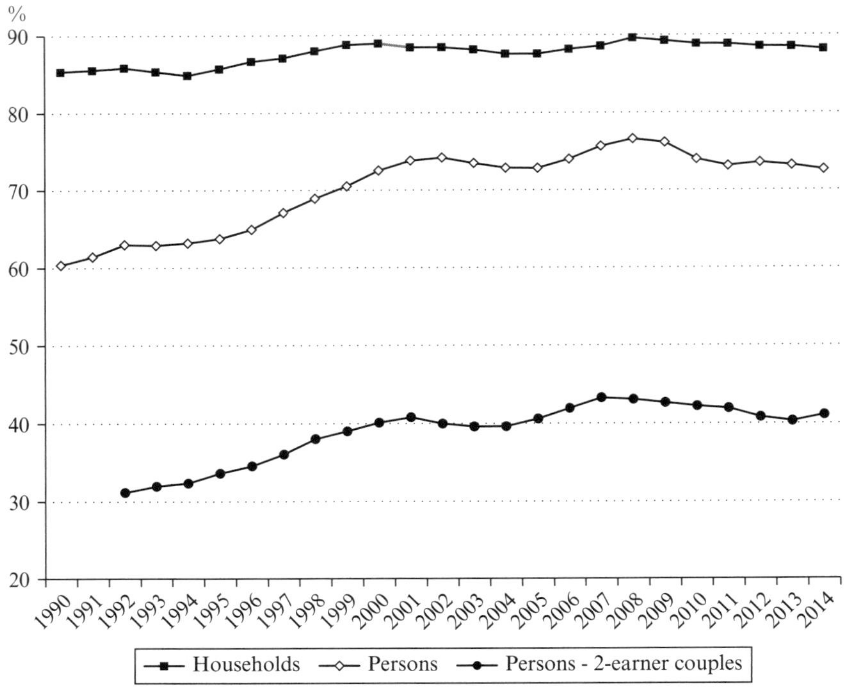

Note: Series break for household rate in 2000–2001.

Source: CBS: Statline (http://statline.cbs.nl/statweb/), Labour Force Survey (Personal rate), Arbeidsdeelname; paren met en zonder minder- en meerderjarige kinderen 1992–2013 extrapolated to 2014 using new data for 15–74 age group (dual-earner rate), IPO income statistics (household rate).

Figure 9.12 Employment rates among working-age persons and households, 15–65 years of age, Netherlands 1990–2015

income shares. Figure 9.13 shows total stagnation in the purchasing power of gross incomes for the lower 70 per cent of the distribution. Growth is found from the eighth decile on and in particular in the highest decile, where the average real income increases by €16 000 or 11 per cent.

Figure 9.14 dissects the picture into three panels to link these distributional developments to labour-market outcomes. Figure 9.14(a) compares for each of the ten deciles the absolute changes between the levels of 1990 and 2014, excluding the break between 2000 and 2001. The unmarked line regards the gross incomes that were shown in Figure 9.13, which give a more precise indication of polarisation: clear declines occur in the middle

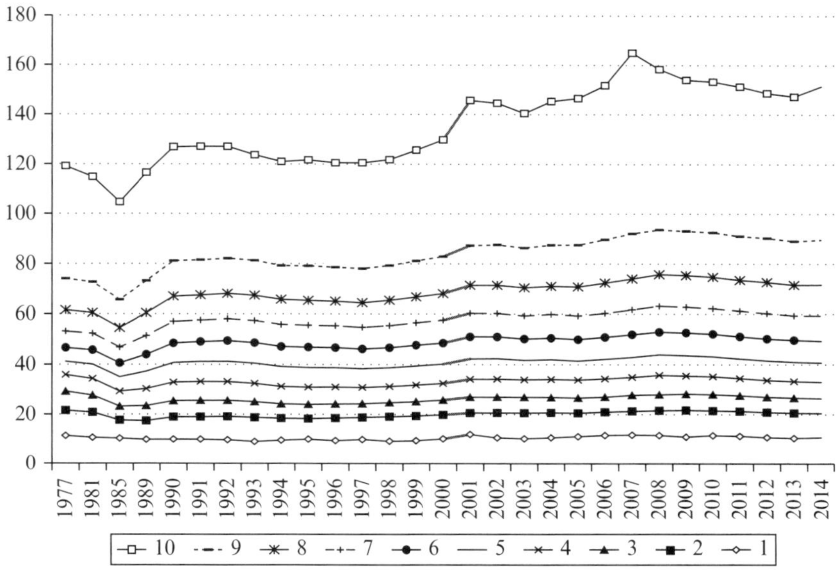

Note: Corrected for series break by excluding employer pension contributions from 2001, and augmenting imputed rent for self-owned housing with help of OECD National Accounts.

Source: Author's update from Salverda (2016b, fig. 10.3).

Figure 9.13 Household gross-income distribution, decile averages, Netherlands, 1990–2014 (€000s, 2014)

(deciles 4 to 6), full stagnation just around this (deciles 3 and 7), little change below (deciles 2 and 1), and clear increases above (deciles 9 and 10). The panel compares these outcomes with the incomes from labour earnings only, which largely drive the gross changes. They show a deeper fall in the middle and a stronger rise for deciles 9 and 10.[34] Labour incomes remain flat at the bottom but rise strongly at the top, gaining €22 000 on average in the tenth decile.

Figure 9.14(b) specifies how the total growth of labour incomes – by 24 per cent or 1 million households and 31 per cent or €63 billion – ranges over the deciles. The distribution of households becomes more polarised: 38 per cent of the rise goes to a very broad middle (deciles 2 to 7), while 18 per cent goes to the very bottom (decile 1) and 44 per cent to the broad top (deciles 8 to 10). This contrasts with labour incomes, which show no such polarisation as they barely change up to the sixth decile and become heavily skewed towards the top. Of the total €63 billion increase in wage

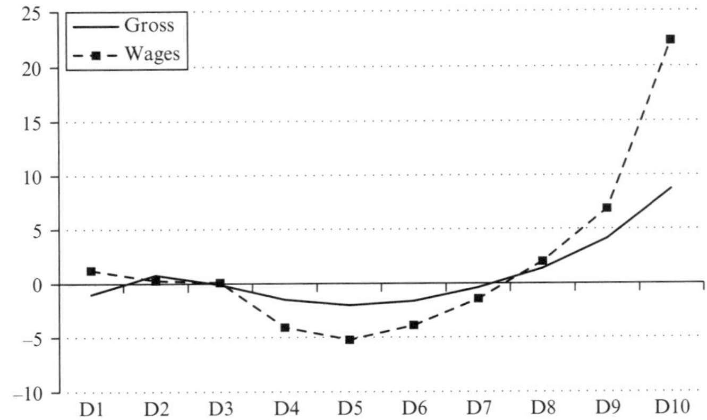

(a) Changes in household gross and market incomes in gross-income deciles (€000s, 2014)

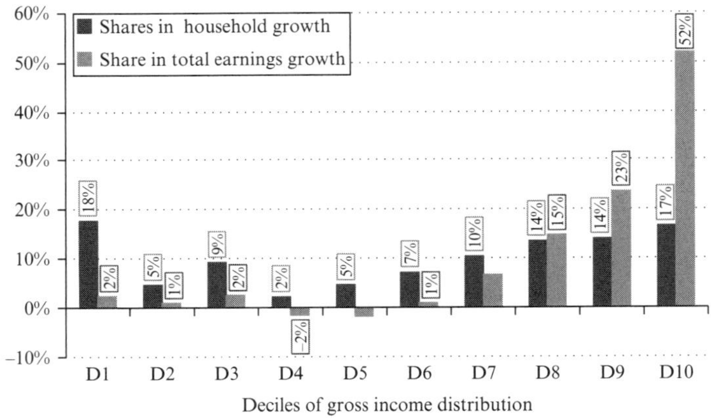

(b) Distribution (percentage) over gross-income deciles of changes for households with a labour income and their earnings (€000s, 2014)

Note: * The shifts exclude the break of 2000–2001. Any household receiving labour earnings is counted; households are allocated over the deciles by their full gross income. Figure 9.14(c) concerns fiscal units: singles and married or cohabitating couples, other persons aged 15 and over in a household are considered separate units.

Source: CBS: Statline, Household income statistics (http://statline.cbs.nl/Statweb/selection/?DM=SLNL&PA=71013NED&VW=T); Salverda and Atkinson (2007), Salverda (2013, 2018b).

*Figure 9.14 Changes in the gross-income distribution, Netherlands, 1990–2014**

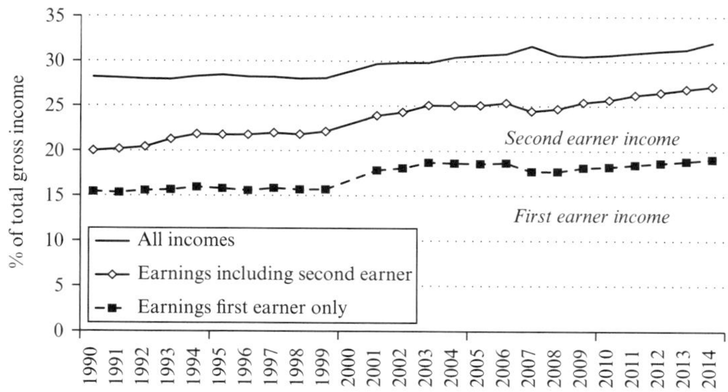

(c) Wage-income contributions to gross income top 10 per cent, percentage of total gross income, 1990–2014

Figure 9.14 (continued)

earnings between 1990 and 2014 no less than 52 per cent is seized by top-decile labour households, while the eighth and ninth decile taken together receive 38 per cent leaving no more than 10 per cent to be shared among the remaining seven deciles. Rising household numbers combine here with increasing average household earnings. However, even the rise of top-10 per cent average, plus 23 per cent, does not match the rise in productivity (see Figure 9.3). The rise rests on the growing role of dual earnings, which is shown in Figure 9.14(c). In the aggregate the top-decile share in the income distribution has grown only slightly, but within this the role of labour incomes has expanded significantly owing to the growing income share of second earners at the top. In 1990 they contributed 4.5 per cent of all incomes, and currently more than 8 per cent.[35] Increasingly, dual-earning households bring together highly educated, high-earning individuals. Thus the muted individual annual earnings changes of the previous section go together with a significant increase in household income inequality, which largely reflects an equally significant shift in the distribution of employment over households.

It is appropriate to consider also the growth of flexible jobs from the household perspective. Figure 9.15 offers some insights into their average annual incomes. Figure 9.15(a) indicates how the earnings of different types of flexible contracts compare with average earnings – reflecting both different working hours, whether weekly or annually, and different levels of hourly pay. The earnings levels spread over a wide range, from on-call contracts at one-fifth of the average up to 85 per cent for probationary

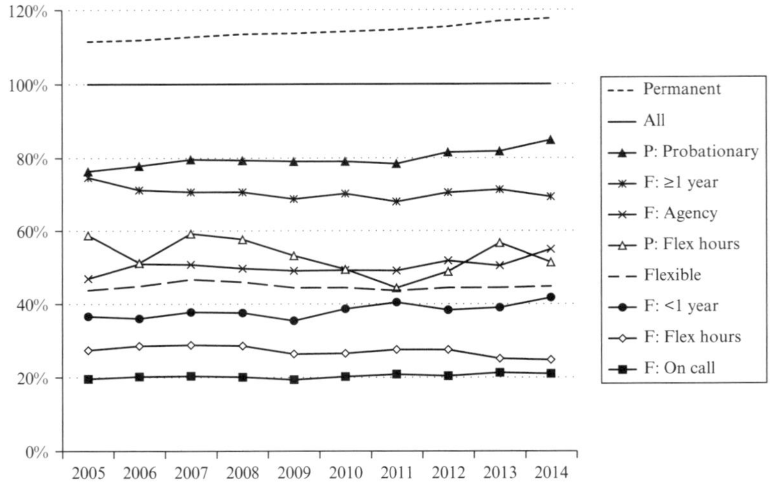

(a) Primary personal income

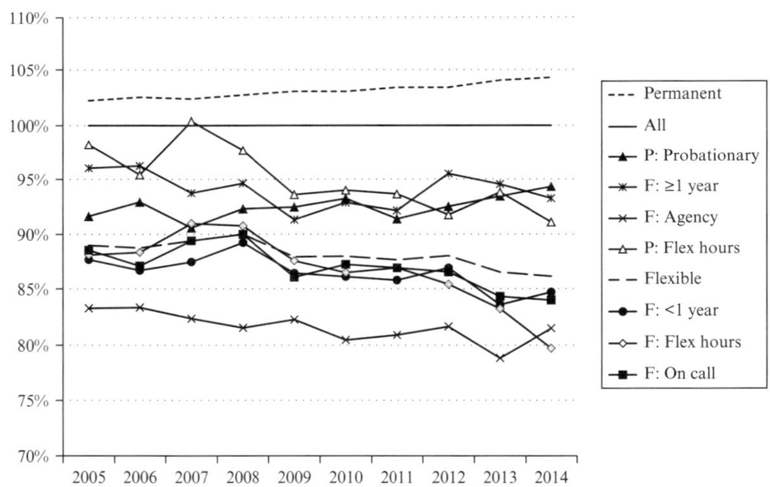

(b) Personal equivalised income

Source: CBS: Statline, Werkzame beroepsbevolking, gemiddeld inkomen (http://statline.cbs.nl/Statweb/selection/?DM=SLNL&PA=83686NED&VW=T); CBS (2016c).

Figure 9.15 Annual earnings by type of contract in the labour market and the household, Netherlands, 2005–14 (percentage of employee average)

positions; permanent positions earn up to 20 per cent more than average. This contrasts with the radically different picture of same incomes after taxation and equivalisation, which is aimed at accounting for the household situation of the individual workers (Figure 9.15(b)). Here the ratios to the average vary over a much narrower range, from a minimum of 80 per cent for agency workers to around 95 per cent for various other types. What it tells us is that many persons undertake flexible work while coming from a household situation close to the average. Indeed, a large majority (85 per cent) of flexible workers are either a partner in a couple or a young or adult child still living at home with their parents. Note, however, that singles and single parents face a higher risk than couples, but they are a smaller group. The difference between the two diagrams is indicative of an important intra-household redistribution. The fact that such redistribution exists does not mean it is readily accepted by the households. After all, 80 per cent of flexible workers are dissatisfied with the flexibility, as we have seen.

Nonetheless, this household background may go some way to explaining the low resistance of individual workers, and thereby perhaps also the unions, to growing flexibility – as it may to low-wage part-time employment too. However, together with the latter, the situation may indicate a negative feedback loop that runs from the household income distribution to the workings of the labour market and affects the nature of job competition, particularly in the low-skill segment. The vast majority of all small jobs (85 per cent) are deeply embedded in a shared household context as they are filled by partners or young and adult children in a household, and, understandably, only very few are held by singles and single parents. Those sharing a household have a great interest in working part-time when it enables them to combine paid labour with other obligations, such as household care or pursuing an education. These jobs play a prominent role in the fragmentation of low-skill jobs, which works against the interest of low-educated workers striving to obtain a living wage. Indeed we find occupants of such jobs in households up to the top decile of the household earnings and income distribution (Salverda, 2016a). It helps us to understand also that the incidence of in-work poverty is far less than of low-wage jobs – most low-paid workers are not a member of a poor household (Salverda, 2018a). Thus the wage earnings of households in the labour market can make an important contribution to the rising inequality of household incomes, in itself and also by means of this feedback effect.

The changing role of labour incomes in the distribution combines with the expansion of the occupational pension system. This is an important accomplishment of the polder model and it is still managed by the social partners, albeit under growing scrutiny from financial authorities. As an analogue to the breakdown of labour-income growth (Figure 9.14(b))

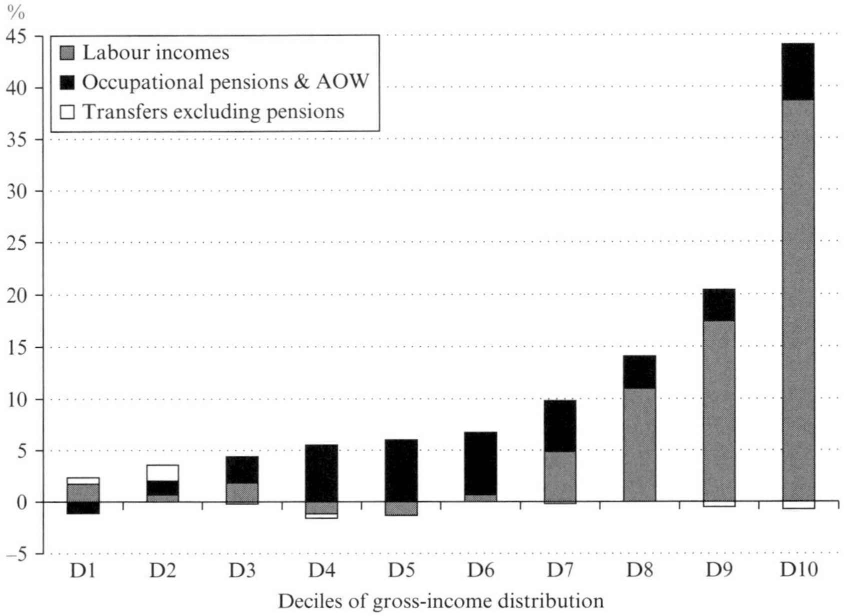

Note: Households locate over the deciles on the basis of their total gross income.

Source: CBS: Statline, Household income statistics (http://statline.cbs.nl/Statweb/selection/?DM=SLNL&PA=70991NED&VW=T; Salverda and Atkinson (2007), Salverda (2013, 2018b).

Figure 9.16 Real (€, 2014) decile changes by income source, Netherlands (percentage of aggregate change in gross incomes)

Figure 9.16 breaks down the €85 billion rise in total gross income since 1990. It shows pension incomes next to labour incomes: the basic public pension, Algemene Ouderdomswet (AOW), and the occupational pensions topping up that AOW. This top up accounts for about 20 per cent of the gross-income growth and, unsurprisingly given their relation to the level and duration of previous earnings, pensions develop in the wake of earnings and clearly move up the income distribution, mostly in the upper half and notably in the tenth decile. Earnings and pensions in the top decile taken together embrace 45 per cent of total gross-income growth between 1990 and 2014. Importantly, Figure 9.16 also shows how simultaneously social transfers are shifting down the income distribution, another aspect of the upward moves. The general evolution of social assistance and other benefits is determined via the net-net-indexation to the statutory minimum wage, which has been stagnating if not declining over much of the period.

The polder model has a noble tradition of taking income inequality into account in its deliberations. However, collective agreement wage formation focuses on individual wages and leaves redistributive policies to the state, whose policy measures also have a strong focus on the individual worker as exemplified by the labour tax credit that is received in full by any worker earning the annual minimum wage or more. This worked fine in the single-earner world, when the distribution of individual labour market earnings was basically identical to that of household incomes. However, this is no longer the case in the much more complex world of combined household labour supply and drastic changes in household formation, such as more singles, fewer couples but more homogamous high-educated couples, and fewer children. The inequality of gross incomes is still reduced by a substantial redistribution of incomes. However, the growth of the former makes the latter harder to realise. Indeed, the inequality of net incomes, after redistribution through taxes and benefits, has tended to increase; after accounting for household needs through equivalisation the increase has been even larger, indicating the effects of thinning households (Salverda, 2014). It is a process that is not well captured by the social dialogue and ensuing policy-making.

5. TWO CASES: THE POLDER MODEL, TO BE OR NOT TO BE?

I briefly consider two cases that may indicate shortcomings of the model vis-à-vis the polder's control of inequalities, one at each end of the wage distribution. Both may be considered potential risks threatening the model: employers taking advantage of government subsidies in the debate over youth minimum wages, and individual employees and employers taking advantage of the room for earnings growth that is left by the long-run moderation of collectively negotiated wages. The former illustrates the possibility that in the polder model one party may extract a rent from the institutionalised bargaining process that the other parties are unable to impede; the latter shows where curtailing the sway of the model might lead individual actors.

5.1 Changing Youth Minimum Wages

The Netherlands has a very long tail of youth minimum wages for each year of age between 15 and 22, ranging from 30 to 85 per cent of the adult minimum wage, which starts at age 23 (Figure 9.17). Against the opposition

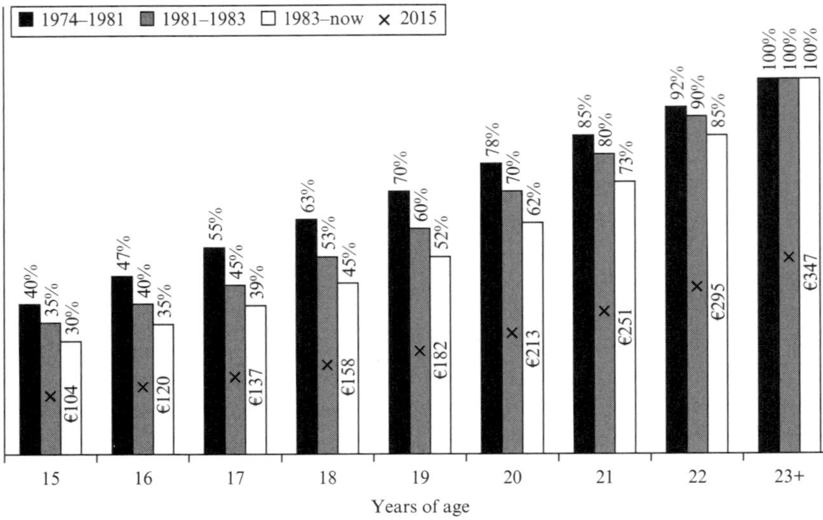

Source: Ministerie van Sociale Zaken en Werkgelegenheid (Ministry of Social Affairs and Employment) (https://www.rijksoverheid.nl/onderwerpen/minimumloon).

Figure 9.17 Youth minimum wages, Netherlands (percentage of adult minimum wage 1974–2017 and level (€ per week, 1 January 2015))

of employers, especially in retail, it was introduced in 1974 by the acting government as an addition to the adult minimum wage. The latter had been enacted in 1969 after the social partners had materially established it in the tumultuous mid-1960s that stopped the intense wage moderation and controls that had been in place since 1945. During the deep economic crisis of the early 1980s the age fractions of the youth tail were lowered twice and subsequently they underwent both the general 3 per cent lowering of 1984 and the subsequent freezes of the adult minimum wage over the 1980s and the two later periods already mentioned (1994–95, 2004–05). As a result the youth minimum wages declined strongly over the 1980s and remained virtually unchanged in real terms thereafter (Figure 9.5(a)), at about €5 in 2014 prices on average for the young age group as a whole. Even if young people are paid above their age-related minimum wage they may still be paid well below the adult minimum wage – an estimated 63 per cent over and above the 17 per cent who do earn the applicable youth minimum wage. Over time, collective agreements have lifted youth pay levels, for example, by applying an older-age minimum wage. However, very little has changed in this respect over the past 15 years (Figure 9.18).

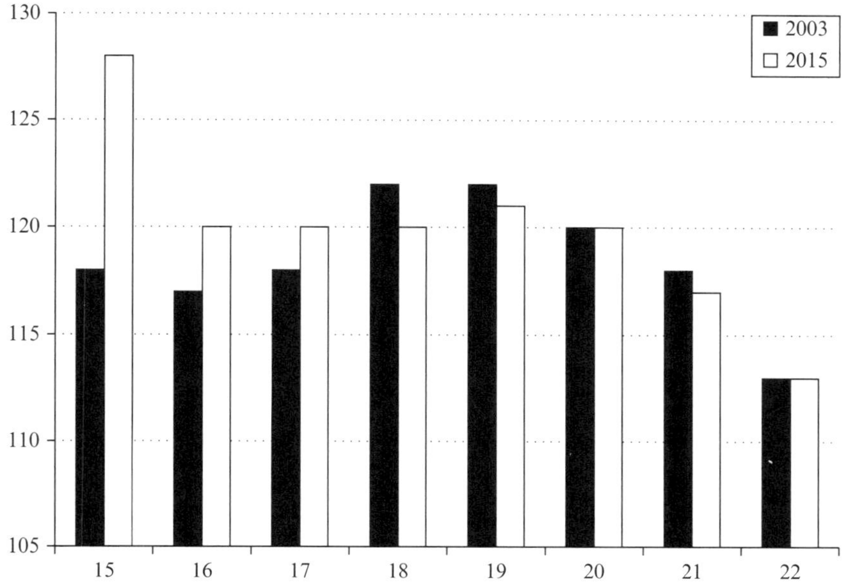

Source: Ministerie van Sociale Zaken en Werkgelegenheid (2003, 2016).

Figure 9.18 Average youth wage scales in collective agreements, Netherlands (percentage of applicable youth minimum wages, 2003 and 2015)

The uplifting for 15-year olds, from 118 to 128 per cent, is the exception confirming the rule; the number of persons affected is very small and the additional 10 per cent of their minimum wage lifts their pay by 28 cents per hour.[36]

As a result the average level of youth pay is very low by European comparison (Salverda, 2015a). By contrast the youth employment rate is high, currently around 60 per cent, but almost half of it consists of small jobs of less than 12 hours a week. Over time and by international comparison, this distorts the youth unemployment rate, which is based on young people seeking substantial jobs, while the Dutch full-time youth employment (13 per cent) is very low and comparable with that of Portugal, Greece and Romania during the crisis. In the meantime retail trade, especially supermarkets, have built their business model on the use of young workers at very low levels of pay and with minimum working hours (Tros and Keune, 2016). Most of them are pupils and students who tend to outcompete their less-educated peers who have already left school and are looking for the same jobs. Even when they succeed they face a situation where at age 18 (the legal age of majority) they will receive less than half the pay of an adult (23+) doing the same work, often with equal responsibilities, and at the same time they have to pay full price for everything, including health care and rent. On that issue of injustice the main Federatie Nederlandse Vakbeweging (FNV) union at the time, Bondgenoten, built a campaign in 2015–16 demanding the abolition of youth minimum wages from the age of 18. It made clever use of the new media and was very successful in getting public support, and managed to convince parliament that youth minimum wages should be adjusted, for the first time in more than 30 years after the lowering in the early 1980s. It was a public campaign outside the social dialogue.[37]

Here is where the polder model and the social dialogue start. It is an old theme of debate for the model's platforms for social dialogue that has never led anywhere. Already in 1990, SER as a whole concluded that youth minimum wages were low by international comparison, but only FNV advocated adjustment (SER, 1990: 33). In 1999 employers agreed to recommend to local collective agreement negotiators that youth-related scales should be replaced with scales based on experience and skill (Stvda, 1999: 2). However, on the occasion of transposing the new European directive against age discrimination into Dutch law in 2004, youth minimum wages were deemed by the minister to provide an objective criterion for differentiation (SZW, 2005: 2). Although in 2015 a majority in parliament was convinced of the need for a change, the minister still asked the advice of SER and subsequently adopted their proposal. The SER drafted what was called an exploratory report, but what effectively reflected the outcome of negotiations with employers, who had to agree to a change. The ultimate outcome is a lowering of the adult age for the minimum wage from 23 to the age of 22 as of 1 July 2017 and to the age of 21 in 2018, conditional on the absence of negative employment effects. In addition, the ratios to the adult minimum wage at ages 18, 19 and 20 will increase from 45.5, 52.5 and 61.5 per cent, respectively, to (ultimately) 50, 60 and 80 per cent. Thus earnings at the age of 18 will after all become exactly half those of adults, and the injustice that resonated so well with the public will remain. The polder model has effectively smothered the campaign.

Most important, however, from the point of view of the workings of the polder model, is that employers – who in retail trade have built a business model on the youth minimum wage that has been profitable for a long time – will now receive a wage subsidy for their employees aged 18 to 20 and earning up to 120 per cent of the relevant minimum wage to compensate for the increase. This will be part of the new subsidy on low pay, LaLo, that the government will introduce in 2018. However, for the young the LaLo's condition that the job shall be for at least 24 hours per week averaged over the year will be dropped. On further scrutiny the subsidy will be financed not by the state, but from additional employer contributions to disability insurance. This means that it will be paid by the employees, as employer contributions are part and parcel of collective wage negotiations, who will then effectively subsidise the continued fragmentation of low-skill jobs.

5.2 Exploding Pay in the Banking Sector and Negotiated Wage Formation

Figure 9.2(b) has shown the narrow range of variation between industries in the rise of collective agreement wages. Figure 9.19(a) details the cumulative rise between 1990 and 2012 for each of the 15 industries, demonstrating that the rise for banking (7 per cent) is not outstanding. This contrasts with the stunning 54 per cent rise found for actual real hourly earnings in banking, more than three times the next highest (government). Figure 9.19(b) shows the evolution over time of both agreed and earned wages for banking: a relentless rise in actual earnings by 60 per cent up to 2007, followed by slightly downward trending fluctuations. This contrasts with average earnings in the total economy, which increased by 11 per cent at the maximum (2009). Equally, collective agreement wages for banks initially lag those for the total economy and ultimately increase up to 10 per cent above the 1990 level in 2009.

Evidently, this large increase in actual earnings might reflect a divergent, strong shift in the composition of banking employment that could have elevated the average. Indeed, employment data for 2003–14 show a substantial increase in the share of the high educated in the banking work force, from 36 per cent to 55 per cent (not shown). However, the same data show even larger increases for the electronics industry (19 per cent to 45 per cent) and utilities (29 per cent to 57 per cent). In spite of this, actual pay for utilities has declined by up to 10 per cent, although its collective agreement wages followed a very similar path since 1990 compared with banking (not available for electronics). This suggests a prime role for pay changes instead of composition effects. The notable difference for banking between the continued rise in collective agreement wages and the simultaneous decline in actual earnings over 2008–09 points in the same direction, suggesting a decrease in bonuses due to the financial crisis. If pay has risen so much, the banking sector has ignored collective agreement wage formation and trade unions in the industry and at the polder model in general. Indeed, actual pay in banking appears to be significantly higher than collective agreement pay over the distribution of wages compared with the total economy, and the gap also increases over the deciles and is particularly large for the top: 172 per cent as against 143 per cent of corresponding

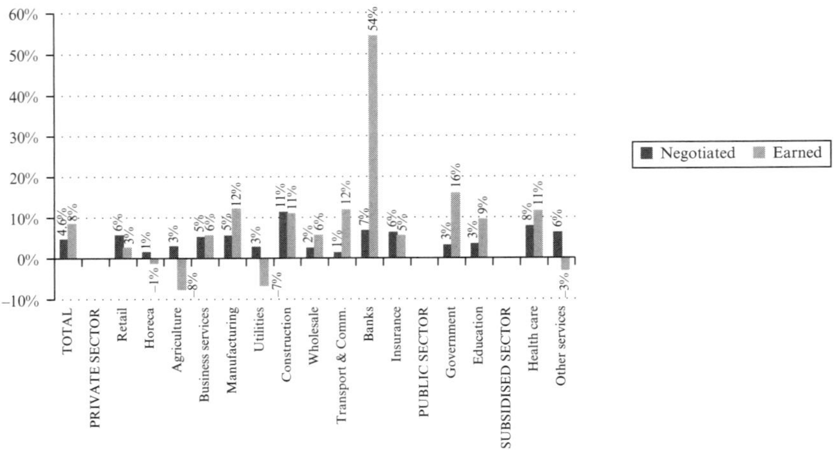

(a) Cumulative change in negotiated and earned hourly wages by sector and industry, 1990–2012, €, 2014

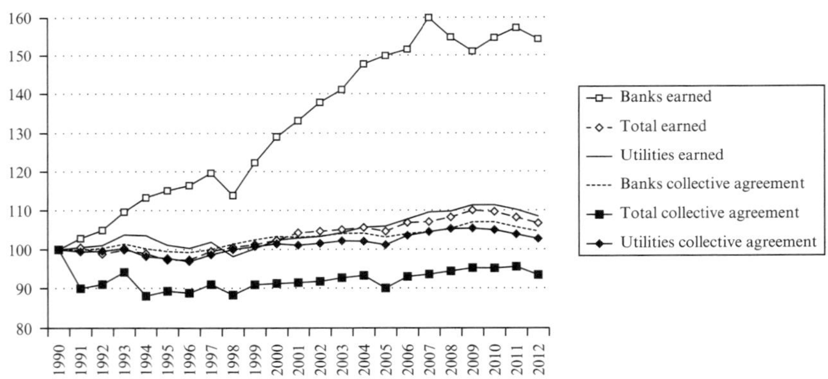

(b) Real change in negotiated and earned hourly wages in banking, utilities and the total economy, 2000 = 100, 1990–2012

Note: Hourly wages including annual payments but excluding employer contributions.

Source: CBS: Statline (http://statline.cbs.nl/statweb/): CAO-lonen 1990–2012 (2000 = 100) and CAO-lonen (2010 = 100); and Labour Accounts; Tros and Keune (2016, tables 4 and 5).

Figure 9.19 Comparative negotiated and actual pay in banking, Netherlands

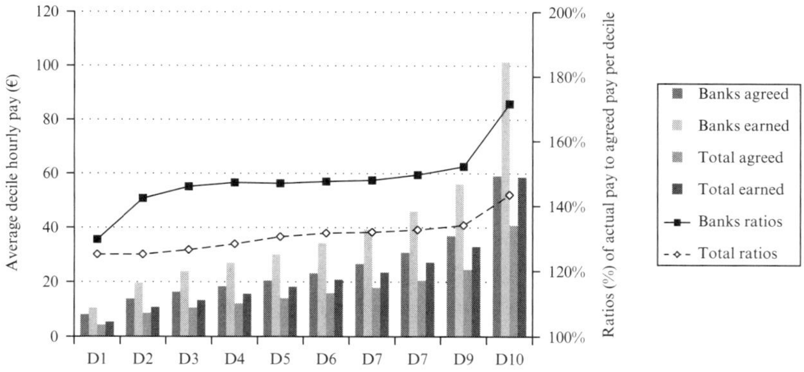

(c) Negotiated and earned hourly wages per decile of the wage distribution, banking and the total economy, 2013

Figure 9.19 (continued)

collective agreement wages (Figure 9.19(c)). Patchy European data suggest that the rise in the Netherlands was as fast as in the banking 'Valhalla' of the United Kingdom between 2002 and 2006, and that the level has maintained itself better in the Netherlands during the financial crisis.[38] In summary, the composition shift towards the highly educated will have been the basic vector of the evolution but it could work out only through much increased levels of pay. This is consistent with a recent paper arguing that 'the best and brightest' have increasingly been drawn into banking since 1980 (Kneer, 2013). Notably the paper adds that this seems to have hurt productivity growth in the economy outside the financial sector.

The polder model has been totally unable to discipline the evolution of wages in the banking industry which has been brought about outside the realm of the polder model's social dialogue. If only for the effects on productivity, the country would do well to discipline the financial sector's wage formation. However, it will likely be helped by expected mass dismissals in banking in the coming years. The new collective agreement 2017–20 recently concluded for Rabobank points in that direction; it is essentially a social plan for upcoming dismissals with tiny and faraway wage increases of only 1 per cent in 2019 and 2020.[39]

6. CONCLUSIONS

The Netherlands has maintained an extensively institutionalised social dialogue for over 70 years. It shows that the results of the dialogue depend on the strength of the parties involved and on the views they may share. Employers have increased their power by obtaining outside options through internationalisation and by their own organisational concentration. Consequently, unions have seen their power decline, but also because of the massive growth of labour supply that has resulted from the rapid expansion of female and student employment participation. Government, the third party of the model, has seen its room for manoeuvre diminish owing to European integration. This has increasingly skewed outcomes to the advantage of employers and reinforced sharing between the actors of views of the Netherlands as a small country riding the waves of globalisation.

As a consequence wage moderation has been practised on a semi-permanent basis in collective wage negotiations, which constitute the hard core of the polder model at the side of the social partners. Thus the purchasing power of collectively negotiated hourly wages has stalled and strongly lagged behind productivity growth. It has led also to a loosening of the grip of collective agreements on actual individual hourly wage formation, which on average has largely but not entirely followed productivity growth – but only if measured in GDP prices, while in terms of consumer purchasing power actual wages have lagged productivity too. Because of its statutory regular indexation to collective agreement wage developments and government interventions which nominally froze it for five out of 25 years since 1990 the real minimum wage has stalled even more than the negotiated wage and has experienced a significant erosion of its position relative to the actual median wage. Ultimately, the social partners have given up in the 1990s their initial post-war goal that the minimum wage should follow the course of prosperity growth and be sufficient for the least paid to maintain a family. They have de facto handed the minimum wage to the state, leaving it to the government to use its measures of income redistribution for turning the (pre-tax) minimum wage into a (post-tax) living wage, or not. As a result the lowest actual wages have stalled as well and the incidence of low pay has grown. This was reinforced by the introduction, under government pressure, in the collective labour agreements of lower wage scales close to or at the minimum wage. This has amplified the inequality of the edifice of collectively agreed wages itself. It implies that the social partners have also let slip away the role of the minimum wage as the base of their own wage formation. Thus the inequality of individually earned hourly wages has grown. Although the stimulus to inequality growth via these lower wage scales may be limited, the continued wage moderation has certainly left ample room to be filled by others, as demonstrated by, for example, the explosive growth of banking-sector pay, with rising inequality as a result. The long tail of youth minimum wages, basically unchanged in real terms since the early 1990s, has played a similar role stretching levels of low pay as far down below the low-pay threshold as in Germany before the introduction of the statutory minimum wage in 2015.

The number of individuals in employment has grown impressively, but almost exclusively in part-time jobs. These now make up more than half of all jobs in the Netherlands and are often strongly linked to low pay, and to flexible contracts. The incidence of the latter has grown considerably, and accounts now for up to a quarter of all jobs – damaging people's job and income security, their training options and career perspectives. Combining employment and hourly pay generates annual individual earnings. At that level, inequality change seems rather modest but data are patchy and allow a rough approximation only. Contrary to individual employment, the rate of households in employment has remained unchanged owing to the expansion of dual-earner households that have absorbed much of the individual job growth. Their combination of individual annual earnings into household incomes has significantly altered the face of income inequality and added the distribution of jobs and hours worked over persons and households as a highly significant new dimension of inequality. Households with earnings have seen their own inequality grow as a significant number of households, normally with a single earner, have shifted down the income distribution while most of labour income moved up the general income distribution. More than half of all wage growth since 1990 has accrued to the top decile of the income distribution, largely by means of growing dual earning. Dual-earner households that include low-wage part-time jobs have spread to the top of the household income distribution. This implies a distortion of job competition in the low-wage low-skill segment of the labour market, a vicious circle of mutually reinforcing inequalities of the labour market and of income. Thus the success of general employment growth in the Netherlands conflicts with the integration into employment of persons and households who have weaker labour-market positions, a recurrent theme of social dialogue where the polder model has made little to no progress over the decades. The focus of the polder model, including the government's tax measures, is almost exclusively on individuals. It has missed out on the radical change in the importance of the household context and the rising inequality of the household employment distribution. There seems a good deal of shared views, between government, employers and unions, behind this. The model has thus fallen behind the curve with regard to growing income inequality.

Finally, two caveats are in place. First, a reminder that this analysis has examined national developments only. In international comparison Dutch inequality levels and inequality growth might still look modest.

Unfortunately, it is beyond the purpose of this chapter to make that comparison. Second, it is not social dialogue and its institutionalisation as such that are at stake here – on the contrary, they offer great advantages in principle, albeit that checks and balances need strengthening – but rather the behaviour of the actors and the views they have come to share.

NOTES

1. The name was derived in the 1990s from the Dutch word for reclaimed land protected by dykes that need collective maintenance.
2. Communist unions were excluded from the start in 1945 and may initially have acted as a potential outside threat that could pick up dissatisfaction among workers, but this petered out soon.
3. This leaves out the 1980s when inequality rose the most after the severe crisis 1980–84 (for example, Salverda et al., 2014).
4. There has been no current balance deficit since 1980, and an average 7 per cent surplus since the introduction of the euro in 2001.
5. The SER's formal prerogatives regarding consultation were legally reduced in the mid-1990s but in practice they sometimes seem even stronger.
6. Also it leaves out employer contributions, which top up employees' gross wages, and occasional (annual) payments.
7. The ministry's monitoring of collective labour agreements has gathered information since 2012 about the highest scales of certain agreements, but only for the sake of comparing the seniority profiles of the lowest scales. For a set of 65 collective agreements it seems to suggest an increasing distance between lowest and highest wage between 2012 and 2015, but the material seems too shaky to warrant firm conclusions.
8. In EU (2003) former Dutch Prime Minister Wim Kok projected the Dutch policy motto onto the European Union. See Salverda (2005).
9. The basis of the index gets renewed about every ten years. Data are now based by CBS on a sample of 250 collective labour agreements comprising about 95 per cent of all employees covered by such an agreement. The total number of agreements is 1100, of which 250 concern industries while the remaining 850 are enterprise based (accessed 20 November 2017 at https://www.cbs.nl/nl-nl/onze-diensten/methoden/onderzoeksomschrijvingen/korte-onderzoeksbeschrijvingen/cao-lonen-indexcijfers--reeks-2010-100--).
10. On a monthly basis their evolution is slightly more limited owing to the fact that the monthly hours worked decreased in the early 1990s.
11. Note that the second case study focuses on the banking industry.
12. The correlation of annual increases in collective agreement wages with those of actual wages across 15 industries over 1990–2012 appears to be surprisingly small ($R^2 = 0.061$). The same holds for the cumulative changes over the entire period 1990–2012.
13. A rough estimation using the ratio of employer contributions to wages from the national accounts but corrected for imputed contributions (*inter alia* continued wage payments to sick employees), which do not lift negotiated wages and are still subject to normal employer contributions, and for the shift in 1998 from employees towards employers of contributions to disability insurance, which was compensated in gross wages and, apparently, is also left out from the negotiated wages index.
14. Note that a similarly strong preceding decline had brought the share back already to the level of the mid-1960s.
15. The peak of 2009 was caused by erroneous predictions by CPB of price and productivity changes for 2009 which are normally used by union federations as a starting point for formulating their wage demands – an accident waiting to happen.

16. Note the decline in 1998 which points to the shift of disability contributions from employees to employers.
17. The inclusion of self-employed hours is the only deviation from this simple identity: (Hourly wages) / (Hourly labour productivity) = (Sum of wages / Sum of hours) / (Sum of gross value added / Sum of hours) = (Sum of wages) / (Sum of gross value added) = Wage share in GDP.
18. Tentatively corrected for the two series breaks. Figure 9.5(a) shows a 12 percentage-points decline from 69 to 57 per cent.
19. Tentatively corrected for the two series breaks. Figure 9.5(b) itself shows a 7 per cent decline for P10 (11.06 to 10.66) but comparable growth for P50 and P90.
20. The employment incidence of the adult minimum wage (including young people earning between the applicable youth minimum wage and the adult minimum wage) is around 10 per cent.
21. Uncorrected growth in Figure 9.5(c)is 11.4 to 19.0 and 14.5 to 18.2 respectively.
22. For the 1000 largest enterprises the ratio of the average pay of the five best-paid individuals to the (annualised) median wage has grown from 5.5 times to 6.1 between 2010 and 2015 (CBS, 2016a). Note that the median wage never was more than twice as high as the minimum wage.
23. However, the introduction of a corporate governance code in 2003, in a sense a branch of the polder model, has not prevented the 2007–08 surge nor lowered the general level.
24. Salverda (2008) discusses the growth of part-time and flexible jobs between 1970 and 2005 and discusses the relevant measures taken by the government and the social partners during that period.
25. Revised employment statistics put the levels before 2006 higher and therefore reduce growth since 1991 (for example, only 1.5 million in total), but unfortunately those data cannot be combined with wage data which remain unrevised. Plausibly, most of the difference concerns small low-wage jobs.
26. Note that also a considerable fraction of workers prefer to work fewer hours, especially those working full-time.
27. It implies also that the series breaks of 1995 and 2006 affected the categories roughly equally.
28. Compare Salverda (2010) for the role of part-time jobs at the minimum wage.
29. They include also temporary jobs with a probationary period until the decision is taken about a permanent contract, and jobs that are permanent but have indeterminate, flexible hours.
30. Similar ratios are found for small and large part-time jobs separately.
31. See Figure 9.15.
32. Full-year incomes show stability and the decline is driven by incomes received only part of the year while their number also falls, which may point to reduced mobility.
33. One-third up to the year 2000, one-quarter thereafter owing to the changed measurement of primary incomes.
34. The data are derived from income tax records; they are taken at face value, although it is likely that enterprise and wealth incomes are not as well observed as labour incomes, which may lead to an overestimation of the role of labour incomes.
35. Interestingly, the combination of different earners in a household actually reduces the individual earnings inequality between the persons involved, as long as their (annual) earnings within the household are not 100 per cent correlated (Salverda and Checchi, 2015); at the same time, however, it shifts dual earners as a group away from other households (Salverda and Brals, 2016).
36. In the mean time, however, youth scales may have been abolished in a number of agreements (not known).
37. Note that campaigning is a costly affair especially for the low-wage segment, as the Bondgenoten union has learned from it campaigning in the cleaning sector. This involved several long drawn-out strikes. Although crowned with success in the sense that

the lowest wage scales have moved up from the minimum wage (Been et al., 2017), it was disappointing for the union in terms of new membership registrations.

38. Hourly pay from Eurostat, European Structure of Earnings Surveys 2002, 2006, 2010 and 2014.
39. Accessed 20 November at https://www.rabobank.com/nl/press/search/2016/20160923-cao-rabobank.html.

REFERENCES

Been, W., P. de Beer and W. Salverda (2017), 'The interplay between the minimum wage and collective bargaining in the Netherlands: a case study of three sectors', paper for 'Mindestlöhne im Ländervergleich' Project, Hans-Böckler-Stiftung, Düsseldorf.

Berkhout, E. and W. Salverda (2012), 'Development of the public–private wage differential in the Netherlands 1979–2009', Discussion Paper 71, SEO Economic Research, Amsterdam, accessed 20 November 2017 at http://www.seo.nl/en/page/article/development-of-public-private-wage-differential-in-the-netherlands-1979-2009/.

Centraal Bureau voor de Statistiek (CBS) (1994), *Arbeid en Lonen 1993*, Voorburg: CBS.

Centraal Bureau voor de Statistiek (CBS) (1996), *Arbeid en Lonen 1994*, Voorburg: CBS.

Centraal Bureau voor de Statistiek (CBS) (2013), 'Personen van 15 jaar en ouder, uitgesplitst naar baan-, uitkerings- en persoonskenmerken', 15 November, accessed 20 November 2017 at https://www.cbs.nl/nl-nl/maatwerk/2013/26/werknemers-van-15-jaar-en-ouder-naar-baan-uitkerings-en-persoonskenmerken-op-15-november-2011.

Centraal Bureau voor de Statistiek (CBS) (2016a), 'Grootste duizend bedrijven: aantal bedrijven en gemiddelde loonkloof naar bedrijfstak', accessed 20 November 2017 at https://www.cbs.nl/nl-nl/nieuws/2016/39/loonkloof-tussen-top-en-gewone-werknemer-gegroeid.

Centraal Bureau voor de Statistiek (CBS) (2016b), '1 op de 5 flexwerkers heeft voorkeur voor flexibel werk', accessed 20 November 2017 at https://www.cbs.nl/nl-nl/nieuws/2016/20/1-op-de-5-flexwerkers-heeft-voorkeur-voor-flexibel-werk.

Centraal Bureau voor de Statistiek (CBS) (2016c), 'Grote inkomensverschillen tussen flexwerkers', accessed 20 November 2017 at https://www.cbs.nl/nl-nl/nieuws/2016/44/grote-inkomensverschillen-tussen-flexwerkers.

Central Planning Bureau (CPB) (2016), 'Flexibiliteit op de arbeidsmarkt', Policy Brief 2016/14, The Hague.

De Beer, P., W. Been and W. Salverda (2017), 'The interplay between the minimum wage and collective bargaining in the Netherlands: an overview and a case study of three sectors', AIAS Working Paper 173, Amsterdam Institute for Advanced Labour Studies, University of Amsterdam, accessed at http://www.uva-aias.net/nl/working-papers/aias/2017/the-interplay-between-the-minimum-wage-and-collective-bargaining-in-the-netherlands.

EU (2003), 'Jobs, jobs, jobs', report of the Employment Task Force chaired by Wim Kok, Brussels, accessed 20 November 2017 at http://www.weceurope.org/fileadmin/templates/eurociett/docs/Kok_Report_2003_Jobs_Jobs_Jobs.pdf.

Houwing, H. (2010), 'A Dutch approach to flexicurity? Negotiated change in the organization of temporary work', PhD thesis, University of Amsterdam.
Kneer, C. (2013), 'Finance as a magnet for the best and brightest: implications for the real economy', DNB Working Paper No. 329, De Nederlandsche Bank, Amsterdam.
Ministerie van Sociale Zaken en Werkgelegenheid (SZW) (2003), 'Najaarsrapportage CAO-afspraken 2003', October, accessed 20 November 2017 at http://cao.minszw.nl/pdf/175/2003/175_2003_13_1023.pdf.
Ministerie van Sociale Zaken en Werkgelegenheid (SZW) (2005), 'Onderscheid naar leeftijd in CAO's', The Hague.
Ministerie van Sociale Zaken en Werkgelegenheid (SZW) (2013), 'Letter to Parliament on the Results of the Social Dialogue 11 April', with enclosure survey of policy measures to be taken, The Hague.
Ministerie van Sociale Zaken en Werkgelegenheid (SZW) (2016), 'CAO-afspraken 2015', June, accessed 20 November 2017 at http://cao.minszw.nl/pdf/174/2016/174_2016_13_237282.pdf.
Salverda, W. (2005), 'Low pay and wage flexibility in Europe: what does the taskforce offer?', Beiträge zur Arbeitsmarkt- und Berufsforschung No. 239, 35–50.
Salverda, W. (2008), 'Labor market institutions, low-wage work, and job quality', in W. Salverda, M. van Klaveren and M. van der Meer (eds), *Low-Wage Work in the Netherlands*, New York: Russell Sage, pp. 63–131.
Salverda, W. (2009), 'The bite and effects of wage bargaining in the Netherlands 1995–2005', in M. Keune and B. Galgóczi (eds), *Wages and Wage Bargaining in Europe; Developments since the mid-1990s*, Brussels: ETUI, pp. 225–54.
Salverda, W. (2010), 'The Dutch minimum wage: minimum wage fall shifts focus to part-time jobs', in D. Vaughan-Whitehead (ed.), *The Minimum Wage Revisited in the Enlarged EU: Issues and Challenges*, Cheltenham, UK and Geneva: Edward Elgar and ILO, pp. 299–339.
Salverda, W. (2013), 'Extending the top-income shares for the Netherlands from 1999 to 2012: an explanatory note', accessed 20 November 2017 at http://wid.world/document/wid_methodology_notes_2013_4_netherlands/.
Salverda, W. (2014), 'De tektoniek van de inkomensongelijkheid in Nederland', in M. Kremer, M. Bovens, E. Schrijvers and R. Went (eds), *Hoe ongelijk is Nederland?* Amsterdam: Wetenschappelijke Raad voor het Regeringsbeleid (WRR) and Amsterdam University Press, pp. 39–58.
Salverda, W. (2015a), 'Lager opgeleide jongeren: Geen werk, geen uitkering, geen beleid', in S. Boumans (ed.), *WTFACT – De feiten over werkende jongeren in Nederland*, Amsterdam: FNV/Young & United, pp. 30–42.
Salverda, W. (2015b), 'Individual earnings and household incomes: mutually reinforcing inequalities?', *European Journal of Economic and Economic Policies*, **12** (2), 190–203.
Salverda, W. (2016a), 'The tsunamis of educational attainment and part-time employment and the change of the labour force 1960–2010: what can be learned about self-reinforcing labour-market inequality from the case of the Netherlands in international comparison?', Working Paper 16/04, ImProvE project, CSB, University of Antwerp, accessed 20 November 2017 at http://improve-research.eu/?page_id=37.
Salverda, W. (2016b), 'Stagnating incomes and the middle class in the Netherlands 1990–2013: running to stand still?', in D. Vaughan-Whitehead (ed.), *Europe's*

Disappearing Middle Class? Evidence from the World of Work, Cheltenham, UK and Geneva: Edward Elgar and ILO, pp. 396–440.
Salverda, W. (2018a), 'Low earnings and their drivers in relation to in-work poverty', in H. Lohmann and I. Marx (eds), *Handbook of Research on In-Work Poverty*, Cheltenham, UK and Northampton, MA, USA: Edward Elgar (forthcoming).
Salverda, W. (2018b), 'Income inequality in the Netherlands 1914–2014', AIAS Working Paper, Amsterdam Institute for Advanced Labour Studies, University of Amsterdam (forthcoming).
Salverda, W. and A.B. Atkinson (2007), 'Top incomes in the Netherlands over the twentieth century', in A.B. Atkinson and T. Piketty (eds), *Top Incomes over the Twentieth Century: A Contrast Between Continental European and English-Speaking Countries*, Oxford: Oxford University Press, pp. 426–71.
Salverda, W. and N. Beukema (1996), 'Second report on the Netherlands. Member of a Group of Experts on the Role of the Social Partners in Implementing the Conclusions of the Essen and Madrid European Councils', report to the European Commission, DG5.
Salverda, W. and D. Brals (2016), 'Opleiding, deeltijdarbeid en huishouden: Meritocratie op de arbeidsmarkt sinds 1990', in P. de Beer and M. van Pinxteren, ed. *Meritocratie. Op weg naar een nieuwe klassensamenleving?* Amsterdam: Amsterdam University Press, pp. 135–64.
Salverda, W. and D. Checchi (2015), 'Labour-market institutions and the dispersion of wage earnings', in A.B. Atkinson and F. Bourguignon (eds), *Handbook of Income Distribution*, vol. 2B, Amsterdam: Elsevier/North Holland, pp. 1535–727.
Salverda, W., M. de Graaf-Zijl, C. Haas, B. Lancee and N. Notten (2014), 'The Netherlands: policy-enhanced inequalities tempered by household formation', in B. Nolan, W. Salverda, D. Checchi, I. Marx, A. McKnight, I.G. Tóth et al. (eds), *Changing Inequalities and Societal Impacts in Rich Countries: Thirty Countries' Experiences*, Oxford: Oxfrod University Press, pp. 457–87.
Sociaal-Economische Raad (SER) (1990), 'Advies bijzondere verhoging minimumloon', Advice No. 1990/25, The Hague.
Sociaal-Economische Raad (SER) (1999), 'Bijzondere verhoging minimumloon', Advice No. 1999/11, The Hague, accessed 9 November 2017 at https://www.ser.nl/nl/publicaties/adviezen/1990-1999/1999/b17822.aspx
Sociaal-Economische Raad (SER) (2002), 'Sociaal-economisch beleid 2002–2006', Opinion No. 2002/08, The Hague.
Sociaal-Economische Raad (SER) (2006), 'Welvaartsgroei door en voor iedereen. Themadicument Arbeidsverhoudingen', Advice No. 2006/8-II, The Hague.
Sociaal-Economische Raad (SER) (2015), 'The power of consultation. The Dutch consultative economy explained', information brochure, The Hague, accessed 20 November 2017 at https://www.ser.nl/en/publications/publications/informatie brochure-power-consultation-en.aspx.
Stichting van de Arbeid (StvdA) (1992), 'Sociaal-economische beleidsorientaties 1993', no. 1992/10, The Hague.
Stichting van de Arbeid (StvdA) (1993), 'Overwegingen en aanbevelingen ter bevordering van deeltijdarbeid en differentiatie in arbeidsduurpatronen', no. 7/93, September, The Hague.
Stichting van de Arbeid (StvdA) (1999), 'Verklaring ten behoeve van het arbeidsvoorwaardenoverleg 2000/2001', no. 6/99, The Hague.
Stichting van de Arbeid (StvdA) (2007), 'Tripartiete beleidsinzet; 27 juni 2007',

The Hague, accessed 9 November 2017 at https://www.stvda.nl/nl/publicaties/convenanten/2000-2009/2007/20070627.aspx.
Stichting van de Arbeid (StvdA) (2013), 'Perspectief voor een sociaal én ondernemend land: uit de crisis, met goed werk, op weg naar 2020', Social Pact, 11 April, The Hague, accessed at http://www.stvda.nl/en/publication/2013.aspx.
Stichting van de Arbeid (StvdA) (2015a), 'Rapportage stand van zaken betreffende scholing van flexibele werknemers', 26 June, The Hague.
Stichting van de Arbeid (StvdA) (2015b), 'Afronding Sociaal Akkoord 11 april 2013', with enclosure about implementation results, The Hague.
Stichting van de Arbeid (StvdA) (2016), 'Letter to the Minister of Social Affairs and Employment concerning inter alia improving access of flexible workers to industry-level training funds', 12 April, The Hague.
Tros, F. and M. Keune (2016), 'Country report: The Netherlands', Negotiating Wage (In)equality (NEWIN) project for DG Employment, accessed 20 November 2017 at http://moodle.adaptland.it/pluginfile.php/28231/mod_resource/content/1/newin_nl_FINAL%20DEF.pdf.
Vergeer, R. and A. Kleinknecht (2014), 'Do labour market reforms reduce labour productivity growth? A panel data analysis of 20 OECD countries (1960–2004)', *International Labour Review*, **153** (3), 365–93.

10. Changes in inequality outcomes alongside industrial relations transformation in Slovenia

Branko Bembič

1. INTRODUCTION

A gradualist approach to transition from self-managed socialism, a rather selective and cautious approach to foreign capital, a relatively generous welfare state and, most of all, 'inclusive' industrial relations system typically place Slovenia at the neo-corporatist pole (see Bohle and Greskovits, 2012, 2007) or, in terms of the varieties of capitalism approach, in the coordinated market economy group (see Buchen, 2007; Feldmann, 2008). Since the mid-2000s, however, the Slovenian neo-corporatist model has been under increasing strain, which intensified during the financial and economic crisis that reached the economy by the end of 2008 and turned into a sovereign debt crisis by late 2011. This chapter provides an overview of the main industrial relations developments in Slovenia, and their impact on the relations between flexibility and security, as well as inequality.

The chapter is structured as follows. Section 2 presents the main characteristics of industrial relations in Slovenia through the transition from self-managed socialism to capitalism, while section 3 examines the outcomes of industrial relations developments in the post-2008 period in terms of the balance between flexibility and security, as well as inequality. Two case studies are presented in section 4. The first illustrates the importance of sector-level collective bargaining for striking a balance between flexibility and security, and the need for articulation between different levels of industrial relations for good equality outcomes. The other case study points to the potential of collective bargaining for attaining employment equality. Section 5 concludes.

2. INDUSTRIAL RELATIONS IN SLOVENIA SINCE THE EARLY 1990S

The focus of this section is the development of industrial relations in Slovenia, and their outcomes in terms of flexibility and security and, thus, inequality. We distinguish the following three periods of transition in Slovenia: the period of formation and consolidation of the industrial relations system in the context of a transitional balance of forces from the early 1990s until 2004; the 2004–08 period that was marked by accession to the European Union (EU) and the eurozone, during which time material conditions for compromise gradually eroded; and the post-2008 period, which has been marked by the crisis and a collapse of social dialogue at the national level.

2.1 Development of Industrial Relations and Social Dialogue at the National Level

Slovenia is generally considered to have a low level of income inequality, a feature sustained throughout the transition, with an income quintile ratio of 3.6, a Gini coefficient of disposable income of 0.25 and a gender pay gap of 3.7 per cent in 2014 (Eurostat, 2017a, 2017b, 2017c). The literature (see Schulten, 2002; Salverda and Mayhew, 2009; Keune and Vandaele, 2013; Keune, 2015) suggests that this outcome could to a large extent be explained by the structure of industrial relations, in which inclusive multi-employer bargaining and the statutory minimum wage ensured the solidaristic wage policy, while national social pacts entailed trading wage restraint for an active role of organised labour in shaping welfare state institutions.

The decisive role of the early mobilisation and strength of organised labour in shaping the path of Slovenia's transition from self-managed socialism to full-fledged capitalism is well documented (see Crowley and Stanojević, 2011). We add another actor to this account, namely, the emerging national bourgeoisie, which consists mainly of the top management of formerly self-managed enterprises that needed an ally in order to become a proper capitalist class by appropriating what used to be social property, an ally that it found in the working class organised around the trade unions (Bembič, 2013). In what follows we present the main developments of Slovenian industrial relations in the context of the changing balance of forces between these two sides as it materialised in various institutional arrangements and policies.

Given the decisive role of the acquisition of what used to be social property, the first compromise – which Stanojević (2012) terms the 'proto-political exchange' – was struck in a privatisation process that favoured managers and workers over foreign bidders (see Simoneti et al., 2004; Mencinger, 2006).

Furthermore, given Slovenia's dependence on exports and the capacity of social pacts to coordinate wage bargaining across the sheltered sectors and sectors exposed to foreign competition (see Traxler, 2010), it should not come as a surprise that further compromises entailed institutionalised exchange of wage restraint for other concessions to organised labour. National tripartite social dialogue was institutionalised in 1994, when the trade unions accepted the government proposed income policy in exchange for the establishment of the tripartite Economic and Social Council (ESC). This first social pact in Slovenia was followed by a series of other pacts regulating a wide array of areas in which certain measures of flexibility (wage restraint) were traded against security-orientated reforms, such as the establishment of the minimum wage, the pension reform of 1999 and the Employment Relations Act of 2002 (see Stanojević, 2010). Other areas in which the compromise between the two sides materialised entailed macroeconomic policies (especially exchange rates; see Bole, 2002, 2003) and social policies implemented by the state (see Crowley and Stanojević, 2011).

The establishment of social dialogue in these early formative years enabled the trade unions to put a brake on increasing wage inequality at the beginning of the transition process when the egalitarianism of the socialist period broke down. The crucial development in this respect was the establishment of tripartite institutions at the national level in 1994 and the institution of the minimum wage in 1995 (see Figure 10.1),[1] which

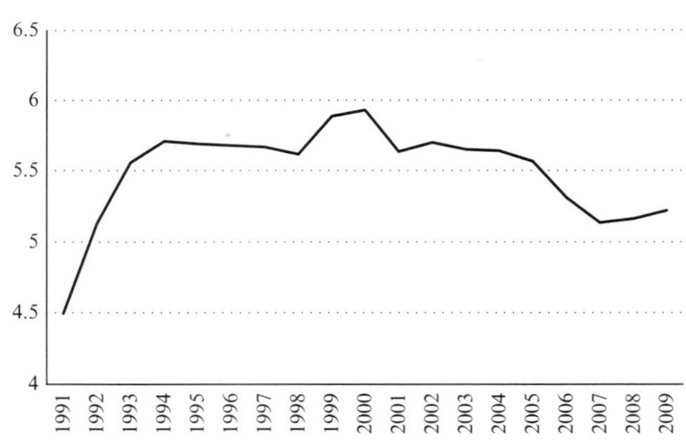

Note: The figure depicts D80/D20 ratio calculated for gross wages. The data include all employees whose wage earnings exceeded general tax allowance and also include (unadjusted) earnings of part-time workers. The data were collected on a yearly basis and do not indicate the time span in which the wage income was created within a given year, which means that even those who worked for only a few months in a given year are included, provided that their earnings exceeded the general tax allowance (cf. Stanovnik and Verbič, 2012).

Figure 10.1 Wage income quintile share ratio, Slovenia 1991–2009

were both a product of social dialogue, while progressive personal taxation further mitigated after-tax incomes (see Stanovnik and Verbič, 2012).

In a relatively short time following EU accession (2004–08), the conditions for compromise eroded significantly, but this was partly masked by a strong economic upswing. Some of the processes dissolving the basis for compromise had been progressing for some time. Workers' ownership was quickly melting away – by the turn of the twenty-first century the phase of concentration and consolidation of ownership was in full swing with workers' ownership declining, while it was increasingly concentrated in the hands of domestic non-financial companies (see Damijan et al., 2004; Prašnikar et al., 2015). Furthermore, as companies found themselves under increasing competitive pressure they resorted to work intensification, as well as working time flexibility (see Stanojević, 2006, 2012). The changes in the state's approach to social partnership in this period – most notably the attempt at neoliberal reform that featured, among other things, the flat-tax rate that nevertheless was never accepted – also signalled that the era of class compromises was drawing to a close. The reform was not negotiated at the tripartite ESC and the unions were pushed into opposition, but they closed ranks and fought back in the winter rally of 2005, deflecting the reform that threatened to sharply increase inequality (see Stanojević, 2015).

Another development of the 2004–08 period – unfavourable from the point of view of work-related inequality – was an acceleration in the trend of precarisation.[2] A considerable part of the increase in temporary employment (Figure 10.2) stemmed from so-called student work, probably the most flexible employment arrangement in the Slovenian labour market, accessible only to those enrolled in secondary or tertiary education which accounted for some 4.9 per cent of all employees in 2008. An even larger share of temporary employment, however, was accounted for by fixed-term contracts, which formally differ from regular employment only by their limited duration. The ballooning of precarious working arrangements that accelerated after 2004 brought about not only increasing wage inequality – the share of low-wage earners among workers on fixed-term contracts was more than twice as large as among those on permanent contracts (Table 10.1) – but also inequality of integration in social security systems, employment security and inequality of access to social dialogue (see Bembič et al., 2016).

Precarisation of work poses a double challenge to trade unions. First, the unionisation of precarious workers is difficult as they work under 'the implicit threat mechanism'; that is, the threat that the employer will not extend the contractual relationship with the employee if the latter does not provide the flexibility required by the former, which

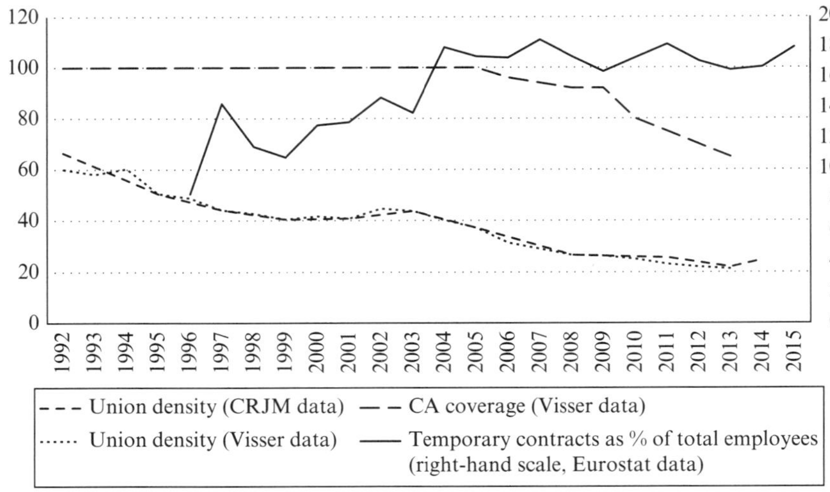

Source: Visser (2015); Broder (2016); Eurostat (2017d).

Figure 10.2 Collective agreements coverage, trade union density and share of temporary employees, 1992–2015

Table 10.1 Share of low wage earners in Slovenia by type of employment

	2006	2010	2014
Permanent	14.80	12.42	14.52
Fixed-term	31.21	29.96	32.89

Source: Eurostat.

might even include renouncing certain rights, for example, the right to unionisation (De Stefano, 2009). Secondly, trade union membership of precarious workers is relatively short lived (Gumbrell-McCormick, 2011) – achieving a certain unionisation rate with a precarious workforce is therefore much more resource intensive than with workers in regular employment. Unfortunately, however, precisely at the time of increasing precarisation of work, which demands a redistribution of resources from core to peripheral union members (Heery and Abbott, 2000), the Slovene unions were faced with an abrupt decline in membership rates (Figure 10.2) and thus a depletion of power capacities to face the challenge.

The period of prolonged crisis (2008–13) saw a further enfeeblement of Slovenian neo-corporatism. Although no major changes in legislation occurred in this period, the crisis severely restricted the room for compromise. With radicalisation of both capital and labour, achieving a consensual decision became increasingly difficult, pushing government into avoidance or narrowing of social dialogue, which in turn eroded its legitimacy (Stanojević and Kanjuo-Mrčela, 2016). Trade union and employers' organisation representatives we interviewed both complained that, with the notable exception of the Ministry of Labour, the role of the social partners is often reduced to briefings offered by the government.

The position of the capital side in social dialogue changed for good. The domestic capitalist class is now firmly in control of certain sections of the economy, and it thus no longer needs a direct alliance with labour as it did at the outset of the transition. Its priorities in the current period mainly concern increasing labour market flexibility and cutting taxes, while maintaining state support for private business, especially the export sector, which, in turn, means cutting public expenditure, preferably through reductions in the public sector wage bill (GZS et al., 2013; GZS, 2014, 2015). Not surprisingly, these demands do not resonate well with organised labour, which, faced with severe losses of membership since 2003, is increasingly turning towards the everyday economic problems of its membership and radicalising its positions in negotiations. At least, at the national level, resorting to popular mobilisation still enables unions to defend certain positions in the tripartite negotiations, while demonstrations and referendums are retained as a fall-back option. Nevertheless, while institutional arrangements of social dialogue remain largely unchanged, labour's influence is incomparable with the 1990s (see Stanojević, 2015; Stanojević and Kanjuo-Mrčela, 2016).

Precarisation of work advanced further during the post-2008 period. Apparently, agency work became much more widespread with the crisis, although reliable data on this trend are lacking. Another form that spread quickly immediately after the first wave of the crisis was self-employment (Figure 10.3) – a development supported by the state, which heavily subsidised the conversion of the unemployed into so-called 'entrepreneurs' (see Bembič et al., 2016). Exit from the formal status of unemployed for these 'forced entrepreneurs' only rarely meant exit from poverty, as is clear from Figure 10.3 which depicts the share of those at risk of poverty among the self-employed which increased after 2008 in step with the increase of the absolute number (not shown in Figure 10.3), as well as the share of self-employed in total employment.

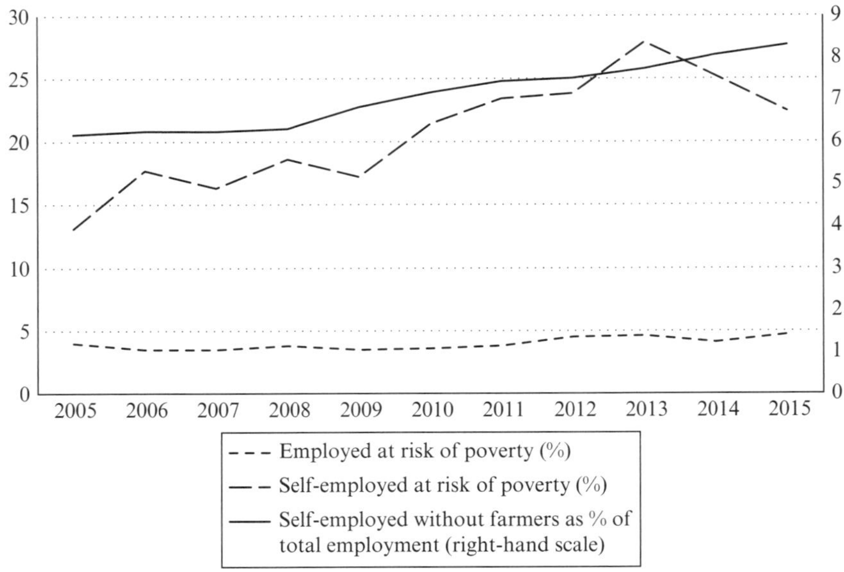

Source: Author's calculation; Statistični urad Republike Slovenije (Statistical Office of Slovenia; SURS, 2017a).

Figure 10.3 Self-employment, Slovenia, 2005–15

2.2 Collective Bargaining at the Sectoral and Company Level

Multi-employer collective bargaining is for the time being – at least formally – firmly established in Slovenia but, according to a union representative we interviewed, the coverage rate is sustained only because collective agreements (CAs) pull sources of potential conflict out of the companies and provide the employers with additional flexibility as deviations from the law can be secured only in sectoral collective agreements (see section 3.2). There are eight trade union confederations, by far the most important being the largest two in the private and public sectors (see Stanojević and Broder, 2012): the Association of Free Trade Unions of Slovenia (Zveza svobodnih sindikatov Slovenije, ZSSS) and the Confederation of Public Sector Trade Unions (Konfederacija sindikatov javnega sektorja, KSJS). Employers are organised in five chambers, two general, two organising the small employers and one sectoral, organising the large trade sector, the largest being the Chamber of Industry and Commerce (Gospodarska zbornica Slovenije, GZS).

Collective bargaining in Slovenia was relatively centralised and highly inclusive from 1990 until 2005. Two separate peak-level agreements covered the public and the business sector separately and were complemented by sectoral- and company-level agreements. Since the membership in the main employer organisation was mandatory the coverage was almost total (Figure 10.2). After 2005, when the general collective agreement for the private sector was abolished, only two agreements for the whole private sector were signed, in 2006 and 2008, that covered wages and wage allowances, but after the latter expired at the end of 2009 only industry- (and company-) level agreements remain. Furthermore, the main employers' organisation turned from a mandatory into a voluntary organisation in 2006 which led to a radicalisation of its positions as it had to compete for members (Stanojević and Klarič, 2013: 222–3). Collective bargaining was thus decentralised to the sectoral level in the period after EU accession, reducing the scope for solidaristic wage policy (Schulten, 2002) across the private sector, while the coverage rate of collective bargaining has decreased significantly (see Figure 10.2), especially in the post-2008 period. The negotiated agreements tend to be increasingly reduced in scope as well as duration, which brings in additional elements of flexibility as the rules are renegotiated after the expiry of the agreement. As regards reduced scope, the collective agreement for non-metal materials (*Uradni list Republike Slovenije – Official Gazette of the Republic of Slovenia* – UL RS, no. 55/2013) offers a case in point – while collective agreements up to 2010, when the last agreement was cancelled, all contained provisions for days of paid leave for examinations, the new agreement, signed in 2013, devolves the responsibility for this issue to the individual contract between employer and employee, which increases flexibility without providing for additional security in this area. Finally, the strength of social dialogue varies strongly across branches of industry, remaining almost intact in some sectors, such as the metal industry and the electro industry, and virtually disappearing in others (Stanojević and Kanjuo-Mrčela, 2016). The latter include the private security industry, where the collective agreement was finally signed in 2016 (UL RS 5/2016), but covers a very limited range of issues; the construction sector agreement (UL RS 101/2015) that was cancelled in 2013 and renegotiated in 2015 but not extended to the whole sector, and the collective agreement for the chemical and rubber industry that was cancelled (UL RS 55/2013) but not renegotiated.

The developments described probably contributed to widening disparities of working conditions and wages between different industries in the private sector. The ratio of highest to lowest wage by activity increased from 1.85 in 2000 to 2.46 in 2007 (Urad za makroekonomske analize in razvoj – Institute for Macroeconomic Analysis and Development – UMAR, 2016: 63). Table 10.2 presents the shares of low-wage earners in

Table 10.2 Share of low wage earners by economic activity in selected branches of economic activity, Slovenia (data for 2014)

Activity	%
Manufacturing	15.88
Electricity, gas, steam and air conditioning supply	0.36
Construction	33.17
Wholesale and retail trade; repair of motor vehicles and motorcycles	25.44
Transportation and storage	17.03
Accommodation and food service activities	39.99
Information and communication	3.37
Administrative and support service activities	54.01
Education	13.80
Human health and social work activities	12.07

Source: Eurostat.

selected industries. While there are barely any low-wage workers in some industries, the depressed construction sector and some service sectors feature shares of between one-quarter and over one-half of employees earning two-thirds or less of the national median gross hourly earnings. Intermediate shares are observed in the relatively prosperous and predominantly export-orientated manufacturing sector, in health care and in education.

Unions are growing weaker at the company level, as argued by Stanojević and Kanjuo-Mrčela (2016: 482) and confirmed by a trade union representative we interviewed in 2017. However, in companies (and sectors) where bipartite dialogue takes place there are reportedly not many concessions as unions try to preserve standards (Stanojević and Kanjuo-Mrčela, 2016: 470). Opt-out clauses are provided for by some sectoral collective agreements, but sectoral unions are trying to prevent them from being used improperly. Still, the swelling of the 'reserve army of the unemployed' and increased employment insecurity, not least owing to the expansion of precarious forms of employment, brought about a major shift in the balance of power in favour of capital. To summarise, it appears that the national-level trade union confederations that are still able to mobilise people around contentious issues related to certain minimum standards, gained in influence in comparison with company-level unions where there are plenty of cases of workers' collectives being rather concessionary in order to avoid redundancies (Stanojević and Kanjuo-Mrčela, 2016: 470, 482). According to a confederation representative we interviewed, the union struggle is almost impossible in

Slovene companies because 'this high unemployment, the awareness that behind your job there are at least 50 candidates meant that workers are willing to work for lower wages, even for minimum wages, if only to keep their job. It is impossible to fight in such circumstances' (interview with a trade union representative, 2014).

3. FLEXIBILITY, SECURITY AND INEQUALITY DEVELOPMENTS IN THE POST-2008 PERIOD

After the mid-2000s the threat of rising inequality was gradually piling up; decentralisation of collective bargaining to sectoral level, decreasing coverage, a decline in the power of trade unions and increasing precarisation probably all worked in the direction of increasing inequality. In addition, it appears that after 2004 and especially after 2012 the Slovene economy has increasingly adopted the downside aspects of the German model of export-led growth, characterised as it is by compression of domestic consumption in parallel with trade surpluses (see Müller et al., 2015), coupled with the emergence of a low paid and precarised service sector that supports the competitiveness of the export sector by providing low-cost services (Hassel, 2014). Most important in this respect were probably the post-crisis economic policies of the central bank, which suppressed the growth of credit after 2010, and government-imposed harsh austerity measures in 2012, impacting both public and household expenditure, which compressed domestic demand (Bole et al., 2015).

Flexicurity is often portrayed as a trade-off between the two opposing poles of flexibility and security (see Wilthagen and Tros, 2004). Nonetheless, since a trade-off implies a zero-sum game, by itself it can hardly constitute a case of flexicurity. Hence, Ibsen and Mailand (2011: 164–5) define two possible cases of flexicurity: either a loss at one pole in a trade-off is supplemented by some compensation at the other pole, or there must be a combination of both elements that results in a win–win pay-off arrangement, making both sides better off. Win–win situations tend to be rare and difficult to achieve owing to antagonisms of interest between labour and capital (see Burroni and Keune, 2011).

In the post-2008 period trade unions retained significant mobilisation capacity at the national level and win–win situations were increasingly rare (the room for compromise was narrowing), therefore, unilateral attempts at increasing flexibility tended to be strongly opposed by the trade unions and eventually rejected in referendums, while legislative solutions that aimed at increasing security with no immediate and corresponding concessions to capital adversely affected social dialogue as employers responded with obstruction. Successfully concluded negotiations in the tripartite institutions resulted mainly in a new combination of flexibility and security.

It must be noted that most of the major developments at the national level in the post-2008 period that we list below do not necessarily involve measures covering both flexibility and security. Rather, most are related to either one or the other but were traded against other measures in a package deal. Often the measures increasing flexibility and those increasing security did not even target the same group of workers. For example, the labour reform of 2013 reduced, among other things, severance pay for regular employees, while introducing the quota restriction on the use of agency work – the two measures are unrelated but were both part of the same package.

3.1 Major Developments in Relation to Flexibility and Security in the Post-2008 Period at the National Level and Outcomes in Terms of Inequality

3.1.1 Anti-crisis measures

The first item of legislation was passed in 2009 with the aim of mitigating the impact of the crisis on employment. It enabled companies to reduce working hours and provided for a subsidy to employers. The social partners in the ESC backed the measure despite the fact that they were only briefed on the government's plans. After a couple of months another measure was adopted, which enabled employers with temporarily redundant workers to place them on 'temporary forced leave' – workers temporarily did not work but were entitled to 85 per cent of their wages (subsidised by the state) and retained work-related rights but had to spend a certain period in an employer-provided training programme. This second measure was coordinated by the ESC (Mandl, 2010; Kavčič, 2014).

Both measures contained several elements of flexibility, as well as security:

- Workers were provided with an opportunity to enhance their employment security through mandatory training, which also provided an opportunity to increase functional flexibility from the standpoint of the employers.
- The measures provided companies with a certain degree of working time flexibility while retaining the skills and experience of the workers.[3]
- In the case of working hours reduction, employers also enhanced labour cost flexibility, as workers accepted reductions even though employers benefited from subsidies.

- Workers enjoyed some employment security at least for the time firms participated in the schemes.
- The income security of workers in the longer term was increased as companies participating in the schemes could not postpone the payment of social contributions.

This was a win–win pay-off arrangement as both measures entailed several flexibility as well as security elements, while the state stood ready to absorb the costs of the deal. However, at least the first measure designed to mitigate the first impact of the crisis probably increased inequality in employment security to some extent since, similar to other EU countries (see Vaughan-Whitehead, 2011), companies' first response to reduced demand was to not renew fixed-term contracts (see Perko et al., 2014).

3.1.2 Minimum wage increase

A wave of wildcat strikes developed in the manufacturing sector as the first blow of the crisis struck in 2009 and brought growing hardship for workers. An official general strike in the metal and electro industry, which constitutes the core of the export sector, followed in November. Responding to the pressure from below, the union confederations demanded an immediate increase in the national minimum wage. In early 2010 the government gave in and the minimum wage was increased by almost 23 per cent, despite the fact that the measure was not agreed by the ESC.

The increase in the minimum wage reduced wage inequality in 2010 and after that date to a considerable extent (see Figure 10.4). With the rate of growth of the minimum wage at 3.9 times the growth of the average wage the cumulative growth of the minimum wage in real terms amounted to almost 30 per cent in the 2008–13 period (see Selan, 2014), which increased the ratio of the minimum wage to average monthly earnings in the private economy from 43.4 per cent in 2008 to 52.4 in 2016 (Eurostat). Also, the wage gap between workers with high and low educational attainments shrank, as did the differences in wages between various professional groups (see Selan, 2014). Other factors also contributed to the evolution of wage inequality in the post-2008 period – the so-called composition effect and the decrease of wages at the upper end of the distribution both contributed to the wage compression during the post-2008 period. Hence, the value of the interdecile coefficient decreased from 3.67 in 2009 to 3.26 in 2014, while the Gini coefficient for wages dropped from 0.283 to 0.258 (see Figure 10.4) in the same period (UMAR, 2016: 63). Wage disparity was reduced more in the private sector where in 2009 the share of total gross wages received by the 10 per cent of employees on the highest wages stood at 24.4 per cent compared with 4.7 per cent received by those in the lowest

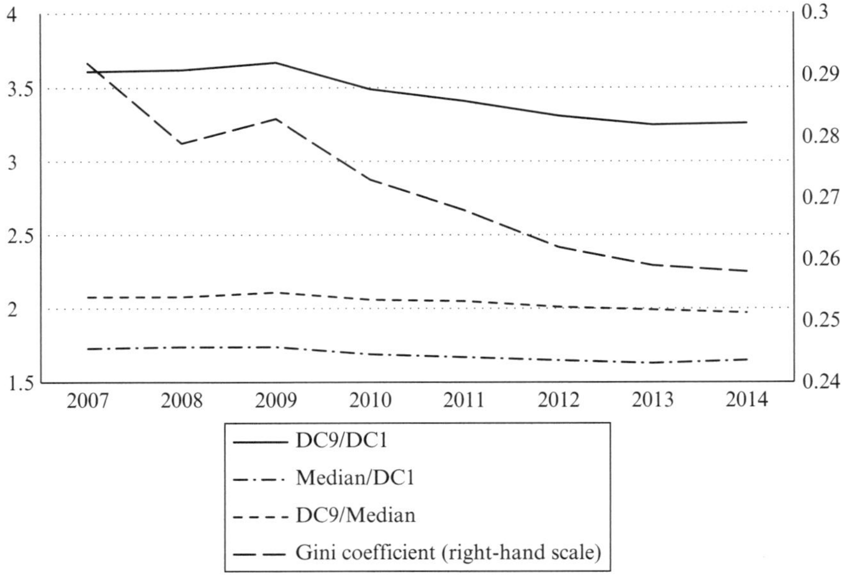

Source: UMAR (2016).

Figure 10.4 Wage inequality in Slovenia, 2007–14

10 per cent, while the difference dropped to 23 per cent compared with 5.4 per cent in 2013. The respective figures in the public sector were 19.7 per cent as against 4.4 per cent in 2009 and 19.4 per cent as against 4.7 per cent in 2013 (Selan, 2014).

The growth of basic wages negotiated in the collective agreements did not match the increase in the minimum wage despite the fact that a large part of the pay grades stipulated in collective agreements were now below the minimum wage (see end note 4 for an explanation). Nevertheless, in some industries, for example in the trade sector, many firms added various bonuses, such as performance bonuses to the minimum wage in order to remunerate their employees. In other industries, for instance in the electro industry, an annex to the collective agreement was agreed that demanded that employers add certain wage supplements to the amount of the minimum wage instead of to a much lower basic wage (UL RS 32/2013). The achievements of the minimum wage in terms of the distribution between labour and capital were, however, much more modest, as the wage share was in 2015 slightly below its 2009 value, although higher than in 2008 (70.2, 70.9 and 68.2 per cent, respectively; AMECO, 2017). More importantly, as Srakar and Verbič (2015) warned, the data in most analyses do not include some of the widespread atypical employment arrangements, which tend to have a much higher incidence of low pay than regular employment arrangements – their inclusion would almost certainly change the picture and make wage inequality more evident.

3.1.3 Mini-jobs and Market Regulation Act

After the hike in the minimum wage, the government adopted a peculiar interpretation of social dialogue according to which either solutions have to be found with some kind of a settlement or, if this cannot be done promptly, the state has the responsibility to take unilateral action. The time had come, according to the government, to meet the demands posed by capital (see Kavčič, 2014: 42–3). A package of reform measures – the pension reform, the mini-jobs law and the law for prevention of undeclared work – were sent to the parliament without the consent of the unions. Closely related to the issues of flexibility and security was the Mini-jobs Act (Zakon o malem delu, ZMD), introducing a temporary and casual form of employment accessible to those in secondary or tertiary education, retired and unemployed persons, amounting to a maximum of 60 hours per month. With lower social contributions, strong external flexibility and without most non-wage costs it would constitute a very flexible form of employment. It had many similarities to the German mini-jobs but introduced some restrictions regarding its use (see MDDSZ, n.d.; ZSSS, n.d.). Employer organisations supported the introduction of mini-jobs. The unions responded by articulating public opposition to the law, building a coalition with the Slovenian Student Union and the civil Movement for Decent Work and Welfare Society and demanding that the law be submitted to a referendum. The Mini-jobs Act was, together with the other two reforms, rejected by a wide margin in a wave of referendums in 2011, which eventually brought down the centre-left government. A part of the same reform package was the Labour Market Regulation Act (Zakona o urejanju trga dela, ZUTD), which had several elements on the flexibility as well as on the security side. For example, job sharing and job rotation that provided for either full or partial replacement of an employee with an unemployed person, as well as the institution of partial unemployment enabling the unemployed to accept a part-time job while retaining a part of unemployment benefit were introduced. The law also added to the security side by easing access to unemployment benefits for those on employment contracts for short periods of time. The Labour Market Regulation Act was discussed in the ESC and although a final consensus was not achieved – the unions opposed certain changes related to retirement contributions for the unemployed (ZSSS, 2012) – it was not submitted to a referendum.

While the Mini-jobs Act promised enhanced external and working time flexibility, as well as considerable wage and non-wage costs flexibility to the employers, it lacked any compensation in terms of security – not a surprising outcome given that no agreement on the law was reached through social dialogue. The 2010 Labour Market Regulation Act, on the other hand, although containing some controversial articles that remained unresolved, introduced several new instruments that could be considered win–win pay-off solutions (job sharing and job rotation, which increased functional flexibility as well as income and employment security, and access to unemployment benefits that improved income security) the costs of which were borne by the state. Although resisting the introduction of mini-jobs did not increase equality directly, it certainly has to be counted as a move preventing a further increase in inequality as the reform threatened to extend the low-paid and insecure form of employment akin to the existing student work to large segments of the population and thus increase pay inequality, as well as inequality of employment security and other aspects of job quality (parental leave, holiday leave, expenses for travel to and from work, a full integration into the social security system and so on). The mini-jobs would probably have become more widespread in some sectors than in others. The brunt would be borne in service sectors such as retail and food services, known for their disproportionate use of student work and employment of women, which would probably increase inequalities in access to regular employment along gender lines. The most important factors in resistance to the introduction of mini-jobs were the mobilisation capacity of Slovene trade unions and the articulation of interests at the national instead of merely the sectoral level.

3.1.4 Austerity measures

After the defeat of the previous centre-left government in a wave of referendums, the sovereign debt crisis started in earnest. Liquidity problems of the state increased the fear of a foreign bailout with strong conditionality. These developments increased the leverage of international actors (EU institutions, the Organisation for Economic Co-operation and Development and international financial markets). The European Commission's recommendations became de facto binding as its signals to the financial markets were of the utmost importance (see Damijan, 2013). During 2011 and 2012 the Commission 'recommended', among other things: to increase fiscal consolidation efforts; to pass the new pension reform; to undertake reform of the labour market, including student work; to ensure that wage growth supports competitiveness; and to resolve the problem of mounting nonperforming loans in the banking sector (see European Commission, 2011, 2012). The European Commission's 'compulsory management' strengthened the position of the new centre-right government in its relations with the trade unions. With the support of the employers' organisations in the ESC, the government proposed austerity measures that were harsh by Slovenian standards. The public sector unions organised a general public sector strike, which resulted in two agreements (UL RS 38/2012; UL RS 40/2012) that ensured that public sector wage cuts were lower and the curtailment of social rights milder than originally announced. Also, the Act that instituted the austerity measures brought lower security for some private sector workers as well, because unemployment benefits were lowered. Moreover, a pension reform similar to that rejected by referendum in 2011 was passed in 2012 with minor concessions to organised labour. Social dialogue in the ESC was used extensively when shaping some of the reforms mentioned above, most notably in the case of pension and labour market reform. For instance, in the case of pension reform the trade unions were able to persuade the government and employers to accept bonuses increasing the accrual rate for those staying in employment longer and to obtain slightly more favourable treatment of children receiving survivor's pensions. The most important achievement was a lower retirement age for those that started work before the age of 18, mothers with children and for years of mandatory military service (Delo, 2012).

Social dialogue in this period was strongly conditioned by external factors that worked mainly in favour of the employers and the state, while workers had few alternatives at their disposal and a form of downward flexibility was simply imposed by the government. The trade unions certainly achieved a more balanced outcome in terms of income inequality and social rights through social dialogue, which nevertheless, as Stanojević and Klarič (2013) rightly underscore, often turned into mere 'concession bargaining'.

3.1.5 The 2013 labour market reform

The basic rationale of the 2013 labour market reform was to lower the legal protection of regular contracts of employment, while introducing new measures for protecting precarious workers. Flexibilisation of regular employment was achieved by shortening the period of notice for open-ended contracts, relaxing dismissal procedures and reducing severance pay for some groups of regular employees, which increased external numerical flexibility for full-time, open-ended contracts of employment. Additional elements of flexibility were the introduction of 'temporary forced leave', the relaxation of provisions related to job demarcations and the introduction of casual and temporary work for pensioners. On the security side, the reform introduced a host of new measures to increase security of workers in precarious arrangements, as well as to de-incentivise the use of these forms of work. As regards fixed-term contracts, the accessibility of unemployment benefits for those on contracts of short duration was further increased, severance pay for fixed-term contracts of employment was introduced, restrictions were placed on the sequencing of fixed-term contracts for a given job (previously for a given worker), and unemployment contributions for fixed-term contracts paid by employers were increased while exempting the employer from payment of contributions for the first two years of open-ended contracts. Agency work was re-regulated by strengthening the provisions for equal treatment of agency workers and introducing quota restrictions for the use of fixed-term agency work. Furthermore, the legal category of dependent self-employed was instituted. The reform widened the possibilities for collective agreements to deviate from the law in certain areas in a way that is less beneficial for workers.

The labour market reform was shaped in the social dialogue. According to a trade union representative we interviewed, the reform was a landmark for the trade unions as it was the first time they had approached labour market reform not by trying to prevent flexibilisation, but rather by accepting changes towards more flexible regular employment in return for increased security and regulation of atypical (and often precarious) employment arrangements. Because the reform enhanced external and working time flexibility and functional flexibility of the regular workers, while at the same time increasing income and employment security for atypical workers, it could be considered a trade-off with compensations.

The impression is that the reform achieved at least some de-segmentation effects, although they seem to have been short lived and weak. As illustrated in Figure 10.5, the share of fixed-term contracts of employment in total number of new jobs (regulated by the Labour Code) was only slightly lower in the year following reform (2014) than in the year of the enactment of the reform (April 2013), although still higher than in the preceding year (2012). The de-segmentation effects of the reform were most notable for the young (15–29 years old), among whom fixed-term contracts are most widespread. The share of such contracts for this age group was lower in the two years following the reform (2014 and 2015) than in the previous year (2012), although in 2015 it was again on the rise (see Figure 10.5; Kajzer, 2015; and UMAR, 2016 for a similar interpretation). Nonetheless, one of the areas in which reform appears to be effective was the quota restriction for agency workers on fixed-term contracts. As depicted in Figure 10.6, the share of regular (open-ended) contracts of temporary agency workers increased from 26 per cent in 2012 to 71 per cent in 2013, but then levelled off to 50 per cent (see MDDSZ and UMAR, 2015). Thus, the reform to a certain extent reduced inequality of access to open-ended employment for

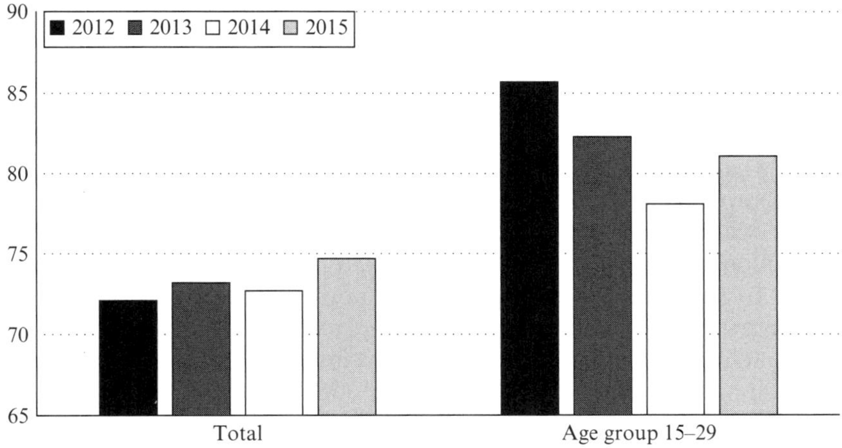

Source: UMAR (2016).

Figure 10.5 Share of fixed-term contracts in total new jobs before and after 2013 labour market reform, Slovenia, 2012–15

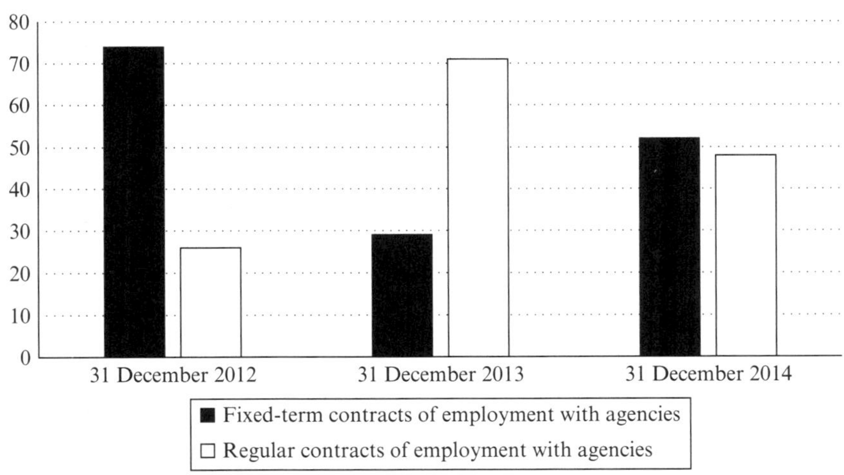

Source: UMAR and MDDSZ (2015).

Figure 10.6 Share of temporary agency workers with permanent and fixed-term contracts of employment before and after the 2013 labour market reform

agency workers and slightly also for the young generation, but these effects were rather weak.

In sum, although the reform of 2013 did not succeed in reversing the trend towards expansion of non-standard and precarious work (see Bembič et al., 2016), it is likely that the process of further proliferation of atypical – and more often than not precarious – forms of employment would progress faster than it actually did if the reform had not been in place, while those employed under these arrangements would enjoy less protection and security. In terms of inequality of access to full-time, open-ended formal work the reform probably prevented a sharper increase in inequality, but did not in general increase equality.

The reform also strengthened provisions for equal opportunities for the training and education of temporary agency workers. According to the law, which is to a large extent shaped through social dialogue, all (Labour Code regulated) non-standard workers enjoy the same rights with respect to training and education as workers on regular contracts. Nonetheless, there seem to be many problems related to adequate provision of training for unskilled workers, according to both trade union and employers' organisation representatives. Perceptions of the causes, however, vary. While the employers' representative argued that the main cause of the low involvement in training programmes of the low skilled is their lack of interest, the trade union representative adds that employers do not bother with preparing the low skilled for new technologies. The latter explicitly pointed to sectoral collective bargaining as the most suitable venue for more equal access to training for those that need it most owing to technology changes and atypical workers, but regretted that development of bipartite dialogue in this area stalled after 2008.

3.1.6 Re-regulation of student work and redefinition of the minimum wage

During the period of economic recovery after 2013, the main developments related to the combination of flexibility and security were the re-regulation of student work in 2014 and the legal redefinition of the minimum wage. The largest part of temporary employment in the 15–24 age group – the highest in the EU – consists of student work. Its re-regulation included the introduction of pension contributions and disability insurance, as well as the establishment of a minimum hourly rate. Since it slightly improved the working conditions for student workers, the measure can be considered an achievement in terms of its effects on inequality. The measure was coordinated with the Slovene Student Organisation and to a certain extent also with the social partners, but it seems that the final agreement with the latter was not achieved.

The redefinition of the minimum wage[4] – that is, excluding some (but not all) supplements from the minimum wage but increasing its sum – was an initiative of the trade unions that strove to tackle the problem within the social pact, but could not reach an agreement with the other side. After unsuccessful attempts to resolve the issue in the tripartite ESC, the seven confederations changed tack – they launched a campaign for a new law and gathered signatures allowing them to demand a referendum. The campaign was largely successful and in late 2015 the parliament endorsed the initiative without a single vote cast against the motion. This, however, prompted three of the four employers' organisations that were signatories of the social pact to withdraw their signatures. Indeed, when asked about the re-regulation of student work, as well as the redefinition of minimum wages, the employers' organisation representative interviewed pointed to the government's decision to adopt the measures and bypass social dialogue as the main problem.

To recapitulate, after 2008 the room for manoeuvre within social dialogue at the national level was severely narrowed and was determined by trade union mobilisation power, on the one hand, and the leverage afforded to the government and the capital side by external factors, on the other. Given the increasing pressures from both internal and external factors the countervailing power of organising labour was of decisive importance for balancing demands for flexibility with some degree of security. With the exception of the beginning of the period when the state was willing and able to support social dialogue with ample funds (this capacity of the state evaporated with the growing public debt), which in turn brought significant results in terms of both flexibility and security, the results of the efforts to sustain social dialogue were quite meagre. When the conditions for a meaningful social dialogue were fulfilled, it resulted in consensual readjustment of flexibility and security elements, but as the antagonism between the interests of labour and capital intensified, these conditions were eroded progressively.

While for readjustments of flexibility and security elements at the national level social dialogue appears essential, for the push towards more equality the sheer power of organised labour appears to be the single most important factor at first. Nonetheless, the share of workers on the minimum wage, the share of precarious forms of employment and so on vary considerably among the sectors of the economy covered by the sectoral trade unions, which means that not all segments of union membership were equally affected by union actions, for example, changes in the minimum wage or the campaign against mini-jobs. The union actions in these cases were not, however, undertaken at the sectoral level but by confederations that were able to universalise the push from below. The exemplary case in this respect was the minimum wage increase that sprang from discontent at a major exporter and was – with the support of sectoral unions – translated into action by confederations at the national level. Thus, the claim that the power of organised labour was crucial for equality outcomes needs to be modified – it was the power exerted through vertically integrated trade unions that allowed the articulation of different levels that really mattered.

3.2 Collective Bargaining Adjusting Flexibility and Security Balance and Tackling Inequality in the Post-2008 Period

Since conditions for collective bargaining differ substantially between sectors it is impossible here to provide a comprehensive general account of developments at this level. Rather, we will first examine the main regulatory changes structuring the conditions for flexibility and security outcomes of collective bargaining and then observe the results in collective agreements of selected industries (see section 4, case study 1).

Surveying the main changes we have to note, first, the gradual decentralisation of collective bargaining from the national level towards sectoral level (see above). Second, this decentralisation took place in a relatively 'organised' (Keune and Vandaele, 2013) manner; that is, the higher-level (sectoral) agreements still determine the framework of rules and standards from which lower- (company-) level agreements could in principle not deviate in a way that would be disadvantageous for workers. The exception to the rule is admissible, though, if the higher-level collective agreement spells out the conditions under which the lower-level collective agreement can deviate from the minimum standards (see UL RS 43/2006). Third, a new phase in this process of decentralisation was reached with the labour reform of 2013, when the Employment Relationship Act (Zakon o delovnih razmerjih, ZDR-1) enlarged the autonomy of the contracting parties at the sectoral level to negotiate in the collective agreements deviations from the law in a manner less advantageous for workers. The areas in which such a deviation is now admissible are the following: job demarcations, permissible reasons for fixed-term employment, the quota restriction for the share of the fixed-term agency workers, working time organisation, introduction of apprenticeships, notification periods in case a worker quits, retirement allowance, disciplinary sanctions and the rate of seniority allowance (ZDR-1).

The flexibility allowed in these areas, as well as other legislative changes prompted a wave of renegotiations of collective agreements (see Stanojević and Kanjuo-Mrčela, 2016). This increase in the social partners' autonomy in relation to legislation should have facilitated the development of solutions balancing flexibility and security (Ibsen and Mailand, 2011:

175). Also, the fact that sectoral collective agreements in Slovenia cover a relatively wide array of issues appears to be conducive to package deals with various combinations of flexibility and security (Ibsen and Mailand, 2011: 175; see also Marginson and Galetto, 2016: 110). Nevertheless, the period after the crisis saw a deterioration in the two conditions facilitating the development of flexicurity listed in the literature – mutual trust and the relative power of bargaining partners. According to the trade union representative interviewed, mutual trust declined after 2008 while the weakened power of trade unions and the decline of membership in employers' organisations adversely affected social dialogue. Nevertheless, given the legislative framework, in the absence of unions that are strong enough to be involved in collective bargaining neither opt-out clauses nor deviations from law can take place as the latter have to be spelled out in the collective agreements, while the former usually require an agreement with the company-level union.

Many collective agreements in the private sector entail provisions on opt-out clauses, which often require notification and sometimes even permission from the sectoral trade union is necessary as well as an agreement with the company-level union. In addition, the majority of sector-level agreements in the private sector make use of provisions allowing deviation from the law listed above. The evidence collected confirms that deviations from the law enable the unions to trade them against various security provisions in other areas of the 'bargaining package' and sometimes even use them in order to bring employers' organisations to the bargaining table, although not all unions perceive these opportunities for trade-offs and compensation in the same way (see Case Study 1).

Owing to a large gap between basic wages and the statutory minimum wage which concentrates a large share of the workforce at the level of the latter, the unions in general do not strive for lower wage inequality but for an overall increase in basic wages and for the elimination of wage supplements from the minimum wage in order to be paid in addition to it. This would increase differences at the very bottom end of the wage distribution, but since many wage allowances add on the low basic wages – which means that for most low-paid workers, they do not count – their elimination from minimum wage (that is, adding them to the amount of the minimum wage) would enhance equality in relation to those in higher pay grades for whom allowances count in any case. Provisions for the elimination of wage supplements from the minimum wage formed a part of collective agreements for the electrical industry until the legal redefinition of the minimum wage in 2015. In addition to basic wages and allowances, collective agreements typically provide for other pecuniary benefits that enhance the income security of workers, such as the solidarity allowance which is paid by the employer when certain conditions are fulfilled and which applies to all employees except student workers.

The law guarantees the right of workers to training and education. Most sectoral collective agreements contain further provisions regarding the financing of education and training, as well as specifying the rights of employees to time off for examinations or attendance of lectures. Since these apply to all (including non-standard) workers except for student workers, they in principle provide for the development of their skills too. However, the problem of implementation remains and the presence of an active and committed union in the company is crucial. As one of our interviewees reports, even when the law explicitly demanded training of workers on subsidised 'temporary forced leave' in 2009–10 (see above), most employers only wanted 'to cash in the subsidy while leaving the workers to stay at home and only sign the attendance list' (interview with trade union representative, December 2016).

There is a variety of provisions relating to working time aimed at enhancing 'combination' security, from additional days of annual leave and for paid leave owing to the occurrence of certain events such as marriage, birth of a child and so on, as well as for unpaid leave. Some agreements strive to reinforce combination security by increasing the predictability of working time. For example, the collective agreement for the hospitality and tourism industry spells out the conditions for temporary rearrangement of working time (UL RS, 17/2016); others, for instance the collective agreement for the trade sector, stipulate that the employer has to present the weekly schedules to the workers a few days before the start of the working week (UL RS, 24/2014). Some agreements contain provisions for monitoring the organisation of working time and advancing suggestions for 'more humane' working time arrangements on a parity basis (UL RS, 104/2011; UL RS 78/2014; UL RS 6/2015). There are various provisions in collective agreements enabling workers to strike a balance between work and family life by strengthening rights related to working time and changes in place of work for parents, single parents, workers with disabled family members, and so on (UL RS, 104/2011; UL RS 17/2016; UL RS 101/2015). Evidently, sectoral collective bargaining can address combination security issues which would otherwise be subject to one-size-fits-all legislation in a very targeted manner and at the same time provide opportunities for more equal access to a proper work–life balance among potentially vulnerable groups (for example, single parents and workers caring for disabled relatives).

Some collective agreements also provide for parity commissions for monitoring reasons for fixed-term employment arrangements in the company and proposing measures for regularisation of their employment status and thus provide a lever for enhancing equality of access to formal open-ended employment to company-level trade unions. Collective agreements for the electrical industry, the metal materials industry and the metalworking industry all entail provisions of this kind, and the latter two also stipulate the duty of the employer to report at least once a year to the trade union on employment policy, which has to take into account 'competitiveness, social inclusion and flexicurity in such a manner that flexibility and security complement each other' (UL RS 78/2014; UL RS 6/2015). In relation to provisions explicitly aimed at addressing employment inequality one has to bear in mind, first, that the sectoral trade union has to be strong enough in order to push for their insertion into the collective agreement (see Case Study 1) and, secondly, that they are but a dead letter if the company-level union is not capable of enforcing them (see Case Study 2).

4. CASE STUDIES

4.1 Case Study 1: Collective Bargaining from the Viewpoint of Flexibility, Security and Wage Inequality in the Collective Agreements of the Trade and Metal Sectors

Concerned mainly with the national-level labour market and welfare arrangements, the flexicurity debate has lately been reproached for not paying due attention to differences in effects of the national regulation on various sectors, occupational groups, companies and so on. In addition, focusing exclusively on national regulation neglects other kinds of regulation, such as collective bargaining (see Burroni and Keune, 2011). In this case study we first illustrate how the sectoral collective agreements provide for readjustment of flexibility and security elements by taking a closer look at two collective agreements in the private sector: the collective agreements of the metalworking sector (roughly C25, C28, C29, C30 and C33) and the trade (G) sector, a large part of which consists of the low paid and precarised retail trade (G47), on which we will focus when making comparisons with the metalworking industry. In addition, the differences in wage developments in both sectors will be examined from the aspect of inequality issues.

4.1.1 Employment conditions and social dialogue in the two sectors

Our choice of sectors tries to reflect difference of conditions that prevailed in various sectors of the economy in the post-2008 period. The metalworking sector and the trade sector together employed some 165000 workers in 2014 (author's calculations from SURS, LFS data), which accounts for

Table 10.3 Employment conditions in metalworking, trade and retail, Slovenia

	Metal	Trade	Retail trade	National average
1 Open-ended contracts of employment (Labour Code regulated)	86.7%	81.9%	79.2%	83.2%
2 Fixed-term contracts of employment (Labour Code regulated)	11.2%	10.6%	11.8%	11.9%
3 Part-time contracts of employment (Labour Code regulated)	1.4%	6.1%	7.3%	5.1%
4 Other forms of work – mainly student work (non-Labour Code)	1.4%	7.4%	9%	5%
5 Self-employment – without farmers (non-Labour Code)	4.6%	8.2%	5.7%	8.1%
6 Average wage (monthly, €)	1476	1395	1184	1540
7 Value added per employee (yearly, €)	36362	36720	30626	39463

Note: Rows 1–4 LFS data; row 5 register data; all data are for 2014; row 7 refers to companies, cooperatives and sole proprietors only.

Source: SURS.

more than a fifth of all employees in Slovenia. However, the two sectors differ considerably in terms of prevailing employment arrangements and wages (Table 10.3). Metalworking is one of the core industries of the Slovenian export sector that was dealt a heavy blow during the crisis of 2009 but saw relatively high rates of growth of both value added and value added per employee thereafter, the latter reaching approximately the same level as the whole trade (G) sector but stood at some 120 per cent of the respective figure for the retail sector (G47) in 2014. This difference was more than reflected in the level of wages in both sectors, with metalworking wages being some 5 per cent higher than wages in the trade sector as a whole, 25 per cent higher than retail wages and 35 per cent higher than wages in the lowest paid retail segment of food retailing (G47, 110) (SURS, 2017b). Differences in employment arrangements point to a much more segmented labour market in retail (and the whole trade sector), though it has to be kept in mind that manufacturing – including the metal sector – is by far the largest user of agency work, which unfortunately does not appear in sectoral employment statistics. Although manufacturing accounts for only some 23.4 per cent of total employment (author's calculations from SURS, LFS data), roughly 63 per cent of all temporary agency workers (TAWs) placements (Ministrstvo za delo, družino, socialne zadeve in enake možnosti, MDDSZ data) were in manufacturing sector (C) in 2015, the respective numbers for the trade sector (G) being 12.1 per cent and 9.4 per cent. Part-time contracts are quite widespread in retail (as well as the whole trade sector) and a large share of these contracts are probably involuntary, while incidence of such contracts is much lower in metalworking. Finally, the share of student work, which is also mostly performed on a part-time basis and is temporary by definition, in the metal industry amounts to less than one-sixth of the figure reported for retail.

Social dialogue in the two sectors is generally considered good. However, industrial relations in the two sectors differ considerably, which also affects the conditions for social dialogue. Following Boyer's (2014) typology, metalworking constitutes an example of the so-called 'polyvalent stability' regime, where the workforce is versatile and possesses firm-specific skills, while firms are exposed to strong international competition, which makes exit options expensive for both workers and management and the bargaining position of labour is relatively favourable. The opposite is true for trade (especially retail trade), which operates in the regime of so-called 'market flexibility', characterised by companies in search of external flexibility that demand more basic and easily transferable skills, while the bargaining position of labour is correspondingly weaker.

The power of the unions operating in the two sectors is also a potentially important factor in the social dialogue. The main metalworking union enjoys a density rate some three times higher than the largest trade sector union. Furthermore, while the metal sector union is capable of bringing employers to the bargaining table and achieving a satisfactory compromise by means of industrial action (the last general strike in the sector was in 2013), the position of the union operating in the trade sector is weaker. According to the trade union representative, the main motivations for the employers to get involved in collective bargaining in the trade sector are to obtain deviations from the law, which can only be secured in the sectoral collective agreement (see section 3.2), and the use of collective agreement provisions in place of internal rules and regulations (which also pulls sources of potential conflict out of the company).

The two sectors also operate in different demand regimes which appears to be of critical importance for their performance in the post-2008 period. The metal sector depends mainly on external demand that dried up abruptly in 2009 but grew steadily thereafter. Trade, however, constitutes the largest part of the market services sector that is orientated to the domestic market which suffered two heavy blows on the demand side in the post-2008 period: first, with the spreading of the crisis from export sectors and construction throughout the economy; and, second, with the imposition of the austerity measures that suppressed domestic demand in 2012.

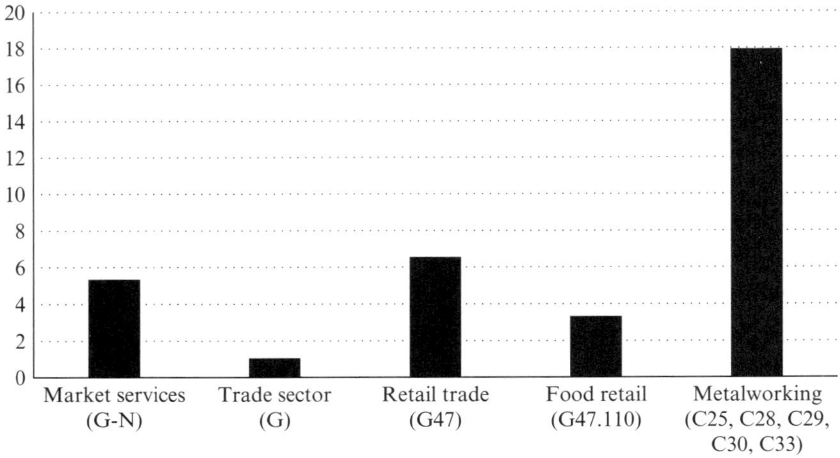

Source: SURS (2017c).

Figure 10.7 Cumulative increase in gross value added per employee, Slovenia, 2008–14

These differences are reflected in the growth of value added per employee in the post-2008 period which was much higher in the metal sector than in the trade sector (see Figure 10.7). It is likely that these disparities in the growth of value added per employee allow companies in the metal sector more room for manoeuvre to accommodate organised labour's demands than their counterparts in the trade sector.

Finally, the attitudes of the sectoral unions differ considerably. Evidence collected reveals that the unions in the export-orientated metal sector are always negotiating bearing in mind the need for competitiveness of the firms in their sector. Hence, in many areas they perceive flexibility adjustments as benefiting not only companies, but workers as well. For example, when discussing the extended reference period for temporary redistribution of working time, the metal sector union representative explains:

> We did it on purpose because during fluctuations the employer will not have to resort to layoffs. The worker will stay at home and make it up later . . . This was on the top of the employer's agenda, but, at the end of the day, of ours too . . . And it is better this way than if we did not accept it, because the employers would then have a temporary surplus of staff or they would resort to layoffs. (Interview with trade union representative, October 2016)

The same applies in the case of other deviations, such as the flexibilisation of job demarcations: 'That is, we accepted it, it might seem, and did a favour to the employers, but it is not true! We did a favour to both of us! The workers will also gain new skills' (Interview with trade union representative, October 2016).

The trade union in the trade sector perceives the flexibility and security readjustments rather differently. As there is no real prospect of skill development (especially in the retail trade), assigning the workers tasks not stipulated in the contract of employment is just 'pushing them around'. The flexibility arrangements are seen as a pure trade-off that has to be compensated with some other part of the package. However, as employers are reluctant to concede on the issue of wages, the union is not willing to cede ground on issues of flexibility:

> We are merchants, everything is on sale. And if you do not want to give in on wages, you'll not get the deviation and you can shoot yourself! . . . We had to give in a bit for the sake of solidarity allowances, you know, and we gave in. OK, not for rises [in wages], but in order to preserve the amount of annual leave, for example, we made a deal on seniority allowance. You try to figure out what you can give away. (Interview with a trade union representative, December 2016)

In summary, unions in the metal sector, where strong international competition prevails and workers with firm-specific skills are tied to companies offering better paying jobs, perceive even some of the flexibility measures as a win–win situation. For unions in the trade sector, especially the retail sector, where wages are lower and firm-specific skills seem less important, virtually every bargain is perceived as a trade-off that requires compensation.

4.1.2 Collective agreements in the two sectors

Being essentially package deals, the two collective agreements do not enable us to identify specific instances of negotiating flexibility against security and corresponding compensations. Rather, elements of flexibility and security will be identified and compared with the two sectoral collective agreements by using the slightly adapted Wilthagen and Tros (2004) framework. The adaptation of the framework consists of the addition of the 'access to social dialogue' category to the security axis and 'procedural flexibility' to the flexibility axis. By 'access to social dialogue' we refer to the conditions for activities of workers' representatives, while by 'procedural flexibility' we refer to stipulations in the collective agreements that enable lower- (company-) level agreements to deviate from sectoral-level agreements or demand the renegotiation of the terms of collective agreements in the future. Finally, we collapse 'job security' and 'employment security' into a single category of 'employment security'.

Flexibility There are relatively few provisions enhancing external numerical flexibility in the two collective agreements, but the deviations from legal regulations are used more extensively in the metal sector collective agreement. Many deviations are allowed by the law with respect to working time flexibility, some of which could also count as labour cost flexibility, such as non-uniform distribution of working time that allows for work in excess of daily norms without the need to resort to (costly) overtime. Deviations in this area are amply used in both collective agreements, but more extensively in the metal sector collective agreement, which also leaves some aspects of working time flexibility to the discretion of company-level collective agreements or the employer (also 'procedural flexibility'). Deviation from the law concerning severance pay in case of retirement (labour cost flexibility) allows more flexibility to employers in the trade sector. The metalworking agreement offers more functional flexibility to employers, as it makes demarcations between jobs demanding the same level of skill or qualifications virtually disappear. Finally the metal sector agreement also enhances 'procedural flexibility' much more than the collective agreement of the trade sector, not least by entailing a provision for opt-out clauses.

Security We were able to identify a few employment security elements in the two collective agreements, the most important being those that refer to training and education (specifying days of paid leave for preparation for examinations, and provisions on lifelong learning) and parity commissions for dealing with the problem of fixed-term employment in the company and turning it into permanent employment. Combination security related provisions in the two collective agreements mostly refer to working time, but the trade sector is much stronger in this respect owing to its detailed stipulations that aim to secure predictable schedules as well as to regulate and compensate workers for unfavourable working hours, Sunday working and holiday working. Elements of income security, such as severance pay in case of retirement, strike pay and solidarity allowance paid by the employer are considerably better provided for in the collective agreement for the metal sector. Security associated with access to social dialogue seems to be stronger in the metal collective agreement that, among other things, provides for better information and consultation rights, although both agreements secure basic conditions for performing trade union functions.

Wages The single most important item in collective bargaining is – according to the representatives of both unions – wages and it is in this area that the differences in the environment in which the two unions operate are most clearly visible. Table 10.4 presents data on collectively

Table 10.4 Basic wages in metal and trade sectoral agreements valid in 2008 and 2015, Slovenia

	Metal CA basic wages 2008	Trade CA basic wages 2008	Trade CA wages/Metal CA wages 2008	Metal CA basic wages 2015	Trade CA basic wages 2014	Trade CA wages/Metal CA wages 2015	2015/2008 Metal CA wages (2008 = 100)	2015/2008 Trade CA wages (2008 = 100)
I	450.66	403.28	89.5	511.56	492.12	96.2	113.5	122.0
II	485.46	438.92	90.4	558.54	511.00	91.5	115.1	116.4
III	534.18	485.26	90.8	617.70	541.36	87.6	115.6	111.6
IV	610.74	535.15	87.6	704.70	594.38	84.3	115.4	111.1
V	666.42	599.28	89.9	769.08	662.53	86.1	115.4	110.6
VI	777.78	706.20	90.8	897.84	776.16	86.4	115.4	109.9
VII	908.28	846.90	93.2	1049.22	925.67	88.2	115.5	109.3
VIII	1.038.78			1198.86			115.4	
IX	1.226.70			1416.36			115.5	

Source: UL RS 70/2008; UL RS 94/2008; UL RS 24/2014; UL RS 6/2015.

agreed basic wages valid in 2008 and 2015 in the trade sector and the metal sector, a comparison of their levels in terms of the latter, and the level of basic wages valid as of 2015 in terms of their value in 2008. The skill and educational requirements for the first seven tariff classes in metal closely match the seven classes in the tariff part of the trade agreement, which makes them comparable. We can immediately notice that negotiated wages in the trade sector collective agreement were lower than those in the metal sector in 2008 and that this disparity grew for all except for the lowest two pay grades in the period between 2008 and 2015. While collective bargaining provided for balanced increases of basic wages across pay grades and thus worked against increases in wage inequality within each of the two sectors, the different rates of growth of negotiated wages between the two sectors – which was nevertheless lower than the difference in growth of value added per employee (Figure 10.7) – did not reduce the wage gap between the two sectors.

4.1.3 Findings and discussion

The so-called autonomy of the contracting parties was, as evident from the above analysis, amply used in both collective agreements. Out of nine areas allowed by the law, deviations took place in six. The same areas were left out in both sectors. Consistent with the findings of previous research (see Ibsen and Mailand, 2011; Marginson et al., 2014; Marginson and Galetto, 2016) is the observed emphasis on internal flexibility (especially working time and functional flexibility) in both collective agreements. Nevertheless, the same areas of deviation from the law and other sources of flexibility were not used to the same extent in the two collective agreements. Thus, provisions related to external flexibility, working time flexibility, functional flexibility and procedural flexibility figure more prominently in the collective agreement for the metalworking sector. Collective agreement for the trade sector permits more flexibility in the area of wage or labour costs with regard to severance payments, which is, however, of minor importance. The metal sector appears stronger in terms of employment security, income security and access to social dialogue, while the collective agreement for the trade sector leads only in terms of provisions for combination security (related to balance between paid work and other commitments).

What do our findings tell us about bipartite dialogue and adjustments of flexibility and security? First, the ample use of both flexibility and security elements in agreements offers strong support for the thesis that collective bargaining can significantly adjust the combination of flexibility and security to sectoral circumstances. Industry-level collective bargaining enables firms to pursue flexibility in the areas where it matters most to them, given the sectoral specifics, instead of relying on one-size-fits-all national legislation and allows trade unions to provide for security according to the needs of workers in a given sector. That is, there is no reason to believe that either the demands of firms for flexibility or workers' needs for security are invariable across the economy. Social dialogue can help to adjust flexibility and security elements according to sectoral specifics. The case of the metal sector shows how the demand of companies for flexible deployment of labour (owing to fluctuations in demand for their products) was satisfied by increasing working time flexibility, as well as functional flexibility instead of external numerical flexibility, which increased workers' employment security. However, turning external flexibility into internal flexibility allows companies to hoard labour and thus retain a skilled and versatile labour force. This is probably the reason why firms in this sector are more likely to invest in workers' skills – the collective agreement of the metal sector is much stronger in the field of training and education than the collective agreement for the trade sector.

Secondly, where there is no bipartite social dialogue or dialogue is weak, workers and firms must rely on the provisions of the law, which means both less security but also less flexibility. Strong and lively collective bargaining at the sectoral level, however, requires strong partners on both sides. According to the literature, trade unions might hesitate to engage in negotiations over flexibility and security when, owing to the power imbalance, the downside risk is too great (see Marginson et al, 2014; Marginson and Galetto, 2016). Bargaining partners in the metal sector, where unions are strong and business conditions are good, were willing and able to strike more comprehensive deals than their counterparts in the depressed trade sector, where unions are comparatively weaker. The metal sector trade unions extended more concessions in terms of flexibility to the employers but also got more in return in terms of security. Nevertheless, even the collective agreement for the trade sector provides much more security and flexibility than collective agreements in industries where unions are virtually non-existent and social dialogue is correspondingly weak, for example, the collective agreement for the private security industry, which contains only a handful of paragraphs with few provisions for either flexibility or security.

What are the outcomes of collective bargaining in the two sectors in terms of inequality? We noted above with regard to wage inequality that the gap between basic wages negotiated in the two sectors increased in the post-2008 period as relatively strong unions in the prospering metal sector (serving the booming German automotive industry) were able to negotiate higher wage growth than their counterparts in the depressed trade sector (selling on the domestic market squeezed by austerity measures). In order to better illustrate the development of business conditions in sectors that depend mostly on the development of the domestic market, we added, in Figure 10.7, the whole market services sector (Nomenclature des Activités Économiques dans la Communauté Européenne – NACE, Statistical Classification of Economic Activities in the European Community – activities from G to N), which also includes the trade sector. For the sake of further exposition we also depict retail and its lowest paid segment, food retailing. As Figure 10.7 shows, the cumulative increase in nominal value added per employee in the 2008–14 period was very low in all of the presented service sectors and subsectors, while it was much higher in the export-orientated metalworking sector. Were wages only to follow the growth of value added per employee, the differences in cumulative wage growth in 2008–14 between the metal and trade sectors would be much higher than the differences observed in negotiated wages (Table 10.4). That is, collective bargaining by itself reduced inequality to some extent.

The actual developments of wages in the observed sectors and subsectors, nonetheless, differed substantially both from negotiated wages and from growth of value added. Figure 10.8 presents the cumulative growth of average wages in selected sectors and the level of wages in 2008 in terms

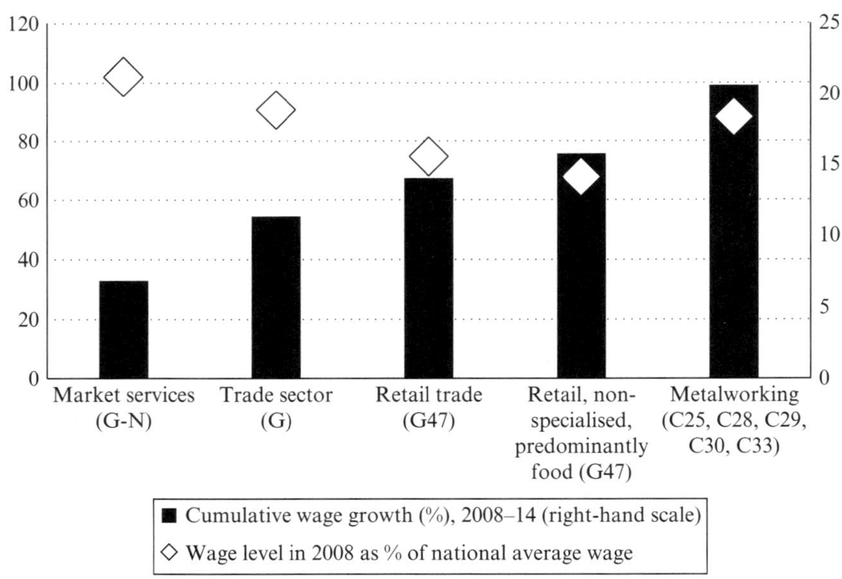

Source: SURS (2017b).

Figure 10.8 Cumulative increase in nominal wages 2008–14 and wage level in 2008, Slovenia

of the national average. A few features stand out. First, the metal sector recorded the highest cumulative growth in wages in 2008–14. However, while the growth in nominal wages in the market services sector as a whole was relatively low and broadly corresponded to the growth of value added per employee, the growth in the trade sector and its two subsectors was unrelated to the growth of value added per employee. Secondly, while cumulative wage growth for the whole trade sector exceeded the growth of negotiated basic wages by only a few percentage points, in retail and especially in the lowest paid food retailing (which has the largest proportion of minimum wage earners), the wage growth fuelled by the increase in the minimum wage surpassed the growth of negotiated basic wages by a wide margin, driving the lowest wages up far beyond what the depressed state of business would allow for. Within the service sector, the growth of wages during 2008–14 becomes increasingly stronger with disaggregation from market services, where the average wage is relatively high, to its lowest paid segments such as food retailing. In summary, while sectoral collective bargaining provided for equality in terms of wage growth within the sectors, wage disparities were prevented from increasing beyond a certain level only by imposing minimum standards (minimum wage) at the national level.

The same goes for equality of access to formal full-time open-ended employment. While there are provisions in the metal sector collective agreement that company-level unions can use in order to foster equality of employment status (the so-called parity commissions), union representatives in the trade sector we interviewed in 2016 claimed that the problem of precarious workers should be dealt with in the sectoral collective agreement but that the price demanded by the employers would be too high. That is, trade unions were too weak to secure the necessary solutions to inequality in employment status by themselves. The national campaign against mini-jobs should be thus understood in a similar way as the minimum wage increase – it upheld certain minimum standards that some weaker industry-level unions would probably be unable to defend by themselves.

No such development at the national level took place in the area of equality of access to training and education. Thus, while the metal sector collective agreement provides for more equal access to education and training provisions, the trade sector workers – where the educational requirements for the key two jobs (shop assistant and shop manager) were deregulated in 2015 – appear to have less equal chances for skill development.

4.1.4 Conclusion

The case study showed the collective bargaining outcomes in terms of flexibility and security and thus inequality in the metal and trade sectors.

We find that collective bargaining can provide for significant adjustments of flexibility and security elements in accordance with sectoral specifics. Sectoral collective bargaining appears more encompassing where social partners are strong and business conditions are good. It can also foster equality in terms of wages, access to full-time, open-ended formal employment, skill development and education at the sectoral level, but close articulation between company-, sector- and national-level industrial relations structures is necessary to address disparities between sectors. Fostering sectoral social dialogue is thus necessary if adjustment of industry-specific elements of flexibility and security, which national-level arrangements fails to address, are to take place and for sustainable equality outcomes at industry level. However, national-level actions and policies are crucial in order to deal with disparities between sectors and reduce inequality.

4.2 Case Study 2: The Potential Effects on Inequality of an Inclusive Union Strategy and the Role of Social Dialogue and Collective Bargaining in the Electro Industry in Slovenia

4.2.1 Introduction

Our second case study presents the industrial relations outcomes for temporary agency workers in terms of equality in a company operating in manufacturing, more precisely, the electro industry in Slovenia. The study should not be taken as a depiction of a typical situation in Slovene companies in general or the electro industry in particular, in which the position of temporary agency workers leaves a lot to be desired despite the efforts of the sectoral trade union functionaries to persuade company-level union leaders to organise atypical workers (Bembič et al., 2016). Rather, our intention is to point out what a good practice could look like and to underscore the role of legislative environment, which is itself an outcome that unions coordinated in dialogue with the government and employers' organisations at the national level, as well as sectoral bargaining and, last but not least, collective bargaining at the company level, articulated as it is with the higher-level agreements and legislation.

4.2.2 The company and worker representatives

The company under investigation employs about 1100 workers in Slovenia and about 500 in subsidiaries abroad. Most of the production is exported, with the greatest share going to European markets and approximately one-tenth sold on the domestic market. Interestingly, until recently, workers, their families and retired employees held approximately half of total company shares, with management holding an additional 10 per cent. These shares were acquired during the first wave of privatisation in the mid-1990s (see above), but were sold in the second half of 2016 to a foreign-owned company. More than 60 per cent of the workforce are assembly workers. Workers in production are relatively easily replaceable because assembly work is mostly broken into simple tasks. The value added per employee is below the average level of the branch. Wages of production workers are slightly above the minimum wage.

There is only one union in the company and the union density exceeds 60 per cent of the total workforce, with members recruited from all departments. There is a works council and the union-nominated candidates are well represented. Three out of six members of the company's supervisory board are appointed by the works council. All workers' representatives collaborate and hold meetings every week. The last strike in the company was the general strike in the sector organised by the sectoral union in 2013.

4.2.3 Provisions for flexibility, security and equality in the collective agreements

While applying many of the provisions for enhancing flexibility, such as allowing night-shifts for women, and deviations allowed by the law – including an increase in quota restrictions for the temporary agency workers from 25 to 35 per cent – the sectoral collective agreement features articles aimed at enhancing security as well as equality. One such item refers to duty of the employer to enable work in the most favourable working time for parents of small children without the possibility for daily care, single parents of school age children, parents of handicapped children, adults with family members that need attendance and help, and spouses of long-term sick persons. Also, single parents of children up to 9 years old and those with a scheduled doctor's appointment have the right to decline overtime work. Although its validity expired with partial redefinition of minimum wage (see above), one of the most interesting items was that which demanded adding some of the wage supplements directly to the minimum wage (instead of to a much lower basic wage) in cases when more than 5 per cent of workers received the minimum wage. The most important from the point of view of union inclusiveness towards agency workers was undoubtedly the provision mandating the establishment of parity committees to monitor the expansion of fixed-term contracts and advancing proposals for their conversion into permanent contracts.

The company-level collective agreement also entails some provisions enhancing combination security of workers by allowing them to decline to work abroad due to educational reasons or family responsibilities, upgrades the sectoral collective agreement in the area of annual leave and defines the order of priority for collective redundancies; that is, the criteria for determining which workers are laid off first. Although education and skills required for the job, work experience, past performance and seniority are overriding criteria in case of collective redundancies, account is also taken of the medical condition of the worker, especially in case of occupational illness or irreversible damage owing to an accident at work and social conditions. Special protection in the case of collective redundancies is afforded to parents of school-age children, parents of handicapped children and single parents, while those with alternative sources of income, such as craft activity, farmers and owners of companies, have negative priority (that is, are laid off first). Furthermore, the agreement specifies the design and working of the parity committee for working time and temporary employment which found its way into the company collective agreement via the sectoral agreement. Finally, the agreement contains a quota restriction on all non-standard employment arrangements, such as agency work, fixed-term and part-time work, which is set at 10 per cent of the workforce but can be increased to 15 per cent under special conditions.

4.2.4 Agency workers and the union

The company began to use temporary agency work in 2009, when the quota restriction was already inscribed in the company collective agreement but not yet in the law. Agency workers in general perform the same tasks as other production workers and are 'permanently' integrated into the company's workforce.

During the first months of their work, the company tried to put agency workers in an unequal position vis-à-vis regular workers by allocating annual leave not in one piece but in twelfth parts and by paying them a lower holiday allowance. When temporary agency workers turned to the union, the latter swiftly intervened and successfully demanded equal treatment guaranteed by the law. Demanding equal treatment convinced the agency workers that the union is a trustworthy institution and encouraged them to become members. The foundations for the union attitude towards temporary agency workers and vice versa were therefore laid (see Matoz, 2016).

The next step that the union took was to improve employment security for agency workers by using the parity committee for temporary employment and working time that featured in the company and sectoral collective agreements. The committee then met regularly on a monthly basis in order to discuss the reasons for using temporary agency workers. In the committee the union pushed for regularising the employment status of temporary agency workers. According to the first arrangement, the agency workers were offered a permanent contract with the user company after three months of work at the premises. In this way about 100 agency workers became employed directly with the user firm. After the new labour law which stipulates the quota restriction for agency workers on fixed-term contracts was passed in 2013, a new compromise was struck according to which the firm checks the employment status of the agency workers every three months and demands that the agency offer them a permanent contract.

As well as improvements in employment security and thus equality of temporary agency workers, they also get the same opportunities for education and skill development. The company uses competency matrices which are the same for regular employees and for agency workers. Promotion is at least in part dependent on skill development and temporary agency workers are promoted according to the same criteria as regulars. Thus, the equal treatment of temporary agency workers seems beneficial to the user firm, too. First, by stabilising the workforce, skill development becomes more viable. Secondly, by blocking a low-road strategy in which temporary agency workers would be treated unequally as a measure for cost-cutting and undercutting regular workers the union forces the management to focus more on productivity, innovation and product quality issues.

Another crucial step needed for the inclusion of peripheral workers (Heery and Abbott, 2000: 170–73) – namely, reform of the structure of union governance at the company level with the aim of reflecting the presence of temporary agency workers in the workforce – was achieved in 2016. The internal rules of the union were adjusted, reserving two out of 15 seats for the representatives that agency workers elect among themselves. The interest among agency workers was considerable and several candidatures were advanced. The two newly elected members of the union's executive board enjoy the legal protection and all the benefits pertaining to other union representatives.

4.2.5 Findings and discussion

The evidence collected indicates that the union in the company treats temporary work agencies in an exclusionary way (quota restriction), while it adopted an inclusionary approach towards their workers (see Heery, 2009). Agency workers in the company examined are treated virtually in every aspect, except for employment security, on equal terms with their counterparts employed in the user company. They receive the same wages, bonuses and benefits, are refunded for work-related costs (commuting expenses and reimbursement for meals during work), and they progress along the same skill ladders as regular workers. They are represented in the governance structures of the union in the company and are entitled to financial assistance from the mutual funds managed by the union. Even as regards their employment security, the union pushes for their immediate employment on a permanent basis, although now with the agency.

What could explain the position of the agency workers in the studied company? First, it has to be noted that although other firms in the branch operate under the same institutional arrangements (legislative and collective bargaining), outcomes vary considerably from company to company. Indeed, while the policy of the sectoral union (Sindikat kovinske in elektroindustrije Slovenije, SKEI – Trade Union of Metal and Electro Industry of Slovenia) is decisively inclusive towards agency workers – though not necessarily agency work as an employment arrangement – the reality often contrasts starkly to the official line as permanent workers (union members) perceive agency workers as unfair competition, which in turn poses an obstacle to their inclusion and organisation (see Bembič et al., 2016: 25). However, the threat of competition was also present in the company observed, but the trade union decided to struggle for equal treatment partly in response to this threat:

> We have to demand it from the employer to make this clear and we also have to say it out loud from time to time. They [the agency workers] have the right to work, to be treated equally, they have equal rights . . . This is our role and it is an important role. In our heads and so on. And, of course, to demand it from the employer. For if the trade union is not going to demand it, who will? . . . When they [i.e. management] once try with less and see that it works, then it will also work with a little less, and even less, you know. We are lowering the standards by that, you know, because then they will say: 'Look, she works for €400 and you for €600.' We'll shoot ourselves in the foot by thinking like that. (Interview with a trade union representative, December 2016)

It appears that the implications of the threat of competition from peripheral workers to union inclusiveness are ambiguous and subject to strategic choice – although undoubtedly important, the institutional environment cannot by itself explain the outcomes. Secondly, as management attempted to treat temporary agency workers differently in the early stage of the company's use of them, equal treatment was not a self-evident outcome but had to be enforced by the union. Finally, as testified by one of the temporary agency worker union representatives, before the current union president was elected the union 'existed only on paper'. This indicates that a strategic choice was made and that there is room for a 'political factor' or agency.

Nevertheless, once the political choice is made, the tools and capacities had to be in place in order to use them. Caught as they are in a company with comparatively low value added per employee and without scarce skills that would grant them structural power, the production workers had to rely on associational power (see Wright, 2000; Silver, 2003). However, while the union president lists membership rates as an essential precondition for any union action, she is deeply aware that causation goes both ways; the union was able to unionise the agency workers only by standing up for them and their rights. The decision to reform the governance structure is already paying off – according to the TAWs union representative agency, workers are more prone to join the union when approached by 'one of them'. A comparison with retail provides further support for the claim that union power matters for union attitude; in retail, where unions are considerably weaker, the representatives of two different unions agreed that collective bargaining is an appropriate tool for regulation of atypical employment, but that (weak) unions would have to sacrifice too much if they were to regulate the conditions of peripheral workers.

The necessary conditions for successful regulation of precarious work, however, were legislation and collective bargaining. These 'institutional factors' were the tools that the union had at its disposal when it had to respond to the management's unequal treatment of temporary agency workers. First, from the very first intervention the union in the company could count on the law, which demands equal treatment and does not allow for deviations in this area. Secondly, it was the collective agreement that provided the tool, that is, the parity commission which the company-level union had at its disposal in order to deal with the problem of employment inequality of temporary agency workers. The fact that the sectoral collective agreement stipulated the establishment of parity committees as mandatory gave the union in the company an opportunity to raise the issue with the management relatively easily. Also, no matter how strong the company-level unions, they simply do not possess the research capacities which would enable them to design such tools by themselves – but the sectoral union does. Hence, in our case the provision of tools and capacities on the part of the sectoral union were a condition sine qua non, although they were not sufficient for achieving good outcomes in terms of equality. However, the converse also holds. For instance, the practice of adding the wage allowances to the minimum wage instead of to the much lower basic wages (see above) – a practice that puts even those in the lowest pay grades with basic wages far below the minimum wage on a more equal footing with those better paid – started in some companies, was taken over by the sectoral union and was imposed in an annex to the collective agreement on all companies in the sector. Hence, not only does sectoral collective bargaining establish minimum standards but it also serves as a channel for the transfer of best practices and as a force for imposing these on the whole sector. Thus, similar to our case study of collective bargaining in the trade and metal sectors, articulation between different levels or vertical network embeddedness (see Lévesque and Murray, 2010) seems an indispensable element for equality outcomes.

4.2.6 Conclusions

The case study points to a best practice for achieving good outcomes in terms of equality of access to formal, open-ended employment. We find that the legislative framework and collective bargaining are of crucial importance for providing the company-level trade unions with capacities to bring about improvements in terms of equality and can function in this regard as a channel for the transmission of best practices. To be sure, other factors, such as the strength of the trade union at the company level and agency are important, but encompassing collective bargaining at sectoral level and legislative requirements for equal treatment constitute a necessary condition for good outcomes in terms of equality.

5. CONCLUSIONS

The aim of this chapter was to provide an overview of Slovene industrial relations in view of their effects on flexibility and security and, finally, their outcomes in terms of inequality with special focus on developments during the post-2008 period. Social dialogue in Slovenia functioned well at the national level in the 1990s, but virtually collapsed after 2008. As regards the post-2008 period, adjustments of flexibility and security elements were achieved in the first year of the crisis when social dialogue at the national level was functioning relatively well and financial support from the state was forthcoming. After that the room for compromise narrowed significantly and most industrial relations developments regarding rearrangement of the elements of flexibility and security were not achieved consensually. Although tripartite dialogue at the national level formally persisted, it became more difficult to reach consensual conclusions, which induced the state to often bypass social dialogue, reducing it to briefing social partners on reform processes. Enfeeblement of tripartite social dialogue, coupled with the weaker bargaining position of the trade unions in comparison with the 1990s brought about unbalanced outcomes in terms of security and flexibility, such as the mini-jobs law, the first attempt at pension reform, and so on. When social dialogue took place in a meaningful way, a compromise was achieved with more balanced outcomes. The labour market reform of 2013 was one such rare occasion of a readjustment of flexibility and security elements achieved by consensus, but even in this case the final outcome seems to be much more significant on the side of flexibility than security.

Sectoral collective bargaining still constitutes the main level of bipartite dialogue and can – as shown by the first case study – bring about major rebalancing of flexibility and security at the sectoral level. In order to fight inequality and overcome the disparities of power among workers in different sectors, however, trade union action and social dialogue in general must be coordinated at various levels (company, sector and national), as both of our case studies illustrate. Trade union action and collective bargaining at company level can bring about significant improvements in terms of equality for atypical or precarious workers, such as agency or fixed-term employees, but here too the interaction between company-level and sector-level collective bargaining and legislation is a necessary condition for success.

NOTES

1. It has to be noted that the data on wage inequality presented in Figure 10.1 inevitably do not capture the incomes of certain groups in atypical employment arrangements, such as students, bogus self-employed or 'entrepreneurs'.
2. We use the term 'precarious work' following Kalleberg and Hewison (2013: 271) who point to: '*uncertainty*, *instability*, and *insecurity* of *work* in which *employees bear the risks* of work (as opposed to businesses or the government) and *receive limited social benefits and statutory entitlements*' (original emphases).
3. Throughout this text we use the term 'working time flexibility' to denote flexibility of both number of working hours and schedules.
4. The sectoral collective agreements usually set a considerable part of basic wages at a level far below the value of the minimum wage. For example, in the appendix to the collective agreement for the trade sector there are seven wage levels of which only the highest determines a basic wage (€925.67) above the value of the minimum wage in 2016 (€790. 73). Although the employer is bound by law to pay wages that cannot be lower than the legally mandated minimum wage, the pay supplements stipulated by the law and collective agreements do not add to the minimum wage but to the basic wage, which means that in most cases they do not count at all until the sum of basic wage and pay supplements exceeds the minimum wage level. Thus, until the minimum wage was redefined only overtime pay was added to the value of the minimum wage, while other allowances and supplements were added to the value of the basic wage agreed in the collective agreement, which could be very low indeed. After redefinition some (but not all) extra payments related to unfavourable distribution of working time were excluded from the minimum wage, which means that now they have to be added to the value of the minimum wage (see MDDSZ, n.d.). All in all, although the minimum wage is relatively high in Slovenia – when calculated as a percentage of average monthly earnings the Slovenian minimum wage in 2014 was the highest among all the EU member states for which data are provided (Eurostat) – the employers really do get a lot of flexibility for the price they pay.

REFERENCES

Annual Macro-economic Database of the European Commission's Directorate General for Economic and Financial Affairs (AMECO) (2017), 'Adjusted wage share: total economy: as percentage of GDP at current factor cost (compensation per employee as percentage of GDP at factor cost per person employed)',

accessed 12 November 2017 at http://ec.europa.eu/economy_finance/ameco/user/serie/SelectSerie.cfm.
Bembič, B. (2013), 'Kolikšna je bojna pripravljenost socialnega partnerja?', in S. Hajdini (ed.), *Prvotna akumulacija med zgodovino in konceptom*, Ljubljana: IDŠ, pp. 82–95.
Bembič, B., M. Stanojević, M. Hrženjak, M. Ignjatovič and M. Breznik (2016), 'PRECARIR Project Report, Slovenia', CELSI, Bratislava, accessed at http://www.celsi.sk/en/publications/research-reports/
Bohle, D. and B. Greskovits (2007), 'Neoliberalism, embedded neoliberalism and neocorporatism: towards transnational capitalism in Central-Eastern Europe', *West European Politics*, **30** (3), 443–66.
Bohle D. and B. Greskovits (2012), *Capitalist Diversity in Europe's Periphery*, London and Ithaca, NY: Cornell University Press.
Bole, V. (2002), 'Disinflation and labor market distortions: lessons from Slovenia', The wiiw Balkan Observatory Working Papers 020, accessed 12 November 2017 at http://www.wiiw.ac.at/disinflation-and-labor-market-distortions-lessons-from-slovenia-dlp-3306.pdf.
Bole, V. (2003), 'Managed floating as a second best option: lessons from Slovenia', EIPF Working paper No. 6, accessed 12 November 2017 at http://www.eipf.si/uploads/tx_tspagefileshortcut/wp-eipf-06-en.pdf.
Bole, V., J. Mencinger, F. Štiblar and R. Volčjak (2015), So banke odvečno breme, ki ga je treba prodati, dokler so še banke? *Gospodarska gibanja*, (479), 6–27.
Boyer, R. (2014), 'Developments and extensions of "regulation theory" and employment relations', in A. Wilkinson, G. Wood and R. Deeg (eds), *The Oxford Handbook of Employment Relations*, Oxford: Oxford University Press, pp. 114–55.
Broder, Ž. (2016), 'Sindikalno gibanje v Sloveniji od osamosvojitve do danes', MSc thesis, Fakulteta za družbene vede, Ljubljana.
Buchen, C. (2007), 'Estonia and Slovenia as antipodes', in D. Lane and M. Myant (eds), *Varieties of Capitalism in Post-Communist Countries*, Basingstoke, UK: Palgrave Macmillan, pp. 74–5.
Burroni, L. and M. Keune (2011), 'Flexicurity: a conceptual critique', *European Journal of Industrial Relations*, **17** (1), 75–91.
Crowley, S. and M. Stanojević (2011), 'Varieties of capitalism, power resources, and historical legacies: explaining the Slovenian exception', *Politics and Society*, **39** (2), 268–95.
Damijan, J.P. (2013), 'Prisilna uprava iz Bruslja', *Večer*, 13 May.
Damijan, J.P., A. Gregorič and J. Prašnikar (2004), 'Ownership concentration and firm performance in Slovenia', LICOS Discussion Paper 142/2004, Katholieke Universiteit, Leuven, accessed 12 November 2017 at http://feb.kuleuven.be/drc/licos/publications/dp/dp142.pdf.
De Stefano, V. (2009), 'Smuggling-in flexibility: temporary work contracts and the "implicit threat" mechanism', Bocconi Legal Studies Research Paper No. 1433350, Bocconi University, Milan.
Delo (2012), 'Pokojninska reforma je sprejeta', *Delo*, 4 December.
European Commission (2011), *Recommendation for a Council Recommendation on the National Reform Programme 2011 of Slovenia and Delivering a Council Opinion on the Updated Stability Programme of Slovenia 2011–2014*, Brussels: European Commission.
European Commission (2012), *Recommendation for a Council Recommendation*

on Slovenia's 2012 National Reform Programme and Delivering a Council Opinion On Slovenia's Stability Programme for 2012–2015, Brussels: European Commission.
Eurostat (2017a), 'Gini coefficient of equivalised disposable income', accessed 12 November 2017 at http://ec.europa.eu/eurostat/data/database.
Eurostat (2017b), 'Gender pay gap in unadjusted form', accessed 12 November 2017 at http://ec.europa.eu/eurostat/data/database.
Eurostat (2017c), 'Income quintile share ratio (S80/S20) by sex', accessed 12 November 2017 at http://ec.europa.eu/eurostat/data/database.
Eurostat (2017d), 'Temporary employees as percentage of the total number of employees', accessed 12 November 2017 at http://ec.europa.eu/eurostat/web/products-datasets/-/tesem110.
Feldmann, M. (2008), 'The origins of varieties of capitalism: lessons from post-Socialist transition in Estonia and Slovenia', in B. Hancké, M. Rhodes and M. Thatcher (eds), *Beyond Varieties of Capitalism: Conflicts, Complementarities and Institutional Change in European Capitalism*, Oxford: Oxford University Press, pp. 328–50.
Gospodarska zbornica Slovenije (GZS) (2014), *Business Memorandum: Diagnosis of the Situation in Slovenia.* Ljubljana: GZS, accessed 12 November 2017 at https://www.gzs.si/LinkClick.aspx?fileticket=711liaZZ-Sg%3D&portalid=55.
Gospodarska zbornica Slovenije (GZS) (2015), *Industrial Policy Manifesto*. Ljubljana: GZS, accessed 12 November 2017 at https://eng.gzs.si/Portals/English/Vsebine/novice-priponke/manifest%205.0%20ENG_web.pdf.
Gospodarska zbornica Slovenije (GZS), Association of Employers of Slovenia, Slovenian Chamber of Commerce, the Chamber of Craft and Small Business of Slovenia and the Managers' Association of Slovenia (2013), *Kisik za gospodarstvo*. Ljubljana, accessed 12 November 2017 at https://www.gzs.si/pripone/Kisik%20za%20gospodarstvo%20(2).pdf.
Gumbrell-McCormick, R. (2011), 'European trade unions and "atypical" workers', *Industrial Relations Journal*, **42** (3), 220–320.
Hassel, A. (2014), 'The paradox of liberalization – understanding dualism and the recovery of the German political economy', *British Journal of Industrial Relations*, **52** (1), 57–81.
Heery, E. (2009), 'Trade unions and contingent labour: scale and method', *Cambridge Journal of Regions, Economy and Society*, **2** (3), 429–42.
Heery, E. and B. Abbott (2000), 'Trade unions and the insecure workforce', in E. Heery and J. Salmon (eds), *The Insecure Workforce*, London and New York: Routledge, pp. 155–80.
Ibsen, C.L. and M. Mailand (2011), 'Striking a balance? Flexibility and security in collective bargaining', *Economic and Industrial Democracy*, **32** (2), 161–80.
Kajzer, A. (2015), 'Prvi učinki sprememb regulacije trga dela iz leta 2013 na segmentacijo in fleksibilnost tega trga v Sloveniji', *IB Revija*, **49** (2), 37–44.
Kalleberg, A.L. and K. Hewison (2013), 'Precarious work and the challenge for Asia', *American Behavioral Scientist*, **57** (3), 271–88.
Kavčič, F. (2014), *Ekonomsko-socialni svet 2004–2014*, Ljubljana: Uradni list.
Keune, M: (2015), 'The effects of the EU's assault on collective bargaining: less governance capacity and more inequality', *Transfer*, **21** (4), 477–83.
Keune, M. and K. Vandaele (2013), 'Wage regulation in the private sector: moving further away from a "solidaristic wage policy"?', in J. Arrowsmith and V. Pulignano (eds), *The Transformation of Employment Relations in Europe:*

Institutions and Outcomes in the Age Of Globalisation, New York: Routledge, pp. 88–110.
Lévesque, C. and G. Murray (2010), 'Understanding union power: resources and capabilities for renewing union capacity', *Transfer: European Review of Labour and Research*, **16** (3), 333–50.
Mandl, I. (2010), *Slovenia: Partial Subsidies of Full-Time Work and Partial Reimbursement of Payment Compensation*, Dublin: Eurofound.
Marginson, P. and E. Galetto (2016), 'Engaging with flexibility and security: rediscovering the role of collective bargaining', *Economic and Industrial Democracy*, **37** (1), 95–117.
Marginson, P., M. Keune and D. Bohle (2014), 'Negotiating the effects of uncertainty? The governance capacity of collective bargaining under pressure', *Transfer*, **20** (1), 37–51.
Matoz, M. (2016), 'Sindikat si sam postavlja pravila!', *Delavska enotnost*, **75** (24), 15.
Ministrstvo za delo, družino, socialne zadeve in enake možnosti (MDDSZ) (n.d.), *Primerjava nemškega Sistema 'mini job' in Zakona o maled delu*, accessed 14 November 2017 at http://www.mddsz.gov.si/si/delovna_podrocja/trg_dela_in_zaposlovanje/malo_delo/primerjava_minijob_malo_delo/.
Ministrstvo za delo, družino, socialne zadeve in enake možnosti and Urad za makroekonomske analize in razvoj (MDDSZ and UMAR) (2015), *Drugo poročilo Delovne skupine za spremljanje učinkov sprememb v regulaciji trga dela*. Ljubljana: MDDSZ and UMAR.
Mencinger, J. (2006), 'Privatization in Slovenia', *Slovenian Law Review*, **3** (1–2), 65–81.
Müller, T., T. Schulten and S. Zuckerstätter (2015), 'Wages and economic performance in Europe', in G. Van Gyes and T. Schulten (eds), *Wage Bargaining under the New European Economic Governance*, Brussels: ETUI, pp. 259–82.
Perko, M., A.S. Tršelič and A. Kajzer (2014), 'Prilagajanje trga dela v Sloveniji v obdobju 2008–2013', *IB Revija*, **48** (3–4), 21–31.
Prašnikar, J., P. Domadenik and M. Koman (2015), *Skrivnost državne lastnine v Sloveniji*. Ljubljana: EF, accessed 12 November 2017 at http://webv3ef.ef.uni-lj.si/_documents/wp/Skrivnost_drzavne_lastnine_v_Sloveniji.pdf.
Salverda, M and K. Mayhew (2009), 'Capitalist economies and wage inequality', *Oxford Review of Economic Policy*, **25** (1), 126–54.
Schulten, T. (2002), 'A European solidaristic wage policy?', *European Journal of Industrial Relations*, **8** (2), 173–96.
Selan, A.T. (2014), *Prilagoditev plač in spremembe plačne neenakosti v Sloveniji v obdobju krize*. Ljubljana: UMAR, accessed 12 November 2017 at http://www.umar.gov.si/fileadmin/user_upload/sporocila_za_javnost/2014/december/Prilagoditev_plac_in_spremembe_placne_neenakosti_v_krizi_dec14.pdf.
Silver, B. (2003), *Forces of Labor: Workers' Movements and Globalization since 1870*, Cambridge: Cambridge University Press.
Simoneti, M., M. Rojec and A. Gregorič (2004), 'Privatization, restructuring and corporate governance', in M. Mrak, M. Rojec in C. Silva-Jáuregui (eds), *Slovenia: From Yugoslavia to the European Union*, Washington, DC: World Bank, pp. 224–43.
Srakar, A. and M. Verbič (2015), 'Dohodkovna neenakost v Sloveniji in gospodarska kriza', *Teorija in praksa*, **52** (3), 538–53.
Stanojević, M. (2006), 'Mobilising human resources to improve work inten-

sity', in I. Svetlik, and B. Ilič (eds), *HRM's Contribution to Hard Work: A Comparative Analysis of Human Resource Management*, Berne: Peter Lang, pp. 157–81.
Stanojević, M. (2010), 'Vzpon in dezorganizacija neokorporativizma v Republiki Sloveniji', in V.U. Vehovar (ed.), *Neosocialna Slovenija: smo lahko socialna, obenem pa gospodarsko uspešna družba?* Koper: Annales, pp. 107–39.
Stanojević, M. (2012), 'The rise and decline of Slovenian corporatism: local and European factors', *Europe-Asia Studies*, **64** (5), 857–77.
Stanojević, M. (2015), 'Sindikalne strategije v obdobju krize', *Teorija in praksa*, **52** (3), 394–416.
Stanojević, M. and Ž. Broder (2012), 'Trade unions in Slovenia: historical development and the current situation', *SEER*, (3), 303–13.
Stanojević, M. and A. Kanjuo-Mrčela (2016), 'Social dialogue during the economic crisis: the impact of industrial relations reforms on collective bargaining in the manufacturing sector in Slovenia', in A. Koukiadaki, I. Távora and M. Martínez Lucio (eds), *Joint Regulation and Labour Market Policy in Europe during the Crisis*, Brussels: ETUI, pp. 441–97.
Stanojević, M. and M. Klarič (2013), 'The impact of socio-economic shocks on social dialogue in Slovenia', *Transfer*, **19** (2), 217–26.
Stanovnik, T. and M. Verbič (2012), 'Porazdelitev plač in dohodkov zaposlenih v Sloveniji v obdobju 1991–2009', *IB Revija*, **46** (1), 57–70.
Statistični urad Republike Slovenije (SURS) (2017a), 'At-risk-of-poverty rate by most frequent activity status, Slovenia', annually, register data, accessed 11 November 2017 at http://pxweb.stat.si/pxweb/dialog/statfile1.asp.
Statistični urad Republike Slovenije (SURS) (2017b), 'Povprečne mesečne plače in indeksi povprečnih mesečnih plač po dejavnostih (SKD 2008), Slovenija, mesečni podatki do oktobra 2015', accessed 12 November 2017 at http://pxweb.stat.si/pxweb/dialog/statfile2.asp.
Statistični urad Republike Slovenije (SURS) (2017c), 'Gross value added per employee in companies, cooperatives and at sole proprietors by size (Nace Rev. 2), Slovenia', annually, accessed 12 November 2017 at http://pxweb.stat.si/pxweb/dialog/statfile1.asp.
Traxler, F. (2010), 'Corporatism(s) and pacts: changing functions and structures under rising economic liberalism and declining liberal democracy', in P. Pochet, M. Keune and D. Natali (eds), *After the Euro and Enlargement: Social Pacts in the EU*, Brussels: ETUI, pp. 45–82.
Urad za makroekonomske analize in razvoj (UMAR) (2016), *Development Report 2016*, Ljubljana: UMAR.
Uradni list Republike Slovenije (UL RS), various issues, Ljubljana.
Vaughan-Whitehead, D. (2011), 'Introduction: has the crisis exacerbated work inequalities?', in D. Vaughan-Whitehead (ed.), *Work Inequalities in the Crisis: Evidence from Europe*, Cheltenham, UK and Geneva: Edward Elgar and ILO, pp. 1–37.
Visser, J. (2015), 'ICTWSS Data base. Version 5.0', Amsterdam: Amsterdam Institute for Advanced Labour Studies (AIAS).
Wilthagen, T. and F. Tros (2004), 'The concept of "flexicurity": a new approach to regulating employment and labour markets', *Transfer*, **10** (2), 166–86.
Wright, E.O. (2000), 'Working-class power, capitalist-class interests, and class compromise', *American Journal of Sociology*, **105** (4), 957–1002.
Zveza svobodnih sindikatov Slovenije (ZSSS) (n.d.), 'Malo delo – gola dejstva',

accessed 8 August 2016 at http://www.zsss.si/malo-delo-gola-dejstva-kaj-nam-ponuja-vlada-z-malim-delom-in-kaj-lahko-od-malega-dela-pricakujemo/.
Zveza svobodnih sindikatov Slovenije (ZSSS) (2012), *Poročilo o delu Zveze svobodnih sindikatov Slovenije med 5. in 6. Kongresom*, Ljubljana: ZSSS.

11. Industrial relations and inequality in the Spanish labour market: Resilience and change

Rafael Muñoz de Bustillo and Fernando Pinto Hernández*

1. INTRODUCTION

The internationally acclaimed success of Spain's transition from dictatorship to democracy at the end of the 1970s (Edles, 1998)[1] owes plenty to the role played by the trade unions. Although illegal until 1977, the underground trade union movement was able to colonise the official workers' associations of the dictatorship, known as vertical trade unions, carrying out limited labour action in firms, although at the risk of being imprisoned.[2] In the unstable years of the transition, when everything was being questioned and the trade union movement had the capacity to control the streets and bring the economy to a halt (see Figure 11.1 in section 2.2), trade unions played a crucial role in facilitating a peaceful transition, contributing to the rise of a new democratic order. As we will see in section 2.2, among other things, the trade unions' role was crucial in 1977 in controlling what could have easily developed otherwise into hyperinflation, backing the so-called Pactos de la Moncloa signed by major political parties. Probably as a result of the key role played by the social partners in this process of social transformation, the Spanish Constitution includes, in its preliminary title, an article stating the important socio-economic role played by trade unions and employers' associations:

> Trade unions and employers associations contribute to the defence and promotion of the economic and social interests which they represent. Their creation and the exercise of their activities shall be unrestricted in so far as they respect the Constitution and the law. Their internal structure and operation must be democratic. (Article 7)

The role of the trade unions recognised by the Spanish Constitution resulted in the development of an institutional structure of social dialogue, including the creation in 1990 of an Economic and Social Council formed by trade unions and employers' organisations (as well as representation of the so-called 'third sector') as a counselling body to the Spanish government (Article 132.1 of the Spanish Constitution) and the strengthening of the institutional role of trade unions and employers' organisations. In this spirit, the new Labour Code of 1980 consecrated the role of collective bargaining.

Three decades later, the difficulties of the Spanish economy in achieving full employment and the massive increase in unemployment resulting from the economic recession of 2008–13 led to a revision (spurred by the European Commission, the Organisation for Economic Co-operation and Development, the International Monetary Fund and the European Central Bank) of many of the core elements of the Spanish system of industrial relations, including collective agreements. This chapter reviews the role played by the system of industrial relations and collective agreements in the working of the Spanish labour market, paying special attention to the levels of security and flexibility achieved and its impact on inequality. With that aim, section 2 briefly reviews the main characteristics of the Spanish system of industrial relations with its impacts on inequalities in the world of work. This section also addresses the role played by social agreements and social consultation. Visser (2016: 3) wrote: 'The Great Recession has not been kind to collective bargaining'; for that reason, section 3 presents the major changes introduced in the system of industrial relations during the economic crisis, both in terms of labour (de)regulation and in terms of the changing power relations between workers and firms resulting from the massive increase in unemployment. Section 4 studies the impact of the system of industrial relations on the functioning and outcome of the labour market in terms of job security and income inequality. As a complement to the quantitative analysis, this section provides two successful equality-enhancing examples (case studies) of social dialogue. Section 5 presents the main conclusions of the chapter.

2. STYLISED FACTS OF THE SPANISH SYSTEM OF INDUSTRIAL RELATIONS: STRENGTHS AND WEAKNESSES

Our necessarily brief account of the Spanish system of industrial relations focuses on (1) the legal nature of the system of collective agreements, (2) the characteristics of the actors involved (trade unions and employers' associations) and (3) the role played by social dialogue at the national level.

2.1 The Spanish System of Collective Agreements and Social Dialogue Up to the Crisis

The main characteristic of the Spanish system of collective agreements is its universal nature: the principle of *erga omnes* applies. According to this principle, once a collective agreement is signed, its provisions are extended automatically to all employees working in the relevant area, beyond those belonging to the signatory organisations. As from the signing of a collective agreement its content is generally binding to all employees, in Spain all employees are covered by a collective agreement except under two circumstances: (1) employees working in sectors excluded from collective bargaining, such as civil servants or household services, and (2) if there is no collective agreement in force in the sector. Before the reform of 2012 this last circumstance was rare, owing to the existence of the principle of automatic time extension (*ultra-actividad*) of collective agreements, according to which expired collective agreements were enforceable until a new one was signed.

The automatic extension – *ex lege* – of collective agreements explains their broad coverage in Spain, even in a context of low affiliation rates (see the next section). As we can see in Figure 11.1, which presents the percentage of total employees covered by collective agreements, in 2015 (the last year with available definitive data) 69 per cent of Spanish employees were

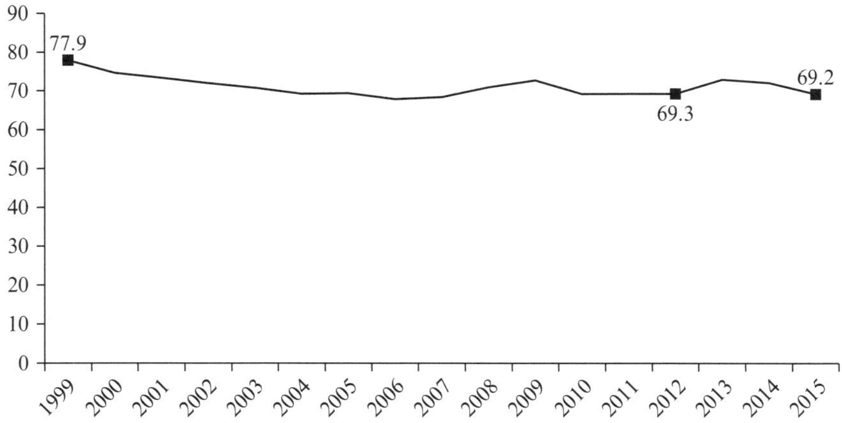

Source: Authors' analysis from EPA and Estadística de Convenios Colectivos de Trabajo, various years.

Figure 11.1 Non-adjusted collective agreement coverage rate, Spain, 1999–2015 (percentage of total employees)

covered by collective agreements.[3] Although there is a 'soft' long-run trend of decrease in the coverage rate, so far the data do not show a radical change in coverage resulting from the Great Recession of 2008–13 and the changes in labour regulation triggered by it. As we will see further on, the large coverage of collective agreements has an equalising impact in terms of wages and working conditions.

As already mentioned, some public employees, among them those with civil servant status (*funcionarios*, accounting for around 61 per cent of total public employees),[4] are excluded by law from negotiating collective agreements. In any case, civil servants have their own system of bargaining, with different regulations and restrictions (Rivero Lamas and De Val Tena, 2007).

Collective agreements can be bargained at the level of the firm or higher: national, regional, sectoral and so on. In 2015, there were 1149 collective agreements higher than firm level and 4493 at the firm level. Most employees covered by collective agreements (92 per cent) were covered by agreements higher than firm level.[5] As we will see in the next section, one of the goals of the labour reforms of 2011 and 2012 was to incentivise collective bargaining at the firm level by changing the hierarchy between collective agreements bargained at the firm level and the rest. Until 2012, in case of concurrence between firm and higher than firm collective agreements, priority was given to those at a higher level. The 2012 reform gave priority to the firm level collective agreements in most of the items bargained (wage, overtime, working time and work–life balance). The intention behind this change in regulation was to adjust the bargaining – and the resulting collective agreement – to the individual firm and its economic circumstances, based on the view (without much empirical backing to our knowledge) that collective agreements were often decoupled from the specific circumstances of firms, acting as straightjackets that reduced their survival rate, especially in a context of economic crisis. In Figure 11.2, the existence of collective agreements at the firm level has a very unequal distribution among firms according to their size: while only 15 per cent of small firms (from 5 to 49 employees)[6] have a firm-level collective agreement, in large firms of 500 employees of more, the percentage is almost 40 per cent.

To sum up, in the Spanish system of collective agreements, often characterised in the literature as centralised at an intermediate level, collective agreements by sector and regional or provincial level prevail, although national collective agreements are also important. In 2014, 35.2 per cent of employees had collective agreements at the province level, 21.3 per cent at the regional level and 32.2 per cent at national level.[7] Therefore, the spatial and economic scope of many agreements is relatively narrow. This bargaining scheme corresponds, at least partially, to the structure of the Spanish economy (Pérez Infante, 2011) as roughly half of all

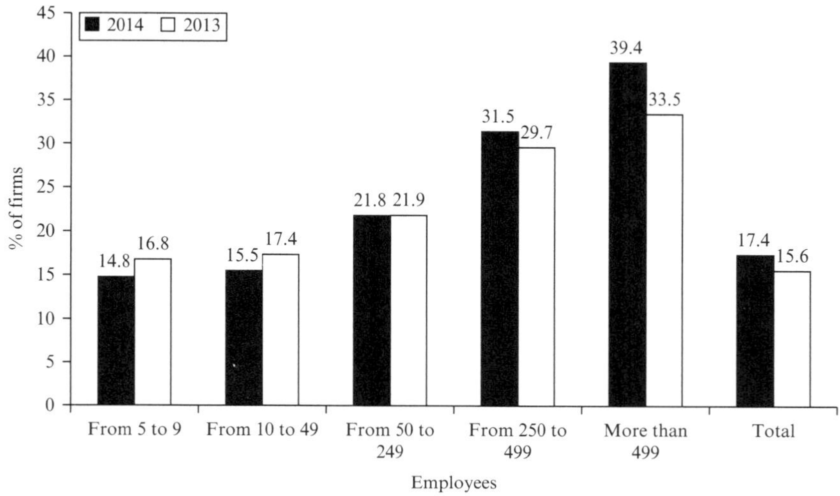

Source: Authors' analysis from Encuesta Anual Laboral, 2013, 2014.

Figure 11.2 Firms with collective agreements at the firm level, Spain, 2013–2014

employees work in firms with fewer than ten workers, where negotiation is likely to be difficult and bargaining power is not balanced. For instance, there is no legal mandate for having employees' representatives for such establishments.

Along with the level of centralisation, a new wave of economic analysis of collective agreements has called attention to the importance of the level of coordination in determining their ultimate impact on economic performance. Calmfors and Driffill (1988) argued that there was a U-like relationship between economic performance and centralisation of collective agreements, according to which decentralised and centralised agreements are associated with better economic performance (lower inflation and unemployment rates) than those with intermediate levels of centralisation. However, the latest wave of analysis in this field argues convincingly that as important as the level of centralisation is the level of coordination of the different bargaining units intervening in collective bargaining, both in terms of horizontal coordination, understood as coordination among the bargaining units in different sectors/regions, and vertical coordination, understood as the capacity of trade unions and employers' associations to guarantee discipline among their members in applying the guiding principles to local bargaining (Traxler, 2003; Traxler and Brand, 2012).

In Spain, usually – although not always – the two major trade unions (Comisiones Obreras, CCOO, and Unión General de Trabajadores, UGT) and the Spanish Confederation of Business Organisations (Confederación Española de Organizaciones Empresariales, CEOE) agree on the general lines of collective bargaining in a document. Such is the case of the Third Agreement for Employment and Collective Bargaining (III AENC) signed in 2015, laying down the guidelines to the bargaining units for 2015–17 regarding wage growth, training, gender wage gap and so on. It can be argued (Cruz Villalón, 2015) that when the impact on these types of agreements is taken into consideration, the Spanish system of collective agreements presents a much higher level of centralisation and coordination than is usually the case.[8]

A final element to address in this section is the range of items considered in collective agreements. Almost all deal with wage setting, but most usually go beyond that to include other items, such as working time, overtime, employment and non-discrimination. As the range of items considered in collective agreements is very large, Table 11.1 presents a selection of the most common items (those present in collective agreements affecting at least 40 per cent of employees covered).

As seen in Table 11.1, the majority (77 per cent) of collective agreements – in terms of employees affected – deal with irregular distribution of working time, one of the items in which firms have shown more interest in the recent past. The same applies to overtime – including type of compensation – and the classification of jobs. However, what is usually not included in collective agreements is as informative as what is included. In this regard only 22 per cent of employees have collective agreements that include provisions on the transformation of temporary into open-ended contracts and only 21 per cent benefit from limits on the maximum number of temporary contracts. Clauses on outsourcing are also rare, affecting only 18 per cent of employees.

2.2 Actors: Trade Unions and Employers' Associations

In order to get a closer view of the nature of the Spanish system of industrial relations it is important to get to know the social partners negotiating them. First, this is because the strength of social partners in terms of knowledge of the sector or bargaining skills is vital in order to result in collective agreements that address workers' problems without compromising competitiveness. Secondly, it is because the legitimacy of collective agreements will depend on the level of representativeness of the social partners negotiating them.

Table 11.1 Most frequent items included in collective agreements, Spain, 2015

	Employees affected	(%)
Wage structure	3 548 975	98.6
Working time		
Irregular annual distribution of working time	2 742 211	77.3
Participation of trade union representatives in irregular distribution of working time	1 711 766	48.23
Measures to improve work–life balance	1 816 204	51.2
Paid leave for family reasons improving on statutory law	2 629 369	74.1
duration of leave	2 420 741	68.2
new leaves included	2 279 686	64.2
Accumulation of lactation hours in full working days	2 594 409	73.1
Overtime		
Compensation of overtime with money	2 398 880	67.6
valued more than a standard hour	1 909 023	53.8
Compensation of overtime with time	2 047 323	57.7
Employment and contracts		
Clauses regarding contracts	2 863 973	80.7
temporary contracts for productive reasons	1 894 634	53.4
training contracts	2 193 361	61.8
Training		
Training	2 130 752	60.0
Professional classification and functional mobility		
Professional classification by definition of group functions, categories, etc.	3 213 913	90.6
	3 057 156	86.1
	1 523 816	42.9
	1 498 972	42.2
Retirement		
Clauses regarding retirement	1 423 499	40.1
Complements to public social benefits		
Complements to different public social benefits	3 175 280	89.7
sick leave	2 247 000	63.3
labour accident and professional leave	2 831 953	79.8
Trade union activity		
Accumulation of trade union hours in a single employee	2 486 462	70.1
Application and interpretation of collective agreements		
Procedure to solve controversies derived from the application of collective agreements	3 342 741	94.5

Source: Authors' analysis from Estadística de Convenios Colectivos de Trabajo 2015.

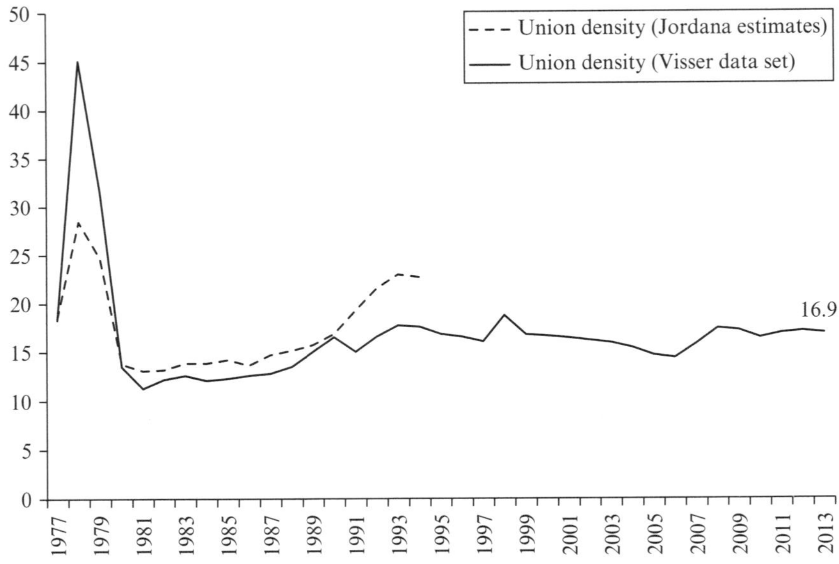

Note: * Jordana estimates are based on trade union affiliations (members paying union dues, excluding retired workers); Visser's estimates are bases on survey data.

Source: Authors' analysis from Jordana (2007: 216), and Visser (2015).

Figure 11.3 Evolution of trade union density rates, Spain, 1977–2013 (percentage)*

2.2.1 Trade unions in Spain

As mentioned in the introduction, trade unions in Spain were illegal until 1977. After their legalisation, trade union affiliations showed two trends (Figure 11.3). During their first few years of legal existence there was a short-lived explosion of affiliations. As argued by Jordana (2007), this increase was largely exaggerated as a result of the fierce competition among trade unions in the early days (and the consequent inflation of their affiliation rates in order to show greater power) and the lack of a clear concept of affiliation. In any case, the first few years of legal trade unions mark the highest and lowest affiliation rates. According to Jordana (2007), several factors colluded to produce this result, including the economic crisis and the intense industrial restructuring that followed, the increase in unemployment, a weak trade union culture, the system of employee representation adopted (decoupled from trade union coverage and based on the results of union elections) and the trial and error behaviour of workers, testing to what extent affiliation to a trade union was worthwhile.

After the correction of the big increase of the late 1970s, affiliation rates show a surprising stability compared with their behaviour in the rest of the European Union (EU) 15. In this sense, we can say that Spain has low but stable affiliation rates. That is, low compared with the Scandinavian countries (near 70 per cent) or Belgium (55 per cent), and stable, as Spain is one of the few EU countries in which affiliation rates have been unaffected by the general declining trend: since 1980 affiliation rates have decreased by 50 per cent in the United Kingdom, by 57 per cent in France and by 48 per cent in Germany, for example.[9]

Two issues have to be taken into consideration for the proper interpretation of affiliation rates in Spain in terms of the legitimacy and strength of trade unions. The first, of a more general nature, are the problems related to the narrow definition of affiliation (paying union dues) compared with other wider concepts, such as workers' sympathy with the union movement. The second, of a more country-specific nature, is that, according to Spanish labour legislation, trade union representativeness is determined by the outcomes of union elections every four years. The role given to elections in the workplace and the general extension of collective agreements has the effect of decoupling, both from the union and the workers' sides, trade union legitimacy and strength from affiliation rates. On the trade union side, their role as workers' representatives is related to the electoral outcome, not affiliation. On the workers' side, and due to the automatic extension of collective agreements, the advantages related to the existence of an agreement are identical for affiliated and non-affiliated workers. For this reason, in order to address the issue of trade union legitimacy, we have to turn to the results of union elections as well as to the presence of workers' representatives in the firms.

According to Spanish regulations, the representation of employees in firms of between 10 and 49 employees is performed by *delegados de personal* (shop stewards) – from one to three, depending on size of firm. Representation in larger firms is assumed by *Comités de Empresa* (works councils). Smaller firms (from six to nine workers) can also elect *delegados de personal* if decided by a majority of employees. The election of works council members and *delegados de personal* takes place in country-wide trade union elections every four years. The elected members have a right to a certain number of paid hours for trade union activities (from 15 to 40 hours per month, depending on size of firm) which can be accumulated by a single person.

All firms with ten or more employees (six or more if decided by the employees) have the right to hold trade union elections, but not all firms have them, as it is necessary to present candidates. In this respect, the presence of a trade union in the firm is central to the holding of elections. Figure 11.4 reproduces the process of narrowing down the total number of

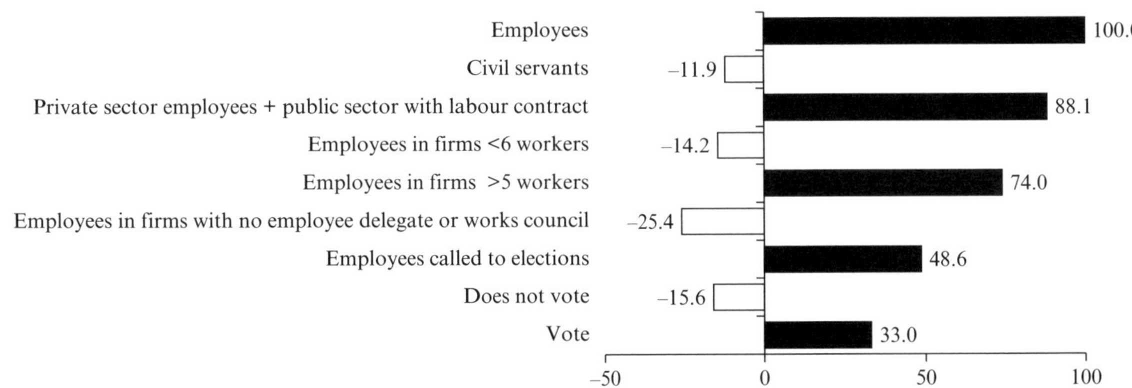

Source: Authors' analysis from Alós et al. (2015: 101).

Figure 11.4 Employees participating in trade union elections, Spain, 2012

employees until reaching the percentage of employees actually voting. In order to reach this number first we have to deduct civil servants (with their own representation bodies and elections), then employees in firms with fewer than six workers (14.2 per cent), after that, employees working in firms without delegates or works councils, that is, with nobody to call the elections (25.4 per cent).[10] In total, 48.6 per cent of employees are called on to vote in elections. After discounting those not voting (around one-third), we arrive at the total number of employees voting in trade union elections: 33 per cent of total employees (37 per cent not taking into consideration civil servants).

There are two different ways of reading Figure 11.4. The first, positive, reading is the relatively high participation rate of 67 per cent; two-thirds of eligible employees vote. The second perspective, clearly less positive, is that only 37 per cent of all employees (excluding civil servants) vote for the trade unions involved in collective bargaining. Even taking the less advantageous perspective, the percentage of involvement in trade union elections is twice as high as the affiliation rate. From a different perspective, according to the European Company Survey 2013, more than half (57.5 per cent) of firms of ten employees or more had trade union representation, well over the EU average of 32 per cent, in line with countries such as Belgium, the Netherlands or France, although below countries such as Denmark (78 per cent) or Finland (70 per cent).

Regarding the demography of trade union affiliations, employees with open-ended contracts have higher affiliation rates, at 20.4 per cent compared with 13 per cent among temporary employees (average rate, 16.4 per cent). Affiliation rates are also higher among men (17.8 per cent) compared with women (14.8 per cent) and in activities dominated by the public sector such as public administration and social security (33 per cent), education (25 per cent) or health and social services (22 per cent). Finally, affiliation rates are also much higher in large firms (250 employees or more), at 29 per cent, compared with small and medium-sized enterprises (SMEs): 6 per cent in firms with fewer than 10 employees, 12 per cent in firms from 10 to 49 employees.[11]

To conclude this section, we should point out that the Spanish trade union landscape is dominated by two main trade unions: CCOO and UGT,[12] with more than 70 per cent of trade union delegates elected at the last elections (Table 11.2). Moreover these two trade unions practise, at least at the level of their confederations, what is called *unidad de acción* (unity of action), presenting more often than not a unified bargaining position vis-à-vis employers and the state. Programmatically speaking, both trade unions have among their aims the reduction of inequalities in the world of work, and in society in general. For instance, in a major

Table 11.2 Distribution of trade union delegates in the past three elections, Spain, 2003, 2007 and 2013

	2003	2007	2013
CCOO	38.8	38.8	37.4
UGT	36.5	36.9	35.1
Generalist trade union	5.0	5.0	5.6
Corporatist trade union	6.0	6.1	7.3
Nationalist trade union	6.3	6.5	6.3
Rest	4.7	4.8	6.3
Non-trade union	2.7	2.0	2.0
CCOO + UGT:	75.3	75.7	72.5

Source: Authors' analysis from Alós et al. (2015: 114).

CCOO document (CCOO, 2016a: 103–4) we can read: 'The general strategy of the trade union has to be based in promoting a social U-turn . . . and the improvement of living conditions for workers . . . and society as a whole (tax reform, social benefits, fight against poverty and inequality, fight against gender inequality, . . .)'. Likewise, in the evaluation report of the 2011–15 legislature, the UGT argue in favour of a new strategy to confront the growth of inequalities in different spheres of life and the growth of poverty pockets (UGT, 2015).

2.2.2 The other side: employers' organisations

The development of employers' associations in Spain has been affected by two things. The first is the lack of a culture of association, the legacy of a dictatorial regime in which firms profited from the state's control over workers' demands, but in which they lacked direct, organic representation (Aguilar, 1985). The end of the dictatorship caught firms without an organisation to defend their interests in turbulent times and without their natural ally.[13] The second is the highly atomised structure of Spanish firms. Out of the 3.1 million firms registered in Spain in 2015, 55 per cent had no employees. Of those with employees, 83 per cent had from one to five employees. In contrast, only 0.8 per cent had 100 or more employees. In absolute terms, in 2015 there were 1727 firms with more than 500 employees. This implies that there is a highly polarised panorama of firms, with millions of businesses with fewer than ten employees, on one side, and very few large firms, on the other (less than 1000 firms with more than 1000 workers).

As argued by Aguilar (1985), the initiatives to organise Spanish firms followed different strategies, ranging from the revitalisation of old structures such as the Catalonian employers' organisation Fomento del Trabajo Nacional, created in 1889, to the development of new associations related to the old vertical trade unions and the creation of new structures connected to entrepreneurs enjoying dominant positions in given sectors or regions. Drawing from all these groups, in 1977 the CEOE was created. The CEOE started with more a reactive than a proactive mandate, to defend the position of business in highly turbulent times, when business was reproached for its connivance with the old regime. Half a century later, business organisations have normalised their position in society and developed to become a central part of the system of industrial relations, now with a clearly proactive position. According to the CEOE, the confederation is made up of more than 4000 base associations, including SMEs, represented by their own confederation, Confederación Española de la Pequeña y Mediana Empresa (Spanish Confederation of Small and Medium Enterprises, CEPYME), integrated in the CEOE.

In terms of the participation of firms in business organisations, as we can see in Figure 11.5, which presents the association rates of Spanish firms with five or more employees (17 per cent of firms with employees), association rates are higher in larger firms, while overall only one-quarter of firms belong to business organisations. The aggregate association rate for the whole universe of firms (with employees) is smaller (as probably the association rate of firms with fewer than five employees is much lower).

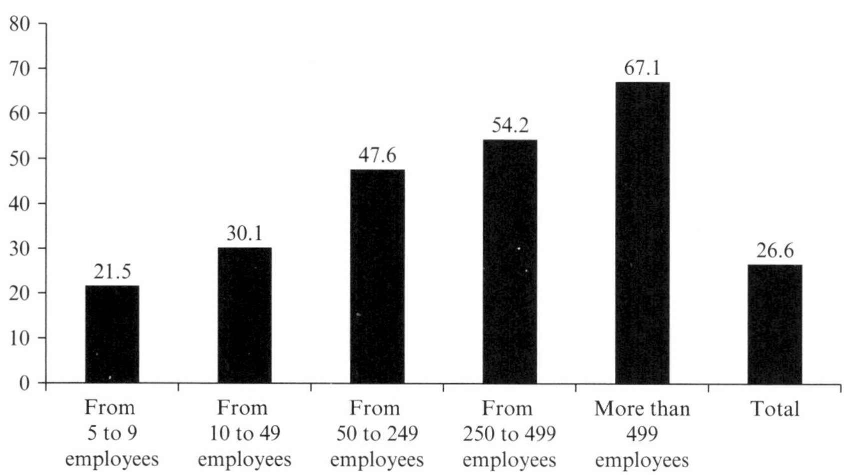

Source: Authors' analysis from Encuesta Annual Laboral 2014.

Figure 11.5 Firms belonging to business associations, Spain, 2014

Looking at the decreasing association rate as we reduce the size of the firm we could speculate (assuming an association rate of 10 per cent for firms with fewer than five employees) an overall rate of association of 12 per cent.[14]

2.3 Beyond Collective Agreements: Social Dialogue from a Long-run Perspective

As mentioned in the introduction, since the democratic transition – '*la Transición*' – Spain has managed to develop a long, although winding and discontinuous, history of social dialogue under different configurations. This is remarkable considering the lack of tradition in this area and the sharp confrontation between social agents existing in the late 1970s, after 40 years of lack of freedoms, including the freedoms of speech or association. The importance given to the role of social dialogue in the years of construction of the new democratic Spain is reflected in the introduction in the Constitution of 1978 of Article 131.2 mandating the creation of a council, of a tripartite nature, to advise the government on economic and distributional issues. With that aim, in 1991 the Consejo Económico y Social (Social and Economic Council) was created, formed by representatives of trade unions (20 councillors), employers' organisations (20 councillors) and the 'third sector' (14 councillors representing agriculture and fishing organisations, consumers' organisations and the 'social economy', and six socio-economic experts).

In order to give an idea of the output, in terms of social pacts, of these 40 years of social dialogue, Table 11.3 presents the major national wide agreements reached during three broad phases of social dialogue in Spain.[15] The first roughly goes from the democratic transition to the joining of the European Economic Community. It was a period of strong institutional change, economic and social uncertainty and growing unemployment. The agreements reached in this first phase present all possible combinations (García Laso, 1992): bilateral (in the first part of the period only with the participation of the UGT), trilateral or even of a political nature with indirect backing of the trade unions, as in the Moncloa Pacts. These social pacts were developed with the direct or indirect involvement of governments of the centre-right (Unión del Centro Democrático, UCD, 1977–82) and social democracy (1982–86). Paradoxically, the first crisis of social agreements came when the economy was finally recovering from the long economic crisis associated with the transition. The years of economic growth and rising employment of the second half of the 1980s and until the crisis of 1993 witnessed an increase in industrial unrest and strikes and confrontation between the trade unions and the government.

Table 11.3 Main social agreements or social pacts in Spain, 1977–2015

Year	Party in government	Denomination	Signed by	Main aspects
Phase I. The age of the Grand Pacts: 1977–86				
1977	UCD	Pactos de la Moncloa	Political parties (backed by trade unions)	Diverse measures of economic policy: fiscal reform, social security, etc./new mechanism of wage growth based on expected and not past prices to control inflation (1977–78)
1979	UCD	Acuerdo Básico Interconferderal, ABI	CEOE and UGT	Elements of regulation of labour market later included in the Labour Code (Ley 8/1980)
1980	UCD	Acuerdo Marco Interconfederal, AMI	CEOE and UGT (+USO)	Items dealing with wage policy, working time, union rights, etc. (1980–81)
1981	UCD	Acuerdo Nacional de Empleo, ANE	Government, CEOE, CCOO and UGT	Income policy, employment, and unemployment benefits (1981–82)
1983	PSOE	Acuerdo Interconfederal, AI	CEOE-CEPYME, CCOO and UGT	Income policy, productivity, absenteeism and retirement
1984	PSOE	Acuerdo Económico y social	Government, CCOO, UGT and CEOE-CEPYME	Diverse measures of economic policy, income policy, productivity, absenteeism and conflict solving instruments (1984–86)
Phase II. Crisis in social dialogue: 1987–94				
1990	PSOE	Acuerdo sobre aspectos relacionados con el empleo y la concertación social	Government, CCOO and UGT	Information rights to employees' delegates (in a context of concern about the growth of temporary employment)

Table 11.3 (continued)

Year	Party in government	Denomination	Signed by	Main aspects
1990	PSOE	Acuerdo en materia de pensiones	Government, CCOO and UGT	Improvement in non-contributory retirement pension. Compromise to increase retirement pensions by CPI
1992	PSOE	Acuerdos en materia de formación continua	CCOO, UGT and CEOE-CEPYME + government	Development of a system of continuous training
Phase III. The age of diminishing expectations: specific agreements 1995–2015				
	PSOE	Acuerdo para la solución extrajudicial de conflictos laborales, ASEC	CCOO, UGT and CEOE-CEPYME	Promotion of mediation and arbitrage through the Servicio Interconfederal de Mediación y Arbitraje (SIMA)
1996	PP	Acuerdo tripartito sobre formación profesional	CCOO, UGT and CEOE-CEPYME	Main lines of vocational training
	PP	II Acuerdo nacional de formación continua	CCOO, UGT and CEOE-CEPYME	Development of a system of continuous training (follow-up of the 1992 agreement)
	PP	Acuerdo interconfederal para la Estabilidad en el empleo, AIEE	CCOO, UGT and CEOE-CEPYME	New open-ended contract with lower dismissal costs. Unification of part-time contracts. Relaxation of fair dismissal regulation
1997	PP	Acuerdo interconfederal sobre negociación colectiva, AINC	CCOO, UGT and CEOE-CEPYME	Content of collective agreements, right to information and consultation
	PP	Acuerdo interconfederal sobre covertura de vacios, AICV	CCOO, UGT and CEOE-CEPYME	Solution of issues related to the derogation of pre-democratic labour regulation (*ordenanzas laborales*)

2000	PP	II Acuerdo nacional de formación continua	CCOO, UGT, CIG, CEOE-CEPYME, Ministry of Labour	Development of a system of continuous training (follow-up of the 1996 agreement)
2001	PP	Acuerdo para la solución extrajudicial de conflictos laborales, ASEC-II	CCOO, UGT and CEOE-CEPYME	Promotion of mediation and arbitrage
2002	PP	Acuerdo interconfederal para la negociación colectiva, AINC II	CCOO, UGT and CEOE-CEPYME	Guidelines for collective bargaining
2003	PP	Acuerdo interconfederal para la negociación colectiva, AINC 2003	CCOO, UGT and CEOE-CEPYME	Guidelines for collective bargaining
2004	PSOE	Acuerdo para la solución extrajudicial de conflictos laborales, ASEC-III	CCOO, UGT and CEOE-CEPYME	Promotion of mediation and arbitrage
2005	PSOE	Acuerdo para la solución extrajudicial de conflictos laborales, ASEC-III	CCOO, UGT and CEOE-CEPYME	Follow up of SEC-I
	PSOE	Acuerdo interconfederal para la negociación colectiva, AINC 2005	CCOO, UGT and CEOE-CEPYME	Guidelines for collective bargaining
2006	PSOE	Acuerdo sobre mejora del crecimiento y el empleo, AMCE	CCOO, UGT and CEOE-CEPYME + Government	Promotion of permanent employment, limitation of chain temp contracts, increase in resources of Labour Inspectorate, improvement of unemployment protection
2007	PSOE	Acuerdo interconfederal para la negociación colectiva, AINC 2007	CCOO, UGT and CEOE-CEPYME	Guidelines for collective bargaining
2010	PSOE	Acuerdo para el empleo y la Negociación Colectiva, AENC	CCOO, UGT and CEOE-CEPYME	Guidelines for collective bargaining for 2010–12

Table 11.3 (continued)

Year	Party in government	Denomination	Signed by	Main aspects
2011	PSOE	Acuerdo para la Reforma y el fortalecimiento del Sistema Público de Pensiones	CCOO, UGT and CEOE-CEPYME + Government	Reform of retirement pensions: increase in retirement age (67), increase in the number of working years used in the calculation of pension rights, etc.
2011	PSOE	Acuerdo para el empleo y la Negociación Colectiva, II AENC	CCOO, UGT and CEOE-CEPYME	Guidelines for collective bargaining for 2012–2014
2013	PP	V Acuerdo sobre Solución Autónoma de Conflictos Laborales (Sistema Extrajudicial)	CCOO, UGT and CEOE-CEPYME	Promotion of mediation and arbitrage
2015	PP	Acuerdo para el empleo y la Negociación Colectiva, IIIAENC	CCOO, UGT and CEOE-CEPYME	Guidelines for collective bargaining for 2015–17

Source: Authors' analysis from Moreneo et al. (2015).

These were the days of the demand for a 'Social Turn' (*Giro Social*), which encapsulates the demands for compensation, in terms of wages and further development of the welfare state, for the sacrifices endured by workers and the population in general during the long years of growing unemployment and stagnation. A successful general strike on 14 December 1988 facilitated the few social agreements produced during this period. Among them was the only major social policy programme developed since the consolidation of the welfare state in the early 1980s, the creation of a universal (means-tested) system of non-contributory pensions in 1990 and the compromise to index old age pensions to the Consumer Price Index (CPI). This agreement is a good example of how social dialogue contributes to higher equality, exceeding the area of narrowly defined labour issues to cover other areas, such as social protection.

It is also worth highlighting that social agreements were signed under governments of different ideologies, with no simple relationship between the political ideology of the government and the intensity and richness of the agreements. During the first, more fruitful period, the party in power was the centre-right UCD. The coming to power of the Socialist Party (Partido Socialista Obrero Español, PSOE), in theory closer to the trade unions (and with a 'brother' trade union the UGT), did not lead to an intensification of social dialogue. Quite the opposite, it practically ended the traditional close relations between the party and the trade unions and cost the government three general strikes (1985, 1988 and 1992). Although it could be argued that the purely bipartite agreements signed among trade unions and employers' associations are largely free from political upheavals, often the social partners' willingness to negotiate is related to their level of closeness to the party in government. A clear example of this is the CEOE's lack of interest in negotiating labour issues during the recent economic crisis.

The change of government of 1996, from socialist to conservative (Partido Popular, PP), is another good example of the non-linearity of the relations between social dialogue and government ideology, as it led to an intensification of social agreements in what was been called 'the third conservative way' (Hamann, 2005). The honeymoon lasted only one mandate, as in the second mandate, then with an absolute majority in parliament, the position of the government became much more confrontational.[16] The years of the Great Recession witnessed a stalemate with regard to social agreements, especially after the unilateral approval of two consecutive labour reforms in 2011 and 2012. Nevertheless, the channels of dialogue remained open. Among the agreements reached, we highlight the social agreement on pension reforms signed, *in extremis*, by major trade unions, backing the first of the two pension reforms approved during the crisis. Following a trade union proposal, the reform introduced the recognition of extra years of social contributions to working mothers to compensate for their temporary abandonment of the labour market. Also in the field of social protection, trade unions campaigned all through the crisis in order to prolong the duration of unemployment assistance for the long-term unemployed. As a result, in 2014 an agreement between the government and social actors was reached extending (means-tested) unemployment assistance through a new Programme of Activation to Employment (PAE).

Before concluding this section, it is worth looking at labour conflict in Spain to see whether the intensity of social dialogue and collective bargaining is reflected in lower rates of such conflict; one of the goals of social dialogue is to take confrontation between social partners from the streets to the bargaining table. The relation is not always straightforward, as strikes might be used as instruments of pressure to improve the trade union bargaining position, to show their strength. Figure 11.6 presents the evolution of labour unrest using as indicator total number of working days lost to industrial action per 100 000 employees. Figure 11.6 shows the transition in the late 1970s from a regimen of repressed labour conflict, as

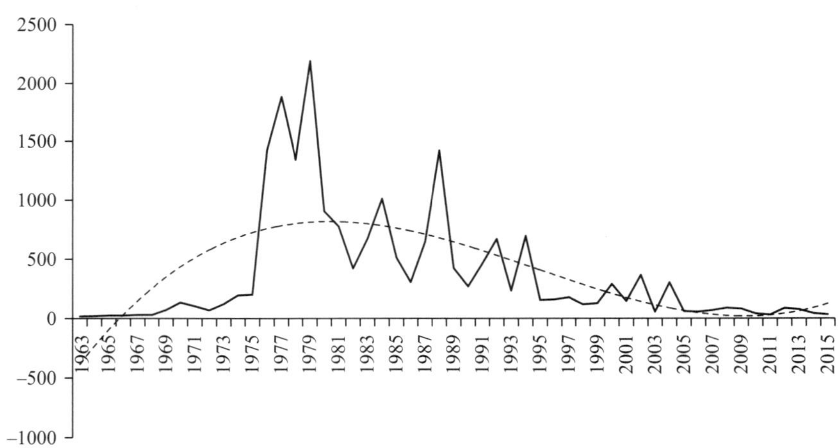

Note: * The data corresponding to 2010 are not included due to the lack of data on the strikes by public employees of 8 June and the General Strike of 29 September.

Source: Authors' analysis from Luque (2013: 267–8), EPA and Estadística de Huelgas y Cierres Patronales.

Figure 11.6 Labour conflict, Spain, 1963–2015 (days of work lost per 100 000 employees)*

a result of the lack of political and labour rights, to a high labour conflict situation, as the political transition opened the 'pressure cooker'. After a first few years of extensive confrontation, the choice in favour of the path of social dialogue facilitated the reduction of labour unrest. This reduction was halted by the crisis of social dialogue in the second half of the 1980s, but the trend was resumed with the new decade (Luque, 2013). The start of the crisis and, more specifically, the second part of it related to the change of economic policy from a countercyclical fiscal policy to austerity, led to a change in this panorama, although at a much lower scale of conflict. This time, much of the social unrest was articulated outside the workplace and through popular citizens' movements, in many cases with trade union participation, but not necessarily led by them. The different natures of these protests and demonstrations means that they are not included in Figure 11.6. To give an idea of their dimensions, according to the European Social Survey (ESS), in 2012 as many as 26 per cent of Spaniards (the highest among the countries included in the ESS) participated in lawful public demonstrations, compared with an EU average of only 7 per cent.

3. CHANGES IN COLLECTIVE AGREEMENT REGULATION AND SOCIAL DIALOGUE DURING THE GREAT RECESSION: RATIONALE AND IMPACT

The permanent high level of unemployment of the Spanish economy since the transition has led, almost since the enactment of the Labour Code in 1980, to a quasi-permanent state of labour regulation reform. Although the huge increase in unemployment of the period 2008–13 (from 7 to 26 per cent) was clearly a by-product of the Great Recession (Muñoz de Bustillo, 2014a, 2014b) and the collapse of construction, one of the most labour-intensive sectors in the economy,[17] the second (approved in 2010–11 under a socialist government) and third packages (approved in 2012 under a conservative government)[18] of policy measures aimed at addressing the crisis included important elements of labour market deregulation. The rationale behind them was twofold. On the one hand, measures were taken to reduce the employment protection gap existing between employees with open-ended and those with temporary contracts, reducing the redundancy costs of the former and increasing the termination costs of the latter. On the other hand, measures were taken aimed at the flexibilisation and decentralisation of collective agreements. The declared purpose of these measures was to facilitate the adaptation of collective agreements to the specific situation of the firms operating in different economic contexts, as well as facilitating the use of other adjustment mechanisms than dismissals.

Before briefly explaining the measures taken and their impact on the system of collective agreements and the agreements themselves, it is important to know to what extent firms were satisfied with the state of affairs. Figure 11.7 presents the results of the *Encuesta Anual Laboral* (Annual Labour Survey) run by the Ministry of Employment and Social Security in 2013 and 2014 on a sample of firms (with five or more employees) regarding, among other things, their level of satisfaction with the collective agreements in force. As we can see, a large majority of firms, of all sizes, declared themselves quite or very satisfied with their collective agreement.[19] Although the data correspond to the years after the reform was enacted, as most collective agreements are multi-annual, in most cases we are talking about agreements that were already in force before the reform. Moreover, when asked why they do not have an enterprise agreement, most firms – 77 per cent – answered that it was because the sectoral agreement suits their needs.

The two labour reforms conducted during the crisis affected the regulation of collective agreements with regard to the following:

- Firms are given the option of halting the implementation of the collective agreement in force in areas such as wages, working conditions and so on. Although the non-implementation of specific aspects of the collective agreement has to be justified and negotiated with employees, in case of a lack of agreement the decision is taken by an Arbitration and Mediation Committee in which trade unions are in the minority.[20] So far, firms do not seem to be making much use of this possibility. According to the Encuesta de Formación de Salarios (Salary Training Survey; Izquierdo and Jimeno, 2015), in 2014 only 3.7 per cent of those firms with sectoral collective agreements made use of it (1.9 per cent of those with a firm level collective agreement). For 2015, the administrative data of the Ministry of Employment (Estadística de convenios colectivos de trabajo, Statistics of Collective Bargaining Agreements) record 1437 cases of non-implementation, in 1254 firms, affecting 43 173 employees. In most cases such a process was agreed (91 per cent).
- Although not directly related to collective agreements, the first of the labour reforms eased the terms on which firms can modify working conditions (Article 41 of the Labour Code). In the opinion of the trade unions this option, on which no data are available, is being widely used by firms to change working conditions, as it is less costly and regulated than derogation from collective agreements. Often

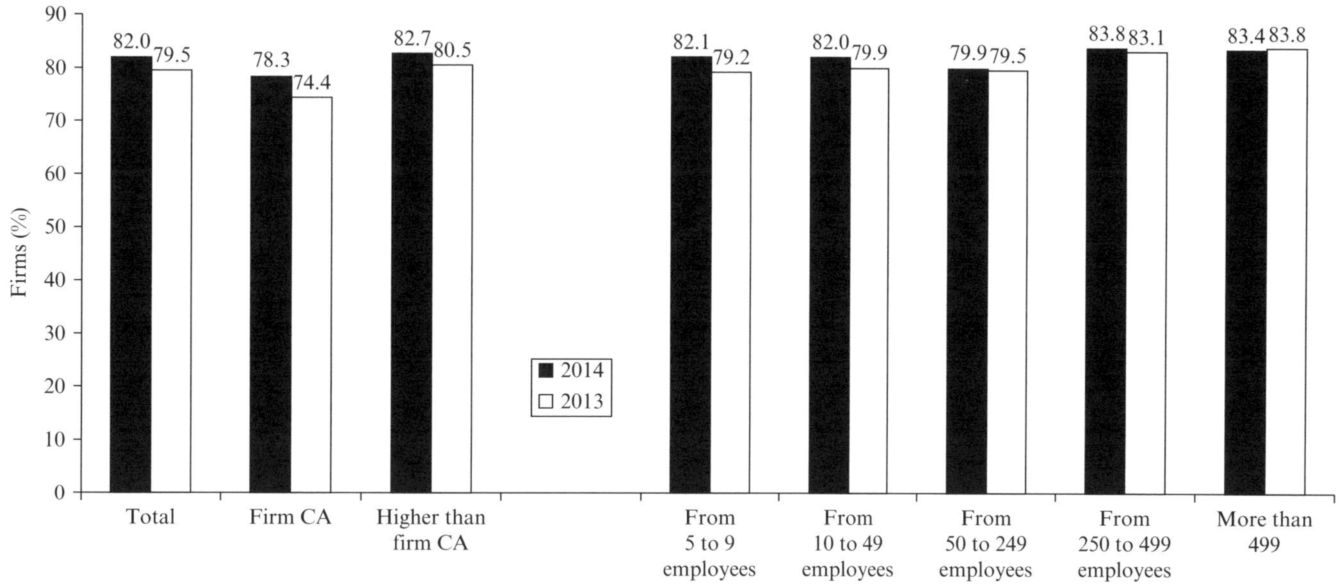

Note: * Only firms with five or more employees.

Source: Authors' analysis from Encuesta Anual Laboral.

Figure 11.7 Firms quite satisfied or very satisfied with their collective agreements, Spain, 2013–14*

both measures are taken simultaneously, the former addressed to those elements of working conditions set above the collective agreement and the latter addressed to those laid down in it (Peñas and Aguilera, 2016).

- Pre-eminence is given to firm-level collective agreements. Since the reform, working conditions set in collective agreements at firm level have priority over those laid down at higher levels. The pre-eminence of firm collective agreements includes most major labour issues dealt with in agreements: (1) basic salary and extra allowances, (2) allowances related to firm performance, (3) overtime and shift allowances, (4) working time and working time distribution, (5) professional classification, (6) contract policy and (7) work–life balance.
- When a collective agreement expires, its conditions will only be applicable for one year. If another collective agreement is not signed during the following year, the working conditions of the firms in the sector will follow whatever other higher level agreement is in force (or the Labour Code, if there is none). Before the reform, the principle of *ultra-actividad* (application beyond expiry) warranted the automatic time extension of the conditions set in the expired collective agreement until a new one was signed. Faced with the risk that in July 2013, after the end of the transitory period included in the reform, many sectors and workers could lose the protection of their already expired collective agreements, the social partners signed an agreement in order to allow, by mutual accord, the extension of the period.[21] This agreement is indicative of the will of the social partners to continue negotiating even when the new regulation allowed firms to benefit from the phasing out of existing collective agreements. In any case, the end of 'application beyond expiry' had a profound impact on the power leverage of employers vis-à-vis employees. As argued by a representative of Confemetal, the employers' confederation of the metal industry: 'Nobody is interested in the decline of the agreement. Another issue is that, from a business point of view, the disappearance of application beyond expiry is being used to obtain other benefits; it is used as a bargaining strategy' (Fernández Rodríguez et al., 2016: 32).

However, equally as important as these changes is that, for the first time, the reform of collective agreements was decided without effective consultation and agreement with the social partners. The reform of 2012 was passed just ten days after the publication of the Second Agreement on Employment and Collective Bargaining signed by major trade unions and employers' organisations setting the guidelines for collective bargaining for

2012–14. The warm embracing of the reform by employers' organisations has not contributed to a spirit of loyal bargaining among social actors, thereby weakening the process of social dialogue and producing a feeling of despair among trade unions. After all, what is the point of engaging in long negotiations if the results are completely wiped out by unilaterally approved legislation?

These changes in the regulation of collective agreements were accompanied by a reduction of subsidies to trade unions and employers' organisations (around a 60 per cent reduction according to CCOO, 2016a) and a withdrawal from trade union agreements with the public administration at different levels to allow for free working time for union delegates (above the legal requirements) to reinforce trade union structures.[22] In a completely different sphere, but also affecting trade union action, there has been a hardening of the position of the Public Prosecutor's Office regarding the role of trade unionists in strikes and the limits on picketing, leading to an unprecedented rise in the number of trade unionists taken to court. According to Morillo (2015), in 2015, 260 persons faced prison sentences for a total of 120 years for strike-related actions; in 2016, 300 trade unionists were on trial for participating in picketing.

To summarise, although it is certainly too soon to present an evaluation of the reforms, we can say that so far there has not been a major change in the structure of collective agreements. The level of coverage, as far as we know with the limited data available (until 2014), has not been much affected (see Figure 11.1), the structure still favours collective agreements of higher than firm level (although firm-level agreements are on the rise), social actors, as in the past, have maintained their collaboration in terms of approving a general framework for collective bargaining, and withdrawal from collective agreements has been kept at a low level, partly owing to the limits set by the judiciary. However, that does not mean that things are 'business as usual', as the main impact of the reform has been on the content of collective agreements. The elimination of many of the existing checks and balances has led to the emptying of collective agreements (Cruces Aguilera et al., 2016), especially regarding wages, to a position of defensive bargaining by trade unions aimed at maintaining the collective agreements in existence. According to a trade union representative, the reforms have changed the attitude of firms at the bargaining table from trying to give as little as possible to trying to obtain as much as possible (Cruces Aguilera et al., 2016).

One way of looking at the impact of the reform in this regard is by comparing in a given year the wage growth of collective agreements signed in previous years, in the current year and in the following years (with retroactive effects). As we can see in Figure 11.8, the wage growth

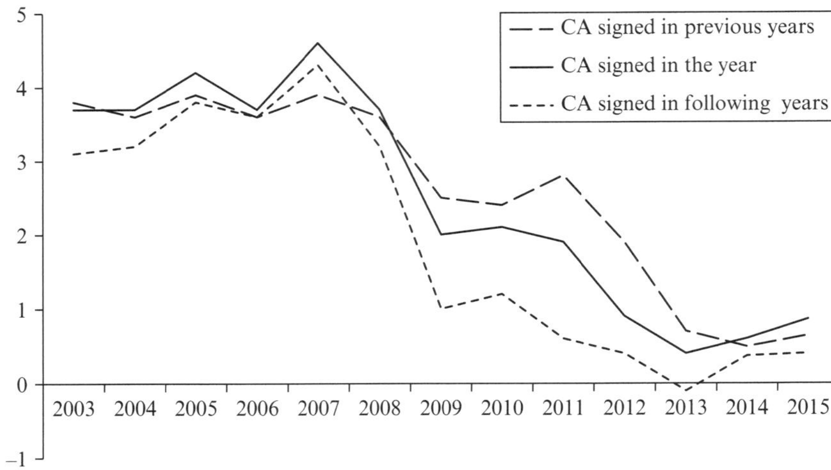

Source: Authors' analysis from Estadística de convenios colectivos de trabajo, various years.

Figure 11.8 Wage growth bargained by year of signing a collective agreement, Spain, 2003–15

bargained in collective agreements signed after the reform is lower than that bargained before it. We have to be cautious when interpreting these results, as probably the results have also been affected by the intensity and duration of the crisis (9.3 per cent drop in gross domestic product in five years, from the second quarter of 2008 to the second quarter of 2013) and the growth in unemployment (from 8.2 per cent in 2007 to 26.1 per cent in 2014). Another major change is the reduction in the number of workers benefiting from collective agreements with compensation clauses for higher than expected inflation, the so-called *garantía salarial*.[23] In 2008, 67 per cent of employees covered by collective agreements enjoyed such a clause; in 2015, the percentage was down to only 12.5 per cent. In any case, it has to be acknowledged that this trend predates the labour reforms of 2010 and 2012.

From the perspective of inequalities, we could say that the aim of the reform was, precisely, to increase inequality, as the policy of 'coffee for all' exemplified by higher than firm-level collective agreements was considered, in the interpretation of the legislator, to be an important element behind the alleged lack of flexibility of Spanish firms. The increase in facilities given to firms to opt out of collective agreements and change working conditions is, in itself, a source of inequality among workers. A different question is to what extent such increases in flexibility have contributed to saving jobs.[24]

4. EFFECTS OF THE SPANISH SYSTEM OF INDUSTRIAL RELATIONS ON INEQUALITY AND SOCIAL SECURITY

Collective agreements can affect job security and inequality through direct and indirect mechanisms. The direct mechanisms are provisions on working conditions, including wages, employment policy, restrictions on part-time employment and subcontracting. The indirect mechanisms are those affecting inequality and social security through the impact of collective agreements on overall employment and job security.

4.1 Collective Agreements and Wage Inequality

The automatic extension of collective agreements in Spain makes it difficult to study their impact on any of the above-mentioned areas of working conditions from a national perspective. As most workers are covered by collective agreements, it is difficult to test, nationally, how having one affects inequality in the labour market. The traditional approach to this question has been to compare wage inequality and collective agreement coverage across nations. Figure 11.9 presents the results of such an exercise for a sample of Organisation for Economic Co-operation and Development (OECD) countries just before the crisis. As we can see, the level of collective agreement coverage is clearly and inversely related to wage inequality (as measured by D9/D1 ratio).[25]

Complementarily, Table 11.4, which presents the pairwise correlations between wage inequality and other variables of the labour market that from a theoretical perspective could also have an impact on wage inequality, shows how the correlation between collective agreement coverage and wage dispersion is more intense than between any other pair of variables, making collective agreement coverage a central variable in the explanation of wage inequality. This result has been largely confirmed by the empirical literature of the economic impact of collective agreements.[26]

From a different perspective, the positive role of collective agreements in reducing wage differences has also been suggested in a recent analysis of part-time full-time wage differences in Spain (Ramos et al., 2016).

Of less interest, but nevertheless related to the impact of collective agreements on inequality, is the analysis of the differential effects of different types of collective bargaining – at the firm, sectoral or central levels – on

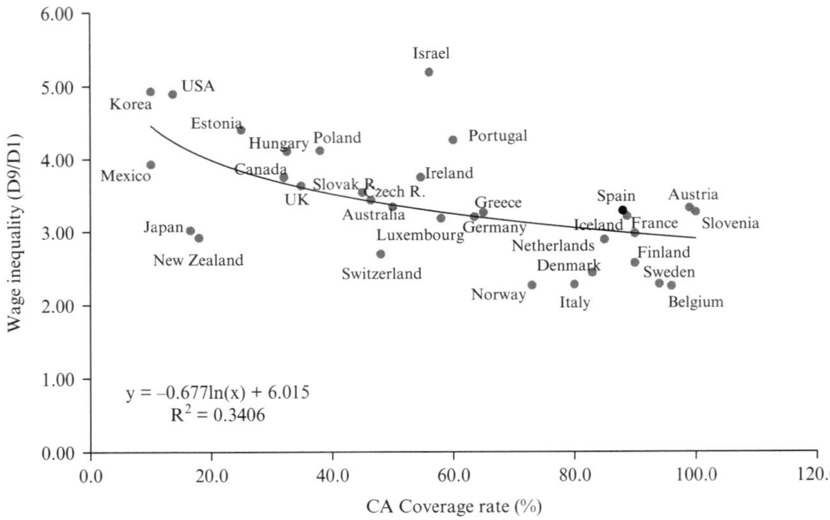

Source: Authors' analysis from OECD Labour Database and Visser (2015).

Figure 11.9 Wage inequality and collective agreement coverage rate before the crisis, Spain, 2008

Table 11.4 Correlation matrix between collective agreement coverage, minimum wage level, trade union density rate and unemployment rate, Spain, 2008

	D9/D1	Trade union density	Minimum/ median wage	Collective agreement coverage	Unemployment 2007	Temporary rate
D9/D1	1					
Trade union density	–0.544	1				
MW/median wage	–0.494	0.392	1			
Collective agreement coverage	–0.610	0.577	0.508	1		
Unemployment 2007	0.103	–0.424	–0.052	0.131	1	
Temporary employment rate	0.045	–0.126	–0.089	0.183	0.284	1

Source: Authors' analysis from OECD Labour Database and Visser (2015).

working conditions, especially wages. In this case, as employees are covered by collective agreements bargained at different levels, it is possible to produce national estimates of the effects on wages and wage inequality at different bargaining levels. The available literature on the subject suggests that firm-level collective bargaining has some differential effects when compared with systems with a higher level of bargaining centralisation, such as the Spanish case: lower wage increases, higher wage dispersion and higher gender pay gaps.[27] As mentioned elsewhere (Muñoz de Bustillo and Antón, 2015), empirical literature for the Spanish economy, which could guide our insights on the likely effects of the reforms favouring firm-level collective bargaining, is inconclusive and problematic. As we have seen, collective bargaining at the firm level was not the default option until the changes implemented in 2012. As a result, Spanish workers under firm-level collective agreements were often those belonging to large firms where they had strong bargaining power, which made it advantageous to sign a firm agreement with more favourable conditions than those agreed at higher bargaining levels. In this context, the causal effect of the level of bargaining centralisation is difficult to gather, because one has to disentangle the relevant selection bias. In general, available studies tend to confirm the higher level of overall wage dispersion associated with firm-level collective agreements (Abellán et al., 1997; Izquierdo et al., 2003; Canal Domínguez and Rodríguez Gutiérrez, 2016), as well as a higher gender wage gap (Amuedo-Dorantes and De la Rica, 2006; De la Rica and González, 2007; Card and De la Rica, 2004).[28]

In order to test the role played by the type of collective agreement in force in a given firm on wage inequality, we resorted to the recently available wage data of the Spanish Structure of Earnings Survey 2014 (SES).[29] After calculating different indexes of wage inequality of the firms in the sample, we estimated the determinants of intra-firm wage inequality, as measured by the Gini index. The variables considered in the analysis are: demographic (gender and age composition of the firm), educational composition and seniority of the labour force, type of contract (open-ended versus temporary contract, full-time versus part-time), size and type (public vs private) of firm, activity, geographic location, type of demand (local, national, European or rest of the world) and type of collective agreement regulating working conditions at the firm. The survey identifies five types of collective agreement: (1) sectoral at national level, (2) sectoral at lower level: regional, provincial, local, (3) firm level, (4) establishment level and (5) other. We are interested in testing if, after controlling for the above-mentioned variables related to the characteristics of employees and firms, the type of collective agreement has any effect on wage inequality at the firm level, as well as its size and direction.

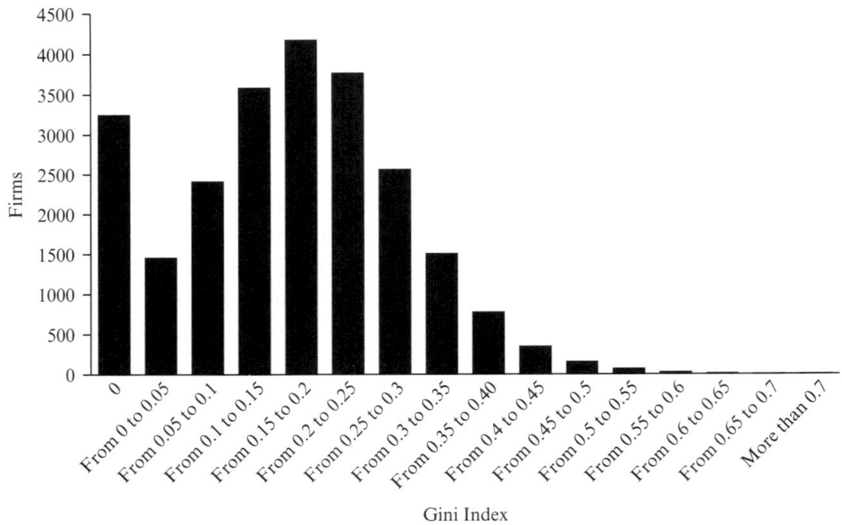

Source: Authors' analysis from SES 2014 microdata.

Figure 11.10 Distribution of wage inequality at the firm level, Spain, 2014

Before presenting the results of our exercise, it is worth mentioning the relatively high dispersion of wage inequality – as measured by the Gini index – of Spanish firms, with values going from 0 (firms with one employee) up to .713 (see Figure 11.10).

Table 11.5 presents the results of the regression using the Gini index of wages of the firm as dependent variable, and the above-mentioned items as independent variables. The same analysis was performed using alternative indexes of inequality (P90/P10; P90/P50; P50/P10 and so on), obtaining similar results. Focusing on the question posed above, after controlling for the characteristics of firms and employees, compared with firms with collective agreements at regional or provincial level, those firms with a collective agreement at the firm level have higher wage inequality. In contrast, having a collective agreement at national level has an even higher compressing impact on wage inequality, although the relationship is not statistically significant. One possible reason behind such a result, as argued by Dahl et al. (2013) for Denmark, could be that the individual characteristics of workers (and firms) are more likely to enter into the process of wage setting in the context of firm-level collective bargaining, generating higher returns to skills (especially in the upper part of the distribution) and leading to higher intra-firm wage inequality.

Table 11.5 Variables affecting wage inequality (Gini index) of Spanish firms (2014): estimation results

	Coefficient	Sig.	Robust standard errors		Coefficient	Sig.	Robust standard errors
% Women in the company	0.007	**	(0.003)	Public sector	–0.012	***	(0.003)
% Temporary jobs	0.047	***	(0.003)	Extractive industries	0.011		(0.008)
% Part-time jobs	0.030	***	(0.003)	Textiles and food industry	0.009	**	(0.004)
% Foreign workers	0.000		(0.005)	Wood and paper industry	0.004		(0.006)
% Below 19 years old	0.155	**	(0.063)	Graphic arts	0.014	**	(0.007)
% 20–29 years old	0.024	***	(0.005)	Chemical and petroleum derivatives industry	0.008	*	(0.005)
% 40–49 years old	–0.003		(0.004)	Mineral and non-metal products industry	0.004		(0.006)
% 50–59 years old	0.002		(0.004)	Metal industry	–0.001		(0.005)
% Above 59 years old	0.030	***	(0.008)	Industrial computing	0.004		(0.005)
% Short tenure workers	0.005	*	(0.003)	Other manufacturing industries	0.003		(0.005)
% Firm size (1–49 workers)	–0.058	***	(0.002)	Energy sector	–0.021	***	(0.008)
% Firm size (49–200 workers)	0.001		(0.002)	Water purification recycling and waste treatment sector	0.021	***	(0.005)
% Below primary education	–0.017	**	(0.007)	Construction and building engineering	–0.002		(0.004)
% Primary education	0.002		(0.003)	Wholesale vehicles sector	0.009	*	(0.005)
% Upper secondary education	0.008	***	(0.003)	Retail vehicles sector	0.020	***	(0.005)
% Vocational training education	0.009	**	(0.004)	Transport services sector	0.003		(0.006)
% BA	0.030	***	(0.005)	Postal services and storage services	0.012	**	(0.006)
% Master's/doctoral	0.039	***	(0.004)	Horeca	0.035	***	(0.006)

Table 11.5 (continued)

	Coefficient	Sig.	Robust standard errors		Coefficient	Sig.	Robust standard errors
North-West	–0.016	***	(0.002)	Information, cinematography and TV services	0.007		(0.004)
North-East	–0.007	***	(0.002)	Real estate activities	–0.037	***	(0.009)
Madrid	0.006	**	(0.002)	Firm advising and consulting services	0.004		(0.004)
Centre	–0.023	***	(0.002)	Renting services	0.020	***	(0.004)
South	–0.017	***	(0.002)	Public administration, social security and defence	0.006		(0.006)
Canary Islands	0.000		(0.004)	Education services	0.038	***	(0.006)
National level	–0.001		(0.002)	Health care services	0.037	***	(0.005)
Firm level	0.004	*	(0.002)	Artistic activities	0.045	***	(0.006)
Establishment level	–0.006		(0.004)	Other services	–0.006		(0.005)
Other type	–0.004		(0.003)	Constant	0.176	***	(0.005)
Local and regional market	–0.022	***	(0.002)	Observations			24062
EU market	0.001		(0.003)	R-squared			0.160
World market	0.003		(0.002)	F(58, 23989)			80.95

Notes:
Reference categories: age = % 30–39 year old; firm size = over 200 employees; education: lower secondary education; region = east; market = national; sector = finance and so on.
Weighted data. *** $p < 0.01$, ** $p < 0.05$, * $p < 0.1$.

Source: Authors' analysis from SES 2014 microdata.

As regards the effect of the control variables on intra-firm wage inequality, we find few surprises: firms with more women not only have lower wages, but higher wage inequality; the same applies in firms with temporary employees and part-time jobs. In contrast, having more foreign employees on the payroll does not have an impact on wage inequality. In relation to age, firms with a higher percentage of young employees (under 30 years old) have more wage inequality. The size of the firm also matters for inequality as small firms (1–49 employees) have lower inequality compared with large firms (over 200). Education also contributes to wage inequality as firms with a more educated workforce have a higher wage Gini index (compared with the category, lower secondary used as reference). Finally, public sector firms have lower wage inequality. Before concluding it is important to highlight that, as we cannot assume that having a firm level collective agreement is a matter of chance (only a minority of firms, 12 per cent of the sample, usually large firms, have firm-level collective agreements), the above-mentioned results have to be interpreted cautiously, and in terms of correlations and not causation.

Summing up, the Spanish system of collective agreements, based on higher than firm level bargaining, so far has had a compressing effect on wage dispersion, contributing to lower levels of wage inequality, at least until the labour reforms adopted during the crisis.[30] Moreover, the sparse evidence available points to the pro-inequality effect of firm-level collective agreements. In this respect, the lower presence of this type of collective agreement in the Spanish labour landscape may also have contributed to lower levels of wage inequality. This result is consistent with the lesser role played by market inequality in overall disposable income inequality in Spain in relation to other EU countries (Muñoz de Bustillo, 2016). In this regard, the move towards increasing the role of collective agreements at the firm level of the 2012 labour reform, if successful, could contribute in the future to growing levels of wage inequality.

4.2 Collective Agreements and Job Security

A second important element to be discussed in this section is the relationship between social dialogue – and more specifically collective agreements – and job security. As regards this issue, the Spanish record can hardly be more dismal. Spain was, in 1984, a pioneer in the liberalisation of the use of temporary contracts and after that it became the leader among OECD countries in terms of its temporary employment rate, to the extent that before the crisis one-third of employees were working on temporary contracts. Only with the crisis and the concentration of employment destruction in this segment of the labour market has Spain conceded this position to Poland. Fortunately, temporary employment rates decrease with the age and labour record of the worker. For instance, in the second quarter of 2016, when the overall temporary employment rate was 25.7 per cent, employees 20–24 years old faced a temporary employment rate of 69 per cent, and those from 25 to 29 years of age, 47 per cent, compared with 27 per cent of those in their thirties and 21 per cent of those in their forties. Nevertheless, a significant percentage of temps are workers in their thirties or forties owing to the larger sizes of those cohorts (more than half, 55.2 per cent, of all temporary employees belong to this age group).[31] Whatever merits collective agreements may have in Spain, it is clear that an increase in workforce stability is not among their achievements. This development is important for two reasons. First, because its mere existence exemplifies the failure of the system of collective agreements to address a major concern of Spanish workers: the high level of job insecurity. Secondly, because the trade unions and the system of collective agreements itself, have often been blamed for the existence of such a large share of precarious employment.

As we can see in Table 11.6, although provisions regarding the use of temporary employment by firms are not absent from collective agreements,

Table 11.6 Clauses related to temporary employment included in collective agreements, Spain, 2012 and 2015

	2012		2015	
	CA	Workers	CA	Workers
	%	%	%	%
Transformation of temporary contracts into open-ended contracts	12.8	28.7	12.9	21.6
Maximum number of temporary contracts	8.0	30.8	8.8	21.4
Control of chain temporary hiring	6.1	19.5	6.3	30.7
Use of TAW	9.4	15.2	8.8	25.3
Outsourcing of specific activities	3.0	11.2	3.5	17.8
Type of jobs that can be performed by temporary employees	9.4	25.2	10.5	28.8
Limits to temporary employees/total employees	3.4	16.5	3.5	6.8
Clauses related to PT employment	10.8	26.2	11.5	33.3
Increase of number of complementary hours for part-timers	2.8	1.6	4.9	15.1

Note: CA = collective agreement; TAW = temporary agency worker; PT = part-time.

Source: Authors' analysis from Estadística de convenios colectivos de trabajo, various years.

their presence can be considered, at most, modest.[32] Of those collective agreements with qualitative information about their content, only around 13 per cent, affecting roughly one-fifth of employees, include provisions on the conversion of fixed-term contracts into open-ended contracts, while less than 5 per cent of collective agreements establish limits on the ratio between the number of temporary employees and overall labour force.[33] The percentage of collective agreements providing some kind of control of chain temporary hiring (to prevent the hiring of a given worker over time using consecutive temporary contracts) is also very low, at around 6 per cent. To summarise, looking at the information provided by Table 11.4 we can say that, at least in terms of results, trade unions have not managed to use collective agreements as a tool for labour force stabilisation. However, it has to be acknowledged that the presence of these types of provisions in collective agreements at the firm level is even lower. For example, in 2015 only 7.4 per cent of employees with firm-level collective agreements benefited from limits on the maximum number of bouts of temporary employment (compared with 21 per cent of those covered by collective agreements).

The unusually high level of the temporary employment rate in Spain is the result of an early change of labour regulation, adopted in 1984, aimed at fighting unemployment by facilitating temporary employment.[34] After the reform, Spanish firms quickly used the newly available temporary contracts almost as the default contract type. In the new regulatory context, firms' flexibility to confront changes in the economic environment was obtained by increasing or decreasing, very rapidly, the number of temporary employees, often on quite short contracts. The adoption of this new culture of 'fungible employees' made possible a very high level of flexibility (numerical flexibility), generating an idiosyncratic system of flexi-security: open-ended employees were reasonably secure in their jobs as flexibility relied initially on temporary employees.

In this context, the lack of emphasis of collective agreements on reducing the temporary employment rate shown in Table 11.4 – probably for reasons related more to the consideration of employment policy as a prerogative of firms and their refusal to reach compromises in this area than to a lack of interest on the part of trade unions (at least from a programmatic point of view) in reducing temporal employment rates – has not made it possible to extend the benefits of collective agreements in terms of lower wage inequality to the area of job security.

This status quo has been often interpreted in terms of a simple insider–outsider model. According to such a model, insiders are able to obtain better working conditions than those granted by the economic situation, as the cost in terms of redundancies of such overshooting would fall on temporary employees. In what follows we explore what is the actual level of

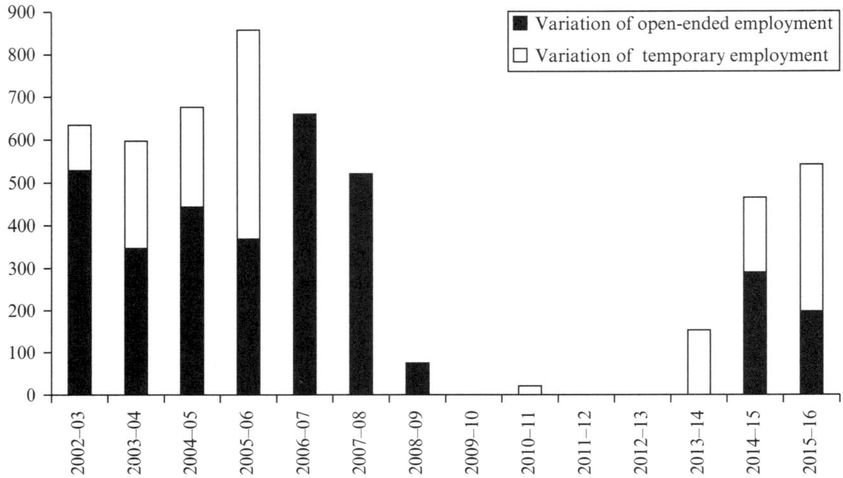

Source: Authors' analysis from Spanish Labour Force Survey (Encuesta de Población Activa, EPA).

Figure 11.11 Allocation of dependent employment change between temporary and open-ended employees, Spain, 2002 (first quarter) to 2016 (first quarter)

security of open-ended employees, that is, the extent to which open-ended employees are really 'permanent' employees. In order to do so we first look at how (dis)employment change has been allocated between temporary and open-ended employment since the beginning of the crisis. In Figure 11.11, in the first year of the crisis, 2009, the role played by temporary employment as a flexibility tool by firms is crystal clear, with a reduction of temporary employment of almost 1.1 million, while open-ended employment was still growing (albeit marginally). In 2009 temporary employees took the full force of the crisis, while the rest were left untouched, but for the period 2009–14 things changed, as open-ended employment accounted for more than 60 per cent of total employment destruction. For the whole period of employment destruction (2008–14), open-ended employment accounted for 39 per cent of total employment destroyed (*circa* 1.2 million), certainly less than their share in total employment at the beginning of the crisis (*circa* 70 per cent), but more than the notion of open-ended employment as quasi permanent would suggest. In the terms used by Toharia and Malo (2009: 21), renowned Spanish labour economists: 'If someone thinks that having an open-ended contract is a guarantee of permanence, he is totally wrong. The data simply refute such a belief.'

Another ingenious approach to gauge whether the burden of insecurity ends when workers finally get an open-ended contract is to compare the number of open-ended contracts signed during a given year with the increase in the number of employees with open-ended contracts with less than one year on the job. In a context of zero rotation of open-ended employees, this ratio would be 1: every new open-ended contract signed would match a new employee. In contrast, an index higher than 1 would mean that some of the new workers hired on an open-ended contract would not remain employed at the end of the year. According to CCOO estimates, before the crisis, 2006, the index was 1.23, while in 2014 it was 1.54 (CCOO, 2016b). This means that while before the crisis, in 2006, roughly 19 per cent of open-ended contracts signed were not in being by the end of the year, after the crisis the percentage was 30 per cent.[35]

Finally, in terms of overall dismissals of open-ended employees (Gómez Jiménez, 2016), the analysis of quarterly transitions from Labour Force Survey data estimates an incidence of separations (from open-ended employment to unemployment) of around 5 per cent for 2005–14, only about 15 per cent of the equivalent for temporary employees, but nevertheless far from nothing.

These results, indicating the lack of full job security among open-ended employees, is confirmed by looking at the broader picture of the total number of open-ended contracts signed since the beginning of the Great Recession (2008–15), 10.9 million, and the total variation of employees with open-ended contracts during the same period, namely –0.9 million. Comparison of the huge number of new contracts signed with the total number of employees with open-ended contracts (almost 1 million lower) shows the high level of rotation of allegedly stable employees, even when we allow for retirements and voluntary termination of open-ended contracts by employees moving to a different job.[36]

Taking this information into consideration it is fully understandable that, according to the Eurobarometer (2011), in 2011 as many as 71 per cent of the workers interviewed (almost three times higher than the existing temp rate) declared themselves worried (15 per cent) or very worried (56 per cent) about losing their job. This result is certainly difficult to match with the portrayal of employees with open-ended contracts as carefree people who, having a secure job, use their market power to improve their working conditions without taking into consideration the economic situation.

To conclude this section we explore another indirect way by which collective agreements might affect job security. The combination of collective agreements lasting several years (in order to minimise bargaining costs and uncertainty for both firms and employees)[37] and unforeseen changes in the economy might lead, in the face of major economic downturns, to a situation in which bargained wages are higher than what the economic conditions would allow, increasing the risk of dismissals. If that is the case – an unforeseen economic crisis not accounted for at the time of negotiating the agreement – collective agreements might contribute to higher unemployment, that is, lower employment security. In this regard, according to the analysis of the impact of the downward rigidity of wages at the onset of the Great Recession of Díez-Catalán and Villanueva (2014), the probability of job losses among those workers covered by collective agreements signed before the start of the Great Recession (signposted by the fall of Lehman Brothers) was 1 per cent higher than among those with agreements signed afterwards (explained mostly by the impact on employees with wages closest to the minimum bargaining wage). This negative impact on employment is confined to the commercial service sector, as the authors could not find similar dynamics in industry.[38]

4.3 Improving Working Conditions through Social Dialogue: Two Case Studies

Before concluding this section, we address the role of social dialogue in fighting inequality using a different approach, based on the study of specific cases in which social dialogue made the difference in terms of inequality and working conditions. With that aim we look at two completely different instruments of social dialogue. The first exemplifies the potential of traditional social dialogue, using the standard tool of the collective agreement, for improving the working conditions of precarious workers. The second focuses on a different approach to social dialogue: the utilisation of a popular legislative proposal by a major trade union to fight the high rate of labour accidents in construction related to the use of subcontracting in the sector.

4.3.1 Fighting low hours through collective agreement: the case of mass catering

In 2016, for the first time ever, the representative trade unions CCOO and UGT signed a national collective agreement for mass catering (*I Convenio Estatal de Restauración Colectiva*). This is important in itself, because the new regulation of collective agreements reviewed above was intended to incentivise firm-level agreements, a road not taken by signatories who considered it more convenient to fix the rules governing labour relations in the sector at the national level. Moreover, Article 9 of the collective agreement emphasises that firm-level agreements should not ‘play a destabilising role’ nor be used as a ‘formula to lower working conditions’. This collective agreement is also important because it was signed after a long period of stalemate in collective bargaining and in a context not auspicious at all for social dialogue, owing, among other things, to the labour reforms of 2011 and 2012.

Although the collective agreement covers different categories of workers, from cooks and waiters to cleaning and administration personnel, the feature we would like to highlight in the context of this chapter is the agreement to increase the minimum number of weekly hours of monitors ('dinner ladies'). Before the signing of the collective agreement, such monitors often worked nominally as little as 45 minutes per day. The collective agreement sets a minimum of ten hours per week, which for many monitors doubles their take-home pay. This is a major improvement in a context, such as the Spanish one, in which involuntary part-time work affects as much as 60 per cent of part-time employees, being a major source of earnings inequality. It is also a measure with an important gender impact, as most monitors are women. Within the context of moderate low wage increases, the collective agreement also represents a substantial wage increase for monitors: 1.5 per cent for 2016 (compared with 1 per cent) and 2.5 per cent for 2017 and 2018.

The collective agreement also includes interesting references to the general hiring principles that should inform firms' hiring policies, addressing another of the major sources of precariousness in Spain, temporary employment. These principles include the promotion of open-ended employment and the transformation of temporary contracts into open-ended contracts, the promotion of proper use of the different types of contracts available and so on.

This case shows how social dialogue can improve the working conditions of some of the worst-off employees, even in an unfavourable context.

4.3.2 Exploring new avenues in the improvement of working conditions: the fight against accidents at work in construction

Outsourcing of the so-called 'non-core' productive or ancillary activities is now one of the stylised facts of the organisation of firms. Although the phenomenon of working conditions in subcontracted activities in Spain has not been much studied owing to the lack of data, the available studies, such as Zimmermann Verdajo et al. (2010), conclude that employees of subcontracted firms face worse working conditions. Thus, the increase in subcontracting is likely to be a source of growth of inequality in terms of wages and working conditions.[39] Construction is a sector in which outsourcing has become the norm, among other things because of the possibilities it offers for separating out different activities.

The growth of construction in Spain in the 1980s, associated among other things with the upgrading and new development of large-scale infrastructure co-financed by the EU Structural Funds and with two major events in 1992 (the World Fair in Seville and the Olympics in Barcelona), led to a significant increase in fatal labour accidents in the sector, often related to subcontracted activities. In order to confront such developments, in 1998 one of the major Spanish trade unions, CCOO, started a campaign to limit the number of successive times that a given construction activity could be subcontracted ('chain subcontracting'), as a means to improve safety. With that aim, CCOO presented – for the first time in Spain – a Popular Legislative Initiative dealing with labour issues to the Spanish Parliament, backed by 600 000 firms. In doing so, the trade union showed how innovative forms of collective action could be pursued when the more traditional mechanisms were not viable (due to the existence of differences among trade union priorities, for example). Although the progress of the initiative was frustrated by the opposition of the ruling party (conservative), the campaign was not abandoned. In March 2001, a general strike in construction was called by major unions to protest against the refusal to proceed with the project of regulating chain subcontracting. The campaign was re-launched in 2004, this time with the backing of the other major trade union, UGT, and supported by demonstrations all across Spain. The change in government in 2004 finally facilitated the proposal's approval, and in September 2006 the Congress approved the Law for Regulating Subcontracting in Construction (LRSC), effective from April 2007. The resulting text, in the words of the then Secretary General of the construction federation of CCOO, FECOMA, Fernando Serrano: 'while *not the one that the trade union would have approved, nevertheless has very positive elements to start rationalising the construction sector*' (cited in Vilela, 2006: 5, original emphasis).

The law restricted chain subcontracting in construction to three levels, established criteria for subcontractors operating in construction (a minimum share of open-ended employees, a Register of Accredited Subcontracted Firms and a Subcontracting Book), recognised information rights to employees' delegates regarding subcontracting firms, and established the principle of collective responsibility for contractor and subcontracting firms in case of non-fulfilment of the above-mentioned requirements.

Ten years after the enactment of the new regulation the results have been dampened by the crisis of the construction sector associated with the Great Recession and the growth of the share of very small firms in the sector, among which compliance with the regulations is much lower. In the words of the Secretary General of the Federation of Construction and Services, CCOO:

> those areas out of reach of the trade unions and the Labour Inspectorate are like the jungle, and now a much more dangerous jungle as such construction projects often rely on contracting own-account workers . . . we think the law is good, but the problem is the lack of resources to guarantee a high level of compliance.[40]

5. CONCLUSIONS

The evidence presented in this chapter shows how the structure of collective agreements previous to the reforms of 2011 and 2012 has contributed to the reduction of wage inequality in Spain. The comparatively low levels of wage inequality found in Spain are a product of the existing high level of coverage of collective agreements. The same could be said of other sources of inequality, such as gender inequality or overall job quality, not covered in the study for reasons of space. Moreover, as proven by the econometric analysis performed with employee–employer match data of 2014, collective agreements at higher than firm level (precisely those characteristic of Spanish industrial relations) appear to be well suited towards this aim, as *ceteris paribus* firms with their own collective agreements also have higher wage inequality. In this regard, the move toward firm-level collective agreements promoted by the labour reform of 2012 could lead to an increase in wage inequality.

In contrast, collective agreements have not been able to address with similar success what is probably the main problem of the Spanish labour market: the high rate of temporary employment (that is, high level of inequality in terms of job security). As we have seen, only a minority of collective agreements deal with this issue, usually by including limits on the absolute or relative number of temporary employees in relation to the total labour force of the firm, or plans to transform temporary into open-ended contracts. Although programmatically the reduction of temporary employment rates has been a key aim of Spanish trade unions, the results have been dismal. Moreover, the failure to address this issue has also limited the capacity of collective agreements to reduce wage inequality, as temporary employees usually have lower wages, among other things, owing to their difficulties in accumulating seniority and the prevalence of seniority wage supplements in most collective agreements (61 per cent of workers under collective agreements had this kind of supplement). As seen in the econometric exercise presented in section 4.1, those firms with a higher proportion of employees with temporary contracts also have higher wage inequality. High temporary employment rates are another factor behind the predicament of trade unions regarding affiliation rates, as temporary workers are more difficult to reach and show lower attachment to trade unions, not so much in terms of satisfaction with existing agreements or unions (Fernández-Macías, 2003), but in terms of affiliation rates and knowledge about the existing mechanisms of representation in the firm.

In this chapter we have argued that the dichotomy open-ended or fixed-term should not be interpreted in terms of permanent versus flexible employment. Although numerical flexibility often relies on temporary employees, in section 4.2, using different approaches, we have shown how this type of employment is far from permanent. In this regard, insecurity is not only an attribute of temporary employees. The existing culture of hire and fire also affects open-ended employees, albeit with a lower intensity.

From a different perspective, it has been argued than the multi-annual nature of most collective agreements could lead to higher employment losses in the event of unforeseen changes in demand (such as the Great Recession). The existence of flexible mechanisms to review collective agreements could help to neutralise such unintended effects but, if unilaterally applied, could also create uncertainty about collective agreements and diminish their role in reducing inequality. Moreover, a successful renegotiation of existing collective agreements would require a high level of trust among social partners and information sharing. It is difficult to conceive how a unilateral reform of collective agreement regulations, such as the two reforms reviewed in this chapter, can foster such requirements.

NOTES

* The authors wish to acknowledge the contributions to the chapter, in different phases of its making, of José Ignacio Antón-Pérez, Ángeles Rodríguez, Fernando Rocha, Ana Hermoso, Antonio Gonzalez and Vicente Sánchez.

1. 'If there is one thing that the Spanish left and right can agree on, it is that the country's transition from dictatorship to democracy in the late 1970s was a singular political triumph' (T. Buck, *Financial Times*, 12 August 2014).
2. In 1972, the leadership of one of the illegal trade unions, *Comisiones Obreras*, was arrested by the police. One year later, the leaders of the trade union were given prison sentences ranging from 12 to 20 years. In 1975 the trade unionists were granted a pardon by the new head of state, King Juan Carlos I.
3. This index is lower than the coverage rate normally used in the literature as the ratio is calculated in relation to all dependent employment, and not only those employees who are entitled to collective bargaining. According to Visser's (2015) estimates, the adjusted coverage rate for 2013 for Spain was 78 per cent.
4. *Boletín Estadístico del Personal las Servicio de las Administraciones Públicas*. Registro Central de Personal, July 2015.
5. *Estadística de Convenios Colectivos*, definitive data 2015 (table CCT-II.2).
6. Firms with fewer than five employees do not have employee delegates or works councils and thus lack the capacity to negotiate collective agreements. Calculated from register data: *Estadística de Convenios Colectivos de Trabajo*, 2014.
7. The remaining firms had collective agreements bargained at the level of the group of

firms, either at the provincial or at the regional and interregional level. Calculated from registry data, *Estadística de Convenios Colectivos* (table CCT-II.2), 2014.

8. In Visser's ICTWSS data set version 5.0, in comparative terms, Spanish wage bargaining coordination system is considered to be 'medium-high', with a value of 3.6 (in a scale from 1 to 5). The value is reduced to 3 for the period 2010–2014 as result of the option in favour of firm-level collective agreements of the reforms of 2010 and 2012.
9. 'Trade union density', OECD labour database, Paris, available at http://www.oecd.org/std/labour-stats/.
10. This is a major weakness affecting trade union participation. Two out three firms with six or more employees do not have delegates or work councils and therefore do not hold trade union elections (the so-called 'white firms').
11. *Encuesta de Calidad de Vida en el Trabajo*, 2010.
12. The UGT, since its creation in 1888, has traditionally been connected with the Spanish Socialist Worker Party (PSOE). Since the 1980s the trade union has reduced its links with the party, although it still has close ties with it. The CCOO (officially Confederación Sindical de Comisiones Obreras) is a much newer trade union; the first groups of Comisiones Obreras were created underground in the 1960s by members of the Communist Party.
13. In the very explicit words of a former president of CEPYME, a business confederation of small and medium-sized enterprises, 'the coming of the new democratic regimen caught business owners "in their underwear", as the saying goes. For obvious reasons there was no type of underground active associative militancy' (*El País*, 25 January 1980, as quoted in Aguilar, 1985: 60).
14. According to the Eurofound European Company Survey 2013 (ECS), with data for EU companies with ten or more employees, in Spain 41.9 per cent of firms were members of an employers' organisation that participated in collective bargaining (the EU15 average is 48.5 per cent). Using the distribution of employment by enterprise size category of the *Encuesta de Coyuntura Laboral* 2012 (last year available) we estimate that these firms employ a minimum of 46 per cent of employees (subsample of more than ten employees). The results are similar using the ECS and the *Encuesta Annual Laboral*.
15. From 1987 on, as a spin-off of the decentralisation of public administration and the development of a quasi-federal state known as the State of Autonomous Regions, social dialogue provided a new venue at the regional level, resulting in the development of social agreements – with different timing – in all 17 Spanish Autonomous Regions. For more details see Aragón et al. (2008) or Moreneo et al. (2015, ch. 10).
16. The result was a major labour reform, not negotiated with social actors, that was withdrawn after a successful General Strike in 2002.
17. According to the estimates of Uxó et al. (2016) between 2007 and 2014, 69 per cent of the jobs lost were directly or indirectly related to construction (82 per cent between 2007 and 2009).
18. Real Decreto-ley 10/2010, de 16 de junio, de medidas urgentes para la reforma del mercado de trabajo, Real Decreto-ley 7/2011, de 10 de junio, de medidas urgentes para la reforma de la negociación colectiva and Real Decreto-ley 3/2012, de 10 de febrero, de medidas urgentes para la reforma del mercado laboral.
19. The same applies in terms of sector, as the sector with lowest percentage of firms quite or very satisfied with the collective agreement is administrative activities, with 77 per cent, and region, as even in Madrid, the region with the lowest percentage of firms quite or very satisfied with the collective agreement, the percentage is almost 77 per cent.
20. Such as the National Commission of Collective Agreements (Comisión Consultiva Nacional de Convenios Colectivos) or equivalent commissions at regional level. These are tripartite organisations with representation of firms, trade unions and the government.
21. *Acuerdo de la Comisión de Seguimiento del II AENC sobre Ultra-actividad de Convenios Colectivos* (Agreement of the Follow-up Commission of the II AENC on Ultra-activity of Collective Agreements) 23 May 2013 (*Boletín Oficial del Estado*, 14 June 2013).

22. Although according to the trade unions (CCOO, 2016a) public subsidies are a minor part of their overall budget (around 15 per cent), the coincidence of such reductions with the drop in affiliation owing to rising unemployment has strained the capacity of the organisation to face the growing challenges of the crisis and the labour market reforms.
23. The 'wage guarantee clause' is activated when the CPI is higher than the forecast CPI taken into consideration when negotiating the wage increase. In that case employees are compensated for the unexpected increase in prices.
24. From the point of view of security, not covered in this section as the changes in regulations in this area are not related to collective agreements, the reforms reduced the redundancy payments of employees with open-ended contracts, a measure considered to reduce job security.
25. Similar results are obtained when using D9/D5 (R^2 of 0.174) and D5/D1 (R^2 of 0.419) wage ratios.
26. See, for example, Aidt and Tzannatos (2002, 2008), Blau and Kahn (2002), Teulings and Hartog (1998), Wallerstein (1999), Fernández-Macías and Vacas-Soriano (2015) or OECD (2004), among others. In the terms used by the OECD (2004: 166): 'overall earnings dispersion tends to fall as union density and bargaining coverage and centralisation/co-ordination increase'.
27. See, for example, Rowthorn (1992), OECD (1997, 2004), Blau and Kahn (1999, 2003), Elvira and Saporta (2001) and Aidt and Tzannatos (2002).
28. Felgueroso et al. (2008) find a different effect depending on the place occupied by women in the wage distribution, with women at the bottom of the wage distribution being subject to lower wage gaps when covered by higher than firm collective agreements, while the opposite occurs for those in the upper part of the wage distribution.
29. The SES 2014 is an employee-employer survey with a sample size of 27 339 firm units and 227 830 employees, covering all activities except agriculture, public administration (partially) and domestic service.
30. In 2008, according to Statistics on Income and Living Conditions (SILC) data the Spanish level of wage inequality as measured by the Gini index was 0.277. The same year Denmark, the country with lowest wage inequality among the 24 EU countries analysed, had an index of 0.216, while the highest index, that of Portugal, was 0.366. The average of the country Gini indexes was 0.296 (Fernández-Macías and Vacas-Soriano, 2015: 35).
31. Spanish Labour Force Survey, second quarter of 2016.
32. For a detailed discussion of this issue see Rocha Sánchez et al. (2006).
33. For example, the 2011 provincial CA of offices of Salamanca sets a minimum limit of 60 per cent of employees with open-ended contracts. A similar minimum percentage (65 per cent) is considered in the national collective agreement of security firms of 2015.
34. *Ley 32/1984, de 2 de agosto, sobre modificación de determinados artículos de la Ley 8/1980, de 10 de marzo, del Estatuto de los Trabajadores.* This law put an end to the principle of causality that governed temporary contracts until then. According to this principle, this type of contract could be used only for jobs of a temporary nature (for example, a lifeguard in a summer swimming pool).
35. Calculated as open-ended contracts signed during the year minus growth in open-ended employees with less than one year on the job in the last quarter of the year, divided by contract signed during the year (percentage), based on data of Gabinete Económico of the CCOO (2016b).
36. The estimated number of retired open-ended employees – calculated using the open-ended employment rate of older workers – for the period is around 1.4 million. Regarding transitions from open-ended employment to open-ended employment, the estimates produced by Gómez Jiménez (2016), based on flow quarterly data of the Labour Force Survey for the period 2005–14, point to very low probabilities (transitions/stock) around 1 per cent.
37. The average duration of collective agreements in Spain is around 2.5 years, with lower duration in agriculture and industry (around 1.5 years) (Du Caju et al., 2009).

38. Another interesting result obtained by Díez-Catalán and Villanueva (2014) is the lack of difference in terms of the detected impact of the date of signature of collective agreements on job losses between employees with open-ended contracts and fixed-term contracts, both types subject to similar employment losses. This result, unexpected by the authors, confirms the above argued non-permanent feature of open-ended contracts.
39. An example of the concern about working conditions of employees of subcontracted firms is the 9 September 2016 proposed bill to guarantee equal working conditions for employees working in subcontracted firms vis-à-vis the employees of the firm subcontracting the activity.
40. Interview with the author, April 2016.

REFERENCES

Abellan, C., F. Felgueroso and J. Lorences (1997), 'La Negociación Colectiva en España: Una Reforma Pendiente', *Papeles de Economia Española*, **72**, 250–60.

Aguilar, S. (1985), 'El asociacionismo empresarial en la transición postfranquista', *PAPERS, Revista de Sociología*, **24**, 53–84.

Aidt, T.S. and Z. Tzannatos (2008), 'Trade unions, collective bargaining and macroeconomic performance: a review', *Industrial Relations Journal*, **39** (4), 258–95.

Aidt, T.S. and Z. Tzannatos (2002), *Unions and Collective Bargaining. Economic Effects in a Global Environment*, Washington, DC: World Bank.

Alós, R., O. Molina, P. Beneyto, P. Jódar and S. Vidal (2015), 'La representación sindical en España', report, Fundación 1° de Mayo, Madrid.

Amuedo-Dorantes, C. and S. de la Rica (2006), 'The role of segregation and pay structure on the gender wage gap: evidence from matched employer–employee data for Spain', *B.E. Journal of Economic Analysis & Policy*, **5** (1), doi:10.1515/1538-0645.1498.

Aragón J., M. Blanco, L. de la Fuente, L. Liceras, F. Puig-Samper, F. Rocha, et al. (2008), 'La Concertación social territorial en España. Una aproximación a los acuerdos autonómicos', Working Paper No. 2/2008, Fundación 1° de Mayo, Madrid.

Blau, F.D. and L.M. Kahn (1999), 'Institutions and laws in the labor market', in O.C. Ashenfelter and D. Card (eds), *Handbook of Labour Economics*, vol. 3, pt B, Amsterdam: North-Holland, pp. 1399–461.

Blau, F.D. and L.M. Kahn (2002), *At Home and Abroad. U.S. Labor-Market Performance in International Perspective*, New York: Russell Sage Foundation.

Blau, F.D. and L.M. Kahn (2003), 'Understanding international differences in the gender pay gap', *Journal of Labor Economics*, **21** (1), 106–44.

Calmfors, L. and J. Driffill (1988), 'Bargaining structure, corporatism, and macroeconomic performance', *Economic Policy*, 3 (6), 13–61.

Canal Domínguez, J.F. and C. Rodríguez Gutiérrez (2016), 'Collective bargaining, wage dispersion and the economic cycle: Spanish evidence', *Economic and Labour Relations Review*, **27** (4), 471–89.

Card, D. and S. de la Rica (2004), 'The effect of firm-level contracts on the structure of wages: evidence from matched employer–employee data', IZA Discussion Paper No. 1421 December, Institute of Labor Economics, Bonn.

Confederación Sindical de Comisiones Obreras (CCOO) (2016a), 'Repensar el Sindicato', Comisiones Obreras, Madrid.

Confederación Sindical de Comisiones Obreras (CCOO) (2016b), 'La reforma laboral hace más inestable el empleo indefinido durante la recuperación', Gabinete Económico, 23 January.

Cruces Aguilera, J., M. Lago Peñas, R. Moreno Preciado, F. Rocha Sánchez and E. Sanz Bernal (2016), *El impacto de la reforma laboral de 2012 en la negociación colectiva (2013–2015)*, Madrid: Editorial Lefebre El Derecho.

Cruz Villalón, J. (2015), 'El diálogo social en España y las aportaciones del III AENC', *Gaceta Sindical,* **25** (December), 55–72.

Dahl, C.M., D. le Maire and J.R. Munch (2013), 'Wage dispersion and decentralization of wage bargaining', *Journal of Labor Economics*, **31** (3), 501–33.

De la Rica, S. and A. González (2007), 'The impact of firm-level contracting on wage levels and inequality: Spain 1995–2002', Department of Foundations of Economic Analysis II Working Paper No. 7, University of the Basque Country, Lejona.

Díez-Catalán, L. and E. Villanueva (2014), 'Contract staggering and unemployment during the Great Recession: evidence from Spain', Working Paper No. 1431, Banco de España, Madrid.

Du Caju, P., E. Gautier, D. Momferatu and M. Ward-Warmedinger (2009), 'Institutional features of wage bargaining in 23 European countries, the US and Japan', *Ekonomia, Cyprus Economic Society and University of Cyprus*, **12** (2), 57–108.

Edles, L.D. (1998), *Symbol and Ritual in the New Spain. The Transition to Democracy after Franco*, Cambridge: Cambridge University Press.

Elvira, M.M. and I. Saporta (2001), 'How does collective bargaining affect the gender pay gap', *Work and Occupations*, **28** (4), 469–90.

Encuesta Anual Laboral, various years, Ministerio de Empleo y Seguridad Social, Madrid.

Encuesta de Población Activa (EPA), various years, Instituto Nacional de Estadística, Madrid.

Estadística de Convenios Colectivos de Trabajo, various years, Ministerio de Empleo y Seguridad Social, Madrid.

Estadística de Huelgas y Cierres Patronales, Ministerio de Empleo y Seguridad Social, Madrid

Eurobarometer (2011), 'Employment and social policy, job security, and active aging', Eurobarometer 76.2 (September–November), Luxembourg.

European Company Survey 2013, Eurofound, Dublin.

Felgueroso, F., M.J. Pérez-Villadóniga and J. Prieto (2008), 'The effect of the collective bargaining level on the gender wage gap: evidence from Spain', *Manchester School*, **76** (3), 301–19.

Fernández-Macías, E. (2003), 'Job instability and political attitudes towards work: some lessons from the Spanish case', *European Journal of Industrial Relations*, **9** (2), 205–22.

Fernández-Macías, E. and C. Vacas-Soriano (2015), *Recent Developments in the Distribution of Wages in Europe*, Eurofound, Luxembourg: Publications Office of the European Union.

Fernández Rodríguez, C.J., R. Ibáñez Rojo and M. Martínez Lucio (2016), 'The reform of collective bargaining in the Spanish manufacturing sector with reference to the metal and chemical sectors: legacies and risks in the reform of regulation since 2008', Project Social dialogue during the economic crisis: the impact of industrial relations reforms on collective bargaining in the manufacturing sector (incorporating social dialogue in manufacturing during the sovereign debt crisis),

Employment, Social Affairs and Inclusion, DG Industrial Relations and Social Dialogue, Manchester.
García Laso, A. (1992), 'La dinámica salarial de los años ochenta. De la política de rentas al'pacto de competitividad', *Información Comercial Española*, **705**, 181–99.
Gómez Jiménez, A.L. (2016), 'Protección del empleo y flujos del mercado de trabajo en España: efectos de las reformas de 2010 y 2012', *Revista de Economía Laboral*, **13** (1), 34–62.
Hamann, K. (2005), 'Third Way conservatism? The popular party and labour relations in Spain', *International Journal of Iberian Studies*, **18** (2), 67–82.
Izquierdo, M. and F. Jimeno (2015), 'Un análisis de los resultados de la última Encuesta de Formación de Salarios de la empresas españolas', *Boletín Económico*, Banco de España, October, 55–65.
Izquierdo, M., E. Moral and A. Urtasun (2003), 'Collective bargaining in Spain: individual data analysis', Occasional Paper No. 0302, Banco de España, Madrid.
Jordana, J. (2007), 'Reconsidering union membership in Spain, 1977–1994: halting decline in a context of democratic consolidation', *Industrial Relations Journal*, **27** (3), 211–24.
Luque, L. (2013), 'La forma de las huelgas en España, 1905–2010', *Política y Sociedad*, **50** (1), 235–68.
Moreneo, J.L., A.L. De Val Tena, J.A. Maldonado Molina, M.N. Moreno Vida and R. Muñoz de Bustillo Llorente (eds) (2015), *La concertación social en España: una evaluación de su trayectoria en la perspectiva de los cambios socioeconómicos*, CES Colección Estudios 233, Madrid: Consejo Económico y Social de España.
Morillo, L. (2015), *Las huelgas en España durante 2014*, Informe, Madrid: Confederación Sindical de Comisiones Obreras.
Muñoz de Bustillo, R. (2014a), 'La crisis del nunca acabar. El comportamiento macroeconómico español 2008–2013', in N.E. García and S. Ruesga (eds), *¿Qué ha pasado con la economía española? La Gran Recesión 2.0 (2008–2013)*, Madrid: Ed. Pirámide, pp. 55–82.
Muñoz de Bustillo, R. (2014b), 'Questioning the myth of expansionary austerity: European macroeconomic policy during the crisis and its aftermath', in J. Bilbao Ubillos (ed.), *The Economic Crisis and Governance in the European Union. A Critical Assessment*, Abingdon: Routledge, pp. 114–33.
Muñoz de Bustillo, R. (2016), 'Algunas consideraciones generales sobre la desigualdad de ingresos en el caso español', *Tiempo de Paz*, **121** (Summer), 51–8.
Muñoz de Bustillo, R. and J.I. Antón (2015), 'Turning back before arriving? The weakening of the Spanish welfare state', in D. Vaughan-Whitehead (ed.), *The European Social Model in Crisis: Is Europe Losing Its Soul?* Cheltenham, UK and Geneva: Edward Elgar and ILO, pp. 451–506.
OECD (1997), *Employment Outlook 1997*, Paris: OECD.
OECD (2004), *Employment Outlook 2004*, Paris: OECD.
OECD, OECD Labour Database, Paris, accessed 14 November 2017 at http://www.oecd.org/std/labour-stats/.
Peñas, J.M. and J. Aguilera (2016), 'Estrategias De los interlocutores sociales', in J. Cruces Aguilera, M. Lago Peñas, R. Moreno Preciado, F. Rocha Sánchez and E. Sanz Bernal (eds), *El impacto de la reforma laboral de 2012 en la negociación colectiva (2013–2015)*, Madrid: Editorial Lefebre El Derechopp, pp. 189–291.
Pérez Infante, J.I. (2011), 'La negociación colectiva y los salarios en España: un análisis agregado', *Cuadernos de Relaciones Laborales*, **29** (2), 261–302.

Ramos, R., E. Sanromá and H. Simón (2016), 'The part-time wage penalty: does bargaining coverage outweigh regional differences in Spain?', *Economics and Labour Relations Review*, **27** (3), 1–19.
Rivero Lamas, J. and A.L. De Val Tena (2007), 'El derecho a la negociación colectiva de los funcionarios públicos', *Revista del Ministerio de Trabajo y Asuntos Sociales*, **68**, 197–236.
Rocha Sánchez, F., A. Colado León and J. Aragón Medina (2006), 'El papel de la negociación colectiva en la regulación de la contratación temporal', Ministerio de Trabajo y Asuntos Sociales, Madrid.
Rowthorn, R.E. (1992), 'Centralisation, employment and wage dispersion', *Economic Journal*, **102** (412), 506–23.
Structure of Earning Survey (SES) (2014), Encuesta de Estructura Salarial 2014, Instituto Nacional de Estadística, Madrid.
Teulings, C. and J. Hartog (1998), *Corporatism or Competition? Labour Contracts, Institutions and Wage Structures in International Comparison*, Cambridge: Cambridge University Press.
Toharia, L. and M.A. Malo (2009), '¿Qué se puede esperar de las reformas del mercado de trabajo?', Circunstancia No. 20, Instituto Universitario de Investigación Ortega y Gasset, Madrid.
Traxler, F. (2003), 'Coordinated bargaining: a stocktaking of its preconditions, practices and performance', *Industrial Relations Journal*, **34** (3), 194–209.
Traxler, F. and B. Brand (2012), 'Collective bargaining. Inter-sectoral heterogeneity and competitiveness: a cross-national comparison of macroeconomic performance', *British Journal of Industrial Relations*, **50** (1), 73–98.
Unión General de Trabajadores (UGT) (2015), 'Balance de Legislatura 2011–2015 Cuatro años de regresión social y económica', Comisión Ejecutiva Confederal de UGT, Madrid.
Uxó, J., E. Febrero and F. Bermejo (2016), 'Crisis, unemployment and internal devaluation in Spain', in M. Myant, S. Theodoropoulou and A. Piasna (eds), *Unemployment, Internal Devaluation and Labour Market Deregulation in Europe*, Brussels: ETUI, pp. 127–68.
Vilela, N. (2006), 'Aprobada la ley que regula la subcontratación tras ocho años de lucha sindical', *Madrid Sindical*, **102** (May), 5.
Visser, J. (2015), Data Base on Institutional Characteristics of Trade Unions, Wage Setting, State Intervention and Social Pacts, 1960–2014 (ICTWSS). Version 5.0, Institute for Advanced Labour Studies AIAS. October 2015. Amsterdam.
Visser, J. (2016), 'What happened to collective bargaining during the great recession', *IZA Journal of Labor Policy*, **5** (9).
Wallerstein, M. (1999), 'Wage-setting institutions and pay inequality in advanced industrial societies', *American Journal of Political Science*, **43** (3), 649–80.
Zimmermann Verdejo, M. and F.J. Pinilla García (2010), 'Estudio de los sectores económicos en los que se recurre habitualmente a la contratación y subcontratación de obras y servicios', Instituto Nacional de Seguridad e Higiene en el Trabajo (INSHT), Madrid.

12. Shaping the future of work in Sweden: The crucial role of social partnership

Dominique Anxo

1. INTRODUCTION

A central pillar of the 'Swedish model', the industrial relations system plays a fundamental role in regulating the labour market and shaping the development of employment, skills and wage structures. Powerful and autonomous social partners, a high union density coupled with a high rate of coverage of collective agreements and a developed and institutionalised social dialogue are the constitutive elements of Swedish industrial relations. These elements, together with a centralised and coordinated two-tier bargaining system, create a favourable institutional environment for the emergence of negotiated compromises aimed at balancing flexibility and security in the labour market. Sweden thus constitutes a good illustration of a flexicurity regime based on negotiated flexibility, in which the social partners are extensively involved in determining the necessary framework, encompassing working conditions, wage formation at the industry and company/local levels, vocational training and the social protection system (notably pensions and unemployment benefits). Furthermore, notwithstanding increasing income inequality, Sweden remains a country with low inequality in absolute terms, regarding both equality of outcomes and of opportunities and there is a continuing high degree of social justice. According to the European Social Justice index, which covers six dimensions (poverty prevention, equitable education, labour market access, social cohesion and non-discrimination, health and intergenerational justice), Sweden was in first position in 2016 – a position it has maintained since 2008 – followed by Finland and Denmark (see Schraad-Tishler and Schiller, 2016).

Against this background, the main objective of this chapter is twofold: first, to analyse the Swedish industrial relations system and how it interacts with inequality issues; and, second, to explore the complex relationship between the main components of the Swedish flexicurity regime, on the one hand, and the industrial relations system, on the other.

This chapter is structured as follows: after a short description of the main features of the Swedish industrial relations system in section 2, section 3 examines the main transformations of the Swedish industrial relations system and how it interacts with inequality issues. Section 4 describes the constitutive elements of the Swedish flexibility regime and the fundamental role played by the social partners. Illustrating the role of social dialogue as a productive factor, section 5 examines the extent to which social dialogue during and after the 2008 Great Recession has contributed to the Swedish recovery and has limited the development of inequalities. In sections 6 and 7, we present two case studies: the crucial role played by the industrial relations system in promoting productivity-enhancing structural changes and favouring skills upgrading (case study 1); and the job security councils and transitional agreements as an illustration of the Swedish flexicurity regime (case study 2). The last section provides some concluding remarks.

2. THE SWEDISH INDUSTRIAL RELATIONS SYSTEM AND ITS IMPLICATIONS FOR INEQUALITY

The Swedish industrial relations system is characterised by a strong contractual tradition based on the existence of powerful social partners enjoying considerable autonomy from the public authorities. Essentially bipartite, another feature of the Swedish model of industrial relations is the crucial role played by the social partners in mechanisms for regulating the labour market, notably wage formation and working conditions. With few exceptions trade unions and employers' organisations in Sweden are structured along sectoral/industry lines. In spite of a clear tendency to a decentralisation of wage determination at the company/organisation levels in the past two decades, the Swedish bargaining system remains fundamentally a two-tier system in which bargaining takes place, first, at the industry/sectoral level and afterward at the company/organisation levels. It should also be emphasised that, by international standards, this two-tier bargaining model remains centralised and coordinated.

Despite a recent and significant decline, the average union density in Sweden remains one of the highest among modern economies (see Table 12A.1 in the Appendix to this chapter and section 2.1), at around 70 per cent in 2014.[1] The coverage rate of collective agreements is also high and at the same date stood at around 90 per cent (84 per cent in the private sector and 100 per cent in the public sector, see Table 12A.2 in the

Appendix). It should be noted that the high coverage rate of collective bargaining in Sweden is not related to the existence of legal provisions for mandatory extension of collective agreements but to the high-density rate of employers' associations and the strong presence of trade unions at the firm/organisation level.[2] Sweden is characterised by well-established and strong employer organisations.[3] In 2013, the density rate of employers' organisations, measured as the share of dependent employees working in workplaces affiliated to employers' associations reached 87 per cent, a density rate significantly higher than union density (see Kjellberg, 2015).

Social dialogue is institutionalised and well developed; regular consultations take place with the social partners[4] and are a key element in the government's policies related to employment and social policies. Even though consultations and information sharing regarding labour market issues between the government and the parliament and the two sides of industry have a long tradition and are a common feature of the political process, it should be stressed that the nature of industrial relations in Sweden remains essentially bipartite. The state is involved in social dialogue in its capacity as employer at the central and local authority levels, but through the respective local bodies and trade union organisations. Tripartite talks do exist and are favoured in Sweden, resulting in either encompassing collective agreements or laws or regulations.

It should also be emphasised that Swedish labour law is limited by comparison with labour legislation in other European Union (EU) member states, and it is for the most part 'optional'; that is, most provisions of labour market legislation may be, wholly or partly, amended by collective agreements. The bipartite and contractual nature of labour market regulation, coupled with the high union density and high coverage rate of collective bargaining, create a favourable institutional environment for the emergence of negotiated compromises aimed at balancing flexibility and security in the labour market. As stressed in Anxo (2013), Sweden constitutes therefore a good illustration of a flexicurity regime based on negotiated flexibility, where the social partners are extensively involved in the regulation of working conditions, wage formation at the industry and company or local levels, the shaping of vocational training but also the social protection system, such as pensions (complementary pension) and unemployment benefits.

By international standards, the extent of wage and income inequality is low in Sweden. The Swedish wage structure remains compressed despite a tendency since the mid-1990s to rising wage dispersion (see Figure 12.1). The lower wage dispersion in Sweden, the lowest among Organisation for Economic Co-operation and Development (OECD) countries according to Paccagnella (2014), can be attributed to a series of interrelated factors: a centralised and coordinated wage bargaining system limiting

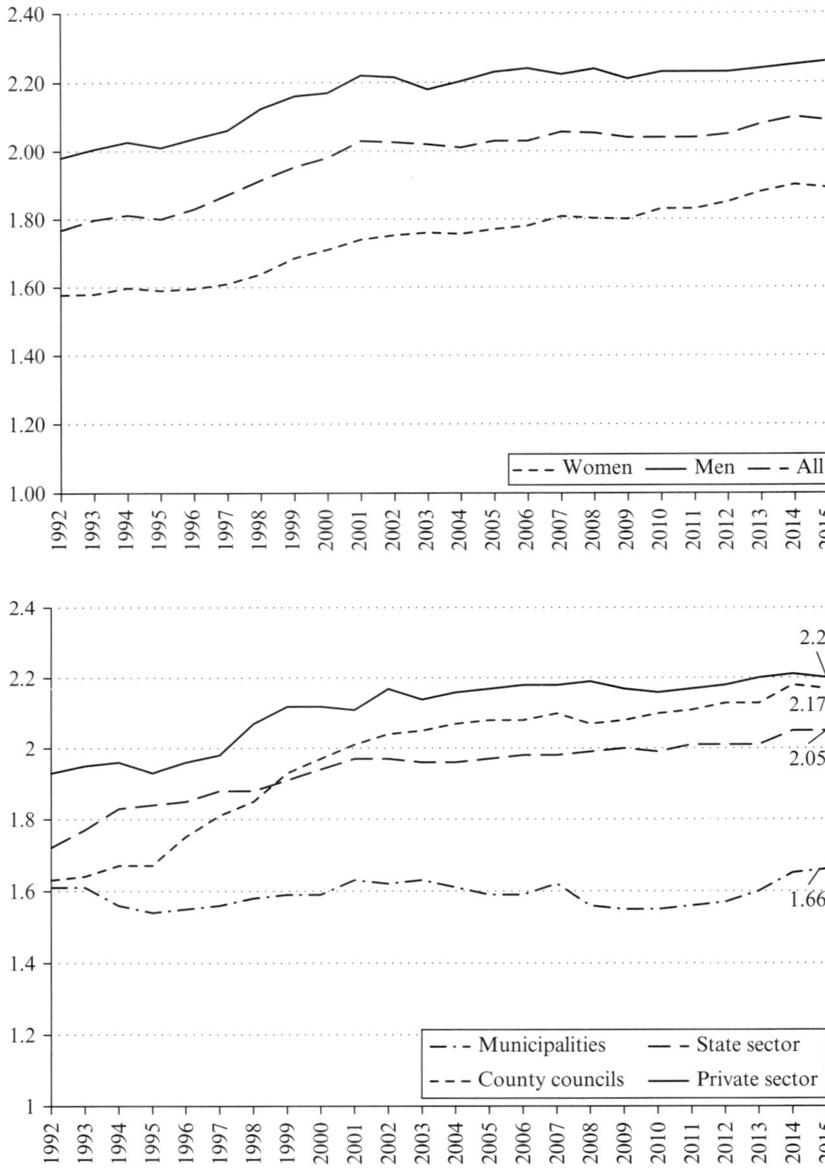

Source: Statistics Sweden (2016).

Figure 12.1 Trends in wage dispersion (P90/P10) by gender (upper panel) and sectors (lower panel)

wage disparities between firms and industries, relatively high collectively agreed wage floors and last but not least the strong bargaining power and implantation of Swedish trade unions, both at industry and company levels, favouring a more balanced outcome regarding wage structure and wage development. This more balanced outcome is not limited to wage structure but also concerns working and employment conditions. The role of the social partners is also central as regards lifelong learning and training facilities and occupational mobility, as illustrated by their active involvement in the shaping of traditional (passive and active) labour market policies or by the so-called security councils and transitional collective agreements aimed at limiting the detrimental consequences of structural changes and collective redundancies (see case studies 1 and 2).

Against the backdrop of the severe economic crisis of the early 1990s and the implementation of several structural reforms, income inequality has been on the rise in Sweden. While it is true that these reforms are aimed at enhancing work incentives and securing the long-term sustainability of the social protection system, it is also clear that they have strengthened the role of the market, reduced the degree of decommodification of the Swedish welfare state and contributed to an increase in income inequality in Sweden (see Anxo, 2015, 2016a). While the reduction of the generosity of the social protection system, the reform of taxation, in particular capital taxation, and the growth of financial markets[5] might explain part of the rise in income inequality, other factors might also have contributed to the widening of income distribution since the mid-1990s, such as the changes in industrial and wage-setting systems. In section 3 we attempt to link the development of income inequality in Sweden with the main transformation of the Swedish industrial relations system.

3. TRANSFORMATION OF THE SWEDISH INDUSTRIAL RELATIONS SYSTEM AND DEVELOPMENT OF INEQUALITIES

3.1 Level of Centralisation and Coordination

From the mid-1950s to the early 1980s, the Swedish industrial relations system relied on highly centralised and coordinated collective bargaining. In 1983, Sweden experienced a rupture in the three decades of a centralised and coordinated system. Following the abandonment of national inter-industry agreements in the mid-1980s collective bargaining in both the private and public sectors nowadays takes place at two levels: industry or sector and enterprise or organisation.

The weakening of mechanisms for coordinated collective bargaining, the resurgence of industrial disputes during the 1980s (see Figure 12.3 in section 5), the threat of state intervention, high wage inflation and the dramatic increase of unemployment during the recession of the early 1990s all had a decisive impact on the emergence of new compromises regarding industrial relations. The three main trade unions[6] in the sector exposed to international competition asked their employer counterparts to consider the possibility of setting up a new procedural rule that fostered both industrial peace and wage increases guaranteeing balanced growth and a return to full employment. The ensuing talks culminated in the signing of an 'Industry Agreement' on Cooperation on Industrial Development and Salary Formation in 1997 (*Industriavtalet*). One of the main innovative features of the Industry Agreement, apart from its tendency to re-coordinate collective bargaining, is that it explicitly regulates the conduct of negotiations and the resolution of disputes. If there is any risk of industrial action, the social partners concerned are obliged to notify the 'impartial chairs' before the start of the notice period for a strike or lockout (see Anxo and Niklasson, 2006). These changes in industrial relations also re-established the pace-setting role of the sectors exposed to international competition and favoured wage adjustments in line with productivity developments. Also worth noting is that these modifications in wage setting led to a perceptible increase in real wages, in contrast to the previous period (mid-1970s to the end of the 1980s), which was characterised by real-wage stagnation. The significant changes in the orientation of monetary policy[7] – namely, the complete autonomy of the Swedish Central Bank and the introduction of a clear inflation target[8] in the mid-1990s – in conjunction with the above-mentioned re-coordination mechanisms in wage setting, also without doubt had an impact on wage formation and wage developments. The social partners in both the private and the public sectors were aware that wage developments not compatible with productivity growth and macroeconomic balance would not, as previously, be accommodated by devaluations, but lead to the implementation of a restrictive monetary policy (interest rate increase), with a potential negative impact on employment and unemployment.

We may argue that this reorientation of monetary policy played a crucial role in wage development by deterring excessive wage increases and wage inflation. It encouraged wage moderation (but still real-wage increases), and rising employment up to the 2008 Great Recession. However, the reformulation of economic policy in the mid-1990s – that is, the priority given to fighting inflation and ensuring fiscal consolidation measures – clearly reflects a weakening of the political commitment to the goal of full employment, as illustrated by unemployment rates well above those experienced during the Golden Age of the Swedish model. We may therefore argue that the higher level of unemployment since the mid-1990s changed the balance of power between the two sides of industry in favour of capital and weakened the bargaining power of trade unions and contributed to the increase of income inequality in Sweden. In other words, if the increase in income inequality can partly be ascribed to the weakening of the bargaining position of trade unions and partly to the decline of union density (see next section), the deterioration of the situation in the labour market, with high and growing unemployment, is a determining factor of this evolution.

In addition to the establishment of new procedural rules aimed at ensuring industrial peace and a re-coordination of wage bargaining at the industry level, we have witnessed since the second half of the 1990s a clear tendency towards a decentralisation and individualisation of wage setting and working conditions at the company or organisational level. This has been the case in both the private and public sectors. That is, the above-mentioned tendency to re-coordinate collective bargaining at the industry level should not be viewed as a weakening of the role played by enterprise-level or organisation-level negotiations. Negotiations at the company or organisation level play a central and growing role in the setting of wages, as well as in the terms and conditions of employment. Enterprise or organisation-level bargaining has tended to gather strength in the past decade, particularly in the public sector (see Anxo, 2013). The acceptance of a more individualised type of wage formation based on individual skills or characteristics and performance or productivity rather than on job characteristics, as had been the case in the past with the application of the 'solidaristic wage policy',[9] testifies to societal changes regarding wage norms and fairness standards among both private and public employees and their representatives. The marked tendency towards decentralisation, differentiation and individualisation of wages and terms and conditions of employment coincides with a wider dispersion of the wage distribution (see Figure 12.1). It is worth noting, however, that the still strong and powerful trade union organisations and high union density at company/organisation level in Sweden lead to negotiated forms of wage individualisation and differentiation. It is also worth highlighting that the modification of the Swedish bargaining system was the outcome of a long process that began as early as the mid-1980s, and the 2008 severe economic downturn did not entail changes in collective bargaining mechanisms. However, the dramatic deterioration of the situation in the labour market induced a series of initiatives and agreements from the two sides of industry aimed at limiting the negative consequences of the economic downturn (see section 5).

The long-term decline in low-skilled jobs and the concomitant increase in demand for high-skilled jobs, combined with the higher return to education witnessed during the past two decades, help to explain this increase in wage inequalities, because wage formation among high-skilled occupations is more individualised and differentiated. There are therefore strong reasons to believe that the tendency towards more decentralised and individualised wage setting has increased wage dispersion, particularly for high-skilled white-collar workers. As stressed by Anxo (2016a, 2016b), if the reduction in the size of the middle class and the corresponding increase in the size of lower- and upper-income groups explain the increased income inequality and polarisation of Swedish society, the decline in the demand for low-skilled jobs (see section 5) and the increase in relative wages for high-skilled workers might have contributed to this development.

3.2 Trends in Union Density

Over the past two decades Sweden has experienced a significant decline in union density. Several factors help to explain the fall of trade union membership in Sweden by almost 12 percentage points between 1990 and 2014 (see Appendix Tables 12A.1 and 12A.2 and Figure 12.2). Parallel to this development the coverage rate of collective agreements has also shown

Source: Mediation Office (2014) and Kjellberg (2015).

Figure 12.2 Trends in union density, 1990–2014, Sweden (percentage)

a slight tendency to decline, from 94 per cent in 1995 to 89 per cent in 2013 (see Appendix Table 12A.3).

It is important to distinguish between long-term transformations related principally to major changes in employment and occupational structure and short-term factors linked to specific measures or the business cycle. In particular, the reduction of employment in manufacturing industry[10] and the public sector owing to fiscal consolidation measures and budget cuts initiated in the 1990s, combined with changes in societal norms (individualistic values) explain part of the long-term decline of union density. The successive reforms of the employment protection system in Sweden, in particular the introduction of short-term contracts not requiring justification from the employer, combined with the deregulation of employment intermediation in the early 1990s, has contributed to a significant increase in employment instability and growing duality in the labour market between insiders and outsiders. The rise of short-term contracts has also contributed to the decline of union density in Sweden; union density is significantly lower among people on fixed-term contracts compared with those on open-ended contracts (74 per cent compared with 47 per cent). Even though structural factors explain the long-term decline of union density in Sweden, the acceleration of this decline after 2006 is closely related to policy measures, in particular the reform of the unemployment insurance system initiated by the centre-right government in 2007 and 2008. This reform resulted in a notable reduction in the generosity of the Swedish unemployment insurance system; the income replacement rate fell from 80 to 70 per cent after 200 days of unemployment and the maximum duration for receiving unemployment benefits was reduced to 300 days. Furthermore, the financing of unemployment insurance was modified: the contributions of the various unemployment funds administered by the trade unions (the Ghent system[11]) were dramatically increased and differentiated according to the unemployment level in the sector or industry concerned. That is, a system of experience rating was introduced, and individual unemployment insurance contributions increased or decreased depending on whether unemployment grows or declines in an industry. This reform entailed a large rise in individual monthly contributions; in some cases, unemployment insurance fees paid by individuals tripled.[12] The consequence was both a large decrease in union membership and a dramatic decline in the number of dependent employees covered by the unemployment insurance system: *circa* 500000 employees left the system between 2007 and 2008.[13] As reported by Kjellberg (2015), the decline of union density in the aftermath of the unemployment insurance reform was unprecedented and as a whole dropped by 6 percentage points (from 77 per cent in 2006 to 71 per cent in 2008). The main objectives of the government with these unemployment insurance reforms were to enhance job seekers' work incentives and to indirectly influence the outcome of wage bargaining by weakening the bargaining power of trade unions and thereby to induce wage restraint.

The 2008 financial crisis particularly hit sectors exposed to international competition and blue-collar workers (see Anxo, 2011; section 5 in this chapter). Against this background, the reform of unemployment insurance financing had a strong impact on union density among Swedish Trade Union Confederation (Landsorganisationen i Sverige, LO) members, in particular within manufacturing industry, but also in low-skilled and low-paid sectors, such as hotels and restaurants and retail, with high labour turnover and large shares of short-term contracts. There are therefore strong reasons to believe that a significant part of the recent decline of union density in Sweden was a consequence of this reform. Also worth noting is that while the crisis did not break the fall of union density among blue-collar workers, the reverse is true for white-collar workers. If the reform of the unemployment insurance system also affected white-collars between 2007 and 2009, union density of these workers increased again in the aftermath of the crisis, reaching the same level as in 2006. In early 2014, the centre-right coalition government again changed the rules concerning unemployment insurance financing, restoring individual monthly unemployment insurance fees to their 2006 level.[14] Against this backdrop, the number of unemployment insurance members has increased during the past two years by almost 55 000, but still remains below its 2006 level. More recently, the Social Democratic–Green coalition government that took office in September 2014 increased the unemployment insurance income replacement rate. There are strong reasons to believe that these two recent measures will contribute at least to stabilising and, at best, to increasing again the level of union density in Sweden and limit the negative impact of the reform of the unemployment insurance system on the development of income inequalities.

4. FLEXICURITY *À LA SUÉDOISE*: THE CRUCIAL ROLE OF THE SOCIAL PARTNERS

Developed during the 1990s and early 2000s, the concept of flexicurity (see Auer, 2010; Madsen, 2002; Wilthagen and Rogowski, 2002; Wilthagen and Tros, 2004) is a broad concept covering areas such as labour legislation, labour market policy, social protection system and skills development. The flexicurity approach, which was espoused by the EU Commission in the mid-2000s, can be considered a policy strategy aimed at 'enhancing the flexibility of labour markets, work organisation and labour relations on the one hand, and to enhance security – employment security and social security – notably for weaker groups in and outside the labour market, on the other' (Wilthagen and Rogowski, 2002: 240). According to this definition, it appears that flexicurity is a central component of the Swedish model. Three constitutive elements of the Swedish flexicurity model can be distinguished: industrial relations system, active labour market policy and training system, and a modern social security system, which combines the provision of adequate income support with the need for labour market mobility and flexibility.

4.1 The Crucial Role of the Industrial Relations System

As already stressed, one of the basic elements of the Swedish model is a strong contractual tradition and the crucial role played by the social partners in mechanisms for regulating labour market working conditions and wage formation. As also previously mentioned, Swedish labour law is limited in comparison with labour legislation in other member states, and it is for the most part 'optional'; that is, most provisions of labour market legislation, such as working time regulation, employment protection and so on, may be, wholly or partly, amended by collective agreements. This distinctive feature coupled with the high union density provides for considerable leeway for the emergence of flexicurity arrangements based on collective agreements at the industry and local/company level, and makes it possible to better adapt the regulatory framework (statutory laws) to firms' productive constraints and workers' preferences as regards working conditions. That is, any assessment of the impact of labour market regulations in Sweden must, in addition to statutory law, consider both the relationship between law and collective agreements and the content of collective agreements at both the industry and firm levels.

A first illustration of the Swedish flexicurity regime concerns the Employment Protection Act (SFS 1982). International comparisons of employment protection indicate that Sweden has fairly restrictive legislation, although it does not stand out as extreme by European standards. Swedish employment protection legislation dates back to the 1974 Employment Protection Act (*Lagen om Anställningsskydd*, LAS; SFS, 1974). The law presumes that, unless otherwise stipulated, an employment contract is open ended. When terminating the contract the employer must provide a valid reason and advance notice. Since the mid-1990s several amendments to the Employment Protection Act have been made. In 1997, the parliament ratified a new bill leading to the creation of new forms of fixed-term contract designed to increase flexibility in the labour market.

The employer got the opportunity to hire, for a limited duration, without having to specify a particular reason. However, an employer could only use a maximum of five such contracts and a particular individual could not be employed under such a contract for more than 12 months during a three-year period. The most important element of the 1997 law is that the Employment Protection Act may now be amended by a company-level agreement without having to pass through a validation procedure by central organisations, provided that the parties had a central agreement in other matters. In both respects, Sweden is fairly unique. In most countries, statutory law is a floor of guaranteed minimum workers' rights upon which collective agreements may build, but not erode, further protection for the employee. In Sweden, however, for instance the Working Time Act and several paragraphs of the Employment Protection Law permit bargaining outcomes that may entail not only higher but also lower levels of protection.

Traditionally, employment adjustment owing to structural and technological changes in Sweden, with the consent or support of the trade unions, has mainly taken the form of external numerical flexibility, combined with active labour market policy measures. The Swedish social partners since the mid-1970s have negotiated security and transitional agreements to help displaced workers to find new jobs quickly, by way of adjustment measures and financial support. (See Table 12A.4 in the Appendix for a list of agreements.) By supplementing the role of local public employment agencies, these agreements, covering nowadays around 75 per cent of employees, help to improve the security of employees and to enhance matching efficiency in the labour market, and have played an important role in ameliorating the deep economic downturn of 2008. Sweden is in this way unique in that the social partners assume the responsibility of a major part in active employment policy measures. These agreements reinforce also the social legitimacy and the positive attitude of trade unions towards structural changes. These negotiated flexicurity arrangements are a good illustration of the Swedish regime of flexicurity and constitute one of our case studies (see section 6.2).

Another illustration of negotiated flexicurity arrangements in Sweden concerns the regulation of working time. The Swedish Working Hours Act (1982) appears to be particularly flexible and has, since the late 1950s, also left the social partners free to negotiate and draw up industrywide agreements on working hours. Hence, the Working Hours Act is also optional and can be partly or entirely replaced through collective agreements at the industry and/or and plant level.[15] Besides the obvious effect of protecting individuals not covered by collective bargaining and limiting the externalities coupled with longer hours, the optional nature of the law has encouraged the social partners to negotiate flexible working time arrangements at the industry or firm level. To illustrate, most of the bargaining areas encompassed in the above-mentioned 'Industry Agreement' apply a yearly working time norm. Also an innovative working time arrangement called 'Life working time' (*Livstidsarbetstidspremie*) allows for 0.5 per cent of labour income per year to be saved in a working time account. The time savings account can be used to take a leave of absence or reduce working time, or may be taken out in cash (except in the engineering sector). It has been estimated that this account can give rise to a working time reduction of 50 hours per year. According to the same agreement, there is also the possibility of introducing a working time bank, which seems to be quite common within this bargaining area.

4.2 Labour Market and Education Policies

The second pillar of the Swedish flexicurity model is active labour market policy programmes (ALMPs). Since the early 1950s, labour market policy has been a central element of Swedish stabilisation policy and has played a crucial role in maintaining a high level of employment and economic growth by easing the redeployment of workers from low to highly productive sectors. Swedish labour market policy comprises a fairly generous unemployment insurance system administrated by the trade unions (Ghent System) and a wide range of active labour market programmes. Similar to the Danish flexicurity model (see Madsen, 2002), one of the salient features of the Swedish flexicurity regime is the emphasis on active labour market policy (activation). The preference for employment promotion programmes has always dominated over benefit options for the unemployed. As previously noted, the early 1990s were notable for a sharp deterioration in the employment situation, with unemployment rising to its highest level since the 1930s (almost 10 per cent in 1994). The early 1990s saw also a re-orientation of the ALMPs, emphasising measures designed to improve efficiency and develop occupational and geographical mobility. The number of participants in vocational training programmes and/or practical insertion courses rose quickly, while traditional measures focusing on labour demand remained at a much lower level than during previous recessions (Anxo and Niklasson, 2006). During 1997–2002, the Swedish government also implemented a new major adult education programme called the Adult Education Initiative or 'Knowledge Lift', with the explicit objective of raising the educational attainment of low-skilled workers to the level of three years of upper secondary school. Participants were eligible for the same grants and loans as for ordinary adult education, and special education support was given to participants receiving unemployment insurance benefits. The size of the programme was unprecedented; during 1997–2002 more than 10 per cent of the labour force was enrolled in 'Knowledge Lift'.[16]

During the recession (2008–11) the volume of participants in the various ALMPs was also gradually increased and supply-orientated and matching measures were emphasised, in particular labour market training and better monitoring of search activities. In the aftermath of the global economic crisis the Swedish government also increased the number of places in post-secondary vocational training and in upper secondary education for adults, as well as the number of places at universities and colleges. The government also extended possibilities for early school leavers to complete their education by participating in training programmes. The growing role of matching measures and vocational training in ALMPs during the past two decades is therefore evidence of the importance that successive governments and the social partners have attached to occupational mobility and to the development of skills over the life course. The re-orientation of ALMPs towards traditional labour market training and adult education can therefore be considered an attempt to upgrade the skills of the labour force in light of the extensive restructuring that the Swedish economy experienced during the 1990s.

Statutory leaves of absence in Sweden are not confined to the existing generous and flexible parental leave system, which allows better reconciliation between work and domestic or care activities. Since 1974, employees have been able to take career breaks to pursue training or study. The legislation on training leave is particularly flexible and gives individuals considerable leeway in their choice of studies. Access to training leave is also promoted by a system of public loans with highly subsidised interest rates and other repayment terms. The Employee's Right to Educational Leave Act (SFS, 1974) had two aims; to encourage social and occupation mobility and to facilitate access to education for employees with the lowest levels of compulsory education. The Act is exceptionally liberal in allowing all workers with at least six months' service to follow the training of their choice, with no restriction on either the type or length of training which may, therefore, be in a field completely unconnected with the worker's job. The arrangements for taking leave are also very flexible: absence may be on an hourly basis (several hours a week combined with normal work) or taken in a block. As with the other forms of statutory leave of absence, the right to training leave is backed by a full employment guarantee; employees are reinstated in their jobs with the same working conditions and the same pay.

Another characteristic of the Swedish education system is the major opportunity it provides to complete education,[17] either through adult education[18] or a training course within the framework of labour market policy. At the workplace level, access to on-the-job training or the opportunity for an employee to further develop their skills is an important component of the Swedish lifelong learning system. Development in the area is also largely a matter for the social partners.

4.3 Modern Social Protection Systems

Despite the above-mentioned reforms of the welfare state, which reduced the extent of its decommodification, the Swedish social protection system remains clearly universal and inclusive in nature and still enjoys a high level of political and public support across the board. The Swedish welfare state remains a societal model based on a generous social protection system, egalitarianism, proactive policies for promoting gender equality and fighting against discrimination and social exclusion, as well as strong public and political involvement in the provision of a wide range of services (see Anxo, 2013, 2015). The generous and comprehensive Swedish social protection system appears to be a constitutive and crucial element of the Swedish flexicurity regime, reducing the cost of mobility and transitions across the life course. High-quality and subsidised childcare facilities, combined with large statutory opportunities to adapt working time over the life course, through various forms of income, compensated legal absenteeism (parental leave, leave for sick child or relatives and study leave) with complete employment guarantees and a reversible time option allow more flexible management of work, investment in human capital and family commitments over the life cycle. Taken together, this policy configuration appears to be an efficient tool to secure individuals' labour market integration, foster employment continuity over the life course and improve gender equality. In my view, the Swedish social protection system constitutes an integrated and coherent system of time and income management over the life course, combining security and flexibility. It should also be stressed that collective agreements at the industry level, and even at the company level, often extend and improve the statutory universal basic social protection in the form of higher replacement or compensation rates, or longer period of entitlement, for example, regarding unemployment and sickness benefits, parental and training leaves and pension (occupational pensions). That is, the role of the social partners is not limited to the regulation of the labour market *stricto sensu* but extending these amendments of the statutory regulations to the realm of social protection via collective agreements constitutes an important element and crucial characteristic of the Swedish flexicurity system[19] (see Palmer, 2014; Sjögren-Lindquist and Wadensjö, 2006; Svenskt Näringsliv, 2016).

5. THE ROLE OF THE SOCIAL PARTNERS AND SOCIAL DIALOGUE IN THE SWEDISH RECOVERY

As a small, export-orientated economy strongly exposed to international competition, Sweden was hard hit by the 2008 global financial crisis. In the wake of that crisis, the Swedish economy started to deteriorate rapidly in the second half of 2008, and in 2009 real gross domestic product (GDP) decreased by 5.0 per cent. With this severe drop in aggregate demand and output, employment decreased by around 100 000 between 2008 and 2009 (an employment rate decrease of 2.1 percentage units from 80.3 per cent in 2008 to 78.2 per cent in 2009) and an increase in the unemployment rate from 6.2 to 8.3 per cent. The fall in output and employment was marked in manufacturing, in particular in the male-dominated export-oriented industries, with a decrease of 14 per cent.

However, sound public finances, owing to, among other things, early fiscal consolidation measures and structural reforms initiated during the 1990s, gave the Swedish government room for manoeuvre in conducting a so-called 'Keynesian' macroeconomic policy in order to maintain aggregate demand and limit the negative impact of the crisis on employment, household income, consumption and welfare. In order to counteract the rise of unemployment, in particular long-term unemployment, the number of participants in the various ALMPs was gradually increased, from 171 000 in 2008 to 314 200 in 2014 (see Swedish Public Employment Service, 2015). While it is true that the above-mentioned reinforcement of ALMP measures and the various activation policies and education measures (in particular the lifelong learning facilities) do not per se create new jobs in the short run, they remain good instruments for securing transitions from unemployment to employment and improving the allocation of resources between sectors. These policy measures, by increasing labour market participation, have favoured social inclusion and have limited the development of long-term unemployment, which remains very low by international standards.

The Swedish economy recovered quickly with a 6.6 per cent increase in real GDP in 2010 and one of 2.6 per cent in 2011 (4.1 per cent in 2015). Employment also increased by 25 000 in 2010 and on average 1.4 per cent between 2011 and 2015. Sweden's relatively rapid recovery from the financial crisis in 2009–10 can be ascribed to several intertwined factors: the expansionary fiscal policies conducted by the Swedish government, more favourable macroeconomic conditions with a quick upturn of exporting industries thanks to an expansionary monetary policy and a floating exchange-rate regime, but also social dialogue and wage moderation.

Regarding the development of social dialogue during the 2008 global financial crisis, the recession had no negative impact on industrial relations[20] and the period 2008–11 remained characterised by industrial peace (see Figure 12.3) in sharp contrast to the situation during the previous recession in the early 1990s.[21] Since the bulk of labour market regulations, working conditions and wage setting in Sweden are determined and regulated by collective agreement, an analysis of measures initiated to combat the impact of the economic crisis on employment and macroeconomic balance cannot be limited to government action. In contrast to other countries, with weaker industrial relations systems and unbalanced bargaining power between the two sides of industry, the specificity of the Swedish industrial relations system also implies a more balanced sharing of the cost of the crisis in terms of both working conditions and inequalities at work. An analysis of the past two waves of the European Working Conditions Survey conducted by Eurofound in 2005 and 2010 (see Anxo, 2013) did not reveal a significant deterioration of working conditions in Sweden in the aftermath of the recession. Working time did not undergo large adjustments, work intensity remained almost unchanged and work satisfaction and work–life balance opportunities seem even to have increased during the period.

As far as wage setting is concerned, experience from the deep economic crisis of the early 1990s shows that wage moderation had characterised wage developments during the second half of the 1990s and early 2000s. There were therefore strong reasons to expect that, in the wake of the current and severe economic and financial crisis, wage agreements would also be concluded in order to preserve employment stability and limit further increases in unemployment. An analysis of collective agreements shows that wage moderation, and not wage cuts as in some other member states, characterised the rounds of collective bargaining during and after the crisis. The depreciation of the Swedish currency owing to an expansionary monetary policy, combined with wage moderation, resulted in a slowdown in the rate of increasing labour costs. This slowdown helped to alleviate the negative effects of the recession on output and employment. The bulk of the adjustment in the public sector took also the form of wage moderation (see Anxo, 2013), with the public sector following the same moderate wage developments as in the private sector. According to short-term wage statistics from the Swedish Mediation Office (2015), the rate of wage increases in 2009 and 2010 for the economy as a whole was 3.3 and 2.5 per cent, respectively, significantly below those recorded in 2007–08 in both the private and the public sector. The stable nominal wage increase continued also during the post-crisis years 2010–15, when wage agreements concluded remained in the range of 2.5–3.0 per cent. In my view, these developments

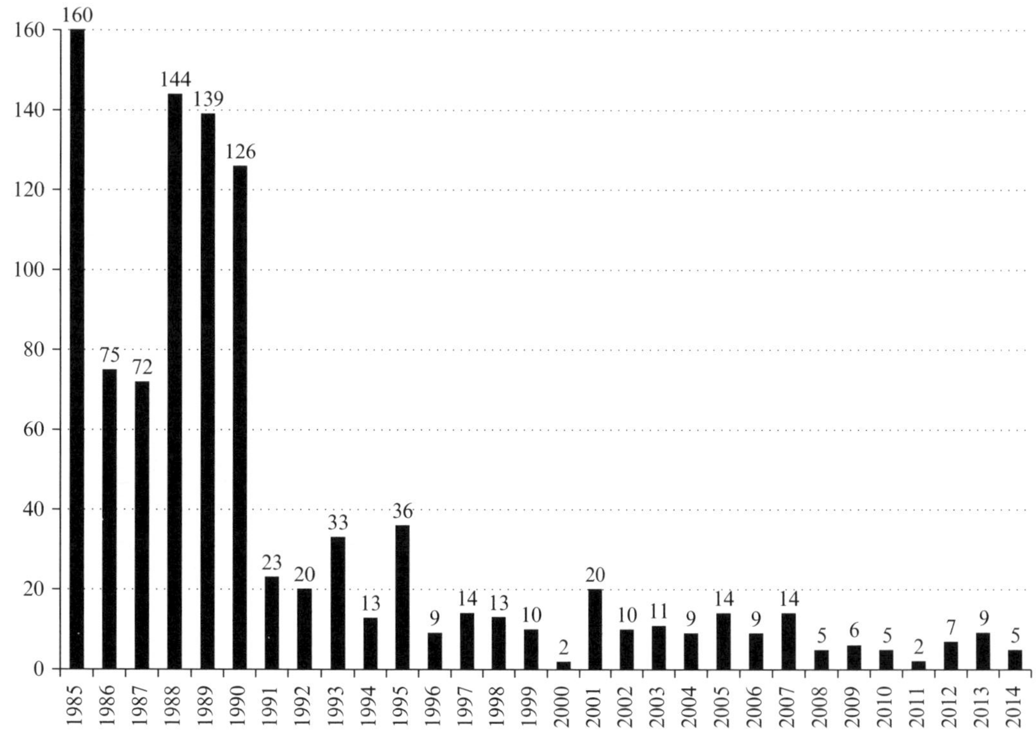

Source: Swedish Mediation Office (2014).

Figure 12.3 Industrial conflicts, 1985–2014, Sweden (number of conflicts)

illustrate well the extent of Swedish negotiated wage flexibility during a recession, and the willingness of the two sides of industry to share more equally the burden of the crisis and limit the potential impact of the recession on employment, wage distribution and inequality.

As already stressed, in line with the core elements of the Swedish flexicurity model, economic downturns and structural changes in Sweden have seldom been accommodated by public measures aimed at protecting jobs and have mainly taken the form of external numerical flexibility, combined with active labour market policy measures. Following this tradition, the Swedish adjustment process in operation during the 2008 global economic crisis was a mix of negotiated numerical flexibility and active support of dismissed workers through active labour market policy measures and/or negotiated agreements helping redundant workers to find new jobs rapidly or to enhance their employability (see case study 2 and Appendix Table 12A.4 for a list of related collective agreements).

However, even though there was no government measure for maintaining employment by means of short-time working schemes during the early phase of the 2008 global financial crisis, as for example in Germany, initiatives were taken by the two sides of industry. By way of illustration, the trade union federation IF Metall and the Association of Swedish Engineering Industries concluded a framework agreement on temporary layoffs, wage adjustments and training in March 2009. The agreement was valid until 31 March 2010, with a three-month notice period. To be valid, the agreement had to be endorsed by local agreement between the employer and the union. Under the agreement, a person temporarily laid off from work could receive at least 80 per cent of their usual monthly wage. The Swedish Industrial and Chemical Employers' Association, the Employers' Association of the Steel and Metal Industry, the Employers' Association of Swedish Mine Owners, the Employers' Federation of Welding Engineering and IF Metall signed a temporary redundancy pay agreement on 2 March 2009, enabling local partners at firm level to conclude agreements on temporary layoffs. This agreement is similar to the agreement between IF Metall and the employers in the Association of Swedish Engineering Industries. Some 400 companies affiliated to the Association of Swedish Engineering Industries concluded such agreements. Most of them covered both manual and non-manual workers. On average, these short-time working agreements included an 18 per cent reduction in working hours and a 13 per cent reduction in wages. The average duration of these agreements was a little over six months.[22] In the wake of the tripartite talks initiated by the government in 2011, the Swedish Parliament (Riksdag) adopted a new law on short-time working in December 2013 (SFS 2013). According to the law, it is possible to implement a state-subsidised short-time working scheme in a severe economic recession. State support is restricted to companies in the private sector covered by a collective agreement at industry level on short-time working. The rules regarding short-time working must be stipulated by a collective agreement at company level. As further stipulated by the law, the state, the employers and the employees (through wage reduction[23]) will share the cost of short-time working, the contribution of the state being one-third.

6. CASE STUDY 1: TECHNOLOGICAL CHANGES, SKILL STRUCTURE AND INEQUALITIES: THE ROLE OF INDUSTRIAL RELATIONS AND FLEXICURITY ARRANGEMENTS

As many modern societies, during the past half-century Sweden has undergone large structural transformations. The long-term trend in employment by broad sectors shows a large decline of employment in agriculture and manufacturing, and a significant increase in the service sector. The shift from a traditional industrial society towards a modern welfare state and knowledge-intensive service economy in Sweden has also had important implications for the development of the skills and occupational structure.

Figure 12.4 gives a graphical representation of the modification in the distribution of jobs and employment structure between 1985 and 2011, distinguishing between periods of job creation (Figure 12.4, upper panel) and job destruction (Figure 12.4, lower panel). As shown by Figure 12.4, the patterns of job creation and destruction during the past three decades indicate a significant diminution, both in absolute and relative terms, of jobs in the lower tail of the job distribution and a clear increase in jobs in the upper tail of the distribution. Contrasting with 'liberal' market-orientated economies, such as the United States and the United Kingdom, which have experienced a polarisation of their job structures during the past half century, Sweden has experienced a consistent and pervasive pattern of skills upgrading over time. This pattern of occupational upgrading has taken the form of a shift of aggregate employment from the lower tail of the job distribution to the top, with an absolute decline of low-skilled, low-paid jobs and an absolute increase in high-skilled jobs. This has also been particularly marked during recessions, in particular the dramatic economic downturn of the early 1990s that resulted in a massive destruction of jobs in the middle and lower tails of the job distribution and a weak increase in jobs in the upper tail of the occupational structure. This pattern of job upgrading has also characterised the current economic crisis, as shown in Figure 12.4 (lower panel), with a clear destruction of jobs in the

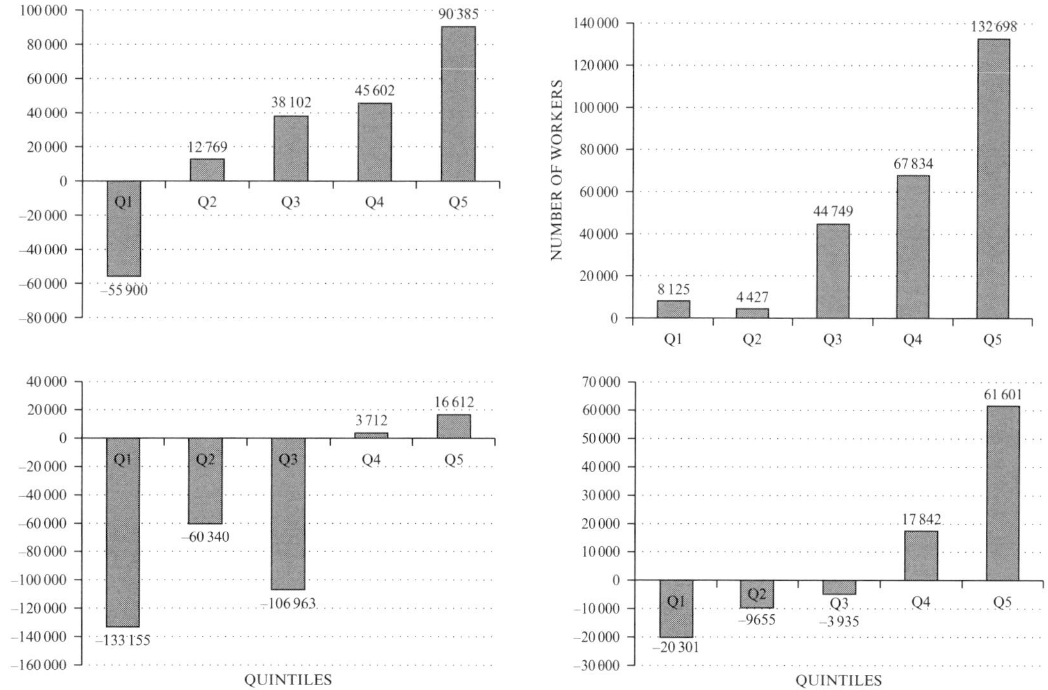

Source: Anxo (2016a).

Figure 12.4 Long-term changes in occupational structure, period of job creation (upper panel) and period of job destruction (lower panel); average annual absolute change in job-wage quintiles, Sweden, 1985–2011

lower tail, but also a significant increase in high-skilled, high-paid jobs. It is also interesting to note that the 2008 global financial crisis did not entail an increase in the polarisation[24] of the occupational structure (see Figure 12.4, lower panel). The 2008 crisis predominantly implied a destruction of low-skilled and low-paid jobs, while high-skilled, high-paid jobs have increased.

If anything, there are reasons to believe that the skill upgrading process during the last crisis has slightly increased wage and income inequality, but the Gini coefficient remained almost unchanged between 2009 and 2015 (from 0.267 to 0.270 in 2015). While cuts in the social protection system and taxation reform – in particular, capital taxation and the growth of financial markets – explain part of the rise in income inequality in Sweden since the mid-1990s, the changes in industrial relations and wage-setting systems might also have contributed to the widening of income distribution. The shift towards more decentralised and individualised wage setting has led to an increase of wage dispersion, particularly among high-skilled white-collar workers. Despite the tendency for rising wage inequalities (see Figure 12.1), the centralised and coordinated collective bargaining system and a still compressed wage structure, with the lowest wage dispersion among OECD countries (see Paccagnella, 2014) have prevented the development of low paid/low-skilled jobs in Sweden and, instead, have boosted policies favouring an upgrading of skills. In effect, large investment in labour saving technologies and research and development and the associated increase in demand for high-skilled jobs,[25] the well-developed lifelong learning and training system, the expansion of tertiary education during the past three decades, as well as a more balanced bargaining power between the two sides of industry have limited the tendency towards job polarisation found, for example, in 'liberal' market-orientated economies. That is, the specificity of the industrial relations system favouring a relatively compressed wage structure with high collectively agreed wage floors has promoted productivity-enhancing structural changes, limited the development of low-paid or low-skilled jobs and contributed to the development of a high-skilled knowledge-intensive workforce. However, the reduction of demand for less qualified jobs has also impacted negatively on the possibility for low-skilled or low-educated workers to get a job and increased their propensity to become unemployed. The limited impact of structural/technological changes and economic crisis on inequality in Sweden can be largely explained by massive investment in human capital and the existence of lifelong learning or training facilities, ALMPs (in particular labour market training schemes) and, last but not least, the existence of job security agreements covering more than 75 per cent of the labour force, aimed at limiting the negative individual consequences of structural changes and economic downturns. (See case study 2.)

7. CASE STUDY 2: JOB SECURITY COUNCILS AND TRANSITIONAL JOB AGREEMENTS

7.1 Introduction

The specificity of the Swedish industrial relations system, together with the contractual nature of labour market regulation, creates a favourable institutional environment for the emergence of negotiated compromises aimed at balancing flexibility and security in the labour market. This specific institutional environment has resulted in innovative practices and solutions for dealing with job losses and structural changes. Particularly notable are the creation during the early 1970s of the so-called job security or transitional job agreements that were established by the social partners on a bipartite basis to support employees and companies affected by restructuring. In the context of the 2008 economic crisis, these innovative instruments appear to be particularly interesting.

In the case of collective redundancy owing to restructuring or individual notice owing to shortages of work, the Swedish social partners have negotiated security or adjustment agreements in order to help workers who have been given notice to find rapidly new jobs by way of adjustment measures[26] and financial support. By supplementing the role of public employment agencies, these agreements, covering about three-quarters of the labour force, contribute to improving the security of employees and enhancing the matching efficiency and geographical and occupational mobility in the labour market. These agreements reinforce also the social legitimacy and the positive attitude of trade unions towards structural changes. The support programmes are administrated by organisations – the so-called job security councils (*trygghetsråd*, TRR) and job security foundations (*trygghetsstiftelser*, TSL) – specially designed for this purpose. The employers finance the various activities by paying a contribution amounting to 0.15 to 0.3 per cent of the wage bill. All employees covered by these agreements are included in the activities, regardless of whether they are union members or not.

The main objective of this section is to identify the key instruments used by the Swedish social partners to accommodate and manage structural changes, namely, through the setting up of the aforementioned job security councils or similar 'transitional agencies' aimed at reducing the negative consequences of restructuring on employees, firms and society as a whole.

7.2 History

The first job security councils were established in 1974, in a context of declining economic growth and significant job losses, as well as important waves of industrial restructuring (textile, shipyard industries and so on). During this period, the main instruments used to address labour market imbalances were traditional active labour market policies, implemented by the Public Employment Service (PES). The PES was responsible for delivering labour market training for blue-collar workers, although at the time it was increasingly criticised for not providing adequate support to displaced white-collar workers. Also, the PES would rarely get involved in ongoing restructuring processes because its primary target group was unemployed jobseekers rather than employees affected by restructuring. One of the rationales behind the development of these innovative transitional practices and the creation of the first job security councils was therefore that the services provided by the public employment agencies were regarded as inadequate and ineffective to meet the requirements of dismissed white-collar workers (Diedrich and Bergström, 2006). For a long time, job security councils and transitional job agreements – that is, agreements between social partners on active measures and financial support for job transition during restructuring – have primarily covered white-collar employees in the private and public sectors and employees in the cooperative sector. Corresponding arrangements have existed for state employees (TSL) and for employees in banking and finance (the Employers' Association of the Banking Institutions, BAO) since the early 1990s. In 2004, a job transitional agreement (*Omställningsingsavtal*) was concluded between the Swedish Trade Union Confederation (LO), and the Confederation of Swedish Enterprise (Svenskt Näringsliv), encompassing almost 1 million blue-collar workers in the private sector and administered by the job security foundation. More recently, in 2010 municipal and county council employees were also covered by new job security agreements between, on the one hand, the Swedish Association of Local Authorities and Regions (SKL) and, on the other, the Municipal Workers' Union (Kommunal), the Public Employees' Negotiation Council (OFR) and the Academics Alliance (AkademikerAlliansen).

There are currently 16 different job security councils in Sweden, covering about 3 million out of approximatively 4.5 million dependent employees (see Table 12A.4 in the Appendix for a description of the main job security councils).

7.3 Organisation, Implementation and Funding

The job security councils were established in order to administer and perform the various support activities stipulated in the respective job security agreements. Each job security council has a supervisory board of representatives of the social partners involved in the agreement, with membership on a parity basis. The board decides upon the scope and content of the support that is to be granted. The job security councils' employees – both advisers and consultants – have a high degree of freedom to prepare, based on the decisions made by the supervisory board, the individual support for each redundant employee. This possibility of providing support tailored to the needs of the individual is considered to be one of the strengths of the Swedish job security councils. Their activities are financed by the employers through an annual contribution amounting to 0.3 per cent of a company's wage bill.

The types of organisation that provide and implement the support activities also vary between the various job security and job transitional agreements. Some job security councils have created their own organisation with 'in house' advisers or consultants, while others – entirely or partly – engage private providers operating in the 'transitional job or labour market' that emerged in Sweden in connection with the deregulation of outplacement and the end of the public monopoly of job placement in 1993.[27] To illustrate, the TRR job security council (see Table 12A.4 in the Appendix) for white-collar employees in the private sector has created its own structure, TRR outplacement, designing and performing support activities 'in house', including guidance and training activities. However, the largest council in terms of affiliated employees, the job security council (TSL) for blue-collar workers in the private sector, outsources all support activities and has signed contracts with nine suppliers of outplacement services. Based on the contract signed between the TSL and its suppliers, the local partners can order specific, tailor-made restructuring programmes, which are then implemented in the workplace. It should also be noted that the cooperation between these actors and the councils – the restructuring activities – may start as soon as the notice of dismissal is given.

7.4 Support Activities and Measures

The job security council plays an important role at different stages in the restructuring process. In the initial stage of the process, counsellors provide the employer as well as trade union representatives with expertise related to the restructuring process per se. Once the decision has been taken on which

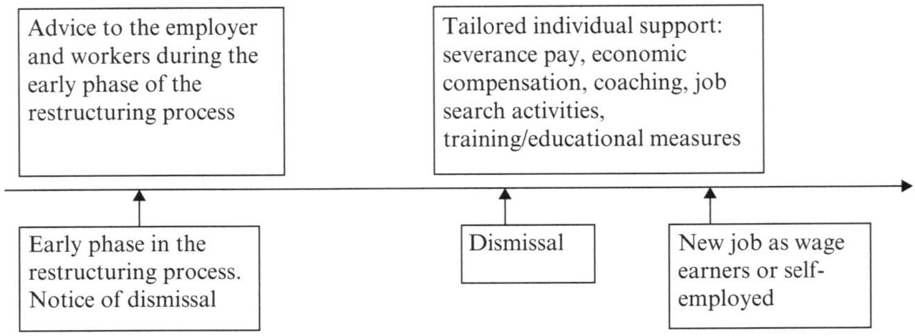

Figure 12.5 The timing of interventions and support activities

restructuring strategy to pursue, the second phase involves guidance and support to the employees affected by restructuring (Figure 12.5).

The Swedish approaches are strongly focused on providing support for workers already affected by restructuring, namely curative and compensatory measures; to date, preventive measures have been limited even though the various forms of support usually start in the early phase of the restructuring process. The support measures offered by the job security councils take several forms, including severance payments and complementary unemployment compensation above the standard unemployment benefit in order to guarantee a decent level of income during the transitional period. According to individual rights stipulated by the various job security agreements, financial support can be ensured through paid leave, earnings supplements, sponsorship enabling individuals to try out a new job to see if it suits both parties, extended occupational health services, early retirement and pension benefits. Some job security agreements also provide a wage differential between the wage of the previous job and the wage of a new but lower-paid job (Diedrich and Bergström, 2006).

In addition to financial support and economic compensation, individual plans are designed and developed through a number of meetings with the advisers appointed by the job security councils. The first step is often an assessment of the worker's skills and requirements. Redundant workers are assisted in drawing up a professional training path aimed at enhancing their employability and promoting their occupational mobility. The most recurrent measures for individuals affected by redundancy include the following readjustment measures: information about labour market and training possibilities both locally and globally; personal guidance, advice and counselling (advice on education and career choices); coaching on job search processes; personal development activities individually or in groups; financial support for further education and training; and support in finding new employment through the councils' own channels or other routes, or support in starting a new business. The measures provided are flexible and the support activities are tailored to the needs of the individual, taking into account their qualifications and professional interests, as well as personal concerns. The relationship between the displaced worker and the job security council adviser continues as long as the person remains a client. A typical average duration is six to eight months (Diedrich and Bergström, 2006).

According to statistics collected by the Job Security Foundation (Trygghetsråd, 2016), the various job security agreements have included approximately 18 500 restructuring projects and has supported more than 100 000 dismissed employees between 1990 and 2009. Around 75 per cent of these workers found new employment, while 25 per cent remained unemployed. In 2015, nine out of ten of dismissed jobseekers found a new job or became self-employed within seven months following their first contact with the job security foundations. Among the displaced workers, around 10 per cent start their own company and 80 per cent remained in business after two years. Furthermore, around 70 per cent of the displaced workers obtained an equal or higher salary in their new job (Bergström, 2009; Trygghetsråd, 2016).

One possible explanation of the relative success of the job security councils in limiting the negative individual consequences of structural changes, in particular, is the significant degree of flexibility and freedom concerning the choice of measures implemented to help redundant workers. Being a comparatively small organisation also makes it easier for these transitional agencies to intervene quickly; rapidity of intervention is crucial for a successful transitional process. It should also be stressed that the job security agreements, by regulating severance payments and redundancy compensation, may make it less costly for an individual employer to restructure. These lower costs might also explain why restructuring processes seems to be shorter in Sweden than in other EU countries (Sjögren-Lindquist and Wadensjö, 2006).

8. CONCLUSION

With its strong negotiation tradition, the Swedish industrial relations system remains the archetype of a bipartite agreement-based model, in which the social partners play an essential role in determining the mechanisms for regulating the labour market, working conditions and wage formation. Despite a small decline in union density during the past two decades, both sides of industry remain firmly in control of labour market regulations and wage setting. As previously explained, Swedish labour law is limited in comparison with labour legislation in other EU member states and most provisions of labour market legislation may be – wholly or partly – amended by collective agreement. This distinctive feature, coupled with high union density, gives rise to considerable leeway for the emergence of flexicurity arrangements based on collective agreements at the industry and local or company level, making it possible to better adapt the regulatory framework to firms' productive constraints and workers' preferences as regards working conditions. The specific features of the Swedish industrial relations system, characterised by a relative balance of power between the two sides of industry, also helps to explain why Sweden, despite a tendency to increasing income inequality and increasing class polarisation, remains a country with a compressed wage structure, low income disparities and extended social justice.

The centralised and coordinated collective bargaining system and a still compressed wage structure with relatively high wage floors and the lowest wage inequality among OECD countries have also prevented the development of low-paid or low-skilled jobs in Sweden and instead have boosted policies favouring upgrading skills. In effect, large investment in research and development, a well-developed lifelong learning and training system, the expansion of tertiary education during the past three decades, as well as a more balanced bargaining power between the two sides of industry have limited the tendency towards job polarisation found, for example, in 'liberal' market-orientated economies. In this context, the Swedish job security councils and transitional job agreements have played a fundamental role in alleviating the detrimental consequences of structural changes on individuals, in particular by limiting long periods of unemployment, which we know are a crucial determinant of social exclusion and increased inequality. These agreements constitute a good illustration of a regime of flexicurity and negotiated flexibility, combining individual security for employees and flexibility for employers with regard to necessary restructuring and readjustment measures. The joint management structure of the social partners appears also to be a clear advantage, reinforcing the social legitimacy as well as the positive attitude of Swedish trade unions towards structural and technological changes and productivity-enhancing restructuring.

The Swedish industrial relations system and its well-developed social dialogue have also played a determinant role during the last recession, and helps to explain why the cost of the crisis has been more evenly distributed between different socio-economic groups. Contrasting with other member states, the 2008 economic downturn has not adversely affected employment conditions through wage cuts, longer working hours, higher workloads and increased work intensity, as has been the case in other EU member states. The Swedish experience thus remains a good illustration of the positive role played by developed social dialogue based on a balance of power between the two sides of industry in mitigating and absorbing the negative impact of external macroeconomic shocks, as well as in limiting the development of income inequalities and favouring social cohesion.

NOTES

1. The Swedish trade union landscape features three confederations: the Swedish Trade Union Confederation (LO), organising blue-collar workers, the Swedish Confederation of Professional Employees (TCO) organising white-collar workers and the Swedish Confederation of Professional Associations (SACO) organising university graduates.
2. In contrast with some other EU member states, wage earners are represented by local union 'clubs' and not by separate works councils. Workplace representatives have a mandate to negotiate. Since the mid-1970s the law on co-determination in working life in Sweden (SFS 1976) stipulates that, prior to any decision regarding significant changes in employment and working conditions, the employer has the obligation to inform and consult the trade union organisation(s) in charge of concluding collective agreements.
3. Sweden has three main employer associations: in the private sector, the Confederation of Swedish Enterprise (Svenskt Näringsliv, SN) and two employer associations in the public sector, the Swedish Association of Local Authorities and Regions (Sveriges Landsing and Kommuner, SKL*)* for local authorities and for the government sector, the Swedish Agency for Government Employers (Arbetsgivarverket, Agf).
4. Social partners are usually represented on parliamentary and government committees responsible for drawing up employment and social policies. In this way, the social partners exert significant influence on the contents of labour market legislation.
5. The stock market flourished during the second half of the 1990s and equities became a common means of saving for an increasing share of Swedish households. By the end of the 1990s around 60 per cent of all households were shareholders (see Gustafsson and Palmer, 2002).
6. The Swedish Federation of Blue-Collar Workers in the Engineering Industry (IF, Metall), affiliated to LO; the Swedish Federation of White-Collar Workers in Industry (Unionen), affiliated to the TCO; and the Swedish Association of Graduate Engineers (Sveriges Civilingenjörförbundet, CF).
7. In particular, the change of monetary regime (floating rate) in the early 1990s was a clear signal that the central bank would no longer conduct an accommodative monetary policy via devaluations, as in the past.
8. That is, 2 per cent per year, within a range of plus or minus 1 per cent.
9. The 'solidaristic' wage policy involved not only the application of the principle of equal pay for equal work (irrespective of sectors, regions or the profitability of companies) but also efforts to reduce wage differentials between jobs, that is, to promote a more compressed wage structure. The primary motivation for the implementation of this wage norm was not only fairness and equity, but even economic efficiency by fostering and promoting productivity-enhancing structural changes through the closure of unproductive plants and/or rationalisation at the company level.
10. The propensity to join a trade union being traditionally higher in these two sectors.
11. The Swedish unemployment insurance system is a so-called Ghent system based on voluntary membership subsidised by the state. Different trade unions covering different industries administer the unemployment insurance funds.
12. To illustrate, between 2006 and 2009 the individual monthly unemployment insurance fees for construction workers increased from SEK116 (€11.9) to SEK455 (€46.6), for workers in engineering industries from SEK93 (€9.9) to SEK384 (€40.9) and for employees in hotels and restaurants from SEK97 (€9.9) to SEK430 (€44.0) (see

Kjellberg, 2014). If you add the normal affiliation fee for being a member of a trade union, the monthly cost increase was significant.
13. The share of the workforce covered by unemployment insurance decreased from 80 per cent to 67 per cent between 2007 and 2009.
14. Two main reasons explain this change: new general elections and that the reform of unemployment insurance implied that a large number of wage earners, in particular low-paid or low-skilled employees with unstable employment conditions, lacked sufficient protection in case of unemployment, which amplified the risk of social exclusion.
15. For example, the dispositions contained in the collective agreement between the Swedish Metal Workers' Unions (Metallarbetareförbund) and the Association of Swedish Engineering Industries (Versktadssföreningen) entirely replaces the Working Hours Act (1982). Furthermore, this agreement enjoins the social partners to negotiate agreements at the plant level, which favours a more efficient use of equipment and greater individual working time flexibility.
16. To illustrate, in 1999 a maximum of 228 000 persons were enrolled in the Knowledge Lift programme; by comparison the number of pupils attending regular upper-secondary school was 300 000 at the same date. An evaluation of the outcomes by Albrecht et al. (2005) shows that the impact of Knowledge Lift on the probability of obtaining employment was on average significantly positive.
17. In relation to, for example, early drop out from the education system.
18. Adult education in Sweden has a long tradition and has expanded markedly since the end of the 1960s.
19. Around 90 per cent of employees are covered by collectively agreed insurance schemes with higher compensation in case of illness, work injury, parental leave and loss of job. To illustrate, public social insurance provides 80 per cent income replacement for loss of income due to own sickness, child sickness or injury. Generally collectively agreed occupational insurance provides an additional 10 per cent earnings replacement above social insurance's 80 per cent replacement rate.
20. Currently, there are in Sweden more than 650 central collective agreements on wages and general terms and conditions of employment. It should be noted that the 2008 crisis per se did not impact negatively on the number of agreements, union density or the coverage rate of collective bargaining.
21. The deep recession of the early 1990s took the form of a dramatic employment crisis. In just three years – from 1990 to 1993 – the rate of employment decreased by more than 10.5 percentage points to about 73 per cent, and the rate of open unemployment increased nearly fivefold, from less than 2 to around 10 per cent of the labour force. Furthermore, the government's annual budget deficit increased from about zero to some 14 per cent of GNP, while public debt increased from 38 per cent to 76 per cent between 1990 and 1995.
22. According to IF Metall these agreements helped to safeguard between 12 000 and 15 000 jobs.
23. The wage reduction is 12 per cent in case of a working time reduction of 20 per cent, 16 per cent in case of a working time reduction of 40 per cent and a maximum of 20 per cent in case of a working time reduction of 60 per cent.
24. By polarisation of the job structure we mean here a concomitant increase of both low-skilled and high-skilled jobs and a destruction of jobs in the middle layers of the occupational structure.
25. Due in particular to a strong complementarity between skills and new technologies.
26. It can be anything from simple advice, such as how to improve a CV, to more far-reaching measures, such as changing occupation or starting a business.
27. The actors performing the support activities range from private temporary work agencies, public and private outplacement consultants, regional organisations working with restructuring, private insurance companies, web-based services and the job security councils.

REFERENCES

Albrecht, J., G. van den Berg and S. Vroman (2005), The knowledge lift: the Swedish adult education program that aimed to eliminate low worker skill levels', IZA Discussion Paper No 1503, Institute for the Study of Labour, Bonn.

Anxo, D. (2011), 'Negotiated flexibility in Sweden: a more egalitarian response to the crisis?', in D. Vaughan-Whitehead (ed.), *Work Inequalities in the Crisis: Evidence from Europe*, Cheltenham, UK and Geneva: Edward Elgar and ILO, pp. 445–73.

Anxo, D. (2013), 'Early fiscal consolidation and negotiated flexibility in Sweden: A fair way out of the crisis?', in D. Vaughan-Whitehead (ed.), *Public Sector Shock: The Impact of Policy Retrenchment in Europe*, Cheltenham, UK and Geneva: Edward Elgar and ILO, pp. 543–75.

Anxo, D. (2015), 'The Swedish social model: resilience and success in turbulent times', in D. Vaughan-Whitehead (ed.), *The European Social Model in Crisis: Is the European Model Losing Its Soul?*, Cheltenham, UK and Geneva: Edward Elgar and ILO, pp. 507–52.

Anxo, D. (2016a), 'The rise and fall of the Swedish middle class?', in D. Vaughan-Whitehead (ed.), *Europe's Disappearing Middle Class? Evidence from the World of Work*, Cheltenham, UK and Geneva: Edward Elgar and ILO, pp. 542–85.

Anxo, D. (2016b), 'Upskilling to avoid job polarisation and growing income inequalities: the Swedish experience', *Economia and Lavoro*, **50** (10), 13–24.

Anxo, D. and H. Niklasson (2006), 'The Swedish model in turbulent times: decline or renaissance?', *International Labour Review*, **145** (4), 339–71.

Auer, P. (2010), 'What's in a name? The rise (and fall?) of flexicurity', *Journal of Industrial Relations*, **52** (3), 371–86.

Bäckström, H. and J. Otosson (2006), 'Government job policy and collective job transitions', in J. Olofsson and M. Zavisic (eds), *Routes to a More Open Labour Market*, Stockholm: National Institute for Working Life, pp. 137–48.

Bergström, O. (2009), 'Anticipating and managing restructuring, Sweden', report, International Training Centre, ITC/ILO, Turin, accessed 9 November at http://www.bollettinoadapt.it/old/files/document/9538ARENAS_27_09_201.pdf.

Diedrich, A. and O. Bergström (2006), 'The job security council in Sweden, MIRE project', Institute of Management of Innovation and Technology, Gothenburg.

Gustafsson, B. and E. Palmer (2002), 'Was the burden of the deep Swedish recession equally shared?', *Review of Income and Wealth*, **48** (4), 537–60.

Kjellberg, A. (2014), 'Vilka hoppade av a-kassan eller avstod från att gå med', working paper, Department of Sociology, Lund University, Lund.

Kjellberg, A. (2015), 'Kollektivsavtal täckningsgrad samt organisationsgrad hos arbetgivarförbund och fackförbund', working paper, Department of Sociology, Lund University, Lund.

Madsen, P.K. (2002), 'The Danish model of flexicurity: a paradise – with some snakes', in H. Sarfati and G. Bonoli (eds), *Labour Market and Social Protections Reforms in International Perspective: Parallel or Converging Tracks?* Farnham: Ashgate, pp. 243–65.

Paccagnella, M. (2014), 'Skill and wage inequality, evidence from PIACC', OECD Directorate for Education and Skill, Paris.

Palmer, E. (2014), 'Financial sustainability of Swedish welfare commitments,

Policy Research Institute, Ministry of Finance, Japan', *Public Policy Review*, **10** (2), 253–75.
Schraad-Tischler, D. and C. Schiller (2016), 'Social Justice in the EU', Index Report 2016 Social Inclusion Monitor Europe, Bertelsmann Stiftung, Gütersloh.
Sjögren-Lindquist, G. and E. Wadensjö (2006), 'Complementary benefits in connection with loss of income and their effect on the work principle', in J. Olofsson and M. Zavisic (eds), *Routes to a More Open Labour Market*, Stockholm: National Institute for Working Life, pp. 129–36.
Statistics Sweden (2016), *Statistics on Disposable Income*, SCB, accessed September 2016 at http://www.scb.se/en_/Finding-statistics/Statistics-by-subject-area/Household-finances/Income-and-income-distribution/Distributional-analysis-system-for-income-and-transfers/Aktuell-Pong/113180/226029/.
Svensk författningssamling (SFS) (1974), *Lag om arbetstagares rätt till ledighet för utbildning*, 1974:981, accessed September 2016 at http://www.riksdagen.se/sv/dokument-lagar/dokument/svensk-forfattningssamling/lag-1974981-om-arbetstagares-ratt-till_sfs-1974-981.
Svensk författningssamling (SFS) (1976), *Lag om medbestämmande i arbetslivet*, 1976:580, accessed September 2016 at https://www.riksdagen.se/sv/Dokument-Lagar/Lagar/Svenskforfattningssamling/Lag-1976580-om-medbestamman_sfs-1976-580/.
Svensk författningssamling (SFS) (1982), *Lag om anställningsskydd, LAS Employment Protection Act*, 1982:80, accessed September 2016 at https://www.riksdagen.se/sv/Dokument-Lagar/Lagar/Svenskforfattningssamling/Lag-198280-om-anstallningss_sfs-1982-80/.
Svensk författningssamling (SFS) (2013), *Lag om stöd vid kortidsarbete*, 2013:948 accessed September 2016 at https://www.riksdagen.se/sv/Dokument-Lagar/Lagar/Svenskforfattningssamling/Lag-2013948-om-stod-vid-kor_sfs-2013-948/?bet=2013:948.
Svenskt Näringsliv (2016), 'Statutory and collective insurance schemes for the Swedish labour market, 2016', accessed October 2016 at https://www.svensktnaringsliv.se/migration_catalog/Rapporter_och_opinionsmaterial/Rapporter/statutory-and-collective-insurancepdf_641713.html/BINARY/Statutory%20and%20collective%20insurance.pdf.
Swedish Mediation Office (various years), 'Wage statistics', various years, Stockholm, accessed September 2016 at http://www.mi.se/.
Swedish Public Employment Service (2015), Statistics database, accessed October 2016 at www.arbetsformedlingen.se.
Trygghetsråd (2016), 'Job security foundation, statistics', accessed in January 2017 at http://www.trr.se/om-trr/statistik/.
Wilthagen, T. and R. Rogowski (2002), 'Legal regulation of transitional labour markets', in G. Schmid and B. Gazier (eds), *The Dynamics of Full Employment: Social Integration through Transitional Labour Markets*, Cheltenham, UK and Northampton, MA, USA: Edward Elgar, pp. 233–73.
Wilthagen, T. and F. Tros (2004), 'The concept of flexicurity: a new approach to regulating employment and labour markets', *Transfer*, **10** (2), 166–87.

APPENDIX

Table 12A.1 Trends in union density by industries, Sweden, 1990–2014

	1990	1996	2006	2008	2010	2014	Var. 2008–06	Var. 2010–08	Var. 2014–10	Var. 1990–2014
Blue-collars										
Manufacturing industries	89	92	84	81	79	76	–3	–2	–3	–13
Construction	90	90	81	73	71	67	–8	–2	–4	–23
Retail	68	74	64	57	57	53	–7	0	–4	–15
Private services	70	77	67	58	57	53	–8	–1	–4	–17
Public services	92	96	87	83	83	77	–4	0	–6	–15
All	84	87	77	71	69	64	–6	–2	–5	–20
Non-manual/white-collars										
Manufacturing industry	82	83	80	75	77	80	–5	2	2	–2
Retail	60	63	62	56	61	62	–6	5	2	–2
Private services	66	73	65	60	63	65	–5	3	2	+1
Public services	94	93	89	85	86	89	–4	1	–2	–5
All	81	83	77	72	73	77	–5	1	1	–4
All sectors/occupations	82	84	77	71	71	70	–6	0	0	–12

Source: Swedish Mediation Office (2014) and Kjellberg (2015).

Table 12A.2 Coverage rate of collective bargaining, Sweden, 1995–2013 (percentage of dependent employees)

Sector	1995	2005	2007	2010	2013	Var. 2013–2007	Var 2013–1995
Private	90	89	86	84	84	–2	–6
Public	100	100	100	100	100	0	0
All	94	93	91	89	89	–2	–5

Source: Swedish Mediation Office (2014) and Kjellberg (2015).

Table 12A.3 Share of workers covered by collective agreements, Sweden, 1995–2013 (private and public sectors, percentage)

	1995	2005	2008	2009	2010	2011	2012	2013
Private	90	89	84	85	84	84	85	84
Public	100	100	100	100	100	100	100	100
Both sectors	94	93	90	90	89	89	90	89

Source: Swedish Mediation Office (2014) and Kjellberg (2015).

Table 12A.4 Main job security councils and job security foundations (case study 2)

Name of the council/agreement (date of the latest agreement)	Number of organisations/ firms involved and number of salaried employees covered by the agreement	Sector/industry; category of dependent employees	Social partners involved in the agreement
Trygghetsfonden, TSL Job Security Fund, 2004 (2004) (http://www.tsl.se)	Approximately 1 million dependent employees and 100 000 companies	Manufacturing industries and trade; blue-collar employees in the private sector	Svenskt Näringsliv (Confederation of Swedish Enterprise) – Swedish Trade Union Confederation (LO)
Trygghetsrådet TRR, Job Security Council 1974 (1998) (http://www.trr.se)	Approximately 700 000 employees and 32 000 companies	Manufacturing industries and trade; mainly white-collar employees in the private sector	Svenskt Näringsliv (Confederation of Swedish Enterprise) — Federation of Salaried Employees in Industry and Services (PTK)

Table 12A.4 (continued)

Name of the council/agreement (date of the latest agreement)	Number of organisations/ firms involved and number of salaried employees covered by the agreement	Sector/industry; category of dependent employees	Social partners involved in the agreement
Trygghetsstiftelse TS, Job Security Foundation, 1990 (1998) (http://www.tsn.se)	245 000 employees and 250 public companies and organisations	Central government employees	Arbetsgivarverket (Swedish Agency for Government Employers) – Public Employees' Negotiation Council (OFR), Confederation of Professional Associations (SACO-S), Union for Service and Communications Employees (SEKO)
Trygghetsfonden BAO/ Finansförbundet, BAO/Financial Sector Union Employment Security Foundation 1992 (1997) (http://www.trygghetsfonden-bao-finansforbundet.se)	Approximately 45 000 dependent employees and 150 companies (banks, brokers companies and other financial institutions)	Banking and financial sector; white-collar employees	Swedish Employers' Association of the Banking Institutions (BAO) and Finansförbundet (Financial Sector Union)
KFO-Handels Employment Security Agreement for Salaried Employees 1974 (1982) (http://www.kfo.se)	Approximately 35 000 salaried employees	Cooperative businesses and non-profit organisations; shop assistants, warehouse workers, hairdressers, white-collar employees	Cooperative Employers' Association (KFO) and the Handelsanställdas förbund (Commercial Employees' Union)
KFS-Companies' Employment	Approximately 30 000	Services and communications,	Organisation for Local Enterprises

Table 12A.4 (continued)

Name of the council/agreement (date of the latest agreement)	Number of organisations/ firms involved and number of salaried employees covered by the agreement	Sector/industry; category of dependent employees	Social partners involved in the agreement
Security Fund 1994 (1994) (http://www.kfs.net)	employees, 500 municipal/ county owned or privately owned municipal-related companies	health education, etc.; both blue- and white-collar employees	(KFS) Municipal Workers' Union, Union of Commercial Employees, Union for Service and Communications Employees, Association of Health Professionals, Teachers' Union, Association of Graduated Engineer and Local Government Officers.
Trygghetsrådet TRS Employment Security Foundation (1974) 2004. (http://www.trs.se)	Approximately 400 companies/ organisation and 30000 employees	Culture and non-profit organisations; mainly white-collar employees	Arbetsgivarealliansen (Employer Alliance), Svenskt Scenkonst (Swedish Performing Arts Association) and Federation of Salaried Employees in Industry and Services (PTK)
Omstälningsfonden, 2010 (http://omstallningsfonden.se/in-english/)	More than 1 million employees	Municipalities and county councils (white-collars)	Sveriges Kommuner and Landsting and Employers' organisation Pacta LO-Kommunal, OFRs förbundsområden and AkademikerAlliansen

Source: Bäckström and Otosson (2006); Diedrich and Bergström (2006); Trygghetsrådet (2016).

13. Inequality at work in the United Kingdom: How perforated industrial relations worsen inequalities and hold back progress on equalities

Damian Grimshaw and Mat Johnson

1. INTRODUCTION

The United Kingdom is one of the emblematic cases in Europe where inequalities between the better off and worse off have widened during two generations of trade union decline. There are serious problems of long-term austerity policy measures, too many sectors trapped in a low-productivity/low-skill cycle and damaging short-term business fixes caused by 'maximising shareholder value' strategies. At the same time, the United Kingdom's perforated industrial relations model, characterised by fragmented collective bargaining structures and limited workplace mechanisms for worker voice, also shares some of the blame for the failure to generate a fairer distribution of economic gains among the workforce. Inequalities take many forms and include differences in pay levels (by occupation and by gender, for example), as well as unequal status caused by employment contract, associated with differences in rights to employment protection and social protection. A further feature of inequality is related to the complex and often opaque organisation of services and manufacturing along supply chains, involving practices of subcontracting that often place some workers in more precarious positions of employment than others. Judging by the media attention, questions of inequalities in employment may be considered today's grand 'social question' and demand urgent efforts, through the joint actions of unions, employers and government, to make labour markets more inclusive and more equal by extending employment rights and welfare state protections to all workers and addressing biases in the wage distribution.

The aim of this chapter is to investigate the relationship between industrial relations and inequalities. It starts by identifying four core features of the

United Kingdom's industrial relations model and considers the interaction with inequalities over the past two decades, with a focus on the post-crisis years. The next section considers the outcomes for modes of flexibility and security with a focus on the strong unilateral managerial prerogative that arises from the United Kingdom's perforated industrial relations system and its relatively weak framework of employment rights. These issues are subsequently analysed in detail through the lens of two case studies. The chapter concludes with recommendations for policy and practice.

2. INDUSTRIAL RELATIONS TRENDS AND INEQUALITIES

Comparative cross-national research on the interrelationship between industrial relations institutions and patterns of inequality displays two narratives. On the one hand, it often seeks to uncover relatively stylised bivariate correlations drawing on quantitative data. On the other hand, it looks at the societally idiosyncratic, changing and contingent factors that shape the institutional effects on inequalities. Both narratives are helpful in informing our analysis of the United Kingdom case. Quantitative comparative analyses have for many years supported the hypothesis that more centralised and coordinated wage bargaining on the whole displays a monotonic and negative relationship with the level of wage inequality (for example, Dahl et al., 2013; Dell'Aringa and Pagani, 2007; Hayter, 2015; Jaumotte and Buitron, 2015). A sub-set of studies also show that the same is broadly true with respect to measures of gender wage inequality (Blau and Kahn, 1992; Rubery et al., 2005) and shares of low-wage employment (Gautié and Schmitt, 2010; Salverda and Mayhew, 2009). Such analyses for Europe place the United Kingdom at an extreme of country outcomes. Figures 13.1(a) and 13.1(b) show that its decentralised wage bargaining, low collective bargaining coverage and weak union density are associated with relatively high indicators of wage inequality and a high incidence of low-wage employment compared with other countries in Europe. However, Figure 13.1(c) suggests that the relationship with the average gender pay gap is not so clear. On the one hand, the United Kingdom has lower collective bargaining coverage than the EU average (30 per cent and 55 per cent, respectively) and registers an above-average gender pay gap (18.3 per cent and 14.9 per cent, respectively), but on the other hand there is little evidence of a cross-country pattern in Figure 13.1(c).[1]

At the same time, the more detailed institutionalist accounts show that there are multiple, changing contingencies – related to welfare state policy, the production system (demand for high-skill or low-skill jobs), education

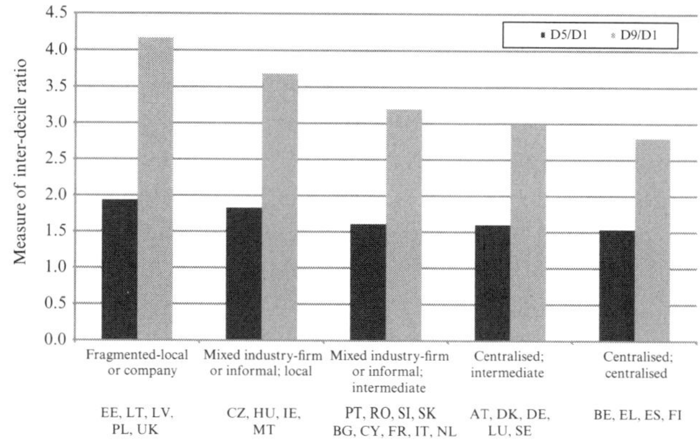

(a) Collective bargaining model (coordination type and bargaining level) and inter-decile wage inequality

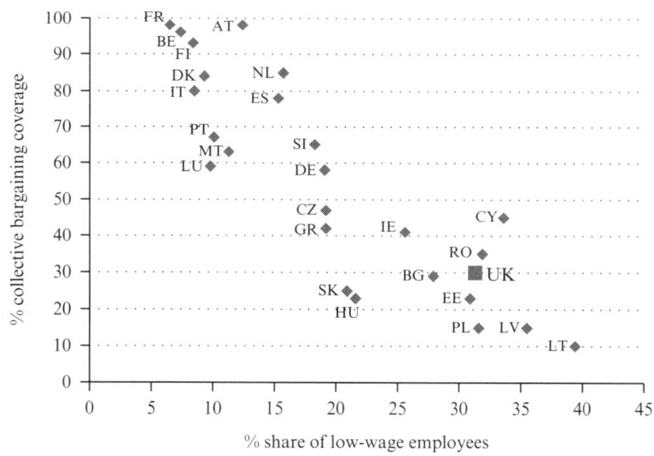

(b) Collective bargaining coverage and low pay incidence

Source: (a) Eurofound country classification scheme (Eurofound 2015: fig. 9) combined with interdecile gross earnings from the OECD database (www.oecd-ilibrary.org/employment/data); (b) collective bargaining coverage from Visser (2016) and low-wage data from Eurostat (Structure of Earnings survey 2010, share of all employees earning less than two-thirds of median hourly earnings); (c) same for collective bargaining coverage and gender pay gap data from Eurostat (difference in average gross hourly earnings all paid employees, 2014, except Greece 2010, Ireland 2012), accessed 10 November 2016 at ec.europa.eu/Eurostat/index.php/GenderPayGapStatistics.

Figure 13.1 The United Kingdom in European comparison: industrial relations indicators and wage inequalities

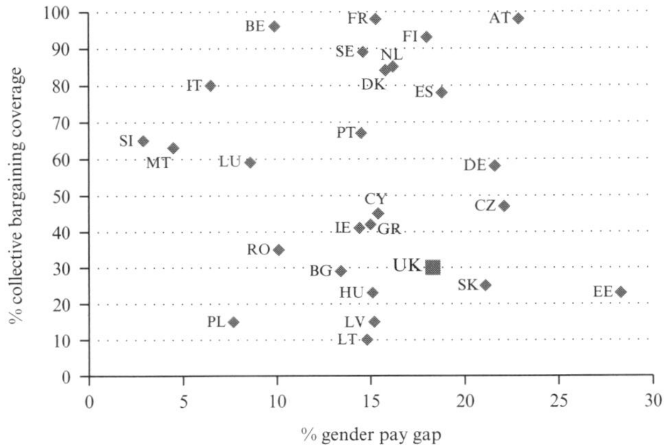

(c) Collective bargaining coverage and gender pay gap

Figure 13.1 (continued)

and training, gender relations, corporate governance and macroeconomic conditions – that shape the inequality effects of industrial relations institutions, such as collective bargaining. For example, during a period of restrictive macroeconomic fiscal policy, traditional wage bargaining institutions are likely to be severely curtailed in their effects on wage equalities. While centralised public sector pay systems may ordinarily be equality enhancing, during a period of public spending restrictions when governments impose restrictions on job hires and wage settlements, the same pay systems can quickly have adverse consequences for equality – particularly gender equality, given women's over-representation among public sector workers (Karamessini and Rubery, 2013). Also, institutions of collective bargaining may be at risk of being crowded out by an active minimum wage policy where there is insufficient role for social dialogue in minimum wage fixing and/or inadequate attention to problems of low pay among employers and trade unions (Grimshaw and Bosch, 2013). Recent research on the ways in which new ownership structures extract wealth from corporations demonstrates that the effects on returns to executive pay, levels of skills investment and pay prospects for workers mostly remain outside the traditional spheres of industrial relations influence and require broader coalitions of stakeholders in collective counter-actions, including, for example, representatives of pension funds and progressive tax bodies (Appelbaum and Batt, 2014; Watt, 2008). As such, concern for inequalities among workers needs to be complemented by attention to what is happening to the share of aggregate income earned by labour relative to capital.

In our account of the United Kingdom, we incorporate examples of these kinds of contingencies where they have been shown to shape the effects of industrial relations on inequalities. Our framework builds on the approaches of Crouch (2010, 2015) and Marginson and Sisson (2006) in setting out a list of governance features associated with the United Kingdom's model of industrial relations (Table 13.1). This approach covers collective bargaining (distinguishing the private and public sectors) and union representation at workplace level, as well as management regulation and government legislation, because it is the combination of these features, arising from state, employer and union interests and actions, which shape the employment relationship. The following discussion assesses each of these governance features in turn, the associated character of social dialogue and worker voice, and the consequences for inequalities and equalities. The analysis considers the current state of play (2010–16) in a context of trends over two decades.

2.1 Limited Collective Bargaining in the Private Sector Drives Inequality and Exploitation

Compared with the mid-twentieth century, when for two decades or so multi-employer bargaining was a stable and comprehensive means of regulating employment in private sector workplaces (Brown, 2010: 257), the early twenty-first century is characterised by very low collective bargaining coverage that leaves the vast majority of private sector workers (84 per cent in 2015) outside jointly regulated protection.[2] It is now a highly perforated national system. Over the two decades since 1995, union membership in the private sector has fallen from 26 per cent to 15 per cent among men and from 15 per cent to 12 per cent among women (14 per cent total). Because the United Kingdom does not use mechanisms to extend the scope of those collective agreements in place (as in France, for example), the share of private sector workers protected by a collective agreement has dropped in close parallel with falling unionisation, from 23 per cent to 16 per cent. There is nevertheless a wide range of experience, especially by sector and employment type: for example, in 2015 the share of employees whose pay was set by a collective agreement varied from a high of 50 per cent in the privatised utilities (gas and electricity) to a low of just 5 per cent in accommodation and food services; and while 17 per cent of employees in full-time employment were covered, this falls to 13 per cent for part-time employment and 12 per cent for temporary employment.

Separating out the private sector from the public sector, Figure 13.2 draws the trends in union density and collective bargaining coverage alongside three indicators of earnings inequality – P90/P10, P90/P50 and P50/P10

Table 13.1 Four industrial relations governance features in the United Kingdom and their inequality effects

Industrial relations governance features	Social dialogue/ worker voice features	Evidence of inequality effects (2010–2016)
1. Weak/absent collective bargaining (private sector)	Majority of workers uncovered Single employer bargaining dominates, shift from negotiation to consultation rights	*Strong evidence of inequality* – High earnings inequality – Falling real wages – High share of low-wage employment – Exploitation of workers in NSFE
2. Strong quasi-collective bargaining (public sector)	Mix of tripartite pay review bodies and collective bargaining, two-tier structures Well-developed systems of workplace representation and employer associations Strong state interventions post-2010 to reduce pay and conditions, privatisation and outsourcing	*Reversal of pre-2010 equality effects* – More equal wage structure than private sector (low–high, male–female) – Relatively harmonised rights for NSFE – Adverse austerity effects for gender equality
3. Single channel workplace representation	Union representatives (shop stewards), no works councils Growth in non-union representatives (many not elected)	*Mixed inequality outcomes* – Enhanced employee rights and more inclusive approach to NSFE at workplace level – Limits of union structures in context of myriad forms of subcontracting across workplace or organisation boundaries
4. Statutory employment rights – for example, minimum wage	Independent tripartite Low Pay Commission, but recent government intervention curtails influence Isolated from collective bargaining structures	*Bottom-weighted equality gains* – Eliminates employer practices of exploitative pay – Persistent high share of low paid ('minimum wage job contours' especially problematic for women)

Note: NSFE = non-standard forms of employment.

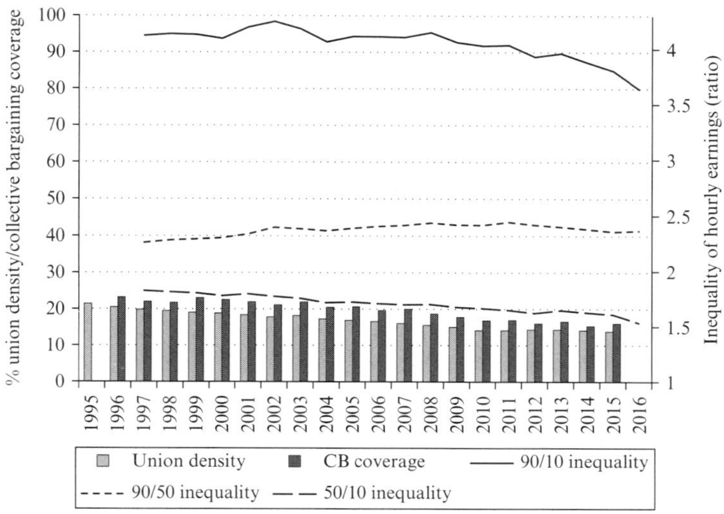

(a) Private sector

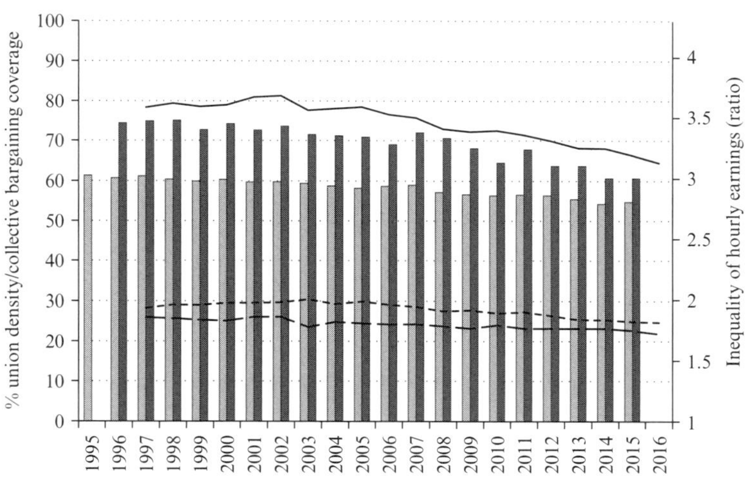

(b) Public sector

Source: Earnings data from Annual Survey of Hours and Earnings (ASHE) published data ('Public and private sectors, table 13'), accessed 10 November 2016 at www.ons.gov.uk/datasets/; union density and collective bargaining (CB) coverage data from Department for Business, Innovation and Skills (BIS, 2016).

Figure 13.2 Trends in union density and collective bargaining coverage and earnings inequality, United Kingdom, 1995–2015

– with reference to gross hourly earnings excluding overtime. Earlier studies showed that the fall in union density in the 1980s was a key factor associated with the rise in wage inequality following a decade of incomes policies, high union density and a compressed wage distribution (Gosling et al., 1994). Since then, the continued fall in union density and collective bargaining protection in the private sector has bolstered the persistently high level of wage inequality. Top decile earnings (P90) were more than four times bottom decile (P10) earnings for most of the period shown. However, the inter-decile measure of inequality has reduced significantly since 2013, due to a compression of earnings in the bottom half of the wage distribution: median (P50) earnings fell from 1.65 to 1.54 as a ratio of bottom decile pay (see below on changing minimum wage policy). The pattern of inequality contrasts strongly with that of the public sector workforce (Figure 13.2b). Here we find inter-decile inequality is considerably lower (ranging from around 3.6 to 3.1 over the period). Also, the gap between the highest paid (P90) workers in the public sector and middle earners (P50) is smaller than in the private sector. Finally, the relative range of the upper half wage distribution (P90 to P50) and the lower half wage distribution (P50 to P10) has remained relatively stable over the two-decade period in the public sector.

Parallel with the high level of private sector earnings inequality is a persistent high share of workers in low-wage employment. As we saw in Figure 13.1, the United Kingdom is an outlier among western European countries. It displays greater commonality with a group of central and eastern European countries – namely, Bulgaria, Estonia, Latvia, Lithuania, Poland and Romania – all with low collective bargaining coverage and a high incidence of low-wage employment. It is the private sector, with its highly perforated collective bargaining and weak union protection, which contributes the largest share of low-wage work in the United Kingdom.

Table 13.2 records estimated levels of low-wage work in the private and public sectors at points in time during the period 1997–2016; low-wage work is defined as hourly earnings less than two-thirds of median pay for all employees (gross and excluding overtime). Around one in four private sector workers were low paid over the period (a high of 27 per cent in 2010), compared with less than one in ten public sector workers. Jointly agreed and regulated pay scales for public sector workers provide a strong defence against the proliferation of low wages witnessed in the private sector where collective agreements are rare in low-wage sectors (although see Box 13.1 for exceptions, as well as Case study 1 below). Other factors are also relevant, however, including composition effects (a higher share of jobs in the private sector requiring limited skills or qualifications) and the outsourcing of low-wage public services work to the private sector (including security, catering, cleaning and care work) (Cunningham and James,

Table 13.2 The incidence of low-wage employment in the private and public sectors, United Kingdom, 1997–2016 (percentage)

	1997	2005	2010	2016
Private sector employees	25.8	26.4	27.3	24.3
Public sector employees	14.5	11.1	< 10	< 10
All employees	22.1	21.6	21.4	19.1

Notes: Authors' estimation of low wages based on published decile earnings levels; an estimate of less than 10 per cent is reported where the bottom decile earnings are higher than the labour market threshold for low wages defined as two-thirds of median earnings, gross hourly pay excluding overtime, all adult employees.

Source: Annual Survey of Hours and Earnings, tables 1 and 13, accessed 10 November 2017 at www.ons.gov.uk/datasets/.

2009; Lloyd et al., 2013; Grimshaw et al., 2015); Table 13.2 shows that the fall in low-wage work in the public sector during 1997–2010 coincided with a rise in the private sector.

2.2 Stronger Joint Wage Regulation in the Public Sector Delivers a Better Record on Equalities

Unlike most European countries, union membership and workplace union presence are very much stronger in the United Kingdom's public sector than in the private sector. Three features contribute to this relatively strong position. First, formalised and largely centralised systems of wage-setting arrangements (with explicit provision for arbitration) have proven for the most part resilient, despite recurrent political campaigns to fragment and decentralise wage-fixing. Wage setting is most likely to occur at national level in the form of separate sector agreements, covering the majority of schools, for example, or local authorities or public hospitals. Unilateral management wage setting is the exception; just 9 per cent of public sector workplaces used this for some workforce groups compared with 53 per cent of private sector workplaces (2011 WERS data).[3] Secondly, the public sector enjoys relatively well developed systems of workplace representation: 92 per cent of public sector workplaces have recognised unions compared with only around one in ten in the private sector (9 per cent in private manufacturing and 12 per cent in private services). A third contributory feature is that there are well-organised employer associations in the public sector, with separate bodies for the higher education sector, National Health Service (NHS) employers, local government employers and fire and rescue services, among others.

BOX 13.1 TWO EXAMPLES OF PRIVATE SECTOR COLLECTIVE AGREEMENTS IN LOW-WAGE SECTORS

Despite low collective bargaining coverage in the United Kingdom's private sector, there are many significant examples of collective agreements. In low-wage sectors such as retail, security and business cleaning, such agreements do influence the level and character of low-wage work but tend to focus on a specific equality issue, such as youth equalities or bottom-weighted settlements for the very lowest paid.

For example, more than 300 000 workers in the United Kingdom are employed by the multinational retail chain Tesco and are covered by a collective agreement with the Union of Shop, Distributive and Allied Workers (USDAW), the main retail union. Two issues are notable. First, the union has successfully improved pay for young workers and harmonised youth and adult rates in 2010 following six years of campaigning. This means that young workers at Tesco earn considerably more than statutory minimum wage rates: 16–17-year-olds earned almost double the minimum in 2016–17 (£7.62 and £4.00 per hour, respectively). Second, the collective agreement has been less successful at maintaining a wage premium for adult workers (aged over 21) above the minimum wage. When the minimum wage was introduced in 1999, the collectively negotiated base rate of pay was 23 per cent higher. Over the years this has steadily shrunk, down to just 10 per cent by 2015–16. With the introduction in April 2016 of a new, higher minimum wage for workers aged 25 years and over, the wage gap has shrunk even further for older adults, to just 6 per cent for 2016–17.

A second example concerns the global security company G4S and the GMB trade union. G4S has a workforce of around 30 000 in the United Kingdom and conditions are covered by two collective agreements, one for cash transit services and one for regular security. The force of collective negotiation (and strikes) has been more effective for cash transit services workers among whom union membership is close to 100 per cent and product market competition less intense. In a landmark five-year pay settlement (2005–10), workers won a cumulative 35 per cent pay rise, double that of the cumulative 17 per cent rise in the statutory minimum wage during this period, raising their base rate of pay to 72 per cent higher than the minimum wage. By contrast, union efforts to improve pay for regular security services workers have been less effective. The main obstacle is that G4S UK refuses to negotiate a single company-wide agreement because it argues this conflicts with its business model of balancing wage costs with income streams across the different outsourcing contracts for security services. The result is that workers providing services on a construction site might be paid the minimum wage while others securing one of the Royal Bank of Scotland offices might earn considerably more. Even across different RBS sites, G4S workers are paid differently to do the same job – earning £8.36 per hour at one of the London sites and £7.54 per hour in Birmingham in 2016. The strong connection between contract pricing and pay rates undermines union efforts to address low pay and wastes resources on hundreds of pay negotiations for each contract which could be better invested in a single overarching company-wide agreement.

Source: Company and union documentation available online.

Despite its relative strengths, the spirit of voluntarist, multi-employer collective bargaining in the public sector is hampered for two reasons: (1) the government has exercised considerable authority since 2010 in imposing first a pay freeze (2011–13), then a 1 per cent cap on annual settlements for most public sector workers (ongoing at the time of writing in early 2017); and (2) most workers are covered by a quasi-form of collective bargaining, a pay review body,[4] in which members are appointed by government and make recommendations to government (on the basis of union, employer and government evidence) and then government exercises the right of veto.

The greater centralisation of pay arrangements in the public sector compared with the private sector in the United Kingdom is associated with a more compressed wage structure and a better record on gender pay equity. Moreover, especially during periods of public sector employment growth (for example, 1999–2010), the public sector can be expected to have made a significant contribution to offset further widening of wage inequality across the economy as a whole and, reflecting the high share of relatively well paid female employees, to have contributed to the overall narrowing of the average economy-wide gender pay gap. Analysis for the period 1986–95, a period of public sector restraint similar to the post-2010 period, showed both that the increase in wage inequality in the United Kingdom was largely associated with changes in dispersion in the private sector and that the reduced share of women working in the public sector as opposed to the private sector had a negative effect on overall gender pay equality (Grimshaw, 2000).

The diverse patterns of gender pay equity in the public and private sectors are shown in Table 13.3. Whether for full-timers or for all employees, we find a higher gender pay ratio in the public sector than the private sector. It is notable that while for full-timers the difference narrowed in the private sector over the 1997–2016 period, for all employees the gap between sectors remains wide owing to the poor wage position of female part-timers in the private sector compared with the public sector; this means that the gender pay equity situation in the private sector today is only slightly better than the public sector was almost two decades ago.

These differences are amplified when we consider women's gains in pay in the public sector relative to the economy-wide benchmark for all male full-timers. Table 13.3(b) shows that women's median full-time earnings in the public sector increased to 7 points higher than median earnings for all male full-timers, compared with a negative gap of more than 20 points in the private sector. The position of part-timers in the public sector has improved significantly more than in the private sector and from an already higher level in 1997; indeed, the earnings position of female part-timers in the public sector has caught up over the period with female full-timers in

Table 13.3 The gender pay ratio and women's relative pay in the public and private sectors, United Kingdom, 1997–2016 (percentage)

(a) Gender pay ratios (median hourly earnings) within sectors

	1997		2005		2010		2016	
	Public	Private	Public	Private	Public	Private	Public	Private
Full-timers	86.5	76.3	90.1	80.0	90.1	80.3	88.7	83.4
All employees	73.2	67.2	78.4	71.6	81.0	72.5	81.7	75.5

(b) Women's pay relative to median male full-time pay in all sectors

	1997		2005		2010		2016	
	Public	Private	Public	Private	Public	Private	Public	Private
Female full-timers	99.9	71.6	105.3	75.3	108.3	75.0	106.8	78.2
Female part-timers	65.1	50.5	70.8	52.5	75.2	53.5	78.4	56.6
All female employees	82.5	61.6	90.1	63.8	95.8	63.8	97.4	66.7

Note: Gross hourly earnings excluding overtime.

Source: Authors' estimations from ASHE published data, table 13.6a, accessed 10 November 2017 at www.ons.gov.uk/datasets/.

the private sector. For all female employees, Table 13.3(b) shows a dramatic closing of the pay gap in the public sector (from 17 to just 3 points) compared with marginal change in a considerably wider gap in the private sector (38 to 33 points). These results can be explained in part by the preceding argument that the more centralised wage-setting arrangements in the public sector are more conducive to addressing gender pay equity. In contrast, decentralised wage determination and patchy joint regulation in the private sector is associated with less positive results; to borrow Blau and Kahn's (1992) phrase from 25 years ago, women are still 'swimming upstream' in the United Kingdom's private sector.

The stronger representative capacities of unions and employers in the public sector compared with the private sector also potentially means that many other features of equalities aside from basic pay can be addressed more effectively. Reforms of sector agreements for health workers and for local government workers established 'single status' terms and conditions so that former inequalities between blue-collar (manual) and white-collar (non-manual) workers were eliminated. The reforms were especially beneficial for women since they accounted for a majority of workers in part-time, manual roles. There is also a higher rate of adoption of equal opportunities policies and practices in the public sector; 2004 data register a formal equal opportunities policy in almost all public sector workplaces (and covering 99 per cent of employees) compared with around two-thirds of private sector workplaces (and 84 per cent of employees) (Kersley et al., 2006: table 9.1). Equal opportunities policies are important for several reasons, one of which is that they encourage employers to implement a range of supplementary practices, such as positive actions to recruit disabled workers, ethnic minorities and women (more than twice as likely in the public than the private sector). Public sector workplaces are also far more likely to promote equalities for working mothers. This includes greater provision of childcare facilities and financial support – 18 per cent of public sector workplaces provide some form of support compared with 5 per cent of private sector workplaces – as well as more generous paid maternity leave (Kersley et al., 2006: 243–58).[5]

2.3 Single-channel Workplace Representation Risks Exclusive Forms of Representation

As well as diminishing coverage in the private sector, the influence of collective bargaining on equalities has also weakened as a result of a shift in the form of workplace representation from negotiation to consultation. There has also been a rising trend of non-union representation. Moreover, while union representation in the United Kingdom still plays an important role in enforcing employment standards and encouraging a more inclusive approach both towards non-standard forms of employment (see Grimshaw et al., 2016) and workers from potentially vulnerable groups (such as migrant workers, Connolly et al., 2014), single-channel, workplace-bound structures limit its effectiveness in addressing inequalities and segmentation caused by myriad forms of subcontracting (including with subcontracted employees, agency, posted and genuine and false self-employed workers), opening the door to a potentially more exclusive and unequal approach to representation.

In stark contrast to most European countries, the United Kingdom's model of employee representation (in the private sector) has long been characterised by a 'single channel' of union representation at enterprise and workplace levels, with very limited representation at industry (multi-employer) level (Terry, 2010). Works councils are present only in workplaces that belong to organisations with operations in more than one country (under EU directive rules), with a share of 16 per cent in

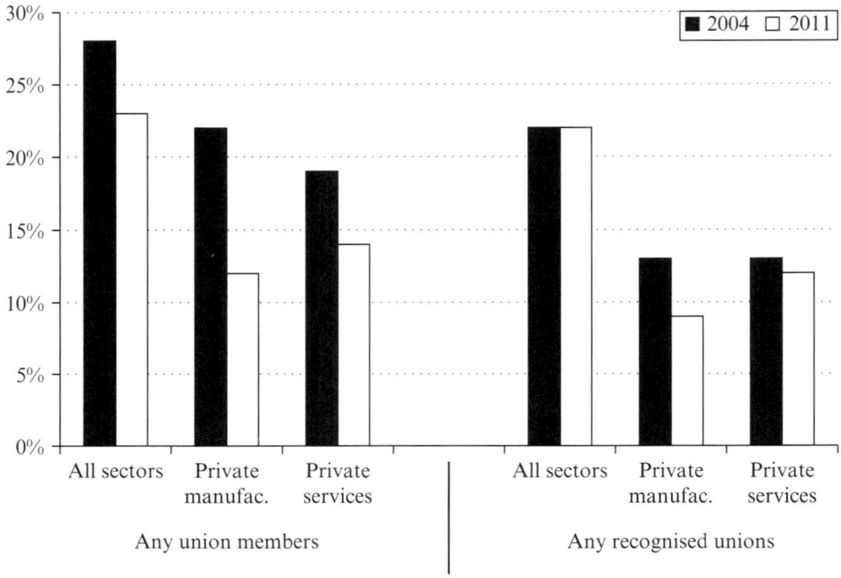

Note: Data refer to workplaces with five or more employees.

Source: Workplace Employment Relations (WERS) data, published in Van Wanrooy et al. (2013); authors' compilation.

Figure 13.3 Workplaces with a union presence, United Kingdom (percentage)

2011 (Van Wanrooy et al., 2013). The share of workplaces with any union members declined from 28 per cent to 23 per cent during 2004–11 and the drop was particularly large in private manufacturing (22 per cent to 12 per cent) and private services (19 per cent to 14 per cent) (Figure 13.3). Of these, only around a quarter (27 per cent, no change since 2004) had one or more on-site lay union representatives (Van Wanrooy et al., 2013). A small proportion of workplaces set up joint consultative committees (JCCs) (around 5 per cent in the private sector in 2011) and these may have union and/or non-union representatives, although in the private services sector it is more common to find JCCs at a higher corporate level (covering 15 per cent of workplaces). Finally, a rising share of private sector workplaces have appointed stand-alone non-union representatives, from 6 per cent to 10 per cent from 2004 to 2011, continuing an earlier trend (Moore et al., 2008).

One of the concerns among observers is that even where union representation has been sustained, workplace activities have become a 'hollow shell' characterised by a diminished substantive and procedural role, with less time spent on collective bargaining (as well as on the exercise or threat of coercive power) and more on representing individual members (Charlwood and Forth, 2009, cited in Terry, 2010). So, for example, while half of all workplaces in 2011 had introduced or upgraded new technologies and one-fifth (19 per cent) of these said this presented the most important consequences for employment, only 7 per cent of the latter group had negotiated changes with a staff representative compared with 45 per cent that had engaged in some form of consultation (Van Wanrooy et al., 2013). The one area in which workplaces registered a similar orientation was for the introduction of performance-related pay (PRP), with 35 per cent registering a negotiation process and 45 per cent consultation (considering those workplaces that stated the introduction of PRP was the most important factor shaping employment changes, 2011 data) (Van Wanrooy et al., 2013) (see further discussion in section 3).

While unionised workplaces continue to campaign for more equal and inclusive workforce conditions in the United Kingdom (see case studies 1 and 2 in this chapter), the lack of union structures crossing workplace and organisational boundaries poses increasing obstacles. Several studies of outsourcing point to the inability of United Kingdom unions to gain a foothold in subcontractor organisations. This is particularly a problem where unions see members moving out of well-organised public sector organisations into the private sector. Nevertheless, other studies indicate unexpected outcomes. A case study of outsourced services at a public hospital highlights the challenges unions faced in seeking to move into powerful, private sector, specialist outsourcing services firms, but also found that the need for the subcontractor to resolve problems of unequal pay, to harmonise disciplinary procedures and to combat a looming industrial dispute eventually led to a union recognition agreement (Bach and Givan, 2010). The living-wage campaigns, as well as wider research on corporate social responsibility (for example, Wright and Brown, 2013), have highlighted the need for redirecting unions' wage justice campaigns towards the client organisation, what Wills (2009: 444–5) calls the 'real employer':

> The nature of short-term contracts and increased competition means that subcontractors are forced to cut back on employees' pay and standards of work. Moreover, given that they are no longer directly employed, these workers have no industrial relations contact with their 'real employer' . . . Subcontracting works to break the mutual dependency between workers and employers that has been so central to the labor movement in the past. When a company directly employs the staff on whom they depend, there is the potential to negotiate over matters of work. Each needs the other, and they have to co-operate, to at least some extent.

The problem, however, with this new focus is that it means unions must now work with multiple third parties (so-called 'real employers') for the workforce of each subcontractor organisation, gaining recognition agreements and then negotiating collective agreements that satisfy all parties. The fragmentation of organising and negotiating across different workplace sites and varying service contracts thus raises significant challenges.

Furthermore, because 'union representation is often coterminous with employment' (Heery et al., 2004: 23), workers in a subcontracting situation of potential 'false' self-employment face significant risks of exclusion and inequalities of treatment. Union campaigns to better represent false self-employed workers have been particularly vocal in the construction sector and platform (gig) economy, notably through efforts by the construction union, the Union of Construction, Allied Trades and Technicians (UCATT) (Boheim and Muehlberger, 2006), and the general union, the GMB. The GMB successfully challenged the claimed self-employment status of Uber taxi drivers in 2016, arguing that drivers ought to have the legal rights of workers (see section 3), although falling short of winning full rights associated with 'employee' status in the United Kingdom, as justified in recent legal analyses (see Rogers, 2016). The case has potential repercussions for many other employers in the platform economy who have traded employee rights for a self-professed 'libertarian' vision of flexibility, trumpeted by the corporate leaders of the powerful Silicon Valley gig economy firms, such as Upwork, Taskrabbit and others (Hill, 2016). The union for media workers, BECTU,[6] has a long tradition of organising freelance workers (who account for around two-fifths of its members, see Heery et al., 2004), a subset of whom are likely to be false self-employed. In response to union campaigns, especially the highlighting of lost tax revenues, in 2014 the government set out clearer criteria for the treatment of persons as employed by the agency or payroll company ('onshore employment intermediaries'). The trade union UCATT responded that this was a first step but a better policy would require that 'if a worker satisfies the conditions to be in receipt of "employment income", then he or she should be acknowledged to be an employee and gain all of the entitlements and obligations which an employee has'.[7]

2.4 The United Kingdom's Statutory Minimum Wage Alone Cannot Address Low-pay Problems

The introduction of a national minimum wage in 1999 was a much delayed response to the need for protection against exploitative pay in large areas of the economy where unions had no effective presence. It is generally perceived as having been successful both in establishing trust in the procedures of the Low Pay Commission (the independent tripartite body charged with researching, evaluating and fixing the minimum wage each year) and in gradually raising the minimum wage's value against the median wage (Brown, 2009). The Commission tends to consider price inflation, average earnings growth and the general state of the labour market in recommending the annual raise, but has at times also pursued the redistributive goal of upgrading the minimum wage relative to median earnings. While relatively successful, the minimum wage nevertheless acts as a relatively isolated wage-fixing instrument in the United Kingdom, particularly in the private sector where there is very limited collective bargaining. This creates problems, especially the widespread misuse of the minimum wage by employers as the 'going rate of pay' for many low-paid jobs and compression of wages in the bottom quartile of the wage distribution as employers squeeze pay differentials (Grimshaw et al., 2014), although see Box 13.2 for a counter-example.

The process for fixing the minimum wage was changed in 2016 when the government announced it would unilaterally introduce a premium rate, referred to erroneously as a 'national living wage', from April 2016, which applied to adults aged 25 years and over. Two issues motivated the reform. First, the United Kingdom's economy had witnessed a jobs recovery without real earnings growth, so the message from government was that 'Britain deserves a pay rise'. Second, and more importantly, the minimum wage rise was intended to justify reduced public spending on in-work tax credits that top up low wages for workers with low household income levels. Analysis by the Institute for Fiscal Studies shows that because the government has simultaneously cut welfare transfers the net effect for many minimum wage workers in low-income households has been negative, with an increasing number of working households falling below the 'minimum income standard' defined as needed for an acceptable standard of living (Belfield et al., 2015). Moreover, because tax credits and minimum wages are not perfect substitutes, those who benefit most from the minimum wage rise are not the same persons who lose most from tax credit cuts; thus, it is not the case, as the government has claimed, that its reforms are moving people from in-work benefits onto a 'living wage' (Belfield et al., 2015).

This intervention was the first time government has bypassed the Low Pay Commission's tripartite process. The government fixed the new minimum wage premium rate at a level 50 pence higher than the normal adult rate (£7.20 per hour versus £6.70 per hour) and also proposed initially to continue raising the premium to 'over £9.00 by 2020', which at the time was forecast to be equivalent to 60 per cent of median earnings and would have represented an average estimated annual rise of 5.7 per

BOX 13.2 NEGOTIATING POSITIVE SPILLOVER EFFECTS FROM A RISING MINIMUM WAGE

Where social partners are convinced of the merits of an egalitarian pay strategy, then collectively negotiated pay structures can foster positive spillovers from a rising minimum wage in two ways. The first mechanism is to raise base rates of pay by at least the rate of growth in the statutory minimum wage. The second is to ensure pay differentials among job roles in the lower rungs of the organisation or industry are sufficiently protected (although perhaps not completely) as base rates of pay increase.

A good example of this type of strategy in the United Kingdom is the sector agreement for public sector health workers. Unions and employers agreed a new harmonised pay structure in 2004 which boosted the lowest rate of pay (earned, for example, by hospital cleaners) from 2 per cent to 18 per cent above the statutory minimum wage. Since then, despite significant rises in the minimum wage, base rates of pay for public hospital workers kept up until the major minimum wage rise in 2016; in 2015 the gap over the minimum was still 16 per cent, but it shrank to 9 per cent in 2016 (Table 13.4). Union strategy also focused on securing bottom-weighted pay deals (mostly through paying a fixed cash sum to the lowest paid and eliminating use of bottom pay points). Nationally implemented pay bands, gender-proofed via job evaluation, assured pay differentials were sustained to a large extent, albeit somewhat narrowed.

Table 13.4 Egalitarian pay changes in the public hospitals sector pay agreement

	Base rate as % of national minimum wage*	Bottom weighted pay deals:		Pay differential
		Enhanced pay rise?	Low paid covered?	Band 3 top as % of Band 1 bottom
2003	102.4	–	–	n.a.
2004	117.7	–	–	142.6
2005	116.6	–	–	142.6
2006	112.9	–	–	142.6
2007	111.1	£400 (= 2.9–3.4% versus standard 2.5%)	Pay points 1 to 7	141.7
2008	112.0	–	–	141.7
2009	117.1	5.7% (versus standard 2.4%)	Pay point 1 (all uprated to point 2)	129.7
2010	118.0	£420 (= 2.3–3.2% versus 2.3% standard)	Pay points 1–12	136.1

Table 13.4 (continued)

	Base rate as % of national minimum wage*	Bottom weighted pay deals:		Pay differential
		Enhanced pay rise?	Low paid covered?	Band 3 top as % of Band 1 bottom
2011	117.3	£250 (= 1.6–1.8% versus standard 0%)	Pay points 1–5	135.4
2012	117.3	–	–	134.8
2013	116.2	–	–	134.8
2014	112.8	–	–	134.8
2015	115.5	5.6%	Pay point 1	128.9
		3.1%	Pay point 2	
		1% + £200 (5 2.1–2.3%)	Points 3–8	
		1%; 0%	Points 9–42; 43–54	
2016	108.6	–	–	128.9

Note: * Minimum wage for adults (21+ years) as of April each year, except 2016 for 25+ years, April; hospital sector pay rates April each year (except November in 2007).

Source: Pay bands and pay settlements available online, accessed 17 January 2017 at http://www.nhsemployers.org/your-workforce/pay-and-reward/pay/pay-and-conditions-circulars/; authors' original compilation.

cent up to the end of the current parliament.[8] An uplift to £9.00 per hour by 2020 would have given a massive uplift to low-wage workers. However, this has been quietly dropped in favour of the 'more prudent' target of 60 per cent of median earnings because this better reflects changed economic circumstances, especially the slower than forecast earnings growth (Low Pay Commission, 2016: ix, 60–61). Given that the 2016 premium minimum wage (April 2016) already measured 59.5 per cent of gross hourly median earnings for all employees (overtime excluded), what the government appeared to be implementing was a four-year plan of aligning the minimum wage with median earnings growth. However, the Low Pay Commission has shifted the goalposts slightly by changing the denominator for the calculation of the 60 per cent ratio so that the estimate of median earnings covers adults aged 25 and over. With this revised calculation the 2016 ratio was 56.4 per cent.[9] Overall, as Figure 13.4 demonstrates, employees aged 25 or over have already experienced a major boost in the wage floor and this will continue until 2020 at a rate

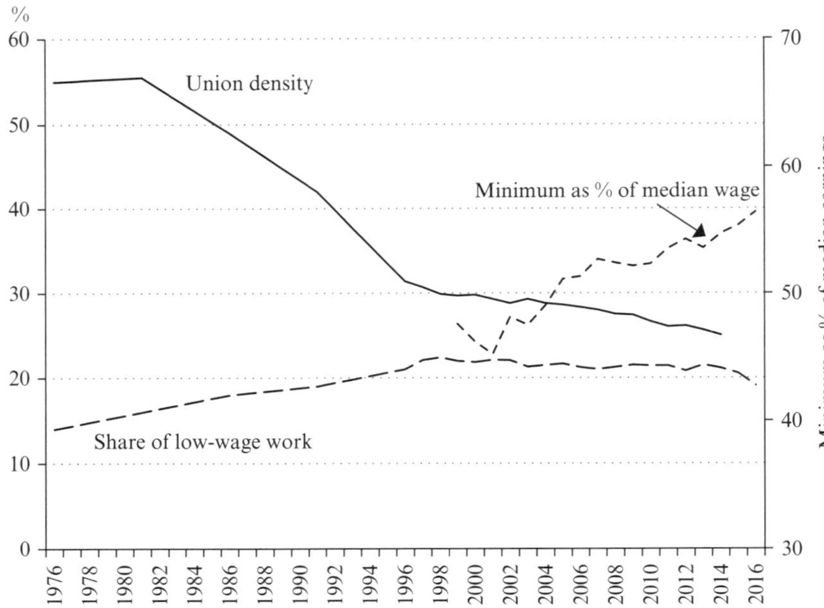

Notes: Median earnings are gross hourly excluding overtime for adult employees aged 25 or over.

Source: Low Pay Commission (2016: fig. 2.4).

Figure 13.4 Minimum wage relative to median earnings for adult employees aged 25 or over, United Kingdom

higher than median earnings growth. Combining all minimum wages, 2016 saw a major increase in numbers affected up to 1.9 million (7.1 per cent of all employees aged 16 or over), which is double the share when the minimum wage was introduced in 1999 and considerably higher than the 1.4 million affected in 2015 (Low Pay Commission, 2016: 55).

The minimum wage is a relatively isolated wage-fixing instrument in the United Kingdom, but it is also relatively inclusive as a labour market rule. It is significant that (similar to working-time rules and anti-discrimination legislation) the minimum wage applies to all 'workers', not just employees. This means it covers casual labourers, agency workers, part-time workers, homeworkers and trainees, for example. However, self-employed workers are not covered. Other excluded categories include workers on government programmes (such as Work Programme job entry schemes or Job Centre work trials), workers aged under 16, students on work placements of up to 12 months, members of the armed forces and prisoners. There are separate rates for young workers (aged 16–17, 18–20 and 21–24) and apprentices.

3. WHAT OUTCOMES FOR FLEXIBILITY AND SECURITY IN THE UNITED KINGDOM'S LABOUR MARKET?

In the absence of joint regulation and effective forms of social dialogue in many of the United Kingdom's private sector workplaces, workers must face changes implemented unilaterally by managers. In United Kingdom laissez-faire policy-speak, this is lauded as 'flexibility' and said to be responsible for the United Kingdom's allegedly positive record on job creation by 'freeing up' employers' capacity to hire and fire and deploy labour on whatever contracts are thought to fit with patterns of demand and cost competition. Thus, while some facets of labour market flexibility in a different societal context may be conducive to worker preferences for hours flexibility (for example, to fit around childcare) or workers' ability to extract higher wages (for example, via increased skill investment, performance bonuses or job redesign), in the United Kingdom too much of what is experienced as 'labour market flexibility' is concentrated on what meets employers' needs, with a particular emphasis on delivering irregular hours and lower labour costs (Fleetwood, 2007; Rubery et al., 2016).

Against a background of relatively weak employment and welfare protections, these management practices generate major inequalities in employment status. The core exploited groups to have emerged in recent years are those with zero-hours contracts, agency workers and bogus self-employment. Where workers do negotiate flexible hours, to suit family commitments say, the price is typically lower remuneration as experienced by many women in part-time jobs. If the purpose of twenty-first century society is to develop a high value-added, high investment and equitable economy then it appears that the United Kingdom has fostered the 'wrong type' of labour market flexibility, with too many workers experiencing 'protective gaps' – namely, gaps in employment rights, in access to social protection, in representation and in enforcement (see Grimshaw et al., 2016).

Basic core protections for the United Kingdom's workforce are on the whole relatively weak compared with other European countries with similar gross domestic product (GDP) per capita. While the United Kingdom scores around average in terms of its statutory minimum wage protection (level and enforcement) and income assistance to unemployed individuals with families to support (OECD 2014 data),[10] it provides only very limited protections for individual employment protection, unemployment support and maternity leave. Employment protection rights have been reduced considerably since 2010 from an already low level: reforms cut notice periods from 90 to 45 days, doubled the period from 12 to 24 months for eligibility to rights, and introduced fees of £1200 to take a case to the employment tribunal (for example, on sex discrimination); although the UK Supreme Court subsequently ruled the latter government reform illegal following a legal challenge by the public services union, Unison. Also, unemployment support has been considerably toughened to a degree that basic income security in the United Kingdom is now not guaranteed despite a person's entitlement through social security protection contributions. Unemployment claimants today face a strict regime of sanctions that causes many individuals and families to lose owed income when they fail to meet strict performance rules. A sanction involves the halting of benefits for four weeks and can be imposed in response to perceived problems with an individual's punctual attendance at Job Centres, ability to meet target numbers of job applications, or problems accepting voluntary (unpaid) 'back to work' jobs, although this was ruled unlawful in 2016. Staff working in Job Centres have been found to be themselves managed by a strict performance management system that halts pay rises where insufficient sanctions have been made.[11] Ken Loach's 2016 film, *I, Daniel Blake*, has been commended as a precise portrayal – and damning indictment – of the injustices wrought on claimants by the current system and serves as a valid and vivid reference point.

Against this backdrop of low and patchy protections for United Kingdom workers, the inequalities generated by unilateral, 'flexible' management practices impose high costs on workers and their families. One major area of economic and social concern since the crisis is the increased use of non-standard employment forms, especially (bogus) self-employment and zero-hours contracts. Numbers of 'self-employed' have expanded dramatically since the economic crisis – by around 25 per cent – compared with less than 5 per cent overall growth in the number of employees (2008–16; Figure 13.5). This means that of the approximately 2 million additional persons in employment since the second quarter of 2008, almost half (0.96 million) were categorised as 'self-employed'. Combined with evidence of falling weekly income among the self-employed, the changing balance of employment forms raises questions about the ability of the United Kingdom's economy to share out the spoils of the resumed economic growth.

Part of the growth in self-employment is attributable to the gig economy and the tendency of many logistics/information technology (IT) firms to rely on sophisticated IT platforms designed to enable self-employed

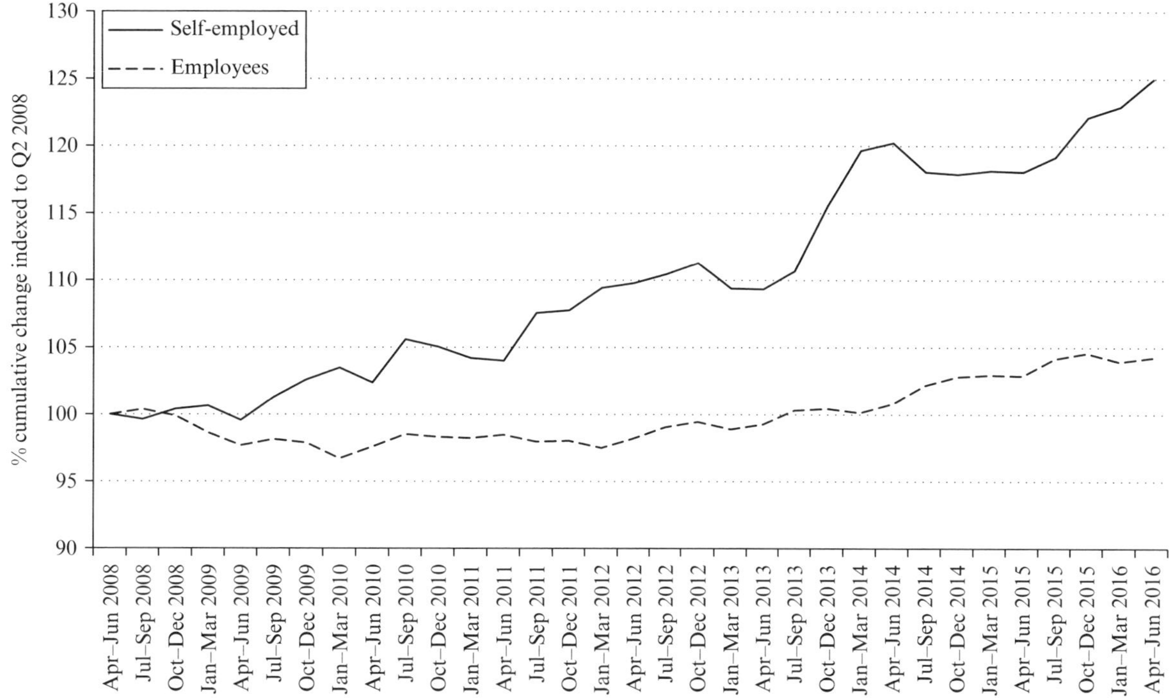

Source: Office for National Statistics (ONS) employment data, accessed 10 November 2016 at www.ons.gov.uk/datasets/, authors' compilation.

Figure 13.5 Trends in numbers of self-employed and employees, United Kingdom, 2008–16 (cumulative percentage change indexed to 100 in Q2 2008)

individuals to subscribe and seek job tasks from one day to the next (Newsome et al., 2016). However, this model was ruled illegal in a 2016 court ruling against the taxi firm Uber. Uber takes a commission from earnings of its 40 000 drivers operating in the United Kingdom and fixes the terms and conditions on which trips are offered and provided. The court ruled that it therefore exercised a degree of control over drivers. At the time of writing, Uber is appealing the employment tribunal decision. If the drivers win the status of 'worker', then they would enjoy minimum wage protection, statutory paid holidays and protection against unlawful discrimination. However, because a 'worker' is not the same as an 'employee', they would not have protections against unfair dismissal, redundancy compensation, right to flexible working and maternity, paternity and parental leave. Several delivery firms were also investigated during 2016, including Deliveroo, Hermes and Yodel, all of which rely on a self-employed workforce despite each company controlling fees per delivery (by weight or size) and performance bonuses (Box 13.3).[12]

Also of concern is the explosion in the number of workers on zero-hours contracts, perhaps the 'scarlet letter' of the United Kingdom's 'flexible labour market'. The latest data for 2016 show a sustained rise to more than 900 000 workers, almost 3 per cent of the workforce[13] (Figure 13.6). These contracts are used for all types of jobs and span various groups of workers. Usual average hours are around 25 per week, compared with 37 for all workers, with a mix of full-time and part-time hours reported. Young people are over-represented, but numbers of zero-hours contracts among core age groups (35–49 and 50–64) also increased significantly, by around 70 000 and 80 000, between 2013 and 2016. Women are also over-represented: zero-hours contracts account for 3.4 per cent of women's employment compared with 2.4 per cent of men's. Also, non-United Kingdom workers (by nationality or country of birth) are more likely to have a zero-hours contract than United Kingdom workers, with figures of 3.2–3.3 per cent and 2.8 per cent, respectively. As well as targeting vulnerable workforce groups, a far higher share of workers on zero-hours contracts say they want more work;[14] 31 per cent compared with less than 10 per cent of people employed on a non-zero-hours contract. Also, a far higher proportion of zero-hours contract workers are employed on a temporary contract – 32 per cent – compared with around 4 per cent among other workers (2016 data).

At the other extreme of the United Kingdom's model of high inequality is the problem of high and rising executive pay, an issue that appears to be out of the reach of social dialogue. In 2015, the highest paid chief executive in the United Kingdom was Martin Sorrell at WPP, who received £70 million. Among all FTSE 100 firms, chief executive officers (CEOs) were

BOX 13.3 EXPLOITING THE FALSE SELF-EMPLOYED AT HERMES

Hermes, a global delivery firm, has experienced substantial growth in its courier business in the United Kingdom thanks to the boom in online retail, from £261 million in 2011–12 to £442 million in 2014–15, average annual growth of around 20 per cent. Gross profits have also ballooned, from £38 million in 2011–12 to £68 million in 2014–15. This successful business model is founded on the deployment of a body of around 10500 couriers who are all classed as 'self-employed' and paid according to a piece-rate system. By classifying its workforce as self-employed, Hermes avoids making pension or social security contributions, and does not guarantee basic employment rights, such as paid holidays, sick leave and a minimum wage. Use of a crude piece-rate system – said to be 55 pence per parcel delivered in 2016 – means that couriers must make 16 deliveries per hour to meet the basic minimum wage, although fuel and other vehicle expenses (tax, insurance and maintenance) also need to be deducted.

Investigations into Hermes's practices by the BBC in 2010 (*Newsnight*) and a report co-authored by the chair of the Work and Pensions Select Committee (Field and Forsey, 2016) brought to light a raft of exploitative practices that led to the company being referred in 2016 to the tax office's compliance department because of an abuse of the status of self-employment (owing to evidence of mutuality of obligation between Hermes and the couriers and Hermes exerting control over work practices). Based on direct testimonies from couriers, the two investigations highlight key areas of exploitation, including:

- unpaid working time while waiting for parcels to arrive at a depot, loading parcels into their vehicle and programming the handheld monitoring device;
- fixed piece rate regardless of the number of times needed to attempt a delivery and no scope for individual negotiation of the delivery rate;
- couriers are required to report to the depot at fixed times on prescribed days, use Hermes equipment to track deliveries and wear Hermes uniforms;
- couriers face the threat of loss of work imposed by a Hermes field manager or compliance manager if they take time off for illness or a family emergency and are expected to organise their own temporary cover;
- Hermes generates the invoices for couriers and sends them a pay statement each month;
- Hermes imposes reductions in piece rates arbitrarily and also adjusts the applicable package weights.

It would appear the couriers enjoy none of the benefits of self-employment, namely, the freedom to negotiate fees, take charge of working patterns and set the pace and control of work. Instead, they sit in the informal economy and face high risks of exploitation in varied forms, including pay, job insecurity, discrimination and bullying.

Source: ONS employment data, accessed 10 November 2016 at www.ons.gov.uk/datasets/, authors' compilation.

Figure 13.6 Trends in zero-hours contracts, United Kingdom, 2000–2016

paid on average 183 times more than the average employee, up from 160 times more in 2010 (High Pay Centre, 2015). In the absence of employees able to represent worker interests in executive pay decisions, there is growing dissatisfaction and frustration with the size of pay at the top. The professional body for human resource managers reported survey findings that around seven out of ten (71 per cent) employees believe that CEO pay is 'too high' or 'far too high'; only a third (32 per cent) believe their CEO's pay is in line with the company's performance; and three-fifths (59 per cent) say that high CEO pay demotivates them at work (CIPD, 2016). High pay levels are driven by the extreme form of flexible management prerogative in the United Kingdom in line with its corporate governance model based on 'maximising shareholder value'. This generates many moral hazard problems, one of which is the growing tendency for public companies to engage in share buybacks (Lazonick, 2014) in order to push up short-term share prices and gain from share options (raising income among the highest paid) at the cost of long-term investment growth, which hampers the United Kingdom's capacity to sustain high-wage employment growth.

The high use of PRP in United Kingdom workplaces (around two-fifths of private sector jobs during 2005–12) generates a potentially interesting balance of flexibility and security since managers may choose to align wage change with organisational performance in order to provide greater job and working hours' security. Stokes et al. (2014) assess this proposition for the pre- and post-crisis years and point to three key results. First, bonuses exhibited greater flexibility than fixed wages in response to pre- and post-crisis economic trends, rising more before 2009 and falling more after 2009. Second, accounting for total pay, workers in receipt of a pay bonus were more likely than other workers (controlling for various other factors including firm performance) to receive a nominal pay cut during the recession year of 2009–10. Third, working hours fell less among workers earning pay bonuses than other workers during 2009–10 and job tenure is longer.

In a high-inequality model, the United Kingdom's fusion of employer-led flexibility and weak employment and welfare protections generates adverse circumstances for high value-added growth and societal cohesion. It is well known that a model of work organisation characterised by high staff turnover, flexible contracts and weak social dialogue runs counter to the conditions required to nurture production systems that are less reliant on low-wage, low-skill labour markets. For the United Kingdom today this is a longstanding problem, which nags more than ever in policy-makers' minds when faced with persistent high levels of low-wage employment, low levels of research and development (R&D) spending, low productivity growth and insufficient numbers of leading high-technology employers. Where competitive strategies are based on flexible employment forms, the risk is that employers neglect investments in training and avoid building mechanisms for social dialogue that would strengthen employee motivation, raise productivity and improve pay prospects. More than a decade ago, Michie and Sheehan (2003) commented on their survey of medium and large-sized manufacturing firms in the United Kingdom to warn of a significant negative association between the use of flexible employment and process innovation:

> The more innovative firms have been those that have passed up the use of these newly – or at least more readily – available 'flexible' labour practices, resulting from labour market deregulation, and instead have pursued the sort of functional flexibility associated not with short-term and temporary contracts but, on the contrary, with employment security. . . (Michie and Sheehan, 2003: 136, 139)

More recently Zhou et al. (2011) found that firms with higher shares of temporary contracts performed significantly worse in sales of 'innovative products', defined as first to market. They argue that instead 'functional flexibility in internal labour markets has advantages for the continuity of (organizational) learning, and strengthens the historical memory of firms' (Zhou et al., 2011: 960). The labour market flexibility strategy, combined with insecure employment and shaped by weak social dialogue, is therefore in contradiction with a policy goal of shifting out of low value-added business segments into higher productivity activities.

4. CASE STUDIES

The following two case studies were selected with the aim of investigating how processes of industrial relations and social dialogue in the public and private sectors shape the balance of outcomes between security and flexibility with attention to equal outcomes for all workers. The first case concerns a relatively successful national sector-level initiative by the public services union, Unison, to improve working conditions among the subcontracted, private sector social care workforce. The second case explores obstacles to union efforts to improve pay and conditions for temporary agency workers and permanently employed staff who work at a large distribution warehouse as part of a global pharmaceuticals retail company. Interview details are listed in Table 13.5.

4.1 Case Study 1: Can Unions Leverage Public Procurement to Improve Standards?

While local authorities in the United Kingdom are responsible for the delivery of social care to the elderly, the bulk of work is subcontracted to the private profit and non-profit sectors. This means that most care workers fall outside the protection of the local authority sector-level collective agreement and mainly have pay and conditions fixed unilaterally by their private sector employer. The Low Pay Commission identifies social care as one of the major low-wage sectors in the United Kingdom, with specific problems of illegal non-payment of travel time a particular concern. It is also a sector in which use of zero-hours contracts is very high.

Like other subcontracted services, most studies show that the practice of public procurement generally exerts strong downward pressure on wage costs, working hours and other terms and conditions (for example, Colling, 2005; Cunningham and James, 2009). Despite this, there is some evidence that some public bodies may be willing to leverage their position as monopsony buyers to improve job quality under the auspices of 'social value', for example by including living wage criteria in service contracts (Druker and White, 2013). In this spirit, the public services union, Unison, launched a voluntary 'charter'[15] designed to establish a minimum

Table 13.5 Details of the two case studies, United Kingdom

Case study	1. Local authority outsourcing	2. Temporary agency work
Sector/ industry	Care work	Warehousing/logistics
Issues of inequality	– Low wages – Subcontracted workforce – Zero-hours contracts	– Low wages – High use of temporary agency work – Access to stable shift patterns and permanent work controlled by agency
Industrial relations system	Sector-level collective bargaining for directly employed care workers in local government Low levels of membership density and highly perforated social dialogue for subcontracted workforce in private sector	Company-level agreement for basic pay and conditions, but gradually downgraded over time Local-level union recognition with comparatively high density, but limited success at incorporating large share of temporary agency workforce
Interviewees	2 national union representatives 1 NorthCity Union representative 2 NorthCity care commissioners 1 NorthCity provider	2 EuroAgency managers 2 PharmaCo warehouse workers 2 EuroAgency workers 1 PharmaCo local union representative 1 PharmaCo manager

framework for conditions for local authorities to incorporate into their commissioning of care services. The key points of the charter for our focus on achieving a better balance of flexibility and security are:

- domiciliary care workers should be paid for travel time between visits;
- zero-hours contracts are not to be used in place of full- or part-time permanent contracts;
- all care workers should receive a full living wage (£8.80 per hour in London and £7.65 per hour outside London at the time).

Because the charter was a voluntary initiative it required mobilisation of union members at local level and the political willingness of local authorities to implement the changes to procurement practices. At the time of research, the process was proving to be slow due to severe spending cuts imposed by central government:[16] in 2016 just 13 local authorities out of 375 in the United Kingdom had officially adopted the charter. One of the

13 is a local authority in the north of England, labelled here NorthCity. NorthCity is led by the Labour Party, covers a local population of around 750 000 and has an annual budget of approximately £1 billion. It began the process of outsourcing care homes and domiciliary care in the mid-2000s (later than most local authorities) and signed up to Unison's care charter in 2015.

4.1.1 Establishing a commitment to 'high-road' contracting through political lobbying

For the local trade union branch, upgrading pay and working conditions in the private sector was a moral imperative, which at the same time could be used as a means to slow down the privatisation of the remaining in-house care services (as the differential in pay of directly employed staff over contracted staff would narrow). For NorthCity commissioners, working with fewer providers and stabilising contract volumes over the medium term were needed to develop quality and capacity in the local market, while also reducing the bureaucracy associated with frequent 'spot' contracting (for as little as 20 hours of care for a single client). Unions also impressed on managers the notion that improving staff pay and conditions could be a means to improve the reputation of both the care profession and NorthCity local authority, while also contributing to the continuity of care by reducing staff turnover. For the trade union locally, persuading the council to sign the charter was the result of three years of persistent lobbying of politicians: 'We kept banging on about ethical care, banging on about travelling time, banging on about zero hour contracts, banging on about 15 minutes [the maximum time allowed for many care visits] . . . In the end . . . I think they just got fed up with us' (NorthCity union representative)

Once unions had secured the political commitment to fund improved care standards, the strategy shifted to considering how the redesign of contracts could best support improved workforce standards, as proposed in Unison's care charter. The process of negotiating contract redesign involved extensive social dialogue in the form of a 'working group'. This group consisted not only of the usual local union and employer representatives, but also a wider group of stakeholders, including NorthCity politicians, service user groups and care providers. After extensive discussions over 18 months the working group established the key features of the new contract, which involved higher fixed hourly fees (to cover increased wages and payment for training and travel time) and the redesign of contracts to allow for greater stability in contract volumes (designed primarily to reduce the need for zero-hours contracts).

4.1.2 How can better contract design reduce precarious work?

The multi-stakeholder 'working group' identified three key problems of precarious work, namely, non-payment of travel time, zero-hours contracts and low pay. Through negotiations, the group sought to address each problem through better contract design.

Paying care workers for their travel time Under the old framework, the union argued that although no specific provisions were made for the payment of travel time, it was generally assumed that providers did pay workers for travel time. However, as fees were low and the council did not check, very few actually did: 'One of [the providers] actually said, "Look, there's people in this room who don't pay travelling time, we do, but I know for a fact some people sat in this room don't"' (NorthCity union rep.).

This reinforced the need to pay for travel time directly in the form of a new specification in the contract for care services. The required practice nevertheless depended on a major uplift in fees and this proved the major point of negotiation in the working group. Prior to the reform, NorthCity paid about £12 per hour for domiciliary care, well below the 'reasonable rate' of £15.74, recommended by the national monitoring body (United Kingdom Homecare Association, UKHCA), which factors in the average time taken by domiciliary care workers travelling from one client to another. Negotiations eventually resulted in a major uplift from the £12 fee, although it fell short of the recommended level for most workers. Revised fees were: £14.41 per hour for urban zones, £15.98 for rural zones (suburbs and outlying commuter villages) and £16.26 for 'super rural' zones (the outer parts of the local area containing open countryside). Overall, the new fees added about £2.5 million to the total annual contract values for domiciliary care of £27 million (met from NorthCity reserves). The higher rates for rural zones were an explicit acknowledgement of the greater time needed to travel from one residence to another. In practice, however, most providers only received the lowest rate of £14.41 since four-fifths of all contract hours are allocated in the urban zones.

Eliminating zero-hours contracts The problem of zero-hours contracts was tackled in a different manner. The key problem recognised via the process of dialogue in the working group was too many providers competing for too many low-volume, short-term contracts, which generated uncertainty in staffing arrangements. Provider managers were clear that zero-hours contracts were the fault of spot contracts as they did not guarantee sufficient volumes of work or pay retainers when clients did not require visits: 'I don't want to use zero-hour contracts, [but] in some cases, I really haven't got a choice, and that's not me being a nasty capitalist to rip loads of profit out of the business, . . . that's the nature of it' (NorthCity provider).

The solution was to restructure contracts into six geographical zones delivered by only four primary providers, thereby reducing the number of providers, increasing the volumes of work each received and injecting more stability in contract volume. Under the new contract, the care provider investigated said it would offer to move staff from zero-hours contracts to a standard 16 or 37 hours per week basis. Zero-hours contracts would still be available for those workers who chose them but now with rotas issued four weeks in advance and flexibility for workers to increase and decrease hours.

Paying a living wage For the trade union, the main prize of implementing its ethical care charter was the living wage. The legality of 'mandating' a higher wage rate in the contract specification was debated within the council but ultimately it was seen as worth the risk:

> You hear debates coming out from councils, from procurement, that you're not allowed to do that. We were advised that there may be a risk and we said, 'Fine, we will take that'. And [so] we wrote into the document we are at risk of challenge and well, no one's challenged us . . . (NorthCity Commissioner 1)

The higher fees (described above) were the main contractual instrument for achieving this. Despite the fees for care services in urban zones falling short of the recommended rate for the industry, all care providers were nevertheless instructed in the contract to pay their workforce a minimum of £8.01 per hour (gross, basic rate). For the union, this was a significant achievement of social dialogue. It fell short of the actual living wage of £8.25 at the time, but was a considerable improvement on the minimum wage paid to many care workers of £6.70. Moreover, the new base rate of £8.01 was approved by the working group as 'a stage' in moving towards a full United Kingdom living wage of £8.25 and was agreed as a condition of the new social care contracts at a cost of about £1.2 million.

4.1.3 What are the limits to a contract-led approach for addressing equalities?

While this case demonstrates the value of social dialogue in reducing precarious work through better contracting, it is nevertheless limited by the fact that trade unions were unable to follow through with further pay negotiations with care providers owing to their absence from pay bargaining. This generated a key problem for wage inequalities in the case study. The new contract required payment of an uplifted basic wage and payment of travel time, but it did not specify appropriate enhancements for unsocial hours and weekend working, nor did it recommend that providers ought to develop or maintain pay differentials between care workers and supervisors. NorthCity managers recognised that the sharp uplift at the bottom could impact on the internal wage structure of providers. However, because some providers had attempted to invoke differentials to leverage wage increases all the way up to management grades, NorthCity dismissed all claims for the restoration of differentials: 'I understand the differential in a care home where your cleaner now ends up being paid the same as the care staff. Maybe, yeah, there's something there. But you know what, if you're paying your area manager £70,000 a year, that's nothing to do with me' (NorthCity Commissioner 1).

The trade union was therefore unable to use the higher base rate as a springboard for bargaining the restoration of pay differentials with higher job grades. Instead, care provider managers were able to exercise sole authority over higher pay rates. Other research suggests this is likely to lead to a compression of pay between care worker and more senior grades. Data from a major survey of care providers show that most providers do not reward experience or years of service, not even between entry and normal rates of pay, and those that do pay no more than 50 pence extra for senior grades (Rubery et al., 2013). The care provider we investigated did offer one form of compensation for more experienced workers, a bonus that increased with years of service and shares owned. However, this only added up to a maximum of 5 per cent of the total wage. Overall, therefore, without a presence in pay negotiations in care provider organisations, trade unions will not address the problem of low pay in the industry through better contracting alone.

4.1.4 Summary

This case demonstrates how even in the United Kingdom's perforated industrial relations model, well-designed national initiatives can have considerable local success in improving pay and conditions of job security for low-paid workers. This case certainly serves as a positive model for other attempts to improve employment standards for subcontracted workers through better procurement. A note of caution is nevertheless needed because public bodies across the United Kingdom – and especially local authorities – have suffered major spending cuts since 2010 as the result of a government ambition to reduce the scale of the welfare state. Despite repeated calls for increased public expenditure to save social care from collapse, the government remains firmly committed to its goal of welfare state retrenchment.[17] The challenge for trade unions and local authority employers, via their respective collective representative bodies, is therefore to organise a more effective campaign of collective action against central government. With increased public expenditures, trade unions and employers can establish better contracting among a wider range of public bodies, and unions will also be in a better position to mobilise new members among the subcontracted workforce.

4.2 Case Study 2: Can Unions Prevent the Levelling Down of Standards through High Use of Agency Work

This case study concerns union efforts to combat an employer's high use of agency workers and the risks this posed for standards enjoyed by permanent workers. Ultimately, the union was unsuccessful, but the case raises useful lessons for social dialogue and efforts to forge a more inclusive approach to staffing that better balances flexibility and security concerns.

The case study covers two organisations: a major temporary employment agency, 'EuroAgency', and a warehouse belonging to a large client retail company, 'PharmaCo', as well as a local union branch present at PharmaCo. PharmaCo is a large employer in the local labour market where the case study was conducted, with 6500 staff working across 20 buildings on a 300-acre site. EuroAgency became the on-site agency provider in 2014 and exclusively handles all recruitment (temporary and permanent). The union was recognised by PharmaCo for collective bargaining over pay and conditions at company level, and at local level was involved in consultation with management over staffing levels, hours and working practices. At the local site, union density was around 43 per cent (around 850 members out of a 2000 strong workforce) and the vast majority were permanent PharmaCo staff (just 40 members were said to be agency workers). The union representative was a permanent employee of PharmaCo and argued that most local issues were dealt with successfully through informal social dialogue without the need to escalate up to a higher level.

The number of agency staff was 1100 and around 100 employees were converted to a permanent PharmaCo contract each year. The number and share of agency workers varied in different warehouse locations across the site, and across seasons. For example, in the goods inbound building there were 273 agency workers and 424 directly employed staff (a share of 39 per cent), whereas in the order-picking building agency staff outnumbered directly employed staff by 686 to 606 (a 53 per cent share). Numbers of agency workers in order picking could reach over 1000 during the lead up to Christmas. Four out of five agency workers were said to be from Eastern Europe (mostly from Poland); they were relatively young (late twenties or early thirties) and most were men (although observation of the day shift in the warehouse suggested a more even split of men and women).

4.2.1 Hard work and performance surveillance

Attendance, timekeeping and hard work were all prized 'worker characteristics'. In terms of screening suitable workers, EuroAgency managers focused on the physical demands of the job: 'We try and drum into them that they can walk up to four miles on a shift, there's lots of lifting, bending, stretching . . . Some people get into the job and the sheer physicality of it is far too much for them and they just can't cope with it' (EuroAgency manager 2).

Performance management was a dominant theme in management–labour relations and the warehouse was designed in such a way as to support both the movement and monitoring of workers; items for picking were organised in long, straight lines with good visibility down aisles. Individual attendance and performance data were displayed on noticeboards around the warehouse with green–amber–red colour coding to shame those workers who were falling behind in attendance, punctuality, order-picking pace and accuracy. The noticeboards also displayed photographs of items found on staff members during exit searches in order to remind workers that attempts to steal would almost certainly be detected by security staff. The practice of conducting lengthy body searches and scanning at the end of shifts after workers have already 'clocked-off' has also been identified as a cause of workers at other warehouse sites being paid below the statutory minimum wage since the search time is typically unpaid (notably at Sports Direct and JD Sports).[18]

> It's not just about performance but attitudes, behaviours, timekeeping . . . absence counts against you straight away . . . We do support people who have got potential . . . We've done it the last two weeks – there is a girl down there and the way she works is so smart, and we spoke to her and said, 'You know we've been watching you and it's a credit to how well you work . . . really thorough.' (PharmaCo manager)

The individual nature of order-picking work and the noisy and mechanical working environment does not lend itself to interpersonal interaction, thereby limiting the scope for the seeds of 'collectivism' to take root, or for mobilisation against common grievances to be initiated. One permanent worker observed that working routines and management–labour relationships were structured on purpose so as to discourage interaction between workers, regardless of status:

> There are no formal barriers between us [permanent and agency staff] but you kind of come in, get on your station and get on with it . . . There are people floating around keeping an eye on you and you're not encouraged to speak so it's not very social . . . You don't get much chance to talk about issues or what is going on. (PharmaCo worker 1)

4.2.2 Union strategy towards temporary agency workers: strategic engagement, exclusion or tactical indifference?

Despite the high share of agency workers at the PharmaCo site, a legacy of negative relations between the union and agency and union perceptions of 'exploitative' employment practices meant that formal interactions between the union and the on-site agency managers were limited. However, rather than a deliberate strategy of exclusion, this could perhaps be characterised as indifference towards the agency and agency workers so that the union could prioritise the needs of PharmaCo employed members. Such a strategy is not inevitable in the United Kingdom context. Heery (2009) reports a range of more successful union practices that involve an 'upscaling' of union representation beyond the workplace. The union did attempt to recruit agency workers during their induction period and used the on-site canteen to advertise the union and engage with workers, but the temporary nature of agency work and the transient nature of some parts of the workforce posed barriers to organising. The union branch official and the union health and safety representative suggested that for those workers who did not know whether they would stay with the client or agency, or remain in the local area, the motivation to join a union based at one site was negligible. The result was very low membership among agency workers; agency workers made up less than 5 per cent of union members in the two warehouse buildings despite making up nearly half the local workforce.

The informal division within the union strategy between organising agency workers and servicing permanent workers is a difficult issue to resolve as there are undoubtedly differences in the needs and priorities of groups of workers engaged under such fundamentally different employment conditions. However, the union's acknowledged failure to engage with temporary agency workers who had been in post for nearly four years is an indicator that union efforts to 'bring the agency in' were not achieved. Similarly, that the agency controls access to all jobs (both temporary and permanent) within PharmaCo suggests that the union has to do more to attract members from within the EuroAgency workforce if it is to preserve its relatively high level of membership density.

4.2.3 Segmentation of regular and irregular working time

A first substantive area of unequal employment practice where social dialogue unfortunately had no impact concerned the use of regular hours for permanent staff and irregular hours for agency workers. The balance of flexibility and security was thus divided between workforce groups in the form of a classic dualist strategy. While permanent staff received guaranteed shift patterns, agency workers received rotas one week in advance with no guarantees of the volume of hours from one week to the next and even from one day to the next. Analysis of working hours suggests a more sensible system of annual hours could in principle be applied since demand was relatively stable across the year and agency workers averaged a working week of 33–34 hours per week, compared with full-time hours among permanent staff of 37.5 hours.

Managers instead preferred to exercise unilateral power to call in workers and send them home as demand dictated. A PharmaCo line manager made clear that a key benefit for the company of having a 'significant' pool of agency workers was that all workers on the rotating shift pattern could take one Saturday off in three but, more importantly, the company was less exposed to the risk of paying staff for unproductive time:

> There is a cost advantage but there is also the flexibility that if the work does dry up . . . We are in a very automated environment here and we would try and keep people but if something breaks down we can't keep people . . . It's a last resort but you need that flexibility. (PharmaCo manager)

The fact that permanent staff and managers were not sent home when demand falls suggests that the risk was borne exclusively by the agency workforce, something which perhaps helped to protect permanent workers from reduced hours or job losses. For agency workers, the cost of irregular hours was significant:

> The hours are okay although recently on two days I have had half days [instead of full days] . . . The rota comes out a week in advance and this Friday I have only got four hours . . . So it's a bit of a knock in the pay packet which isn't great when you've got kids . . . But it goes like that sometimes. (EuroAgency worker 2)

4.2.4 Union efforts to prevent the levelling down of pay and conditions

A second area where the local union struggled to make an impact concerned the imposition by PharmaCo in 2011 of a downgraded offer of pay and conditions to newly hired permanent workers. PharmaCo management reduced basic pay and premium rates of pay for weekend working, shifts and night work, and replaced paid breaks with unpaid ones. The loss of paid breaks reduced weekly basic pay by 6 per cent[19] and further cuts were associated with the 'normalisation' of hours worked on public holidays and weekends (Table 13.6). Workers were not happy, but the union was unable to translate this into sufficient bargaining power and ultimately could not overturn the decision. The workforce was now characterised by a second division, that between new hires and incumbent staff with permanent contracts: 'You could have two people working next

Table 13.6 Working-time schedules and pay premiums for all workers at PharmaCo

Work schedule	Pattern	Paid hours	Shift premium	Weekend premium	Overtime premium
Rotating early-late shifts	Five days out of six, Monday to Saturday 06.00–14.00, 14.00–20.00 (with occasional 01.00 finish)	37.5 hours	No	No	No
Night shift	Sunday to Thursday 22.00–03.00	30 hours	Yes £1.17	No	No
Weekend night shift	Friday and Sunday 22.00–06.00	15 hours	Yes £1.17	No	No

to each other on three or four pounds difference in pay. That's caused a lot of bad feeling over the years' (PharmaCo Union representative).

The union challenged the change in pay and conditions through negotiation and also explored the legality of the new contract in terms of both equal pay and the contractual entitlement to weekend shift premiums. However, in the end PharmaCo management imposed it, albeit with a small cash settlement to workers (£600) to reflect the move to more flexible working patterns and loss of unsocial hours' premiums.

The reduced pay and conditions meant that contracts for temporary and permanent workers since 2011 have been harmonised, a perverse example of 'equality via levelling down'. Hourly rates of pay for new starters, whether on temporary or permanent contracts, were £7.20 on entry (equivalent to the statutory minimum wage for workers aged 25 plus during 2016) and £7.70 after 12 weeks' experience whether or not the agency worker transitioned to a permanent contract. It is possible both PharmaCo and EuroAgency managers wished to respond to the 2011 Agency Work Regulations, which require equal pay between temporary and permanent staff after 12 weeks, although the spirit of the regulations suggests levelling up of agency workers' conditions not the levelling down of permanent workers' conditions. However, the temporary workers were directly employed by EuroAgency on a pay-between-assignments basis and therefore have no legal right to equal pay according to the Swedish derogation (see Forde and Slater, 2016).

4.2.5 Summary

Our second case study reveals the risks for workers' employment standards of too high use of temporary agency work in a context where unions, even where present, do not enjoy sufficient bargaining power. The local union did not enjoy high representation among agency workers and, despite very high membership density among PharmaCo workers, the union had insufficient power resources to confront PharmaCo, a powerful US-owned multinational retail company. Over time, PharmaCo's very high use of temporary agency workers and a failure of the local union to prevent this led to an aggressive management imposition of worse conditions for its directly employed permanent staff that aligned with the poor conditions of agency workers. A significant lasting benefit for permanent workers is the greater regularity of working time, although it is unclear how sustainable this is.

5. CONCLUSIONS

Persistent high inequality in the United Kingdom is a function of its dual aspect in the labour market. It is both an outcome of labour market functioning and is instrumental in its evolving character. All too often, inequality is treated simply as another indicator of economic performance or a signal of fairness in society. However, it also plays a strongly instrumental role, especially at high levels, in shaping the character of work and employment, particularly norms governing flexibility and security.

In the United Kingdom, while the rate of job growth during the current recovery has beaten all records and unemployment is relatively low, these performance indicators veil an ongoing series of qualitative shifts in the labour market in protections for workers and in the nature of work. These shifts both reproduce high-level inequality and feed off workers' unequal socio-economic conditions. Understanding this two-way interrelationship is becoming increasingly critical to our analysis. Sandler (1998) warned that in a highly unequal society many people enter the labour market and seek to improve their working life under conditions of economic coercion. In the United Kingdom's perforated industrial relations system, a person's ability to negotiate a fair deal with his or her employer – on pay, hours, holiday entitlement or job security – is undermined by a weakened bargaining position caused by, for example, poor alternative job opportunities or risk of sanctions and loss of welfare benefits.

The problem for the United Kingdom is that for many years there has been too much inequality in society. Too many employers design jobs paid at or just above the minimum wage while mid-pay jobs in the manufacturing and public sectors are downsized and the very high earners enjoy accelerated pay rises. This leads to too many low-paid jobs, too many workers dependent on top-up welfare benefits, too much job insecurity caused by zero-hours contracts, outsourcing and self-employment, and overly limited pay and career prospects over the longer term. While for many years this problem has plagued low-income households, the past decade has also witnessed its extension to people in the middle of the income spectrum (see Vaughan-Whitehead, 2016). The future for the United Kingdom requires a radical change of mind-set and a new political acceptance that workers require more than the ad hoc interventions of government – on minimum wages, for example – and rather a commitment to joint regulation of pay and conditions of work. Without collective bargaining it is difficult to imagine how the United Kingdom can move towards a fairer distribution of the rewards from work. As Willy Brown has argued:

> the process of collective bargaining is at the heart of a pluralist approach to employment, one that expects management to make a case for changing workers' lives, and for those workers to have some opportunity to argue about it. Its decline is likely to diminish popular experience of the exercise of citizenship at the place of work and to reduce the capacity to achieve negotiated adjustments to change. (Brown, 2010: 272)

NOTES

1. The correlation between variables of collective bargaining coverage and the gender pay gap is negative but very small, just –0.08. Removing the two country outliers, Austria and Poland, increases the size of the correlation to –0.28.
2. All data on union membership and collective bargaining coverage are derived from the Labour Force Survey, accessed from the Office for National Statistics (ONS) (see BIS, 2016).
3. 'Workplace Employment Relations Study' data reported in Van Wanrooy et al. (2013).
4. This form of wage-setting was first used for the separate groups of senior civil servants, judges and senior military, for doctors and dentists and for the armed forces. Since the 1980s other groups have come under the umbrella of pay review bodies, including health-care occupations (a major expansion in 2004 with a modernised national framework known as 'Agenda for Change') and school teachers.
5. The workplace data refer to sample of workplaces with ten or more employees.
6. Broadcasting, Entertainment, Cinematograph and Theatre Union.
7. http://www.ucatt.org.uk/false-self-employment (accessed 10 November 2016).
8. Government documents describe its intervention as setting a 'premium' for experienced workers (defined as 25 years of age or over) that will provide a 'national living wage' (BIS, 2016). As many commentators have observed, however, this is merely political rhetoric. The imposed rate will fall short of the real living wage, which is set by the Living Wage Foundation; for the period November 2014–October 2015 it was fixed at £7.85 per hour outside London and £9.15 in London, considerably higher than the £7.20 announced for 2016–17. It would seem that the government has confused the target of fixing the minimum wage at 60 per cent of the median wage (by 2020), as specified in the new remit for the Low Pay Commission, with the notion of a living wage.
9. The difference is caused by the higher level of median earnings among workers aged 25 or over, namely £12.77 compared with a figure of £12.10 for all adult employees (Annual Survey of Hours and Earnings, 2016).

10. See benefits and wages statistics accessed 10 November 2016 at www.oecd.org/els/benefits-and-wages/.
11. According to documents obtained by the PCS union and reported in the *Guardian* newspaper (Patrick Butler, 3 February 2015), Job Centre staff must meet specified targets and also deliver target 'off-flows' which refer to moving people off benefits altogether.
12. Evidence from Hermes delivery drivers reported in a special report for the *Guardian* newspaper on 18 July 2016, accessed 10 November 2016 at https://www.theguardian.com/business/2016/jul/18/how-hermes-couriers-shoulder-insecurity-of-internet-shopping-boom.
13. Second quarter of 2016, see https://www.ons.gov.uk/employmentandlabourmarket/peopleinwork/earningsandworkinghours/datasets/zerohourssummarydatatables (accessed 10 November 2016).
14. More work is in the form of 'additional job', 'replacement job with additional hours', or 'more hours in current job' (ONS Labour Force Survey).
15. Available at https://www.unison.org.uk/content/uploads/2016/08/22014.pdf (accessed 10 November 2016).
16. The problem of spending cuts is a major issue and reflects the United Kingdom government's explicit ambition to reduce central government funding for municipalities for ideological reasons: 'Austerity is Thatcherism's logical end-point, effecting simultaneously the destruction of local government as a potentially rivalrous state-within-a-state, and the marketisation of nearly every aspect of public policy. Since 2010 the Conservative leadership, following the example of Thatcher and Blair, has diminished local democracy in order to entrench the gimcrack democracy of the free market' (Crewe, 2016: 9).
17. In the 2016 budget the government promised no additional expenditures to compensate for post-2010 cuts to the social care budget. Professional bodies and trade unions are united in calling for new investment.
18. *Guardian* online, 15 December 2016.
19. Working hours remained 40 hours per week but paid hours were reduced to 37.5.

REFERENCES

Appelbaum, E. and R. Batt (2014), *Private Equity at Work: When Wall Street Manages Main Street*, New York: Russell Sage Foundation.

Bach, S. and R.K. Givan (2010), 'Regulating employment conditions in a hospital network: the case of the Private Finance Initiative', *Human Resource Management Journal*, **20** (4), 424–39.

Belfield, C., J. Cribb, A. Hood and R. Joyce (2015), *Living Standards, Poverty and Inequality in the UK: 2015*, London: Institute for Fiscal Studies.

Blau, F.D. and L.M. Kahn (1992), 'The gender earnings gap: learning from international comparisons', *American Economic Review*, **82** (2), 533–8.

Boheim, R. and U. Muehlberger (2006), 'Dependent forms of self-employment in the UK: identifying workers on the border between employment and self-employment', IZA Discussion Paper No. 1963, Institute of Labor Economics, Bonn.

Brown, W. (2009), 'The process of fixing the British national minimum wage, 1997–2007', *British Journal of Industrial Relations*, **47** (2), 429–43.

Brown, W. (2010), 'Negotiation and collective bargaining', in T. Colling and M. Terry (eds), *Industrial Relations: Theory and Practice*, Chichester: Wiley, pp. 255–74.

Charlwood, A. and J. Forth (2009), 'Employee representation', in W. Brown,

A. Bryson, J. Forth and K. Whitfield (eds), *The Evolution of the Modern Workplace*, Cambridge: Cambridge University Press, pp. 74–96.
Chartered Institute of Personnel and Development (CIPD) (2016), 'The view from below: what employees really think about their CEO's pay packet', CIPD report, London, accessed 10 November 2016 at https://www.cipd.co.uk/knowledge/strategy/reward/ceo-pay-report.
Colling, T. (2005), 'Managing human resources in the networked organisation', in S. Bach (ed.) *Managing Human Resources*, Oxford: Blackwell, pp. 90–112.
Connolly, H., S. Marino and M. Martinez Lucio (2014), 'Trade union renewal and the challenges of representation: strategies towards migrant and ethnic minority workers in the Netherlands, Spain and the United Kingdom', *European Journal of Industrial Relations*, **20** (1), 5–20.
Crewe, T. (2016), 'The strange death of municipal England', *London Review of Books*, **38** (24), 6–10.
Crouch, C. (2010), 'British industrial relations: between security and flexibility', in T. Colling and M. Terry (eds), *Industrial Relations: Theory and Practice*, Chichester: Wiley, pp. 29–53.
Crouch C. (2015),'Labour market governance and the creation of outsiders', *British Journal of Industrial Relations*, **53** (1), 27–48.
Cunningham, I. and P. James (2009), 'The outsourcing of social care in Britain', *Work, Employment and Society*, **23** (2), 363–75.
Dahl, C.M., D. Le Maire and J.R. Munch (2013), 'Wage dispersion and decentralization of wage bargaining', *Journal of Labor Economics*, **31** (3), 501–33.
Dell'Aringa, C. and L. Pagani (2007), 'Collective bargaining and wage dispersion', *British Journal of Industrial Relations*, **45** (1), 29–54.
Department for Business, Innovation and Skills (BIS) (2016), 'Trade union membership 2015: statistical bulletin', Department for Business, Innovation and Skills, London.
Druker, J. and G. White (2013), 'Employment relations on major construction projects: the London 2012 Olympic construction site', *Industrial Relations Journal*, **44** (5–6), 566–83.
Eurofound (2015), *Pay in Europe in Different Wage Bargaining Regimes*, Luxembourg: Publications Office of the European Union.
Field, F. and A. Forsey (2016), 'Wild West workplace: self employment in Britain's "gig economy"', accessed 10 November 2016 at http://www.frankfield.co.uk/upload/docs/Wild%20West%20Workplace.pdf.
Fleetwood, S. (2007), 'Why work–life balance now?', *International Journal of Human Resource Management*, **18** (3), 387–400.
Forde, C. and G. Slater (2016), 'Labour market regulation and the 'competition state': an analysis of the implementation of the Agency Working Regulations in the UK', *Work, Employment and Society*, **30** (4), 590–606.
Gautié, J. and J. Schmitt (eds) (2010), *Low-Wage Work in the Wealthy World*, New York: Russell Sage Foundation.
Gosling, A., S. Machin and C. Meghir (1994), 'What has happened to men's wages since the mid-1960s?', *Fiscal Studies*, **15** (4), 63–87.
Grimshaw, D. (2000), 'Public sector employment, wage inequality and the gender pay ratio in the UK, 1986–1995', *International Review of Applied Economics*, **14** (4), 427–48.
Grimshaw, D. and G. Bosch (2013), 'The intersections between minimum

wages and collective bargaining institutions', in D. Grimshaw (ed.), *Minimum Wages, Pay Equity and Comparative Industrial Relations*, London: Routledge, pp. 50–80.

Grimshaw, D., G. Bosch and J. Rubery (2014), 'Minimum wages and collective bargaining: what types of pay bargaining can foster positive pay equity outcomes?', *British Journal of Industrial Relations*, **52** (3), 470–98.

Grimshaw, D., J. Cartwright, A. Keizer and J. Rubery (2015), 'Market exposure and the labour process: the contradictory dynamics in managing subcontracted services work', paper presented at the Regulating for Decent Work conference, Geneva, 8–10 July.

Grimshaw, D, M. Johnson, A. Keizer and J. Rubery (2016), 'Reducing precarious work in Europe through social dialogue: the case of the UK', report for the European Commission, European Work and Employment Research Centre, University of Manchester.

Hayter, S. (2015), 'Unions and collective bargaining', in J. Berg (ed.), *Labour Markets, Institutions and Inequality: Building Just Societies in the 21st Century*, Cheltenham, UK and Geneva: Edward Elgar and ILO, pp. 95–122.

Heery, E. (2009), 'Trade unions and contingent labour: scale and method', *Cambridge Journal of Regions, Economy and Society*, **2** (3), 429–42.

Heery, E., H. Conley, R. Delbridge and P. Stewart (2004), 'Beyond the enterprise: trade union representation of freelances in the UK', *Human Resource Management Journal*, **14** (2), 20–35.

High Pay Centre (2015), 'The state of pay: high pay centre briefing on executive pay', accessed 15 November 2017 at http://highpaycentre.org/files/The_Pay_Today_draft.pdf.

Hill, S. (2016), 'The California challenge: how (not) to regulate disruptive business models', FES study, Friedrich Ebert Stiftung, Berlin, accessed 10 November 2016 at http://library.fes.de/pdf-files/id-moe/12797-20160930.pdf.

Jaumotte, F. and C. Buitron (2015), 'Linkages between labour market institutions and inequality', International Monetary Fund, accessed 10 November 2016 at http://www.imf.org/external/pubs/ft/survey/so/2015/int071015a.htm.

Karamessini, M. and J. Rubery (eds) (2013), *Women and Austerity: the Economic Crisis and the Future for Gender Equality*, London: Routledge.

Kersley, B., C. Alpin, J. Forth, A. Bryson, H. Bewley, G. Dix and S. Oxenbridge (2006), *Inside the Workplace: Findings from the 2004 Workplace Employment Relations Survey*, London: Routledge.

Lazonick, W. (2014), 'Profits without prosperity', *Harvard Business Review*, **92** (9), 46–55.

Lloyd, C., C. Warhurst and E. Dutton (2013), 'The weakest link? Product market strategies, skill and pay in the hotel industry', *Work, Employment and Society*, **27** (2), 254–71.

Low Pay Commission (2016), *National Minimum Wage: Autumn 2016*, Cm9272.

Marginson, P. and K. Sisson (2006), *European Integration and Industrial Relations: Multi-Level Governance in the Making*, Basingstoke: Palgrave Macmillan.

Michie, J. and M. Sheehan (2003), 'Labour market deregulation, "flexibility" and innovation', *Cambridge Journal of Economics*, **27** (1), 123–43.

Moore, S., A. Tasiran and S. Jeffreys (2008), *The Impact of Employee Representation upon Workplace Industrial Relations Outcomes*, London: Department for Business, Enterprise and Regulatory Reform.

Newsome, K., S. Moore and C. Ross (2016), 'Supply chain capitalism, parcel delivery

workers and the degradation of work', paper presented at the International Labour Process conference, Berlin, 4–6 April.
Rogers, B. (2016), 'Employment rights in the platform economy: getting back to basics', *Harvard Law and Policy Review*, **10** (2), 479–519.
Rubery, J., D. Grimshaw and H. Figueiredo (2005), 'How to close the gender pay gap in Europe: towards the gender mainstreaming of pay policy', *Industrial Relations Journal*, **36** (3), 184–213.
Rubery, J., D. Grimshaw and G. Hebson (2013), 'Exploring the limits to local authority social care commissioning: competing pressures, variable practices and unresponsive providers', *Public Administration*, **91** (2), 419–37.
Rubery, J., A. Keizer and G. Grimshaw (2016), 'Flexibility bites back: the multiple and hidden costs of flexible employment policies', *Human Resource Management Journal*, **26** (3), 235–51.
Salverda, W. and K. Mayhew (2009), 'Capitalist economies and wage inequality', *Oxford Review of Economic Policy*, **25** (1), 126–54.
Sandler, M.J. (1998), 'What money can't buy: the moral limits of markets', Tanner Lectures on Human Values, Brasenose College, Oxford, 11–12 May, accessed 20 August 2009 at www.tannerlectures.utah.edu/lectures/documents/sandel00.pdf.
Stokes, L., A. Bryson, J. Forth and M. Weale (2014), 'Who fared better? The fortunes of performance-pay and fixed-pay workers through recession', NIESR Discussion Paper 440, National Institute of Economic and Social Research, London.
Terry, M. (2010), 'Employee representation', in T. Colling and M. Terry (eds), *Industrial Relations: Theory and Practice*, Chichester: Wiley, pp. 275–97.
Van Wanrooy, B., H. Bewley, A. Bryson, J. Forth, S. Freeth, L. Stokes, et al. (2013), *Employment Relations in the Shadow of Recession: Findings from the 2011 Workplace Employment Relations Study*, Basingstoke: Palgrave.
Vaughan-Whitehead, D. (ed.) (2016), 'Trends in the world of work: what effects on inequalities and middle-income groups?', Report presented at the European Commission, Brussels.
Visser, J. (2016) 'ICTWSS database 5.1', AIAS, University of Amsterdam.
Watt, A. (2008), 'The impact of private equity on European companies and workers: key issues and a review of the evidence', *Industrial Relations Journal*, **39** (6), 548–68.
Wills, J. (2009), 'Subcontracted employment and its challenge to labor', *Labor Studies Journal*, **34** (4), 441–60.
Wright, C.F. and W. Brown (2013), 'The effectiveness of socially sustainable sourcing mechanisms: assessing the prospects of a new form of joint regulation', *Industrial Relations Journal*, **44** (1), 20–37.
Zhou, H., R. Dekker and A. Kleinknecht (2011), 'Flexible labor and innovation performance: evidence from longitudinal firm-level data', *Industrial and Corporate Change*, **20** (3), 941–68.

Index